THE
BYRDS
OF
VIRGINIA

OTHER BOOKS BY ALDEN HATCH

We Nehrus

A Man Named John

The Mountbattens

Ambassador Extraordinary

The Wadsworths of the Genesee

THE
BYRDS
OF
VIRGINIA

BY
ALDEN HATCH

Holt, Rinehart and Winston

NEW YORK   CHICAGO   SAN FRANCISCO

Grateful acknowledgment is made to the following publishers and persons for permission to reprint portions from their publications:

Reprinted by permission of G. P. Putnam's Sons from *Skyward* by Richard E. Byrd. Copyright 1928 by Richard E. Byrd; renewed 1956 by Richard E. Byrd.

Reprinted by permission of G. P. Putnam's Sons from *Little America* by Richard E. Byrd. Copyright 1930 by Richard E. Byrd; renewed 1958 by Richard E. Byrd.

Reprinted by permission of G. P. Putnam's Sons from *Discovery* by Richard E. Byrd. Copyright 1935 by Richard E. Byrd.

Reprinted by permission of G. P. Putnam's Sons from *Alone* by Richard E. Byrd. Copyright 1938 by Richard E. Byrd; renewed 1966 by Marie A. Byrd.

Portion of Articles by Richard E. Byrd in the National Geographic Magazine reprinted by permission of the National Geographic Association.

Reprinted by permission of Louis B. Wright from *The Secret Diary of William Byrd of Westover*. Copyright 1941 by Louis B. Wright and Marian Tinling. Printed by Dietz Press, Richmond, Virginia.

Reprinted by permission of Louis B. Wright from *The London Diary of William Byrd of Westover*. Copyright 1958 by Louis B. Wright and Marian Tinling. Published by Oxford University Press.

Reprinted by permission of Estate of Maud H. Woodfin from *Another Secret Diary of William Byrd of Westover (1739-1741)*. Edited by Maud H. Woodfin. Translated by Marian Tinling. Copyright 1942 by Maud H. Woodfin and Marian Tinling. Printed by Dietz Press, Richmond, Virginia.

Designer: Winston Potter

SBN 03-066420-9

Printed in the United States of America

ACKNOWLEDGMENTS

A writer's working life is often referred to as a lonely vigil. Fortunately, this cliché does not apply to the work of one who tries to probe and reflect history. Always in a book of this nature many people generously contribute their knowledge and expertise to the finished product with no motive of gain or ax to grind, but simply from a desire to expound the truth as they see it and expand man's knowledge of his fellow man. To all those who have assisted me in writing this book I am profoundly grateful. One of the fringe benefits of such an undertaking is the stimulus of associating with first-rate minds and the joy of making fine new friendships.

In particular I should like to express my appreciation for the assistance of the family of the late Senator Harry F. Byrd of Virginia, not only for the invaluable information they supplied and their help in tracking down elusive facts, but also for their admirable restraint in not pressuring me to reveal what I have written about their beloved progenitor. Among these are Senator and Mrs. Harry F. Byrd, Jr., Mr. and Mrs. B. Beverley Byrd of Westwood, Mr. and Mrs. Richard E. Byrd of Rosemont and Mr. Harry F. Byrd, III.

I am also under great obligation to Mrs. Richard E. Byrd, the widow of Admiral Byrd, and his son Commander Richard E. Byrd, Jr. Others who were of great assistance to me include Mr. and Mrs. William Byrd, Mr. and Mrs. Gray Beverley, Miss Elizabeth Tab, Mrs. Henry M. Stimson, former Senator A. Willis Robertson of Virginia, Congressman William M. Tuck, Judge Howard Smith, Colonel Francis Pickens Miller, Rear Admiral Lewis L. Strauss, Doctor Paul A. Siple, Doctor James Mooney, Doctor Louis B. Wright, Arthur Krock, Mr. and Mrs. Joseph A. Massie, Jr., Mrs. James Thompson, Colonel M. J. Menefee, E. Blackburn Moore, Alexander McKay Smith, Jesse Johnson, Mr. and Mrs. Thomas H. Reynolds, Senator Homer Ferguson, John Walklet, Thomas E. Schlesinger, Doctor Edward M. Riley, Mrs. Bruce Crane Fisher of Westover, Dudley B. Ball of the Library of Congress, Leonard Grant of the National Geographic Society, Miss Martha Cropp, Mr. and Mrs. E. I. Williams, Mr. and Mrs. Richard Harkness, Mr. and Mrs. W. Nelson Page, George Burwell and Colonel Harold E. Byrd.

April, 1969   Alden Hatch

FOR ALLENE

CONTENTS

Sixteen pages of photographs follow page 248

P R O L O G U E

A family tradition of public service is rare in America. Both our system of government and our traditional dislike of political dynasties have made it so. In addition, during most of the nineteenth century and part of the twentieth, politics was regarded as "a dirty business" whose meager rewards and evident uncertainties hardly compensated for the risk of defamation and the necessity for compromising principles, for wheeling and dealing, and for conveniently overlooking dishonesty on the part of one's associates.

Fortunately, a few families were traditionally willing to accept these disadvantages in order to serve their fellow Americans in public office. The Adamses, Lodges, Cabots, Tafts, Roosevelts, Harrisons, and Lees come to mind. These, however, served but two, three, or four generations. The Byrds of Virginia are unique: For two hundred and ninety-nine years every generation but one has served the public.

The Byrds entered the American scene with a flourish. William (1652–1704), the first to come to the colonies, became a prominent figure within two or three years of his arrival in 1670. He was helped by a good marriage and an uncle's legacy of money and land, but it was wild frontier land at the Falls of the James River where Richmond now stands. The land would not have done it without the good sense and drive which made older and far richer men follow William's leadership against the Indians and in the affairs of the colony.

In the early eighteenth century his son, the second William, (1674–1744) was so cultivated, effulgent, and powerful that Charles and Mary R. Beard in their *Basic History of the United States* chose him as the archetypical planter-aristocrat whose birth and wealth forced him to uphold the prerogatives of his class. The evidence seems to refute this view. He played an important role, not only in governing the Dominion, but also in defending the liberties of the colonists by his diplomatic dexterity and his determination as agent of Virginia at the Courts of Queen Anne and King George I of England. All Americans in all the colonies benefited by Byrd's refusal to compromise the rights of Virginians, under the Royal Charter, to appoint their own judges and levy their own taxes.

His son, the third William (1728–1777), was also a leading figure in colonial times. He successfully commanded the Second Virginia Regiment—there were only two, with George Washington in command of the First—in the French and Indian War; he was one of the commissioners who negotiated vitally important treaties with the Catawba and the Cherokee Indians; and he was an influential member of the Governor's Council, which was both the senior legislative body and the High Court of the Dominion.

Unfortunately this Byrd had two weaknesses. One was self-indulgence for which he spent almost all of the great patrimony (179,400 acres of land) his father bequeathed to him; he was, besides, a singularly inept businessman, a born sucker for fly-by-night, get-rich-quick schemes. Loyalty was his second failing, though it is a virtue if practiced on the winning side. Unfortunately, Byrd was loyal to King George III. This, together with his other proclivities, completely wrecked the family fortunes and their prestige in what, despite his efforts, became the United States of America.

For a period of one hundred and fifty years, the Byrds played comparatively minor roles while their contemporaries were signing the Declaration of Independence, driving the British out of the Colonies, drawing up a Constitution, and guiding a new nation through the crises of childhood and adolescence to greatness. Nevertheless, there was at least one Byrd fighting for his country in all the wars including the Revolution; one son of the third William defied his father and became an officer in the Continental Line. In the Civil

War they fought for the Confederacy, which was their country. Every generation of Byrds but two served in the Virginia General Assembly. If the Colonial General Assembly and Council are considered as a continuing body in the present legislature the family has served in it for a total of one hundred and twenty-seven years.

Between 1776 and 1925, they did not achieve national recognition. Then suddenly, in the twentieth century, two Byrd brothers simultaneously shot up close to the apex of national life, and each in his own special way took up the making of American history where his ancestors left off. Admiral Richard E. Byrd became a national hero, not by luck or one brief flash of valor, but because he had the stuff of which authentic heroes are made—determination, ruthless pursuit of an objective, mysticism, and a bellyful of guts. He was the first man to fly over both the North Pole and the South Pole, and he made the incredibly inhospitable, storm-wracked Antarctic Continent, where the temperature on an average winter day is —70°, his personal fief for as long as he lived. His brother, Senator Harry Flood Byrd, less picturesque, but more substantial, stayed at home. His fief was the Commonwealth of Virginia. He ruled it benevolently for forty years, first as Governor, then as Senator and boss of the Byrd Machine, and became, at last, the leader of conservative opinion in the United States.

In personality they were as different as brothers could be. The Admiral was thin as a flagstaff and tempered like a Damascus blade. His finely drawn features, deep-set burning eyes, and wavy brown hair made him one of the handsomest men alive. But this was just the flashy exterior of the man. So, too, was his gung-ho attitude toward danger, though that was real enough to make him face death a dozen times without any visible tremor. Beneath it all was a deep spiritual mystique. He believed ardently in God and the divine order of the universe. But his God was not the sort to get one out of trouble brought on oneself by carelessness or miscalculation. Even in Byrd's own writings there is no record of his trying to pray his way out of difficulties. According to his creed this could be found only by using your God-given intelligence and never, never giving up so long as you could still move the little finger of your left hand. There came a time when, alone at his Advance Base during the South Polar winter night, the Admiral, stricken by carbon-monoxide poisoning from his oil heater, had barely that much strength left. Yet he refused to call the Main Base in Little America for help lest his men be lost facing the howling gales of the ice cap in an attempted rescue. Little by little he regained enough strength to make himself a cup of soup and when he vomited that up, forced himself to drink another and another until he could crawl to the radio transmitter and broadcast the flagrant lie that everything was "O.K. at Advance Base." No man could, by stamina alone, have survived that monstrous ordeal, which lasted for one hundred and thirty-six, twenty-four-hour nights. It required soul strength—that mysterious indefinable quality by which the human spirit can repeal the laws of probability and confound the most intricate computers that human ingenuity can build. Yet this same mystic—who in a little icebound hut emulated the spiritual fortitude of an ascetic—could come home to take a boyish delight in the trinkets that various governments gave him to wear on the breast of his uniform and to have a wonderful time dancing all night with adoring debutantes at the Richmond Cotillion.

Senator Harry Flood Byrd was more earthy. He tended to be a bit rotund in face and figure. Instead of challenging earth's bleakest plateau, he loved the fertile fields and the sweet, apple-scented air and forested hills of Virginia. He enjoyed growing things and mingling with people. He also like to influence the course of history, and this he did in no small measure.

In England, some of the families who were national leaders before Virginia was more than a geographical expression are still prominent in government and other fields of leadership. Even in America, some descendants of the old New Englanders have played a leading role in modern life. This lends to the history of a nation a certain continuity that is not without value. The fact that the Byrds—by a sudden, startling upsurge of ability and with no noticeable help from their forebears—have refurbished what was once a great and then almost-forgotten name makes them worth remembering.

Many of them were daring and ribald adventurers, or extremely elegant but equally effective technicians of power politics, and almost all of them were individualistic to the point of eccentricity. This makes them as interesting as they are important.

BOOK ONE

The First William

I · TO VIRGINIA

THE LETTER from America, which arrived late in 1669, must have caused a considerable flurry in the house of John Bird, goldsmith, of London. It was from his wife's brother, Captain Thomas Stegge,[1] who had large estates in Virginia. Since Captain Stegge had no children, he offered to make Bird's seventeen-year-old son, William, his heir, provided the boy would come to the Dominion. There is no record of what John Bird thought of this proposal, but one may suppose he thought well of it. After all he had another son, Thomas, who would inherit the business and most of his money.

However, Mrs. Grace Stegge Bird may have had motherly tremors, since her father, Captain Thomas Stegge, senior, had been lost at sea returning from a government mission to Virginia. That she was a devoted mother is indicated by her extravagance in having a portrait painted of William at the age of four or five. It is the only record there is of his appearance and it now hangs in the Library at Westover, the great house on the James River in Virginia which his son built. William is shown as a chubby little boy with an abundance of golden curls. He is dressed in a tunic with a small cloak over his shoulders and strange boots on his feet. He is holding a small dog on

1. Spelling of all names follows the records of the College of Arms, London.

a chain. A cherished, happy little soul, he looks nothing at all like the strong, sagacious man he became.

Whatever his mother and father thought of Thomas Stegge's offer, the one fact that is known is that young William jumped at it. He went off on the first available ship to join his uncle.

William Byrd [2] was that kind of man. All his life he saw the main chance plain and aimed for it. He was a conservative gambler, shrewd and courageous, willing to stake his life to advance his prospects in the New World or the Old.

He knew very well that his prospects in the Old World were not brilliant. The Bird family, though in very comfortable circumstances, had gone downhill quite a bit. William's great-grandfather had been Thomas LeBrid, a direct descendant of Hugo LeBrid who fought with the conqueror at Hastings in 1066 and had the right to a heraldic coat of arms; [3] but his grandfather, Thomas Bird, had been apprenticed to Henry Sacheverell, vintner, in 1608 and admitted to the Freedom of the Vintners Company in 1616. Thomas married his first cousin, Elizabeth Bird, daughter of his uncle, John Bird, "Citizen of London." Thomas did not have time to sell much wine, for he died at twenty-three. His second son, John—also a Citizen of London and William's father—became a goldsmith. In short, though well-off and respectable, the Birds were hopelessly middle class.

Young William knew that in the rigid hierarchy of seventeenth-century England it was very difficult to climb up again if a man remained in London. The quickest road from the old city to the Palace at Whitehall was a long detour via Virginia. It was also the shortest road to fortune.

William sailed for America in one of the small cranky vessels [4] that beat their painful way across the Atlantic ever more frequently as trade with the growing colonies expanded. Though still short of eighteen years of age, he probably enjoyed the rough winter voyage, for he never minded danger or discomfort and in the worst storms he could lash himself in his hammock in the smelly hold and dream of his uncle's promised heritage and great adventures in the New World.

2. William Byrd seems to have changed the spelling of his last name. Possibly he thought the Y looked more aristocratic.

3. Certified in 1927 from the records of the College of Arms, London, by H. F. Burke, Garter King of Arms.

4. The largest ship built in the seventeenth century, the *Sovereign of the Seas*, was only 127 feet long.

Seventeenth-century Englishmen viewed Virginia through a romantic haze engendered by the flamboyant prose of Captain John Smith, augmented by the appearance at Court of John Rolfe with his lovely Princess Pocahontas, and maintained by glowing letters written home by the colonists. The main object of these letters and articles, which constantly appeared in London newspapers and handbills, was to induce more men, women, and boys to come over and settle in the vast empty land of which the leading planters had already acquired huge acreages. Most of the land they owned, except for a thin sliver along the coast, was still primeval wilderness of no use to anyone except Indians until it was cleared and settled. Therefore they wrote idyllic accounts of the beneficence of the climate, the fertility of the soil, the possibilities of gold and silver ore deposits beyond the mountains, and the opportunities for advancement. It was all true enough as far as it went—except for the mythical gold and silver—but what they never wrote about was the plague of flies and mosquitoes, the rigorous boring winters, and the miasma of the swamps which laid virtually everyone low with the ague, as they called malaria. Nor did they mention the discouraging statistic that only about one in four of the early settlers survived the perils of disease and Indian massacres.

Byrd knew little or nothing about these disadvantages, nor, in all probability, would he have turned back if he had. What he did know was that his Grandfather Stegge had gone to Virginia sometime in the 1630's and had made quite a considerable fortune that enabled him to keep residences on both sides of the ocean. In fact Byrd had been born in his grandfather's comfortable London house which Captain Stegge, senior, had left to his daughter, Grace Bird, while leaving all his Virginia property to his son.

Furthermore, Byrd knew that his grandfather had attained such eminence that Cromwell's Parliament had appointed him a Royal Commissioner in 1651 to treat with the rebellious Virginians who refused to acknowledge the rule of "regicides and tyrants." In fact, on the execution of King Charles I, Governor Sir William Berkeley of Virginia, with the approbation of the colonists, had proclaimed the late King's son, Charles II, "King of Virginia" and invited the exiled monarch to come and reign in his colony. The young King was so touched that ever after he fondly referred to Virginia as "My Old Dominion," a name Virginians have cherished ever since.

Captain Stegge and his associates had finally succeeded in persuading the colonists to submit to Cromwellian rule by giving them numerous concessions in the way of local self-government that considerably advanced the liberties of Virginians. Apparently the fact that Stegge was so well liked and trusted by the colonists contributed greatly to the success of the Commission. That it was on the return from this mission that Captain Stegge had disappeared at sea seems not to have bothered Byrd in the least.

The exact date of William Byrd's arrival in Virginia is unknown, but the fact that his uncle's will is dated March 31, 1670, offers a good clue. Captain Stegge was evidently carrying out his part of the bargain. So it is likely that some time in March, 1670, Byrd's ship passed between Cape Henry and Cape Charles and sailed up Chesapeake Bay. Some sense of the great size of the New World would strike a man because of the distance between the capes and the extent of the great bay which he could not see across. As the ship coasted along the Virginia shore, young Byrd could see the thickly forested land beyond the salt marshes, broken in a few places by the corduroy brown fields, newly plowed for the spring tobacco planting. The trees were still bare except for the black green of the enormously tall primeval pines, and the landscape was leeched of color by winter's cold. As the ship swung into the broad James River, Byrd would have noticed that the forest had been driven back and the plowed fields came down to the water's edge. Wharves ran out into the still river where an occasional ship was moored. Gaunt, gray wooden tobacco barns stood starkly against the hazy sky. To an eye accustomed to the neat, green English countryside it must have looked rather ragged, though deceptively peaceful.

Higher up the river on a swampy island connected to the mainland by a sandspit was the damp, unhealthy village of Jamestown. It was a poor place to be the capital of so great a territory. There were perhaps forty or fifty houses, a church, and a statehouse that was no larger than an English schoolhouse. The village's only defenses were two or three small cannon pointing toward the land. Those early Virginians refused to build proper towns, let alone cities, to the disgust of sophisticates like their first historian, Robert Beverley, who believed that civilization flourished only in cities; and to the despair of officers of the Crown who had to collect the excise taxes and export duties. But why should the Virginians huddle in towns? Every large plantation was a self-sustaining unit which raised its own food and had a carpenter, mason, butcher, baker, candlemaker and blacksmith, and its own wharf on deep water from which produce could be shipped directly to England. Even a decree from King Charles II in 1665, ordering that forts be built at the mouths of the great rivers and that all ships should be loaded under them instead of at the plantation wharves, had no effect. Some little breastworks were built and cannon mounted, but the people paid no attention to the King's command. That was their custom when they did not like a royal decree even in 1670.

Beyond Jamestown were the great plantations of Berkeley and Shirley, fine manor houses, made of brick with walled English gardens and tree-shaded lawns running down to the river. But in March the trees were bare of leaves and the lawns like rusty straw. The mansions were built in the style of English country houses, yet had a stark, somewhat forbidding look in keeping with the character of a new, still-savage land whose uncertainties were emphasized by the loopholes under the eaves of Berkeley in case of an Indian attack.[5] In the plowed fields on either side of the great houses white indentured servants and a few Negro slaves worked side by side.[6]

William Byrd must have landed at one of the plantation docks, for the big ships did not usually go much farther upriver. There he either took a river sloop or, more likely, mounted a horse and rode over the twenty-odd miles of wilderness trail between huge boles of sky-scraping trees in shifting, endless files to infinity. Hardly anything but ferns and moss could grow on the sunless forest floor.

So he came to his uncle's house. The prospect was as savage as the lower James River had seemed peaceful. Steep hills reared abruptly out of the plain and, cutting through a rocky gorge, the James roared and tumbled over the falls and down rock-strewn rapids in the exuberance of the spring freshet.

Captain Stegge and his young wife lived in a square, two-story stone house with one chimney in the exact center of the roof. The house was built on a flat meadow where the river made a broad bend below the cliffs and it was more fortress than dwelling. For this place, where Richmond now stands, was the very spearpoint of civilization beyond which the untouched, savage forest stretched for thousands of

5. Various embellishments were added to these famous houses in later times.
6. At this time there were fewer than two thousand Negroes in the whole colony.

miles. In 1670, cultivation and habitation stopped dead at what was called the Fall Line—the line stretching from northeast to southwest across the colony where the alluvial plain ended in a sharp upthrust of land. Here the tides from the sea stopped as did navigation by ship on all the great rivers of Virginia—the Potomac, the James, the Appomattox, the York, and the Rappahannock. This Fall Line effectively halted the advance of civilization for the first hundred years of Virginia's history.

The edge of the forest was a perilous place to live. A man never knew when the friendly Indians would suddenly get tired of trading furs for rum, guns, and gewgaws and decide to take their country back. Less than fifty years before, in 1622, they had nearly succeeded.

The early spring of that year had been a pleasant time for the colonists. The abundant land had at last provided enough to eat in addition to a fine cash crop of tobacco. The great increase of the people and the long quiet they had enjoyed, ever since the marriage of Pocahontas to John Rolfe in April, 1614, had smoothed interracial relations and made the colonists no longer afraid of the Indians. In fact the colonists welcomed Indians into their homes in the hope of converting them to Christianity. Never had the friendship between the races seemed warmer than on March 21, 1622, the eve of Good Friday. That day the Indians brought presents of deer, turkeys, fish, and fruits to their English friends. Many of them spent the night outside the settlers' houses and turned up for breakfast.

Then at eight o'clock on Good Friday morning, when most of the men had gone out to work in the fields, the Indians in all the scattered settlements and lonely cabins up and down the James for one hundred and forty miles suddenly attacked their hosts. The lucky ones never knew what hit them; those less fortunate lived to see their children's skulls cracked before their eyes, their wives mutilated and themselves tortured.

The Indians acted on orders from their head chief or emperor, Opecancanough, who, made uneasy by the large number of settlers pouring in, had organized the great conspiracy in utter secrecy and with extraordinary efficiency. As Robert Beverley wrote in *The History and Present State of Virginia* (1722): "[He took] indefatigable pains to engage in so horrid Villany all the Kings and Nations bor-dering upon the English settlements on the western shore of Chesapeake."

The entire colony might have been annihilated had it not been for Chanco, a Christian Indian, who got wind of the massacre the night before and warned his master, Richard Pace. Pace rowed across the river at night to alert Governor Sir Francis Wyatt in Jamestown, who spread the alarm as far as possible before the Indians' attack. Thousands of lives were saved, but at least three hundred and forty-seven colonists were killed.

A great deal of sympathy has been expended on the American Indians. In fact, today, almost every American feels a twinge of guilt when he thinks about them. But in writing about the early colonists it is only fair to consider their point of view. They saw themselves as clinging to the thin edge of a mighty continent whose unchartered spaces contained unknown thousands of savages. Their scalp-lock tonsures, the gaudy spots, blotches, circles, and squares of their war-paint were designed to terrify their enemies. Though they did not frighten the settlers out of the colony, they did scare them out of their wits in the sense of impairing their judgment as to the best and fairest way to treat the Indians.

The idea that a country might belong to its aboriginal inhabitants had scarcely been broached by the most humanitarian of philosophers. On the contrary, the early settlers—from the Spaniards in Peru to the Puritans in Massachusetts and the French on the St. Lawrence—genuinely believed that they were doing the heathen Indians a good turn by exposing them to the blessings of Christian civilization, even including smallpox, measles, and tuberculosis. They felt themselves to be on firm moral ground.

As to the particular relationship between the Virginians and the Indians, any possibility of real friendship and trust between them vanished in the smoke of burning houses, the cries of small children beneath the scalping knife, and the shrieks of men and women suffering unspeakable tortures in the massacre of 1622. After that there could never be anything more than an armed truce, frequently broken by both sides. The Virginians adopted the Roman maxim, "Faith is not kept with heretics," to excuse their own frequent acts of treachery.

The truth is that even by ethical standards less rugged than those of the colonists the Indians were, by and large, cruel and un-predictable. The latter fault was perhaps their worst in English eyes. The colonists could have understood a deliberate policy aimed at driving them out, or cruelty practised for a purpose such as obtaining information or punishing a transgressor; but war by whim and cruelty, apparently simply for the fun of it, was pure savagery to them. Though Virginia had grown enormously in the fifty years since the massacre, even in the most populated areas the colonists kept a wary eye on the receding forests; and in the lonely outposts eternal vigilance was still the price of survival.

Such was the condition in which William Byrd found his uncle and his young aunt living. This was by their own choice. Stegge had inherited fom his father a nice piece of land in Charles City County among the settlements, but he had sold it and bought eighteen hun-dred acres at the Falls of the James. This apparently insane act had a sound commercial reason behind it. The Stegges were not primarily planters and cared not at all for the prestige of great land holdings. They were merchants who had made their fortune trading with the Indians and with their fellow colonists. From this point of view the location of Captain Stegge's property was ideal. The forest trails ended at the Falls and goods were shipped from there by water. The Indians came there with pelts to sell in exchange for goods from England; and thence the Captain's white traders went out like ped-dlers with their packs on horse or mule back over the long dangerous wilderness paths four hundred miles or more southwestward to the rich country of the Catawbas and Cherokees. If the Indians were feeling frisky, the traders did not come back; but more often than not they returned with their pack trains loaded down with fine furs, especially the beaver skins which were in tremendous demand in England for beaver hats. In the entire colony this trade was second only to tobacco for bringing in cash, and the man at the edge of the forest got the cream of it.

Thus William Byrd's heritage was not so much the eighteen hundred acres of land as a flourishing trade empire. If it was rather less grand than he had anticipated, it provided considerable sums of the hard cash so difficult to come by in Virginia where tobacco often was used as currency.

On the plantation, Byrd found an object of curious interest. It was a great rock thrust from the soil, bearing indentations about five feet apart like the footprints of a gigantic man. The rock was sacred to the Appomattox Indians, who said these were the footprints of their god. Because of this, Captain Stegge might have had difficulty holding the land, except that there were so few Appomattox left. Contact with civilization had reduced the tribe to seven families whom Stegge—and later William Byrd—allowed to live in huts in his pasture within sight of their sacred relic.

Of additional benefit to Byrd was the eminent position the Stegges had won in the colony. Thomas, senior, had been an early settler and by 1637 was a respected merchant. He became a member of the House of Burgesses and was elected its Speaker in 1643. The following year he was appointed a member of the King's Council, the senior governing body and high court of the colony. During the reign of the Roundheads in England, Thomas Stegge and his son managed to keep on friendly terms with both the Parliament and the cavaliers who came streaming into Virginia by the shipload to escape the rigors of Puritan rule. In those days of religious fanaticism and intense emotions the Stegges' neutrality was an extraordinarily nimble performance.

Building on his father's political dexterity and his deserved reputation as an honest merchant, the son had attained a fine position in the colony as a member of the Governor's Council, a colonel of militia, and a close friend of the Governor and Captain General, Sir William Berkeley.

William Byrd arrived at a time when Virginia's golden age was dawning, but before the conscious effort of the great planters to found an aristocracy had stratified society. The social position his uncle bequeathed him was not the least of his heritage.

Captain Stegge did not keep his appointed heir waiting long to meet Virginia society. He had barely time to show young Byrd the techniques of the business before the wedding of the sixty-four-year-old bachelor Governor Berkeley to a beautiful young widow, Frances Culpeper Stevens, gave him an opportunity to present his nephew to practically every person of importance in the colony. It was the first really lavish extravaganza of the new Virginian aristocracy. Men and women dressed in fine brocades poured into Jamestown for the occasion. The men wore their dress swords and the long ringleted periwigs which were the latest fashion from London. After the ceremony, trumpets sounded, cannon saluted, and the whole company adjourned to Sir William's nearby plantation, Green Spring, the first of the great mansions of Tidewater Virginia, for a splendid wedding feast.

Having assured young William's social position, Captain Stegge died in the spring of 1671. His will was proved by his executor on May 15, 1671. He had bequeathed fifty pounds to Sir William Berkeley, Knight; a hundred pounds to each of his nieces and nephews, and provided something for his wife. But Stegge left all of his lands, goods, and business in Virginia and England to his nephew, William Byrd. Thus, very early, did the principle of primogeniture begin among the Byrds. They meant to found a family and they followed the English custom for assuring it.

Captain Stegge also wrote into his will a little advice for his nephew: William is "not to be led away by the evil instructions he shall receive from others, but to be governed by the prudent and provident counsel of his aunt, the testator's loving wife." [7] The first part of this sentence is sound, the second could have been disastrous. The "prudent and provident" Widow Stegge promptly married Colonel Charles Grindon of Charles City County. Then she got herself involved in Bacon's Rebellion of 1676 and was referred to in a bill passed in 1677 by the House of Burgesses—of which Byrd was by then a member—as "a great assister and encourager of the late horrid rebellion." However, she managed to escape going to jail.

In 1684, Mrs. Stegge's second husband died at sea on his way home from England and she quickly married a newcomer named Edward Braine. Byrd described her act bitterly in a series of letters to his relations in England: "My cuz Grindon, in the flower of his age, died the 10th. 8 br. [October] lost at sea, and the old woman, not enduring to lie alone, married about the latter end of January to one Edward Brain [sic], a stranger here."

In a letter to a Mr. Gower he writes: "Sir—yours of the 8th of August came safe to my hands though the poor gentleman that was to bring it died at sea, 10th. of 8 br., much lamented by all his friends. The old gentlewoman seemed mighty disconsolate some short time. However, she married again about the latter part of January and is now mighty earnest to get all the estate into her hands and I daily expect a writ against Capt. Randolph and myself, ex. rs

7. W. G. Stannard, *Beau Monde* (a weekly) edited by W. Cabell Trueman, April 7 and April 14, 1894.

[Executors for Grindon] here for her bond of £1900–11 which I fear will in a manner carry away all the estate here."

Byrd loathed Mr. Braine, whom he described as arriving in Virginia with "thirty servants and a thousand pounds worth of goods." Since he usually liked the rich, one must conclude that Braine was indeed an unpleasant character.

Had Captain Stegge known his nephew better, he would have realized that he had no need of advice to be prudent. William Byrd kept his eyes fixed on his own ambitious purpose and played the splendid cards which fate and Uncle Thomas had dealt him close to his handsomely embroidered waistcoat. He took over the business with a firm hand, and sent the caravans of traders out even farther than his uncle had; sometimes they numbered fifteen men and a hundred horses. Nor did he try to cheat the Indians. He insisted that sound goods be delivered to them and would put up with no shoddiness. In letters to his British agents, Perry and Lane, he constantly warned them against sending him inferior goods—"Kettles with holes" and "hoes that are too small"—and demanded the best cotton cloth, "mostly dark blue." Also "Pray speak to the gunsmith that the dogs of all the gun locks have good hold, otherwise the Indians will not buy them."

Neither did Byrd sit at home counting his money. A few months after coming into his patrimony he organized an expedition that penetrated as far west as the Allegheny Mountains. Perhaps he wanted to explore the possibility of extending his trading empire to the Sapony and Totera Indians, or maybe he simply wanted to see what the wild western lands were like. At any rate, we know he went, because an official expedition—sponsored by Major General Abraham Wood in September, 1671, and headed by Thomas Batte, Thomas Woods, and Robert Fallam—crossed his trail.

In the Toteras' town at the foot of the mountains, Robert Fallam recorded in his journal that they were given "news of Mr. Byrd and his great company's Discoveries three miles away."

In *The Story of Virginia's First Century*, Mary Newton Stannard [8] states that, "William Byrd, . . . who though but a youth of nineteen, was regarded as General Wood's chief rival in the attempt to open the great western country. After Wood's death, Byrd was re-

8. J. B. Lippincott Company, Philadelphia, 1928.

garded as the best informed man in the colony concerning western matters."

That was high praise for a young neophyte who had been in the colony less than two years, and it may well be exaggerated. However, Byrd was in an excellent position to learn about the wild lands from the traders who went out with his caravans as well as from personal observation. For example, he learned that there was not an unbroken wilderness. On the level uplands and in the rich valley of the river, called Shenandoah (Daughter of the Stars), the Indians, in the dry seasons, deliberately set the woods afire. Before the burnt-out trees could grow up again, the thick blue-green grasses that flourished in the flatlands spread over the blackened earth turning it into a lush prairie on which buffalo, deer, and elk came to feed and multiply rapidly, providing the Indians with excellent hunting.

In running his business, Byrd did not neglect the needs of the colonists. Many of them ordered goods directly from England, but these did not always arrive as specified and there were often unforeseen items needed in haste. Byrd could keep a stock of goods on hand in the warehouse he built at Shacco Creek. By the 1680's we find him writing to Perry and Lane for duffels, cotton goods, window glass with lead and solder, and ten boxes of "Lockyer's pills."

Nor did Byrd hesitate at trafficking in people. "If you could send me six, eight or ten servants, men or lusty boys, by the first ship and the procurement might not be too dear, they would much assist in purchasing some of the best crops, they seldom being bought without servants. Help me to a carpenter, a bricklayer or a mason, I would be willing to pay somewhat extraordinary." In another letter he complains that an apprentice boy he had ordered had not arrived, adding, "They may be had from ye hospital [orphanage] at any time as I am confidently informed."

He referred there to white indentured servants who signed a contract to serve for a stated length of time, often five years, in return for their passage to America.

But Byrd also dabbled in the increasingly profitable slave trade. He writes to a Mrs. Gadlier in Barbados, ordering 1,200 gallons of rum, 3,000 pounds of muscovado sugar, 1 barrel (200 lbs.) of white sugar, 3 *tons* of molasses—to make more rum—and four Negroes.

And again to Perry and Lane, with a shipment of eighty-nine hogsheads of tobacco and two of furs and skins, he writes, "I should have been glad to know whether we might expect any Negroes or not, that we might, if ye project have failed, have provided otherwise."

By 1684 he is blackbirding in a big way. In a long letter to Perry and Lane in which he complains about everything from the expense of chartering ships to a bed tick not received he says, "Servants [white] at the rate you mention . . . cannot be worthwhile." Then in a postscript he adds: "If you send the Pinke [9] to Barbadoes on our account, I would have by her 506 Negroes between 12 and 24 years old, about 1,000 gallons of rum, 3,024 L. sugar [Muscavado] and about 200 L. of ginger." [10]

There was no taint attached to the slave trade in the seventeenth century. True, the Quakers objected to it, but everyone knew that Quakers were subversive of law and order. Yet slavery took hold slowly in Virginia. Twenty Negroes, who arrived aboard "a Dutch Man Of Warre" in 1619, were at first treated like the white indentured servants. However, though a few did gain their freedom, their period of servitude usually ended only at death. Gradually, Negroes became chattels, recognized as such by about 1640. At first they were in small demand, these wild, frightened, surly people who spoke only an unintelligible African dialect, and had never seen a plow or planted a crop. But there was a constant labor shortage in Virginia, partly due to the aristocratic background of its cavalier colonists. Captain John Smith wrote in his famous *Historie:* "In Virginia a plaine Soldier, that can use a Pick-axe and spade, is better than five knights."

As the land-hungry planters extended their holdings to tens of thousands of acres and the Negroes produced a second generation, English-speaking and tamed to servile ways, the demand for them increased and the price went up from twenty pounds or so for a strong young buck to sixty-three pounds or more at the turn of the century. During the early seventeenth century the slave trade had been monopolized by the Dutch, but a few English naval victories in mid-century opened the way for British participation in this increasingly lucrative business.

At first William Byrd owned no slave ships but was happy to play the trader's role, receiving slaves on consignment and selling

9. A small, flat-bottomed ship.
10. *Virginia Historical Magazine,* Vol. 25.

them at a handsome profit. However, when, in 1697, the British Government broke the monopoly of the Royal African Company and allowed private persons to enter the slave trade, William Byrd became principal owner of a slaver named the *William and Jane*. She was captured by a French privateer while about her business off the coast of Africa. Thus, it was no qualm of conscience that stopped Byrd from the ultimate act in this noisome commerce; just very bad luck.

II · ROYAL BLOOD, MASSACRE, & REBELLION

For a young man who intended to found a family in a new country the first necessity was a wife. One was not that easily come by. As Byrd once remarked, "A spinster here is so rare a sight as to be ominous as a blazing star."

The woman shortage was worse than the labor shortage in the colony. In 1621, Sir Edwin Sandys, Treasurer and chief promoter of the Virginia Company, which founded the colony, sent shipload after shipload of "maids for wives" to the settlers, taking care "to provide them with young, handsome and honestly educated maids, whereof sixty are already sent to Virginia; such as were specially recommended to the Company for their good bringing up . . . which maids are to be disposed of in marriage to the most honest and industrious planters, who are to defraye and satisfye to the adventurers [stockholders] the charge of their passage and provisions." [1] So eager were the planters for wives that although cash was very hard to come by, the chosen planters met the ship to claim their brides with fistfuls of money to pay the fare. [2]

According to historian Robert Beverley, the problem could have

1. Records of the Virginia Company, July 16, 1621.
2. Some paid as much as 100 pounds for "a deserving wife," according to Robert Beverley in *The History and Present State of Virginia* (1722).

been easily solved if the colonists had taken Indian brides. Intermarriage was proposed by the Indians, who said the English "were not their friends if they refused." Beverley writes, "I can't think but it would have been happy for the country if they had embraced this proposal. . . . In all likelihood many if not most of the Indians would have been converted to Christianity by this kind method. The country would have been full of people . . . besides there would have been a continuance of all those nations of Indians that have now dwindled away to nothing . . . or have fled to other parts."

The colonists were less broadminded than Beverley. They refused to wed the Indian maidens, who, though beautifully formed, did smell rather strongly because of the bear's grease they rubbed on their supple skins. The pious English also feared that their souls might be imperiled by taking heathen as brides, though this did not stop their sleeping with them.

Even as late as the 1670's the woman shortage continued. Unlike America today, when the ladies' life spans outrange the men's, women died very young in colonial Virginia. It was not unusual for a man to take three and even four wives, losing them by disease or in childbirth.

Thus young Byrd had a problem. No mail-order bride would satisfy him, or even the daughter of a small planter. He intended to put himself on equal terms with the British aristocracy; if he could not quite make it himself, at least his children would. So his bride must be at least as well born as he, and have a little money of her own as well.

Against the odds, he found one. Considering the competition, this seems proof that in addition to courage, sagacity, and the magnetism that made him a born leader, he must have been a fine-looking young fellow. Mary Horsmanden, a widow of twenty-one, had been briefly married to Samuel Fillmer, the third son of Sir Robert Fillmer of East Sutton, Kent. Her husband had left her his whole estate, probably not very large, with her father, Colonel Warham St. Leger Horsmanden, and her uncle, Antony Horsmanden, as "overseers" (trustees).[3]

Colonel Horsmanden was a cavalier who found Cromwell's rule so distasteful that he fled to Virginia from his native Purleigh in Essex. The Horsmandens were lords of the manor in Purleigh. It was

3. *Virginia Historical Magazine,* Vol. 25.

they who gave the Reverend Lawrence Washington the rich living of Purleigh Church, and in that vicarage young Lawrence and John Washington lived as boys before they emigrated to Virginia.

Colonel Horsmanden became quite a figure in the colony, being elected to the House of Burgesses in 1657 for a two-year term. But after the restoration of Charles II he headed for home, leaving his daughter in America.

If the Byrds traced their ancestry back to one of William the Conqueror's knights, Mary Horsmanden's pedigree was much more effulgent. Her maternal grandmother had been Ursula St. Leger, whose family was well-known enough to have a classic horse race named for them. The St. Leger line went back to the Earl of Westmoreland, who married the daughter of John, Duke of Lancaster, a descendant of King Edward III of England. From there it took off in a royal flight back through the female line to King Charles II of Naples and many kings of Hungary, and through them to Baldwin III, Emperor of the East, various kings of France, and finally to Charlemagne himself. Thus William Byrd could happily contemplate the fact that his children would be kin to practically every royal family in Europe. The Byrds still like that idea.

Mary Horsmanden Fillmer married William Byrd in 1673, when he, too, was twenty-one. The following year, on March 28, 1674, their son William was born in the fortlike stone house at the Falls of the James. Things were not easy for Mary; she seems to have found love but certainly not security. The year 1674 was a troubled one in Virginia, with worse to come. Discontent was bubbling beneath the surface. The price of tobacco was very low. King Charles had made two huge grants of land to some of his favorites; these were contrary to the Charter of the Colony and included some already settled plantations. Taxes were oppressively high. Then, early in 1675, the Indians went on a rampage. On a sunny Sunday morning, a group of people on their way to church in Stafford County on the Potomac, passing the house of Robert Hen, saw that unfortunate gentleman lying in a pool of blood in his doorway beside a dead Indian. With his final breath Hen gasped, "Doegs! Doegs!" ·

There was no church service that Sunday. Instead the parishioners grabbed muskets and, led by Colonel Giles Brent and Colonel George Mason, started after the Doegs, a fierce Maryland tribe which seldom ranged as far south as Virginia. With thirty men the colonels pursued the Indians up the Potomac and across it into Maryland. They caught them in two log cabins. Brent shot the Doeg king and captured his small son. The Indians in the other cabin took off like antelopes with the colonists after them, shooting wildly. One Indian turned back and called out "Susquehannocks. Friends!" and Colonel Mason yelled, "For the Lord's sake shoot no more! These are our friends the Susquehannocks."

But the damage had been done. All up and down the thinly settled frontier, Indians took revenge on colonists in isolated cabins. Finally Maryland and Virginia raised a thousand men to fight the Indians. The Virginians, under the command of Colonel John Washington, formerly of Purleigh in Essex and future great-grandfather of George Washington, besieged the Susquehannocks in their fortress town in Maryland. When six chiefs were sent out to talk peace terms with them, a radical, raging group of the besiegers thought they recognized them as having been involved in the attacks on their homes and murdered five out of the six.

That did it. The main body of Susquehannocks got away in the night and flitted across country to the James, murdering every colonist they saw. In a speech in the House of Burgesses poor Sir William Berkeley said in a shaky voice, "Even if they had killed my grandfather and grandmother, my father and mother and all my friends, yet if they had come to treat of peace they should have gone in peace."

From then on the Susquehannocks were on the warpath. None of the outlying plantations were safe and the planters, abandoning them, crowded into Jamestown. Over three hundred colonists were killed. William Byrd thought it best to send his wife and little son to England to visit "Father Horsmanden" as he called his father-in-law.

The Governor seemed incapable of action. He raised an army and then dismissed it without a fight. Unlike most of his contemporaries he had always tried to give the Indians fair treatment and the last thing he wanted was to make war on them. The poor man did not know what to do.

Sir William had been a popular governor back in 1645 when he was young and energetic. He was really interested in the welfare of the country that he came to consider his home. Of course he had always been very conservative. Once when the Board of Trade in London inquired as to schooling in the colony, he replied, "I thank God that there are no free schools or printing presses; for learning has brought disobedience, and heresy and sects into the world, and printing has divulged them. . . . God keep us from both!" [4]

On the other hand he had dealt firmly with an Indian uprising, had dared to defy Oliver Cromwell and his Roundhead Parliament, and had tried to diversify the economics of the colony by encouraging the raising of silkworms, flax, and hemp. But all this was long ago. Now he only wanted the peace and quiet that his sixty-nine years demanded.

The colonists cried out for a punitive expedition against the Indians. Sir William refused to commission anyone to lead them. The best he would do was to build eight forts along the frontier in March, 1676. These did no good at all because their garrisons were forbidden to fire on the Indians without special permission from the Governor. Sir William also forbade trading with the Indians in the hope of alleviating one cause of friction. The colonists were very angry.

In the spring of 1676, Indians attacked at the Falls of the James, and killed three of Byrd's servants. They also made the dire mistake of raiding the plantation at Curles Neck twenty miles lower down the river, which was owned by a newcomer to the colony named Nathaniel Bacon. "If the Redskins meddle with me," Bacon roared, "damn my blood, but I'll harry them, commission or no commission."

Bacon was a firebrand who in three years had made a name for himself in Virginia. He was a belated cavalier of gentle blood and a fine education, who had studied the humanities at Cambridge and law at Grey's Inn, as well as traveled on the continent of Europe. Sir William appointed him to the Council soon after his arrival in Virginia, saying, "Gentlemen of your quality come very rarely into this country, and therefor when they do come they are used by me with all respect."

According to the report of the Royal Commission, later sent to investigate the "horrid rebellion" of 1676, Bacon, who was twenty-nine years old, was slender and black-haired with "an ominous, pensive melancholy aspect." His spirit was wild and proud and he was a superbly flamboyant orator, who could sway men to his own passionate purpose.

In the early spring of 1676, Virginia was seething with fury and

4. Hening, "Statutes," II, 57.

frustration. All over the colony men armed with muskets and swords gathered together and milled aimlessly around for lack of a leader. One sunny day a small group of gentlemen, whose plantations on the upper James had suffered severely, met to discuss the situation. Bacon was there and Captain James Crews of Turkey Island, Henry Isham, and William Byrd, whose lands had not only suffered, but whose pocketbook had been badly hit by the Governor's ban on trading with the Indians.

Across the river at Jordan's Point they could see a crowd of colonists gathered in arms and fury surging around with no one to lead them and no place to go. It is said to have been Captain Crews who first told Bacon that he should lead the volunteers in a campaign against the Indians. The other gentlemen joined in. Byrd, unusually reckless with rage, offered to lead a company under Bacon.

That born revolutionary needed little urging. The gentlemen rowed across the river to be greeted by joyous shouts of "A Bacon! A Bacon! A Bacon!" The volunteers, anxious to join up, crowded around the slim, vibrant figure. Bacon made them sign on a big sheet of paper in circles so that no one could tell who were the ringleaders. Then in his own words "having conjured them into this circle" he "gave them brandy to wind up the charm." [5]

From there Bacon went on to other counties, raised an army of about three hundred men and led them into the forest. True to his word William Byrd was at the head of a company. He knew that to campaign without the Governor's commission was an illegal act for which he might be severely punished—even executed. But for once he must have been too mad to care.

Back in Jamestown, Sir William was also in a fine fury. He fired Bacon from the Council and declared him and his men to be "rebels and mutineers." With a force of three hundred men the Governor started out to quash the rebellion, but when he reached the Falls of the James, Bacon was already deep in the woods on his daring raid against vastly superior numbers of Indians in their own bailiwick.

How far Byrd went with him is not known, but probably all the way to North Carolina, where they found the Ockinechee Indians encamped on an island in the Roanoke River with a large band of Sus-

5. Mary Newton Stannard, *The Story of Virginia's First Century.* J. B. Lippincott Co., Philadelphia, 1928.

quehannocks not far off. Somehow Bacon persuaded the Ockinechees to join him against the Susquehannocks and defeated the latter, killing thirty braves and all their women and children.

Then, when the Ockinechees refused to give him food for his starving men, Bacon attacked them. Shoulder deep in the river, holding their muskets and powder over their heads, Bacon's men moved close under the palisade surrounding the Indian village so the savages could not shoot at them. Then, poking their muskets between the stakes of the palisade, they fired and fired again all night long and into the next day. Hardly an Indian, man, woman or child, was left alive. Bacon only lost eleven men.

Bacon and his men returned the heroes of all Virginia. Berkeley called an election of a new assembly, and Bacon and Captain Crews were elected delegates from Henrico County. Not trusting Berkeley's intentions toward him, Bacon sailed down to Jamestown early in June in a ship with forty armed men.

Byrd parted company with Bacon right there. It was one thing to fight Indians without the Governor's permission and quite another to fight the Governor. All through the long generations, with few exceptions, the Byrds have been conservatives in politics—above all, loyal to their King and, later, to their state. The first William Byrd was no exception. He hurried to make his peace with Sir William and thenceforward was on his side, as were most of the aristocratic planters. In this case loyalty was also good judgment.

Meanwhile, in England, Mrs. Byrd was praising Bacon to the skies and criticizing Berkeley's donothingness, *not* having heard of her husband's switch of allegiance. Since her connections were so high, this doubtless swayed the Court against the Governor, but it did Byrd no harm in the end.

The contest between Nathaniel Bacon and Sir William Berkeley, Governor and Captain General of Virginia, was both tragic and wildly comic. To appease the colonists Berkeley at first offered to restore Bacon to the Council provided he ask forgiveness. Before all the Council, whose President was his own cousin, Nathaniel Bacon, senior, Bacon begged forgiveness on his knees, and Sir William said loudly, three times, "God forgive you! I forgive you! God forgive you! I forgive you! God forgive you! I forgive you!"

Under Bacon's influence the Burgesses and Council prepared for a large expedition against the Indians. But Berkeley would not give Bacon his commission as "General." Indeed, he plotted to have him assassinated, or so Bacon believed. Getting wind of the plot, Bacon fled upcountry, where the countrymen rallied around him. On June 23, Bacon returned to Jamestown at the head of four hundred men. Berkeley, with only thirty men, put on a melodramatic act. Facing the rebel leader outside the State House at the head of his Council, he tore the ruffled shirt from his breast, shouting, "Here! Shoot me! Fore God, a fair mark! Shoot!"

Then the seventy-year-old Governor drew his sword and challenged Bacon to single combat.

Smiling gently, Bacon said, "Sir, I came not, nor intend, to hurt a hair of Your Honour's head, and as for your sword Your Honour may please put it up. . . . I came for my commission against the heathen who daily, inhumanly murder us and spill our brethren's blood and no care is taken to prevent it." Then, passion flaming up, he shouted, "God damn my blood! I came for a commission and a commission I will have before I go!" [6]

Berkeley turned back to the State House followed by the Council. Its windows were soon filled with anxious faces framed by the ringlets of periwigs; Councilors on the lower floor, Burgesses above. Losing all patience, Bacon swore he'd kill every one of them including the Governor, and ordered his men, in hunting shirts and homespun knee breeches, to take aim. Up went the muskets, their firelocks clicked as they were cocked. The men shouted in unison, "We will have it! [The commission.] We will have it!"

Frightened Burgesses waved white handkerchiefs and shouted, "You *shall* have it. You *shall* have it!"

So Bacon finally got his commission, grudgingly signed by Sir William, and went off on another Indian hunt. Meanwhile, in three days, the Burgesses passed a whole hatful of bills liberalizing the colony's laws and restricting the power of the Governor. On June 26, the Governor dissolved the Assembly and again declared Bacon a rebel. Now at the head of thirteen hundred men, Bacon started back for Jamestown. Sir William left town in a hurry. Bacon turned again toward the wilderness. The Governor hurried back to Jamestown and on to Gloucester County, which he heard was loyal to him. There he

6. *Ibid.*

raised an army supposedly to fight against the Indians, but really to put down Bacon. When his militiamen got wind of this, they tramped off the field in cadence with their shouts of "Bacon! Bacon! Bacon!" The report of the Royal Commission states that the poor old Governor fainted in his saddle for "very grief and sadness."

Bacon conducted a raid against the Pamunkey Indians, which was successful except that his men nearly starved to death. He had only one hundred thirty-eight tattered followers when he reached Green Spring on his way back to Jamestown. Gathering them around him, probably in one of Sir William's own fields, he indulged in perhaps his finest oratorical flight. "Come on my hearts of gold," he shouted. "He that dies in the field lies in the bed of honour!"

Thus inspired, the "army" marched on Jamestown and took it after a short siege, while Sir William fled to the Eastern Shore of Chesapeake Bay. Some authorities say that Byrd went with him; others, that he hibernated in the Stone House. Meanwhile the rebels burned Jamestown to keep Berkeley from using it as a base. Mr. Richard Lawrence, in an excess of patriotism, started things off by setting fire to his own house.

Now, in September, 1676, Bacon held all of Virginia except the Eastern Shore. Exactly a hundred years before the Declaration of Independence the Government of the English King had been successfully defied. But it did not last long. On October 1, Bacon, worn out by his frenzied summer, died of dysentery in Gloucester County. "Where he was buried was never yet discovered; though afterward there was a great Enquiry made with Design to expose his Bones to publick Infamy."[7]

Bacon's was essentially a one-man show, and when the man went, the rebellion collapsed. Sir William sent Robert Beverley, the historian's father, across the bay in command of one of the Governor's most ruthless contingents. Every rebel leader he caught was promptly hanged. Colonel Nathaniel Bacon, senior, came over with another force. Finally Sir William himself returned. The last of the rebels to hold out was William Drummond. He was captured in Chickahominy Swamp. When he was brought before the Governor, Sir William bowed and said, "Mr. Drummond, you are welcome. I

7. Robert Beverley, *The History and Present State of Virginia* (1722).

am more glad to see you than any man in Virginia. Mr. Drummond, you will be hanged in half an hour."

"As Your Honour pleases," said Mr. Drummond.[8]

If Sir William was vindictive to the rebels, he was most grateful to the few who had stood by him, so William Byrd profited pleasantly from his change of allegiance. In January, 1677, months after the rebellion had collapsed, a British fleet with a thousand soldiers sailed up the bay to quell the uprising. They were accompanied by a Royal Commission to inquire into its causes. One of the commissioners, Sir Herbert Jeffreys, was empowered to replace Berkeley as Governor. Sir William irritably told them that he had no need of their troops nor any place to put them; and he refused to recognize Jeffreys as his successor. Instead he summoned a new assembly to meet at his plantation of Green Spring, since the State House in Jamestown had burned with the town. William Byrd was elected to this Assembly.

Thoroughly cowed, the Green Spring Assembly repealed all the liberal laws of its predecessor. Having put his house in order and rewarded the faithful, Sir William sailed for England to give the King his version of the outbreak. He knew that King Charles II took a jaundiced view of both the rebellion and the stern reprisals. Probably he had heard of the King's quip: "That old fool hanged more men in that naked country than I did for the murder of my father."

The sea voyage on top of all his other exertions was too much for the old knight. Shortly after landing in England he died without ever having seen the King.

With all those British troops on hand spoiling for a fight, the danger from the Indians seemed over. William Byrd sent for his wife and son, who returned in the summer of 1677. Byrd was now flying high. As a true loyalist, he profited by the reaction that inevitably follows such a forward leap. He was twice elected to the House of Burgesses and, in 1680, achieved his first ambition, when he was appointed to the King's Council by Governor and Captain General Lord Culpeper.

The Council was the most important arm of government in Vir-

8. Mary Newton Stannard, *op. cit.*

ginia. It consisted of twelve men appointed for life by the King; therefore collectively the Council was more powerful than the royal governors who came and went. In fact, the Council was usually able to get rid of any governor it did not like. It was also more powerful than the House of Burgesses for a number of reasons. For one thing the Burgesses had to get themselves elected each time a new assembly was called, and the Councilors, being usually great landowners, could exercise tremendous pressure on their tenants as to how they would vote. Then there was the power of patronage. The Councilors usually appointed one of their own members to key offices such as Receiver General, Surveyor, Secretary of Virginia, and so on. Lesser jobs were given to supporters and relatives. Finally the Council, sitting as the General Court, performed all the functions which in England were divided among the courts of Chancery, the King's Bench, Common Pleas, Exchequer, Admiralty, and the ecclesiastical courts. Thus they not only judged themselves, but held the power of life and death. It was a tremendous responsibility which, in general, they exercised throughout the years with diligence, fairness, and mercy.

However, in their other capacities the councilors often used their power to line their pockets. Byrd, appointed to the Council at the age of thirty, thus became one of the ruling oligarchy of Virginia.

III · WESTOVER

SOON AFTER Byrd was elected to the House of Burgesses, he rented what he called "a chamber" in Jamestown to live in during the frequent meetings of the Assembly and the Council. According to Bassett,[1] he added to its original simple furnishings "a desk, inke, glasses and a hogshead of claret." He was becoming more and more a politician, and claret was the necessary lubricant for political machinery in those days. In addition, according to Beatty,[2] he plied his guests with canary that had "twice doubled the Cape," which voyage was supposed to improve the quality of the wine. With Burgesses and Councilors, and frequently the Governor, sitting around puffing tobacco in long clay pipes and scheming for the advantage of the colony and their own advancement, Byrd's chamber may well have been the original smoke-filled room of American politics.

Those days saw several trials of strength between the Burgesses and the governors. Major Robert Beverley, a highly educated Yorkshireman who had come to Virginia in 1663, was Clerk of the Assembly. Though he had fought vindictively against Bacon's rebels, Beverley often courageously defended the liberties of Virginians.

1. John Spencer Bassett (ed.), *The Writings of Colonel William Byrd of Westover in Virginia.* New York, 1901.
2. Richard Croom Beatty. *William Byrd of Westover.* Houghton, Mifflin, 1932.

When Berkeley's successor, Sir Herbert Jeffreys, demanded the journals of the House of Burgesses in 1677, Beverley defied him and refused to give them up without the consent of the House.

Later, in 1682, when the price of tobacco fell very low, he supported the planters against the Governor, when they passed a law calculated to raise the price by restricting the crop. This cost Beverley his job. Finally, in 1686, when Lieutenant Governor Lord Howard of Effingham proposed to levy a tax without the consent of the Assembly, Beverley incited the Burgesses to refuse it.

That was too much. At Lord Howard's request King James II wrote: "It is our will and pleasure that he [Robert Beverley] be declared incapable of holding any office of public employment in our colony of Virginia." This pretty well finished Beverley, who died in 1687.

There is no record of how Byrd stood on these matters, but it is probable that he was on the same side as Beverley in the tobacco controversy. However, in 1686, Byrd, then a member of the Council and a close friend of Lord Howard, had certain fish to fry at the English Court, and probably stood with the Lieutenant Governor against the Burgesses and Beverley. But Byrd and Beverley remained good friends, with mutual respect and admiration.

During this period Byrd put interesting schemes afoot to improve his financial and social condition. In 1679, after the British troops had gone home, the Indians again began harassing the outlying plantations. Byrd did not wait for a commission from anyone. He called up the militia and, according to one account, "attacked the Indians boldly. . . . He soon overcame them, after some resistance, and put all of them to the sword without sparing anyone. He also destroyed their settlement and whatever they owned. . . . Those Indians, who were not at home, or escaped, still camp during the summer not far from their former home." [3]

Secretary of the Assembly Nicholas Spencer strongly disapproved of the precipitate action. In spite of his opposition Byrd got a bill passed by the Assembly and approved by the Governor, giving him land on both sides of James—a total of six thousand acres—in return for his agreement to maintain fifty men there to protect the frontier. The grant was disapproved in England, but Byrd seems to have hung on to some of the property. He was also made Comman-

3. *Virginia Magazine of History and Biography*, Vol. 26.

der in Chief of the militia in charge of the defense of Henrico County. From then on he was known as Colonel Byrd.

His next project was even more ambitious. He proposed to Governor Lord Culpeper that, if he were given a monopoly of the Indian trade, he would compose all the differences between the Indians and the Virginians, would see to it that the King's annual tribute was promptly paid, and would explore the country west of the mountains. He also agreed to pay the King a hundred pounds a year provided he was guaranteed permission to transport his Indian wares to England. Lord Culpeper transmitted Byrd's proposition to the Lords of Trade in London, who turned it down. That was the last he ever heard of it.

Byrd's ambition blazed more for his children than himself, or rather for himself through his children. He had a somewhat sketchy education, as can be noted from the consistent misspelling and eccentric grammar of his letters. When had he had time for learning? Nevertheless he valued it and sought it. He often wrote to John Clinton of London, ordering books: "Either Mr. [Robert] Boyle's or any other English author [on stones and minerals], and Salmon's 'Polygraphicae.' " He also ordered many books on theology—he was deeply religious—and, as a change of pace, he desired Clinton to send him *The Turkish Spy*. One order for books alone came to £35-14, almost a thousand dollars by today's standards.

Byrd was also keen on introducing plants from the Old World to the New. In 1688, after his one trip back to England, he wrote to his friend, Jacob Bobart, head of the Botanical Gardens at Oxford, thanking him for the kindness shown during the visit, as well as for the plants he sent in "such fine condition," and offering any possible service in return. He was also very proud of his friendship with John Banister, the leading naturalist of Virginia.

He recognized his own lack of education, regretted it, and sought to remedy it. Furthermore, he was absolutely determined that his children should have the best education in the world. This certainly was not to be had in Virginia, where there were no schools and children were gathered in some plantation house or other and taught by the local clergyman. That was not good enough for William Byrd's children. In 1681, when his little son, William, was seven years old, he was put aboard a ship with a cargo of tobacco and skins consigned to Perry and Lane. William was consigned to "Father

Horsmanden." The tobacco and furs would pay for the finest education England could give. This was a genuine sacrifice on Byrd's part,
for he saw the son, on whom all his hopes and love centered, only
twice more in his life.

Having done her duty by the Byrd line first thing, Mary Horsmanden Byrd thereafter had three girl children—Susan, Ursula, and
Mary [4]—followed by another son, Warham Byrd, who died in infancy. Unlike most Virginia fathers of his time, William Byrd was
determined that his daughters should also have a good education. So
one by one, as they reached the proper age—four or five—they, too,
were sent off alone on that terrifying sea voyage to Father Horsmanden. It was rough on them and perhaps even harder on their mother,
but it was remarkably unselfish of both parents.

There is one rather charming letter from Byrd to Warham
Horsmanden which explains his point of view. It was written early in
1685, when Ursula was only four years old: "My wife hath all this
year urged me to send little Nutty [Ursula] home to you, to which I
have at last condescended and hope you will please excuse the trouble. I must confess she could learn nothing good here in a great family of Negroes." [5]

There are two sidelights cast by this letter: Byrd now had many
slaves and few if any white servants; and, despite fifteen years in Virginia, England was still "home."

Ursula went off in the ship *Culpeper*, followed by a whole spate
of anxious letters from Byrd to his friends and relations in England,
begging them to be kind to "my little Nutty if she should call on
you."

Young William, put in Felsted Grammar School in Essex to
study the classics under its famous headmaster, Christopher Glassock,
did brilliantly. Susan and Ursula were placed in a good girls' boarding school at Hackney, where, as can be sensed from Byrd's later correspondence, they did not get along well. Probably after their easy,
though perilous, life in Virginia, with slaves to wait on them and

4. Byrd's daughter Mary is a rather nebulous figure. According to some authorities she married against her father's orders. Introduction to *The London Diary
of William Byrd II*. Edited by Louis B. Wright and Marion Tingling (Oxford University Press, New York, 1956) says that she married a James Duke. Her father left
her £300 in his will.

5. These were mostly newly imported slaves, wild and dangerous, except for
the house servants.

adoring parents to spoil them, the rigors of a seventeenth-century English boarding school were too drastic a change.

William Byrd was very fond of children and got along with them beautifully. He knew exactly what they wanted. About this time he sent his son a present that must have made "Will," as he was called, the envy of every little boy in England. It was an authentic Indian warrior's dress that Byrd procured from "neighbor Indians" and consisted of "a flap of belly clout," stockings, moccasins and some shells to put around the neck. There was also a bow with some arrows tied to it.

Despite his dignity and honors, Byrd was still living in the old Stone House at the Falls. In 1685, the James River evicted him. A letter to his brother-in-law in England describes it:

"Dear Sir—I wrote you last by the *Culpeper*, by whom I sent my little Nutty, and hope that ere this is safely arrived. My wife is fair for another because she will not be behind her sister.

"About the latter part of April here happened about the greatest flood was ever known [which] flowing all our lands came into my dwelling house and did us infinite mischief. . . ." [6]

The flood "raised our river upward of 20 foot above an ordinary tide" and "almost drowned," the Byrd family. It decided William to move to higher grounds. Mary Horsmanden Byrd doubtless pushed him upward. It was too much to expect any woman with a new baby in her womb to go sloshing around in several feet of water in her parlor and bedroom. Byrd built a fine new house on nearby Oregon Hill, which he named Belvidere.

That same year, according to Bassett, he was sent to Albany, New York, as Virginia's representative to negotiate a treaty with the powerful Iroquois Confederation who were becoming a menace to the southern tribes and so, of course, to the Virginians. The Treaty ended incursions by the Iroquois for many years.

Byrd's next scheme for advancement paid off. He set out to be named Receiver General of the King's Revenue and Auditor of Virginia. This was a convenient arrangement for the holder of the two offices, since it meant that he audited his own accounts. It was also quite lucrative as the Receiver General received 5 per cent—later 7½ per cent—of all the money he collected for the King. Lord Culpeper had gone home to England, leaving the government in the hands of

6. *Virginia Magazine of History and Biography*, Vol. 26.

Lieutenant Governor Lord Howard. It became quite customary for the titular Governor to stay home enjoying both the emoluments of the office and life at Court while his deputy did all the work. The receiver generalship was also an absentee job. James Blathwayt was Auditor General of all the colonies. His deputy in Virginia was Nathaniel Bacon, senior. But Bacon was getting old and, having quite enough to do as President of the Council, was willing to give up his second office—for a consideration.

William Byrd, who had no trouble reaching an agreement with Bacon, was also on friendly terms with Lord Howard, as many Virginians were not; he got the acting Governor's enthusiastic backing. But the decision would be made in England; so off to England Byrd went in 1687 to bring all the influence he could muster to bear on the Lords of Trade, and, incidentally, to see his children.

Byrd's trip was highly successful. There was still a sort of glamour about a gentleman from Virginia and he was welcomed in great houses that John Bird, Goldsmith, could never have entered except on business. Byrd, though he never met King James II, operated on the fringes of the Court. By energetic lobbying, working every friend he had at Court and, undoubtedly, by some judicious bribery, he got the job—subject to a hereditary claim of the Aleway family. When the case came up before the Lords of Trade, who were still responsible for the affairs of the colony under the King, those gentlemen in a Solomon-like decision ordered that Mr. Robert Aleway should be given possession of the office—if he would execute it in person in Virginia; otherwise Byrd could have it and Aleway could seek redress in the courts.

Since Aleway was horrified by the idea of going to Virginia and was less than confident of winning his case in court, Byrd had no trouble in negotiating with him a deal whereby Byrd was to be Aleway's deputy for two years, presumably splitting the fees; after that Byrd would be Receiver General and Auditor.

Judging by the letters of thanks written after returning to Virginia, Byrd had the time of his life in England. Though to nostrils accustomed to the sweet Virginia air the stinks of London—with its open sewers, its narrow cobbled streets slippery with slops and horse dung and reeking with the smell of half a million unwashed bodies—should have been appalling, Byrd seems not to have noticed them. Perhaps they reminded him of his youth. Of far more importance was the hospitable "condenscention" (to use one of his own words) of the noblemen which that boy of long ago had hoped to enjoy someday. He made many friends who were to be immensely useful to young Will.

Not the least of his delights must have been renewing his acquaintance—it was hardly more—with his son. Will was now thirteen years old, a slim, elegant boy with exquisite manners, who was already at ease in Latin and Greek and could quote the latest French authors. In fact, he was already far better educated than his father ever would be. Thus Byrd had a father's rarest satisfaction, that of seeing his son turning into exactly the sort of man he hoped the boy would become.

The matter of Byrd's appointment as Receiver General was settled on December 4, 1687, and despite the attractions of England he rushed straight back to Virginia, where he arrived on February 24, 1688. He did not even wait to say good-bye to his many friends or even members of his family, so anxious was he to get back to business and consolidate his new position.

Unlike his uncle, who had cared little about land, Byrd was hungry for it, not only as the basic form of wealth, but for the status it conferred. He had already acquired six thousand acres at the Falls of the James, and was steadily buying other large pieces of Virginia. In 1688, right after his return from England, he made his most famous purchase.

Westover was a plantation of about two thousand acres in Charles City County on the James, adjoining Berkeley about midway between Jamestown and the Falls. Francis West had selected it in 1619 from the lands granted to his brother, Lord De La Warr, the first Royal Governor, whose timely arrival with a fleet in 1610 had saved the colony from being abandoned by its first starving settlers. Six people were killed at Westover in the massacre of 1622, and Francis West had then abandoned it as too exposed.

Westover—or Westopher as it was sometimes spelled—was next granted to Thomas Pawlette, a kinsman of Governor Berkeley, in 1638. He left it to his brother, Sir John Pawlette in England, who gave part of it to one Otto Southcoat and in 1665 sold the remaining twelve hundred acres to Theodorick Bland for £150. Bland left it to his sons, Theodorick and Richard.

In 1688, William Byrd bought it from them for £300 and ten thousand pounds of tobacco. The deed was for twelve hundred acres, but an actual survey showed it to be somewhat less. A tract of two hundred acres right in the middle of it belonged to James Minge. Byrd bought that also. Westover was a lovely piece of land just west of Ducking Stool Point, where the broad and tranquil James made a wide bend. Byrd described it as being "two miles above where the great ships ride." He intended to make his home there. However, he did not begin to build at once.

The troubled year 1688 was the last of the brief reign of King James II. Intrigue and counterintrigue disturbed the Government. The English were violently agitated by what they imagined were their Catholic King's "popish plots," and when the honorable but bumbling James published his decree of religious toleration, lifted the ban against Catholics holding public office, and appointed a number of them to key positions in the Government, the uproar became deafening. In staunchly Protestant Virginia the people were even more hysterical. Ridiculous rumors swept through the colony, one being that the Papists of Maryland had incited the Seneca Indians to murder all the Protestants, and that ten thousand Senecas and nine thousand Nanticokes had landed in Virginia. There were not that many braves in the whole backwoods of both colonies.

Lord Howard sailed for England and the President of the Council, old Nathaniel Bacon, became *de facto* Governor. It was said that Lord Howard got out just before the angry Virginians threw him out. The turmoil increased with settlers rising in arms against they knew not what. As William Byrd wisely remarked, "When the body is disturbed its members must needs be afflicted; therefore we can expect no settled times 'till England is in peace." [7]

The disturbance of the body was put right when the English revolted against James II and installed his daughter Mary and her husband William, Prince of Orange, a grandson of King James I, as joint rulers of Britain early in 1689. The news that England was once more safely in the hands of a Protestant King and Queen was greeted in Virginia with wild enthusiasm—bells ringing, cannon firing salutes, and protestations of loyalty and relief. Byrd certainly

7. Wendell Holmes Stephenson, *A History of the South*. Louisiana State University Press, 1927. Vol. 1, p. 224.

shared this feeling, for he was a devout Anglican who regarded Catholics as but one degree above the devils from hell. In fact, he appeared to hate them rather more than he did Indians.

In 1690, William and Mary made everything in Virginia legal again by sending over Colonel Francis Nicholson as Lieutenant Governor—Lord Culpeper was still titular Governor. In his first term the new Governor was very well liked. According to Beverley: "He studied Popularity . . . [and] made his Court to the People by instituting Olympick Games, and giving prizes to all those that shou'd excel in the Exercises of Riding, Running, Shooting, Wrestling and Backsword." He also enthusiastically backed the proposal for a college to be built in Middle Plantation, foreseeing that it would make him popular with the powerful bishops of the Anglican Church in England. The Assembly was so enamored of him that it voted him a gift of £300, an act of untypical generosity by the tight-fisted Burgesses; Nicholson gave £150 to the college. He also proposed to the Assembly a law to encourage the manufacture of linens and the leather trade—tanning, currying, and shoemaking. In addition, according to Beverley, he got the Assembly to pass "a Law for Cohabitation and Improvement of Trade."

Governor Nicholson had come to Virginia with James Blair, who had been appointed Commissary of the Bishop of London and head of the Anglican Church in Virginia. William Byrd was enthusiastic about both appointments. The poor man was unable to foresee that he and his son would be fighting Nicholson for most of the remainder of his life, and that Byrd's son would be engaged in controversy with Blair until a year before the second William died.

The good news of William and Mary's accession to the throne was quickly followed by bad. In May, 1689, England went to war against King Louis XIV, who was backing James II's attempt to recover his throne. This was of vital import to Virginians, for the French had forts on the Mississippi and Ohio rivers, and the colonists feared that they would incite the western Indians to attack the English colonies and perhaps even form a French expedition against them. It was no idle fear. For over seventy years, until the final defeat of the French in the 1760's, the danger threatened.

Byrd suffered heavy financial losses during this time of turbulence, and he was also anxious about the political situation. This is probably the reason he did not begin building at once. In a letter to his father-in-law, dated July 25, 1690, he told about his troubles:

Worthy Sir:

I received two from you this year which gave us great satisfaction in hearing of all your healths at Purleigh amidst ye late amazing revolution, and truly I must acknowledge that it seems apparent to me that none can be so happy or contented as those that are retired from public business or geat traffic. Experience of ye trouble and danger in both cases I have had last year though I hope with the help of some more gold to secure my first station. As for my losses, I thank God, I can bear with patience, though a few such would put me out of danger of losing so much again. . . .

My wife and family, I thank God, are indifferent well, only I had lately one murdered and two carried away by the Indians within this twelve months. I hope to get settled at Westopher [sic], which I bought last year, where at least ourselves will be out of danger. . . .[8]

Byrd began building the first house at Westover late in 1689 or early in 1690. Very little is known about it, so completely was it erased by his son when he built the superb brick mansion that still stands. There are no pictures of the earlier house, nor is its exact location known, though as to that there are certain clues. Mrs. Bruce Crane Fisher, the present owner of the Westover mansion, points out that the beautiful formal garden west of the house is laid out with an avenue of ancient box that goes nowhere. It makes sense only if one assumes that the original house stood at the end of it. This seems to be confirmed by another fact. Located there is a dry well, fifteen feet deep, with arched doorways leading into two underground rooms about eight feet square and paved with brick. An escape tunnel ran from these rooms directly under the garden to the river. Byrd had so many close calls from Indian attacks that he evidently did not feel safe even in the midst of the settlements. His son apparently also liked to have a way out, for a second tunnel leads from the underground Indian-raid shelter to the west wing of the present house.

The original house was made of wood, and must have been quite large, judging by the number of people William Byrd II entertained there. It was certainly far more handsome than the Stone House or even Belvidere.

8. *Virginia Magazine of History and Biography,* Vol. 26.

As Byrd moved down the river, he moved upward in elegance. That summer of 1690, he sent his old silver-hilted sword to England to be exchanged for a fashionable rapier, and one of his periwigs to be remade in the latest fashion. But even as he moved upward socially, he retained his merchant's sense of values. He did not simply order a new sword and a new wig as he could have well afforded.

His thriftiness, which his heirs did not inherit, is further emphasized in an order he placed for furniture for his new house. It was to be good but not extravagant—a dozen Russian-leather chairs; one small, one middling, and one large oval table; and "a looking glass for a chamber to be handsome and neat but cheap."

On the same day that he wrote to Warham Horsmanden, he wrote more fully and frankly to his brother-in-law, Daniel Horsmanden. After speaking of Daniel's forthcoming marriage, he says:

Only lately I had one killed and two carried away by Indians. If the French come not with them we may be in hopes of continuing able to endure a small incursion now and then from the Indians alone. However, I design, God willing, to remove down the river about 20 or 30 miles where I am now building and hope you will send us, according to your promise, your's with your fair Lady's picture to adorn my new house. . . .

I likewise ordered Mr. Perry to take the girls from Hackney, but how to dispose of them I know not, London being no fit place for them and I have no relations in the country. Sister Nutty has girls enough of her own. I would be glad, if you and your Lady think fit, that you should take one or both, unless someone else may offer, for some time and I would willingly pay what you should reasonably desire. I paid the old Gentleman [Warham Horsmanden] £20 per Mr. Perry since I came away. . . .

Please give my best respects and service to all friends and accept the same to yourself and Lady with my utmost good wishes from

Your obliged loving Brother and
humble Servant
William Byrd.[9]

The Daniel Horsmandens were conned into taking Susan and Ursula into their household, which they soon regretted, according to some acerbic correspondence of which only William Byrd's side has survived. Perhaps the girls were simply lonely and miserable; possi-

9. *Ibid.*

bly they were spoiled little hellions. In any event a letter evidently arrived at Westover in 1691 from Daniel Horsmanden complaining about their conduct and the expense and trouble of maintaining them. Byrd was obviously furious at both complaints, for his irritation pierced the fashionable flowery language of his reply like thorns in a bouquet of roses:

June 2, 1691.
Sir: I received one from you this year and am glad to hear of your's and your Lady's good health which I heartily wish you may both long enjoy and may see a numerous progeny who may live happily in the world without troubling their relations.

I'm sorry my children have been so troublesome to others, chargeable I hope not, since I paid whatever was charged on me, though had the money been left by Sir Edward Fillmer and fairly accounted for, there might have been no occasion for that. Hereafter, I shall endeavor to provide other ways for them and as soon as the war [with France] is over remove them far enough.

I'm sorry I had occasions for this and that reflections have passed which might deserve more. However, upon all occasions I shall be ever ready to express myself, dear Sir, your humble obliged servant
William Byrd.[10]

It is perfectly evident that Byrd felt neither humble nor obliged. He had long been discontented with Antony Horsmanden's handling of the Fillmer estate which his wife had inherited. There is only a faint implication that Antony might have dipped his fingers in it; but as a very good businessman and an impeccable trustee of other people's money, Byrd, probably rightly, considered that his wife's uncle was a careless and incapable executor. The very next day he wrote to Perry and Lane to remove Susan and Ursula from the Horsmandens and "Put out the girls for their most advantage without unnecessary charge."

Susan never did return to Virginia. She was married in England to John Brayne of London. Ursula came home when she was about thirteen. A little before her fifteenth birthday she made the kind of marriage that was highly satisfactory to her ambitious father. Her husband was Robert Beverley, Jr., the son of Byrd's old friend and sometime opponent, Major Robert Beverley. He was a year older than Byrd's own son and like him had been educated in England. He

10. *Ibid.*

was Clerk of the General Court, Clerk of the Council, and Clerk of the General Assembly, thus serving the government in three functions, and very much a member of the establishment. He had inherited two fine estates from his father, Porototank Plantation in Gloucester County and Beverley Park in King and Queen County, where he took his bride to live.

The happiest year of William Byrd's life was probably 1696. His dear little Nutty was safely married to Robert Beverley. His son William was home on a visit from England, and the family was settled at last in beautiful Westover. Its garden, which Byrd had carefully planned, was a thing of special beauty. Surrounded by a low brick wall, it was laid out with gravel paths lined by pungent box. In it all the flowers of England grew bountifully along with some that flourished only in the New World. Byrd's son-in-law, Robert Beverley, speaks of it in his *History:*

"Have you pleasure in a garden? All things thrive in it [in Virginia]. . . . Besides your Eyes will be saluted by the charming colors of the Humming Bird . . . a glorious, shining mixture of Scarlet, Green and Gold. Colonel Byrd in his garden, which is the finest in the country, has a Summer-House set round with Indian Honey-Suckle which all the Summer is continually full of sweet Flowers in which the Birds delight exceedingly. Upon these Flowers, I have seen ten or a dozen of these Beautiful Creatures together, which sported about me so familiarly, that with their little wings they often fanned my Face."

One likes to picture William Byrd on a fine summer evening, sitting in his summer house with his wife Mary, little Nutty and her charming husband, and, best of all, with his tall, dashing son, dressed in the latest London fashion, so slim and elegant as to make the neighbors' boys look almost cloddish. Briefly they talk and laugh and are happy in that enchanted garden while the hummingbirds' little wings fan their faces.

IV · AMBITION ACHIEVED

WILLIAM BYRD II's stay in Virginia was even shorter than he had expected. Before he came, he had completed reading law at the Middle Temple in London and had been called to the English Bar. Early in 1697, the Assembly chose to send him back to England as Virginia's legal representative to present an address to the new Board of Trade on their behalf. Sadly but proudly his father said good-bye to him and continued about his own ever greater affairs.

Among these was his position as a trustee of the proposed college for which he was an ardent worker and probably a substantial subscriber. Whatever his faults, Francis Nicholson, in his first brief term as Lieutenant Governor (1690–92), had given the necessary impetus, and quite a lot of his own money, to get it started. Mr. Blair, returning to England for that purpose, had persuaded the King and Queen to endow the college generously with an outright gift of £1,985.14.10 from the quit rents, twenty thousand acres of choice land whose income was to be used to maintain it, and the revenue from the tax of one penny per pound on tobacco exported from Virginia and Maryland to the other American colonies. Their majesties were pleased with the pious plan for the college, which was to give free instruction in a "Grammar School to teach Latin and Greek, a Philosophy School for Philosophy and Mathematics, and a Divinity

School for the Oriental Languages and Divinity." The college was designed especially to be a "Seminary for the breeding of good ministers." [1] The English archbishops and bishops were as delighted by the idea as Nicholson had foreseen; the Virginians too, were enthusiastic. The Assembly voted considerable sums for building and maintenance, and clinched the deal by naming the college William and Mary after their sovereigns. They also decided to establish it at Middle Plantation—later known as Williamsburg. The college—first proposed in 1620 and abandoned after the great massacre two years later—was finally off the ground.

An unexpected addition to the endowment was made by some pirates whose ship was captured in the mouth of the Chesapeake by a British man-of-war. They surrendered upon terms of the "King's mercy." Three of the pirates were not included in this amnesty, but James Blair, always alert to collect money for his college, offered to get them off if they would contribute £300 to William and Mary. They did.

In 1692, Nicholson was made acting Governor of Maryland and was replaced by Governor and Captain General Sir Edmund Andros.[2] Andros, who had been Governor of New York and of the temporary Dominion of New England, had so infuriated the citizens of those colonies by his pomposity and dictatorial ways that, when the overthrow of James II gave them an excuse, the New Englanders clapped him in jail. He was a poor choice to govern the touchy Virginians. Almost everything good that Nicholson had done, Andros tried to undo. This was particularly true of the college. The trustees had trouble collecting the monies assigned to it, and the new Governor obstructed it in other ways.

Part of the trouble was due to a clash of personalities between the arrogant Governor and the peppery Scot, James Blair, who had been elected President of William and Mary in addition to being Ecclesiastical Commissary and a member of the Council. The Governor thought Blair was getting too big for his breeches and Blair thought the Governor was interfering with his great project. As a result, Andros removed Blair from the Council on the ground that, being a Scot, he was ineligible.

1. Instructions of the Assembly to Mr. Blair.
2. Lord Culpeper had died in 1689.

Sir Edmund, always foolishly tactless, should never have taken on Blair. Through his influence with the bishops of England, Blair brought charges against the Governor before the Archbishop of Canterbury at the Lambeth Conference in London in December, 1697. He accused the Governor of obstructing progress on the college and misfeasance concerning its endowment, and made the charges stick despite Sir Edmund's counter charges. This resulted in the removal of Andros as Governor in November, 1698.

Yet Andros did some good things for Virginia. He encouraged the production of cotton, the setting up of fulling mills, and, being "a great lover of method and dispatch," he reorganized the Secretary of State's office in Jamestown, where the records of the colony, land patents, deeds, and other public papers were in a terrible mess, lying about loose in a room in the State House "dirtied, torn, and eaten by moths and other insects." [3] He had them all put in order and copied into new books. But the poor man was always unlucky. Hardly was this done than the State House burned down in October, 1698, destroying many of the records; and all his good work had to be done again by others.

Though Sir Edmund Andros was generally and deservedly unpopular, William Byrd and his son-in-law became his great friends. The Byrds, being always conservative and sometimes more royalist than the King's representative, were usually close to the Royal Governors (with the exception of Colonel Nicholson and, later, Colonel Alexander Spotswood), a tendency which served them well until the American Revolution, when it almost wrecked the family. So warm was the friendship between Byrd and the Governor that Andros actually chose young William to defend him before the Lambeth Conference.

Despite these political hassles, work went forward on the college. Wanting nothing but the best, the Virginians ordered plans from the famous English architect, Sir Christopher Wren, and then altered them somewhat to suit the conditions of the country. The result was a serenely classic Georgian building of mellow brick and white trim that faced Duke of Gloucester Street in Williamsburg. William Byrd took his job of trustee very seriously and had a tremendous pride in the new college. It got under way even before the building was com-

3. Beverley, *op. cit.*

pleted with a president and six masters instructing students in a little schoolhouse nearby.

Though there was still no newspaper, there were by now free schools in almost every parish in Virginia—Governor Berkeley must have been quivering with indignation in his English grave—and plenty of young men equipped to appreciate higher education. By 1699, two sides of the proposed quadrangle were completed. (It never was finished.) These contained rooms for the president, the masters, and a full complement of one hundred students. There were a great hall and a lecture room, and all the conveniences for cooking, baking, brewing, and so forth. William and Mary was a going concern, the second college in the colonies, Harvard being the first.

In 1697, George Hamilton, Earl of Orkney, was appointed Governor in Chief of Virginia, though he never set foot in the Dominion; and upon the removal of Andros, Colonel Nicholson came back as Lieutenant Governor. He had changed for the worse since his first tour of duty, being now, by all accounts, despotic, cantankerous, and inconsistent. On one occasion, when the Virginians protested that he had invaded their rights derived from the laws of England, he replied that they had no right at all to the liberties of English subjects and that he would hang anyone who presumed to oppose him, "with the Magna Cartar about their necks." [4]

Another example of his choler was when he fell madly in love with Miss Martha Bunwell of whom William Byrd II wrote, "Her eyes have fire enough to inflame the coldest saint; and her virtue is pure enough to chill the warmest sinner." Martha turned him down in favor of another suitor, whereupon the Governor swore that if the marriage took place, he'd cut the bridegroom's throat and that of the officiating minister, too. Martha went ahead with her wedding and no throats were cut. But people passing by the Governor's residence that day noticed that His Excellency was making a "Roaring noise." [5]

Nicholson started his second term rather well. Taking office soon after the State House and prison at Jamestown burned down, the Governor proposed to the Assembly that the capital be moved to

4. Beverley, *op. cit.*
5. Matthew Page Andrews, *Virginia, The Old Dominion*. New York, Doubleday, 1937.

Middle Plantation, which he suggested be rechristened Williamsburg in honor of King William III. Queen Mary had died in 1694. Beverley referred to this as, "The wild project of Governor Nicholson," but Beverley was not unprejudiced; he owned a lot in Jamestown. It was, in fact, a very wise move. Middle Plantation was a hamlet on a comparatively high plateau, traversed by deep ravines, between the James and the York rivers. Near it were two navigable creeks, each running into one of the rivers, a very important thing for the transport of goods. There were also springs and rivulets of pure water. Most important of all, its elevation made it far healthier than swampy, mosquito-ridden Jamestown.

The Assembly, meeting in the great hall of William and Mary College on June 6, 1699, passed the Act establishing the City of Williamsburg. Nicholson promptly got to work planning the new capital, one of the first and most successful efforts at city planning in America. Possibly working from plans drawn by Wren for the rebuilding of London after the great fire of 1666—which unfortunately were not followed there—Nicholson drew up a beautiful design for the new capital. It consisted of a very broad main avenue (one hundred feet wide) which was named Duke of Gloucester Street after the little son of Princess Anne, later Queen Anne. At one end was the graceful Wren Building of the College and at the other was to be the new State House or Capitol. A few side streets crossed Duke of Gloucester Street and, equidistant between the Capitol and the College, a wide grassy mall flanked by roadways ran north to the site chosen for the Governor's House.

The whole layout was meticulously planned, including such modern innovations as zoning laws. No house could be built on less than one-half acre of land and there were even such stipulations as: "Whosoever shall build in the maine Street of said City of Williamsburg . . . shall not build a house less than tenn foot pitch [distance from ground to second floor] and the front of each house shall come within Six foot of the street and not nearer and the houses in the Severall lots in the Said main street shall front a like. . . ." [6]

Slowly the little city, which never had more than two thousand permanent residents, rose according to this plan. The Capitol became the most splendid "Fabrick" in the American colonies. The general specifications, embodied in the Act passed by the Assembly in June,

6. Act Establishing the City of Williamsburg, June 6, 1699.

1699, directed that it be made in "the form and figure H. . . . The length of each Side or parte . . . shall be seventy five foot. One end of each Part or Side of which Shall be . . . Semi-circular and the lower rooms . . . fifty foot long." There were to be "a handsome Staire Case," and "Great folding gates to each Porch." The roof was to be "a hip roof with Dormand windows." Finally "A Cupulo to surmount the rest of the building which shall have a clock placed in it and on top of the said Cupulo Shall be put a flag on occasion." [7] Henry Cary, the "carpenter" or "overseer," was authorized to contract for five hundred thousand bricks for the Capitol.

Working within these specifications, and possibly from a Wren-inspired plan, Cary produced a building that, while classically Georgian in feeling, was both strikingly original and surprisingly functional. Its twin wings were joined by a central section over a colonnade. The oval ends of the wings stood like medieval bastions, giving a sense of strength and permanence, while grace was attained in the soft rose brick of its construction, the white trim around the many windows, and the tall, slender cupola with Queen Anne's bright flag flying from the high flagpole.

Within, it provided spacious rooms for the different arms of government—a luxurious, paneled chamber for the Governor and Council; a commodious courtroom; and a long, narrow chamber for the House of Burgesses, with high-backed benches running lengthwise, which gave it a symbolic resemblance to its English forerunner and pattern, the House of Commons. There were comfortable committee rooms and, in the bar of the H, a conference room where the Councilors and Burgesses could meet to iron out their differences on neutral ground. Altogether the Capitol was worthy of the comment of the Reverend Hugh Jones that it was, "The best and most commodious pile of its kind I have seen or heard of." [8]

William Byrd did not live to see the Capitol completed, but, presiding as President of the Council, he had the satisfaction, when it was partly finished, of sitting in the tall-backed wooden Chair of State with the Royal Arms blazoned above his head at the oval end of the courtroom, its unique round windows like the portholes of a gigantic ship.

7. Act of the General Assembly, June 7, 1699.
8. David Hawke, *The Colonial Experience*. The Bobbs-Merrill Company, Indianapolis, 1966.

The misfortunes of age overtook Byrd comparatively early in life. The first of these was the loss of his favorite daughter. Poor little Nutty did not long enjoy the splendid new domain she had acquired by her marriage. When she was less than sixteen, she gave her husband one son, named William for her father. She died a year later. Beverley never married again and remained the devoted friend of William Byrd and his son all his life.

Ursula was buried in the cemetery of the little old church in Jamestown, but her tomb sank into the marshy ground and completely disappeared. However, her epitaph was preserved in the Beverley family papers:

Here lieth the body of Ursula Beverley, late wife of Robert Beverley, daughter of the incomparable Col. Wm. Byrd, Departed this life the last day of October, 1698, being much lamented of all who knew her. Aged 16 years, 11 months and 2 daies.[9]

Not long afterward Byrd was again bereaved by the death of his wife in November, 1699, at the age of forty-seven. Mary Horsmanden Byrd had been a splendid pioneer woman in spite of her very blue blood and aristocratic upbringing. Neither storms, floods, sea voyages, Indians, nor childbirth had dismayed her; and in her husband's frequent absences she had competently managed his ever-increasing household, which at the time of her death included two mansions, about twenty thousand acres of land and over a hundred slaves.

That so little has been written about her is due to her virtues, not her lack of character. For Mary lived in a time when Virginia society was organized on a patriarchal basis. The husband was head of the family, with almost autocratic powers over the whole establishment, whether it was great or small. Only bad wives were greatly noticed; a good one lived in her husband's shadow, sharing good fortune or bad, happiness or peril; bearing his children, watching over his affairs, running his household, perhaps helping him in his career, but always *inconspicuously*. Mary was a good wife to William Byrd.

Byrd's health, too, began to fail quite early. In 1700, he was excused from attendance at the Council because of a bad attack of gout. He must have been extremely lonely with no members of his family

9. John McGill, *The Beverley Family of Virginia*, R. L. Bryan Company, Columbia, South Carolina, 1956.

in his big houses, yet he never seems to have thought of interrupting his son's brilliant career in England by sending for him. The old man, like the youth he had been, was a stoic.

Byrd still kept a tight rein on the trading business and made frequent trips to the Falls to see how things were going there. His son-in-law, Beverley, describes an amusing incident of one such trip at about this time. There had been a long drought, and Byrd knew that his tobacco crop was in poor shape. However, his overseer came riding all the way to Westover to tell him it was saved. The man explained that an Indian conjurer had come to him and offered to make it rain for two bottles of rum. Seeing not a cloud in the sky, the overseer took him up, whereupon the Indian went into a *Pauwawing,* or conjuration, throwing himself into convulsive postures, straining and gasping and shouting unearthly supplications to his god. Sure enough, within half an hour a black cloud climbed up the sky and dumped its contents squarely on Byrd's lands, with only a few drops left over for his neighbors.

When Byrd next went to the Falls, the conjurer came to demand his two bottles of rum. Byrd teased him by pretending to know nothing about the conjuration. The Indian explained at great length. Byrd smiled knowingly and said, "You're a cheat. You saw that cloud coming and took advantage of my overseer."

The Indian seemed to have very hurt feelings. "Why then," he asked, "did not such a one or such a one [naming the neighbors] also have rain? For they lost their crops, but I loved you, and therefor I saved your's."

Byrd teased him a while longer, but finally gave him the two bottles of rum. He preserved his own intellectual integrity by making sure that the conjurer understood they were a free gift and not because of the bargain with the overseer.

Despite his illness, Byrd had one more public service to render, and one more ambition to achieve. The first was the assistance he gave to the Huguenots who fled to Virginia from increasing persecution by the most Catholic King Louis XIV. In 1699, three hundred of them arrived on ships furnished by King William III. The following year another two hundred came and, in all, largely as a result of the arguments presented by young William Byrd to the Board of Trade, between seven and eight hundred settled in Virginia.

The first batch were advised to settle on the south side of the James about twenty miles above Byrd's plantation at the Falls. The land was partially cleared because the once-powerful Monácan Indians had lived there. The Assembly was very sympathetic to these Protestant refugees from France, giving them large donations of money and food, and exempting them from all taxes for several years until they could make a new start.

The Huguenots were an enterprising lot, who quite soon acquired stocks of cattle which, because they bred and tended them more assiduously than the English colonists, produced more milk than was usual. They even experimented in cross-breeding them with buffalos, though this did not work. The Huguenots also raised cotton and manufactured their own clothes, and, being French, started making brandy and wine from the small wild grapes which grew profusely in the woods.

William Byrd took a tremendous interest in the Huguenots who had come with letters of introduction from his son. He was also drawn to them partly by his ardent anti-Catholicism and also because he liked to help those who so ably helped themselves; besides, it was good business. In the 1705 edition of his *History,* Robert Beverley wrote of "the Goodness and generosity of Colonel Byrd toward these distressed Huguenots."

Beverley goes on to say, "Upon their first Arrival in that country, he [Byrd] received them with all the tenderness of a Father, and ever since has constantly given them the utmost assistance . . . employing all his Skill, and all his friends to advance their interest both publickly and privately. . . . What Liberties has he not all along allowed them on his own plantations to furnish themselves from thence Corn and other necessaries? His Mills have been at their Service to grind their Corn toll-free. . . . With what Zeal did he represent their Cause to the Assembly? And with what earnestness did he press all his Friends in their favor?"

Beverley believed that the Huguenots would hardly have survived without Byrd's help because, as he cynically points out, "When several hundred Families of Men, Women, and Children are set Ashoar Naked and Hungry in a strange Land," they not only have to contend with nature itself but with the zenephobia of the inhabitants who dislike strangers and think they have come "to eat the bread out of their mouths."

According to Beverley, "All these Difficulties befell these poor

Refugees at their first Arrival there; but God Almighty rais'd up this Gentleman, not only to succor them with his own Charity, but to solicit the Liberalities of other People. . . ."

In fact, right up to the end of his life Byrd continued fighting for the rights of his beloved Huguenots in the Assembly where he favored the bill granting them title to the lands which they had settled and cleared in Monácan Town, as it was now called. They had, indeed, a powerful champion for, by then, Byrd had achieved his final ambition.

President of the Council was at that time the highest post to which a Virginian could aspire. Besides the influence its prestige brought, the office carried with it the Chief Judgeship of the court if the Governor were not present. Also, in the absence of the Governor, the President exercised the executive power of the King's Government as well. The Presidency was held neither by appointment nor election, but by seniority; the oldest Member of the Council in terms of service was automatically its President.

Old Nathaniel Bacon, senior, had been President for over thirty years, beginning long before Byrd was appointed to the Council. In 1703, he finally died, and Byrd, the senior member, though only fifty-one, succeeded to the office. Ill and exhausted though he was he must have taken immense satisfaction in it. For, even if he had been given a head start by the tangible and intangible legacies of his uncle, he had come to Virginia as an unformed youth and had won the greater part of his wealth and, especially, the confidence of his peers and of the people as well, by his own ability, integrity, sound sense, and courage. Best of all was the thought of the fine legacy he would leave his son, who, he knew, was worthy of it. The goldsmith's grandson would mingle on easy terms with the nobility of England and be welcome in the Palace of Queen Anne who, since the death of King William III, reigned in England. Furthermore, he would have money enough to do so without embarrassment, and 26,231 acres of land [10] —more than many a peer could boast.

Yet, it was a lonely old man who lay dying at Westover in November of 1704. Not that he was old in years as we reckon it, or even by com-

10. Bassett, *op cit.*

parison with such stalwarts of his time as Sir William Berkeley or
Nathaniel Bacon. He was just plain worn out. The doctors diagnosed
his ailment as gout; God knows what it really was, for that was their
universal name for any affliction of the joints and vascular system.
Perhaps they may even have been right, though William Byrd was
no high liver, and had always been more interested in getting on than
in getting drunk. In any event, he was dying and he knew it.

Besides the many slaves, there were only two people with him in
the big house he had built on the banks of the James. They were not
relatives or any of his grand acquaintances, but servants who were
also his friends—his housekeeper, Mrs. Joanna Jarrett, who had
nursed him these last dreary months, and his valet, Jean Marat, who
by his name might have been one of the Huguenots.

There was no doctor. Byrd had no more use for them than his
son-in-law who wrote: "Virginians have the happiness to have very
few doctors." Robert Beverley, who would have been with him, was
in England.

On the stormy morning of December 3, 1704, the charcoal-gray
river whipped white by wind and rain, the bare branches of the tall
trees stark above the sodden turf, Byrd suddenly knew that he did
not have much time left. He called Marat and ordered a boat sent
through the howling winter wind to Turkey Island for Colonel Randolph.[11] Randolph arrived in the winter dusk, dripping with rain and
spray from his rough passage. He found Byrd unable to move but
absolutely clear of mind.

They talked together about Byrd's will, and Randolph received
final instructions concerning a number of business matters with which,
as acting executor in the absence of Byrd's son, he would have to
cope. Once Byrd tried to raise himself to sign a codicil giving £10 to
Mrs. Jarrett, who had cared for him so faithfully, but he had not the
strength. Sometime the next morning, December 4, 1704, William
Byrd died.

William Randolph proved Byrd's will on February 3, 1705. In
it he left £100 to his daughter Susan Brayne in England, £300 to
the almost mythical Mary Byrd (Duke), and £50 to his little grandson, William Beverley. All the rest of his lands, his slaves, his mills
and ships, his money and the trading business, which had been the

11. William Randolph, the founder of the famous Randolph family of Virginia.

foundation of his fortune and which was still flourishing, he left to his son, William.[12]

Byrd was buried in the churchyard at Jamestown beside his wife, Mary, and little Nutty. Whether his son or Colonel Randolph composed his epitaph is not known. It was probably Will, for it was written in elegant Latin:

Here are buried the ashes of William Byrd, Armor Bearer of the King, and Treasurer of the Province, who exchanged this life for eternity on the IV day of December, MDCCIV after he had lived LII years.

12. *Westover Title Book.*

BOOK TWO

The Black Swan
of Virginia

I · THE EDUCATION
OF A VIRGINIA
ARISTOCRAT

WILLIAM BYRD II had grown up as an Englishman, though he never forgot that he was also a Virginian. In fact, to his mind, there was not a very sharp distinction between one and the other; for all Virginians were Englishmen, loyal to the King and claiming the same rights as his other subjects under English law, which had been imported to the colony almost intact. All attempts by royal governors, like Nicholson, to make the colonists second-class citizens were violently contested. This sense of Englishness was particularly strong in young Byrd who had spent twenty-two of his first thirty years abroad.

The little boy who sailed for England in 1681 could have had only scattered recollections, like fading snapshots, of the old Stone House which had been his Virginia home. His real home, for his first eight years in England, was Felsted Grammar School, with brief holidays spent at the Horsmandens' house at Purleigh, where his uncle, Daniel Horsmanden, was now Rector of Purleigh Church.

Unlike his sisters, Byrd evidently liked school and thrived there. His grandfather, Warham Horsmanden, had chosen Felsted because of the towering reputation of its headmaster, Doctor Christopher Glassock, as a classicist. Oliver Cromwell had sent his sons there, which hardly recommended it to a royalist like Horsmanden, but the Protector had chosen it for the same reason Horsmanden did—it was the best. William made the most of his opportunities. He drank up knowledge like a thirsty elephant. In a long life he never got enough of learning and was at great pains not to let what he had learned get rusty from disuse while reaching out for more. Had he not been inhibited by his wealth and his equally strong desire to conform to the code of what a gentleman could or could not do, he might have made an even greater name for himself as a writer or scientist than he did as a leader of the governing class in Virginia. By the time he was fifteen, he was accomplished in Hebrew, Greek, and Latin, and quite able to render a publishable translation of certain works of Petronius.

William's father yanked the boy out of the academic life in 1689. The first Byrd did not want his son to be a scholar but an all-around man. Despite his acres and his political eminence, he was also a merchant; and his son would inherit not only the plantations, which were themselves big business, but also the trading business at the Falls, which still brought in more ready cash than the crops. Then, and even into the twentieth century, the Dutch were considered the best merchants and bankers in the world; so Will was sent to Holland to learn their methods at first hand.

He did not like it. Some of his biographers have opined that it was too foreign, that he felt lonely and homesick; but that is quite out of character. Lonely he undoubtedly was, but not because of the foreignness of the Dutch. Byrd would not have been unhappy in France or Italy, meeting kindred spirits and compatible minds. More probably the Dutch bored him. They looked so dismal in their somber clothes and peaked hats; and they took everything so seriously, especially their business and their, to him, dreary Reformed religion —almost as abhorrent to a good Anglican as the Church of Rome. The naughty snap and crackle of Restoration wit, which William had already savored, was totally missing; so was the elegance he loved. The Dutch burghers were hopelessly middle class, which was just what the Byrds, father and son, were trying to escape. He wrote his father to please take him away from there.

That indulgent gentlemen quickly complied. In July, 1690, in a letter to Warham Horsmanden he said, "I have wrote to Mr. Perry to send for my son for London and there to put him into Business and let him learn what may be wanting yet to accomplish him for that Purpose." [1]

1. *Virginia Magazine of History and Biography*, Vol. 26

Young Byrd stuck out two years of clerking at Perry and Lane's. It was certainly not pleasant. The hours were long, the work was dull —sitting on a high stool copying figures into ledgers—but he undoubtedly profited by it as, in spite of his dislike of the country, he did from Holland to the extent of learning Dutch, which he kept up by reading it to the last year of his life. Byrd never let go of anything.

When the two years were up, William persuaded his father to let him read law at the Inns of Court. He had no trouble being accepted at the Middle Temple—all one needed was a knowledge of Latin, a sufficiently good social position, and £140. Byrd qualified brilliantly on the first two counts; his father cheerfully put up the money.

If Holland had been boring, and Perry and Lane drudgery, the Temple made up for it all. It was probably the gayest time of William Byrd's life. Considering his extraordinary lifetime record in these matters, it is doubtful that William had retained his virginity to this point, but forty years later he fondly reminisced by letter with his boon companion, Benjamin Lynde of Salem, who was by then Chief Justice of Massachusetts, about "the naughty jades" whose favors they had enjoyed.[2]

Apparently the Inns of Court were like an aristocratic club and reading law was secondary to raising hell all over London. Byrd's companions in profligacy included Charles Boyle, later the fourth Earl of Orrery; Charles Wager, who became First Lord of the Admiralty; John Campbell, who inherited the Dukedom of Argyll; and many other future English leaders. One year ahead of Byrd was his friend, Robert Walpole, who was to be Prime Minister of England for over twenty years (1721–41). Since Byrd never relinquished a friend except to death itself, the names of these men appear again and again throughout his life and portraits of some of them later hung on the walls of Westover. His intimacy with them was to contribute not only to his own advantage but to that of Virginia as well.

There was also in the Temple what might be called the intellectual clique, except that the first group, in addition to being great roisterers, were likewise highly intellectual. Brains were in fashion. So the second lot might be classified as men who wrote their names in history with their pens and not with the sword or politics or by inher-

2. Bassett, *op. cit.*

itance. They included the famous Restoration dramatists William
Wycherly and William Congreve, and the first great Shakesperean
scholar, Nicholas Rowe. The Inns of Court had a traditional, if unexpected, liaison with the theater. As far back as Queen Elizabeth's
day, the members had produced plays for the amusement of the
Court and amateur theatricals were a regular extracurricular activity
for generations of young law students. Association with such men as
these not only sharpened Byrd's wit, but gave him a critical appreciation of the theater which lasted throughout his life.

What with prowling the streets of London in search of naughty
jades, fencing with words, or reading *The Spectator* in the famous
coffeehouses, which were like private clubs, one wonders when, if
ever, these young men studied law. Byrd certainly did, though it
took enormous energy and a quick mind to combine it with his other
activities. In order to be admitted to the bar he had to prepare and
plead at least twelve cases before the Bencher who was assigned as his
tutor. He accomplished this rather quickly, all things considered, for
he was admitted to the bar on April 12, 1695.

Of all the friends whom William Byrd made in England, the dearest
to him was Sir Robert Southwell. Just how or where they met is not
known. Presumably they were introduced at one of the great houses
to which Byrd's companions of the Temple invited him, or possibly it
was arranged by his father or the Horsmandens. Southwell was a
much older man, who was not only Principal Secretary of State for
Ireland, but also President of the Royal Society (the leading society
of scientists of England). Southwell apparently took an immediate
liking to the young Virginian. It could not have been just his youthful charm; London was full of attractive young men. Most probably
it was due to Byrd's intense excitement about science, which topped
all his numerous other interests. This was, of course, reinforced by his
complete devotion to Southwell, who became like a father to him, far
closer and more companionable than his own father had the time to
be. Sir Robert introduced William to the best scientific minds of the
day, among them Sir Hans Sloane, with whom he corresponded for
forty years.

In 1696, when Byrd was only twenty-two, Southwell got him
elected a Fellow of the Royal Society. This was an honor Byrd treas-

ured above most of those that came to him, and he tried to pull his weight in that intellectual galley. On his return from a trip to Virginia in 1697, he contributed a paper entitled, "An account of a Negro Boy That Is Dappled in Several Places of His Body with White Spots," by Will. Byrd, Esq. F.R.S., which was published in *Philosophical Transactions XIX*. London. 1698. When he went to live permanently in Virginia, Byrd sent the Royal Society a steady flow of observations on the zoological and botanical phenomena of the New World.

Southwell's house was always open to Byrd, and the younger man repaid his friend and patron with the sort of adoration that few men ever get from the young. In a character sketch of Southwell, to whom in the fashion of the time, he gave the fictitious name of "Cavaliero Sapiente," Byrd wrote:

> While he was young he was wise enough to instruct the old and when he came to be old, he was agreeable enough to please the young. All that had the honor of his conversation, confesst that he had the peculiar talent of mixing delight with information. Religion appeared in all her charms when he was practiceing it; he had Zeal without bitterness, Devotion without hypocracy and charity without ostentation. His Principles were so firmly riveted that he was able to converse in a corrupt Court above 30 years, without any prejudice to his integrity. . . . He had a mighty fund of knowledge. . . . He was so uncorrupt, so untainted with Vice and folly, that whoever was intimate with him, had the nearest prospect of Innocence that he can ever meet without of Paradise.[3]

Forty years after Sir Robert's death, Byrd had engraved on his own tombstone that he (Byrd) had been educated in England, where, under the care and direction of Sir Robert Southwell:

> *And ever favored with his particular instructions.*
> *He made a happy proficiency in polite and varied learning.*

In 1696, Byrd sailed home to Virginia, probably expecting to remain for some time. His father was undoubtedly enraptured by his son's polish and learning, which was combined with a few aristocratic vices. Of the young man's penchant for gambling, his father said

---

3. William Byrd's *Notebooks*, University of North Carolina.

that Will gambled merely as a fashionable amusement, "avarice being a passion alien to his breast." This was just as well because the Byrds, with the possible exception of the present generation, were remarkably poor gamblers. The fashionable amusement could be costly. That sporting parson and President of William and Mary, James Blair, once recorded winning £192.8 from the younger Byrd at Westover.[4]

Immediately after his son's return, William Byrd, Sr., used his influence to have him elected to the House of Burgesses as a member from Henrico County, an early manifestation of the "Byrd Machine." He must have given his son a piece of land to qualify him. In October, 1696, young William took his seat in the old State House of Jamestown.

The first act of this Assembly was to pass a resolution castigating the recent plot in England to assassinate King William III and restore James II to the throne, as "a horrid and detestable conspiracy of Papist and other barbarous and bloody traitours in the Kingdom of England . . . ." and proclaiming that, "We whose names are hereunto underwritten, the Burgesses Assembled at James City in his Majesties Dominion of Virginia, do heartily, Sincerely and Solemnly profess, Testify and declare that his present Majesty, King William is our Rightful and Lawful King, and we do hereby mutually promise and engage to Stand by and assist each other to the utmost of our power, in the Supporting, defending and keeping this Government for his Majesty against the late King James and his adherents . . ."[5]

This Act of Association was signed by all the Burgesses. Byrd certainly signed with a will; he was fully as anti-Catholic as his father.

After this burst of unanimous loyalty the debates got more acrimonious and exciting. These were the days when Governor Andros and James Blair were contending over the funds for William and Mary and for power in Virginia. Feeling ran high against Andros, but William, a true Byrd, was on the Governor's side.

Nevertheless, by the end of the session young Byrd had made such an impression on the Assembly that, as has been noted, in the spring of 1697 they engaged him to go back to England as the legal

4. Paul Wistach, *Tidewater Virginia*, Bobbs-Merrill Company, Indianapolis, Ind., 1929.

5. Act of Association. Virginia Assembly, October, 1696.

representative of Virginia to present an address stating their hopes, needs, and discontents to the new Board of Trade which had been formed by King William to administer the affairs of the American Colonies.

One may guess that, after a snow-and-mud-bound winter at Westover with not a single peer, wit, playwright or naughty jade to pass the time with, young Byrd was delighted to be off. Besides it was a singular honor; and if he performed his function well, it could be a steppingstone to political power in the Dominion when he eventually returned to claim his heritage. For this latter reason his father, William I, must also have been pleased. Whatever sadness he felt at seeing his son sail away, he was never a man to let sentiment stand in the way of advancement.

Hardly was Byrd back in England when he received that challenging brief of which we've already heard. He was asked to defend Governor Andros against the charges brought by James Blair that the Governor was blocking efforts to improve the Virginia clergy and to build the College of William and Mary. The hearing opened before the Archbishop of Canterbury at Lambeth Palace on December 27, 1697. The atmosphere was hardly conducive to impartial justice in that huge room, hung with the purple and gold of the Established Church, with the Archbishop majestic on his episcopal throne in his splendid medieval vestments, the Bishop of London beside him, and the other prelates gathered around. James Blair was the Bishop of London's own man. Even if Byrd's case had been a good one, he would not have had a chance—but it was not.

Though he knew in his heart that he was defending a lost cause, Byrd valiantly took the offensive. Dressed in his handsomest, long-skirted brocade coat with fine French lace at his waist and throat and the long black ringlets of his periwig framing his aquiline face, Byrd conducted Andros' case with grace, wit, and ingenuity. In regard to the clergy he said that Blair had filled Virginia's pulpits with Scots, to the detriment of the Church. He charged him with unfairly accepting £150 a year from a college that did not even have a roof on it as yet. He then maintained that Andros was a true friend of the college and that Blair himself was responsible for its difficulties. He also accused Blair of exaggeration and misrepresentation, saying that he operated on the principle that if you "throw a lot of dirt some of it will stick." He added that Blair's war against Governor Andros was due to his desire "to worm him out of his government," in order to "get his righteous patron, Mr. Nicholson, to succeed him."

In answer, Blair proved that the Bishop of London had himself appointed the Scots, several of whom were actually Englishmen with Scottish names. As to the £150 pounds a year, Blair showed that he had been obliged to give up his own church living to raise funds for the college and that, furthermore, the Virginia Assembly had given him permission to accept the salary.

With the first part of his case shot down, Byrd tried to defend Andros against Blair's charges. In a ringing declamation he demanded proof that Andros had obstructed the interests of the college and had committed the other anti-clerical acts.

Unfortunately, he got proof aplenty. It was shown that Andros had systematically prevented the collection of funds pledged to William and Mary; that he had allowed people, without payment to the college, to settle on the twenty thousand acres that King William and Queen Mary had given it as an endowment. Furthermore, Andros had tried to browbeat the trustees, including Byrd's own father, into approving his actions. It was clear as daylight that the Governor had acted from spite and jealousy of Blair's growing power and prestige in the Dominion.

All Byrd's charm and eloquence did not fool the adamantine churchmen for a minute. They brought in a report that, added to other Virginia discontents, caused King William to recall Andros and replace him with Nicholson. When Byrd heard this, he prophesied that Blair would soon be at loggerheads with Nicholson.

Though Byrd lost the battle, he gained reputation. People are always sympathetic to a brilliant and courageous effort by an underdog, which Byrd surely was in Lambeth Palace. As a result, and also due no doubt to his father's valiant lobbying on the home front, Byrd was appointed Agent of Virginia at a salary of about £100 a year.

Before his new appointment came through, Byrd made a trip to France, where King Louis XIV received him at his splendid court in Versailles. Byrd was so proud of this social coup that he had the fact engraved on his tombstone, along with the reference to his patron, Southwell.

Byrd's first formal appearance in his new office was in a far more popular cause. In 1698, he went before the Board of Trade in the matter of those Huguenots who became his father's final charge. King William, bored by the conflicting clamor for the Huguenots by Virginia and North Carolina, had decided to give them a colony of their own in a swampy area of land to which both colonies laid claim. Byrd argued that this would be bad both for the Huguenots and the two colonies because the French Protestants would probably sicken and die in that forsaken hole, and because a small sparsely settled enclave between the colonies would be an open invitation to criminals and runaway slaves to seek refuge there. As to North Carolina's claims for the Huguenots, he slyly pointed out that "between a plantation belonging to ye King [Virginia] and another belonging to proprietors [North Carolina] the first ought always, in duty and by virtue of ye perogative, to be preferred." [6]

Finally Byrd grew really lyrical in describing the advantage of the fine climate and good land on the upper part of the James River and proposed that the Huguenots be settled there. (Of course he did not add that such a settlement would be advantageous to his father's business and plantation at the Falls.)

Good sense and logic prevailed. In March, 1699, King William reversed himself and ordered the Huguenots to be settled in Virginia; not, however, on the upper James, but in Norfolk County in the lower Tidewater. This did not bother Byrd a bit. Having gotten the French ordered to Virginia, he gave them a letter of introduction to his father. There the King's wishes did not have much force, and, as we have seen, the Huguenots headed straight for the upper James and settled in Monácan Town.

It was not long before Byrd was embroiled with Governor Nicholson. In 1701, the intermittent war with France was clearly about to be renewed, and the British Government ordered the colonies to prepare to defend themselves. New York, as usual, demanded that Virginia help out by sending money and men. Governor Nicholson transmitted to the Assembly an order from England that they assist New York financially, and himself fixed the proper amount at £900. Instead, the Burgesses and Council voted to send an address to the

6. Records of the Board of Trade, 1698.

King, explaining the impossibility of raising money or sending troops to help New York, which they regarded more as a rival in the lucrative Indian trade than as a friend in need.

Byrd's father sent him the address and told him that the Assembly wished him to explain the matter to the Board of Trade and carry the address to the King. While the younger Byrd was making the necessary arrangements, King William died, on March 8, 1702, and James II's younger daughter became Queen Anne. The pomp of a royal funeral and the excitement of a new reign were the talk of the mansions of his friends and the coffeehouses where he gathered with the intellectuals. At the same time Byrd was drafting a petition to Queen Anne, requesting that she allow him to present the address to her. He did not succeed in getting an audience. Instead, the Privy Council read the documents and referred them to the Board of Trade.

When Governor Nicholson in Virginia heard of the attempt of the Assembly to bypass him, he went into one of his finest furies. Not only did he refuse to sign the voucher for Byrd's salary, but he sent to London an emissary of his own, Dionysius Wright, to confound Byrd and confuse the issue. Wright succeeded in getting the Privy Council to advise the Queen to order that all communications from the colonies to the throne be sent through the royal governors. This infuriated not only the Virginians but the other colonists as well, and was a milestone on the road to revolution.

Byrd argued Virginia's case before the Board of Trade, showing that New Yorkers were always crying for help. In the last ten years they had received £2,500 from Virginia. The reason they could not keep peace with the Indians, he said, was that the New York merchants were so greedy. He humbly pointed out that the frontiers of Virginia were just as exposed as those of New York and even harder to defend because the population was scattered and not concentrated in cities. He craftily showed that if men were sent to New York from Virginia, the Queen would lose £20 per man every three months because they could not grow tobacco and fight at the same time.

But Byrd had as much chance with the Board of Trade as he had in Lambeth Palace. Later, reinforced when his able brother-in-law, Robert Beverley, came to England, he made complaint against the Governor for trying to discourage Virginians from raising cotton and flax and weaving their own clothes. Beverley said that the Governor wanted the Virginians "to go naked." Naturally the powerful London merchants, who wanted to sell to the colonists, opposed them on this issue. Byrd lost his case and his job as Agent of Virginia.

War between France and the Grand Alliance, led by England, began in 1702. The great Duke of Marlborough was made Captain General of the Allied Forces. As word came of his early victories at Venloo and Liége the young bloods of London burned with patriotic fervor and dreams of glory. Byrd evidently caught the fever and thought seriously of joining the army, with a commission of course. In a self-portrait he described himself as "charmed with the Glory of serving in the Army and thought it a shame for a fellow to live at home in ease when the Libertys of Europe were in danger, but before he had provided his Equipage, he was discourag'd by the confinement, dependence and barbarity of that service." [7] Whether this means that he had actually undergone training or only heard about its rigors is not known. But he had almost committed himself to serve under one of his noble friends and only extricated himself in a subservient letter in which he pleaded that his uncle, Daniel Horsmanden, had begged him not to go, and that he must obey his uncle's wishes. It was a fine piece of hypocrisy, as Byrd was never known to give up doing anything simply because his uncle Daniel wanted him to.

In the summer of 1703, Byrd went down to Oxford to see "The Act," when the candidates for degrees read their theses in public. From his account of it, the students were even more raucous than those of today. They sneered at the masters and their wives in far from witty lampoons and were apparently as filthy in body as in mind. Byrd wrote, "I was perfectly Sick of the confusion and impertinence of the place and thought every day a Month 'til I cou'd return hither to my hermitage." [8]

Hermitage was hardly the *mot juste*. Throughout this entire period Byrd was constantly involved with women. He was a strikingly handsome man, tall and very slender—he only weighed one hundred forty pounds. His features were almost classically perfect

7. Byrd *Notebooks.*
8. *Letters to Facetia.* Published privately by Thomas Fortune Ryan in 1914.

and in his portrait of this time Godfrey Kneller has caught the glint of devilment in his eyes. He was intensely passionate and uniformly successful—except when he was really in love. He was constantly falling in love. As he wrote of himself: "Never did the sun shine upon a Swain who had more combustible matter in his constitution than the unfortunate Inamorato. Love broke upon him before his Beard, and he cou'd distinguish sexes long before he cou'd the difference between Good and Evil. . . . 'Tis well he had not a Twin sister as Osyris had, for without doubt he would have had an amourette with her in his mother's belly. . . ." [9]

However combustible Byrd may have been, he never fell seriously in love with a girl who was not well born and reasonably rich. In these cases he was extraordinarily unsuccessful which, considering his charm, would be hard to believe had he not explained the cause himself. In the remarkably frank self-portrait which, in a curious mixture of Italian and French he called *Inamorato L'Oiseaux* [10] (Enamored The Bird), he wrote that when he was looking for a wife, "he'd work himself violently in love with some nymph of good sence. . . ."

He goes on:

And when he was in love no man ever made so disingageing a figure. Instead of that life and gaiety, that freedome and pushing confidence which hits the Ladys, he wou'd look as dismal as if he appear'd before his Judge, and not his mistress. Venus and all the Graces wou'd leave him in the lurch in the critical time when they shou'd have assisted him most. When he ought to have had the most fire he had the most flegm. . . . He wou'd look like a fool, talk like a philosopher when both his Eys and his Tongue should have sparkled with wit and waggery. He wou'd sigh as rufully as if he sat over a dead friend and not a live mistress.

No wonder this awkward conduct was without success.

Whenever his bashfulness gave him leave to declare his mind something wou'd rise in his throat and intercept the untimely Question. A Woman is more at ease delivered of a huge boy, than he was of the painful secret. His Ey-balls wou'd roul with as much gastliness as if he had been strangled. 'Twas melancholly to see how his heart panted, his spirits fluttered, his hands trembled, his knees knockt against one another, and the whole machine was in deplorable confusion. You may

9. *Inamorato L'Oiseaux*, Byrd *Notebooks*.
10. *Ibid.*

guess how ingageing a Declaration must be that was attended with so many sorrowful symptoms. It moved the nymph to pity at least, if it cou'd not move her inclination. If she cou'd not be kind to a man to whome she had created such disturbance, yet she cou'd not forbear being civil. Thus whenever Inamorato lost a mistress, he got a friend by way of equivalent, and so Providence made a good Bargain for him when he wou'd have made a wofull one for himself. . . .

The principal object of Byrd's affection in 1702–03 was the Lady Elizabeth Cromwell. She was the only child and heiress of the fourth Earl of Ardglass, Viscount Lecale and Baron Cromwell. At the time Byrd was courting her, her father died, leaving her £2,000 a year. She called herself the Baroness Cromwell because, though the earldom and viscounty descended only through the male line, she believed that the barony was not so entailed. Later she found she was mistaken about that. In his letters Byrd called her "Facetia" and signed himself "Veramour" which could be translated as Truelove.

Lady Betty appears to have been a gay and charming person, though a bit wild as so many Restoration ladies were. She had a sparkling wit. Byrd did not have much difficulty "working himself up" to being violently in love with her. So were half the beaux of Queen Anne's Court.

Byrd was nothing like as laggard in his letters to his loves as he was in person. Early in 1703, he wrote to Facetia: "The minute your coach drove away, Madame, my heart felt as if it had been torn up by the very roots, and the rest of my Body severed limb from limb. I cou'd not have shed a Tear, if I might have gained the Universe. My Grief was too fierce to admit of so Vulgar a demonstration. . . ." [11]

Veramour wrote fifteen such passionate letters to his love. He also wrote an extraordinary piece entitled *To Facetia in the Bath* when his love was at Bath, the famous English watering place, which apparently was only slightly more moral than the Baths of Caracalla. The letter begins:

The Bath had need be prepared with all the sweets you mention to protect you from being offended by your own perspiration just as the elegant Mr. S-ms lys with his head in a sweet bag to secure him from the Incence of his own F--ts. How can you or the Tawny Nymphs that are with you in the Bath pretend to be Ivory Palaces, when each of you is an eye-witness how great a shade nature has cast upon your skins?

11. *Letters to Facetia.*

The Learned Dr. Burgess hath lately prescribed a Bath to the female saints of his flock to wash the dirt off their imaginations; this wou'd be of sovereign use to you & your companions. . . .

For myself I can give it under my hand that I am as sweet as any one can be that perspires 4 Pounds a day, because you know I make vigorous love to a lady with a Nose truly Roman that smells as quick as a Vulture, tho for very different ends, this to pursue, but she to avoid any thing like carrion.

Adieu.

What a love letter! And yet, according to his own account, when, on a country weekend, his host repeated rumors of some scandalous adventure of Lady Betty, Byrd leaped to his feet and burst forth in impromptu verse:

"By heaven and earth and that one God that formed
This beauteous world, each word you've spoke is false.
And spawned of hell that cursed forge of lies,
Where spiteful fiends contrive with pois'nous breath
To blast the Fame of Saints they can't corrupt." [12]

Having delivered himself of this mouthful (which he probably thought up afterward), Byrd mounted his horse and galloped furiously back to London in the middle of the night.

Lady Betty turned Byrd down. Perhaps his ineptitude when he was with her was the cause, though she was probably after bigger fish. She found one in the person of Edward Southwell, Secretary of State for Ireland and son of Byrd's dear friend and Patron Sir Robert Southwell. She married him that summer.

Despite his ardent passion for Facetia, Byrd took it lightly. He wrote of himself: "The miscarriage of an honerable amour never disturb'd him so much, but that he wou'd sleep and look much better in his dispair than he did in the hottest of his Expectation. He was not in half the jeopardy of hanging himself when he lost a mistress that he was while he was in danger of getting her. . . ." [13]

At any rate, he wrote a charming letter of congratulation to the bridegroom in which he said, "I firmly believe your Joys will outlive the common Term of conjugall Happiness, because the Nymph you have married has variety enough to satisfy the inconstancy of any

12. *Ibid.*
13. *Inamorato L'Oiseaux.*

man liveing. She comprehends all the agreable qualitys of her sex and consequently will give you neither provocation nor excuse to go abroad for change." [14]

So they all remained good friends and Byrd often went to their hospitable house. However, the remembrance of his passion and her present kindness did not prevent him from writing her asking for the repayment of some money he had lent her. The letter was couched in his most flowery style with protestations of eternal love and admiration and was signed, "Your Slave." It was nevertheless a dun.

Having lost his job as Agent of Virginia and lost his love (and probably several more as well), Byrd was at a loose end, and so thoroughly bored with the diversions of London that even such amusements as the raffish theaters and St. Bartholomew Fair, with its three-legged chickens and three-breasted women, failed to lighten his mood. He wrote that the Fair had "got together such a frightful collection of nymphs that one would swear . . . that they're all Citizens' daughters lawfully begotten. . . ." [15]

The letter that came from Virginia in the winter of 1705, telling him of his father's death, was opportune, though sad. Even in death the old gentleman obliged his son. Byrd dallied yet awhile in London and then sailed for Virginia.

14. Byrd *Notebooks.*
15. *Ibid.*

II · LORD OF WESTOVER

WILLIAM BYRD II sailed up the James River in August, 1705.
The trip was quite different from his father's first arrival. Instead of a
hammock in the hold of the ship, he was undoubtedly accommodated
in a cabin in her towering carved and gilded poop, as became a gentleman of distinction who owned 26,231 acres of land and nearly two
hundred slaves. It was full summertime when the trees were heavy
with leaves and the fields were golden with wheat or dark green with
tobacco plants full-leaved and tall. He probably landed at his own
dock to be greeted by his people and walk across the lawn and
through his English garden to the big, comfortable wooden house his
father had built.

There were, however, certain drawbacks. For one, Byrd, having
been away so long, had no real friends except Robert Beverley, who
had been with him in London. Acquaintances, yes; the planters, especially those with unmarried daughters, were eager to entertain him,
and their sons were anxious to hear the latest gossip from London
and get on good terms with this very rich young man. For wealth is a
magnet that draws the wellborn as strongly as the ill-bred. Friendship takes longer.

Another source of annoyance was the "disorder" in which he
found his estate. For eight months it had been neglected because

Colonel Randolph was too busy with his own affairs to do much more than prove the will. Byrd took matters strongly in hand. The overseers of the different plantations were brought up sharply; lazy slaves were well whipped. Byrd made a thorough study of the condition of the land and the crops thereon. He made many trips to the Falls and reorganized the trading business, refurbished his mills and planned new ones, and generally set matters to rights in an efficient, businesslike way.

Most irksome of all, the Lord Treasurer of the Colonies required Byrd to file a complete re-audit of his father's seventeen years' accounts as Receiver General and Auditor of Virginia. Thanks to his boring experiences in Holland and with Perry and Lane, he was able to do it; and thanks to his father's integrity, the accounts came out right to the penny. Governor Nicholson, in the last weeks of his tenure, and also some members of the Council had suspected, and probably hoped, that there would be discrepancies, but Byrd was able to show that the only money owed by his father was for the current year's quit rents and even this was covered by his bond.

Byrd had already been confirmed in his father's place as Receiver General of the Dominion by Queen Anne on April 2, 1705, but through the machinations (as Byrd regarded them) of some fiscal reformers in England, the post of Auditor was separated from it despite the objections of the Council. It was only sensible not to have a man audit himself, but this reduced the income of the Receiver General to only 3 per cent, which was pretty poor pay—less than £75 a year. By complaining bitterly for ten years Byrd finally got the fee raised to 5 per cent.

Byrd also attempted to get his father's seat on the Council, but the Board of Trade remembered him too well to give it to him. He had to wait nearly four years for memories of his energetic defense of Virginia's interests to fade a bit before he achieved this ambition.

Byrd found life in Virginia rather dull at first. He wrote to Sir Hans Sloane at the Royal Society about how little intellectual stimulus he found. There were, he said, no scientists. There were a few men "that are called doctors, but they are generally discarded surgeons of Ships who know nothing above very common remedies. . . ."[1] He

1. *William and Mary Quarterly*, Vol. I, p. 86, 1921.

added that ignorant newspapers described the country as being very unhealthy because there were so many cases of ague (malaria). But, said Byrd, "they are due, in my opinion, to the intemperance with which the people eat fruit."

Despite the dissolute life he led in England, and in Virginia, too, when opportunity offered, Byrd took great care to keep his body in fine condition. Throughout his diaries almost every morning he notes, "I danced my dance," which was some sort of setting-up exercise. That first winter he swam in the James at least twice a week, sometimes running across the snow-covered lawn of Westover and plunging in through a skim of ice near the bank. He firmly believed, and told all his friends, even his girls, that cold baths would infallibly make one proof against catching colds and prevent attacks of ague and fever. According to Byrd they would even cure headaches and give you a fine, ruddy complexion—which last they really do. His neighbors thought he was crazy, but his glowing health and the absence of the perennial colds from which they suffered almost convinced them he was not.

Actually, their first impression was correct, for Byrd was a health faddist. He had strong notions about diet and in an age of gargantuan meals would rarely eat more than one or two courses at dinner because he felt that mixing different kinds of food was worse than mixing liquors.

He also prided himself on his knowledge of medicine. At his death his famous library at Westover contained one hundred and thirty volumes on the subject. He studied them assiduously, and prescribed for all his friends, his family and his slaves, and, of course, himself. His cures for various ailments were not only far worse than the disease, but it is a wonder anyone survived them. An example is a letter to an English friend, who had contracted a venereal disease:

"'Tis a sad story you tell, my Lord. . . . Certainly your wayfareing Phillis must have carry'd a terrible sting in her tail to leave so much poison behind her, or else your Physician must have taken an improper method with you. . . ." After philosophizing on the moral lesson to be learned from "the vast disproportion there is between 3 months pain and one minutes pleasure," he describes the cure: ". . . All the loathings and revilings when you swallow half a dozen Pills in a morning. Don't forget the mortification of Water gruel and soup Maigre, of Balsom, and injections of Basilicum, Sapis Infernalis, & Diet-drinks. . . ."

"Adieu" [2]

For lesser ills Byrd always prescribed "a vomit" and "a purge." He was convinced of the efficacy of bleeding and when he finally got through treating someone, the poor patient had lost everything in his stomach and his bowels, and half his blood. One of the few slaves who ever ran away from him was a Negro youth who was taken ill and fled because he feared his master would try to cure him.

Byrd's greatest medical fad was his faith in the roots of ginseng as a universal panacea. He probably first heard of it through delving into Chinese medicine, as their doctors were great believers in its curative powers. He took it constantly and recommended it to all his friends. Doubtless its demulcent effect on inflamed tissues made him feel temporarily better after a dose of this bitter powder. At the age of sixty-one he expressed the hope of living many years longer with the aid of ginseng. However, he said, it was useless as an aphrodisiac.

With nothing much in the way of diversion and a strong sense of the years going by—he was thirty-one—Byrd was quite frantic to enjoy the comforts and serenity of marriage, and to provide an heir to Westover and all that went with it. Hardly had he arrived in Virginia before he was working himself violently in love again. As usual the object of his passion was well born and, so he thought at the time, rich. She was Lucy Parke, a daughter of Colonel Daniel Parke, who had recently become the fashionable hero of Queen Anne's Court.

Colonel Parke was a violent man, a rapscallion in peace, but a paladin in war, as so many rapscallions are. He came to Virginia and married Jane Ludwell, whose father, Colonel Philip Ludwell, was a member of the Council and had an estate of forty thousand acres, which he had acquired by adding a zero to the grant of four thousand acres which was rightfully his. Parke's behavior hardly made him popular in the Dominion. He was such a notable adulterer that James Blair preached a sermon in Bruton Parish Church in Williamsburg of the evils of adultery directed straight at him. The next time Parke went to church he saw Mrs. Blair sitting alone in Lady Berkeley's pew by her invitation. Parke rushed up and dragged the

2. Byrd *Notebooks.*

poor lady screaming out of the pew, shouting that she had no right to sit there.

This finished him with Virginia society. The icy solitude in which he found himself decided him to return to England, leaving his wife and two daughters in Virginia. Then came the war with France. Parke wangled a commission as aide to the Duke of Marlborough. At the Battle of Blenheim his performance was so valuable and his conduct so heroic that the Duke made him his envoy to bring the news of that great victory to Queen Anne. Parke's fortune was made. The least the Queen could do to show her appreciation was to make him governor of a royal province. There was talk of him being appointed to Virginia. Fortunately for the Dominion, the Queen decided to appoint him to the Leeward Islands. This suited Parke quite well as the Islands had even greater opportunities for graft, and he knew how the Virginians felt about him.

By the time Byrd met Lucy Parke, just after he returned to Virginia in August, 1705, the glory of Blenheim had refurbished her father's reputation. She and her sister, Frances, who was engaged to John Custis of Arlington on the Eastern Shore of Chesapeake Bay, were living with their mother at the Parke plantation on Queens Creek near Williamsburg. Lucy was truly beautiful; brown hair framing an oval face with a slender aquiline nose and slightly tilted eyes. Her voluptuous mouth gave a clue to her passionate nature. As far as one can see in her portrait, her lovely flesh was shaped to man's desire. Byrd did not, in truth, have to work himself up; he just let himself go.

In his courtship letters, Lucy was Fidelia, he again Veramour. They followed his usual artificially ornate style, but perhaps it had a greater impact in Virginia where the beaux were not so highly polished as at St. James's:

" 'Tis above a month by Loves calendar since I had the happiness to see you & methinks the sun loiters in his course. . . . Oh how I grutch the time I am obliged to bannish myself from Fidelia! but I must not call it liveing when my heart is 40 miles off. It will be still a fortnight before I shall come to life again. . . . Pray give your sister as many Kisses as there are lys told at Court and I will thankfully repay you with interest. . . ."

Evidently Byrd saw Lucy two weeks later, probably at the wedding of her sister to John Custis. In his next letter he chides her about being able, in public, "to counterfeit indifference" too well or else have very little love for him. However, she seems to have warmed up in private, for he discreetly says, "After you had the goodness to give me that cordial, my blood began to circulate and my pulse to beat. . . ."

Again he writes of watching two amorous turtle doves and says, "I cant forebear enjoying these innocent lovers for the blessings they enjoy of being always together, while I, poor I, must lament the want of my dear, dear Turtle for many days." [3]

Nor would it seem that Byrd was as inept a lover in Lucy's presence as he had formerly described himself to be. The conditions of courtship were nothing like as straitlaced in early eighteenth-century Virginia as they later became. The young people played kissing games and romping games that warmed their blood; and there were walks in moonlit gardens with no one to see them but the statuary. These two passionate young people had plenty of opportunity and undoubtedly made the most of it. Soon they were unofficially engaged; public betrothal must wait for Colonel Parke's consent.

Dutifully Byrd wrote to him. He made no secret of his love for Lucy, but strongly implied that he expected a generous marriage settlement. Somewhat condescendingly he wrote:

Since my arrival in this country I have had the honour to be acquainted with your Daughters, and was infinitely surpriz'd to find young Ladies with their accomplishments in Virginia. This surprize was soon improv'd into a Passion for the youngest for whom I have all the respect and tenderness in the world. However, I think it my duty to intreat your approbation before I proceed to give her the last testiment of my affection. And the Young Lady her self, whatever she may determine by your consent, will agree to nothing without it. If you can entertain a favorable opinion of my person, I dont question but my fortune may be sufficient to make her happy, especially after it has been assisted by your Bounty. If you shall vouchsafe to approve of this undertaking I shall endeavor to recommend my self by all the marks of kindness to your Daughter. Nobody knows better than your self how impatient Lovers are, and for that reason I hope you will be as speedy as possible in your determination which I passionately beg may be in favor of

Your & C.[4]

3. *Ibid.*
4. *Ibid.*

Colonel Parke in London, preparing to start for his governorship of the Leeward Islands, was speedy enough. He knew all about Byrd's splendid fortune and position in Virginia, and was obviously delighted to have his daughter marry so advantageously. Perhaps he enjoyed the fact that many a one who had snubbed him would have to acknowledge her superior position now. He dashed off a letter giving his consent and promising to give Lucy a dowry of £1,000. This cost him nothing as he never paid it.

William Byrd and Lucy Parke were married on May 4, 1706, less than nine months after his return to Virginia. Byrd's various biographers have called it an unhappy marriage. Certainly Lucy was a tempestuous and neurotic young woman, given to furious tantrums. On one occasion Byrd had to intervene to save her personal maid whom she was belaboring with the fire tongs, and she branded another slave with a hot iron. In fact both Parke girls were spoiled and temperish. Poor John Custis of Arlington had a wretched life with Frances. On one occasion they had a violent quarrel when out driving. In a rage he turned the horses' heads toward the banks of Chesapeake Bay. "Where are you going?" she demanded.

"To hell, Madame!"

"Drive on!" she said. "Any place is better than Arlington."

Age did not soften John Custis' bitterness. On pain of disinheritance he forced his son to engrave on his tombstone:

Beneath this Marble Tomb lies The Body of The Hon. John Custis, Esq. Age 71 years and yet lived but seven years which was the space of time he kept a bachelor's home at Arlington on the Eastern Shore of Virginia.

If Byrd did not find the comfort and serenity he sought in marriage, he got something better. Though he and Lucy fought continually—again and again in his diary Byrd notes, "I quarrelled with my wife"—she never bored him. Her swiftly changing moods were such that, as he had written to Edward Southwell about Facetia, she had "Variety enough to satisfy the inconstancy of any man." Not that she entirely cured Byrd's inconstancy. He continued to have flings with married women and serving girls, but he never stopped loving Lucy. They were both intelligent and gay. Between battles, they read to each other, walked together of an evening in their lovely garden enjoying the flowers and the hummingbirds and the tranquil view across the silver river. She was as ready as he to welcome the platoons of friends who came in six-oared barges rowed by Negroes in livery, by coach, on horseback or on foot to enjoy the flowing hospitality of Westover; and she was equally delighted to exchange country pleasures for the balls, races, and spicy conversation of Williamsburg.

Best of all was their sexual compatibility. Lucy was as hot-blooded as he, ready to make love anytime in any place. The note in the diary, "I rogered[5] my wife," occurs with extraordinary frequency. Most of their numerous quarrels ended, as matrimonial differences should, in a passionate embrace. One passage in particular exemplifies this:

July 30, 1710.
I rose at 5 o'clock and . . . read two chapters in Hebrew and some Greek in Thucydides. I said my prayers and ate boiled milk for breakfast. I danced my dance. . . . In the afternoon my wife and I had a little quarrel which I reconciled with a flourish. Then she read a sermon in Dr. Tillotson to me. It is to be observed that the flourish was performed on the billiard table. . . .[6]

For the first three years of his marriage William Byrd played no great part in public affairs beyond performing his duties as Receiver General of Virginia. He was extremely busy straightening out the tangled affairs of his inheritance and acquiring more land, for which he was even hungrier than his father. Aside from the prestige it gave, Byrd was firmly convinced that land was the only safe investment because everything else was perishable; ships could sink, goods be stolen, and buildings might be destroyed by earthquakes, but the land remained. To work the additional properties that he purchased Byrd had to buy new slaves. In June, 1710, he mentions the arrival at Westover of twenty-six for whom he paid £23 apiece. So his estate in land and humanity increased.

On July 16, 1707, Lucy gave birth to their first child, a daughter whom they named Evelyn. She became the legendary family heroine

5. An early eighteenth-century euphemism probably because a ram was called a roger, hence the verb "to roger."
6. *The Secret Diary of William Byrd of Westover 1709–1712.* Edited by Louis B. Wright and Marion Tingling. The Dietz Press, Richmond, Virginia, 1941.

of the Byrd family. Her father was devoted to her from the first, and may have spoiled her. When she wet the bed at the age of two, he whipped her nurse, Anaka, for allowing it, but not Evelyn.

Early in September, 1709, Lucy was again expecting to give birth. Her labor pains began on September 5. Byrd hastily sent for two neighbors, Mrs. Richard Hamlin and, his wife's cousin, Mrs. Benjamin Harrison, who lived at nearby Berkeley. At ten o'clock he went peacefully to sleep, although matters must have reached the crisis stage in Lucy's downstairs bedroom. At one o'clock someone knocked on his door and he was awake "in a blink." He met Mrs. Harrison on the stairs and she told him it was a boy, "Thanks be to God Almighty!" They all drank some French wine together and Byrd went back to bed.

On September 28, the boy was christened Parke Byrd after Lucy's father. Captain John Roberts of H.M.S. *Southsea Castle* and Captain Cook of H.M.S. *Garland,* who happened to be staying at Westover, were his godfathers, and Mrs. Betty Harrison his godmother. Byrd prayed: "God grant him grace to be a good man."

On September 12, 1709, between the birth of little Parke and his christening, Byrd rode to Williamsburg where he was sworn in as a member of the Council of State, taking the prescribed oath of loyalty and obedience to the Crown and secrecy as to the Council's proceedings. He was idealistically aware of the responsibility he was assuming, for he prayed that God might grant that he distinguish himself with honor and good conscience. Then he took his seat in the paneled Council Chamber.

The splendid new Capitol, despite the beauty of the building and its luxurious furnishings, must have been extremely uncomfortable in cold weather. The Council and the Burgesses were so terrified of being burnt out that there were no hearths to warm it. However, the perquisites of membership in the Council were well worth temporary discomfort. By the time of Byrd's appointment, its power had greatly increased. After the recall of Governor Nicholson, popular Colonel Edward Nott had been appointed Lieutenant Governor. He died in 1706 after serving only one year. In the Williamsburg churchyard the Assembly erected a fine marble monument to him, for which Byrd wrote an elegant epitaph.

Governor Nott was not replaced until 1710. During that four

years Colonel Edmund Jennings, President of the Council, was Acting Governor. With one of their own as chief executive there was no check on the Council's powers, except the Burgesses, many of whom owed their elections to one or another of its members. The Councilors made the laws, executed them, and judged themselves. No one could touch them. Furthermore, they were nearly all related to each other either by blood or marriage, and were not likely to vote against their own interests. As James Blair said in 1707, some of the Councilors had for years tried to reduce the royal governors to a cypher, "And in truth they have in effect gained their point."

The lack of a royal governor did make for tranquility in Virginia politics, and it was during this peaceful era that William Byrd took his seat on the Council. Hardly was he there, than ambition vaulted higher than any Virginian had ever yet aspired. Apparently with the tacit consent of his fellow Councilors, he wrote to Colonel Nathaniel Blakiston, who held his former place of Agent of Virginia in London, to offer Lady Orkney, wife of the absentee Governor of Virginia, £1,000 if her husband would appoint him Lieutenant Governor of Virginia. Lord Orkney was willing—Byrd was undoubtedly the highest bidder—but the Duke of Marlborough ruined the deal by decreeing that no one but a soldier should have the government of a plantation. Byrd was bitterly disappointed, but simply noted, "God's will be done." [7]

However, letters from England cheered him with the news that the Bishop of Worcester believed that in the year 1715 Rome would be burned, that before 1745 the popish religion would be routed out of the world, and that by the year 1790 "all the Jews and Gentiles" would be converted to Christianity and the Millennium would begin. [8]

Nevertheless that was a sad spring at Westover. Many of Byrd's friends were dying—first Uncle Thomas Bird, who had come to Virginia in his old age; then Captain Ned Bolling and another "pretty young" man of smallpox. Benjamin Harrison, their neighbor at Berkeley, was very ill. In February, Lucy had a miscarriage. Byrd wrote that she was so melancholy it made him weep.

Mr. Harrison rapidly got worse. On April 4 the Byrds went to see him and found him so ill that Byrd sent his wife home and sat up

7. Byrd also tried for the governorship of Maryland and was turned down.
8. *Secret Diary* (March 31, 1710).

with his old friend all night. Six days later Benjamin Harrison woke early in the morning and quite clearly asked that the door of his room be opened because he wanted to go out and could not. At the moment the door was opened he died.

The Byrds and all the neighbors and relations gathered at Berkeley for the funeral where they were first served "plentifully" with wine and cake. At exactly one o'clock the cortege started for Westover Parish Church while the ship *Harrison*, lying off Berkeley, fired a gun every half minute. Even in these melancholy circumstances Byrd cynically noted that the minister made an extravagant panegyric in which he not only overlooked all Harrison's failings but endowed him with virtues he had never possessed.

In the soft days of early June the worst blow of all fell upon William and Lucy Byrd. On the morning of June 3, they woke at six o'clock and were told their son was very ill. In his diary Byrd wrote: "We went out and found him just ready to die and he died at 8 o'clock in the morning. God gives and God takes away; blessed be the name of God."

The entry for that day ended almost as usual, "In the evening I neglected to say my prayers, had indifferent health, good thoughts and good humor, thanks be to God Almighty."

Lucy was not as philosophical. All day she wept bitterly while the neighbors came to mourn with her. In the evening she walked sadly with her husband in the rain-sweet garden while he tried to comfort her. Three days later they buried little Parke in the graveyard of Westover Church. The rain poured down so hard that the little group of mourners huddled in the portico of the church while the minister stood alone by the graveside reading the service.

The whole sad three days are described in Byrd's diary in the most matter-of-fact fashion, interspersed with comments about what he ate, the business of the plantation, and the visitors who came. It is a strange thing, perhaps typical of the dawning "age of reason" in which sentiment was suppressed and intellect was all, that a warm and passionate man like William Byrd should have treated the death of his only son and heir so casually. His diary was really secret— written in shorthand supposedly never to be read—so he could have expressed his real sorrow if he felt any, without fear of violating the code of self-control which was the fashion. It is impossible to believe that he was not deeply grieved, nor was he cold-hearted. So the only conclusion must be that either he achieved such a remarkable degree of intellectual detachment by sheer will power in the face of real tragedy that he was able to suppress his emotions, or that he found it impossible to commit his feelings to paper even secretly.

III. LIFE AND LOVE AT WESTOVER

COLONEL ALEXANDER SPOTSWOOD was appointed Lieutenant Governor of Virginia in the spring of 1710. He arrived off Kiquotan with two men-of-war on June 21. That day William Byrd was frightened by seeing in the sky a "flaming star," which he considered a bad omen. The next morning he rode for Williamsburg in the rain, but when he crossed the Chickahominy River on the ferry, he heard that the new Governor was at Green Spring—now owned by his wife's uncle, Colonel Philip Ludwell, II. So he rode to Green Spring, whose great hall, nearly one hundred feet long, was filled with company come to welcome the new Governor. Colonel Spotswood greeted him very courteously, saying that some of Byrd's English friends had recommended him. Byrd decided that Spotswood seemed a good man. (This was the start of the long association between Governor Spotswood and William Byrd, beginning in friendship, degenerating into enmity and ending in friendship again when two old men could reminisce nostalgically of battles long ago.) That evening they danced a sprightly minuet while slapping at swarms of mosquitoes which poured through unscreened doors and windows.

The next morning Byrd bribed Spotswood's valet to shave him, then mounted his horse to join the rainbow cavalcade of ladies and gentlemen who escorted the Governor to Williamsburg. Outside of town they were met by the President of the Council and most of the inhabitants, who flowed after them to the Capitol with cannon firing salutes, pipes squealing, and general rejoicing. The Governor made a charming speech to the Council in which he spoke of his desire to be of service to the Queen and to the Dominion, and hoped that they would aid him in his design. In fact, all the royal governors of Virginia, even the last unfortunate one who fled for his life in the night, were thus warmly welcomed, though most of them were later vilified as they tried to carry out the arbitrary orders of successive British governments and to increase the power of the Crown over the colonists. In Spotswood's case the honeymoon lasted over three years, which was almost a record.

This was due to the fact that an Indian war in North Carolina kept him too busy to try to exercise any royal prerogatives. The Tuscarora Indians had gone on the warpath in that colony, and the North Carolinians were screaming for help from Virginia. As usual the Councilors were not inclined to waste their money and men on rescuing a sister colony, though the House of Burgesses took a more sympathetic attitude. Governor Spotswood sided with the Council, preferring to spend the money putting Virginia's defenses in order rather than wasting it trying to defend the North Carolinians whom he considered scum.

Byrd completely agreed with Spotswood. Both of them regarded the North Carolina Assembly as an utterly worthless group of radicals. Spotswood wrote to the Board of Trade that their election had been made possible by "a defect in the constitution" of the colony, which allowed every man who could purchase half an acre of land a vote equal to that of a gentleman with a large estate. Such a democratic state of affairs was regarded by Byrd much as the Constitution of Soviet Russia is looked upon by the D.A.R.

When, in 1713, the North Carolinians managed to massacre most of the Tuscaroras, Governor Spotswood came forward as a mediator and made peace between them. This was the high moment of mutual admiration between the Governor and the Council, which asked Byrd and William Cocke to draw up an address praising the Governor for his remarkable diplomacy and wisdom.

During this prolonged era of good feeling, William Byrd was on intimate terms with Spotswood. Byrd was frequently in Williamsburg because he took his duties as a Councilor very seriously and hardly ever missed a session or a court. He always dined with the Governor or went with him to inspect progress on the beautiful Georgian residence which was slowly taking shape at the head of the Mall. Spotswood lovingly supervised every detail. He called it "my house," but the townspeople, who thought it wildly extravagant, called it the "Palace," which became its official name. Though imposing, it was not that grand; several plantation houses were larger.

On September 20, 1710, Governor Spotswood came to stay at Westover. Byrd neglected both his prayers and his reading of the classics that morning as he bustled around, making preparations for his important guest and sending his man, John, out to shoot some bluewings for supper. At about five o'clock in the afternoon the sound of guns on the river heralded the Governor's approach in Captain Richard Burbydge's eight-oared barge. Byrd hurried down to the dock to receive him and his party. As Spotswood stepped ashore Byrd "gave him three guns."

They strolled across the tree-shaded lawn and all drank wine together in the house. Then Byrd and the Governor walked in the garden, which was dressed in its fall finery of yellow chrysanthemums and late roses. There was a fine supper of bluewings.

Byrd had been made commander in chief of the militia of Charles City County and Henrico County, so the next morning some of the militia officers came to Westover and they all rode out to review the men who were mustered in a pasture. Just as they started, a heavy shower began, but this did not deter Spotswood. He reviewed the militia in a downpour, then formally presented Byrd to them as their colonel and commander in chief. Afterward all the officers were invited back to Westover. As many as could sit at the big dining table stayed for an excellent dinner; the rest made do with a hogshead of punch in the churchyard.

On the twenty-second, the company were again on horseback, riding in fine weather upriver toward Henrico County where that militia were mustered at Colonel Randolph's plantation. They made a good showing, drawn up in line in their fringed hunting shirts with bell-mouthed muskets sloping over their shoulders. Spotswood drilled them for over two hours, and then, lining them up, presented Byrd as their commander in chief. This time, in the sunshine, the troops gave him a spontaneous hurrah, which delighted him.

All the officers dined with Colonel Randolph. Byrd supplied a hogshead of punch, which he says made them "drunk and fighting all the evening," but no great harm was done.

On the third day of the visit, it was the turn of the French. They came to Westover to have the Governor mediate some quarrel among themselves, which Spotswood straightened out peremptorily. Then the French militia company went through the drill so well that the Governor made them dragoons (mounted infantry) on the spot.

The fourth and final day was Sunday. Byrd rode the short distance to church with the Governor in the coach. Lucy, furious that there was no place for her, sulked in her room. Byrd brought a large group of gentlemen home for dinner. Lucy, after "much persuasion," relented and came to the table with them.

These were the most serene days of Byrd's early life, though a spice of excitement was provided by Lucy's wild moods. One day she would be gentle and melancholy, the next riotously gay and loving, and two days later in a black fury, whipping her maid or ordering other house servants beaten, quarreling with her husband, and threatening to commit suicide. Sometimes he gave her cause as when he romped with Mrs. Charles Chiswell and kissed her at least twenty times, but mostly it was just Lucy's temperament. Once she was angry when he spent an evening talking Latin, which she could not understand, with the Reverend Mr. Dunn. Frequently she did not have even that much cause. On the whole, Byrd handled her with remarkable tact and self-control combined with saving humor; for he truly loved her, and she him. When she threatened to commit suicide, Byrd took it as a joke; he knew she loved life too well.

One thing that upset him greatly was that Lucy refused to be bled when she was ill, but this again was because he loved her dearly.

Despite—or because of—his tempestuous wife Byrd found life in Virginia much pleasanter than before his marriage. In addition to the many guests at Westover and the rounds of visits to neighboring plantations, there were the frequent trips to Williamsburg which was far more amusing than it had been when he had served in the House of Burgesses in 1696. When the Assembly was sitting—which was called "The Public Times"—life was very gay. People had dinner parties and balls almost every night. In October, 1710, the Byrds went to Bruton Parish Church to the christening of Lucy's sister's son, Daniel Parke Custis; Governor Spotswood was the child's god-father. Daniel was destined to become famous by association because he became the first husband of Martha Dandridge, who after his death married George Washington. It was Custis' money that enabled Washington to live in splendor at Mount Vernon.

Genial Governor Spotswood was constantly entertaining at impromptu dinners for men, or formal balls at which Lucy sparkled in all her beauty. She loved Williamsburg and always wanted to be in the latest mode. The Byrds had one tremendous quarrel just before they started for Williamsburg in February, 1711, when Byrd found Lucy plucking her eyebrows. He forbade her to do it, and she said in that case she would not go to the capital with him. In his diary Byrd remarked complacently that he got the better of her and asserted his authority. It is more likely, however, that Lucy had been bluffing.

They spent that night with the Custises at Queens Creek. Byrd had a frightful cold. Though Frances Custis dosed him with sage tea, he had a bad night and woke up feeling too ill to go to Williamsburg for the Governor's ball. Lucy promptly offered to stay with him, which so touched him that he resolved to go if possible. He got up, shaved with a very dull razor and, feeling terrible, started off for Williamsburg on horseback; his wife followed in a coach.

It was well worth the struggle. Like many gregarious people Byrd felt better the moment he got in good company. The ladies arrived; they had a fine supper at the Governor's house and then went in coaches through the pouring rain to the Capitol, which was ablaze with candles, with an orchestra fiddling gaily. Governor Spotswood opened the ball with Lucy in a graceful French dance. Byrd, proud of his wife's beauty, had a glorious time dancing and flirting with all the ladies. Late in the evening the orchestra struck up quick country tunes and they all danced the violently active square dances until, wet with sweat and limp with laughter, they went to another room for a magnificent collation of sweetmeats. At two in the morning it was still pouring, so Spotswood gallantly carried the ladies to their coaches.

Another new amusement at Williamsburg was the races on a course sponsored by that gay churchman, James Blair, who added improving the breed to his other multifarious activities. He was partly responsible for importing some famous thoroughbred sires from England. But Blair also had his cross to bear. Mrs. Blair, the former Sarah Harrison, was a chronic alcoholic. Byrd noted in his diary on March 2, 1709, that Mrs. Blair was drunk, which, he said, was growing pretty common with her, and her relations disguised it under the name of "consolation."

They were a hard-drinking, high-gambling crowd in Williamsburg in those early days. Even the professors at William and Mary were seen drinking and gambling all night in the taverns. Of course, with that example, the students were as rowdy as they could be. On Sunday everybody sobered up and went to Bruton Parish Church; for churchgoing was obligatory by law unless a man had a good excuse, which Byrd frequently found for himself.

In church the congregation sat solemnly in the white-painted pews which they bought or inherited. The Governor occupied his crimson-curtained box with the royal arms above it. The slaves were accommodated in a balcony to the left of the chancel and visitors had one on the right. At the back of the church another balcony was reserved for students of William and Mary. When the service began, a deacon locked them in. There they all sat, Governor, Councilors, Burgesses, planters, riff-raff, slaves, and students for three or four hours while the Reverend James Blair conducted the service, and then, from the high, carved pulpit preached an endless sermon, exhorting them to abstain from the very sins he might have been committing the night before.

It was during this period of serene public life and gay private parties that Byrd, because of his elegance and dash, was called "The Black Swan of Virginia." But even then he had major and minor vexations. One of the latter was an attack of piles with Lucy dutifully "annointing my bum" with soothing ointment. Much more serious was an event which led him into one of the few really stupid actions of his life. He made very few blunders, but when he made one, it was colossal.

On April 12, 1711, Byrd belatedly heard of his father-in-law's death in the Leeward Islands the previous December. Colonel Parke's arrogance, tyranny, and immorality had finally proved too much for the usually submissive Islanders. They rioted, not against England but against him personally, and one of them shot him in the head. Byrd was truly saddened by the news. He broke it as gently as he could to Lucy, and comforted her by the specious argument that Parke had been killed by his enemies to prevent his making their villainy known in England.

A far worse blow came when Byrd read a copy of his father-in-law's will, at which time he probably began to sympathize with the Leeward Islanders. Colonel Parke left all his rich holdings in the Leeward Islands to Lucy Chester, his illegitimate infant daughter by Mrs. Edward Chester, whose complacent husband was agent for the Royal African Company in the Islands. All Parke's lands and money in England and Virginia were left to Frances Custis, but against them were charged his colossal debts. He left Lucy Byrd only £1,000, for which, Byrd said bitterly, "I thank him very much."

Lucy did inherit half the lands in York and James counties, which Colonel Parke's father had left to him for life and then to his heirs who were Frances Custis and Lucy Byrd.[1]

Despite Byrd's fury, his relations with the Custises remained very friendly. In November, they met in Williamsburg and agreed amicably about the division of Grandfather Parke's lands. A little later Frances gave her consent to selling some of Colonel Parke's lands and Negroes to pay his debts. But it was all too pleasant to last. The following year the real nastiness of Frances' disposition began to show. She went back on her agreement to sell the lands, which inspired a quarrel with Byrd in which her husband joined.

However, when the extent of Parke's debts became partially known, it was evident that the real estate would have to be sacrificed. The sale of it required permission of the Assembly, which duly passed an act giving assent.

To use one of Byrd's favorite phrases he was "subject to severe gripeing" at the thought of all that lovely land going out of the family. He wrote to Micajah Perry of Perry and Lane to learn the exact amount of Colonel Parke's debts. Perry replied that they amounted to £6,130.[2] Meanwhile the rift with the Custises was made up and in February, 1712, Byrd rode with them from Williamsburg to inspect the Parke lands at Mount Folly—well named as Byrd found out. They spent the morning riding over the fields which were lush and fertile, well fitted for raising cattle. They ate a picnic lunch of cold roast beef and went on to Colonel Henry Duke's plantation to spend

1. *Westover Title Book*
2. *Virginia Magazine*, Vol. XX.

the night. The Colonel was hospitable, "as far as he was able," but he had only one bottle of wine.

Over that meager potation Byrd proposed to John Custis that he and Frances deed over the Mount Folly lands, the Skimino mill, and the Negroes to him in return for which he would assume all Parke's debts. John and Frances Custis were agreeable to this.

It rained all the next day and Byrd spent most of it figuring up his profits on the proposed purchase, and sitting in front of the fire with the Custises, discussing details of the deal. Byrd's judgment was badly warped by the land-hunger from which all the planters—and he in particular—suffered. The fact that those fair acres had actually belonged to his wife's father and should have been part of her patrimony undoubtedly added an emotional pressure, an anger in his soul, that further clouded his reasoning.

That evening Byrd drew up the document that was to plague him for the rest of his life, and the following morning he and the Custises signed and sealed it:

That said John Custis and Frances his wife shall by sufficient conveyance give all the land, houses, mills and slaves to said William Byrd and his heirs forever which are mentioned in an act of the Assembly. . . .

That everything continue in the plantations to the use of said William Byrd. . . .

That all tobacco sent to England and all tobacco already made . . . and not yet sent to England be and remain to the use of said William Byrd.

That all effects of any sort now in England remain to the use of said Byrd which did belong to the late Collo. Parke. . . .

In consideration thereof said William Byrd doth hereby oblige himself, his heirs, executors, and administrators to pay all the debts due in England from the late Collo. Parke and charged upon his Virginia estate by his last will and testament and thereof shall discharge the said John Custis and Frances his wife and their heirs forever . . ." [3]

Some faint premonition of disaster caused Byrd to add a memorandum to the effect that if any new Parke debts were found *in Virginia,* he and Custis would each pay half. If he had only left out the words "in Virginia"!

Having signed his soul away, Byrd galloped gaily home to Westover to tell Lucy that he had acquired her share of the Parke

3. *Westover Title Book.*

lands. To his amazement Lucy was not pleased. Some instinct, or perhaps a better knowledge of her father's unreliability, informed her that her husband had made a fool of himself.

It was not long before Byrd found out that Lucy was right. In 1713, a further accounting arrived from Micajah Perry, showing Parke's debts to be £8,510—£2,380 more than Byrd had bargained for—which caused him severe "gripeing." Whether or not Perry had deliberately understated the debts originally in order to get them off his hands or had been honestly mistaken no one knows. One thing was quite clear and became even clearer as still further debts turned up: William Byrd had been badly victimized. He immediately applied to the King for leave of absence to go to England to straighten out his confused affairs.

In 1712, the Byrds' second son, Philip William, was born and he died the same year. Lucy had no luck with her boys.

Despite his intimacy with Governor Spotswood, Byrd stood up to him whenever he thought it necessary. An early occasion had been at the Council meeting of December 15, 1711, at which a money bill concerning taxes was sent back from the House of Burgesses who had refused to accept some important amendments proposed by the Council. Several Councilors announced that the Governor wished the bill passed even though the Burgesses had refused the amendments.

With the Governor presiding from his thronelike chair, Byrd rose to say in his most courtly manner that though he must oppose this action he was very ready to oblige the Governor "in anything in which my honor is not concerned."

Spotswood bore no grudge. He and Byrd walked to his house together where Byrd ate boiled mutton and drank French wine until eight o'clock.

A few days later a more serious difference came between them. The Burgesses wanted to levy extraordinary taxes in order to raise £20,000 to be used by the Governor for defense against the Tuscarora Indians and to help the North Carolinians. Byrd strongly opposed the whole idea and remarked to some of his friends that no Governor ought to be trusted with £20,000. Naturally this was repeated to Spotswood, who was furious with Byrd and treated him coldly for the next month. They finally made up, but it was the first rift in their friendship.

The real trouble began over the quit rents of two shillings a hundred acres. As Receiver General, Byrd had been receiving them through the sheriffs of the counties and their deputies who visited the plantations to collect them. Tax dodging was as favored an occupation as in modern times, and the rich, as always, were more efficient than the poor. Through various subterfuges and bribery, many a great plantation paid less than those a third their size. Though the sheriffs were landed gentlemen, the deputies were the highest bidders for the job, so they in turn could easily be bought. Nor were the gentlemen entirely scrupulous. For their own purpose they might inflate their land patents to ten times their original acreage as Ludwell had; but when it came to paying taxes, they deflated them right down again. Another fringe benefit of the Councilors was that the taxes were also payable in tobacco. They could buy it at a discount for six shillings a hogshead and use it to pay their taxes at the going rate of twenty shillings a hogshead.

In 1713, Governor Spotswood demanded a change in the system of tax collections. He said that the existing method was "the grossest mismanagement and the most fraudulent collection of quit rents that was ever known in the revenue," and he offered to prove it, though he did not question the moral integrity of either Byrd or Lucy's uncle, Philip Ludwell, who was Auditor. Byrd agreed that the system needed changing and proposed a plan for appointing four deputy receivers, who would be responsible to the Receiver General—himself —and swear to their accounts before the Auditor. In Byrd's words, Spotswood sneered at the plan, and proposed his own, which was to have the sheriffs collect the quit rents at places appointed by the county courts instead of on the plantations. The sheriffs were then to settle with Byrd at Williamsburg.

After a great deal of discussion and hot words the two plans were presented to the Council in 1714. Here, among his friends, Byrd suffered a staggering defeat: His plan was voted down and the Governor's accepted with only Byrd and Ludwell voting against Spotswood.

That determined Byrd to go to England, not only on the matter of Colonel Parke's debts, but to counter Spotswood's by now open enmity at the source of power, before the Board of Trade and the King himself.[4]

4. Queen Anne died in 1714 and was succeeded by the Elector of Hanover who became King George I.

IV · "PEOPLE DIE STRANGELY . . ."

IN LONDON, Byrd took up his old life almost where he had left it ten years before. He found pleasant lodgings on Beaufort Street off the Strand, with two menservants to look after him, and resumed his round of gaiety with old friends and many new ones. He was welcome at the Court of King George, frequently going to Kensington Palace in the country just west of London where the King preferred to live, although formal court functions were held at gloomy St. James's Palace overlooking the Mall.

The business of Colonel Parke's debts kept Byrd busy going down to the city to consult with old Micajah Perry and his son Richard against whom he seems to have born no grudge despite the misinformation they had given him as to the amount due. More debts kept turning up. In one "gripeing" letter Byrd remarks that he had already paid off £1,000 more than the original estimate. Parke seems to have borowed money from everybody. For the next ten years Byrd continued to pay considerable sums on his account to various noble ladies who dunned him. The debts were, at least, another entrée to London society, for these ladies felt it was only courteous to entertain him in return.

Byrd's increasingly bitter relations with Spotswood do not seem to have injured his standing in London. Soon after his arrival the

Board of Trade sent for him to ask his advice about a war which had broken out between the Yemasee Indians and South Carolina. Byrd told them bluntly that it was the fault of the avaricious South Carolina merchants, who not only cheated and robbed the Indians, but treated them insolently and seduced their women by trickery and even by force.

Among those who threw their houses open to Byrd were his old friends, the Duke of Argyll, who gained new laurels as commander of the King's Army which at the Battle of Sheriffmuir early in 1716 defeated the pro-Stuart Scottish rebels; the Earl of Orrery; John Percival, now Lord Percival; distinguished old Horace Walpole and his nephew Sir Robert Walpole; Sir Charles Wager, and the Southwells. At the Royal Society, Byrd renewed his scientific interests, and the theater was a source of constant delight to him.

In the autumn of 1715, Byrd received the news that he had another daughter whom Lucy had christened Wilhelmina for her absent lord.

With his usual tremendous energy Byrd was conducting not only his own intricate business affairs but also combating a serious threat to Virginia's finances. The new King, pressed for money as all the monarchs of England were until the time of Queen Victoria, tried to get his hands on the surplus revenues of the Dominion. At the request of the Virginia Assembly, Byrd went before the Board of Trade in August, 1715, to argue against this grasping policy, which had been attempted in no other colony and might set a precedent for all.

He conducted the case with logical argument seasoned with the wit and irony so evident in his writings, pointing out that the Dominion's only sources of revenue were the two shillings a hogshead tax on tobacco and the quit rents on land, which together produced only about £5,000 income. Since the expenses of the colonial government were £3,500 the surplus of £1,500 should, he said, be kept in the Dominion as a reserve for defense in war and other emergencies. Spotswood surprisingly backed him up, though like Nicholson he objected to the Assembly's bypassing him and wrote the Board of Trade that they should grant the petition but only as coming from him and not from Byrd. The Board of Trade ruled favorably and the money stayed in Virginia.

Other important cases were coming up, and Byrd realized that his position in England was seriously compromised by the conflict of interest occasioned by his office of Receiver General of Taxes of Virginia. He had been thoroughly bored with the job ever since the Council had accepted Spotswood's plan for collecting the quit rents over his own. He wrote to John Custis that the holder of the office must either fawn on the Governor and do exactly as he was told or else have so much trouble loaded on him that it was not worthwhile: "In short a man must be either his dog or his ass, neither of which stations suits in the least my constitution." [1]

Putting the office up for sale, he found a bidder in John Roscowe who paid him £500 for it. Thus unencumbered, Byrd was able to attack two more of Spotswood's pet projects, which the Governor had pushed through the subservient Assembly of 1714. The first provided for the payment of debts in tobacco in lieu of currency. This had the effect of making all creditors gamblers in the tobacco market without hope of profit, for if tobacco was high, they were paid in money, if low, they got tobacco. They lost either way. The second act provided for the formation of a company to have all rights to the Indian trade. Byrd attacked both these laws before the Board of Trade with vigor; he was probably even more effective on the latter because his inherited trading business was still flourishing. He succeeded in getting both enactments repealed in 1717, thereby contributing to the welfare of Virginia—and his own.

Despite all his activities in the affairs of the Dominion, the Parke debts, and his brilliant social life, Byrd was lonely. In 1716, foreseeing that his stay in England would be prolonged, he sent for Lucy. In this he went against the advice Colonel Ludwell had sent him from London just before he left Virginia. In a letter to his son, Ludwell wrote: "If Will Byrd comes to England advise him not to bring his wife, people die strangely of ye small pox." [2] By that Ludwell meant that native-born Virginians translated from the pure country air of their habitat to the fetid atmosphere of London fell easy victims to the disease.

Lucy arrived in England in the late summer of 1716. She fitted

1. Custis Letters. Virginia Historical Association.
2. Ludwell Papers. Virginia Historical Society.

into Byrd's brilliant world as though she had always lived in it. His aristocratic friends were enchanted by her beauty and spirit, and by her high delight in all the pleasures of London, which familiarity had blurred for them. To see their world anew through her ecstatic eyes was to savor it afresh. Byrd was bursting with pride at her success and Lucy was happier than she had ever been.

Then came a dreadful day, November 23, 1716, when Lucy woke with "an unsupportable" headache and fever. The doctor who examined her took Byrd into another room and gravely told him that Lucy had smallpox. They consulted as to whether she should be told. Byrd made the difficult decision that in good conscience he must tell her so that she might be prepared to face the God in whom they both fervently believed.

One can imagine the fearful anxiety with which he went to her bedside and as gently as such news could be given told her of her danger. Lucy took it gallantly. She was so full of vitality and the joy of living that she did not believe she would die, either then or throughout that long day. In twelve hours she was dead.

Stripped of the affectations of the age by shock and sorrow far more piercing than he had felt at the death of his son, Byrd wrote heartbrokenly to John Custis, telling him the circumstances of Lucy's death. "Gracious God," he wrote, "what pains did she take to make a voyage hither to seek a grave! No stranger ever met with more Respect in a strange country than she had done here from many persons of distinction, who all pronounced her an honor to Virginia. Alas! how proud I was of her and how severely am I punished for it. . . ."[3]

The loss of his wife threw Byrd into a cycle of moral degradation combined with an absurd propensity for falling in love. He was a man who must have women and he took them in high places and low, from the drawing rooms of his friends to the house of assignation called the "Bagnio." Once he called upon a lady known to history only as Mrs. A-L-C. Finding her not at home he "committed an uncleanliness"[4] with her maid, and when Mrs. A-L-C returned, rounded out the evening by going to bed with her. Frequently the

3. Bassett, *op. cit.*
4. *The London Diary.*

irresistible urge came on him late in the evening and he would rush into the street to find a woman, any woman, and, perhaps, "roger" her under the shrubbery in St. James's Park. His regular mistresses were Mrs. A-L-C, who was an amateur; Mrs. A-L-N to whom he gave two guineas a time; and Mary Wilkinson, who also washed his shirts.

But even at his lowest ebb Byrd maintained constant contact with his fine friends; energetically forwarded the interests of Virginia before the Board of Trade and the Court of Requests; and seldom failed to say his prayers, thanking God for His blessing and asking His forgiveness for his almost daily sexual sins, which were, in fact, a release as necessary for his physical well-being as the exercises he continued to perform every morning.

Byrd's juvenile romantics reached a ridiculous climax in his passion for Mary Smith in 1717–18, when he was forty-three years old. The Black Swan of Virginia temporarily became the gray-haired goose of London.

Miss Smith was about twenty-four years old, though she claimed to be twenty. She was the daughter of John Smith, Esquire, a rich merchant and a commissioner of excise, who lived in Beaufort Houses, a fashionable apartment house—then called a "tenament"—right across the street from Byrd's lodgings. Mr. Smith belonged to the new oligarchy that was profiting from England's expansion of trade, and marrying its daughters to members of the old aristocracy —a happy custom that enabled many noble families to live in luxury until the twentieth century when the daughters of American millionaires took up the burden of supporting them.

Mary's father also had pretensions to gentility, for the Smiths were an ancient heraldic family from Lincolnshire. Mr. Smith was extremely proud both of his coat of arms and his wealth, and expected his daughter Mary to make a great match, even though she was getting on in years by the standards of the time. Her sister, Anne, had married Lord Dunkellen, eldest son of the Earl of Clanricarde.

Incidentally, back in 1702, Byrd had engaged the College of Arms to look up *his* pedigree and certify his right to the LeBrid coat of arms, which he used thereafter. Two hundred and twenty-five years later his descendant, William Byrd of New York, did the same thing.

Byrd met Mary Smith at Lady Calverly's house in 1716. He was much taken with her, but, as he put it, "being a married man at that time I cou'd go no further than admire her." [5]

However, within two months of Lucy's death, on January 15, 1717, Byrd wrote the first of a long series of passionate love letters to "Sabina" as he called her and signed it, as usual, "Veramour." In his diary he referred to her as "dear Miss Smith."

That letter was the beginning of a strange romance that lasted for sixteen months. From the windows of his flat Byrd could see the front of Beaufort Houses and the windows of John Smith's apartment. Day after day he must have sat looking down at the street waiting for Mary to come out. It was her custom to smile and wave to him. Nourished by this pleasant amenity, a few chance meetings at the play or some party at mutual friends, and no more than five letters from Sabina, Byrd's romantic love flamed higher, perhaps, than Dante's for his Beatrice with almost as little concrete substance to feed upon. He rhapsodized about her "enchanting form," her humor, and her charm. He posed the rhetorical question, "Tell me, my Dear Sabina, if you could reproach a man for adoreing a Damsel with such irrestible Qualities?" And added, "This is the Picture of the enchanting Nymph that fills all my thoughts by day, and my Fancy by night. . . ."

Knowing that her father disapproved of him, Byrd wrote in invisible ink by arrangement with her. The first effort was a dismal failure as Miss Smith was unable to bring the message to light with her "Decyphering Elixir." Later they appear to have perfected the device.

By July 2, 1717, Byrd was so far gone from his customary cautious attitude toward matrimony as to write that to prove her fortune had nothing to do with his suit, "I declare that I would even marry you tho your Gaoler should be so hard hearted as to deny his Consent, and then T'is a plain case you wou'd not be worth a splendid shilling."

Even in his distraught condition he realized that this was going rather far, for he added, "If an act so very heroique be not sufficient to convince you, I must pronounce you more unbelieving than a free thinker." [6]

5. Letter to John Smith. Byrd *Notebooks*.
6. Byrd *Notebooks*.

Miss Smith turned down Byrd's "very civil offer" because, she said, she would not break the Fifth Commandment and would never marry without her father's consent.

Byrd's letters became more and more passionate if that were possible. Sabina sent them back unopened and finally told him he should write no more and "be wise if you can."

That did not discourage Byrd in the least. He kept on writing of his love and despair. Miss Smith played him like a trout. Some letters she sent back, some she received, and some she even answered. Her occasional replies, months apart, threw Byrd into paroxysms of joy. He swore again and again that she could trust him absolutely, he would never show her letters or even speak of them to anyone.

It is difficult to comprehend Mary Smith's attitude; probably she did not understand it herself. That she was strongly attracted to Byrd is shown by the fact that she refused several other good offers of marriage and that she even advised him to address his letters to her maid to avoid her father's eye. Yet she often cruelly sent his letters back unopened. On the whole she displayed a great deal more common sense than he.

Finally she got tired of his high-flown nonsense and on January 23, 1718, a year after their correspondence began, gave him some blunt advice: "Supposing this Billet to be as Romantick as all the rest, I did not think it worth a sincere woman's while to decypher it. I desire you, if I have any interest in your heart, not to pursue your address in this distant manner: but if you must attaque me, let it be in the forms. A woman is no more to be taken than a Town by randome shot at a distance, but the Trenches must be opened and all the approaches must be regular . . . [then] Tis possible the Garrison may capitulate, especially if the terms be offered that are honourable. 'Tis a sad case when a swain is so intolerably dull, that his mistress must prescribe her own method of being taken. . . ."

Then she advised Byrd to see her brother-in-law, Lord Dunkellen, who was sympathetic, and get him to negotiate this important affair. She ended this remarkable letter by the tart comment: "I expect you'll make the most of this hint, for when a mistress gives her lover [7] advice, she never forgives him if he don't follow it. Adieu." [8]

7. The words "mistress" and "lover" did not have their modern connotations in 1718.

8. Byrd *Notebooks*.

Byrd took the hint or rather obeyed the command. He opened up the trenches and brought up his heaviest artillery. Not only did he begin conversations with Dunkellen, and ask Colonel Blakiston to speak in his favor, he somehow even persuaded his old enemy, ex-Governor Nicholson, to promote his cause with the obdurate Mr. Smith who in Byrd's letters is called "Vigilante." In Leveridge's Coffee House he and Dunkellen concocted a letter to "Vigilante" in which Byrd stated that he owned forty-three thousand acres of land (he had nearly doubled his inheritance), about 220 slaves and "prodigious quantities" of livestock. His income from it varied between £1,500 and £1,800 a year, which he said would be greatly increased if he went home and attended to his own business, though he was willing to promise not to go back to Virginia. He offered to settle his whole estate on Miss Smith except £4,000 for dowries for his daughters, Evelyn and Wilhelmina. As Byrd figured his net worth to be about £33,000 this was a handsome offer.

Lord Dunkellen agreed to be his messenger and advocate. Late in February, Dunkellen took the letter to Mr. Smith one evening. At the opening of his remarks poor Dunkellen suffered such a blast of fury as left him pale and shaken. Smith said that in his opinion "an estate out of this island is little better than an estate on the moon and I wouldn't give a Bermingham groat for it."

Then he reviled Dunkellen for daring to propose such a chimerical match, and spoke darkly of treachery. He would not even read poor Byrd's carefully composed letter.

Dunkellen reported this fiasco to Byrd at Leveridge's, but urged him not to despair as Miss Smith was working on her father. This was confirmed by a letter from Sabina herself.

From then on love's course was down hill all the way. As his hopes faded, Byrd became quite frantic. He wrote to Micajah Perry and tried to borrow £10,000 to settle on Mary Smith. The wise old merchant refused to let him have it.

Byrd was terrified that Mary's father would insist on her marrying someone else. He wrote to her of his fears and his hopes that she would refuse any other match. He even wrote the script for that dramatic scene:

In the very infancy of it [such a proposal] for God's sake throw yourself at his [her father's] feet, and with gushing tears intreat him in terms like these: *I conjure you, sir, by all the tender regards of a Parent to take Pity on me. If you have any respect for the life or any care for the happiness of your child, I beg, I beseech you not to force my inclinations. While you disapprove of any Person I will not marry him though it cost me my life, but on the other side I hope you will never force me to marry a man I cant love. That would involve me in the blackest perjury. . . . I beg you therefor, my dearest Father on my bended knees, if you wont please indulge me in marrying the man I like, that you will permit me at least to mourn away my life in solitude, so that I mayn't make any body miserable but myself.*[9]

Then Byrd asked if his love did not think that such an appeal would touch her father to the quick, soften his obstinacy, and disarm all his resentment.

There is no reason to suppose that Mary Smith went through this absurd charade. Instead she again forbade Byrd to write to her and sent him a message by Lady Dunkellen that she had abandoned hope of softening her father. On March 31, she sent her cousin John Orlebar, a Master of Chancery, to call on Byrd to tell him not to trouble her any more. Byrd received his message with taciturn dignity, "but when he was gone I cried exceedingly."[10]

At this point Byrd became completely demented. All honor cast aside, he wrote Orlebar, describing all the encouragement Miss Smith had given him and the letters they had exchanged. On Lady Dunkellen's advice he continued to write frantic letters to his love, which she returned unopened.

Now his worst fears were realized. On April 26, Dunkellen met him at Will's Coffee House and told him that a proposal to Mary's father had been made by Sir Edward des Bouverie. Sir Edward was a baronet with a rumored fortune of £20,000 a year.[11] Evidently this was too much for Mary's constancy. When Byrd saw her in church next day, she refused to look at him, but blushed in great confusion.

Then on April 29, 1718, Mr. Smith sent Byrd a message that he wished to see him. Downing a whole quart of champagne to raise up his courage, he marched across the street to Beaufort Houses, the only time he ever entered his love's home.

That was a curious confrontation, not as violent as might have

9. *Ibid.*
10. *The London Diary.*
11. In his *Notebooks* Byrd calls his rival "The Chevalier de Booby."

been expected, rather a long discussion in which Byrd repeated almost word for word all the encouragement Mary had given him until at last her father admitted that Byrd had indeed been led up a primrose path. But that made no matter; Mr. Smith was still adamant.

Byrd promised not to oppose the match with Sir Edward.

As Byrd was leaving, he heard the old gentleman rush into the next room and shout at his daughter, "You bitch! You jilt!"

That was not the end of it. On May 5, Lord Dunkellen told Byrd that everything was agreed upon about the marriage settlement. Apparently Dunkellen was still on Byrd's side, for he met him twice that day, and appears to have advised him to move at once or all would be lost. Byrd saw his rival in Will's Coffee House and "dispised him."

The next day he wrote a horrible letter to Sabina, accusing her of leading him on and then betraying him; yet desperately hoping she was too much a woman of honor to go through with her marriage to Sir Edward. Mary showed the letter to her father.

Possibly as a result Sir Edward and his friend, Captain Maurice Wynne, called on Byrd on May 8. They had a long conversation in which Byrd told all in a last desperate hope of discouraging his rival. According to the diary, Sir Edward admitted that Mary was all wrong, but said he intended to go through with the marriage. The meeting led to gossip of a duel between the two men, but this seems to have had no foundation. In a final frenzy Byrd wrote to Sir Edward, repeating all his accusations for the record and ending bitterly: "However I assure you Sir I must own myself much obliged to Mrs. Smith for being so charitable to me as to cure intirely the wounds of her Eys by the imprudence of her Behavior in imitation of the Viper that cures by the Virtues of its flesh the dead bite of its teeth. This makes me easy at least in missing her as you can be in marrying her, and I shall esteem it as just a compliment to wish me joy in loseing as to give it you upon gaining so extraordinary a Prize. I am & c." [12]

So ended the extraordinary affair of Miss Smith. One cannot feel that the poor girl was as dishonorable as her lover chose to think on the basis of the meager encouragement she gave him. Rather that she was pulled and torn between a strange, almost snakelike attraction he had for her and parental duty. Byrd in his inflammatory condition

12. Byrd *Notebooks.*

read far more into everything she did and said than was in it. At the end he seemed almost insane, yet all that time he had continued his normal life, his rounds of noble houses, his work for Virginia; his lechery.

Once cured, he was, as he wrote of himself, relieved, and hardly appreciated the irony of the ultimate result. Mr. Smith spent £1,500 upon his daughter's trousseau and wedding. On the day before her marriage, Smith made his will, leaving his estate equally divided between his two daughters. On July 8, 1718, Mary Smith married Sir Edward des Bouverie in Somerset Chapel. On July 10, 1718, John Smith, Esquire, dropped dead.

Byrd's diary laconically reports:

July 8.

I wrote a letter to Mrs. Perry about the marriage of my mistress, Miss Smith, who was married this day. . . .

July 11. "My neighbor, Smith, died last night. . . .

V · THE CROWN & THE COUNCIL

EVEN WHILE Byrd's passion for Mary Smith was at its peak, he was deeply engaged in a new controversy with Governor Spotswood. Early in 1718, Spotswood was moving vigorously to increase the prerogatives of the Crown in Virginia and Byrd needed all his faculties to combat him. The immediate threat was Spotswood's insistence on his right to appoint judges of oyer and terminer, who would have the power of life and death over Virginians. Back in 1710, in the honeymoon period, the Council had assented to some such arrangement; but as Spotswood attempted to carry it out, they realized the danger. Council and Burgesses alike resolved to fight it. In the spring of 1718, the Assembly met. They fired Colonel Blakiston, who was considered subservient to the Governor, and elected Byrd once again Agent of Virginia in London. Spotswood vetoed the bill, but the Burgesses agreed to pay Byrd's salary out of their own funds.

On November 17, 1718, Mr. James Craggs, one of the principal secretaries of state, officially presented Byrd to the King as the Agent of Virginia. Byrd kissed the King's hand in the traditional ceremony at St. James's—and made another enemy. Lord Orkney, the figurehead Governor of Virginia, was furious. In the King's drawing room immediately afterward, he flew at poor Craggs for daring to do such a thing. Byrd looked on in apparent unconcern, and then went to a tavern and ate hog's feet for supper. Needless to say, when the news reached Virginia, Spotswood was even more enraged than Orkney.

Meanwhile Byrd had presented an eloquent memorial to the Board of Trade against allowing the Governor of Virginia to appoint the judges. He argued that the earliest laws of the colony and the Royal Charter granted by King Charles II expressly forbade it. Furthermore, all criminal cases, by common usage, had been judged by the Council and the Governor, an arrangement which, he said, was founded on reason and justice because the councilors were appointed by the King himself, whereas the other judges would be appointed only by the Lieutenant Governor, "without the advice of anybody, for a particular time and—it may easily happen—for a particular purpose."

Finally he pointed out that governors were "not in the least exempt from human frailty, such as a passionate love of money, resentment against such as presume to oppose their designs, partiality to their creatives and favorites, and many other passions to which men in power are more subject than other people. . . ."[1] Therefore, he said, no man should be given such absolute power over the lives and liberties and whole estates of the King's subjects.

Despite Byrd's logical argument he lost the case; yet, in the end, it was won. The King ruled that the Governor had the power to appoint the judges; but Spotswood was so appalled by the anger this aroused in Virginia that he promised the Assembly not to appoint anyone but councilors as judges. It was a major victory for liberty in America.

But Spotswood had already decided to get rid of Byrd.

In the autumn of 1717, Byrd had brought his ten-year-old daughter Evelyn to England. She arrived "very safe in the care of Captain Wray." It seems strange that he should have taken the risk in view of Lucy's death. However, in his opinion it was so important for Evelyn to have the advantages of an English education, and to acquire the polish that only London society could give, that he considered it well worthwhile. In fact, two years later he asked his friend

1. *Calendar of Virginia State Papers* (edited by William P. Palmer). Vol. 1, pp. 190–193. R. F. Walker, Supt. of Public Printing, Richmond, Virginia, 1875.

Captain Isham Randolph [2] to bring three-year-old Wilhelmina to London. The little girl also made the voyage safely in friendly Captain Randolph's cabin, though she caught "the itch" on the voyage. Randolph offered to keep her in his London house, where Mrs. Randolph, "a pretty sort of woman," would take care of her until she recovered. Byrd gave Captain Randolph twelve guineas for bringing her over.

Neither of his daughters lived with Byrd in London. In his rather small apartment they would have driven this finicky bachelor wild and also indubitably would have dampened his gay life. So he boarded them with respectable families. However, he did not neglect them. Every few days he called on Evelyn and either took her to the park or out to dinner—the noon meal—with one of the ladies at whose houses he was welcome. When Evelyn was thought to have smallpox, he rushed to her bedside regardless of the danger, and was on hand every day until it proved to be a false alarm.

Despite the collapse of Byrd's love affair with Mary Smith and the increasing bitterness of his struggle against the machinations of Governor Spotswood, the summer of 1718 was a gay one for him. On May 15, 1718, just a week after his final break with Sabina, he went for a lovely picnic down the Thames with his cousin Daniel Horsmanden, Jr.; two pretty Horsmanden cousins, Ursula and Susan; Sir Wilfred Lawson and two misses Sands, chaperoned by a Mrs. O-r-t-y. As they were towed down the quiet river in a barge drawn by six horses, followed by a boatload of provisions, they were "very merry," playing commerce and other games. For lunch they had ham, chicken, and salmon. They saw Dagenham Breach where a flood had formed a sandspit half across the river, and walked off their lunch in Greenwich Park. They floated home by starlight, eating lobster and tongue, which they washed down with burgundy and champagne. It was ten o'clock by the time they landed at the Tower Stairs.

Byrd decided to splurge a bit that year. He ordered a "chariot," or coach, made to his order by a leading coachmaker. The chariot was delivered on June 15, a thing of beauty in which Byrd took as much

2. One of the seven sons of William Randolph of Turkey Island.

pride and pleasure as any twentieth-century Byrd ever enjoyed in a brand-new Cadillac. It was certainly as costly, for a description of a similar vehicle notes that it had "a body neatly carved and run with raised beads and scrolls, the upper panel covered with neats leather, japanned and highly polished with plated moldings and painted crest and arms on the doors' panels." The inside was lined with superfine light cloth, windows were made of the best polished plate glass with mahogany shutters. The whole great structure was slung on leather straps to strong iron axle trees.

Proud as a peacock Byrd drove to church at Somerset Chapel in this splendid equipage drawn by six hired horses. The weather was clear and warm, the wind from the west. He drove on to lunch with Mrs. U-M-S and then to drink tea with Edward Southwell[3] and his wife. After tea he invited Southwell to drive in the Park with him. Pride fell mightily. The coachman was dead drunk. Byrd noted that he set the man down at White's Chocolate House[4] in St. James's. What happened to the chariot and six horses he does not say. Perhaps he drove them back to the livery stable himself.

Now that he had his chariot, Byrd frequently went visiting in the country. On June 13, he went to stay with Lord and Lady Orrery in Britwell, their country house near Windsor. Though he only used four horses, he made excellent time over the fine King's Road, originally built to speed the King's progress to Windsor Castle. He arrived at one o'clock, in plenty of time for dinner. It was a charming interlude; walking through "an abundance of pretty lanes," with his host and hostess; riding over to see "the great house at Taplow" (Cliveden) where Lord Orkney lived; and playing bowls, billiards, and piquet—at which Byrd usually lost.

Six days later he returned to London, and took up his usual round of visits to his noble friends, his wenching, business, attendance at Court (which he found very dull), and gay evenings of cards and dancing at the residence of the Spanish Ambassador, the Marquis Monte Leon, who apparently kept open house every night. One of Byrd's favorite pastimes was the public masquerade dances to which anyone could buy a ticket. Everyone went in costumes and masks, which gave them ample opportunity for flirtation or more ambitious

3. Son of Byrd's friend and patron, Sir Robert Southwell.
4. Precursor of the famous Whig Club, which is still one of the most fashionable in London.

carnality. Of course, Byrd was soon in love again, this time with an affluent lady known to history only as the Widow Pierson. He pursued her for nearly a year with his usual vigor and extravagant epistles, matrimony being his object. But he was clearly not as far gone for "Zenobia," as he called her, as he had been for Sabina.

In July, Byrd was off again, this time to Oxford where for a few days he enjoyed more intellectual companionship and appreciated the ancient beauty of its famous buildings. On August 17, he and Daniel Horsmanden, Jr. set out at six o'clock in the morning in his chariot and six horses for the fashionable spa of Tunbridge Wells about twenty miles southwest of Windsor. Stopping for breakfast and dinner, they reached Tunbridge about five o'clock. There, Mrs. Blakiston had taken lodgings for them in a charming cluster of houses on a gentle rise of ground called Mount Zion.

Byrd lost no time going down to the Walk, a broad street paved with tiles in the Dutch manner. It had splendid old trees on one side and the Assembly Rooms, libraries, and shops on the other. Many fine ladies and gentlemen of Byrd's London world strolled through the summer evening in their elaborate dress of laces and silks, fine brocades and jewels. The men all wore the light French rapiers with which fashion had replaced the more serviceable swords of a cruder era, long ringletted periwigs, and blazing decorations—from the Garter on its broad blue ribbon to a galaxy of lesser orders in bejeweled crosses, stars, and sunbursts. The women looked lovely in draped, low-cut gowns that revealed a crescent of pouter-pigeon breasts but concealed their elbows, which it was considered immodest to reveal. Byrd wrote critically of one lady whom he considered fast that, "Her elbows were as bare as Eve's backside." [5] They greeted Byrd and each other with the elaborate courtesy and ornate speech which doubtless gave rise to the old saying, "When quality meets compliments fly."

Tunbridge Wells was, in fact, London Society in a rural setting, less constrained than the metropolis but just as mannered. The principal amusements were strolling down the Walk two or three times a day to see and be seen; sipping an occasional glass of the light, pure chalybeate water from the famous springs; gambling in the Assembly Rooms where Byrd lost almost every time; eating, drinking, and making love. Far exceeding the popularity of all these pastimes put

5. *Letters to Facetia.*

together was gossiping, which for sheer malevolence leavened by cutting wit as far exceeded any modern chitchat as a Ferrari would excel the speed of Byrd's chariot.

Byrd duly made his contribution to the cruel game, for his wit was as lethal as his taste was sometimes dubious. In 1719, he published *Tunbrigalia* by "Mr. Burrard" in which he lampoons one poor "Belinda" in a verse beginning:

> *Belinda bowsy fat and fair*
> *Adorned with Collops greasey*
> *These are Perfections not so rare*
> *Amongst the plump and Easy.* . . .

However, most of the verses in *Tunbrigalia,* addressed to ladies of high degree, are extremely flattering. One example will be quite enough, written to the wife of Byrd's good friend Lord Percival:

> ON THE LADY PERCIVAL
> *Silence were sin, when Percival, thy Name*
> *Should stand the Monument of lasting Fame.*
> *To speak thy Beauty, tell thy pleasing Air*
> *With such perfections as with these compare*
> *Words were but wind, for they express no more*
> *Than what the World would say,* They knew before.
> *But if good sense Perfection may define*
> *Let conversation shew how great's thy Mind.*

A fine example of Byrd's Rabelaisian wit is a verse in his Notebooks, possibly of a somewhat earlier date. It appears that Mrs. Heneage Finch, later the Countess of Winchelsea, wrote a charming little poem called "Upon A Sigh" beginning:

> *Gentlest Air Thou Breath of Lovers*
> *Vapor from a secret Fire*
> *Which by Thee it self discovers*
> *E'r yet daring to aspire.* . . .

This had considerable success until, as Byrd wrote, the lady was cured of her itch to poetry by the following burlesque:

> UPON A FART
> *Gentlest Blast of ill concoction*
> *Reverse of high-ascending Belch*

Th' only Stink abhorr'd by Statesmen
Belov'd and practic'd by the Welch. . . .

Swiftest ease of Cholique pain
Vapor from a secret stench
Is rattled out by th' unbred swain
But whispered by the Bashfull wench.

Shapeless Fart! We ne'er can show Thee
But in that merry Female sport
In which by burning blew we know Thee
Th' Amuzement of the Maids at Court.

In Tunbridge Wells, Byrd moved in the highest social circles among duchesses, maids of honor, ladies of the bedchamber, and all the lesser breeds. In his chariot and six he took his friends driving to see such neighboring sights as a new iron works, where his huge vehicle got stuck in a narrow country lane; and to Penshurst, the great house of the sixth Earl of Leicester, to view his superb collection of pictures. He saw a great deal of the Dunkellens, with whom he maintained his friendship. It was now his turn to comfort Mary Smith's sister, who came privately to him to spill her woes concerning her lord's excessive gambling and drinking.

Then he visited Lord Orrery again; and in October he and Cousin Daniel Horsmanden, Jr., took the Maldon mail coach to Danbury, where his uncle Daniel Horsmanden's chaise met them and took them to his mother's family home at Purleigh.

That was a serene interlude for Byrd, away from the pressures, temptations, and affectations of London Society. He was fond of his aunt and uncle Horsmanden and had grown very attached to young Daniel. A younger brother, Barrington (Bunty), was there as were Susan and Ursula, who, like Byrd's dead sister, was nicknamed Nutty. They were a gay family group. On the first evening after supper they "sat and talked of old stories until ten." The next morning, Sunday, a clear cold day, they went for morning prayers to lovely Purleigh Church standing on a hilltop between Chelmsford and the North Sea. In the afternoon they went to church again, where Horsmanden, Sr., who was the rector, "gave us a good sermon," from the pulpit where Lawrence Washington had once held forth. Then they walked in the garden until evening and after supper went "to romp and eat walnuts."

That was the pattern for the delightful fortnight that Byrd spent at Purleigh. It is evident from his diary that he adjusted easily to rural simplicity and thoroughly enjoyed himself. The presence of two very pretty girls, for whom he may have felt more than cousinly warmth, doubtless contributed to his enjoyment. This ever-youthful man of forty-four liked nothing better than to play the fool with people half his age, nor ever seemed to think of age at all where he was concerned.

One afternoon he notes they took a walk with Ursula and Suky and "romped with them in the fields." The next day a Mr. Humphrey, the beau of one of them, joined them at dinner at Danbury Place, but would not speak to him. Whatever Mr. Humphrey jealously imagined, Byrd was far too honorable to do more than romp with his young cousins.

Byrd's happy summer was followed by a disagreeable winter. As far back as July, 1718, Governor Spotswood had written to Lord Orkney, asking that four of the "most turbulent Council members," Ludwell, Blair, John Smith, and Byrd, be dismissed.[6] Orkney promptly went to the Board of Trade and proposed an investigation. Nothing came of it then, and, as has been noted, in November, Byrd was officially received by the King as Agent of Virginia.

Spotswood was steaming, and after Byrd's brilliant, though losing, argument in the matter of the appointment of judges, he wrote again falsely accusing Byrd of having fled from the Dominion with his records as Receiver General for fear of an inquiry; and stating that "the peace and quiet of Virginia depended upon the dismissal of that implacable gentleman, Byrd."[7] In February, 1719, the Board of Trade agreed with the Governor and recommended that Mr. Cole Diggs be appointed to the Council in Byrd's place.

Byrd was now in terrible trouble. With Governor the Earl of Orkney, the Lieutenant Governor, and the Board of Trade against him, it looked as though he would lose his seat on the Council. Without that distinction, a man of his proud nature undoubtedly felt he could never go home to face the hypocritical condolences of his friends. Life in Virginia would be ended for him. Indeed, life any-

6. Saintsburg Abstracts, Vol. III, p. 720.
7. Bassett, *op. cit.*

where would not be worth living; for he knew that even in England he would lose the prestige he had held as one of the acknowledged rulers of England's greatest dominion; that one by one his fine friends would slip away, and that eventually he would be relegated to the fringe of the society he adored and would become a mere hanger-on at Court.

So he fought back desperately, and he was not without allies. He still had loyal and powerful friends of whom the most powerful was, happily, also the most loyal. The Duke of Argyll, Victor of Sheriff-muir, was a far greater figure and much closer to the King than Orkney. He would do all he could for his American friend, but even his influence had its limits. Beneath him was the phalanx of friends whom Byrd had cultivated so assiduously, both for his own advantage and their usefulness to Virginia; they would also help. But in the end it would be up to Byrd himself, by diplomacy, wit, and, if necessary, by humbling himself, to give them the arguments to save him.

He had previously written a petition to the Board of Trade that no member of the Virginia Council be removed on Governor Spotswood's accusations until he had an opportunity to present his side of the case. Colonel Blakiston brought him the news that the Board "took my letter very ill." Micajah Perry told Byrd that he had gone before the Board which treated him coldly.

During this period Byrd went ever more frequently to Court, keeping his fences mended, never losing a chance to do a favor for someone with influence. One evening at the play he had an opportunity "to do a civil thing" for the Duke of Buckingham, which did his cause no harm. On the credit side he was also willing to do favors for people from whom he expected no return, as when he promised to try to find a place in the Duke of Argyll's household for the son of Lord Orrery's housekeeper. And, despite his personal difficulties, he continued vigorously to represent Virginia's interests before the Court of Requests and to promote a law to encourage the growing of hemp in the Dominion because he knew only too well the dangers of a one-crop economy.

Byrd's first big break came on February 6, 1719, when the Duke of Argyll was given the white staff of Lord Steward of the (Royal) Household. This was not only a signal mark of royal favor, but it put Byrd's patron in a position to see the King almost daily. The next morning Byrd was among a great crowd of people who called to congratulate the Duke.

For many months, however, Byrd's position was still perilous. In an endeavor to placate the Board of Trade, he wrote them a long letter in March, 1719, offering to go to Virginia and use his utmost endeavor to make peace between the Council and the Governor and to "dispose them to a sincere pacification upon the terms of the Governor's own plan." As he set them forth the terms were: Only Council members were to be appointed to courts of oyer and terminer except in an extraordinary emergency; the Act of Assembly giving the Governor power to lay out money for his Palace as he saw fit was to be repealed; the Lieutenant Governor was to be told to let all members of the Council, Court, and House of Burgesses give their opinions frankly "without reproach or ridicule"; and neither Governor nor Council was to complain to the Board of Trade without first giving a true copy of the complaint to the party complained of.[8]

This may have been Byrd's idea of a compromise, but it certainly was not Spotswood's. Had that gentleman seen the document at the time he would have quite literally frothed at the mouth. Byrd was obviously still implacable as far as the rights of Virginians were concerned.

Meanwhile Byrd was also intriguing to have Spotswood removed, and to get the governorship himself if possible. On March 28, he met Madam Kielmansegge, the King's German mistress who was afterward created Countess of Leinster, but he did not follow up that promising lead. Then the Duke of Argyll's son, Lord Islay, a dark and devious fellow quite unlike his open-hearted father, advised Byrd to bribe Baron von Bernstoff, the King's German advisor, in order to get the governorship for himself. That plan never matured.

Byrd's case had been referred to the Privy Council, a sort of super-cabinet, consisting of the sixty most important men in Britain, whose duty it was to advise the King on all matters of government. Legally, the King did not have to take their advice, but as a practical matter, he was obliged to do so, or risk being dethroned like poor James II. The Duke of Argyll, Lord Stanhope, and Mr. Craggs promised to use their considerable influence in the Privy Council in Byrd's favor.

Meanwhile, back in Virginia, Byrd got an unexpected ally. The

8. Public Records Office, London, March 1719.

Governor attempted to interfere with feisty James Blair's right to appoint ministers to the different parishes. Like Nicholson before him, he should have known better than to meddle with that ecclesiastical buzz-saw. Blair gradually mobilized the power of the Church of England against Spotswood.

Byrd's case did not come up before the Privy Council until June 25, 1719. That morning, anxious for a word with the Duke, Byrd was at the Cockpit—a building near Kensington Palace formerly used for cock fighting and then, oddly enough, for the deliberations of the Privy Council. When the case came up, Argyll, a true friend, made an eloquent speech in Byrd's favor. In spite of this, the Privy Council referred the matter to a committee for investigation.

Though Byrd remained on tenterhooks, he had an agreeable summer, walking with Horace Walpole in St. James's Park; discussing philosophy, politics, and literature; spending several weekends with Argyll at Petersham, the Duke's superb country house, strolling in the garden with the Duke and Duchess and discoursing at his charming best. He made two pilgrimages to Tunbridge Wells where he entertained the Duchess of Monmouth, whose unfortunate husband had lost his head for trying to seize the throne from King James II.

As if he were going to live in London forever, Byrd bought a spacious apartment in Lincoln's Inn from Sir George Cooke for £900. He redecorated it lavishly; the superb marble mantelpiece he installed may have been the one he later put in the drawing room at Westover.

Hardly had Byrd moved into his new apartment when, on September 13, he suddenly decided that he must go to Virginia to mend his fences there. One of Spotswood's principal arguments for putting him off the Council was that he had been away so long. From the moment of decision he was in a flurry of preparation. On September 28, he called upon Lord Orkney with Colonel Blakiston and old Mr. Perry to make a proposal of peace. He found Orkney "on the high rope"; but the Earl finally agreed to write a letter for Byrd even though he felt he had been "treated indifferently."

On October 24, dressed in his finest clothes, Byrd went to the Cockpit for his hearing before the committee of the Lords of the Treasury, the inner group who really ran the Government. One may imagine his anxiety as he prepared for the confrontation upon which his whole future depended; and his enormous relief when the Lords were "exceedingly courteous" to him and promised to recommend to the King his retention on the Virginia Council. Thus Byrd won a round against the Lieutenant Governor, which in itself was amazing and showed that his supporters, headed by Argyll, were friends indeed. For the British Government was naturally inclined to support its own appointed governors against any colonial gentleman, however just his cause.

Byrd was not yet easy in his mind, however. To make assurance doubly sure, he determined to carry with him to Virginia a letter from the Duke of Argyll to Spotswood. To this end he wrote the Duke on November 4 a long letter which is important because it clearly states his side of the controversy:

My Lord:
The time now draws near for my Transportation, which makes me repeat my humble Request to your Grace for the letter you was pleas'd to say you wou'd write to Arroganti [Spotswood]. I was so happy as to be in that Gentleman's good graces the first 2 years of his Government, but after that he grew out of humour with me for reasons I am very far from being asham'd of. . . . After that [Byrd's resignation as Receiver General] he was pleased to send over to the Junto de Sapienti [Lords of the Treasury] heavy charges against me. . . . Now my Lord these were sore provocations, but neither they, nor all the bitter things I understand he has been pleas'd to say of me, cou'd ever stir me up to attempt his Removal.[9] All that I have ever done since I came over, has been to get several hardships remov'd w$\underline{^{ch}}$ he graciously intended to lay upon that Country; & the success I have had against him in every particular, notwithstanding the biass the Junto hath toward Governors, is a proof that I have had Justice on my side. He hath managed his matters so politickly that he has 9 of the council and a great majority of the commons against him. . . . Thus I have proceeded against him in the gentlest manner.[10]

Byrd goes on to say that he fears Spotswood's anger will make the Governor continue to do him ill turns when he goes to Virginia and try to prevent him from returning to England. He begs Argyll to use his influence to keep the Governor from harassing him.

From then until he left, Byrd gave Argyll no peace. Finally two days before his departure the Duke gave him the letter.

9. Here Byrd is tampering with the truth.
10. Byrd *Notebooks*.

With Daniel Horsmanden, Hannah, and Annie (two serving maids who had agreed to go with him to Virginia), and his man Tom, Byrd left London on November 24, en route for Dover where he was to board his ship.

For nearly two weeks Byrd sat around in Dover waiting for his ship, which was kept out of harbor by a persistent east wind. On December 13, he boarded her at Deal. Ironically enough her name was the *Spotswood.*

The wind now blew steadily from the south, so for four days more the *Spotswood* lay at anchor unable to beat out of the harbor. Finally on Sunday, December 17, there was a shift to the southeast. The great, unwieldy sails were hoisted up the masts, anchor chains rattled in, and the *Spotswood* cleared the headlands to sail westward down the English Channel at four knots.

The voyage was typical of an early-eighteenth-century Atlantic crossing; faster and more comfortable than when Byrd had crossed as a baby in 1675, but still a rugged experience. The *Spotswood* was a new ship, much larger and with more modern, sleeker lines than those earlier craft. Their absurdly high poops and forecastles, which had caught the wind and made them so difficult to control, had been smoothed away. The main deck ran level to the bow, from which the bowsprit still sprang upward at an acute angle. But it carried modern jibs instead of the foolish little square sails, which were now only used in a fair wind. The poop deck was a vestigial remainder of the old stern castle only a few feet above the main deck. However, it was handsomely carved and gilded, and still had big square windows at the stern.

There was a fair sized dining saloon and Byrd's cabin was comfortable, with windows high enough above the sea to stand open in anything less than a gale. It was undoubtedly handsomely furnished, though everything had to be screwed down because in Atlantic storms ships were still tossed about like eggshells. A few cannon were mounted aft on the poop, and broadside on the gun deck, to stand off pirates or small privateers.

Because of the prevailing winds and wintry weather the *Spotswood* sailed the reverse of a great-circle course, running far to the south, then climbing over the bulge of the earth and sailing northward again before the southerlies. Byrd was a good sailor. Again and again he notes that all his people were seasick, while he continued to enjoy cake and veal broth for breakfast, a hearty one-course dinner, and, perhaps, roasted chestnuts and a bowl of punch with the captain for supper. He was extremely fond of "sea pie," which the captain made himself, but he does not give the recipe. Byrd had brought a great many books with him, and every morning read Greek, Hebrew, or Latin, relaxing with French or English in the evening. Each day he did his "dance" and whenever possible took a brisk walk on deck to keep in condition.

On Sundays, Byrd read prayers to the crew; he frequently wrote his own. He seems to have managed to contain his sexual drive remarkably well, though he occasionally made a few passes at pretty, young Annie. She resisted gallantly, though she finally succumbed at Westover. He was intensely disturbed by "something like an apparition" of his daughter Evelyn; then dreamed she had died of small-pox at that moment. Some days later he dreamed again that he saw Evelyn with only one hand, which he took to mean that one of his daughters was dead, and since the right hand was gone, he was convinced it was Evelyn and was very melancholy.

On January 18, thirty-six days out of Deal, the captain expected to raise Bermuda, but did not see it; so he concluded they were west of it. Though the invention of small, reasonably accurate clocks had greatly improved navigation, it was far from perfect. By January 27, the color of the water changed; the captain ordered soundings taken. When the leadsman reported only twenty fathoms, he ordered the ship to sail east to avoid the sea graveyard of Cape Hatteras. Byrd slept uneasily that night, thinking of its deadly shoals. On January 30, they were fairly between Capes Charles and Henry with Chesapeake Bay stretching welcoming arms, when a terrible northeaster struck and almost carried away the main mast. Out to sea they scudded under bare poles. Byrd noted, "It was a grief to us to take our departure thus from the Cape. However, it is the fortune of the sea." [11]

Almost in sight of land they endured a terrifying twenty-four hours. In a furious sea, with no sails set, the little ship rolled and pitched; climbed gigantic waves toward the sky; corkscrewed down to the windless valleys between and climbed again to be flattened by

11. *The London Diary.*

the blast, while her timbers shrieked in twisting torture. Things flew around Byrd's cabin as he braced himself in his bunk. The violent motion of the ship "carried the captain's quarters and him to leeward and broke his head," and one of the seamen broke a hole through the galley door.

The next evening they managed to get the mainsail set and regained some control over the ship. On February 2, 1720, fifty-one days out of Deal, they lay becalmed on a flat sea, staring avidly at green, unreachable land. Toward evening a breeze came up. They sailed between the capes and seven leagues up the bay, where they anchored. "For which God be praised."

Contrary winds held them near the mouth of the bay for yet another day. Byrd was fuming to get ashore to begin his battle with Spotswood. He offered the captain a draft for £28 to pay for his passage, but that mariner said it was not enough. On February 4, a gentleman came out in a small boat to get the mails. Byrd seized the opportunity to go ashore. He must have given a much larger draft for his passage, because as he left the *Spotswood* the captain saluted him with nine guns.

Byrd spent his first night back in Virginia at the home of Captain Smith of Gloucester County, and woke with a terrible attack of piles. A messenger was sent for Doctor Archibald Blair, brother of Commissary James Blair, who bled Byrd and "annointed" him with oil of marshmallow. He felt easier, but was most unhappy sitting up.

As word of his arrival went out, the clans began to gather. Council member Colonel Philip Lightfoot of Sandy Point and Colonel John Smith came. Lightfoot offered Byrd a lift to Williamsburg in his chariot. They stopped at John Custis' plantation, Queens Creek, where many of Byrd's cronies of the Council came from Williamsburg to greet and advise him. In addition to Phil Lightfoot there were James Blair, Philip Ludwell, Francis Lightfoot, young Ben Harrison of Berkeley, John Randolph, and James Roscowe who was now Receiver General. Together they concocted a letter, which Byrd sent off to the Governor. The next morning John Randolph arrived with an answer from the Governor. It was such a blast of anger as put an end to all Byrd's thoughts of peace.

More conferences were held as Councilors streamed back from

Williamsburg. Byrd was uneasy that his friend Attorney General John Clayton did not come. He supposed it was for fear of the Governor; and decided to force Clayton's hand by sending him a polite note, stating that only illness prevented him from calling on the Attorney General. This "courteous reproach" brought Clayton around by ten o'clock.

In view of the Governor's hostility, Byrd decided not to go to Williamsburg until the orders from the King and Privy Council arrived, confirming his place on the Virginia Council. Instead he went to Green Spring to stay with Philip Ludwell. More of his friends gathered there and talked of politics. Doubtless Spotswood, fuming in Williamsburg, considered it conspiring.

Without going to Williamsburg, Byrd pushed on to Westover in a borrowed coach on February 13. It was high time he came home. His nephew, John Brayne, whom he had put in charge, was a negligent steward. The place had deteriorated. In addition, Brayne had drunk most of Byrd's fine wines and "spoiled" his guns; he was probably too lazy to clean them properly. Byrd reprimanded him, but kept his temper. He walked the bounds of his estate as required by law, freshly blazing the trees that marked its borders.

Then he rode to his trading post at Falling Creek, where he found more evidence of neglect. His gristmill was in such bad repair it would barely turn. He briskly put things to rights and returned to Westover to await the King's orders in Council from England.

For over two months Byrd waited, while it seemed that his whole world came to Westover to confer and to cheer him. There was no question that almost the entire Council and a majority of the Burgesses were on his side; by the alchemy of politics and the errors of Spotswood, it had become Virginia's side, America's side. Finally, on April 23, word came to Westover that the orders in Council had come.

The next morning Byrd rose at six o'clock, read a chapter of the Bible in Hebrew, and some Greek. In the afternoon he rode toward Williamsburg. The weather was warm and clear with a gentle wind from the northeast. White and pink stars of dogwood were glimmering beneath the tall, new-leaved trees in the forest, the sweet-meadow scent of springtime in his nostrils. What a day to ride toward a bloodless victory; a day to turn his forty-six years back to twenty-six, or sixteen, with the surging joy of youth in his blood.

On the way he met Colonel Edward Hill and Colonel William Randolph, who had no news but wished him well. At Green Spring, Colonel Ludwell gaily handed him a letter from his devoted friend Edward Southwell in London. It contained the King's order confirming him to the Council. Commissary James Blair and Major John Holloway of York County were there. "We talked of several things." [12] Did they not!

Byrd read nothing the next morning because Blair came to his room to discuss privately his own controversy with Spotswood. After breakfast Byrd drove with Ludwell in his chariot to Williamsburg, where he found another copy of the King's Order in Council. With a small phalanx of friends he walked to the Capitol. In the great courtroom he presented the King's order to the Governor.

Spotswood was in a predictably disagreeable mood. He greeted Byrd haughtily and said, "I shall obey the King's order; but if you had come without it I would not have admitted you."

Then the Governor let himself go, railing violently at Byrd "before all the people." By Byrd's own account he remained calm and dignified, answering the Governor fearlessly but politely, and "came off with credit." Spotswood could not bring himself to swear him in, so Byrd loitered around until court ended, then dined with the whole Council.

The next morning he went to the Capitol with Commissary Blair, where he was sworn in, presumably by the President of the Council, Colonel Edmund Jenings. He took his place in the court which was then sitting. The following evening he called on Colonel Robert Carter of Corotoman at his lodgings. Nicknamed "King" Carter because of his magnificent manner of living and his huge land holdings of over 330,000 acres, the Colonel was the agent in Virginia for Lord Fairfax, whose family had been granted the whole Northern Neck of Virginia between the Potomac and the Rappahannock rivers. Soon to become President of the Council, Carter was, perhaps, the most influential man in Virginia at this time. Sitting before his fire, he and Byrd whiled the evening away discoursing about "some treasonable matters."

In fact, tension between the Governor and the Council had risen to a dangerous stretch. Far from alleviating it, Byrd's return to Virginia and his defeat of Spotswood had intensified the problem. How-

12. *The London Diary.*

ever peaceful Byrd's original intention may have been, he was now preparing to wage full-scale war against the Governor. The first step was to be a formal complaint against Spotswood, drawn up by Byrd and his adherents. The object of all the meetings, conferences, and lobbying was to secure, if possible, the signatures of every member of the Council. By April 29, Byrd virtually had it in the bag.

That was a strange and stormy morning. The full Council met. The Governor sat in his carved chair at the head of the long table in the luxuriously appointed Council Chamber, surrounded by angry men of whom he was, perhaps, the most enraged. For two hours they traded insults and imprecations, their voices rising in fury until they were bellowing at each other as the Governor pressed a violent attack against Blair and Colonel Ludwell. Fortunately for the peace of mind of the anxious townspeople, the sound was contained by the three-foot walls and heavy walnut doors of that handsome room.

Then, at the height of this storm, when the peace of the Dominion itself seemed lost, "Of a sudden the clouds cleared away and we began to be perfectly good friends, and we agreed upon terms of a lasting reconciliation to the great surprise of ourselves and everybody else." [13]

Viewed from hindsight what appears to have happened was that Spotswood suddenly realized that he was beaten. The defeat of his attempt to unseat Byrd had shown him how precarious his support in London was, how powerful the influence of the Virginians. When his temper was not high, Spotswood was an astute politician who knew how to compromise where force would not serve. Furthermore, he loved Virginia and wanted to remain there even after his tenure of office ended. This would be impossible if he antagonized the leading men of the Dominion beyond hope of reconciliation. His reasoning may well have been that if the King and his Privy Council so little regarded his efforts to assert the royal prerogative over these intransigent colonists and particularly "that implacable gentleman, Byrd," then the hell with King and Council; he would make the best terms he could. So he suddenly and masterfully practiced the art of dissimulation, and won their hearts by an unexpected sweet reasonableness, for which they were totally unprepared.

When the treaty was agreed upon and embodied in a resolution, the Governor invited the whole Council to dinner at his house. They

13. *Ibid.*

walked all together down Duke of Gloucester Street and up the broad green mall that led to the imposing brick façade of the Palace with its steep, dormered slate roof and airy cupola surmounted by a gilded weathercock. It was the first time Byrd had been in the newly completed building. He appreciated its great hall paved in marble and paneled in dark, polished walnut; its charming withdrawing room and the long state dining room with crystal chandeliers and gleaming silver. Chances are that the Governor led them up the splendid stairway to the middle room on the second floor. Its tall windows looked down the Mall, and its walls were hung in hand-tooled Spanish leather. There they could rejoice and drink at ease.

Meanwhile a happy celebration was going on outside. Though the deliberations of Councilors were private and every one of them sworn to secrecy, all the Burgesses and townspeople of Williamsburg had known of the violent quarrel between the Governor and the Council and were fearful of its repercussions and the possibility— even probability—of a breakdown of law and of armed rebellion against the Crown. Their joy was even greater than that of the principals in the drama. While the feast of peace took place in the Palace, guns were fired and there was "illumination all the town over" as the citizens expressed their exhilaration.

The dinner lasted for about seven hours. The Governor sent for musicians to make them more merry; toasts were drunk to everyone and everything from the King, the Dominion, and the Governor to each individual Councilor. In his exuberance Spotswood went around kissing every Councilor and, Byrd noted, "gave me a kiss more than other people." [14]

14. *Ibid.*

VI · "MY ANTICK VIRGIN"

I T IS NOT to be supposed that the leopard had changed his spots in one sunny afternoon, so that thereafter all was love and kisses between Governor Spotswood and the Council of Virginia. The conflicting interests of Crown and colony, plus the clash of ideologies between the conservative government of an Old World country and the thrusting independence of the leaders of a new one, were almost irreconcilable. The gentlemen of Virginia, however much they might ape English modes and manners, were still pioneers at heart, forcing an expanding civilization on a wilderness and influenced in turn by conditions, opportunities, and perils which a group of English politicians meeting in the Cockpit could but dimly apprehend. Under these circumstances, it was the sworn duty of any royal governor to use his utmost efforts to contain and circumscribe the independent spirit which, in hardly more than half a century, would bring about the final break. The only difference between the various men who were charged with upholding the prerogatives of the Crown in the American colonies was that some performed their part more tactfully than others.

Spotswood was more tactful than many and his second honeymoon lasted for almost a year. During that time the old intimacy between him and Byrd was almost renewed. The Councilor was often asked to dine at the Palace and "made merry" with his old enemy.

Though Byrd undoubtedly missed the stimulating life in London and was determined to return there soon, Williamsburg was not too bad. It was becoming much more cosmopolitan. William Livingston, who had started the first dancing academy in Williamsburg, had branched out and built a theater where the latest English comedies were performed, sometimes by English road companies, but mostly by American casts who made up in enthusiasm what they lacked in polish. Byrd often went to the play, though his criticisms were not gentle. Then there were the races at which he usually managed to lose a little money, and, of course, the balls and dinners to which he was invited every night during the "public times."

Another contribution to his content was the great respect in which he was held by the Virginia gentlemen who regarded him as an authority on everything to do with England and who were profoundly impressed by the influence he wielded through his friendships there. One incident shows how effective this influence still was.

On October 22, 1720, Byrd was sitting in Court in the Capitol when the Secretary of State, Doctor William Cocke, had a heart attack and fell dead upon him. This "made a great consternation," for Cocke was very popular (though not one of Byrd's favorites, as he suspected the Secretary of having taken the Governor's part). At any rate, it did not affect Byrd's appetite for the wild duck he had for dinner. He duly went to Cocke's funeral, which, according to the Doctor's epitaph in Bruton Parish Church, "Alexander Spotswood . . . with the principal gentlemen of the country attended . . . weeping."

Cocke's death left a great place to be filled by the ambitious. King Carter asked Byrd to write a letter to the Duke of Argyll, proposing that his son, John Carter, be made Secretary, which Byrd promptly did. Even though Governor Spotswood on the very day of Cocke's death had dashed off a letter proposing Colonel Jenings for Secretary, John Carter obtained the place and made a fine Secretary of State. He paid £1,500 for the post. Its income was about 122,000 pounds of tobacco a year—not a bad deal.

Though Byrd certainly enjoyed life in Williamsburg, he was not too unhappy during his long sojourns at Westover. People poured through its hospitable doors and there were gay parties at the neighboring plantations, where they played the latest games from England or shot with bows and arrows. But it is quite evident that Byrd was lonely living there without a wife—how lonely is shown by his efforts at church each Sunday to induce people to come back and dine with him. He was determined to get back to London and renew his search for a suitable wife. None of the Virginia ladies appears to have met his exalted standards, although he developed a mild affection for King Carter's daughter, Anne, who later married his young neighbor, Ben Harrison.

The summer of 1721 passed pleasantly enough at Westover. Byrd was already beginning his famous library in which he arranged the many books he had brought from England. In August, Governor Spotswood paid him a visit. It went off very well except that on the first night the Governor and another guest fainted at the table. After dinner they drank claret until Byrd noticed that, "The Governor was going to faint again so we put him to bed." [1]

Preparing for his return to England, Byrd engaged young John Banister, the son of the famous naturalist, to live at Westover and manage the plantation for a salary of £30 a year. In November, a newly elected assembly met at Williamsburg, and Byrd had his final conflict with Spotswood. He left for Williamsburg November 1, spending the night at Green Spring. His young cousin Hannah Ludwell was there with her beau, Thomas Lee, whom she eventually married. Lee later became the only native Virginian to serve as royal governor. After Byrd had gone to bed that night at Green Spring, the matchmaking ladies of the house put a drawn sword at his head with a Book of Common Prayer opened at the marriage service so that he would dream of his future wife. He dreamed of Annie Carter.

The next evening the new House of Burgesses met and elected Major John Holloway as Speaker. On November 3, the Governor addressed both Council and Burgesses. They, in turn, presented polite addresses to him. So far all was well. Byrd and Spotswood were on the friendliest terms, frequently dining together.

On December 14, the House of Burgesses once again appointed Byrd as Agent of Virginia "to solicit in Great Britain the subject matter of the address of the Council and Burgesses to His Majesty" and other matters. They proposed to pay him £400 salary and expenses. That put the Governor very much "out of humor." It was his constant endeavor, as it had been Governor Nicholson's, to prevent the

1. *The London Diary.*

Assembly's bypassing his authority by means of an agent in London. He sent a message to the Council, desiring them to amend the Burgesses' resolution of appointment to require that Byrd act only on instructions signed by the Governor and that he be obliged to enter into a bond with the Governor "not to meddle in Great Britain in any other affair of this government. . . ." [2]

Byrd was indignant. The Council, of course, passed the resolution without that amendment. The Governor refused to sign it, and went before the Council to show how reasonable it was to make Byrd promise not to meddle. Council and Burgesses answered him firmly and logically. The Governor still refused to sign.

As the Assembly was coming to an end, Byrd paid a farewell visit to the Governor. They argued the question of the bond face to face. Byrd proudly told the Governor that he would not sign such an agreement "for all the money in the treasurer's hands." That afternoon Spotswood told the House of Burgesses that his object was "to take away temptation from unquiet spirits who might be disposed to sow again the seeds of contention." [3]

On hearing this, Byrd stormed down to the Capitol and melodramatically said to Spotswood, "I had rather my tongue be cut out than it should be tied up from doing my country service." [4]

The end of it all was that Governor Spotswood was, as usual, forced to yield to his implacable adversary and sign the bill.

Probably because of the business of his plantations, Byrd did not leave immediately for England, but spent all the winter of 1721 in Virginia. He occupied himself by writing a very learned treatise, which was published that autumn in London under the title:

A

DISCOURSE
concerning the
P L A G U E
with some preservatives
against it.
By a Lover of Mankind
Printed for J. Roberts near the Oxford
Arms in Warwick-lane. 1721.
1 Shill.

2. Journal of the House of Burgesses. Vol. I, p. 300.
3. *Ibid.*
4. *The London Diary.*

Beginning with a history of the word "plague" as used in Holy Scripture and the Iliad of Homer, Byrd gave an account of the disease from ancient Egypt, Greece, and Rome to seventeenth-century Europe. He went on to a detailed description of the nature of the plague and the treatment and preventatives used by all the various peoples who had suffered from it, with a side dissertation on the Turkish system of vaccination for smallpox, not yet used in England.

Finally Byrd got down to his own preventatives of which the first was "a most humble and sincere repentence of our sins." This was followed by such sensible precautions as "temperance, sobriety and moderation" and the avoidance of violent exercise. He then advised "good courage and cheerful spirits since a terrified and dejected mind will dispose us most unaccountably to suck in the very distemper of which we are afraid," a fact noticed by modern medical philosophy. Some more dubious "preservatives" follow, such as bleeding and a purgative of strong wine and tobacco. He also strongly recommended "an issue," or hole cut on either side of the groin to drain away "the vicious humours." Fires must be kept burning in all the rooms and "if it might not look a little too frantick," it would be a good idea to shoot guns out of the windows and "pistols in our rooms."

With his tenth and final preservative, the planter-author mounted his hobbyhorse and was off flat out in praise of tobacco as the sovereign preventative: "The sprightly effluvia sent forth from this vegetable . . . are by nature peculiarly adapted to encounter and dissipate the pestilential taint. . . ." Byrd described the nature of tobacco and its use in curing ulcers, sores, wounds, the itch and leprosy, the "bite of Scorpion, Viper or Mad Dog."

Coming back at last to his theme, Byrd attributed England's recent freedom from the plague to the vastly increased use of tobacco. Therefore, if there is any danger of this pestilence, "we should provide ourselves with fresh, strong scented tobacco."

We should wear it about our clothes, and about our coaches. We should hang bundles of it round our beds, and in the apartments where we most converse. If we have an aversion to smoking, it would be prudent to burn some leaves of Tobacco in our dining rooms lest we swallow the infection with our meat . . . take snuff plentifully . . . to secure the passages to our brain. . . . The pass to our stomachs should be also safely defended, by chewing this great *Antipoison*. In short, we should both abroad and at home, by night as well as by day, take care to have our sovereign antidote very near us; an antidote which seems design'd by Providence as the strongest natural preservative against this great destroyer.

If Byrd's pamphlet reads like an advertising man's dream copy, let no one think it was a hypocritical way of stimulating the demand for his product. He was far too respectful of medical lore and of the great physicians—virtually all of whose works were well thumbed in his library—to trifle with the truth. He was absolutely convinced that his theory was correct and, allowing for the crude state of medical research, he had as good grounds for his conclusions as the medical profession today has for its condemnation of smoking.

Byrd was so proud of his book that he read passages of it to all his friends during the long winter nights at Westover. He was so convinced of its importance to mankind that it was the only one of his prose writings, except his paper before the Royal Society, that he allowed to be published during his lifetime.

In the summer of 1721, Byrd sailed back to England accompanied by James Blair. He ensconced himself in his apartment in Lincoln's Inn, dragged out the chariot, and took up his vigorous advocacy of Virginia's interests as well as his own frantic search for a wife. If Spotswood was worried about what these two gentlemen might do to him in England, his anxiety was justified. In less than a year he was dismissed.

Alexander Spotswood was one of the new type of professional British administrators, as opposed to the more or less gifted amateurs who had governed the British Colonies in the seventeenth century. He had come to Virginia idealistically determined to do a good job for both Crown and colony; and was genuinely horrified by the shenanigans by which the members of the Council and other great planters escaped taxes and illegally grabbed huge hunks of land. But the planters were too much for him. Frustration and disgust gradually eroded his character. When he found he could not beat the system, he joined it. Shortly before his dismissal he made one of the greatest land grabs of all. He had one piece of twenty thousand and another of forty thousand acres patented in the names of substitutes. When he retired, he took over the sixty thousand acres without ever having qualified for them or followed any of the legal procedures. The only authority that could have caviled was the Council, and they were not about to set any precedents that might compromise their own holdings.

In Spotswood's case the wages of sin were prosperity and contentment. He married Anne Butler Brayne, the daughter of Richard Brayne of St. Margarets, Westminster, and lived happily in what Byrd once called "Colonel Spotswood's enchanted castle," near Fredericksburg on the Rappahannock. Years later Byrd wrote: "My old friend [Spotswood] is very Uxurious and exceedingly fond of his children. This was so opposite to the maxims he used to preach before he was married that I could not forbear rubbing up the memory of him. But he gave a very good natured turn to his change of sentiment by alleging that whoever brings a poor Gentlewoman into so solitary a place from all her friends and acquaintances would be ungrateful not to use her and all that belongs to her with all possible tenderness." [5]

Though Byrd finally got rid of Spotswood, he did not achieve his ambition to succeed him. Colonel Hugh Drysdale was appointed in his place.

Byrd's other object, matrimony, was not forgotten. The first lady he passionately pursued was the Lady Elizabeth Lee, granddaughter of King Charles II and his mistress Barbara Villiers, known to the Court as the Duchess of Cleveland and to the mob as "the French whore." Lady Elizabeth's father was Sir Edward Henry Lee, first Earl of Lichfield. In 1722, she was a widow sixteen years old.

The courting of "Charmante" as Byrd called Lady Elizabeth was fast and furious. While it lasted, during October and November, 1722, Byrd saw his beloved every day, speaking openly of his passion and confirming it with many a tender squeeze of the hand. Of course he wrote her his usual high-flown letters, the most extraordinary of which describes a dream he says he had about "Venus in her Golden car drawn by two innocent turtles [doves] which billed and cooed as they passed along." The goddess was looking over her shoulder. "[She] smiled upon Charmante, who followed in the next car, reaching out her *cestus* full of all the enchantments of her Sex. . . ." Charmante "was clothed in a loose robe of spotless white with her sable tresses flowing in ringlets upon her shoulders. Thus adorned she seemed to rival the goddess so much that the wanton cupids left their mother to frisk and play about her. . . ."

5. Letter of William Byrd quoted in Andrews, *op. cit.*

In Byrd's fantasy those frisky little fellows took him by the hand and led him to Charmante. He joined the procession, which also included a comely dame in azure blue, leading a little dog; a beautiful virgin dressed only in a see-through linen shift; a matron "with an everlasting smile upon her face . . ." and a plump, cheerful damsel, "pouring out of a cornucopia the finest fruit and gayest flowers. . . .

"In this order," Byrd went on, "we marched to the Temple of Honor where a dignified Priest joined our hands and descending angels sang Amen. . . ."

This perfervid prose did Byrd's business for him, though not as he hoped. Lady Elizabeth probably thought she had an old madman to deal with (Byrd was now forty-nine). One can picture her giggling with her young beaux and at the same time feeling a little flattered by the attention of such a distinguished older man. When she got that letter, she may have been somewhat frightened. The next time they met was in a public place. Lady Elizabeth, with a young man to support her, told Byrd plainly and rudely to let her alone. He was so shocked by this transgression of all the rules of etiquette and courtesy that for once he was struck dumb by mortification and astonishment. It was, perhaps, his darkest hour.

But he bobbed up like a cork. Within a few days he was writing to a lady known to history only as "Minionet," protesting undying passion. But she, too, in the end turned him down.

Finally, in 1724, Byrd found love at last. His prize was Maria Taylor, the heiress of the late Thomas Taylor of Kensington, though she does not seem to have inherited much money. While not as beautiful as Lucy Byrd or her daughter, Evelyn, Maria, a widow of twenty-six, was a handsome woman. She had a strong but gentle face, swan-white, translucent skin, high rose color in her cheeks, very blue eyes under delicately arched eyebrows, and a full, voluptuous mouth. For her portrait by Charles Bridges she wore her dark hair piled high in a knot with a carefully careless lock curling on her high forehead. Her dress of pale blue shimmering silk with a deep décolletage outlined an amply feminine figure.

Byrd was strongly attracted to her and when he discovered that she could read Greek, he wrote her a letter in that language and sent it care of a Mr. Ornis at Will's Coffee House:

"When I thought you knew only your mother tongue I was passionately in love with you: but when, indeed, I learned that you also spoke Greek, the tongue of the Muses, I went completely crazy about you. In beauty you surpassed Helen, in culture of mind and ready wit Sappho. It is not meet therefor to be astonished I was smitten by such grandeur of body and soul when I admitted the poison of Love through my eyes and my ears. Farewell." [6]

As far as is known this is the only letter Byrd wrote to Maria, accounting perhaps for the success of his suit. Though her father was dead, Maria had a mother whom Byrd evidently regarded as an ogre —perhaps on her daughter's evidence. Having been disappointed before by the intervention of his mistress's parent, he took no chances, but having won the girl, married her on May 9, 1724, without informing Mrs. Taylor. About two weeks later, on May 26, he wrote to "Medusa," as he called that formidable lady:

I had the honor to marry your Eldest Daughter about a fortnight since & can assure you it shall be the great business of my life to make her happy. She tells me that she acquainted you with it soon after it happened & begg'd your blessing. I humbly join with her in that Petition. . . . I am sensible, madame, how cruelly I have been misrepresented to you both in my character & circumstances. Tis no unusual thing for men going to be married to be painted in malicious Coulors, and so no wonder I have shared that common Fate. However I am the less concern'd, because I know those very spiteful storys, and can without much difficulty disprove them. I shou'd think my self very fortunate, Madame, if you'd please to let me wait on you, and shou'd not dispair of quieting the apprehensions you may have of Your Daughters being unhappily married, and shou'd be happier stil if you wou'd give me leave to call my self what I shall always endeavor to be with the utmost duty and Respect. &c. . . .[7]

There is no record of Mrs. Taylor's reaction.

Shortly before he thus evaded parental opposition, Byrd was, himself, playing the heavy father. In 1723, Evelyn Byrd was sixteen—an authentic beauty by any standard. Byrd had Charles Bridges paint her portrait, for which she wore a low-cut blue-green gown that set off her snowy skin and slender figure. She had slanting, mischievous, dark blue eyes under penciled brows. (Byrd had evidently given up

6. Byrd *Notebooks.*
7. *Ibid.*

trying to keep his women folk from plucking their eyebrows.) Her nose was classically straight, her mouth small and beautifully shaped. Bridges painted her with a flowered ornament in her brown hair and a long corkscrew curl trailing over one white shoulder. She was holding a large straw gardening hat and a little walking cane in her lap. When Evelyn was presented to King George I at a drawing room in the summer of 1723, that susceptible monarch exclaimed, "Are there many other as beautiful birds in my forests of America?" [8]

Evelyn was not only the beauty but the tragic heroine of Byrd family lore. She fell deeply in love that summer but with whom is a tantalizing mystery. The family legend naming the Earl of Peterborough seems most unlikely. In 1723, Lord Peterborough was a man of sixty-four whom Thackeray describes as "that noble old madcap . . . [who] actually had the audacity to walk about Bath with his blue ribbon and stars and a cabbage under each arm and a chicken in each hand." [9] Though Peterborough was a wit, a friend of Pope and other intellectuals, and still had a fine figure, it seems unlikely that a girl of sixteen, who was the belle of the Court, with wealth and beauty and that American springtime look so appetizing to the jaded beaux of St. James's, should suffer a great passion for such an ancient character. Besides, Peterborough was having an affair with the popular singer of the era, Anastasia Robinson, whom he married. Nor does it seem likely that Byrd, who knew Peterborough well, would refer to him as "the Baronet."

So the mystery remains. However, the fact that Byrd broke up Evelyn's first and only love affair rests solidly on two letters he wrote at this time. The first was addressed to "Amasia" (the beloved one) in stern parental tones:

July 20, 1723

To Amasia

Considering ye solemn promise you made me, first by word of mouth & afterward by letter, that you wou'd not from thence forth have any Converse or Correspondence with the Baronet, I am astonisht you have violated that protestation in a most notorious manner. The gracious audience you gave him the morning you left ye Towne & the open conversations you have with him in the Country have been too unguarded to

8. Edith Tunis Sale, *Old Time Belles and Cavaliers*. J. P. Lippincott Company, New York, 1912.

9. *Henry Esmond*.

be denied. Tis therefor high time for me to reproach you with breech of duty & breech of faith and once more to repeat to you my strict and positive Commands never more to meet, to speak or write to that Gentleman or to give him an opportunity to see, speak or write to You. I also forbid you to enter into any promise or engagement with him of marriage or Inclination. . . . And that neither he nor you may be deluded afterwards with Vain hopes of forgiveness I have put it out of my power by vowing that I never will. And as to any Expectation you may fondly entertain of a Fortune from me, you are not to look for one brass farthing. . . . Nay besides all that I will avoid the sight of you as of a creature detested.

Figure then to yourself, my Dear Child, how wretched you will be with a provokt father and a disappointed Husband. To whome then will you fly in your distress . . . ? For God's sake then, my dear child, for my sake & your own, survey the desperate Precipice you stand upon, and don't rashly cast yourself down head long into Ruin. The idle Promises this man makes you will all vanish into smoke, & instead of Love he will slight & abuse you when he finds his hopes of Fortune disappointed. Then you & your children (if you should be so miserable as to have any) must be Beggers, & you may be assur'd all the world will deservedly dispise you, & you will hardly be pity'd so much as by Him who wou'd fain continue, &c. . . .

Hot on this turgid masterpiece of parental objurgation Byrd dashed off a bitterly sarcastic letter to "Erranti," as he dubbed the unfortunate object of his anger, in which he announced his knowledge of the fellow's pursuit of his daughter into the country like "a Knight Errant" with

a pompous Equipage that dos Her & your self much honor. What success these worthy steps have met with in the Girle I know not: but they shall never meet with any in the Father. I fear your circumstances are not flourishing enough to maintain a Wife in much splendour that has nothing, and just such a fortune as that my Daughter will prove if she ventures to marry without my consent. . . . I have made my Will since I heard of your good intentions toward me, & have bequeathed my Daughter a splendid shilling, if she marrys any man that tempts her to disobedience. After giving you this friendly warning, I hope you will have discretion enough to leave off so unprofitable a Pursuit, to which no tears on my Daughter's part, or Intreatys on yours will ever be able to reconcile. &c. . . .

Whoever Erranti was or however much he loved Evelyn, his passion was evidently not as strong as his prudence. The affair was broken up. Early in 1726, Evelyn and Wilhelmina sailed home to Virginia with their father and stepmother. Byrd's famous chariot was in the hold, and so were thousands of pounds of books.

The fact that Evelyn never married gave rise to the whole tragic romance which has brought tears to the eyes of susceptible females of two continents and was even the subject of a costume novel in French. The ghostly tapping of Evelyn's high heels is still supposed to be heard on quiet evenings in the southeast bedroom of Westover.

Though one may doubt that her heart was truly broken, there is good reason to believe that Evelyn was unhappy in Virginia. What girl would not be who had been feted in the brilliant society of eighteenth-century London? In 1727, Byrd wrote to Lord Boyle, son of his old friend the Earl of Orrery:

My young gentlewomen like everything in the Country except the Retirement, they can't get the Play, the Opera and the Masquerades out of their Heads, much less can they forget their friends. However, the lightness of our Atmosphere helps them to bear their losses with more Spirit, and that they may amuse themselves the better they are every Day up to their elbows in Housewifery, which will qualify them effectively for useful Wives and if they live long enough for notable women. . . . [10]

A year later, when Evelyn was twenty-one, Byrd wrote to Lord Orrery: "One of the most Antick Virgins I am acquainted with is my daughter, either our young Fellows are not smart eno' for her, or she seems too smart for them, but in a little Time I hope they will split the difference. . . ." [11]

Those young Virginia squires may well have seemed boorish to Evelyn, or perhaps she truly pined for her lost love in England, though Byrd may have been too cynical or too stubborn to admit it. As she grew older, she seems to have withdrawn from Virginia society and spent whatever time she could with her one dear friend, Ben Harrison's young bride, Mrs. Anne Carter Harrison of Berkeley. Almost every fine afternoon they met in the grove of tall trees that marked the border of the two plantations to talk and work on elaborate embroideries and needlepoint.

In 1737, when she was only thirty years of age, Evelyn died, in all probability of boredom. There is no record of what her last ill-

10. Orrery Manuscripts, Harvard College Library.
11. *Ibid.*

ness was. Melancholy ever since her return from England, Evelyn had a premonition, perhaps a hope, of an early death. She confided in Anne Harrison that after she died she would meet her again in their beloved grove. For a long time after Evelyn's death Anne refused to go to the grove. Finally, thinking her fears foolish or perhaps feeling that she should keep the sad tryst, she forced herself to go that way. "As she walked in sad reflection she felt a presence. Looking up she saw the etherial figure of her departed companion who leaned toward her with a tender smile. Then vanished." [12]

12. Edith Tunis Sale, *Interiors of Virginia Houses of Colonial Times.* Printed by the William Byrd Press, Inc., Richmond, 1927.

VII · RUNNING THE LINE

BYRD'S RETURN to Virginia in 1726 was the beginning of the most serene and useful period of his life. Maria Taylor Byrd was a good wife to him, staunch, uncomplaining, placidly accepting his eccentricities and bearing him strong, healthy children, all of whom lived to grow up and marry—no mean accomplishment in that time and place. If his existence lacked the excitement and sexual ecstasy of living with Lucy, the compensation was matrimonial serenity. He was getting on in years, though he showed no sign of diminishing vigor, and unlike most of his contemporaries kept his body strong, slim, and supple.

Their first child, Anne, had been born in London on February 5, 1725. Lord Orrery was her godfather. The Byrds left her in England with Maria's sister until 1730, when the latter married Francis Otway, an army officer who became Colonel of the Guards. Anne came home to Westover to find two sisters and a brother—Maria born in January, 1727, Jane born in October, 1729; and the third William Byrd, heir to Westover, born on September 6, 1728. Poor little William, the central object of six adoring females and a doting father, had not much chance. It would have taken a far sturdier character than his to surmount such an environment.

That Byrd relished his patriarchal role is shown by a lyrical letter he wrote to Lord Orrery in July, 1726:

Besides the advantage of a pure air, we abound in all kinds of provisions without expense (I mean we who have plantations). I have a large family of my own, and my doors are open to everybody, yet I have no bills to pay and a half crown will rest undisturbed in my pocket for many moons. Like one of the Patriarchs I have my flocks and my herds, my bondsmen and bondswomen and every sort of trade amongst my own servants so that I live in a kind of independence of everyone but Providence. . . . However this sort of life . . . is attended with a great deal of trouble. I must take care to keep all my people to their duty, to set all springs in motion and to make every one draw his equal share to carry the machine forward. But then tis an amusement in this silent country. Another thing, My Lord, that recommends this country very much: we sit securely under our vines and our fig trees without any Danger to our property. We have neither public Robbers nor private, which your Lordship will think very strange when we have often greedy Governors and pilfering convicts sent amongst us. . . . Thus my Lord we are very happy in our Canaans if we could but forget the onions and fleshpots of Egypt. . . .[1]

Perhaps Byrd was only putting a fine face on his situation while he dreamed of the fleshpots. Certainly news from England was the very lifeblood of his mind. Every ship that came in was eagerly pounced upon for letters—"We tear them open as eagerly as a greedy heir tears open a rich father's will"—its captain was royally entertained for the reports he could bring. Those letters from English friends gave Byrd a sense of still belonging to the great world of which America was as yet merely an outpost. Maria was even more eager for word from home. Byrd wrote that the arrival of mail from abroad excited her so that she could not sleep but talked and tossed all night. To preserve his own sacred rest, when letters arrived in the afternoon or evening, he tried to keep them from her until the following morning so that she would have all day to get over their effect.

The business of setting all the springs in motion occupied most of his time for over a year. He was notably more gentle in the management of "my family," as he called his servants and slaves, than in the spirited days of his first marriage when he personally had whipped

---

1. *Virginia Magazine of History and Biography.* Vol. XXXII, 1924.

Negroes and white servants alike if they displeased him. An unruly slave was now often given a vomit, which Byrd found was more efficacious than a whipping. And frequently of an evening he "held converse" with his family, listening to their troubles and illnesses, counseling for one and prescribing, still fearsomely, for the other.

One source of disturbance was the growing tension between Wilhelmina and her stepmother. They had numerous violent quarrels. Unlike his former self, when Byrd saw lightning streaking the domestic skies, he sensibly retired to his library until the storm was over.

But Byrd was far too high-spirited and vigorous to remain inactive long. In 1727, he accepted the most arduous assignment of his life. Virginia and North Carolina had a long-standing quarrel about the dividing line between the colonies, which had never been surveyed. This left a sort of limbo fifteen miles wide in which criminals, run aways, and undesirables squatted. King George I died in June, 1727, and the new King, George II, ordered the Governors and Councils of the two colonies to appoint commissioners to survey the dividing line and make it definite.

Governor Drysdale having died after a year in office, King Carter, President of the Council, acted in his stead. Byrd had one more try at getting the governorship, but Major (later Colonel) William Gooch was sent over. Byrd bore him no grudge and wrote to Lord Orrery, "By a great accident we have a very worthy man to represent Lord Orkney. It is Major Gooch."

The new Governor and Council appointed William Byrd, William Dandridge, and Colonel Richard Fitzwilliam as Virginia's commissioners to run the line. Byrd wrote two accounts of this extraordinary expedition: a formal, document intended for posterity called "History of the Dividing Line betwixt Virginia and North Carolina,"[2] and a short, wickedly witty piece for very private consumption, "The Secret History of the Line." The History was probably the finest piece of writing William Byrd ever did, filled with interesting information concerning the appearance and geographical characteristics of the wilderness through which the line

2. William Byrd's *History of the Dividing Line betwixt Virginia and North Carolina*. Edited by William Byrd, Raleigh, N.C., 1729.

passed, its flora and fauna, and important asides on the character of its inhabitants and the mores and religion of the Indians. In addition, there are enlightened philosophical disquisitions that show the breadth and learning of his mind. Some of his ethical standards were a hundred and fifty years ahead of his time. When he was seriously setting down his thoughts instead of conforming to the cynical, wit-at-any-price fashion of the time, William Byrd emerges as quite a man.

The Secret History is like the diaries, full of wisecracks and outrageous statements. Here Byrd followed his custom of giving the main characters fictitious names. He called Fitzwilliam "Firebrand" and Dandridge "Meanwell," and dubbed himself "Steddy." The surveyors were "Astrolabe" (William Mayo) and "Capricorn" (John Allen). As Capricorn began to realize the dangers and rigors of the business, he backed out. Governor Gooch appointed Alexander Irvin [3] ("Orion") in his place. Irvin was Professor of mathematics at William and Mary, where he had so few scholars he would not be missed. At Byrd's suggestion the Reverend Peter Fontaine, Rector of Westover Church ("Dr. Humdrum"), went along as chaplain to look after the souls of the party who were to pass through "an ungodly country," and to give the inhabitants of the wild border region an opportunity to have their children christened. These gentlemen, with fifteen strong young volunteers, made up the Virginia delegation.

Four commissioners were appointed by Governor Sir Richard Everard of North Carolina: Christopher Gale; John Lovick; Edward Moseley, who was Surveyor General of the colony; and William Little Boyd, the Attorney General. Byrd christened them "Jumble," "Shoebrush," "Plausible," and "Puzzlecause" respectively. As always he chose pseudonymns suited to his idea of a man's appearance or character.

After a stately exchange of correspondence, the two commissions agreed to meet at Currituck Inlet on the coast on March 5, 1728, which they reckoned an auspicious day because Mercury and the moon would be in conjunction.

The Virginia party equipped itself lavishly with provisions for forty days, a large tent and a marquee, and as much wine and rum "as just to enable us and our men to drink every night to the success of the following day." This sounds reasonably comfortable, but even

3. Spelled Irvine by Byrd. Irvin probably correct.

the journey to the meeting place was arduous. The party rode twenty to thirty miles a day over roads that were usually little better than trails. For a man fifty-four years old, no matter how good his condition, this was strenuous, and Byrd was often very weary at the end of the day. He made no complaint and refreshed himself at the hospitable plantations at which the officials spent the night, while the men camped in the grounds. The accommodations varied from John Allen's "elegant seat," a Jacobean manor house known as Bacon's Castle —though Nathaniel Bacon never owned it—to Andrew Duke's cabin where they were forced "to lie in bulk upon a very dirty floor that was quite alive with fleas and chinches. . . ."

Their route led them past the fringes of the Dismal Swamp whose trees "looked very reverend with the long moss that hung dangling from their branches" [4] to Norfolk which "has more the air of a real town than any in Virginia." Twenty brigantines and sloops rode at its long wharves, fine houses stood on the straight streets bustling with the commerce of sea and land. The inhabitants were either ship carpenters and artisans, or merchants. Byrd admired Norfolk, though he thought it a pity that its merchants "contribute much toward debauching the country by importing an abundance of rum which, like gin in Great Britain, breaks the constitutions, vitiates the morals, and ruins the industry of most of the poor people of this country."

On March 5, the Virginia commissioners reached Currituck Inlet at the head of Albermarle Sound, where the breakers "flew over it with a horrible sound and at the same time afforded a very wild prospect." That night they made a circle of cedar branches with a roaring fire in the center of it, and lay around it, feet to the blaze, like the spokes of a wheel.

Only two of the North Carolina commissioners were there, but the rest arrived the following day, "better provided for the belly than business." At their very first meeting a row took place about the exact starting point of the dividing line. However, the Virginians produced their commission from the King, which empowered them to proceed without the North Carolinians in the event of a dispute. This silenced opposition, but for the sake of harmony Byrd proposed conceding two hundred yards to North Carolina. Accordingly they fixed the start that distance north of the inlet and drove a cedar post

4. Byrd, *History of the Dividing Line.* . . .

deep in the sand to mark the spot. From thence the line was to run due west to the western mountains (the Alleghenies).

On the morning of March 7, the surveyors, Mayo and Irvin for Virginia, Moseley and Samuel Swann II of Perquimans County for North Carolina, having carefully calculated the compass variation and the latitude, began to run the line. Byrd soon discovered that however much Professor Irvin knew about mathematics, he was abysmally ignorant of surveying and tartly noted that "he had been much more discreet to loiter on at the College and receive his salary quietly. . . ." Byrd was also generally contemptuous of the Carolina commissioners. John Lovick, he wrote in *The Secret History*, was a merry, good-humored man who had learned "decent behavior" as valet to former Governor Edward Hyde of North Carolina; but William Boyd "had degenerated from a New England preacher, for which his godly parents had designed him, to a very wicked but awkward rake." Of Christopher Gale, Byrd said, "If His Honor had not been a pirate, he seemed intimately acquainted with many of them"; while Edward Mosely "had been bred in Christ's Hospital and had a tongue as smooth as the Commissary [Blair], and was altogether well qualified to be of the Society of Jesus." [5]

The work of running the line was difficult from the first as it went over the sandspits, marshlands, and estuaries near the shore. The surveyors, frequently up to their waists in icy water, painstakingly sighted their instruments and took their bearings; the Virginia crew carried their chains and cleared the way while most of the Carolina men devoted themselves to cooking. The commissioners followed along with them, sometimes on horseback, sometimes trudging through "intolerable quagmires" in which they sank to their knees, and occasionally taking to the water in large Indian canoes called "Peraguas"; camping for the night in the fields of various plantations, drinking up a storm and trifling with the women, though Byrd, according to himself, behaved very well and tried to keep the more raucous within the bounds of decent civility—not always successfully.

The marshy country near the sea was so damp that Byrd declared they became as impervious to water as beavers and otters. But in spite of this he became so enamored of camping that on fine nights he refused the hospitality of an occasional house "to lie in an open field for fear of growing too tender. A clear sky, spangled with stars was our canopy which . . . gave us magnificent dreams."

5. Byrd particularly hated Jesuits.

All the wild border folk turned out to stare at these extraordinary characters whom they considered insane to undertake such hardships and perils. They pointed out the difficulties with relish. One inhabitant said to Byrd, "Ye have little reason to be merry, my masters. I fancy the pocosin [6] you must struggle through tomorrow will make you change your note. . . . Ye are, to be sure, the first of human race that ever had the boldness to attempt it, and I dare say will be the last. If, therefore, you have any worldly goods to dispose of, my advice is that you make your wills this very night. . . ." [7]

Byrd found the border people extremely bizarre, noting their "custard complexions" and the fact that the noses of many of them had rotted away. This, he said, was due to their eating nothing but fresh pork during the winter, which gave them scurvy and yaws. They were too lazy to grow and store vegetables or grain, but subsisted on their herds of swine which ran wild through the woods and required no labor beyond slaughtering.

With his strong religious beliefs, Byrd was shocked and disgusted to find that the Carolinians were, by his standards, practically heathens who boasted of having no parasitic priests to support. Every Sunday the expedition rested; the gentlemen put on their best clothes and clean linen and Fontaine conducted services and edified them with a rousing sermon. Though Byrd saw to it that notices of these services were spread throughout the countryside, few people came and those only from curiosity. Fontaine had little luck with his missionary work. He was allowed to baptize quite a few children, but not one couple accepted his offers to regularize the relationships of men and women with a marriage ceremony.

Byrd was very strict about keeping the Sabbath. He would allow no work to be done that could possibly be avoided; and even when it could not be helped, as in the case of searching for a lost horse or making a march forced by necessity, he was uneasy in his conscience and sought a Biblical excuse.

Just how he reconciled this with the work his slaves were obliged to do for the big Sunday dinner parties at Westover is one of those quirks of conscience which he never explained. Perhaps it never occurred to him.

Despite all the difficulties, the surveyors made very good progress of four to ten miles a day until they came to the Great Dismal

6. A junglelike swamp.
7. Byrd, *History of the Dividing Line.* . . .

Swamp. This putrid place was so feared by the inhabitants that it had never been explored and even its area was unknown. The commissioners were advised that it was completely impassable, but the hardy surveyors and their helpers were willing to try. Byrd, Dandridge, and William Boyd of North Carolina went into the swamp with the surveying party. The other commissioners preferred to "toast their noses over a good fire, and spare their dear persons."

The expedition marched two miles to the edge of the swamp, where Byrd gave the men a pep talk. "Gentlemen," he said, "we are at last arrived at this dreadful place, which til now has been thought impassable, though I make no doubt but you will convince everybody that there is no difficulty which may not be conquered by spirit and constancy. . . . I protest to you that the only reason we don't share your fatigue is the fear of adding to your burdens (which are but too heavy already) while we are sure we can add nothing to your resolution. I shall say no more but only pray the Almighty to prosper your undertaking and grant we may meet on the other side in perfect health and safety."

The men evidently approved his style of oratory, for they gave him three hearty hurrahs. Then, with two men hacking out a path for the surveyors to sight along, they all plunged into the Dismal. Byrd found that the ground was like a thin crust floating on liquid mud. A dense growth of tall reeds thickly interwoven with bamboo briars had to be cut away by the pioneers. In other places juniper trees or large white cedars grew among the reeds or lay blown down by the wind so their huge rotting trunks blocked the way. No living creatures were seen. "Not so much as a Zeeland frog could endure so aguish a situation. . . ." The air in the swamp was so foul and its ascending stench so strong that "not even a turkey buzzard would fly over it."

Byrd, Dandridge, and Boyd struggled along for two hours, during which they made only half a mile. They came to a hummock of firm ground where the exhausted men, staggering under sixty-pound packs, threw themselves down for a brief rest. There the commissioners took their leave after furnishing William Mayo, the most experienced surveyor, with bark and other medicines, "not forgetting three kinds of rattlesnake root made into doses in case of need." Committing the company to the care of Providence, the commissioners trudged back to their base camp.

The surveying party disappeared for nine days. Meanwhile the commissioners marched around the Dismal to Captain Thomas Speight's plantation, where they waited for word from the surveyors. Though the entertainment was good and Byrd might well have enjoyed the rest after an arduous journey, he was very uneasy, "quite cloyed with the Carolina felicity of having nothing to do." In addition he was badly worried about his men in the Dismal. He ordered scouts to its edges, beating drums and firing guns, in the hope of a return signal, but not a sound broke the deadly silence. On the ninth day, Mr. Swann appeared in "a very tattered condition," but with the welcome news that all the Dismalites were safe. He told a hair-raising tale of their hardships, which included sleeping in water every night, ploughing through stinking jungled morasses, running out of food, and enduring fevers and chills brought on by the miasmas.

From that point on the work proceeded rapidly as they reached the uplands. It was still a matter of driving the line straight through a wilderness broken only by occasional plantations, but after the Dismal nothing seemed very difficult. However, dissensions among the commissioners made up for that. Byrd had always disliked Colonel Fitzwilliam, who appears to have been a real troublemaker. He was well named "Firebrand," for he continually started quarrels and found more pleasure in the company of the Carolinians than his own people, which made Byrd suspect his loyalty to Virginia. It appears to have been a clash of personalities, for both men were dictatorial, arrogant, and absolutely sure they were right. In addition, "Firebrand" Fitzwilliam swore a great deal, which surprisingly upset Byrd, who could curse like "a trooper in His Majesty's Guards" if the occasion called for it. In the close quarters of the tent where they camped "Firebrand" kept them awake all night by alternately snoring and cursing in his sleep.

By April 5, they had reached Isle of Wight County on the Meherrin River, seventy-three miles and thirteen chains [8] from their start. Since it was a hot, dry spring, the rattlesnakes were beginning to swarm out of their holes, endangering both men and horses. The commissioners in a rare burst of unanimity decided to halt there and resume operations on September 10. They parted company with feelings of mutual relief. Colonel Fitzwilliam and Professor Irvin headed straight for home; Byrd, Dandridge, Fontaine, and the other

8. A surveyor's chain was four rods or sixty-six feet long.

Virginians decided to pay a visit to the famous Nottaway Indian town, a little over fourteen miles away.

Sending a runner ahead to announce their visit, they marched toward the town. Indian girls, acting as scouts, announced their coming with yells and whoops, which brought the braves out in a body to escort them in. The town was enclosed by a square palisade about a hundred yards on each side with loopholes at intervals. Within it were enough bark cabins to shelter the remnants of the whole Nottaway tribe, once powerful but now numbering only two hundred, including women and children. Yet they were the only tribe of any consequence left in Virginia. The braves escorted their guests to the best cabins, which were very sweet and clean with new mats on the floors.

That evening the young men—their faces hideous with vermilion, black, and white war paint—entertained them with a war dance, singing to the beat of their drums while gesturing with all-too-realistic ferocity.

The Indian women were dressed in their best for the occasion, wearing "red and blue match coats thrown so negligently about them that their mahogany skins appeared in several part, like the Lacedaemian damsels of old. Their hair was braided with white and blue peak [9] and hung gracefully in a large roll on their shoulders. . . . Though their complexions be a little sad-colored, yet their shapes are very straight and well proportioned. Their faces are seldom handsome, yet they have an air of innocence and bashfulness that with a little less dirt would not fail to make them desirable. Such charms might have had their full effect upon men who had been so long deprived of female conversation but that the whole winter's soil was . . . encrusted on the skins of those angels. . . ." [10]

Despite the bear's grease and dirt, the Reverend Mr. Fontaine was horrified next morning to observe, from the soiled ruffles of some of the less squeamish members of the party, that they had enjoyed the Indian maidens' favors.

At this point in his *History,* Byrd indulged in some interesting observations on English-Indian relations. He noted that only the Indian boys used bows and arrows any longer; all the men had guns. Byrd thought this was a good thing for the English for two reasons: It bound the Indians to them by the chains of trade; secondly, in a

9. Beads made of conch shells used for both money and ornament.
10. Byrd, *History of the Dividing Line.* . . .

forest fight, arrows were much more deadly because the Indians could fire a great number of them swiftly and silently, but because of the difficulty of reloading they usually fired a gun only once and then ran away.

Byrd agreed with his brother-in-law Robert Beverley's opinion that the early settlers were foolish not to marry Indian girls, not only because it was the best way to reclaim them from "barbarity" and convert them permanently to Christianity; but also because, had they done so, the country by now "had swarmed with people more than it does with insects."

Byrd pointed out that a policy of intermarriage had been approved by the Most Christian King, Louis XIV, in Canada and Louisiana. In an extraordinarily enlightened passage Byrd wrote:

It was certainly an unreasonable nicety that prevented their [the English] entering into so good-natured an alliance. All nations of men have the same natural dignity, and we all know that very bright talents may be lodged under a very dark skin. The principal difference between one people and another proceeds only from different opportunities of improvement. The Indians by no means want understanding and are in their figure tall and well proportioned. . . . I may safely venture to say that the Indian women would have made altogether as honest wives for the first planters as the damsels they used to purchase from aboard the ships. Tis strange, therefor, that any good Christian should have refused a wholesome, straight bedfellow when he might have had so fair a portion with her as the merit of saving her soul.[11]

On leaving Nottaway Town and crossing the Nottaway River to Colonel Henry Harrison's plantation, they congratulated each other "upon our return to Christendom." After washing off the Indian dirt and putting on fresh linen, Byrd drew the men up in line and "harangued" them:

Friends and fellow travellers, it is a great satisfaction to me that after so many difficulties and fatigues you are returned in safety to the place where I first joined you. I am much obliged to you for the great readiness and vigor you have showed in the business. . . . You have not only done your duty but also done it with cheerfulness and affection. Such a behavior, you may be sure, will engage us to procure for you the best satisfaction we can from the Government. And besides that you may

11. *Ibid.*

depend on our being ready at all times to do you any manner of kindness. You are now, blessed be God, near Your own dwellings . . . I heartily wish you may, every one, find your friends and your families in perfect health, and that your affairs may have suffered as little as possible by your absence.

The men appeared touched by this speech and replied, thanking their leaders for their "affectionate care." In the general upswell of emotion Byrd notes: "It was as much as we could do to part with dry eyes." [12]

Byrd made straight for Westover where he found all his family in good health and Maria doing well in her third pregnancy. He rested there a week before going to Williamsburg to report to the Governor and Council. Colonel Fitzwilliam and Professor Irvin had been there before him with all sorts of complaints of his conduct of the expedition. James Blair was in a froth over the alleged mistreatment of these favorites of his. With Dandridge and others backing him up, Byrd had no trouble convincing the Governor that their complaints were baseless.

However, the infighting continued off and on all summer. Whatever Byrd wanted, Fitzwilliam opposed. The Carolina people proposed putting off the resumption of running the line until September 20. This suited Byrd very well, as he hoped Maria would have her child by then. Fitzwilliam, backed by Blair, held out for the tenth. But the start was postponed. Then Fitzwilliam and Blair proposed that only ten men be taken; Byrd wanted twenty. He pointed out that there must always be five men on duty, the chain carriers, the markers, and the man to carry the instrument after the surveyors. In thick woods two more were needed to clear the way. He said the rest were needed to handle the riding and pack horses. In addition, he pointed out that during the next stage they would be far beyond human habitation and the dividing line would cross the great trail down which the war parties of the northern Indians came to attack their Catawba enemies. Twenty men would be needed to hold them off if, in an excess of martial ardor, they attacked the English. In fairness he admitted that the North Carolinians would add to their numbers, but, he said, "They will bring more eaters than fighters."

Governor Gooch thought this was good sense, and put it to a vote

12. Byrd, *The Secret History.*

of the Council. They upheld Byrd. So Fitzwilliam and Blair were defeated on all counts but one. Byrd attempted to get rid of "Firebrand" altogether. In this he failed, but, as the senior commissioner, he was given direct command of the men.

Promptly on time William Byrd III was born at Westover on September 6, 1728. He was a fine sturdy child and it was with a high heart that Byrd again rode into the wilderness. He took with him twelve hundred pounds of bread on six pack horses, but he proposed to hunt for meat in that upland country where game abounded in the fall.

The commissioners met on September 20, at a Mr. Kinchen's house. Almost everyone got drunk on cheap brandy they bought from their landlord. Mrs. Kinchen barricaded herself in her room armed with "a chamberpot charged to the brim with female ammunition." The maid in the kitchen was not so foresighted and "would certainly have been ravished if her timely consent had not averted violence."

In spite of this spree, the surveyors got off to a good start in the morning. Byrd's plan for getting their meat off the country worked out very well. Noticing that his own men were poor shots, he hired Ned Bearskin and another Sapony Indian to do the hunting. They brought in plentiful supplies of wild turkeys, deer, and quite a few fat bears. This was Byrd's favorite meat; he declared it had a high relish and rested easily on the stomach. The greatest delicacy was the bear's paws if one were not put off by the fact that, when skinned, they looked like a human foot. Byrd warned, however, that bear "is not a very proper diet for saints [because] it makes them a little too rampant. . . ." After eating it, "one is sure to dream of a woman or the devil or both." Despite this, the Reverend Peter Fontaine enjoyed it so much that "he growled like a wild cat over a squirrel, as he ate." [13]

It was inevitable that among men who disliked each other to begin with tensions must rise in the wilderness. The division was the same as before—Fitzwilliam, Irvin, and most of the Carolinians on one side; Byrd, Dandridge, Mayo, and the Virginia men, almost all of whom had been on the first expedition and adored Byrd, on the other. However, in the fine weather and comparatively easy going of the upland country the enmity remained latent for the time being.

The line roughly paralleled the Roanoke River, crossing many

13. *Ibid.*

rivulets which ran into it. These, the commissioners gaily named according to their fancy: Sable Creek, whose water looked black; Nutbush Creek; Bluewing Creek; a branch of the upper Roanoke was named Fitzwilliam River in honor of "Firebrand"; another for Professor Irvin. Byrd named a particularly violent little stream Matrimony Creek because it was so noisy and impetuous.

Sometimes the surveyors were held up by thick underbrush and only made two or three miles in a day. At others, the ground was clear beneath the dense foliage of tall, huge-boled trees and they went ten miles or more. There were abandoned Indian fields and savannas of high, rich grass where Indians had burned off the forest. Along the rivers grew canes tall enough to hide a man on horseback. Byrd fell in love with the country, and afterward bought twenty thousand acres along the Dan River for £200 from one of the North Carolina commissioners who had been granted it in payment for his services. Byrd called it "The Land of Eden."

Despite the idyllic conditions, tension was growing between the rival camps. It reached its peak on October 5, a few days after they crossed the Roanoke River. The North Carolina commissioners announced that Governor Everard had instructed them not to carry the line more than thirty or forty miles beyond the river. Byrd replied that Governor Gooch had ordered the line carried to the western mountains and he intended to do it. Fitzwilliam, as usual, joined with the Carolinians and tempers got hot. Fitzwilliam wrote out a minute, accusing Byrd of various faults. In return, Dandridge jokingly said he would write a minute against Fitzwilliam, and began to do so.

Suddenly "Firebrand" blazed up. He broke off a leg of the table big enough to stun an ox and started for Dandridge. Quick as a lynx Byrd leaped to intervene, knocking the table over on poor John Lovick. Dandridge jumped up, yelling at Fitzwilliam that he was a son of a whore. For a moment it looked like a general donnybrook, with "Firebrand" and Dandridge roaring at each other!

Then Byrd assumed command. He told Fitzwilliam that if he did not quiet down, he would put him under arrest.

"You have no such authority!" Fitzwilliam yelled furiously.

He was quite right, but Byrd intended to take it whether or not. "If you will not be easy I'll soon convince you of my authority," he answered.

Backing him up were the Virginia pioneers, ready to obey his command. The sight of them doused "Firebrand's" flames. The quarrel was settled, and Fitzwilliam departed with the North Carolina commissioners after everyone had signed the surveyors' plat. Thereafter harmony reigned.

From that place on, the expedition was far beyond any habitation. As the country rose toward the Alleghenies, it became wilder and more rugged. Panthers stalked the woods at night; wolves howled at the moon. They had one bad Indian scare when one of the hunters reported finding a camp abandoned by a large war party of northern Indians with the ashes of their campfire still warm. That frightened some of the party and even Byrd was quite concerned. He tightened the perimeters of their overnight camps and posted sentries. To soothe his nervous companions he made light of the matter in his inimitable way, saying cheerfully that the Indians would probably not attack them, but if they did, the company would have the satisfaction of fighting to the last man. It is doubtful if this comforted them very much.

No more was seen of the Indians, however. One night, Byrd, who was deeply interested in religion, had an interesting talk with Ned Bearskin about his people's beliefs. Bearskin believed in a Supreme Being who had created the world and who protects and prospers the good people and punishes the wicked. After death all people follow one great road until it forks. Here the good are parted from the bad by a flash of lightning and take the right-hand road, which leads to a fine, warm country where every month is May. Just as the year is always young, so are the people. The women are "beautiful as stars and never scold"; there are plenty of fat deer, and the trees bear delicious fruit all year round.

The unfortunate ill-doers who are forced to take the left fork come to a land where it is always winter and everyone is old, ugly, and toothless, but very hungry. The women are hideous but very passionate. With long, sharp, pantherlike claws, they attack the men who repulse their obscene overtures. On the border of this Indian hell sits a hideous old woman with rattlesnakes for hair and "a tongue twenty cubits long, armed with sharp thorns." This she uses like an elephant's trunk to throw the bad people over a "vast high wall," where still another crone sentences them to punishments that fit their crimes. When their sentences have been served, they are thrown back over the wall for another chance on earth. "If they mend their manners," they eventually reach the Indian heaven.

Soon after this conversation Byrd had another of his elaborate dreams. In it the three Graces appeared to him in "all their naked charms." He chose Charity and had an intrigue with her.

On the party went, over the ever-steepening hills and valleys toward the western mountains, which one morning opened suddenly to their view. Those to the north rose in four ridges, one above the other, to a great height; to the south were individual peaks, one of which was "so vastly high it seemed to hide its head in the clouds." The western end of this range "terminated in a horrible precipice" which they called "Dispairing Lover's Leap." As Byrd stood there staring at the ultimate limit of the English world thus far, he must have been an extraordinary sight himself; he was dressed in British outdoor fashion, with high soft leather boots, a long-skirted coat fastened with golden buttons, and a ruffled shirt. An alien, apparently fragile figure, he should have been overwhelmed in that primeval wilderness, but he had never a doubt it would be conquered, if not by him, by others like him.

For one more day the commission pushed on up hill. Then on October 26, Byrd decided that they had gone far enough to satisfy His Majesty's commission and somewhat farther than prudence would prescribe. The season was getting late, and "we had reason to apprehend the consequences of being intercepted by deep snows and the swelling of many waters between us and home." In addition, their supply of bread was running out and their horses, not being able to eat bear meat but relying on uncertain fodder, were in such bad shape they could not possibly climb the steep hills that rose in their path.

At the end of their long journey they blazed a red-oak tree and all the trees around it to mark the place where the dividing line ended temporarily. According to the Charter of North Carolina, it should extend due westward "to the South Sea." No one then, nor for half a century, had the faintest idea of how far that would be, or that the "240 miles 230 poles" [14] they had traveled in a straight line from the sea was a mere sliver of the vast land mass to the west.

The return journey to "Christandom" was almost as arduous as the forward march. The poor horses were no more than skeletons cov-

14. Byrd, *History of the Dividing Line*. . . . In another place he gives slightly different distances.

ered with skin. Several lay down and died. Byrd, who was by now as lean and fit as an Indian, walked more than half the way back to spare his beast. In this, he was unlike his fellow countrymen who, he said, had so great a passion for riding "that they will often walk two miles to catch a horse in order to ride one. . . ." For meat the expedition finally had to resort to "fire hunting," which Byrd considered most unsporting. The men set a ring of fire in the woods to burn inward and drive the deer toward its center, where they were easily killed. Byrd says, "This sport . . . is much practiced by the Indians and some English as barbarous as Indians."

Despite the discomforts and perils of this long journey through a totally untouched wilderness, Byrd brought his entire party back in glowing health without the loss of a single man. He did not take credit for this but gave it to God. In his farewell speech to the expedition, when they were safely back across the swelling rivers, he said:

> You will give me leave to put you in mind how manifestly Heaven has ingaged in our preservation. No distress, no disaster no sickness of any consequence has befallen any one of us in so long and dangerous a journey. We have subsisted plentifully on the bounty of Providence and been day by day supplied in the barren wilderness with food convenient for us.
>
> This is surely an instance of divine goodness never to be forgotten, and, that it may be more complete, I heartily wish that the same protection may have been extended to our families during our absence. . . .[15]

The people standing around him listened glumly, for they had heard a rumor, which they were careful to keep from him, that his little son had died at Westover. Fortunately the rumor was unfounded. When Byrd received a letter from his wife, telling him that everyone at home was well, the whole company burst out with joyful congratulations. Byrd was deeply touched by this, and by the fact that thirty people—"three of them women"—had managed to keep word of the rumor secret, out of their affectionate care for his peace of mind.

15. Byrd, *The Secret History.*

VIII · THE LAND
OF EDEN & A CITY
IN THE AIR

RETURNING from his adventures, Byrd was met a day's journey from home by a chair [1] in which rode his eager wife and Evelyn. His daughter obligingly mounted a borrowed horse to ride home so that William and Maria could travel in the chair together to the river bank where boats were waiting to take them to Westover. Everyone there was well and Maria had managed the place splendidly in his absence, for all of which he devoutly gave thanks to Providence.

Safely home, with time on his hands, Byrd began to plan the greater, more beautiful Westover which stands beside the James today. His old wooden house must have bulged with his growing family—five daughters and a son, the son that made it all worthwhile. Besides, all the great planters were stepping up their scale of living. Berkeley, of course, already stood next door with tall chimneys towering above a steep slate roof; its great hall and lofty ceilings, its large beautifully paneled rooms, ancient trees shading the lawn, and its garden famous for "Anne Harrison's Rose." Green Spring was almost as it had been when grandiose Sir William Berkeley built it. A short distance from Westover, Secretary of State John Carter was embellishing Shirley, a big, almost square, brick

---

1. Possibly a two-seated chaise.

house; very plain, almost forbidding outside, but spacious, luxuriously paneled and furnished within. King Carter had Corotoman; his son, Colonel Landon Carter, was completing Sabine Hall high on a hilltop overlooking the Rappahannock.[2] Former Governor Spotswood was planning his "castle" at Germanna; the Lees had Stratford; the Beverleys, Blandfield; and other great houses were springing up all along the Tidewater rivers and even beyond the Fall Line. Could Byrd be left behind? Given his proud temperament and love of elegance, that was inconceivable, even though that foolish old Parke debt still kept him pinched for ready money.

In the building and furnishing of the second Westover there was no such parsimony as Byrd's father had used in the first. Everything was the finest obtainable; the Second William was a perfectionist. Nor was it done hastily. Several years elapsed while bricks were being made of just the rich red hue Byrd wanted; slate was accumulated for its steep dormered roof with two tall thin chimneys at either end; marble and granite were quarried for trim; wood was carved by craftsmen for paneling; and while all this was going on, plans were drawn and redrawn. Though he undoubtedly employed one or more architects, it is a fair assumption that Byrd himself was the master builder.

When Westover was finally finished in about 1736, it was, though not the largest, perhaps the most classically beautiful of the great Tidewater houses; at least the Marquis de Chastellux rated it as such in his *Memoires*, written in 1782.

Approaching it from the landward side, the Byrds' guests passed between brick gateposts topped by marble urns and pineapples, the symbol of hospitality. Half a mile of driveway, curving between an avenue of trees, brought them to another pair of tall wrought-iron gates, with the entwined initials W.B. hung between high stone pillars. These were decorated with the Byrd coat of arms and angry lead eagles faced toward the house. Seen from the river across the sweep of turf, the great house stood three tall stories high. Its façade was of dark red brick trimmed with white. Low stone steps led up to the marble-framed doorway with a scroll pediment in the style of Sir Christopher Wren. The slate roof rose steeply to a great height enlivened by the dormered windows of the third floor. The central section was flanked on either side by buildings which were smaller, one-

2. Robert "King" Carter died in 1732.

and-a-half-story replicas. That on the west was the kitchen, completely separate from the main building; the one on the east housed the famous library and was also used as a ballroom; though a small building, it made a large room.

The paneled hall, eighteen feet wide, ran right through the house, a little off center. Its principal features was the splendid stairway, which mounted upward to the second and third floor. It had broad, easy steps and mahogany banisters, brought from England, and supported by hand-turned, finely carved spindles. Opening off the hall to the east were two large parlors. The one overlooking the river through three deeply recessed, very tall windows was centered on the famous Italian mantelpiece of black and white marble. This may have been the one from Byrd's flat in Lincoln's Inn.[3] The room's fifteen-foot-high gilded ceiling was decorated with ornate scrolls. There were in the corners medallions of classic heads of Homer and Virgil. The classical theme was carried through by the fluted pilasters on either side of the doorways.

On the west side of the hall were two somewhat smaller rooms—since knocked together—one of which may have been the Byrds' downstairs bedroom. All the rooms were handsomely paneled, probably in dark, lustrous wood in Byrd's time, though it is now painted over. There were eight bedrooms, four each on the second and third floors. These were only for family and guests as all the servants were quartered in separate buildings.[4]

Byrd had the finest furnishings and splendid silver shipped over from London. Never one to accept shoddy goods, he wrote a sharp reproof to his London Agent:

[I] beg you will employ your interest with the tradesmen not to send all the refuse of their shops to Virginia. Desire them to keep them for the customers that never pay them. Tis hard we must take all the worst of their people and the worst of their goods too. But now shopkeepers have left off their bands and their frugality and their spouses must be maintained in Splendor, tis very fit the sweat of our Brows should help support them in it. Luxury is bad enough among people of quality, but when it gets among that order of men that stand behind counters, they

3. Credence is given to this theory by the fact that it is somewhat too small to heat so large a room but just right for a flat.

4. Some historians speak of Byrd's having remodeled the old Westover. Since the walls of the new buildings are three feet thick and of brick, it seems improbable that the old wooden house was rebuilt.

must turn Cheats and Pickpockets to get it and then Lord have mercy on those who are obliged to trust to their honesty. . . .[5]

Byrd made the great hall into a portrait gallery in which he could fondly recall his English friends. There hung Argyll in his steel corselet and crimson mantle; Sir Robert Southwell, Byrd's first and steadfast friend in London; the Earls of Orrery, Albermarle, and Egremont; the Marquis of Halifax, Sir Charles Wager, now First Lord of the Admiralty; Sir Wilfred Lawson; and Sir Robert Walpole, Prime Minister of England, to whom Byrd sent supplies of ginseng and good advice, including the wise warning to keep the Navy strong.

"A great superiority at sea," he wrote, "will secure us from invasion, and at the same time enable us to insult the enemy's coast and interrupt its fleets. It is to the interest of Great Britain to decide all her disputes upon her own element, and leave the people on the Continent to fight their own battles." [6]

Most of the portraits were painted by Godfrey Kneller at the height of his form; though some, including Byrd's own family, were by Charles Bridges, who came to Virginia in 1735. Byrd's collection became so famous that Mr. Walpho, Clerk of the House of Burgesses, went off and had his portrait painted, then offered Byrd a diamond ring to hang it among the great men in his hall. Never one to turn down an honest acquisition, Byrd accepted the deal.

Always intensely interested in botany, Byrd made the garden even more beautiful than it had been in his father's time. He imported all the flowers of England and rare bulbs from Holland to plant in beds beside the gravel walks. At any time of the year, except the dead of winter, it was gay with blooms that changed with the season. And even in mid-winter the dark green of splendid English box made the spot a refuge from the leached fields and frost-seared lawns. A low brick wall covered with honeysuckle enclosed the garden and extended down the western edge of the lawn to the river.

Perhaps the greatest glory of Westover and its most lasting contribution to Virginia culture was the superb library which Byrd had been collecting throughout the years. Its 3600 volumes contained the essence of Western man's accumulated knowledge and artistic endeavor. There were 250 works on history and biography; 150 law

5. *The London Diary.*
6. Letter to Walpole August 30, 1739.

books; 130 books on medicine arranged historically from the aphorisms and commentaries of Hippocrates (in Greek) down through the ages to John Jennent's *Epistle to Mead* published in 1737. These medical books bore the marks of intensive reading. All the great names of English literature to that date were represented in poetry, novels, and plays; there were 300 books in Latin and Greek; at least 200 in French, Dutch, and Italian. Hobbes, Descartes, Boyle, Locke, and the best of the ancients represented philosophy. Theology included sections in Hebrew, Greek, Latin, and the European languages, in addition to English. Of course there was a large number of works on science and mathematics, and many books on architecture from Vitruvius to Palladio and the contemporary English architects. Treatises on drawing and painting and collections of music were in another section of the room. Still another contained many books on travel and discovery. Books on the miscellaneous shelves were on agriculture and gardening, cookbooks and works on distilling, even books on etiquette—including such precursors of Mrs. Emily Post as *The Courtier's Calling* and *The Gentleman's Recreation*.

Byrd's was certainly the largest privately owned library in America, and probably, after Harvard's, the most complete in the whole continent. Its very existence had a snowball effect on education in the Dominion; for if Byrd had such a collection of books, other Virginia gentlemen felt obliged to imitate him, though none surpassed him in his lifetime or for many years thereafter. In addition, its owner made it free to all who came to his hospitable house; and no one knows how many young Virginians first savored the delights of literature in that annex of Westover.

About the time Byrd moved into the new house he engaged the Reverend Mr. Procter, fresh from England, as full-time librarian. He was lodged in a small tenant house and supplied with "all the genteel conveniences" as well as having his clothes ordered from England with Byrd's own shipments. However, on one occasion Procter wrote his master a letter complaining that the allowance of one candle a night was not sufficient to enable him to pursue his studies, to which Byrd replied in his most facetious vein:

Most Hypocondriack Sir:
  I have your list of complaints . . . as for your being forced, like mad people, to sit in the dark without a candle . . . orders have been given

from the beginning to furnish you with one every night. . . . But I understand the candles are not big enough for you. I am sorry we have not wax, or at least mould candles big enough, to light you in your lucubrations. Had your dear friend Mr. Stevens supplied us with more tallow, perhaps we might have been better able to light up the white house with bigger candles. In the meantime, if such as you have, by the judgement of two good men, will burn for an hour and a half, that is full long enough to read by candle light which is not good for the eyes, and after that, meditation and devotion might fill up the rest of the evening. Then as to the calamity of your wanting those useful implements of tongs and poker, that I must own is a very compassionate case. But I can clear myself of this impeachment, too, for I remember I ordered the Smith to make a pair of tongs on purpose for you, and if you or your chamberfellow unluckily destroyed them, it was by no means the fault of

> Yours,
> *Wm. Byrd* [7]

Despite an occasional brush with the penuriousness which frequently strikes the rich in unexpected places, Mr. Procter was happy at Westover and liked Byrd whom he described as "a very honerable and virtuous master." They had long, interesting conversations and Byrd was fond of teasing this serious young man. He gave Procter the expectation of eventually getting him appointed to a parish. When the librarian appeared ambivalent as to whether he wanted to continue in the ministry or take up some land to farm, Byrd laughingly asked, "Why don't you try being at once a planter and a parson?" [8]

By the time they moved into the new Westover the Byrds no longer had to wait for a ship from England or a visit from the neighbors to get the news of the wide world. In 1736, a four-page weekly newspaper called the *Virginia Gazette* was started. It prospered, grew, and soon became a daily. At that, Virginia was behind almost all the other colonies. The first newspaper in America was the *Boston News-Letter,* founded in 1704; and Pennsylvania, Maryland, New York, Rhode Island, and South Carolina all had newspapers before Virginia. Perhaps the fault lay with the conservatives, clinging to old Sir William Berkeley's distaste for the press.

7. Bassett, *op. cit.*
8. *Ibid.*

The mellow and kindly Lord of Westover had changed considerably from the rather arrogant, waspish, and passionate young heir who had come to claim his heritage in 1705. There were no domestic brawls to tighten his nerves; and his public life was also more peaceful, under the tranquil administration of good Governor Gooch.

In later years he began to have grave doubts about the institution of slavery on which his fortune was partly founded. In a letter written in 1736 to Lord Egremont, who was a partner of General James Edward Oglethorpe in founding the Colony of Georgia, Byrd approved the plan to prohibit slavery and rum in the new colony, though he was afraid they would find it difficult to do so.

He wrote:

For the saints of New England, will find out some trick to evade your Act of Parliament. . . . These foul traders import so many negroes hither that I fear this Colony will sometime or other be confounded by the name of New Guinea. . . . I am sensible of many bad consequences of multiplying these Ethiopians among us. . . . They blow up the pride and ruin the industry of our white people who, seeing a rank of poor creatures below them, detest work for fear it should make them look like slaves. . . . Another unhappy effect of many negroes is the necessity of being severe, numbers make them insolent and then foul means must do what fair will not. . . .

On rum he wrote in the same letter:

I entirely agree with your Lordship in the detestation you seem to feel for that diabolical liquor, Rum, which does more mischief to people, industry and morals than anything except gin and the Pope. Thrice happy Georgia if it be in the power of any law to keep out so great an enemy to health and industry and virtue. The new settlers had much better plant vineyards like Noah and get drunk with their own wine.[9]

Though his life was comparatively serene and his attitude benevolent, Byrd was far from relapsing into semi-retirement. He was full of energy and continually propounding schemes for the advancement of his country and the improvement of his finances. One of his most remarkable plans was to drain the Dismal Swamp, which would have added an area of some three hundred square miles of fertile land to North Carolina and have given the back country a waterway to the sea. He worked it out in great detail, proposing a joint stock company

9. *Virginia Magazine of History and Biography*, Vol. IX.

with £4000 capital, half to be raised in England, half in Virginia. The labor would be done by slaves. He thought ten of both sexes should be enough to start with and their "breed would supply the loss from death." They would raise their own food and, with the addition of their offspring and small yearly purchases, could be counted on to increase the proprietor's wealth in addition to the valuable land which would emerge as the waters were channeled out of the swamp. This scheme fell through because British investors, having recently taken fearful losses from the bursting of the South Sea Bubble, were in no mood to venture capital in chimerical colonial enterprises.

While he was building Westover, Byrd went on more journeys through the country and wrote about them in charming narratives of adventure. "A Progress to the Mines" described a pilgrimage he made, in the autumn of 1732, to the iron furnaces at Fredericksville and Fredericksburg on the Rappahannock to learn about the business of smelting iron, which he planned to enter with his own mines on the original land at the Falls of the James.

After inspecting his properties at the Falls and giving everyone hell for their poor management, he proceeded to Mr. Charles Chiswell's plantation. Mrs. Chiswell was the lady whom he had kissed so ardently in 1709 that Lucy wept from jealousy. Byrd had not seen her for twenty-four years and sadly recorded that "Alas! [the years] had made great havoc with her pretty face and plowed deep furrows in her fair skin. It was impossible to know her again, so much had the flower faded." [10]

Mr. Chiswell, who owned the iron mines and furnace at Fredericksville, was a fine source of information, which he poured out to Byrd, giving him all the facts and figures in the course of a three-day visit and showing him over the entire mining operation.

From there, Byrd went to visit his old enemy, Colonel Spotswood, at his "enchanted castle" at Germanna on the Rappahannock, where Mrs. Spotswood kept two tame deer that wandered like lap dogs through the house. Colonel Spotswood, who had a much larger mining operation than Chiswell, "very civilly" agreed to tell him all the secrets of the business and even agreed to visit Byrd's mines on the James and give him the benefit of his opinion. The Colonel lec-

10. "A Progress to the Mines" by William Byrd. Republished in *The Prose Works of William Byrd of Westover*. Edited by Louis B. Wright. The Belknap Press, Harvard University Press, Cambridge, 1966.

tured for hours while Byrd meticulously noted down everything he said: how rich ore must be smelted with a poorer grade lest the iron be too brittle; how much limestone to mix with it, though oyster shells would do; the proper location and cost of building a smelter (£700); the best wood to make charcoal; the number of slaves required (120); white employees—founder, mine raiser, collier, stocktaker, smith, carpenter, wheelwright; the logistics of carting the iron to water transport; the cost of shipment, duties, and expected sale price per ton in England . . . on and on. Byrd absorbed knowledge like a dry sponge. Then they visited the mines so that Byrd could see the whole operation and compare it to Colonel Chiswell's. Before he was through, Byrd, with his retentive memory and capacity for organizing facts, was a first-rate theoretical ironmaster.

Thence Byrd went to see Augustine Washington's [11] mines near the Potomac; then home by easy stages.

In September of the following year, Byrd traveled to his new properties on the Roanoke and Dan Rivers, of which he wrote a lyrical account in *Journey to the Land of Eden*. On this trip he took a large party, including John Banister and Major James Mumford of Prince George County—"I was the more obliged to him . . . [for] leaving the arms of a pretty wife to lie on the cold ground for my sake"—as well as Major William Mayo, who had surveyed the Dividing Line; also Colonel Drury Stith, Peter Jones, five woodsmen, three Negroes, three Indians, twenty horses, and four dogs.

In some ways, Byrd loved these newly acquired lands of his better than Westover. One tract ran ten miles along the Roanoke, and in the middle of the river were three big islands on which he was already raising cattle. In the old fields, where the Indians had lived, the grass grew as high as a horse and rider. On Bluestone Creek, whose bottom was filled with small blue rocks, Byrd had built a cabin which he magniloquently called "Bluestone Castle." A little higher up river was Banister Creek, which Byrd had named for his young friend whom he persuaded to file a claim for land nearby.

From Bluestone, through the wilderness and along the old Dividing Line, whose markings were already beginning to dim, the party rode to Byrd's property on the Dan River. It began on the eastern bank of Sable Creek where it emptied into the Dan. "Six paces from the mouth and just at the brink of the River Dan," he wrote,

11. Father of George.

"stands a sugar tree, which is the beginning of my fine tract of land in Carolina called the Land of Eden. I caused the initial letters of my name to be cut on a large poplar tree and beech for more easy finding it another time."

They then began the survey. Byrd's line ran from the sugar maple due south for a mile, then a little south of west (84½°) a mile, then westerly for about fifteen miles, crossing the Irvin River. Here Byrd plunged into the icy water—it was October 1—to cure a "small cold." He was entirely cured.

Much of the land had been cleared by the Sauro Indians before they abandoned it. Byrd wrote: "It must have been a great misfortune to them to abandon so beautiful a dwelling where the air is wholesome and the soil equal in fertility to any in the world. The river is about eighty yards wide, always confined within its lofty banks and rolling down its waters, as sweet as milk and clear as crystal. . . ."

As the party started homeward, Byrd could hardly bear to leave his edenic land; again and again he turned back for one last look at the lovely countryside, one final glimpse of the western mountains "which still showed their towering heads."

As usual, the way home was more arduous than the high-hearted advance. Following Byrd's custom they were living off the country except for bread carried by the pack horses. The bread began to run out; meat was scarce because the local Indians were fearful of hunting far afield lest they should meet a Catawba war party. However, a lonely young buffalo provided a splendid feast. In the eastern savannas, buffalo did not roam in herds as on the western prairies, but pursued a more or less solitary existence. One day when they were loaded down with a young bear and two deer, they came upon a solitary old bull buffalo, which, instead of turning in crashing flight, boldly stood his ground. Byrd wrote, "We spared his life on the principle of never slaughtering an innocent creature to no purpose."

They did, however, set the dogs on him for amusement. Even then he would not flee, but "ran at them with great fierceness, cocking up his ridiculous little tail and grunting like a hog. The dogs . . . only played about him, not venturing within reach of his horns. . . ."

Byrd injured one knee when his horse brushed it against a tree and hurt the other a few days later. Though they pained him severely, he writes, "I broke not the laws of traveling by uttering the least complaint." Even more painful was "an impertinent tooth." With no "tooth drawers" in the wilderness, Byrd got rid of his troublesome companion by "cutting a caper." He fastened one end of a piece of twine around the tooth and the other end to a log. Then, "I bent my knees enough to enable me to spring vigorously off the ground. . . . The force of the leap drew out the tooth with so much ease that I felt nothing of it. . . ."

With his penchant for embodying useful information in everything he wrote, Byrd added that an undertooth could be drawn by standing on a log, fastening the tooth string to a branch overhead, then jumping off. "The weight of your body added to the force of the spring will force out your tooth with less pain than any operator on earth could draw it."

Despite such misadventures, the party came safely home. Byrd, as usual, gave fervent thanks to his Creator.

With all the exploring, surveying, and planning that went on, the most important thing Byrd and his companions did on the trip had nothing whatever to do with the Roanoke Country. On September 19, 1732, while they were still staying in Bluestone Castle, Byrd recalled: "When we got home [to Bluestone], we laid the foundation of two large cities.[12] One at Shacco's, to be called Richmond, and the other at the point of Appomattox River to be named Petersburg. These Major Mayo offered to lay out into lots without fee or reward. The truth of it is, these two places, being the uppermost landing of James and Appomattox Rivers, are naturally intended for marts where traffic of the outer inhabitants must center. Thus we did not build castles only, but also cities in the air."

True to his promise, though a little tardy, Mayo, in 1737, laid off the ground at Shacco Creek into thirty-two squares, four wide and eight long, each square containing four lots of one-half acre. Byrd priced these lots at £7 each in Virginia currency. The cross streets began at what is now Seventeenth Street, which was called First Street, and ran to the present Twenty-Seventh Street. Byrd named the city

12. On his Tidewater land.

Richmond because its situation reminded him of Richmond on the Thames.

A good many lots were sold. At a vestry meeting of Curles Church in Henrico Parish, it was agreed that "a church be built on the most convenient spot of ground near ye spring on Richardson's Road on the south side of Bacon's Branch on the land of the Hon. William Byrd, Esquire."[13] The church was to be sixty feet long, twenty-five broad and fourteen feet pitched. It was to be finished in "a plain manner" like Curles Church. The contractor, Richard Randolph, Gent., agreed to finish it by June 16, 1741, for the sum of £317.10 of current money, which was to be raised by a levy of twenty thousand pounds of tobacco on the Parish.

Apparently no one had previously asked Byrd for the land, because on October 12, 1740, he wrote to Randolph:

Sir,

I should with great pleasure oblige the Vestry and particularly yourself in granting them an acre to build their church upon, but there are so many roads already through the land that the damage to me would be too great to have another of a mile cut through it. I should be glad if you would please think Richmond the proper place and considering the great number of people that now live below it would pay their devotions there, that would not care to go much higher. . . . If they [the vestry] will agree to have it there I will give them two of the best lots that are not taken up, and besides give them any pine timber that they can find on that side of Shacco Creek and wood for burning brick into the bargain.

I hope that the Gent. of the Vestry will believe me a friend of the church when I make this offer and that I am both theirs, Sir, and your most humble servant.

W. Byrd

The vestry accepted this generous offer. So Richmond got its first church. It was called St. Johns.

In May, 1742, an act was passed by the Assembly, establishing the town of Richmond in the County of Henrico and allowing fairs to be held there. The act also stated that "the Hon. William Byrd intends speedily to lay out other parts of his adjacent land into lots and streets . . . and he is willing that part of his land situated between the said town and Shockhoe's [sic] Creek and the river shall

13. Records of Henrico Parish.

remain and be ours and for a common for the use of the inhabitants of the said town forever. . . ." [14]

As, coming from the east, one raises the tall towers of Richmond standing high above the James, it does indeed look like Byrd's "city in the air."

14. Asbury Christian, D.D., *Richmond, Her Past and Present*. Manufactured by O. H. Jenkins, Richmond, Va., 1912.

IX · THE FIRST GENTLEMAN OF VIRGINIA

U

NLIKE MOST agings, the last years of William Byrd were, perhaps, his happiest. Never until near the day of his death were there any indications of diminishing vigor. He could still "play the fool with Sally," the maid.[1] When his hair turned to snow, it was still the fashion to wear wigs, though no longer the long corkscrew curled ones of his youth, so this indication of age was concealed. In all else he had the body of a man ten to twenty years younger, which he attributed to his frequent use of ginseng. He still danced his dance; occasionally forgot to say his prayers; and frequently ducked going to church—from disinclination to be bored by tedious sermons, rather than from any physical inability or weakening of his strong religious convictions.

Though with age and personal serenity he certainly became more tolerant, this did not apply to his prejudice against Catholics, New Englanders, and Quakers. He never forgave the last named for slicing Pennsylvania from what he considered the rightful lands of Virginia. In this connection he repeated some delightfully malicious gossip about William Penn, which appears nowhere else in history.

In his preamble to *The History of the Dividing Line*, he re-

---

1. *Another Secret Diary of William Byrd of Westover 1739–1741*. Edited by Maud H. Woodfin. Translated by Marion Tingling. The Dietz Press, Richmond, 1942.

marked that it was surprising that a Quaker should have managed to get a royal grant "from a popish prince." Byrd's explanation was that Penn had not always been a Quaker but in his youth a man of pleasure with a very charming way with women; so pleasing had he been that he had an affair with a mistress of the Duke of Monmouth by whom he had a daughter. According to Byrd, this daughter "had beauty enough to raise her to be a duchess. . . . But this amour had like to have brought our fine gentleman in danger of a duel had he not discreetly sheltered himself under this peaceable persuasion." [2]

With tongue in cheek Byrd added that he only mentions this piece of secret history "to wipe off the suspicion of [Penn's] having been popishly inclined." It was his opinion that Penn's high connections, especially with the Duke of York (later King James II), enabled him to get the royal grant of Pennsylvania, after which, Byrd comments with disgust, "The Quakers flocked over to this country in shoals, being averse to go to heaven the same way with the bishops."

Byrd stated his own religious creed very beautifully in his notebook: "I believe that God [made] man . . . and inspired him with a reasonable soul to distinguish between Good and Evil, but the law of nature taught him to [follow] the good and avoid the evil because the good tends manifestly to his happiness and his preservation, but the evil to his misery and destruction. . . ." Byrd affirmed his belief that Christ came down from "Heaven . . . to redeem mankind from the punishment of their sins;" and without further mentioning Heaven or Hell he wrote: "I believe that in God's appointed time we shall be raised from the dead . . . That God by Jesus Christ will judge all Nations and Generations of men . . . That those who have led good and holy lives here will be rewarded with unspeakable happiness hereafter, but those who have obstinately and impenitently Rebelld against God and their own conciences shall go into a State of Sorrow and Misery." [3]

Doctor Louis B. Wright, who is the most profound student of William Byrd II, appears justified in concluding that though his religion was not a deeply mystical experience, he truly believed in Christ and the Resurrection, and that the Anglican Church was the most perfect expression of Christianity.

What Wright does not say, but which seems explicit in Byrd's

2. Byrd, *History of the Dividing Line.* . . .
3. Huntington Diary quoted in Byrd's *Secret Diary.*

secret thoughts confided to the diaries, is that, though he was not a mystic in the great manner of the saints, he felt an intimate relationship with God, a confidence and trust in Him and submission to His will that was so natural and unlabored as to be the essence of true faith. Like a naughty but not a wicked child, he expected to be forgiven his minor transgressions by a loving Father.

In the things that he considered most important, Byrd was conscientious to a high degree. He hardly ever missed a meeting of the Council or a sitting of the Court. In the former, his advice was broadminded and farseeing. He stood up for Virginians as the inheritors of all the liberties and rights that Englishmen had won through the years from the Magna Carta to the "glorious Revolution" of 1688, and he was as ardent in this advocacy when a senior statesman as when he had been the young Agent of Virginia at the Court of King William III. He would have been horrified by the thought of American independence, for he regarded his British citizenship with the same pride with which a Roman of old said, *"Civis Romanus sum."* Yet, had the issue been drawn as sharply in his time as in his son's, it is most probable that his loyalty would have been to Virginia.

In the court he could be severe, but he was always just. He condemned traitors, murderers, and pirates to death, and felons to the loss of a hand, whipping, or branding, without losing sleep or appetite. It was the law and custom of the era, and he made sure in his own mind that the poor wretches, slave or free, were really guilty and not the victims of some gentleman's trumped-up charge.

In one court proceeding, when the other Councilors proposed that a gentleman's word should be absolutely conclusive against a member of the lower classes, Byrd wrote, "This procedure agreed not at all with my notions of justice."

Though he believed that all men were and should be equal before the law and their Creator, those were the only places where this was true. He had not the faintest doubt that he was a superior being; a patrician raised above the ruck of mankind by the grace of God, to rule and guide and enjoy the perquisites of his rank. However, he willingly assumed the responsibilities that went with this position.

These included his duties as a colonel and commander in chief of militia. Though he never served in the field, because the occasion did not arise in his lifetime, he felt responsible for maintaining his command in good order.

In October, 1739, England went to war with Spain again—"The War of Jenkins's Ear." Byrd was enthusiastic about the war. He was keen to throw the Spaniards out of Florida and to liberate the Spanish West Indies, with whom he foresaw great opportunities for trade. General Oglethorpe marched against St. Augustine in Florida with a few hundred men and his Cherokee Indian allies. The General was over-optimistic. His force was simply not large enough to capture that strong Spanish city and they were repulsed.

Meanwhile, a great expedition against the Spanish West Indies and her colonies on the mainland of South America was mounted under the command of Vice Admiral Edward Vernon. The American colonies from New Hampshire to South Carolina were to furnish 3,000 troops, which, for a change, they enthusiastically did.

In the spring of 1740, the Virginia contingent of 300 men were encamped near Williamsburg. On June 10, Byrd rode out with Governor Gooch to inspect them, "such as they were." He was thoroughly disgusted. These were not militia, but men conscripted for foreign service. The draft law had been so rigged that virtually no man who made an honest living was called; only ex-convicts were inducted. In a letter to his brother-in-law, Colonel Otway, Byrd forcefully expressed his opinion of the Virginia troops.

Old Colonel Spotswood came out of retirement to command the Americans [4] under the over-all command of Lord Cathcart. The effort was too much for him and he died at Annapolis, on June 14, on his way north to confer with other governors. Very much saddened by the death of Spotswood, his friendly enemy, Byrd attended the Council meeting which appointed Governor Gooch in his stead and agreed that indestructible Commissary James Blair, aged eighty-five, should, as President of the Council, govern Virginia in his absence.

In a letter to his old friend Sir Charles Wager on May 26, 1740, Byrd blasted the strategy of Admiral Vernon. "I have no great opinion," he wrote, "of embarking landsmen on such distant expeditions. They will all be down with scurvy or something like gaol distemper from being stowed so thick aboard. . . . Instead of attacking Carthagena or Havana it would be happier and more feasible," he thought, "to proclaim the Independence of all the Spanish West In-

4. This is the first war in which the Colonial troops were called—and called themselves—Americans.

dies and keep a sufficient force in those parts to protect them in it." [5]
Byrd was convinced that the inhabitants would like to shake off the
yoke of Spain.

He was right. The expedition was disastrous. Admiral Vernon
chose to attack Spain's strongest fortified city, Cartagena, in what
is now Colombia. He succeeded in running past the forts into the harbor, but his attack on the citadel was thrown back with heavy loss.
While he waited for another opportunity, yellow fever struck.
Scarcely 1,300 Americans out of 3,000 survived to return home. One
of those who did was young Captain Lawrence Washington, George's
half-brother. He so admired the British Admiral, in spite of his mis-
takes, that he named his plantation on the Potomac "Mount Vernon"
in his honor.

After the defeat at Cartagena, Byrd poured out a stream of letters to England, warning of the danger of the French encirclement of
the American Colonies. Up the St. Lawrence, through the lakes, and
down the Mississippi to New Orleans, they had built an enormous
semicircle of forts—five thousand miles of forts—which cut off from
the rich interior the thin strip of coastal land, of English land. Byrd
predicted that the French would try to seize the passes of the Alleghenies, establish an active alliance with the Indians of that region,
and bar to the inhabitants of the crowded seaboard any western advance. He advised the British Government to fortify the passes
through the mountains.[6] Vast as it was, so much vaster than Byrd
realized, there was not room for France and England on the American continent. He knew it and he shouted the danger. His son would
face it bravely.

In spite of his huge holdings of land, Byrd was hungry for more. In
addition to his successful promotion of Richmond, he was busy right
up to the end of his life on his biggest real-estate venture of all.
From the Assembly, he secured a grant of one hundred and five
thousand acres of land on the south side of the Roanoke River on
condition that he settle one thousand families upon it. This was in

5. Letter to Sir Charles Wager. *Virginia Magazine of History and Biography*,
Vol. XXXVII.
6. Bassett, *op. cit.*

addition to the Land of Eden in North Carolina, to which he had added six thousand acres, giving him one hundred and thirty-one thousand acres which he hoped to sell to the prospective settlers at £5 per hundred acres.

He began writing to a Mr. Ochs in Switzerland, who was contemplating bringing over a boatload of Swiss immigrants. Byrd praised to the skies the quality of the land, mentioned the possibility of silver mines in the western mountains, and the necessity of forestalling the French whom he feared were moving in from the west. He ended his letter with the characteristic comment: "I had much rather have to do with honest Switzers than the mixed people that come from Pennsylvania, especially when they all are to be conducted by so prudent a person as yourself." [7]

Byrd disliked the Scottish and Irish settlers who were pouring into the American Colonies "like the Goths and Vandals of old." But when the Switzers failed to arrive, he put out feelers for people from Pennsylvania.

Finally, a shipload of two hundred and fifty Swiss set sail, only to be wrecked in a violent storm on the shores of their promised land. All their leaders and most of the settlers were drowned, their possessions smashed and washed sodden upon the roaring beaches. A few, virtually naked, survived and, as Byrd wrote, "are gone upon my land to make a beginning." [8]

Byrd remained pressed for ready money. He still owed a considerable amount in England. Some biographers think this was the old Parke debt, but it seems more likely that he had contracted further obligations by his lavish expenditures on Westover. He was forced to sell a few hundred odd acres of land here and there and he tried desperately to get his wife's inheritance from England, but he was stymied in this endeavor by his all-too-durable mother-in-law. He also strove to get a government job, preferably that of Governor, but even the post of Surveyor of Customs, worth £500 a year, would help. In a fit of gloom he even tried to sell Westover, and thought of moving to Bermuda. Fortunately, nothing came of it.

In the end, Byrd succeeded in balancing his budget. By 1743, he appears to have paid off his debts or at least reduced them to insignificant proportions.

7. *Virginia Magazine of History and Biography,* Vol. IX.
8. *William and Mary Quarterly,* Vol. VI.

Byrd served once more as Commissioner for Virginia in 1736, when Governor Gooch appointed him to conduct the survey of the land in the "Northern Neck" between the Rappahannock and Potomac Rivers, which had been granted to Lord Culpeper by King Charles II and inherited through the female line by Thomas, Lord Fairfax. A sharp dispute with Fairfax resulted in two separate commissions making the survey, one headed by Byrd, the other by a creature of Fairfax's.

In his report to the British Government, Byrd strongly contested the legality of the whole grant, and particularly Lord Fairfax's claim to additional lands in his survey of the line. The avaricious nobleman claimed no less than 5,282,000 acres of the finest land in Virginia, some of it already settled. Fairfax had too much influence with the British Government and the King for Byrd's report to prevail. He succeeded in establishing his colossal land grab.

That was Byrd's last service to Virginia beyond his duties as a Councilor, Judge, Colonel of Militia, and trustee of William and Mary. Thereafter, he spent a great deal more time at Westover and was happy there. He was certainly not in retirement, however, as the account of his activities indicates. Nor was there any settling into the diminishing social activities of the elderly. Quite the contrary. After the sadness of Evelyn's death in 1737 had passed, Westover was gayer than ever. Though Byrd was moving toward seventy, the house was full of the noise and frolic of his children who were young enough to be his grandchildren. In 1740, Mina was only twenty-five, soon to be married to Thomas Chamberlayne of North Kent County. Anne was fifteen; Maria, thirteen; William, twelve; and Jane, eleven. Annie, as her father called her, had been a beauty and a belle from childhood. Her portrait, probably painted by Charles Bridges when she was about ten years old, shows a merry little girl with tilting blue eyes. Wearing a filmy dress and with flowers pinned in her hair, she stands barefoot, patting a spaniel.

In 1739, when Anne was not yet fifteen, Philip Johnson of King and Queen County came courting her. Byrd either thought her too young, or had higher aspirations for her, because he sent her suitor away with a "gentle denial."

Two years later Anne's step-cousin, dashing Daniel Custis, came "with the intention of making love to Annie." It was an excellent match and Byrd was in favor of it. So was Colonel Custis, and negotiations began between the one time brothers-in-law. Though very rich,

Colonel Custis was very stingy and very irascible. He constantly inveighed against everything from his wife to the "damn confounded pretended post office"[9] in Williamsburg. He absolutely refused to come up with what Byrd considered a suitable settlement. After a long and heated correspondence, during which the two young people were apparently not consulted at all, Byrd wrote rather sadly to Daniel how he greatly regretted his father's "impracticability." Though he said he preferred Daniel to all others, "I cannot trust to such a phantome as Colonel Custis's generosity."[10] So Daniel married Martha Dandridge instead.

In September, 1741, Maria, at the age of fifteen, beat her older sister to the altar, marrying the widower, Colonel Landon Carter of Sabine Hall. His house stood amid several thousand acres on the Rappahannock River, cut from his father, King Carter's, great estate. Still intact, it is one of the great classic Virginia houses. At the large round table in its library, nearly forty years after his marriage, Colonel Carter is said to have conferred with George Washington about the Morristown Campaign.[11]

Annie, however, was not far behind her sister. Christmas of that same year was probably the merriest ever at Westover, for Anne suddenly married Maria's brother-in-law, Charles Carter of Cleve. Though it was a spur-of-the-moment wedding, and quite unexpected by Byrd, he was highly delighted. Next to his own, he regarded the Carters as the first family of Virginia and what could be more suitable than that two of his daughters should marry into it? Though he did not live to see it, his beloved son capped the alliance by marrying Elizabeth Hill Carter, daughter of Secretary of State John Carter, Esquire, of Shirley.

What with the weddings and the other activities, Westover was thronged with guests whenever the Byrds were at home. There were regular "dancing days when Mr. William Dering came from Williamsburg to instruct the young people of Westover and nearby plantations in the newest French manner." The elders joined the young people in a courtly minuet, a gavotte, the lively Saraband, and the Sir Roger de Coverley, which metamorphozed into the Virginia Reel. Nor did such gaiety wait on Mr. Dering. Guests would come from

9. Custis Letters.
10. Letter to Daniel Custis quoted in *The London Diary.*
11. Sale, *Interiors of Virginia Houses.*

across the river in eight-oared barges; up the road from Williamsburg or down from the interior in the lumbering chariots, which were
becoming more popular as the roads improved; or they would gallop
up on the highly bred horses which both men and women rode with
practiced skill. Then Byrd would call in the plantation musicians and
everyone would dance, morning, afternoon, and evening, until exhaustion forced them to stop. In his diary entry for June 20, 1741,
Byrd wrote: "I settled some accounts and read latin till dinner when
abundance of company came from the other side of the river and I
ate chicken and bacon. . . . The company danced in spite of the
weather. It rained and I prayed."

He must have meant that he prayed after the gaieties, for he
never lost his love of dancing and bodily contact with beautiful
women.

A new enjoyment imported from London was "a certain game
upon the cards called whist.[12] . . . It was engaged by the men of
all ages to keep company with women more than anything did before. Tis apparent there are much stronger charms in cards than any
the female sex can boast of." [13]

With relaxation from financial pressure finally achieved, his children growing up handsome and well-mannered, and Westover bloom-
ing in the beauty of its classic design and lovely gardens, "gripeing"
was replaced by the sheer joy of living. Ambition, too, achieved a
final goal when Commissary Blair finally died in 1743 in his eighty-
ninth year, and Byrd became President of the Council. He had, in
effect, been acting head of it as far back as 1740. When Governor
Gooch was away commanding the American troops of the Cartagena
expeditionary force, Blair had been too feeble to do much more than
sit in the chair of state at the head of the table nodding at words he
was too deaf to hear and catching catnaps as the business of the
Dominion was conducted around him. In the court, too, Byrd acted as
Chief Judge because the Commissary could not hear a word of the
testimony. Now he was President in fact, and it was not too late for
him to savor the honor, though he did not enjoy it long.

In the summer of 1744, his health failed rapidly. True to the
conventions of the Age of Reason, he showed no fear of death, but

12. Ancestor of Bridge.
13. Mrs. Taylor to Byrd. *Virginia Magazine of History and Biography*, Vol.
XXXV.

affected to regard it with a certain nonchalance. Hearing that his old friend, Patrick Coutts, owner of the ferry at Richmond, was desperately ill, Byrd, probably struck by the fact that Charon was also a ferryman, sent off a courier to tell Coutts not to hurry, but to wait for him.

Coutts, raising himself in bed, said to the messenger, "Tell Colonel Byrd that when Patrick Coutts makes up his mind to die he waits for no man." [14]

There can be little doubt that Byrd enjoyed a last chuckle at this flash of wit.

On August 26, 1744, in his beautiful house, surrounded by his handsome children and still youthful wife, proud of his position and the services he had rendered to his country, and confident of a future life, William Byrd died as happily as any man can, facing eternity.

With all his foolishness and his sometimes tawdry sinning, despite the artificiality of many of his cherished conventions, the egotism and arrogance inherent in his character and way of life, he was a good man. He had been a loving and understanding husband and father, a conscientious and imaginative public servant, a force for good in the forming of America, and finally—most important of all to his way of thinking—a man of honor.

Reckoning up his great land holdings; his house and library; his elegance, intelligence and wit; his panache; and his faithful public service in the highest offices of the Dominion, it must be conceded that he had the right to say, as in fact he did: "I am the First Gentleman of Virginia." [15]

EPITAPH

William Byrd was buried, undoubtedly at his own request, under a granite pedestal surmounted by a small obelisk, at the head of a path in the garden he loved so well. His epitaph, whoever wrote it (and one suspects he did except for the last few fulsome lines), is one more revelation of his character, since it records the achievements of his life that he considered most worthy of remembrance:

14. Blair Niles, *The James: From Irongate to the Sea.* Farrar & Rinehart, New York, 1945.
15. Louis B. Wright, *First Gentlemen of Virginia.* The Huntington Library, San Marino, California, 1940.

Being born to one of the amplest fortunes in the country
He was early sent to England for his education
Where under the care and direction of Sir Robert Southwell,
And ever favored with his particular instructions.
He made a happy proficiency in polite and varied learning.
By the means of this same noble friend,
He was introduced to the acquaintance of many of the first persons
of his age.
For knowledge, wit, virtue, birth of high station,
And particularly contracted a most intimate and bosom friendship with
The learned and illustrious Charles Boyle, Earl of Orrery.
He was called to the bar in the Middle Temple
Studied for some time in the Low Countries,
Visited the Court of France
And was chosen a Fellow of the Royal Society.
Thus eminently fitted for the service and ornament of his country.
He was made Receiver General of His Majesty's Revenues here.
Was thrice appointed Public Agent of Virginia to the
Court and Ministry of England.
And being thirty-seven years a Member,
At last became President of Council of that Colony.
To all this were added a great elegance of taste and life.
The well-bred gentleman and polite companion.
The splendid economist and prudent father of a family.
With the constant enemy of all exhorbitant power
And hearty friend to the liberties of his country.

BOOK THREE

The Wastrel

I · THE LAST
COLONEL BYRD

U NLIKE HIS father, the third William Byrd was not sent early to England for his education. Most likely his bemused parents thought him too precious to be parted from them. In addition the opportunities for education in Virginia were considerably improved.

The Byrds ran a school at Westover, not only for their own children but for those of their neighbors who cared to attend. In his diary William Byrd II mentions going "to hear the children at their lessons." Colonel William Beverley sent some of his children to stay at Westover and study with them. This produced tragedy, for a young son died there and his father bitterly recorded that it was due to the inhuman neglect of Maria Taylor Byrd.

There is no question that young William was spoiled outrageously. A hint of it is given by his father at the beginning of *A Progress to the Mines* when he writes:

"For the pleasure and good company of Mrs. Byrd and her little governor, my son, I went about half way to the Falls in the chariot. There we halted, not far from a purling stream, and upon the stump of a propagate oak picked the bones of a piece of roast beef. By the spirit which that gave me I was better able to part with the dear companions of my travels and to perform the rest of my journey on horseback by myself."

Mrs. Byrd's "little governor" had apparently made himself master of Westover at four years old.

When his father died, William was sixteen. In accordance with family custom, there was comparatively meager provision for his mother and sisters, and young William inherited the whole great estate, consisting of 179,423 acres of land in plantations scattered from Westover to the Alleghenies; hundreds of slaves, herds of cattle, squadrons of horses and uncountable swine which ran wild through the forests and were not reckoned worth appraising. There were also the mills at the Falls, sloops to transport the produce down river to where the great ships lay and all the appropriate farming tools. There was very little hard money.

In truth, the estate was top-heavy with land, part of it worked out by the drain of tobacco crops which suck the nourishment from the soil, leaving it barren unless properly fertilized. The planters generally neither understood nor bothered about this. It would have taken a very shrewd manager to have made the Byrd estate pay and William, by his own account, was far from that. But it did supply a tremendous base on which to borrow money.

William went to England to finish his education at the Middle Temple in 1746–47.[1] Given his character and apprenticeship in elegance, if not in mathematics, it was probably a costly schooling, though the legend that he lost £10,000 gambling in a single night is ridiculous. In 1748, he returned to Westover and, at the age of twenty, married Elizabeth Hill Carter, who lived almost next door at Shirley. Doubtless she brought a suitable dowry, a thousand pounds or so, which would be a handy pinch of change in William's mind.

In his twenties, William was appointed to the Virginia Council almost as automatically as a hereditary peer takes his seat in the House of Lords. He also became a Colonel of Militia on the same principle, but he earned his right to his military title by becoming a fine soldier. He was also, up to a point in time, a good Councilor.

For William, despite his rightful reputation as a wastrel, was not stupid. He had a good mind, though it was not as polished as his father's, and was equally conscientious in performing the duties of the high offices he held.

1. Records of the College of Arms.

In his youth he was a fine-looking man. Cosmo Alexander painted him in his dress uniform, faced and cuffed with broad bands of heavy gold embroidery, with an embroidered waistcoat, and delicate lace at the throat and wrists. He carried a cocked hat edged with feathers and wore the short curled and powdered wig of the new fashion. He had a full face, not yet jowly, with slanting Byrd-blue eyes under perfect semicircles of dark brows; and a strong straight nose. Only the self-indulgent, full-lipped mouth gave away the weakness of his character.

William spent money like no other Byrd before or since. He loved racing thoroughbred horses and imported from England fine stallions which enriched the blood lines of the American Turf, if not their owner. His famous stallion, Tryal, ran in the historic race at Gloucester Court House on December 5, 1752, against Selina, Jennie Cammeron, and Childers.

As soon as William became a Councilor, he built a little gem of a house on three lots he inherited in Williamsburg. It is now known as "The Byrd-Allen House" because of the family who bought it when William's debts forced his widow to sell it. To the left and right of a small central hall were an exquisite little drawing room and a dining room capable of seating ten at dinner. Each of these rooms had a corner fireplace with a lovely mantelpiece. A narrow curving stairway with pie-shaped steps led to the second floor, which had four pleasant bedrooms. So classically beautiful were its proportions that it is now used as the guest house for V.I.P.'s who visit Williamsburg. Queen Elizabeth II of England and her consort stayed there on their first state visit to the United States.

Even in the 1750's William's house must have cost a pretty pound. Of course, his mother-in-law, the widow of Secretary of State John Carter, had a fine house on the Mall near the Governor's Palace where she entertained lavishly during the Public Days. William wanted his wife to be equally well housed, although his own father and mother had made do with simple lodgings on their many official stays in Williamsburg.

William apparently also refurbished Belvidere on Orchard Hill near Richmond, which had hardly been used since the first William bought Westover. In her letters Anne Carter Byrd frequently refers to the family staying there.

William's best service to his country, and the apex of his career, took place during the French and Indian War which began in 1754 when he was only twenty-six.

As William Byrd II had foreseen, that encircling chain of French fortresses began to hem in the English colonies, and when the French-Canadian forces built several new forts in the Alleghenies, energetic Lieutenant Governor Robert Dinwiddie of Virginia felt they had gone too far. In the autumn of 1753, he sent young Major George Washington to warn the French Commander, Legardeur de St. Pierre, to keep away from English territory in the Ohio River valley. St. Pierre was very polite and much too frank. He told Washington "that it was their absolute Design to take possession of the Ohio, and by God he would do it." [2]

Dinwiddie reacted furiously. He forwarded to England the report of "the gent. I sent"; made the twenty-two-year-old Washington a lieutenant colonel and sent him and Colonel Joshua Fry off with 350 men to chase the French out of the Alleghenies. Fry was killed by a fall from his horse, leaving Washington in command.

The confrontation took place at Great Meadows not far from the new French Fort Duquesne where the Monongahela and Allegheny rivers join to form the Ohio, and where Pittsburgh now stands. The Americans built a ramshackle fortification at Great Meadows which they named "Fort Necessity." Spirited young Colonel Washington pushed ahead with 150 men.

Washington was hardly the tactician he later became. Though considerably outnumbered by the French Canadian troops, he ordered them out of British territory. When they refused to go, he ordered his men to open fire. The battle was a swift disaster. Overpowered by superior numbers, Washington was forced to surrender Fort Necessity. He did not become a prisoner of war because no war had been declared. The French turned him loose and he returned to Virginia in some embarrassment. To his surprise he was given a hero's welcome.

Washington had, indeed, started a tremendous chain of events. As Samuel Eliot Morrison writes in *The Oxford History of the American People:* [3] "That shot in the Western wilderness sparked off

2. Washington quoted in *Encyclopaedia Britannica*, (1952 edition) Vol. XXIII, p. 381.

3. Oxford University Press, New York, 1965.

a series of world-shaking events . . . . Called in Europe The Seven Years War and in America the French and Indian War, it was fought on three continents by seven great nations;[4] and ultimately resulted in the domination of America by the English-speaking peoples."

At first this glorious result seemed highly improbable. As usual, England made sure she would lose the first battles by entrusting command of her armies to brave but blundering British generals. A prime example was General Edward Braddock, who arrived in Virginia with "two of the worst regiments in [the British Army] at half strength."[5] He recruited them up to seven hundred men each, and, with the First Virginia Regiment—"The Virginia Blues"—under Washington, cut a road through the wilderness from Fort Cumberland in Western Maryland to Fort Duquesne.

The French and their Indian allies impolitely declined to wait for the attack. On July 9, 1755, they ambushed Braddock in the forest ten miles from Fort Duquesne. The rigid files of scarlet-coated British had as much chance as ducks in a shooting gallery against the French woodsmen and the screeching, copper-colored savages flitting through the great trees, shooting and running, and shooting again. Braddock, who had five horses shot from under him, was killed bravely trying to rally his men, who broke and ran "as sheep pursued by dogs." Washington had two horses shot under him. With four bullet holes through his best uniform—but none through his skin—he brought up the Virginians who, fighting Indian style, saved from annihilation what was left of the British. Over 900 British were killed or wounded.

Morrison calls Braddock's defeat, "The Pearl Harbor of the Seven Years War." There were other disasters. Governor William Shirley of Massachusetts was defeated before Fort Niagara. William Johnson of New York beat the French at Lake George and was knighted for that meager success, though he failed to take their fortress at Crown Point. The following year, the Marquis de Montcalm captured Fort Oswego on Lake Ontario in New York.

In the autumn of 1755, after Braddock's defeat, Virginia was in a perilous position. The frontier had been driven back a hundred

---

4. France, Spain, Austria, Sweden, Russia vs. England, Prussia and some small German states.

5. S. E. Morrison, *op. cit.*

miles. Washington wrote to Dinwiddie, "The Blue Ridge is now our frontier." The western Indians were joining the French in droves. Their war parties poured into the new settlements in the Shenandoah Valley, scalping and burning, carrying off women and children. Settlers, fleeing for their lives, left behind everything they had toiled to build and cultivate.

To secure the southern borders, Governor Dinwiddie decided to attempt to strengthen British ties with the still-friendly Catawba and Cherokee Indians. On November 6, 1755, he and the Council agreed to send a commission to treat with them and appointed Peter Randolph and William Byrd, who had just become a Councilor, as the commissioners.[6] On December 23, they received their commissions and copies of the speeches Dinwiddie wished them to make on his behalf. The Governor's letter of instruction ordered them to hold themselves in readiness to start immediately for the place of the treaty. Once there: "Having adjusted the necessary forms and ceremonies you are, at the first general and public conference, to acquaint the Indians that you have come purposely to assure them of the kind and friendly disposition of the inhabitants of this Colony toward them. . . ." The commissioners were to incite the Indians against the French and *their* Indians and induce them to destroy French forts and by no means allow any French settlements in their nation. The Catawbas and Cherokees were to watch the passes over the mountains to the Upper Cherokee to prevent surprise. The Governor told the commissioners to make excuses for not sending the Indians arms immediately—the Virginians could spare none—but to give assurances they would be sent later. They were also told to accept any terms they considered reasonable: "You are to conduct yourselves in such a manner as the nature and expedience of the subject matter, time and place may require according to your best discretion."

The Governor enclosed an invoice of presents for the Indians and £250 for expenses. He signed the letter, "Your affectionate and humble servant Robert Dinwiddie. To the Honerable Peter Randolph and William Byrd, Esq."

In effect, the commissioners were given virtually unlimited discretion to form an alliance with the Indians on any terms they could.

6. This account of Byrd's mission and the quotations in it are based on the *Virginia Magazine of History and Biography*, Vol. XIII, p. 228 ff.

In January, Peter Randolph and William Byrd, with their interpreter, William Giles; a secretary, a group of woodsmen and servants; and a train of pack horses rode over the hard, rutted roads and the frozen forest trails toward the border between North and South Carolina where the Catawbas lived. The final stage was a cold and dangerous ride through the silent, interminable columned pine woods.

They came to Catawba Town on the Catawba River in what is now York County, South Carolina, in February, 1756. Once a powerful nation, the Catawbas had been so reduced by smallpox that they could only field about 400 warriors. However, this was still a formidable force to confront in their stockaded citadel.

The conference was held with the dignity and formality the Indians loved. Their leaders decked out in gaudy beads and feathers, or blue coats of English wool, gathered around Heigler, King of the Catawbas. Behind them the braves squatted row on row, while squaws peeped from the cabanes. The commissioners in their finest scarlet coats with gold facings, clean ruffled shirts, and feathered tricorn hats were equally colorful. Byrd, tall, heavy-set but hard-muscled, and with a commanding air, was especially impressive.

First the secretary read the letter introducing Randolph and Byrd, and their commission from the Governor, which were translated and copies given to King Heigler. Then in their best oratorical style the commissioners addressed the gathering:

"Brothers, Kings, Sachems and Warriors of the great Catawba nation!

"Our common father, the great King of England, has been pleased to direct your brother, the Governor of Virginia, to send commissioners to assure you of his affection, and to present you with as many goods in token thereof as it is convenient to send so far at this season of the year. It was his pleasure to appoint us to this charge and at the same time to direct us to deliver a speech to you in his name."

Courteously, but wooden-faced, King Heigler answered, "We shall always listen to everything that comes from our brothers in Virginia with great attention. . . ."

The secretary then read the Governor's speech of friendship and hope for a complete understanding. When the translation was finished the Indians shouted in unison, "*Yo hah!*"

Then the commissioners made their own speech, which they had doubtless labored over by the light of many campfires. They began by commending the Catawbas for their long friendship with the great King George and his children in Virginia; then they got down to the meat of their mission:

"You cannot be strangers, brave Catawbas, to the late unjustifiable steps taken by the French, those crafty enemies of all mankind, to debauch the principles and poison the minds, not only of the Indians, but of all other nations who are in alliance with the great King, our father. . . ."

Just how Giles managed to translate this complicated English into Catawbaese is difficult to imagine, but he appears to have succeeded, for the Indians listened in silent intensity. Byrd and Randolph went on to talk about the French thirst for power and "the dark measures and deceitful practices" they had used to incite the Shawnees and the Delawares to overrun the borders of Virginia, Maryland, and Pennsylvania, and to perform dastardly murders of women and children.

Turning now to the one cheerful prospect in that dark hour, they said, "Our friends, the Six Nations [the powerful Iroquois Confederacy] have taken up the hatchet against the French and joined General Johnson last fall at Lake St. Sacrement [Lake George] where, after a bloody battle it pleased the great gods to bless our arms with victory. . . .

"We are desired by the Governor of Virginia to tell you that we now stand in need of your assistance. And, that you may be encouraged to march against the enemy with greater steadiness, we promise you that your men shall be supplied with arms, ammunition, and everything necessary for war. To confirm the truth of what we have said and to reinforce our request, we give you this belt of wampum."

As Byrd ceremoniously offered the belt of glittering shells to King Heigler, the Indians thundered, "*Yo hah!*"

The next day King Heigler answered, saying that at the Governor's wish he had held his warriors in readiness for this moment. "Now," he said, "since the Shawnees and Delawares have broken the chain of friendship between them and our brethren, the English, we think ourselves bound in gratitude to declare them our enemy and we shall immediately take up the hatchet against them. We have always been supplied with clothes, guns and ammunition by the great King on the other side of the water and have the most grateful rememberance of his kindness to us. . . .

"Our warriors delight in war and our young men are equally pleased that they have the opportunity of going to battle. It is my resolution to lead them wherever the Governor of Virginia desires."

King Heigler spoke of his hopes of getting the Cherokees, Choctaws, and the Chickasaws to join the Catawbas; and gave the Virginians a belt of wampum in token of good faith.

He then asked his warriors to speak for themselves. One after another they rose to declare themselves ready to fight the French and their Indian allies. The most eloquent of them, Chippataw, said, "Brothers, you have put a bright hatchet in our hand which we have accepted and hold fast. You have also directed us where to strike it. I am determined either to dye it in the blood of our enemies or lose my life in the attempt."

After that they got down to bargaining on details. The Indian promises fell rather short of their eloquence. The treaty stated that:

1. The ancient alliance between the English and Catawbas shall be renewed and the old chain of friendship brightened.
2. Any time the French King shall wage war against the English, the Catawbas will make war against the French King.
3. The Catawbas shall march into Virginia forty or more able warriors within forty days. . . .
4. [These warriors] shall be provided with clothes, vittles, arms, and ammunition.
5. Neither Catawbas nor Virginians shall protect disobedient subjects or entertain rebels. . . .

The treaty was signed by Peter Randolph and William Byrd; King Heigler made his mark and all the sachems followed suit.

The commissioners then went on to meet the Cherokees at Broad River, where they palavered in the same fashion with King Old-Hop, his sachems, and warriors. This was a far more important negotiation; for though the Cherokee nation had lost half their strength in the smallpox epidemic of 1738, they could still put 3,000 warriors in the field. They held the land on an east-west course for about one hundred and forty miles from Fort Prince George to the Tennessee

River thirty miles above the present site of Knoxville, and claimed a wide swath of territory in southwest Virginia and the present states of West Virginia, Kentucky, and Tennessee.

Byrd found them much tougher bargainers than the Catawbas, since their strength gave them leverage. There was less yo-hahing and much more discussion. The Cherokees shrewdly refused to sign anything until the commissioners promised that the English would build a fort at the western limit of their territory to protect them against the French. Byrd and Randolph agreed; whereupon a treaty similar to that with the Catawbas was finally signed by all hands.

Their mission accomplished, the commissioners rode home to receive the jubilant acclaim of the Governor and Council. It was William Byrd's first important public service and he had performed it well. There is no question that his charm, his splendid appearance, and his intelligent appreciation of the military problems involved had contributed significantly to the success of the undertaking.

Its ultimate value to the colonial cause was considerably less than was anticipated by the euphoric Governor and Council. Far fewer Catawbas and Cherokees than promised ever came to Virginia to help the English, which was fortunate. For those that did come went on a rampage in the Shenandoah Valley, attacking and scalping English settlers and paying very little attention to the French.

However, the main objective had not been what the Indians could do to help, so much as securing that they would not join the mass movement to the French standard. With this settled, Virginia could disregard the danger from the south and muster all her forces toward the defense of the western settlements.

John Campbell, Earl of Loudoun, became Governor in Chief and Captain General of Virginia in 1756, though Dinwiddie still functioned as Lieutenant Governor until 1758. Lord Loudoun was also made commander in chief of all the British forces in America. Unfortunately for him, the far more brilliant Marquis de Montcalm arrived almost simultaneously to take command of the French. Loudoun, although competent, was unimaginative, cautious; the French general brilliant and daring.

To strengthen Virginia's western defenses Loudoun decided to raise the Second Virginia Regiment. Dinwiddie gave William Byrd command of it.

The First and Second Virginia regiments were not militia. They were regulars like the Continental Line of the Revolutionary armies: subject to rigorous discipline—which the militia would never accept —and proud of it. They were the equal of any troops in the world, and in wilderness fighting proved themselves better than British regulars.

As soon as the Second Virginia, recruited to its full strength of 1,000 men, was whipped into shape in 1757, William Byrd proudly led it to join the First Virginia in the beleaguered Shenandoah Valley under the over-all command of Colonel George Washington. That year things again went badly for the English. Lord Loudoun was no match for Montcalm who, with 8,000 French and Indians, moved down from his strongholds on Lake Champlain to take Fort Henry on Lake George. This was enough to shake the confidence of England's Indian Allies of the Six Nations, who considered switching sides. If they had gone over to the French, all northern New York might have been lost.

In the Shenandoah, Washington and Byrd were desperately fighting off Indian forays. Fortunately the French at Fort Duquesne did not move against them.

In England a change of government at the end of 1757 altered the whole prospect for the American colonies. William Pitt, one of the great Prime Ministers of England, took the helm. With extraordinary perception, considering how close England was to France and how far from America, Pitt decided to reverse British strategy—to hold in Europe instead of attacking there and throw most of England's strength into winning the war beyond the sea. With a self-assurance not unlike Churchill's, he said, "I believe that I can save this nation and that no one else can."

Pitt planned a three-pronged offensive for 1758, and sent young, energetic generals over to implement it, although Loudoun remained for a time as commander in chief. General James Abercrombie was given command on the New York lakes and ordered to take Fort Ticonderoga. Sir Jeffrey Amherst commanded an expedition against the great French fortress of Louisbourg in Nova Scotia, and General John Forbes was given 4,000 British regulars with which to take Fort Duquesne.

William Byrd marched his regiment from Winchester to Fort

Cumberland, which General Forbes, like Braddock, chose for the start through the wilderness. Young Robert Mumford wrote about that march to his uncle, Colonel Thomas Bland of Prince George County, on July 6, 1758:

> *Honored Sir:*
>
> . . . After being delayed at Winchester five or six weeks longer than expected . . . we pushed into the wide ocean.[7] I was permitted to walk every step of the way to this humble fort, to eat little, to lay [sic] hard, over mountains, through mud and water, yet am as merry and hearty as ever. Our flankers and sentries pretend they saw the enemy daily, but they never approached us. A detachment is this moment ordered off to clear a road 30 miles and our company to cover the working party; we are in fine scalping ground I assure you. The guns pop about us and you may see the fellows prick up their ears like deer every moment.
>
> Our Colonel [Byrd] is an example of fortitude either in danger or hardship, and by his easy polite behavior has gained not only the regard, but the affection of both officers and soldiers. He has kindly invited us to his table for the campaign, offered me any sum of money I may have occasion for without charging either principal or interest, and signified his approbation of my conduct hitherto in such a manner as is to my advantage. . . .[8]

Young Mumford's anxiety about the "scalping ground" was not unjustified. Major Grant of the Highland Regiment, leading a flying column of 800 British and American troops against Fort Duquesne, was ambushed and captured in September. As in Braddock's case those who escaped owed their rescue to the Virginians.

Meanwhile General Forbes, who had been delayed in Philadelphia by illness, decided not to use Braddock's old road but to cut a new one broad enough for wagons and artillery through the hardwood forest—the road Mumford's company was guarding. When the General finally arrived at Fort Cumberland, the advance got under way with the Virginia regiments leading the long scarlet and blue snakelike line through the noon-dark wilderness, and also furnishing scouts and flankers. Over that difficult terrain of steep, heavily forested hills and deep gorges progress was so slow that Forbes was about to give up the whole campaign and retreat to winter quarters when unexpected news reached him.

7. Mumford's poetic term for the wilderness.
8. Calendar of Virginia State Papers, Vol. I—1652–1781.

Up on lakes George and Champlain, General Abercrombie had moved forward with 15,000 men. Though Montcalm checked him in a bloody battle near Fort Ticonderoga, the Iroquois were so impressed by British power that, in October, they not only renewed the alliance but promised to call off their wards, the Delawares, who were with the French at Fort Duquesne. A Moravian missionary brought the word to the Delawares, who promptly left the French in the lurch.

Forbes received the news by messenger and moved forward vigorously. At the approach of his army of 6,000 men, Captain de Ligneris, on November 23, ordered his small French garrison to burn the fort and flee. The next day the Virginia regiments, led by Washington and Byrd, charged gaily into the smoking ruins of the stronghold that had so long threatened the western lands of Pennsylvania and Virginia. Forbes rebuilt the fort and rechristened it Fort Pitt.

This was the end of heavy fighting for the Virginia regiments. Washington resigned and ran for the House of Burgesses; but William Byrd remained in command of Fort Pitt while the new commander in chief, General Sir Jeffrey Amherst, made a successful expedition to clear the French out of the New York lakes in 1759. That same year, Pitt ordered General James Wolfe to strike at the jugular vein of the French—the St. Lawrence River. The whole long chain of French forts from Canada down the Mississippi depended for their supplies and reinforcements on that waterway. When, on September 13, 1759, Wolfe took Quebec—and died with Montcalm on the Plains of Abraham—he cut the vital artery. The other French forts withered on the vine; the war in America was virtually over, though peace in Europe was not signed until 1763.

In considering Byrd's military career his salient characteristics were his courage, coolness, easy confidence, and concern for his men. One final example of this is a letter he wrote to the editor of the Virginia *Gazette* on November 30, 1759:

To the Printer:
As Captain Bullet of my regiment has been accused of great misbehavior when he had the misfortune to be defeated and to lose his con-

voy at the Laurel Hill. In May last he applied to General Stanwix for a Court of Inquiry to give him the opportunity to clear up his character or rid the regiment of a bad officer. . . . The following was the sentence which I beg you will publish for the satisfaction of that gentleman's friends.

I am, sir, your humble sevant,

William Byrd.

*　　*　　*

Pittsburg, Oct. 26, 1759. It is the unanimous opinion of the Court that Captain Bullet behaved like a good officer and did everything in his power to repulse the enemy and save the convoy.

Signed by the Court by the General.[9]

Thus Colonel Byrd was thoughtful not only of the welfare of the men under his command but also of their reputations. He did not guard his own as carefully.

His military service was the Third William Byrd's most useful and happiest period, but even that was shadowed by the financial difficulties in which he was already involved. The legend, which has become history through repetition, is that he gambled away his patrimony. Perhaps he did, but there is no concrete evidence to prove it. As has been seen, the Byrds were bad gamblers; and what with his interest in horse racing and the custom of the era of playing for high stakes, William no doubt lost considerable sums of money. But it is improbable that this was the basic cause of his ruin. More likely it was his self-indulgence. He had been brought up to believe that whatever William wanted, William must have, and he bought it with no regard for his ability to pay. This was also a custom of the other planters. According to *The Growth of the American Republic* by Samuel Eliot Morrison and Henry Steel Commager,[10] at the beginning of the Revolution the Virginia planters owed their British agents at least £2,000,000, which some people were snide enough to say was the reason for their ardor for independence. But William, having come into his fortune much too young, was more reckless than almost any of his contemporaries.

9. *Virginia Gazette*, November 30, 1759.
10. Oxford University Press, New York, 1930.

In addition, Byrd, self-admittedly, was an extraordinarily bad businessman, plunging into harebrained ventures, naïvely trusting to the integrity of rascals, good-naturedly loath to press his debtors, and generously giving away money to unfortunates who asked his help. Finally he had damned bad luck in money matters, though good fortune in his family life.

It all began quite early in his career. A little over a year after his marriage to Elizabeth Hill Carter, his young wife presented him with a son, on August 2, 1749—good fortune. Bad followed quickly. The night after the baby was christened—William, of course—the housekeeper was brewing "a lotion" over a brazier on the third floor of Westover. A cotton sheet or curtain touched the coals and in an instant the room was in flames. At the shout of fire, the family and guests assembled in the smoky hall. As William led his wife, carrying their infant son, onto the lawn, they suddenly remembered that her young brothers, Charles and Edward Carter, were asleep on the third floor.

William dashed back into the house, running up the great stairway in great leaps through thickening smoke and crackling flames. He grabbed the boys, half led, half carried them to safety just as part of the roof fell in.[11]

With flames soaring into the chilly night, it looked as if Westover was gone. But though there was no fire department, there was plenty of manpower and plenty of water. Hundreds of slaves, men and women, tumbled half-naked out of their cabins and quickly formed a bucket brigade to the river. Chanting a rhythmic song, they passed the water across the lawn and up the stairs. While William, his guests, and overseers directed them, they flooded the second floor, saving it and the lower rooms as the thick brick walls confined the fire to the upper floor.

Thus was William's fortune—good and bad. His young wife, their son, and all the guests were safe. Westover still stood, stinking of smoke, soaked, half ruined, but still there. However, the rebuilding and refurbishing must have cost an enormous sum, and there was no fire insurance then to cushion the blow. This was probably the first bad crack in the Byrd fortune.

Incidentally, the family chronicler seemed to feel that William's

11. Byrd Letter Book in the possession of William Byrd, of Princeton, N.J.

action in saving his brothers-in-law was particularly noble since, if they had died, his wife would have inherited "an immense fortune." [12]

This unexpected, heavy loss did not stop William from spending money on the things he wanted—the house in Williamsburg; the thoroughbred horses; the finest clothes for himself, Elizabeth, and the children, who arrived every year or so. Following William IV came John Carter, January 27, 1751; Thomas Taylor, January 7, 1752; Elizabeth Hill, November 27, 1754; and Francis Otway (named for his English uncle by marriage), May 8, 1756. A year later when William was preparing to go to war, his three oldest sons, aged eight, six, and four, were sent to Colonel and Mrs. Otway to be educated in England.

William's marriage to his first wife has been called unhappy. The evidence of her letters written to him at Fort Cumberland and on the New York campaign flatly contradicts this notion. That she calls him "Mr. Byrd" is merely the affected formality of mid-eighteenth century. (One can hardly imagine Lucy Parke calling her husband Mister—"What! On the billiard table, Mr. Byrd?") Form aside, Elizabeth's letters are extremely touching in their sincere devotion and anxiety for her husband's welfare:

My dear Mr. Byrd:
I wrote to you the other day, which letter I hope you received by Mr. Robinson. I could give you a token of my affection much oftener if I could get any good opportunity of saluting you. I must tell you how much I am obliged to you for the agreeable epistle enclosed in your epistle from New York. . . . It gives me great comfort that my darling son and his brothers are so happy in having very good friends and relations in England. Your little girl and boy [Elizabeth and Otway] are well and our sweet Betty often mentions her papa. I hope dear Mr. Byrd will fulfill his promise when he returns to carry me to England with my dear children. I hope after this campaign is over I shall have the inexpressible pleasure of having you with me and your babes once more. I heartily wish Lord Loudoun success and pray the Almighty God to preserve your dear person safe. . . . Your horse Valient [sic] has lost the race that Mr. Paige and Mr. Lewis made with Mr. Boothe. My Calista has a very handsome filly.

12. *Ibid.*

I will no longer trespass on the patience of dear Mr. Byrd but conclude by saying that it would give me most infinite pleasure if I have an opportunity to tell him in person how much I am his most obedient and very affectionate

E Byrd.
Belvidere, May 13, 1757.[13]

William's mother also wrote to "My most dear and only son," telling him the news and bemoaning that she will not see him soon as she hears that "Lord Loudoun is hastening up the lake to free what we have lost there." She tells him of the death of "my sister Otway"; and says she has ordered her share of her sister's estate paid to Colonel Otway to reimburse him for the expenses of keeping her grandsons. Also five guineas to Billy and two each to the younger ones and a handsome present for Mr. Cawthern, Headmaster of the Tunbridge School.

"[The Otways] are all charmed by Billy's sweet disposition," she wrote, "and think Jack [John Carter] will make a good boy though at present his temper is not as good as his brother's. . . ." Thomas Taylor was evidently the Otways' favorite: "Little Thomas is a lovely little fellow and shows a most martial genius. The first time his Aunt Baynham saw him she asked who he was. 'I am, Madame, a soldier,' says he. . . .

"The lady and her daughter [Byrd's wife and Elizabeth] at Belvidere are well, but the little fellow [Otway] is a weakling. She has never once been to see me though I offered her the chariot whenever she pleased. . . ." A typical mother-in-law's complaint. Maria became testy with age.

Maria wrote again to her son on November 6, 1757, with more news of her grandchildren in England, who were spending their "Holy Days" at Colonel Otway's country house, River Hill. Significantly she added, "Mr. (Charles) Turnbull is a man I deem most zealous in your interest. He is lately given a statement of your affairs in which he showed me by that calculation tis plain to a demonstration that your estate will be cleared of all incumbrances in four or five years at furthest barring accident. . . ." Perhaps it would have been if William had remained away at the wars.

Meanwhile Elizabeth wrote to him about their youngest son:

13. This and succeeding letters from the *Virginia Magazine of History and Biography*, Vol. XXXVII.

"Poor sweet Otway, poor dear Babe, he is a weakling. He has been sickley for such a number of months that he was incapable of walking without being supported. But, sir, your orders must be obeyed whatever reluctance I find thereby. If the infant lives, which God only knows, . . . I'll send him to his pleasant, old native air of Westover. . . ."

Elizabeth, lonely and forlorn at Belvidere while her dominating mother-in-law held the fort at Westover, was worried that her sons in England would get smallpox: "I shall be in a pannick for them until I can embrace them in my arms again. . . . Never shall I be so happy as to see their dear papa and our sweet family all together, I shall fancy myself in the Elissium Field. . . .

"God Almighty bless you. Adieu, I am yours most affectionately, Eliza Byrd."

Little Billy was worried about smallpox, too. On May 29, 1759, he wrote from England to his grandmother:

Honored Madam:
I received your affectionate letter with greatest pleasure. . . . I wish Westover were nearer that I might pay my duty to you, Madame. . . . Now I give you an account of my brothers and myself. I am 4 feet 4 inches and Jack is half a head shorter than me and Tom is half a head shorter than him. They send their duty. I am very happy with my cousins on Holy Days. I am sometimes at Lyons Square [Otway's town house] sometimes at River Hill. . . .
I am, my dear grandmama, your most dutiful grandson,
William Byrd.
I am very desirous of having the smallpox [vaccination] but my friends in England will not consent without particular orders and I shall be obliged to you, my dear Madame, for your consent.

Billy wrote in equally stately prose to his mother also addressed as "Honored Madame," in which he again begged for permission "to have the smallpox."

On July 25, 1760, when William was still away commanding Fort Pitt, Elizabeth Byrd died at Belvidere. If her side of the marriage was unhappy, it was due to being separated so long from her beloved husband and to the unpleasant characteristics of her mother-in-law, which even Maria's son finally recognized. It had been impossible for the two ladies to live under the same roof, so Elizabeth had retired to Belvidere, a long way by the transportation of those days from her family at Shirley and the friends with whom she had grown up. According to the English custom, which Virginians imitated, she should have stayed at her husband's estate at Westover, and Maria should have moved to another house. But the gentle Elizabeth could not win such a contest, so the widow lived in splendor while the wife lived and died in a kind of exile.

Maria's satisfaction at her daughter-in-law's demise is barely concealed in a letter she wrote to her son on August 15, 1760. After a passing reference to "the death of poor Mrs. Byrd" and the many letters of condolence she had received, she briskly goes on to inform him that she had written to Shirley to let the Carters know that it was her and their father's wish that she should have the care of her "blessed grandchildren." Her satisfaction at having Betty and Frankie, as she called Otway, is plain: "Your daughter is the picture of her brother Billy, and Frankie is exactly what you was at his age. He is my bedfellow. . . . Betty is at this time fingering her needle and Frankie has begun his alphabet. . . ."

It must be admitted that William did not mourn his wife very long. Barely six months after her death, on January 29, 1761, he married Mary Willing of Philadelphia, the daughter of Charles and Anne Shippen Willing. Both the Willings and the Shippens, especially the latter, were among the best families of Philadelphia, whom even Virginians recognized as being almost equal to them in aristocratic lineage and manner of living.

The marriage came as a great shock to Maria. When she opened her son's letter, she cried out, "Good God, is my son married and never acquainted me with it!" However, she soon found out the eminence of Mary Willing's family and hastily wrote all sorts of loving messages to the new bride.[14]

Mary Willing at twenty-one was a very different type from Elizabeth. To begin with she was much prettier and to end with she was far more forceful. It probably was not long before Maria sincerely mourned her late daughter-in-law.

14. Maria Byrd to her son. Feb. 17, 1761. Byrd Letter Book.

II · "THE WORLD TURNED UPSIDE-DOWN"

WILLIAM BYRD was a powerful begetter; he had ten more children by his second wife, making fifteen in all. Their first, Maria Horsmanden, was born in Philadelphia on November 2, 1761; their last, William Boyd Byrd, after his father's death in 1777. Byrd brought his family home in 1762 and Mary took her rightful place as mistress of Westover.

But William was never to have the happiness his father and grandfather had known. Though the hummingbirds still hovered over the honeysuckle on his garden wall, and his thoroughbred horses frolicked in the grassy paddocks, and the world came to dance and be merry at Westover, peace of mind he had not. His debts, instead of diminishing, ballooned to staggering proportions as he continued to gratify his whims, and to spend large sums of money on his children at home and in England. He bought two of his English-bred sons commissions in crack regiments of the British Army and made them handsome allowances. Otway became an officer in the Royal Navy.

Twisting and turning, borrowing here, selling something there, William managed to walk a financial tightrope, carrying the whole elaborate structure on his shoulders for fifteen years more. He went to England in 1767. Immediately upon returning in 1768, he conceived the scheme of the great Richmond lottery. In an advertisement in the *Virginia Gazette* for June 9, 1768, he proposed to raffle off the entire towns of Shockoe (sic) and Rocky Ridge, near Richmond, pointing out that the obstructions through the Falls and other parts of the James River would shortly be removed and navigation thereby extended more than two hundred miles. This would open communication to the western frontier with a portage of no more than sixty or seventy miles to the Ohio River, "so that the immense treasure of that valuable country must necessarily be brought to market to one or other of the above said towns."

Ten thousand tickets were to be sold at five pounds each with 839 prizes and 9,161 blanks. The prizes included a twenty-year lease on the mills; various fisheries; Byrd's Shacco and Watson warehouses; Patrick Coutt's ferry; seventeen improved lots; ten thousand acres of land to be laid off in hundred-acre lots; four hundred unimproved lots and ten islands with a total value of £50,796. In other words, all the original Stegge and Byrd holdings, from which their fortune grew.

The lottery appears to have been a dismal failure. Not enough people bought tickets to clear William's huge debts. After several postponements the drawing finally took place at Williamsburg in November, 1768, under the management of Presley Thornton, Peyton Randolph, Charles Carter, and Charles Turnbull. The lucky winners had a terrible time clearing their titles to the lots and it took several acts of the Assembly to straighten things out.[1]

That the lottery did virtually nothing to relieve the pressure on poor William is shown by a letter from Thomas Adams to his brother, Richard Adams, written less than a year later on July 5, 1769:

You say Colonel Byrd owes you £200. Pray don't advance him another shilling as I fear his affairs soon will be desperate, being informed he must part with his whole estate in a short time, and that it is suspected that it will not do all [cover all debts].

He has desired me to put some tobacco on board on his account which I would not have done had he not been in your debt, but I shall try to get enough to make you whole. . . .

I am sorry to hear you were so unlucky in his lottery which was the

1. *Virginia Magazine of History and Biography*, Vol. V.

case with me, having had tickets to the amount of £150 and got nothing.[2]

Perhaps William's case was not quite as desperate as Mr. Adams thought, for he managed to keep going for eight years longer, selling and borrowing—for example £56.19 from Robert Carter in 1775, which had not been repaid in 1805. Everything was against the frantic gentleman. The year 1772 was a terrible one for tobacco, there being a depression in England; 1773 was worse. The major depression in this product, which began then, lasted right through the American Revolution, although in other trade and manufacturing in the colonies, business was booming.

In addition to these problems, the land was running out. Many of William's fellow planters were trying other crops—flax, hemp, indigo, and cotton. Cereal crops like wheat and corn were the most favored. William himself was raising large quantities of wheat. But with his great money crop in such straits, there was no way of pulling out of the morass of debt on which the interest charges ran from 8 to 10 per cent a year.

Beyond all this, the American colonies were moving rapidly toward their final confrontation with England. And William Byrd was on the losing side.

During the French and Indian War, the British Government had been careful not to antagonize the American colonies, whose full cooperation they badly needed. In the 1760's, with the war won and British rule in America, except for Louisiana, apparently secure, they proceeded to tighten the screws of economic and political bondage. King George II had died in 1760. His successor, King George III, was twenty-two years old, charming, energetic, a good sportsman and, despite most American histories, intelligent. He was at first very popular. His trouble was that he really believed that he had a divine right not only to reign but to rule, and he was less than tactful in asserting this right. This attitude soon sat ill with his subjects in England and even worse with those in America.

England had subsidized the colonies' war effort with £2,000,-

2. *Virginia Magazine of History and Biography,* Vol. 25.

ooo. In order to get it back and to make the colonies pay for their own future defense, Parliament, urged on by the young King, greatly increased duties on goods shipped to America and cracked down on smuggling, which was a way of life for many Americans. Then, in 1765, they passed the Stamp Act, which required that every official paper, such as deeds, court proceedings, wills and even diplomas from colleges, must have an official stamp which cost from 1/2 penny for a newspaper to £2 for a diploma. It was the first time a British Government had ever tried to levy a direct internal tax on Americans, who considered it not only illegal but oppressive. The poorer colonists simply could not afford the impost, and it raised a furor in America that astounded the gentlemen in London, both King and Parliament. Americans were enraged less by the cost than by the violation of the principle that internal revenue could not be raised without their consent. "No taxation without representation!" External imposts such as duties on imports were legal by established custom, Benjamin Franklin said in London, but not internal taxation. All over the colonies men banded themselves together as "Sons of Liberty," a phrase coined by Member of Parliament Isaac Barre in a speech against the Act. In the Virginia House of Burgesses a wild young patriot from the western lands, who possessed the gift of eloquence, made his first great speech: "Caesar had his Brutus, Charles the First his Cromwell and George III [shouts of "Treason! Treason!"] may profit by their example," declared Patrick Henry. The Assembly promptly voted a resolution, declaring that they alone had the power to tax Virginians.

William Byrd undoubtedly regarded Henry as a rabble-rousing radical and felt nothing but disgust for the doings of the Sons of Liberty. What he called them "sons of" in private conversation can easily be guessed, as they aroused the mobs in the seaboard cities, burned the Stamp Act official paper, and for good measure looted and burned the homes of the collectors appointed by the Crown.

Seeing that the Act was unenforceable, Parliament repealed it in March, 1766, which caused great jubilation in America and a surge of renewed loyalty to King George III. However, this ardor was soon dampened by the British Government which, taking Benjamin Franklin at his word, put heavy duties on the export of English goods such as paper, glass, paint and *tea*, to the colonies. This caused another explosion of anti-British feeling in America. With Samuel Adams in Boston and Patrick Henry in Virginia whipping up the spirit of revolt, feeling ran so high that the Townshend Duties—named after Chancellor of the Exchequer Charles Townshend—were repealed in 1770. All, that is, except *the tax on tea*.

The Boston massacre took place that same year. Soldiers of the British garrison fired, without orders, on a mob that was stoning them and killed four Americans, giving the radicals another oratorical handle. Three years later the boycott against the tax on tea reached its climax in the Boston Tea Party when the Sons of Liberty, humorously disguising themselves as Mohawk Indians and Negroes, pitched a shipload of tea into Boston Harbor. King George's tame Prime Minister, Lord North, put through the Coercive Act in 1774, virtually closing the Port of Boston, quartering troops on the inhabitants of colonial towns, and making all Massachusetts officials from the Council down to justices of the peace appointees of the Crown at the King's pleasure.

Americans now really had something to complain about and they reacted strongly. In the Convention in St. John's Church at Richmond, Patrick Henry asked, "Is life so dear or peace so sweet as to be purchased at the price of chains and slavery? . . . I know not what course others may take, but as for me, give me liberty or give me death!" For the first time the colonies joined together to resist British tyranny. On September 5, 1774, the First Continental Congress met in Philadelphia. The stage was set for revolution.

During those years William Byrd was a desperately unhappy man. Not only were his own affairs inextricably mired in debt; his eldest son, charming Billy, was killed in France in 1771 by being thrown from a phaeton. And Otway was so clearly sympathetic to the rebellious radicals that he was writing:

"Honored Sir:

"I am sorry to trouble you again about my leaving the Navy and can assure you was I to remain I should be the most unhappy man in the world. I must therefore beg my Dear Father not to insist on my continuing in a service I so much dislike and shall be obliged to him if he will get me in the Secretary's office. . . ."

William answered that letter in his will, and for the time being, Otway remained in the Navy.

Even more disastrous from William's point of view, the country he truly loved was falling into chaos, misled by men he considered traitors, on a course that might end in repudiating the King to whom he felt his loyalty was due. To his shocked amazement, most of the great planters, his friends and kinsmen, were fired by the spirit of revolt. Peyton Randolph actually became President of The Grand Continental Congress. William felt a growing sense of spiritual and social isolation.

Sometime during those years he had his portrait painted. Why he ever commissioned it, or why, having seen it, he did not destroy it, is unimaginable. For, compared to his youthful portrait, it reminds one of "The Picture of Dorian Gray" in which the ravages of all the vices and dissipations of the subject were magically transferred to his painted image. William stands there on spindly legs which support a huge pear-shaped torso whose waist must measure between four and five feet in circumference. His moon face is fallen into huge jowls and wrinkles, veritable craters and mountain ridges of flesh from which little pig eyes stare dully. This is the ruin of a man.

His soul was as corroded, for on July 6, 1774, he made a will which must be one of the most bitter self-condemnations ever written into a testament.

In the name of God Amen.

I William Byrd of Westover . . . being of sound mind and health of body make this my last will and testament. . . .

In the first place, unworthy as I am, I resign my soul into the hands of its unerring Creator. . . .

Next, I desire my body may be privately buried by the tomb of my sister Evelyn in the old churchyard.

As to the remaining part of the estate which it has pleased God to bless me with, which through my own follys and inattention to accounts, through carelessness of some interested with the management thereof, and the villainy of others, is still greatly encumbered with debts, which embitters every moment of my life . . . it is my will and desire that one hundred Negroes and such part of the plate and household furniture as my wife can conveniently spare, together with the library, and part of the stock of horses, cattle and sheep shall be sold immediately to pay my just debts. And, likewise, debts due me from my trustees, managers and adventurers in the lottery; many of whom are greatly in arrears, shall be immediately collected and applied to the above purpose.

After some minor bequests William left to

. . . my dearest and best of wives for her lifetime Westover and Buckland Plantations, all the remaining Negroes, stock, household furniture that she might choose to keep and the carriage and coach horses.

It is my will that at the death of my dearest wife all my estates whatsoever shall be sold . . . and the money arising from the sales thereof be equally divided among all my children that are alive at the time . . . deducting from a share of those I had by my first wife such sums as they may claim under the wills of my deluded and superannuated mother and my ungrateful son, William, [reaching into the grave to chastise him because he had left his money to his mother's children and not to his father].

My will is likewise that if my son Otway shall quit the Navy before my wife's death that he shall not be entitled to any part of the above said money . . . in that case I give him one shilling sterling.

My will also is that if my son Thomas should marry Susanna Randolph, the daughter of the present Attorney General . . . [he would also get one shilling sterling.]

There are various other bequests: one thousand acres of land in different parts of the country to each son, specific bequests to each daughter, his wife to be sole executrix, but if she finds it too taxing, then John Carter Byrd and "my good friend Patrick Coutts [Jr.]" are appointed executors.[3]

Hopes for a peaceful settlement in Virginia had been aroused by the arrival of the Earl of Dunmore as Governor in Chief on September 25, 1771. His predecessor Lord de Botetourt, who died in 1770, had been the fanciest governor ever. Not only did he build a superb ballroom wing on the Palace, but he brought over a magnificent gilded coach in which he appeared on state occasions drawn by eight white horses (thereby giving George Washington ideas at the time he became the first President of the United States). During the interim (1770–71), President of the Council William Nelson managed to get some revolutionary declarations through the Assembly.

3. *Westover Title Book.*

When Lord Dunmore made his official entry into Williamsburg, the *Virginia Gazette* fairly gushed with good feeling as it described the principal gentlemen of the city—among them William Byrd—going to the Palace to pay their respects and staying to dine with the Governor in the comfortable upstairs drawing room. As night fell, "There were illuminations as a testimony of our joy at His Excellency's safe arrival, and the gratitude to His Majesty for appointing a nobleman of his ability and good character to preside over us. . . ." Everything seemed just as it had been in William's father's time.

In 1774, despite the tightening tensions between the colonies and Great Britain, Lord Dunmore reached a peak of personal popularity. Even that late, the Shawnee Indians had gone on the warpath in the Ohio Valley, plundering, burning, scalping, and taking many colonists captive. Lord Dunmore personally led a force of militia against them, routed them completely, and by treaty moved back the western border of the Indian Reserve, giving the eager pioneers more Indian land to settle, and confining "the Indians to limits that entirely remove the grounds of future quarrels between them and the people of Virginia . . ." [4]

To add to the popular enthusiasm, Lady Dunmore gave birth to a daughter in the Palace the day before her husband made his triumphant return from the foray, which was called Lord Dunmore's War. The *Virginia Gazette,* on December 8, 1774, noted rapturously that "The young Virginian is in perfect health;" and the "city fathers in Common Hall assembled moved an address of congratulations to His Excellency." [5]

It was a brief detente. On November 17, the First Continental Congress had issued a Declaration of Rights of Americans, which proclaimed that Americans were entitled to all the liberties of Englishmen. Then, the Congress proposed an agreement among the colonies not to trade with Great Britain until their grievances were rectified. That hurt the powerful English merchant class in their most tender spot.

Throughout the colonies the Sons of Liberty were· dancing around their Liberty Trees, and, more to the point, Americans everywhere were accumulating caches of arms and gunpowder, and drill-

4. *Virginia Gazette,* Dec. 8, 1774.
5. *Ibid.*

ing systematically against the day that everybody except the hotheads
hoped would never come. Massachusetts was the spearpoint of insurrection; Virginia was second only to her. In April, 1775, before the
news of Lexington arrived, the train was fired by an ill-timed act of
Lord Dunmore.

According to custom fifteen half-barrels of gunpowder from
H.M.S. *Ripon* were stored in the small, octagonal brick magazine at
Williamsburg, a few hundred yards from the Governor's Palace.
Lord Dunmore appears to have been one of those dim-witted gentlemen by whom England so often had the misfortune to be represented
in moments of colonial crisis. The Patriots drilling in the public
squares under his very nose made Dunmore extremely fidgety, the
squealing of their pipes and rattle of their drums exacerbated his
nerves. All he could think of was that gunpowder virtually unguarded in the magazine; theirs for the taking. He decided to do
something about it.

On the night of April 30, 1775, the Governor ordered sailors
from H.M.S. *Fowey* secretly to transport the gunpowder aboard
their ship. At two o'clock in the morning, guarded by a detachment
of bluejackets, wagons with carefully greased wheels, and drawn by
horses with padded shoes, emptied the arsenal. So stealthily was the
operation performed that the citizens of Williamsburg heard nothing
until they woke to find the powder gone.

What a roar of rage, what a hue and cry, what protestation of
injured innocence arose! So great was the clamor that on May 2,
Lord Dunmore summoned the Council to explain and get approval
for his action. A minority of the members attended—six out of
twelve Councilors—among them William Byrd, Thomas Nelson,
Richard Corbin, William Wormeley, Jr., John Page, and John
Gann, Clerk. There was a loyalist majority.

Taking his place in the chair of state under the emblazoned arms
of England, the Governor addressed them portentously:

Gentlemen: Commotions and insurrections have suddenly been excited among the people which threaten the very existence of His
Majesty's Government in this colony; and no other cause was assigned
for such dangerous measures than that the gunpowder which had been
brought from one of the King's ships, to which it belonged, and was de-
posited in the magazine of this city, hath been removed, which it is
known was done by my order under the constitutional right of the
Crown, which I represent. . . .

I acted in this manner as my indispensable duty required to anticipate the malevolent designs of the enemies of order and Government. . . .

Lord Dunmore then called upon the Council for their advice on issuing a proclamation explaining his act and calling on all persons to submit to the legal authority of the Government. . . . The Council asked the Governor for time to think it over and agreed to meet the following day.

As they discussed the Governor's statement that evening, it was clear to William Byrd and a majority of his fellow councilors that Dunmore had acted within his rights and according to his duty. The gunpowder did belong to His Majesty's Ship *Ripon* and not to Virginia. The Governor had a perfect right to send it back to the ship, even if his timing was less than tactful. They resolved to support him.

If William Byrd read the *Virginia Gazette* the next morning in the pleasant dining room of his Williamsburg house, he found some interesting material. The entire front page was devoted to the debate in Parliament on the American question. Lord North had offered to resign, but His Majesty had requested him to remain until the disputes between Great Britain and the colonies had been settled.

There was also a small item on an inside page, written by a wildly excited correspondent in Massachusetts, on April 19, 1775. It stated that 1,000 British troops had marched out of Boston to Lexington, where they had seen a number of men exercising on the Common and, after ordering them to disperse, had fired upon them, killing several. The British troops were marching on to Concord.

A gentleman who had talked with the Express [messenger] from Lexington stated in the same article that another British brigade of a thousand men had been sent across the river and that "4,000 of our troops have surrounded the first brigade, who are on a hill in Lexington, but the action is continuing and there were above 50 of our men killed and 150 regulars, as near as they could determine when the Express came away." [6]

It must have been with a heavy heart but strongly reinforced convictions that William Byrd went that morning to the Capitol, where the rump Council consented to the Governor's issuing the following proclamation—as silly as it was irritating.

After noting that, "Some persons in different parts of this

6. *Virginia Gazette*, May 3, 1775.

Colony have disaffection to His Majesty's Government . . . and are working toward effecting a change in the form of it, covering their wicked designs under the specious appearance of defending their liberties," Lord Dunmore described the removal of the gunpowder and explained it by, "the apprehensions which seem to prevail throughout the whole country of an intended insurrection of the slaves. . . ."

Everyone who read the proclamation knew that this was unadulterated eyewash, and the Governor as good as admitted it by stating: "I chose the night as the proper season because I knew the temper of the times. . . ." He ended with the usual palaver urging the people to trust to, "the goodness and tenderness of our most gracious Sovereign." [7]

Since the majority of Virginians had no faith whatever in King George's goodness and tenderness, the proclamation only infuriated them, and their ire was heightened by a full and surprisingly accurate account of the Battle of Lexington-Concord in the same issue of the *Gazette:* ". . . 1,000 of the best troops, in a very secret manner," had crossed the Charles River and marched to Lexington, where they had fired on the Minute Men and gone on to take Concord. The correspondent wrote, "This alarmed the country so that it seemed as if men came down from the clouds."

The article went on to say that the British, reinforced by a second brigade of one thousand men from such crack regiments as the Welsh Fusiliers, the 4th, 47th, and 38th Regiments, and two fieldpieces, had tried to make a stand on a hill near Lexington but had been forced to continue their retreat. The Boston correspondent gracefully commented, "They did [it] with the bravery becoming British soldiers; but the country was in a manner desperate, not regarding their cannon in the least. . . ."

"I stood upon the hills," he wrote, "and saw the engagement very plain which was very bloody for seven hours. It is conjectured that one half the soldiers at least were killed. [8] They are this morning entrenching themselves on Bunkin Hill [sic] until they can get a safe retreat to this town. . . ."

William Byrd could hardly believe that an armed rabble like those Yankee Minute Men had defeated two thousand crack British

7. *Virginia Gazette*, May 6, 1775.
8. Totally inaccurate. The figure was about one-tenth of the British.

troops. He realized that this stirring account of the American victory would set Virginia afire and vastly encourage Patrick Henry who already had left town to take command of a body of patriots in open insurrection. William's world in the words of that new English song was "turned upside-down."

Throughout May and early June, Byrd continued to live in his pretty house in the capital and to attend Council meetings. The status of Williamsburg remained quo. The Patriots held all the surrounding countryside and the Williamsburg Volunteer Cavalry, in new dark blue uniforms, splendidly mounted on thoroughbred horses, drilled right under the Governor's nose. Lord Dunmore nervously paced the beautiful rooms of his palace and issued a fresh proclamation, declaring Patrick Henry and his followers outlaws and ending with "God Save the King." The Patriots scratched out "Save" and wrote in "Damn."

On May 12, the subservient rump Council voted a humble address to the Governor supporting his actions, to which Lord Dunmore gratefully replied, "Your willingness to concur in measures, which if adopted, will entirely compose the destructive differences between the country and Great Britain and restore the order and tranquillity of the colony, cannot but give His Majesty the most sensible pleasure." This can have given William Byrd very little comfort in view of His Majesty's obvious inability to control events in his Old Dominion.

On Monday, May 29, the Williamsburg Volunteer Cavalry rode gaily out of town, followed by a wagon piled high with baggage and provisions. They went to Ruffin's Ferry to meet Peyton Randolph, who had just resigned as "President of the Grand Continental Congress" and escort him to the capital. Randolph, "an affable gentleman of majestic deportment," reached town on Tuesday, riding down Duke of Gloucester Street between lines of cheering citizens. Byrd in his house could easily hear the horrid sound.

On the night of Saturday, June 3, some young patriots broke into the magazine to see if they could find any arms. As they stumbled around in the dark, there was a blinding flash and a deafening concussion. Choking and retching in the powder smoke, they fled.

What had happened was described in the *Virginia Gazette*. They had been surprised by a gun, "which was so artfully placed, said to be contrived by L——— D———e, that upon touching a string which was in their way it went off and wounded three persons, but not mortally." This incident notably failed to enhance the Governor's popularity.

Dunmore was in an absolute panic. The House of Burgesses met and went about its normal business. On June 6, they even expressed their "humble thanks" to his Lordship for his concern about the colony. This did nothing to alleviate his Lordship's case of nerves.

At two o'clock the next morning, Thursday, June 7, the lights were out in all the little houses on Duke of Gloucester Street. Even Raleigh's Tavern had shut down. The whole town slept. How soundly they must have slept! For no one heard the Governor's coach brought around to the door of the Palace, or the baggage wagons, or the guard of bluejackets from the *Fowey*. In the darkness, with shaded lights, men wrestled with Lord and Lady Dunmore's baggage and boxes filled with magnificent silver plate and piled them on the wagons. Hastily, with starting eyes searching the bushes, the Governor General bundled his wife and children into the coach. At a dead walk, clanking softly, the coach and wagons skirted the silent town; once clear of it, at a dead run, swaying and bouncing, they made for the river. The Governor and his family tumbled into the *Fowey's* waiting cutter. "Up oars! Let fall! Give way with a will!" shouted the coxswain. Eight oar-blades bit the water, eight strong backs pulled in unison; and the cutter foamed away from shore toward the tall-masted man-of-war swinging at anchor in the James. Aboard her, waiting to greet the Governor, was William Byrd's son, Captain Thomas Taylor Byrd of the British Army.

So ended, for all practical purposes, the British Empire in Virginia.

Lord Dunmore's behavior was hardly in the best traditions of the British Army. Though he said he departed, "in order to have the privilege of wearing my head," it was in no danger of severance. However inflammable the patriots were, it never occurred to them to kill a royal governor. Possibly his freedom of action might have been hampered, and he may have thought that he could preserve it by going aboard ship. But if he thought he could govern Virginia from a warship anchored off Yorktown, he was as fatally misled as Lord Cornwallis seven years later at the same place.

Dunmore's poltroonery shattered British prestige, and turned the royal authority into a joke. A small, ironic item in the *Virginia Gazette* for June 10, 1775, indicates the Virginians' attitude: "Last Thursday morning about two o'clock our Governor and his family decamped from the Palace and are now aboard the *Fowey* Man of War at Yorktown. . . ."

Of course, Dunmore left behind one of his inept addresses to the House of Burgesses, in which he excused his action on the ground that he was "fully persuaded that my person and those of my family likewise, are in constant danger of falling sacrifices to the blind and immeasurable fury which has so unaccountably seized upon the minds and understanding of great numbers of people. . . ."

He added that it was not his intention "to give the least interruption to the sitting of the Assembly," and that they should proceed with their business while he would be easily accessible to them. He hoped that "the House will see my proceedings on this occasion as they were really meant. . . ."

The Council and the House did exactly that. Grave-faced they wrote of how hurt "We, His Majesty's dutiful and loyal subjects [are] that Your Lordship entertains any suspicion of the personal safety of yourself or family, as we can by no means suppose that any of His Majesty's subjects in this Colony would meditate a crime so horrid and atrocious as Your Lordship seems to apprehend. . . ."

So for a short time the forms were preserved. William Byrd and other loyal members of the Council and House, called on Dunmore aboard the *Fowey*, urging his return. To no purpose—Dunmore had had enough.

Disappointed and embittered, William Byrd retired to Westover. What he thought of the Governor's conduct he kept to himself, but one can easily surmise. For however much dissipation and self-indulgence had eroded his character, he was never a coward. It is impossible to imagine William Byrd decamping in the night.

Never again did William Byrd play an important role in the affairs of his country. He sat morose and lonely in his beautiful house, despised by most of his fellow Virginians, hopelessly watching the course of events, as Edward Pendleton, Chairman of the Committee of Safety, became Acting Governor; the illegal Fifth Convention of

Virginia met in the Capital; the Second Continental Congress voted to support Massachusetts, and Byrd's close friend, George Washington, rode northward to take command of the Continental Army besieging the British in Boston. Incidentally there is absolutely no substance to the legend that Byrd was considered for that command. His well-known loyalty to the King would have precluded it even if George Washington had not had far better military credentials.

However, according to the memoirs of Nancy Shippen of Philadelphia [9] written after the Revolution, Byrd was offered command of the Virginia Continental Line. This is substantiated by a letter written by Byrd to Sir Jeffrey Amherst, dated Westover, July 30, 1775, in which he said that it is "impossible now to avoid civil war" and that he "has met with insults and been given offense because of his refusal to command the armies being raised by this Convention [the Virginia Convention] to oppose the King's troops." Byrd went on to inform Sir Jeffrey that, "The Southern Colonists have been led to believe by false accounts that they are far superior to the power of Great Britain and by artful schemes have been deluded into rebellion."

Byrd requested that he "may not be considered one of the American traitors as he is ready to serve His Majesty and would be glad of the opportunity to convince the Virginians of their error and bring them back to loyalty and duty." He also requested that the answer "be enclosed to General Gage and thence forwarded to him by boat if no more ships are sent to this colony." [10]

There is no record of any reply.

Meanwhile Lord Dunmore was adding the final insult to the injuries he had done the Virginians. In an act of desperation the miserable man proclaimed Virginia in a state of insurrection and all the slaves free. This infamous attempt to start a slave insurrection must have disgusted Byrd as thoroughly as what he considered the reckless behavior of the Patriots.

9. *Nancy Shippen, Her Journal Book.* Compiled and edited by Ethel Ames. J. B. Lippincott Company, New York and London, 1935.

10. Autographed Letter endorsed H [sic] Byrd to Sir Jeffrey Amherst from Vo. 2. *Manuscripts of the Earl of Dartmouth* published by the Historical Manuscripts Commission, London, 1895.

Lord Dunmore did not feel safe enough on the James and dropped down to Norfolk. With about one thousand former slaves, his marines and sailors, he took the city. After several months, the Patriot militia, among whom was Major Alexander Spotswood, son of the former Governor, drove him out. As he left, he burned Norfolk. After hanging around in his warships for nearly a year, Lord Dunmore gave up and sailed for England in 1776, shouting, "To think I should have come to this!"

The year 1776 was a bad one for William Byrd. The Fifth Virginia Convention officially declared Virginia an independent nation. Byrd's old friend George Mason wrote the Declaration of Rights of the new Virginia Constitution containing such egalitarian sentiments as, "All men are by nature equally free and independent . . . and have certain inherent rights . . . namely, the enjoyment of life and liberty, with the means of acquiring and possessing property and pursuing and obtaining happiness and safety." Patrick Henry was elected Governor of the Commonwealth of Virginia.

To cap it all, on July 4, 1776, the Continental Congress, led by the Massachusetts and Virginia delegations declared the Independence of the United States of America in almost the same words.

To William Byrd's anguish over the radical course his country was taking was added the misery of his personal situation. The one thing left to console him was pride in his son Thomas Taylor, who remained in the British Army. Thomas wrote to his father explaining his attitude in the crossfire of conflicting loyalties:

On board the Dunmore, February 25, 1776.
My dear sir;
I have taken the first opportunity of informing you of my arrival off Norfolk, where my Lord Dunmore expressed a desire to have me with him. . . . So I can talk no other language but that of a Soldier, & am determined to support that character as long as I have the honour to belong to the Army, & consequently to obey every order I receive from my superiors. . . .

Believe me to be your
Most Dutiful Son *T. T. Byrd*

My Lord Dunmore presents his compliments to you and all the family.[11]

11. Byrd Letter Book.

Otway Byrd was considerably less dutiful. Despite the provision in his father's will, he jumped ship (family legend has it that he leaped overboard off the North Carolina coast and swam ashore). He joined the Continental Army, and became an officer on the Staff of General Charles Lee. The brothers came close to shooting at each other on May 13, 1776, when Thomas was commanding a battalion under Lord Dunmore at Norfolk and Otway rode with General Lee to inspect Dunmore's entrenchments.

Otway was with Lee during his successful defense of Charleston, South Carolina, later that summer. Despite his disinheritance, he wrote a properly filial letter to his father after the defeat of the British:

Charleston, July 20, 1776.

My dear Sir, Ever since the departure of the Enemies Army from this place we have flattered ourselves with the pleasing thought of a march northward, but our hopes were frustrated last night by an express from the President of Georgia that a large ship had got over the Bar and several others were discerned in the offing. . . . The General ordered Brigadier General Howe to take command of the Continental Troops and march with all possible expedition to the Province. . . . I am ordered to proceed with Mr. Howe. . . .

He then states that his white servant is going to join his regiment in New England and would William please give him money for the journey as he (Otway) is "almost out of money myself." He goes on:

As you was so kind as to promise to give me a servant . . . I will not put myself to the expense of another.

My love to my Mother, Brothers & Sisters & I am, My Dear Sir, with the greatest respect from your,

Very Aff.
Son
Otway Byrd.[12]

From this it is evident that William maintained an affectionate relationship with his rebel son, though he did not change his will. In fact, Lord Dunmore's outrageous behavior had disillusioned him with the loyalist cause.

As always, the worst of William's troubles was his huge debts. Since the outbreak of war no tobacco or wheat had been shipped to

12. *Ibid.*

England; so no money was coming in and his great tobacco warehouses and granaries were bursting with the rotting produce of his land. The new Government of Virginia was taking stringent measures against the Tories. Men active on behalf of the Crown were declared to be subject to penalties of imprisonment, or death and the loss of property. Though William refrained from any such activities and took a-plague-on-both-your-houses attitude, he could foresee the time—which came the following year—when loyalists would be forced to take an oath of allegiance to the state or face the loss of their right to vote and to sue for debt, and be taxed doubly or triply. At best his patriotism would be suspect.

As the dark skies and dripping clouds of November gave place to the bitter cold of December, William became desperate. The world was passing him by. His peers and one-time friends were walking in glory, however ill-gained he might consider it. As he surveyed the state of the nation and his own affairs, the bile of frustration and bitterness rose in his brain like corroding acid. He could see no chance of recouping, no light of hope in the somber future.

On the morning of January 1, 1777, he awoke at lowest ebb. All the physical and mental ills of his condition enveloped him in black despair. Quite possibly the news of General Washington's defeat of the British at Trenton on Christmas night was the last unbearable weight that tipped the balance of his brain. He could not face the dawning year.

William arose in the frigid darkness, dressed himself, and went to the armory. He selected a beautifully wrought dueling pistol, measured powder, rammed in wad and bullet with particular care. Then he placed it against his temple and pulled the trigger.

III · THE WIDOW
AT WESTOVER

HE SHOT that rang through the dark and silent rooms at Westover was William Byrd's ultimate act of selfishness. In those days of strong religious belief, suicide was considered perhaps more heinous than murder. Not only did it disgrace the entire family of its perpetrator, but his estate might be forfeited to the state. That was the situation in which William placed his children and "the dearest and best of wives," who was pregnant.

Fortunately, Mary Willing Byrd was twice the man her husband had been. It was not for nothing that as a girl she had been advised and taught by her godfather, Benjamin Franklin. Mary realized that the first imperative was to conceal the manner of her husband's death. This she succeeded in doing, with the loyal silence of her household and the connivance of William's friends who, however much they might deplore his politics, rallied to the support of his widow. The only official notice was a small item in the *Virginia Gazette* for January 3, 1777: "Colonel William Byrd died at Westover on January 1, 1777."

Nor did Mary find the responsibility of becoming executrix of her husband's estate too taxing. She felt she could handle the business better than her son or any less interested person. She had been left with eight living children, ranging in age from sixteen to two years old, and she must hold things together for them. In the midst of war and against heavy odds she succeeded.

The house in Williamsburg, together with all its furnishings and plate, was advertised for sale "by the Executrix" and brought a good price. Somehow she unloaded the western lands that her husband had not already disposed of. The superfluous slaves and stock were sold in accordance with his will. The Second William's superb library, to which very few additions had been made since his death, was sold intact to Mr. Robert Bell.

By 1780, Mary Byrd had brought the estate into some sort of order. She had had a rough time. Cotton and silk cloth were very expensive because their import was cut off by the war, so Mary cut up the beautiful brocade curtains of Westover to make clothes for her children, and the curtain linings to make underwear. Despite all her difficulties, she had made excellent matches for two of her daughters. Maria married John Page of Page Brook; and Evelyn Taylor married the contemporary Benjamin Harrison of Brandon.

She put the plantations and her business affairs in astonishingly good shape. Then, just as she might have relaxed a little, another blow fell.

This misfortune could be traced to the day in 1779, when her first cousin, the beautiful, sexy, willful Tory sympathizer, Peggy Shippen, married the most dashing of all the American generals, Benedict Arnold. When Mary Byrd heard the news, she must have been delighted. Not only was Arnold a brilliant match, but by marrying a popular American general, Peggy would help to clear the Shippen and Willing families from the taint of Toryism, which had made things difficult for Mary. Though she had been completely cut off from her Philadelphia relatives during the British occupation of that city, the known fact that they had fraternized with Lord Howe and his officers had made Mary's patriotism suspect in Virginia. From all sources it would seem that such a suspicion was not unfounded. Mary Byrd's sympathies were almost certainly loyalist. On the other hand she had been extremely careful not to say or do anything disloyal. All she wanted was to keep her reputation pure and her children in comfort at Westover.

Then came the attempted betrayal of West Point. Benedict Arnold became the most hated name in America, easily outranking

Judas Iscariot as the symbol of perfidy. And Mary Byrd herself was soon to be personally involved.

From the decampment of Lord Dunmore until 1781, no real battle had been fought on Virginia soil. Massachusetts, Rhode Island, New York, New Jersey, Pennsylvania, Delaware, the Carolinas, and Georgia had all been fought and bled over, had suffered the rigors of enemy occupation and known the ugliness of war at first hand. Virginia remained inviolate, though she stripped herself of men and arms to help her sister states. Now it was Virginia's turn.

On January 3, 1781, news came to Westover that a large British fleet had anchored off Jamestown. The next morning Mary Byrd saw the topsails of a ship coming stately around the bend in the James; then another, and another, until the whole broad blue water was covered with white sails like clouds in a mackerel sky—twenty-seven ships, from tall men-of-war to small brigantines. The children, especially the little boys, Charles and Richard, must have been enchanted by this splendid maritime spectacle. Perhaps Mary's heart was lifted, too. But it must have sunk as she saw the lead ships wear round and head straight for Westover.

In minutes they were all along the shore; the big ships smartly clewing up sails while their anchor chains rattled out; little ones coming alongside the dock and nuzzling up to the low river bank. Scarlet-clad British troops poured out onto the lawn, running toward the house under the glitter of fixed bayonets and the flash of officers' swords. Nobody had much time for Mary, standing on the portico with her children, half-fascinated, half-terrified, as the red tide flowed past them and around the house while Negroes fled to their cabins or cowered under beds.

Meanwhile boats loaded with more soldiers were putting off from the big ships; barges were brought alongside and horses in slings lowered into them. Some small cannon were disembarked. There was a great stir on the flagship; a twelve-oared barge lowered and manned; boatswains' pipes shrilling; the flash and crash of saluting cannon as officers in cocked hats climbed down the accommodation ladder and took their seats in the stern.

The boat, with its oars like a huge many-legged beetle, crawled swiftly across the water to the dock. The officers disembarked and walked across the lawn in a glittering group. Leading them, in the glory of his brand-new scarlet uniform, gold braid, fringed epaulettes, white knee breeches and black jackboots, was the man whom Mary wished least in the world to see—her cousin by marriage, Brigadier General Benedict Arnold of the British Army.

What does one do when a relative comes to call backed by a thousand British soldiers? Does one receive him politely or spit in his eye? Mary well knew that she was damned whichever she did; but the exigency of the moment seemed to call for courtesy. Though she later vehemently denied it, the probabilities are that Mary entertained General Arnold and his staff with Westover's customary hospitality. One can imagine her sitting at the head of the table with Arnold on her right and his officers around the board, while Negroes in livery brought in a spectacular meal and she made small talk with her newly met cousin germane—"How is darling Peggy? She was only a baby when I last saw her. When did you see my brothers Richard and Charles? In Philadelphia in '79?"

"They sent their compliments if I should come this way."

"Thank you, General. Please return mine to them if you should see them again. But of course that is unlikely."

"It's not improbable, Ma'am; the rebellion is in its final fever."

Yes, courtesy was indicated; war was no excuse for bad manners, especially when the enemy was in a position to burn your house, steal your treasure, rape your daughters . . . but they were gentlemen, no danger of that. In fact were they even the enemy? At first, Mary may have been in two minds about it.

After spending two nights at Westover, Arnold pushed on toward Richmond. It had become the capital of Virginia in 1779 because it was more easily defensible than Williamsburg, though it was "quite an insignificant town" with a population of but eighteen hundred people, only half of whom were white. Arnold's plan was to capture Governor Thomas Jefferson if possible, or at least to destroy the American munitions and supplies, and burn the foundry at Westham, which was making cannon for the Continental Army. Arnold took Richmond without a fight, missed Jefferson by a whisker, but succeeded in his other objectives. Then he retreated back down the peninsula.

His second call at Westover was less enjoyable. When this new relative left, he carried off forty-nine of Mary's slaves—a heavy financial loss—all the grain and other supplies he could transport, two ferries, and three fine horses, including Maria Byrd's favorite saddle horse. Then, Arnold fortified himself in Portsmouth opposite Norfolk and waited for Lord Cornwallis, who was coming up from South Carolina with a large army.

As soon as the British left, Mary Byrd was in trouble with the Americans. It seemed very fishy to them that Arnold had chosen to land at his cousin-in-law's plantation. They suspected collusion if not treason. Some wit, playing on her maiden name, called her "Willing Molly." Mary was frantic to get her Negroes back. She invited General Baron von Steuben to Westover and charmed that great German drillmaster of the Continental Army. Not knowing American politics, but appreciating a handsome woman, von Steuben authorized Mary to send a flag of truce through the lines to attempt to persuade the British to return her property. It was carried by Lieutenant Charles Hare, R. N., another Philadelphia relative by marriage. Unfortunately Hare's ship, H.M.S. *Swift*, ran aground, and Mary's letter was captured by Major Tuberville, who was a red-hot, angry patriot and regarded any traffic with the enemy as treason. He forwarded the letter to Jefferson, who also took a jaundiced view of the matter. Whether by Jefferson's orders or on his own initiative, Major Tuberville, with some militia, raided Westover, locked Mary in an upper room, and carried off all her private papers.

Though she realized she was in very bad odor with the Government of Virginia, Mary was still determined to get her Negroes back. She wrote to Governor Jefferson, stating her side of the case:

Westover. February 23, 1781

Sir:

I think I am called on to say something on the subject as a duty to myself, the public in general and you in particular as Supreme Magistrate of this State. . . . I appeal for justice.

I hear Mr. Hare has forfeited his flag and been made a prisoner. . . . Among his papers they have found a letter written by myself; I think in answer to a message received from Captain Evans. I do not recall the contents of the letter but am easy about it. For, as my heart never dictated aught that was dishonerable so my pen could never express anything I could not justify. If policy had not forbid it, I owe too much to my honour to betray my country. . . .

I know a law passed some time ago, which I looked over in a cursory manner, imported what was treason. I never concede that there was an object upriver to lead the enemy near my habitation. . . . When the officers landed I received them according to my idea with propriety. I consulted my heart and my head and acted to the best of my judgement agreeably to all laws human and divine, if I have acted erroneously it was an error in judgement not of the heart. . . . Every good man must have been shocked when they heard of the savage treatment I have met with. This cannot be called liberty. . . .

I am convinced, Sir, that you have had no share in these base actions [nor] that great man Baron Steuben (sic). He was incapable of giving orders that would authorize such rash, indecent, horrid conduct as I have met with.

I have the honour to be, sir, your most obedient humble servant.

M. Byrd.[1]

In spite of this letter, Mary was scheduled to be tried on March 15 for treasonable dealings with the enemy. She knew quite well the law forbade any communication with them, or exchange of goods. However, Arthur Lee wrote that he had reason to believe Mrs. Byrd would never be brought to trial, "means having been taken to keep the witnesses out of the way."[2] Arthur Lee was quite right. The Virginia establishment took care of its own and even Thomas Jefferson could not change that.

Mary Byrd was so disgusted and annoyed that she decided on a drastic step. On April 21, 1781, the following advertisement appeared in the *Virginia Gazette:*

FOR SALE

WESTOVER containing upwards of 1,000 acres of land of which 365 acres is reclaimed meadow about 100 acres unimproved swamp. For terms apply to the subscriber, M. Byrd.

That was a momentary aberration. Luckily there was no time to sell Westover. In July, Lord Cornwallis' British Army of over 8,000 men—having ravaged Virginia as far west as Charlottesville, the temporary capital, nearly capturing the whole Virginia Government

1. *Papers of Thomas Jefferson*, Vol. 4. Julian P. Boyd, Editor. Princeton University Press, 1951.
2. *Ibid.*

—came pouring down the Peninsula. They camped at Westover. Again the house was filled with scarlet coats and golden epaulettes, while the library building was turned into a stable for Lord Cornwallis' horses. Arnold was there, too. Mary charmed Cornwallis as she had von Steuben. After a brief stay Cornwallis moved on to take up a "secure" position at Yorktown.

Despite Mary's close call on a treason trial, she was still determined to get her slaves back. On August 10, 1781, she wrote to the new governor of Virginia, Thomas Nelson:

> You have been so good, Sir, as to show me it would give you the greatest pleasure to grant me a flag. I hope it is now convenient. I have lost forty-nine of my people, three fine horses and two fine ferryboats all of which Lord Cornwallis promised me should be returned to me. Other people have flags granted to them; the Baron assured me I should have one whenever the enemy were inclined to deliver my people. . . .
>
> If I do not recover my people my family are ruined and this, worthy Sir, you have the power of preventing. Shall it be said that because I am a stranger in the country I am not to have justice in any line. I have sent my soldier who has lost his life in the service of his country.[3] I have paid my taxes. . . . My property is taken and I have no redress. . . .[4]

Mary never got her flag of truce; events were moving too fast. Troopers in blue and buff replaced the redcoats at Westover, as the Marquis de Lafayette with 1,200 men of the Continental Line and 3,100 militia cautiously pursued Cornwallis down the Peninsula. Late in September, General Washington himself arrived bringing 4,000 more American troops and General le Comte de Rochambeau with 7,000 white-uniformed French.

They began the siege of Yorktown on September 30, 1781. Nineteen days later Cornwallis surrendered his army—7,241 men, 214 cannon, 457 horses, 30 ships and over £2,000 in cash. The war was over, though peace was not signed until 1783.

The winter of 1781–82 was the gayest ever in Williamsburg. Comte de Rochambeau made his headquarters there; the place was full of titled French officers. There were balls or parties almost every night. Mary Byrd spent a good deal of time in the sparkling little city with

3. None of the Byrds were killed. Perhaps Mary thought Otway had been.
4. *Papers of Thomas Jefferson.*

her two eldest daughters, who dazzled the French with their beauty. Comte de Rochambeau invited them to his elegant parties; he cared not whether their mother was a Tory or a Patriot. In fact, it made little difference to anyone now.

On April 27, 1782, Mary met the Marquis de Chastellux and promptly invited him to visit her. He, too, felt her charm and arrived two days later at Westover. We are indebted to him for a vivid picture of the house and his hostess:

[Mrs. Byrd] is about two and forty with an agreeable countenance and great sense. She has preserved [her late husband's] beautiful house . . . rich furnishings, and a considerable number of slaves and some plantations which she enhanced in value. Her care and activities have in some measure repaired the effects of her husband's dissipation and her house surpasses [all the others] in the magnificence of the buildings, the beauty of its situation and the pleasures of society.

She has, however, experienced fresh misfortune. . . . Her relationship with Arnold, whose cousin German she is, and perhaps, too, the jealousy of her neighbors, have given birth to the suspicion that war alone was not the object that induced the English always to make their descent at her habitation. She has been accused of connivance with them . . . but she has braved the tempest and defended herself with firmness. . . . It does not appear that she will likely suffer any other inconvenience. . . .

Of Westover de Chastellux wrote:

Mrs. Byrd's house, which with its various annexes has the appearance of a small town, formed a most delightful prospect. . . . As I walked by the riverside I saw two Negroes carrying an immense sturgeon and on my asking how they caught it they told me that at this season sturgeon were so common they can easily be taken in a seine. . . . These monstrous fish, which are as active in the evening as to be seen perpetually leaping to a great height above the surface of the water, usually sleep down deep at midday. . . .

As for the humming birds I was seeing them for the first time and never tired of watching them. The walls of the garden and the house are covered with honeysuckle which afforded an ample harvest for these charming little animals. I saw them perpetually fluttering above the flowers; sometimes they perch but never for more than an instant . . . when they are in the sunlight they display the brilliant glaze of their red throats which have all the brilliance of rubies and diamonds." [5]

5. Marquis de Chastellux, "Travels in North America in the years 1780, 1781, 1782." As translated for the Byrd Letter Book.

The first William would have liked to know that his humming-birds were still there.

For all her indefatigable efforts Mary Byrd never received compensation for her property looted by the British, though some of the Negroes may have been returned after the fall of Yorktown. After the war she put in a claim to the British Government for over £6,000 in damages, of which she probably never received a copper penny.

Despite this, she managed to live at Westover for over thirty years after the war in comfort and a serenity her husband never knew. When she died in 1814, at the age of seventy-four, Westover was sold in accordance with William's will, and the money distributed among William Byrd's children then living, except Otway, who did better than they because he received a Federal grant of six thousand acres of land in Ohio for his services in the Revolution.

With Westover gone, the eminence of the family was diminished until two of William's descendants restored the family fortunes in the twentieth century.[6]

6. Westover was purchased by William Carter, who went broke endorsing a note for a friend and sold it to a Mr. Douthat, who had won $100,000 in a lottery. After passing through various other hands and being used as General George B. McClellan's headquarters in the Peninsula Campaign of the Civil War, it was purchased by Mr. Richard Crane, who restored it to its former splendor. It is now the property of his daughter, Mrs. Bruce Crane Fisher.

IV · IN THE SHENANDOAH

THOMAS TAYLOR BYRD returned to America shortly after peace was signed, but not to Tidewater Virginia. Feeling still ran too high for him to be comfortable there. Virginians were willing to accept Mary Byrd despite the suspicion of her patriotism, but not a man who had been an officer in the enemy's army all through the Revolution—even though after 1776 he had not served in America.

His problem of where to live was solved when he was given a thousand acres of land in Frederick County [1] in the Shenandoah Valley by his uncle, Charles Carter of Shirley, one of the young boys his father had saved in the fire at Westover. Because the Scotch-Irish settlers in the Valley were further removed from the harassments of royal governors and had never seen a British redcoat, except when they came to protect them during the French and Indian War, feeling ran less high than in Tidewater Virginia and service in the enemy army was more easily forgiven.

Captain Byrd, proudly wearing the rank he had gained in the British Army, married Mary Anne Armistead of Hesse in Gloucester County and brought her to the Shenandoah Valley. He built a cottage on the land his uncle had given him. Thereafter it was known as

1. Now Clarke County.

"The Cottage Farm." Thus, the main line of the Byrd family moved to the western lands that the second William had loved so much.

It was the main line because Thomas Taylor was the oldest son to have any children. His oldest brother, William, died unmarried and though John Carter Byrd married Molly Page of Cumberland County, they had no children. So devoted was John to his wife that when he was told she was incurably ill, "He in perfect health but from great affliction, took to his bed, turned his face to the wall, and in six weeks Molly Page was a widow, and most ungratefully got well and married Archie Bolling." [2]

Thomas Taylor restored the balance by having eight sons and two daughters. Though he resigned himself to becoming a gentleman farmer—planter was too grand a term for a man with only a thousand acres—Thomas was never wholly reconciled to life in the rural west country. "He was accused of loving England better than his own country," [3] and he probably did. Though from his terrace he could look eastward over rolling fields and orchards to the ever-changing Blue Ridge, or westward to the serrated Alleghenies on the far horizon, Thomas Byrd often dreamed of greener, neater fields beyond the sea.

The only portrait of this member of the family was painted when he was a child in England. The little boy, with hair clubbed back from a high forehead, slanted blue eyes, big nose, and strong chin is wearing a silk coat with deep cuffs over an embroidered waistcoat and ruffled shirt. He is holding a bow and arrow which the artist may have used as an indication that he was American. Apart from that, he looks like the son of an English aristocrat. Nor did he greatly change. In his old age he was described as having, "the appearance and manners of an English nobleman." [4]

When Thomas Taylor came to the Valley in 1786, it was not far removed in time from the frontier. The nearest town was Winchester where, not many years before, his father and Colonel Washington had held the fort against the Shawnees, the Delawares, and the French. Close by was the hamlet of Battletown. The name did not refer to any clash of arms, but to the fact that this town's one street was lined with saloons where the Scotch-Irish settlers got drunk

2. Byrd Letter Book.
3. *Ibid.*
4. *Ibid.*

every Saturday night and, roaring with alcoholic rage, revived their ancient feuds with shelalaghs and broken bottles till their blood spattered the wooden sidewalks and muddy roadway. In more peaceful and decadent times, Battletown was innocuously rechristened Berryville just in time to become a real battleground, as Yankees and Confederates took and retook it, over and over, during the Civil War.

Despite his distaste for the primitive conditions in the Shenandoah Valley, Thomas Taylor became a good citizen. He joined the Anglican Church—it had changed its name after the Revolution to Episcopal—and worshiped in the Old Chapel, which was a glorified log cabin, whose logs were "squared and dovetailed. It was thirty feet long in the clear, twenty-two feet wide . . . and eleven feet high from sill to the wallplate." [5] There were two, tall eighteen-paned windows at front and back. A communion table served as the altar, facing rows of wooden benches. Byrd served as a vestryman of Frederick Parish for over twenty-five years.

Soon after Thomas Taylor came to the Shenandoah, the heirs or younger sons of the Tidewater planters began leaving the worn-out fields for the fresh pastures of Frederick County. Fine houses with high-columned porticos blossomed on every other hilltop. George Steptoe Washington was already there at Harewood, where James and Dolly Madison were married. He was followed by King Carter's grandson, Carter Burwell, who built Carter Hall; Byrd's cousin, dashing Nellie Custis Lewis, came to live with her son, Lorenzo Lewis, at Audley, bringing many mementos of her adoptive father, George Washington. George Norris built beautiful Rosemont, just outside of Battletown. Other kinsfolk came flocking—the Pages, who built a new Page Brook and also Aunefield; Isaac Hite lived at Bellegrove; General Elisha Boyd at Boydsville; Claymont was built by Bushrod Washington; a dozen more great houses sprang up. Life became as gay as it had been along the James, with balls and parties, parlor games, and fox hunting over the lush, grassy fields enclosed by stone walls or zigzag wooden fences; barbed wire, that horror of the sportsman, was yet to be invented.

Fortunately, the old families did not bring their prejudices with them when they moved west, so Thomas Taylor Byrd was accepted for what he was, a conscientious citizen, a brave soldier, and a charming gentleman.

5. Minutes of the Vestry of Frederick Parish.

That he was also an Anglophile did not matter until the United States went to war with England again in 1812. Then, Thomas Taylor noted a certain offishness in his friends: curious glances, sudden pauses, or bright bursts of irrelevant conversation when he entered a room. But they were always courteous, those Virginians. They tried very hard not to be obvious.

All this nonsense stopped when Thomas Taylor's eldest son, John Carter Byrd, was killed fighting the British at North Point in 1814; and his third son, Captain Francis Otway Byrd, was presented with a Sword of Honour by Virginia for his gallant conduct at Fort Erie and Lundy's Lane.[6]

Thomas Taylor lived until 1823. His later years "were clouded by disease" and he was especially "liked and admired for the courage he showed in his infirmity." [7] When he died, his coffin was carried one and a half miles from the Cottage Farm to the Old Chapel Cemetery by weeping slaves, who were joined in their sorrow by most of his fellow parishioners.

It is impossible to follow the fortunes of all the Byrds. They became almost as numerous in the forests of America as their feathered namesakes to whom King George I had referred. William went to Ohio where he probably took up that six thousand acres belonging to his Uncle Otway. Other progeny spread across the land as far as Texas where Micajah Byrd appeared in 1824; a group moved to St. Louis and misguidedly changed the spelling to Burd.

The next member of the family who directly concerns this history is Thomas' sixth son, Richard Evelyn Byrd, who was born on December 29, 1800. Richard grew up during the years of high romanticism that nostalgic literature pictures as the heyday of Southern chivalry. Everyone in the South was reading Sir Walter Scott's novels and trying to emulate his fearless, spotless knights and gentle damsels. A few Gothic castles even made their incongruous appearance on wooded hilltops; and tournaments were held in which young gentlemen on thoroughbred horses rode gallantly down the lists, impaling curtain rings on the points of their lances for the honor of crowning their lady Queen of the County.

6. The sword is now in the possession of Senator Harry Flood Byrd, Jr.
7. Minutes of the Vestry of Frederick Parish.

Richard, however, was a hard-working no-nonsense man. He had to be; for his father never had enough money to support a flock of sons in elegant idleness. He became a lawyer and achieved a fine reputation in the Valley and, indeed, the whole state. He served in the House of Delegates in 1847–49 and in the Constitutional Convention of 1850–51.

Though his roots were firmly planted in the Shenandoah Valley, Richard went back to Tidewater for his bride. Doubtless he often visited his kinsfolk in the great houses on the James. There he met Anne Harrison, the daughter of Benjamin Harrison of Brandon, who was his cousin. This relationship was multiplied by other Harrison-Byrd alliances. The interrelationship does not seem to have damaged future generations. When strong, healthy bloodlines are inbred, the offspring frequently inherit their best features. Cleopatra, the end product of the Ptolemys' custom of brother-sister marriages, was hardly a weakling. Though certainly not that closely related, the Byrd-Harrison line emphasizes the point.

Richard and Anne married on May 18, 1827. They had three sons and a daughter: George Harrison Byrd (1827–1910), the sixth William Byrd (1828–96), Alfred Henry Byrd, and Anne Byrd. They lived to see a far different, sadder world; a world that would have been unthinkable to the gay, gentle people who had played at chivalry on the grassy lists at Carter Hall.

When Richard Evelyn Byrd was in his late fifties, the possibility of war between the Northern and Southern states, which for most of his life had hung like a thunderstorm flashing and rumbling below the horizon, suddenly became imminent. Virginians, especially those in the western counties, were not enthusiastic proponents of slavery. This "peculiar institution," had never been economically viable in the Valley, a land of small farms and hard-working white settlers. Negroes represented less than 2½ per cent of the population. These Virginians watched with dismay as the great slaveholding states of the Deep South and the idealistic but rabid abolitionists of New England moved inexorably toward a bloody confrontation.

It is quite possible that Virginia might never have joined her seceding sisters had it not been for the tragic incident at Harpers Ferry in October, 1859. John Brown, who had gained notoricty by a bloody massacre of peaceful citizens in Kansas, conceived the idea of abolishing slavery by taking over the Government of the United

States. With a group of fanatical followers he seized the arsenal at the Ferry and endeavored to start a slave revolt.

After killing six people, Brown was captured by Federal troops under the command of Colonel Robert E. Lee and Lieutenant J. E. B. Stuart. He was tried at Charles Town, only twelve miles from Berryville. There were no rioting crowds or manifestations of hatred. It was a fair trial with all the forms and safeguards of liberty punctiliously observed. Brown was convicted and hanged on December 2, 1859.

It was not that a fanatical old man had endeavored to raise a slave revolt, however horrid such an act appeared to Southern eyes. What inflamed the people of Virginia was that the Northerners made a saintly martyr of him. When men like Wendell Philips wrote of "the eternal brightness of his glorious deed," and Ralph Waldo Emerson said, "A new saint will make the gallows glorious like the Cross," and ministers in a thousand Northern pulpits called upon God to help exterminate the Southern people, Virginians realized that they were faced by an almost insane hatred of their institutions and their very persons.

In 1860, with the flames kindled at Harpers Ferry still burning fiercely, a Negro woman allegedly murdered her white mistress near Winchester. Whether guilty or not, what chance had she for justice less than thirty miles of the scene of John Brown's revolt? As it turned out, a very good chance.

By the code of English and American law, guilty or not, she was entitled to the advice of counsel. After half the lawyers in that part of the state had turned down the unpopular task of representing her, the most distinguished attorney in the county offered his service free of charge. That she should be condemned without a fair trial evidently did not accord with Richard Evelyn Byrd's notions of justice.

Despite Byrd's best efforts, the defendant was found guilty and condemned to death. However, Byrd got a stay of execution on the ground that she was pregnant. While the matter was still in question, the war began. Federal troops took Winchester and set her free. That she thus got away with murder detracts nothing from the high moral courage of her defender.

Richard Byrd joined the Army of the Confederate States of America and served throughout the war as a colonel on the staff of Major General Montgomery Dent Corse. Byrd died in 1872.

Richard's oldest son, George Harrison Byrd, married Lucy Wickham and went to live in Baltimore, where he established a mercantile business. When the Civil War broke out, Maryland remained in the Union by a close decision. George Byrd, a strong Southern sympathizer, is believed to have used his wide connections on both sides to organize a large-scale smuggling ring, supplying the Confederacy with desperately needed cloth, medicines, and possibly arms in return for contraband cotton and tobacco. This not only satisfied his loyalty to Virginia, but showed a handsome profit.[8]

After the war, George moved to New York and into the big money, becoming the richest Byrd up to that time. He bought Upper Brandon, next door to the famous Harrison place on the James, and inherited the Cottage Farm at Berryville. He and his wife lie in the Old Chapel Cemetery, which he helped to endow.

Meanwhile his brother, William Byrd, ranged much farther afield. After graduating from the Virginia Military Institute and taking a law degree at the University of Virginia he traveled to Austin, Texas, in 1853, where he formed a law partnership with T. Scott Anderson. Politics were in his blood and in no time he became Treasurer of the City of Austin (1856) and a prominent figure in the Democratic Party. In 1859, he further consolidated his political fortunes by marrying Jennie Rivers, daughter of Judge Robert Jones Rivers. Their oldest son, Richard Evelyn Byrd II, was born in Austin in 1860.

That year, the shadow of war, stretching from the Potomac half across the continent, deepened over Texas. After the election of Abraham Lincoln in November, there was not much doubt that Texas would join her eastern sisters in secession. In 1861, Governor Edwin Clark appointed William Byrd Adjutant General of Texas to organize the preparations for war. Though Texas was so distant from the great battlefields, her sons were as eager to fight the Yankees as any firebrand from the Deep South, and more so than many Virginians who, like Robert E. Lee, were troubled by conflicting loyalties to their state and to the Union. Byrd helped to organize the great Texas regiments that—a thousand miles from their homes—played so important a role in both the early victories and the desperate last stands of the Confederacy. That he did his work well would be testi-

8. George Harrison Byrd's grandson, William Byrd of Princeton, New Jersey, in conversation with the author.

fied to by many a Union soldier whose blood was chilled by the high-pitched screams of Hood's Texas Brigade as they charged through the smoke of half a hundred battles from the glory of Gaines' Mill to Antietam, where 82 per cent of them died, to Gettysburg and on to their final defeat in the twilight of the Confederacy.

But William Byrd was not the man to sit at a desk for long, no matter how important his job. In November, 1861, he used his political influence to get into what he supposed would be a fighting outfit. He was appointed Lieutenant Colonel of the 14th Texas Infantry and put in command of Fort DeRussey in Louisiana. There he stayed, doubtless biting his nails from vexation, until March, 1864, when, hopelessly outnumbered by the victorious Federal troops, he was obliged to surrender the Fort, his regiment, and himself.

Soon after the end of the war William Byrd left Texas and returned to Winchester in "Military District One," formerly Virginia. He found it in an appalling condition. The Shenandoah Valley had been the bloody runway of contending armies. Winchester had been taken and retaken seventy-two times. The countryside was ruined, thousands of barns and hundreds of houses burned, fields devastated, livestock slaughtered; the life of the people was reduced to a bare subsistence level.

Of the postwar period, Julia Davis wrote in *The Shenandoah* [9] "Those were lawless years. Throughout the Valley, not a property nor life was safe after dark. Horse stealing reached such a pitch that the death penalty was demanded for it. Livestock of all kinds disappeared. Public property was smashed by vandals. The drifting and embittered Negroes did some of this but more was done by the ex-soldiers. . . . Civil authority commanded no respect for its representatives were removed or appointed at the will of the military. The new county courts were referred to as 'immigrant trains' or 'menageries' ". Union general succeeded general as dictators. A Northerner named Henry Wells was appointed Governor and a Negro from Ohio, Lieutenant Governor. Carpetbaggers purloined whatever the armies had left. "The Valley people were for the most part sunk in apathy or stubborn bitterness. . . ." [10]

The condition of the liberated Negroes was desperate. They

9. Farrar and Rinehart, New York, 1945
10. *Ibid.*

flocked to the Federal camps like trusting sheep until, overwhelmed, the soldiers drove them away, killing a few. After that they trickled into the towns looking for food. The townspeople had not enough to give them. Violence broke out in Lexington and Front Royal. There was a race riot in Charles Town; and in the streets of Winchester the Irish laborers fought with the starving Negroes. The raped body of a white woman was found in a ditch and for the first time in Valley history a Negro was lynched.

This was the condition of the country to which William Byrd returned, bringing his wife, young Richard, and his other children— eventually there were seven, four boys and three girls. Why he chose to do so is something of a mystery. In Austin he had made a fine position for himself, and, though Texas had lost so many of her sons, the state was comparatively untouched physically. It seemed insane to leave such a land of opportunity for a ruined, desperate country; but a man who has gone through a losing war is not usually logical. During long boring years in Fort DeRussey and the miserable months in a Federal prison, William Byrd must often have recalled the lovely valley of his birth, its tilted fields and fragrant orchards and the Blue Ridge standing guard against the outside world. No doubt he was bone-weary; tired of Louisiana's swamps and the flat Texas plains; sick of war without glory and brokenhearted by defeat; longing for the safe, sweet security of home. It could have been just homesickness that brought him back to the Valley, or possibly a quixotic compulsion to help rebuild his devastated homeland. In any event he came. And against the odds he prospered.

Byrd formed a law firm with Captain Lewis N. Hutt, C.S.A. There was plenty of business in those chaotic years, but very little hard cash. However, times slowly improved. Virginians were not allowed to vote in 1868 when General Ulysses S. Grant was elected President, but had they been able to, they should have voted for him. For the magnanimous victor, who at Appomattox had said to General Lee, "Your men can keep their horses. They will be needed for the spring plowing," was very different from the Northern radicals in Congress, who wanted only vengeance upon the defeated South. Soon after his inauguration, President Grant accepted the proposals of the Committee of Nine, organized by Alexander H. H. Stewart of Staunton, for universal amnesty and universal suffrage. This allowed

Virginians to elect their own state officials. In January, 1870, Grant persuaded Congress to pass an act to readmit the State of Virginia to the Union.

Of course, this action did not produce an instant Utopia. Life was still hard in the Valley. In fact, it remained difficult for half a century until the second Yankee invasion. This time the rich Northerners came again, not to conquer but to enjoy the amenities of the Virginia countryside and to pour their dollars into refurbishing long-neglected mansions and recreating a reasonable facsimile of the kind of life they had read about in romantic Southern novels.

With the passing of the worst privations, the settling down of the Negroes, and the eviction of the carpetbaggers, there was a chance for a man of ability to make a little money. The William Byrds lived very comfortably in his father's big brick house on Washington Street in Winchester. It had been built by General Daniel Morgan in about 1780 and stood alone on a block-square lawn with tall trees and terraces dropping down to the street level. The portico was supported by tall pillars with Ionic capitals. The cool, high-ceilinged rooms were paneled; there were exquisite carvings around the doors, windows and mantelpieces done by Hessian prisoners of war during the Revolution. Next door lived Judge Richard Parker, who had condemned John Brown to death.

William's son, Richard, grew up in that house with his six brothers and sisters. He got his schooling at the Shenandoah Valley Academy, and went on to study law at the University of Virginia. Because of his love of books, his preference for quiet evenings at home, and his photographic memory, he was probably the best-educated member of the Byrd family since the second William, and like his ancestor, he read Latin as easily as English. But Richard was no bookworm. He liked strong liquor in his youth; as he grew older, he liked it even better. He was ready to fight any man at the drop of a hat, and often did. Once, in his later years, Mr. Dick, as everyone in town called him, was sitting in his law office overlooking the Courthouse Square with his partner, Judge Thomas W. Harrison, when a minor riot broke out below. Watching the fighting with an appreciative eye he said, "You know, Tom, we've been in a hell of a lot of tight places together."

"Well," said Harrison, "we've been tight in a hell of a lot of places together."

Only a few months before Mr. Dick died, his son, Harry, then running in the Democratic primary for Governor, was due to speak in the hostile area of Blue Mountain. Someone there sent him word, "If you appear, I'll kill you."

"You go on, Harry," said Mr. Dick. "I'll take my little pearl-handled revolver and if that son of a bitch gets up, I'll shoot him." [11]

There is a characteristic photograph of young Dick Byrd taken shortly after he opened his law firm with Tom Harrison. He had a strong, stocky body. Above the batwing collar and stripped gray tie of his formal courtroom clothes is a round, determined face surmounted by a brush of unruly, short-cropped hair. The photographer's flash highlights his determined chin; and his alert eyes give him the look of a terrier ready to pounce.

Almost immediately after graduating from law school, Richard Byrd plunged into politics. He was elected Commonwealth Attorney for Frederick County and held the office for twenty years. In that capacity he had plenty of chance to show his fighting spirit and moral courage. When a murder was committed up in the hills, no one else cared to tackle the mountain folk. Byrd went up there alone in his buggy and brought the murderers to trial by a combination of bluff and moral authority.

On the other hand, he would take on high society as well as hill-billies. One of his grandsons tells the story of how a hot-blooded member of a prominent family from another part of the state killed a minister right in front of his own church. The local district attorney disqualified himself as a friend of both parties, and other state officials boggled at prosecuting the murderer because of the powerful political connections and social influence of his family. Byrd volunteered for the job and secured a conviction. As his grandson says, "He was not afraid of the devil himself." [12]

In 1906, Mr. Dick was elected to the Virginia House of Delegates and two years later became the Speaker of the House— unusually speedy recognition of ability by that conservative body. He served until 1914, resigning to open a law office in Richmond. But he remained a political leader. With his brother-in-law, Henry Delaware Flood, Jr., Chairman of the House Foreign Relations Commit-

11. Mr. Richard E. Byrd of Rosemont in conversation with the author.
12. *Ibid.*

tee, and United States Senator Thomas Martin of Charlottesville, he gathered around him a group of "like-minded men" who eventually became the nucleus of the famous—or infamous—Byrd Machine.

Mr. Dick was a delegate to the Democratic National Convention of 1912, where he opposed the wishes of both Virginia's Senators and other powerful politicians to swing some of Virginia's votes to Woodrow Wilson, whom he had known when Wilson was studying law at the University of Virginia. Wilson was properly grateful, and when he became President, he consulted Byrd about many Federal appointments in his home state, thus giving him the power of Federal patronage. In 1914, Wilson appointed him United States District Attorney for the Western District of Virginia.

Public service and politics were Mr. Dick's delight and avocation, but they were chancy and ill paid. He supported his family mainly by practicing law. As a civil lawyer, he built a tremendous reputation, first in Frederick County and then throughout the state. According to those who remember him at work, no one could trick a hostile witness into damaging admissions more suavely than Mr. Dick, and no one could squeeze tears from a jury's eyes more eloquently. He was a superb orator, far better than his son, Harry, even though the latter climbed much higher up the political ladder. So eloquent was he that when he retired to his cabin on a mountain peak at Skyline for one of his periodic binges, it is said that the legal business of the whole county paused to await his return to the courtrooms.

Even at that, Richard Byrd never seems to have made much money. For one thing, it did not interest him; for another, he was always taking on underdogs' cases, for which he was apt to be paid with a pair of chickens or, if he was very lucky, a fine Virginia ham.[13]

When he was two years out of law school, in 1886, Richard Byrd had married Eleanor Bolling Flood, whom he had met while she was attending the Episcopal Female Institute in Winchester, run by Mr. Pocahontas Smith. Miss Flood's family was even more eminent than the Byrds at that time. Her great grandfather was General Elisha Boyd, who in 1812 built Boydsville, the superb mansion at Martinsburg in what is now West Virginia. Her grandfather, Charles James Faulkner, was Ambassador to France under Presidents Buchanan and Lincoln. Though Faulkner was opposed to slavery, when Virginia seceded from the Union, he regretfully informed the President that

13. *Ibid.*

he must follow his state and resign. President Lincoln replied, "It is a great loss to the Union, but I must respect the sincerity of your convictions." [14]

Faulkner became Stonewall Jackson's Adjutant General.

When a Union general decided to burn Boydsville during the war, Mrs. Faulkner, the daughter of Elisha Boyd, telegraphed Lincoln, who promptly ordered his general to cease and desist.

Miss Flood's father was Henry Delaware Flood. Her brother, Hal Flood, whom she adored, later served as a congressman from Virginia for twenty years. As Chairman of the House Foreign Relations Committee, he introduced the Declaration of War against Germany in 1917.

Eleanor Bolling Flood was a gay and fiery little lady, as much of a fighter as her husband. Having had a lonely childhood on her father's isolated plantation, Selmo, near Appomattox, she delighted in people and parties, good times, good food, and good drink. This may have caused disputation with her reclusive husband, but well-bred people did not air their differences in public in those days. Throughout the countryside she was known as Miss Bolling. The younger members of her family called her Nana.

The Byrds' first son was born in 1887 while Miss Bolling was visiting her family at Boydsville in West Virginia. She promptly named him for her beloved brother, Harry Flood Byrd. A year later another son arrived. "I'm going to name this one," her husband said firmly; and the infant was called Richard Evelyn Byrd, Jr. Since they now had Harry and Dick, it seemed appropriate to both of them the following year to name their third son Tom; so Thomas Bolling Byrd he became.

Miss Bolling was quite conscious of family accomplishments. When her two older sons simultaneously became national figures, she remarked, "Their brains and ability come from the outcross of the Byrds with the Bollings." [15]

14. Charles J. V. Murphy, *Struggle: The Life of Commander Byrd.* Frederick G. Stokes Company, New York, 1928.
15. Richard E. Byrd of Rosemont to the author.

BOOK FOUR

The Admiral

I , FOREVER YOUNG

REAR ADMIRAL Richard Evelyn Byrd, Jr., made himself one of the authentic heroes of the American people. From May, 1925, when he flew over the North Pole for the first time, until he died in 1957, he lived under the searchlight of publicity. Millions of words were written about him and his formidable achievements—the transatlantic flight, the first flight over the South Pole. Also recorded were his more substantial scientific contributions in mapping undiscovered lands and in establishing a year-round base in Little America, from which he and his fellow scientists compiled continuous records of Antarctic conditions, while suffering the ferocious winters where winds of one hundred and fifty miles an hour were not unusual, and temperatures of —70° Fahrenheit, quite normal.

Despite the extensive reporting of his activities, to which he personally contributed several hundred thousand words, Byrd's character has never been well understood. On the surface he seemed to be a plain, straightforward man—honorable, indefatigable, loyal, physically fit, mentally acute, dedicated to the advancement of science, especially aviation, and brave to the point of foolhardiness.

Admiral Byrd was all of those things, but he was not the super-boy scout they seem to imply. Beneath his handsome, deceptively slight exterior was a deep vein of mysticism and extraordinary contradictions of character. His favorite niece, Margaret Byrd Stimpson, who was especially close to him during the brief twilight of his life, thus described him: "He was very sensitive, and as gentle as a woman with people he loved. But he was completely motivated with a one-track mind; when he wanted something he would climb over people. Great men like Uncle Dick have to be more motivated than other people. To accomplish great things you have to walk over a few people.

"There were so many facets to his character. He was soft and hard; handsome and vain and very shy. He could be very sweet and very determined. He was completely unpredictable.

"When we were young we used to stay with him and Aunt Marie at 'Wickyup,' their camp in Maine. Uncle Dick was fun because he was one of us; our leader but not our elder. He enjoyed the games we played as much as we did. My father [Tom Byrd] and the Senator were kind and sweet, but they did not know how to play; they were old when they were young. There was something of the child about Uncle Dick; he was forever young.

"Life exuded from him. He would talk to us about the cosmos. When he would look up at the stars the whole universe was his. . . ."[1]

Though she spoke of it from secondhand, Margaret never really saw the tough side of the Admiral's character, his ruthless destruction of anyone who stood in the way of his ideals or his objectives. He helped, for instance, to destroy General William Mitchell, yet he felt great admiration for him and sorrow at his fate.

But Admiral Byrd was never meanly secretive with his competitors. At Spitzbergen, when Roald Amundsen, the discoverer of the South Pole, and Lincoln Ellsworth, with their dirigible *Norge*, were racing him to be the first to fly over the North Pole, he helped them as they aided him. And at Hempstead, Long Island, when he and Lindbergh were competing to be the first to fly nonstop from America to France, he gave the younger flyer the use of Roosevelt Field and the benefit of his years of study of aerial navigation, together with charts and the navigational instruments without which Lindbergh might never have beaten him to France. This seeming contradiction was due to his code of honor, of good sportsmanship.

That code included the utmost care for the men under his com-

1. Tom Byrd's daughter (Mrs. Henry) Margaret Byrd Stimpson, to the author.

mand, a concern that carried on long after a particular expedition had ended. Any man who had sailed with him to the Polar seas, north or south, could bring his troubles to the Admiral and be sure of help. For them he was the softest touch in town. An example of this comes from one of his former subordinates, who wishes to remain anonymous. In 1954, twenty years after he had sailed with Byrd as a minor member of the First Antarctic Expedition, this man had a complete breakdown and landed in a public hospital in Washington—"a skid row situation." Though no word was sent to Admiral Byrd, two days later he appeared at the hospital in his uniform alight with all his ribbons to call on his "old shipmate." His purpose was to make sure that the man got the special care and consideration he might not otherwise have received.

This did not prevent Byrd from driving his men beyond the limits of human endurance when the chips were down. They knew it and gave him their best. For they also knew that he drove himself farther and harder; and that if there were dangers to be faced, their commander would be ahead of them. Despite the perilous places they followed him and despite his own daring, Byrd never lost a man in any of his expeditions.

For all that he lived most of his life in the glare of fame and loved it, Admiral Byrd was a secret man. Like his father he needed to be alone; and, another resemblance, he sometimes drank a great deal, though never on one of his great expeditions. His people adored him and would follow him to the ninth circle of hell; but they found him aloof. He was always the Captain alone on the quarterdeck. He sought advice from all; but *he* gave the orders.

However, as Mrs. Stimpson recalled, he was never aloof with children. The invincible boyishness which helped him enjoy the honors heaped upon him, and love the shiny bits of metal he was entitled to wear upon his breast, also made him sympathetic to children. Because he had been to the North Pole, hundreds of children wrote to ask him if he had seen Santa Claus. He always answered them seriously, describing Santa Claus and his helpers and ending with a little moral for their edification.

With all its complexities and contradictions, the main ingredients of Admiral Byrd's character were strength, courage, and an old-fashioned concept of honor—due in part to his family heritage, in part to his youthful training, and most of all to the romantic quality of his mind that kept its youthful idealism long after harsh experience would have reduced most of us to a compromise with reality.

Byrd was a great missionary and the faith he taught with fanatic zeal was the future of aviation and the advancement of science. He was a great patriot. America could do no wrong in his eyes; and to him Americans were like the knights of Camelot, ever fighting on the side of right. If the comparison be just, Richard Byrd always rode, or rather flew, in the van. He was no Launcelot with dark amours to stain his gallantry; nor even doubt-troubled Arthur. Rather it was he who sought the Holy Grail. When he found it at the North Pole and the South, he immediately dreamed up another almost unobtainable object and pursued it with undiminished ardor. He was uneasy when he was not on a quest.

This was what his niece meant by being "forever young." But if he never completely grew up, he attained maturity at a remarkably early age. By the time he was twelve years old the main ingredients of his character were formed. Though he grew in depth and wisdom and self-control, he never basically changed thereafter.

II · AROUND THE WORLD TO ANNAPOLIS

Tom, Dick, and Harry Byrd were the terrors of Winchester, and the greatest terror of the three was Dick. The boys lived with their parents in a comfortable Victorian monstrosity of a house on Amherst Street. Built in 1880, it was three tall stories high with a turret tower and a steep mansard roof covered with green fish-scale shingles. It had a wide veranda; large, dark, high-ceilinged rooms; and a huge kitchen with a wood-burning stove. Upstairs there were seven bedrooms. There was an ample yard and, of course, a large stable. Mr. Dick bought the house when he married, and his wife lived in it for seventy-one years until she died in 1957.

Harry, the eldest boy, was the most quiet and companionable. Tom, though the youngest, soon grew to be the biggest. In between, Dick was the smallest and spunkiest, always compensating for his lack of stature by a fighting spirit that was downright foolhardy.

The two great rivals were Tom and Dick. Harry was a bit above the battle unless some outsiders joined in; then the three Byrds fought as one. Gang fights are no new thing in the world. The little city of Winchester had four well-defined gangs who fought each other all over town. There were the Eastern Gang; the Western Gang, to which the Byrds belonged; the Fort Hill Gang, and the Potato Hill Gang—the worst of the lot. On one occasion the Westerners were playing baseball against the Potato Hill crowd. Inevit-

ably the game ended in full-scale war. As the Potato Hillers retreated slowly toward their end of town, one of them heaved a rock
at the victorious Westerners. It hit Harry Byrd in the forehead.
Dick, seeing the blood pour down his brother's face, was off like a
flash with murder in his eyes. Fortunately for the Potato Hiller,
Harry, blinded by blood, was more interested in first aid than vengeance. He yelled to Dick to come back and lead him to Doctor
Love's office. The cut required several stitches, and Senator Byrd had
the scar all his life.

The rivalry between Dick and Tom got fiercer as Tom grew
larger. Dick soon realized that if he were to maintain the ascendancy
of an older brother, he would have to take serious compensatory measures. He deliberately trained to toughen himself; he never stopped
training until he died. At the age of sixty he could still walk on his
hands along the diving board at Rosemont and dive in from that
stance.

Tom had a peaceable humor, and Dick rode him hard—too hard
on one occasion, and Tom's slow burn suddenly erupted into volcanic
rage. He grabbed a carving knife and started after his tormentor.
Dick went up the stairs like lightning; into his room, with the door
locked just in time. Tom, roaring with rage, attacked the heavy door
with the knife. Dick was really worried about his brother. Out the
window and down the drain pipe he went, and ran all the way to
Doctor Love's. "Come to our house quickly," he said. "My brother
Tom has gone crazy."

Mr. Dick gave all his sons boxing lessons and, a crack shot himself, taught them to shoot, graduating them from BB guns to twelve-
gauge shotguns, .30-caliber rifles, and Colt forty-fives. It was during
their BB period that their neighbor, Mrs. Sloanaker, incautiously
bent over to gather up some washing. Presented with so fair a target
what could Dick do but draw a bead? Mrs. Sloanaker's yelp of pain
testified to his accuracy.

The Byrds liked practical jokes and were rather ruthless in
perpetrating them. On one occasion, a horrible concatenation of
squalls, howls, and feline shrieks brought the natives on the run.
They found all the Byrd household cats hanging from the clothesline
by their tails.[1]

---

1. This and other anecdotes of the Byrd boys are from the unpublished memoirs of their cousin, Mrs. J. A. Massie, Jr., and conversations with other close relatives.
Since they hardly reflect credit on their subjects they are probably true.

In spite of this somewhat misguided humor, the Byrds, in general, were fond of pets and had a great many. Most interesting of all was the white cockatoo that Dick brought back from his trip around the world. This bird had the run of the house. Every morning he would wake the boys by hopping upstairs rasping, "I'm coming! I'm coming! I'm coming!" When Mrs. Byrd went downtown, he would accompany her, fluttering from tree to tree as she walked along the sidewalks.[2]

Every summer the three Byrds spent a month at the Flood plantation, Selmo. When their train pulled into Appomattox, they would find three horses tethered to the hitching posts. From there it was a horse race to Selmo. The hot summer month on that run-down plantation gave the boys a taste of country living which they all cherished.

Until they were old enough to enter the Shenandoah Valley Academy they went to a two-room schoolhouse operated by the Misses Jennie and Lizzie Sherrard, whose idea of a good grounding in education was to teach the history of the Civil War. At best, Dick Byrd's early education was spotty; his brother Harry's, almost nonexistent. Had not Dick eventually applied himself to learning with the same intensity with which he pursued every other objective, he could never have achieved the intellectual level he did.

Confounding pedagogical theory on the necessity for maintaining consistent schooling throughout the formative years, Dick decided to take an entire year off at the critical age of twelve, and thereby gained more useful knowledge than ever was taught in the eighth grade.

In 1901, his cousin, Judge Adam C. Carson, was appointed Chief Judge of the Eighth Judicial District in the Philippine Islands, which had been added to the growing imperial possessions of the United States after the recent Spanish-American War. Dick idolized his cousin, whom he had visited in camp in Washington on Carson's return as a captain of volunteers from the Cuban campaign of 1898. Inevitably, the Judge responded to Dick's hero worship with warm affection. He wrote a letter from the Philippines inviting the boy to visit him.

What high excitement must have blazed in Dick's blue eyes as he showed the letter to his mother; in spirit he was already deep in

2. Mrs. Stimson, in conversation with the author.

tropical jungles. Mrs. Byrd reacted as any mother would. "You can't do that," she said. "At your age, it's ridiculous."

Quietly, respectfully, but very determinedly, Dick said, "You can give me your consent or not. I'd rather have it; but I'm going anyway."

Mrs. Byrd knew her son, as should she not, since he was her favorite. Even though Dick was then only twelve years old, the adamantine character which was to conquer both Poles was fully formed. Nothing could deter him once he had made up his mind. Though he had no money and probably only the haziest notion of the difficulties involved, his mother did not doubt that he would do exactly what he had said. She gave in quietly.[3]

There was still the question of money. The Byrds' income did not run to trips to the Orient. But official wires were pulled; friends in Washington written to. Eventually, in 1902, Dick was furnished with a chair-car ticket to San Francisco, and accommodations on the army transport *Sumner* at one dollar a day. His mother took him to Washington to see him off. He looked such a very little boy; his face was swollen from poison oak; his eyes were slits. "My mother was not given to weeping but she wept that day," Byrd once told his friend, Charles J. V. Murphy. "I felt more than a little blue myself." [4]

The trip was all and more than Dick had hoped. He was the sort of boy—and man—who not only seeks adventure but attracts it by a sort of psychological law of gravity. Off Japan the *Sumner* ran into a first-class typhoon—a ninety-knot gale shrieking through the rigging, driving sheets of rain; mountains of water curled over and crashed down on the tired little ship, carrying away the railings, smashing lifeboats, staving in the single funnel. Byrd seems to have spent his time alternately comforting a hysterical schoolteacher in her cabin and dashing up to the bridge to watch the tremendous spectacle. He loved it so much that he mistakenly thought he had found his element. The error was natural, for it would be over a year before the Wright brothers took off at Kitty Hawk.

The Philippines were not exactly tranquil. The United States'

3. Byrd's nephew, Beverley Byrd, in conversation with the author.
4. Charles J. V. Murphy, *op. cit.*

William Byrd II of Westover (1674–1744).

Evelyn Byrd of Westover (1707–1737),
daughter of William Byrd II.

Col. William Byrd III of Westover (1728–1777),
grandson of William Byrd II.

Governor's Palace in Colonial Williamsburg.

Westover

Thomas Taylor Byrd of the Cottage Farm (1752–1821).

Three phases in the life of Rear Admiral Richard E. Byrd. Left: at eight years; Center: as a cadet at the Shenandoah Valley Academy; Right: as a midshipman at the United States Naval Academy.

Commander Byrd's plane at the North Pole, 1926.

Commander Richard E. Byrd and Pilot Floyd Bennett, 1926.

Byrd Expedition to Antarctic: climbing a peak.

*Mrs. Richard E. Byrd and three sons
—Admiral Byrd, Tom Byrd and Governor Byrd.*

Admiral Richard E. Byrd, campaigning for his brother
Harry F. Byrd at the Democratic Convention in 1932.

Rear Adm. Richard E. Byrd is greeted on return to Washington from Antarctica by his wife and brother, Senator Harry F. Byrd.

SENATOR BYRD

Sprung from illustrious progenitors,
One of the wilderness-crying senators,
 Trying to spike
 The raging flood,
 His hand's in the dike
 And his name is mud.
 He fights Inefficiency,
 Wars on Waste,
 And marks Dead Wood,
 However high-placed.
Taxpayers toss him a grateful word,
But otherwise what does he get? The byrd.

From the *Saturday Evening Post*, —ETHEL JACOBSON
April 24, 1943

Senator Harry F. Byrd (foreground) *and some friends hiking up Old Rag Mountain in the Shenandoah National Park,* 1960.

Senator Harry F. Byrd, from a painting by Gib Crockett.

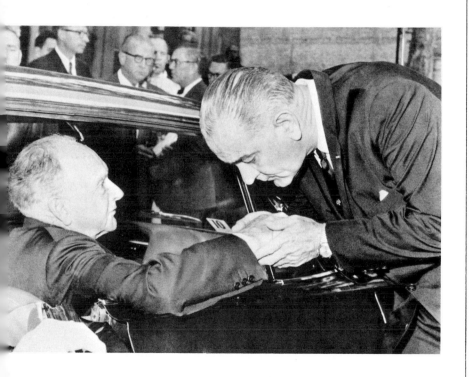

In a gesture of condolence and respect, President Johnson kisses the hand of Senator Harry Byrd after attending funeral services for the Senator's wife, 1964.

"Rosemont," the Byrd family estate in Berryville, Virginia.

Left to Right: *Bradshaw Beverley Byrd, Harry F. Byrd, Jr., and Richard Evelyn Byrd.*

willingness to assume the White Man's Burden on behalf of the natives was so little appreciated that it had taken a full-scale war to convince them of the benevolent intentions of their conquerors. In the southern provinces guerrillas still roamed the jungles. Dick Byrd's letters home, printed in his father's paper, the Winchester *Star*, were filled with such interesting details as:

October 9, 1902; The insurrection is not over in the southern part of the Islands. . . . There are lots of insurrectos in this province [Sargosan] the other day and they killed nine of our men and wounded many others. The other day I went with a captain and some soldiers to a place called Palange, thirteen miles from here, where most of the fighting has taken place, to capture a mayor who stole some money. We got the mayor and on the way back captured a Filipino spy and as he is such a notorious spy who has done the Americans much harm he is going to be hung.

We are at the foot of a volcano, the largest active volcano in the world. It is apt to explode and the other day a great cloud of smoke came out of the top of it. . . .

Doubtless out of regard for his mother's feelings, which can easily be imagined, Dick did not say that he had secretly galloped off on his Filipino pony with a Colt .45 strapped around his waist to join the expedition. While Judge Carson spent an anxious forty-eight hours wondering how to inform his parents of their son's demise, Dick had taken part in a fire-fight with some seventy insurrectos who flitted through the wet, green gloom of the jungle shooting antiquated Spanish muskets and poisoned arrows. Dick came home triumphantly riding herd on a group of prisoners.[5]

In another letter, dated February 1, 1903, he wrote with obvious relish: "In the next room Judge Carson is holding court. . . . There are two men in there whom the Judge is sentencing to be hung, and they take the sentence as if nothing was going on. Their expression does not change. And from my window I can see the scaffold from which six men were hung last year. . . ."

Those were the happy days when small boys and grown men alike had never a doubt of the justice of the American cause nor of the fact that anyone who opposed it deserved hanging. All his life Dick Byrd retained that uncomplicated faith in his country's rectitude.

5. Mrs. Massie's memoirs.

Insurrectos were not the only peril of life in the Philippines. Bubonic plague was also a menace and cholera never far away. One day a Filipino dropped unconscious in the courtyard of the Judge's house. Dick felt his pulse and called for help. That night the man died of cholera and an epidemic soon swept through the native village. The Americans were quarantined on a hilltop, cut off from contact with the outside world—and from food. For Christmas dinner [1902] young Byrd had roasted parrot monkey and canned plum pudding.[6]

When the slackening of the disease permitted the Americans to venture out, Judge Carson evidently concluded that he had acquired enough gray hairs on behalf of his young kinsman. He shipped Dick home on a British tramp steamer bound for Rangoon, Bombay, the Suez Canal, and the Mediterranean. In July, 1903, Dick landed in Boston to be greeted by a dozen reporters—and his first burst of publicity. He savored it then and all the rest of his life. The *Republic Special* of July 12, 1903 printed the following story:

BOY OF TWELVE TRAVELS AROUND THE WORLD [7]

New York, July 11, 1903: American independence and enterprise are typified in Master Richard Evelyn Byrd, Jr., scion of a famous family of Westover, Virginia, who arrived in New York after a voyage around the world alone. He left his home in Winchester on August 9, 1902, to circle the globe. . . .

He went across the continent to San Francisco, there took a streamer for Manila. . . . Judge Carson met him in Manila and under his guidance he passed several months exploring the islands.

General Monreal of the Province of Sargosan made him a deputy sheriff and as such he joined an expedition against troublesome ladrones [thieves]. He met Aguinaldo and says he liked the little Filipino leader very much.

He left Manila for home early in May, journeying back by the Suez Canal . . . and stopping at various places in Europe. He came by the S. S. *Strathard* to Boston and met his mother in this city yesterday.

Such high adventure so early in life could turn an ordinary youth into a wandering bum unable to settle down to the humdrum business of getting an education or earning a living, forever seeking to recapture the zest and rapture of that magic year. Though he was

6. Charles J. V. Murphy, *op. cit.*
7. Richard was actually fourteen.

an adventurer born, Byrd could look ahead and plan and wait. This early experience gave him a goal to strive for, direction to his life. He knew now that he wanted to go to Annapolis and become a naval officer.

As always when he had an objective, Byrd pursued it with almost frightening intensity. He applied his brilliant, facile mind to his studies to such effect that within a year he was prepared to enter the Virginia Military Institute. The usual entering age was sixteen. Though Dick was only fifteen and small for his age, V.M.I. accepted him on the strength of his academic record and character.

Byrd went through V.M.I. in two years. Then he studied for a year at the University of Virginia. Though he only weighed a hundred and twenty-five pounds, he went out for football and became substitute quarterback on the Varsity Squad. His one recorded appearance on the field was less than glorious. Near the end of the game against Washington and Lee, Byrd was sent in to relieve the first-string man. He misjudged a punt which fell within five yards of the goal line. Byrd called for a quick return punt, which was blocked. Washington and Lee secured the ball and crashed over for the winning touchdown.

Given his temperament, his all-or-nothing spirit, it is probable that never again did Byrd taste such bitter gall. He had let down his teammates, the ultimate disgrace. He could not have believed that such a thing could happen to him; yet it had. It was the most valuable lesson he learned at the University—that bad luck and bad judgment can combine to ruin anyone, even Dick Byrd. The capacity for taking infinite pains to forestall disaster which later insured the success of his polar expeditions in part may have stemmed from this trivial incident.

Richard Byrd entered the Naval Academy on May 28, 1908. Though he was such a raging individualist, he accepted the strict discipline cheerfully, as he had at V.M.I. The order, beauty, and tradition of the place accorded with his character. Byrd was an authoritarian. When his time came to command men, he was a martinet, though a thoughtful one. Believing firmly in the military code of absolute obedience, he was prepared to take it—so he could dish it out later.

At Annapolis, Byrd did not shine academically; he worked just hard enough to get by. At that stage he was more interested in athletics, which presented a greater challenge because of his slight stature. In his plebe year he was made captain of the second football team, won the tennis doubles championship, was runner up in the singles, boxed and wrestled, and became chairman of the Athletic Committee. On the summer cruise, he dove off a battleship to rescue a classmate who had fallen overboard.

The next year he made the Varsity Football squad and met disaster. In the game against Princeton, four two-hundred-pounders piled on top of him. When they were pried off, he found that his foot was broken in three places.

That was the beginning of a streak of bad luck that pursued Byrd for years. On the summer cruise to Europe he caught typhoid fever and spent two months in the Royal Naval Hospital at Pulham, England, while his classmates sailed home. Gaunt as a greyhound, he reached Annapolis in time for the football season. That he again made the Varsity was a triumph of spirit over flesh. But there were limits beyond which he could not drive his body. In the game against Pennsylvania he collapsed on the field from sheer exhaustion. The doctors forbade him to play football again that year.

So he became captain of the Navy Gymnasium Team, where weight did not tell against him. Now his burning ambition was to win the Intercollegiate Meet. He devised a spectacular double stunt on the high rings that he was sure would accomplish his purpose. The first part of it was a "dislocate" in which, swinging high and wide with arms at full length, he revolved his rigid body head over heels, forcing his shoulders into a quick jerk that looked as though he had dislocated them. On the next swing, he revolved again with his legs outside his arms, letting go of the rings on the upswing and catching them again as he fell.

The first time he tried it the trick came off. Then in final practice before a big crowd he tried it again. Never had he swung so high in great swoops that carried up to the rafters. Exhilarated and confident he made the dislocate perfectly. Up again, and now the outside somersault, twenty feet above the floor. . . . Timing just a fraction off, catching one ring; grabbing wildly for the other, missing, as the crowd gave a sigh-groan; falling feet first. . . . The crash shook the cavernous gymnasium and echoed from the steel cross beams. Byrd tried to rise and fell back stunned. His bad foot and ankle were shattered again.

In his book *Skyward* [8] Byrd recalls that the Navy Team won the intercollegiate championship without him and comments "Never again, I felt, would I attach an undue importance to myself." But of course he did.

That accident eventually wrecked Byrd's naval career. He missed so much study time that the authorities wanted him to drop back a class. This he would not do, and by a tremendous effort of concentration made up the back work and graduated with his class in June, 1912. In the year book his classmates wrote of him:

"Richard Evelyn Byrd. Athlete. Leader in all right things. Friend. Gentleman. From the time he entered as a plebe until the present Dick has been putting his whole heart into everything he does . . . most of the time Dick moves around with a faraway look in his eye. But go where he may, he cannot hope to find the truth and beauty of which he dreams. He has already lived a life rich in experience. He will live a life richer still, but he must give to life more than he takes." [9]

Fine and true. But that ankle bone never healed properly. When he walked, it clicked. One can imagine him marching in those rigid ranks of blue and gold, forcing himself not to limp, but clicking softly.

Someone told him that if he walked enough he would grate the fragments together and induce the flow of osseous fluid. So he walked and walked, in constant pain. His ankle improved some, but he could not count on it. Standing long watches on the bridge of a ship was sometimes sheer agony. On one occasion, the ankle gave way and he fell down a gangway in the U.S.S. *Wyoming*. The doctors decided to nail the ankle together. For a time Byrd rather enjoyed the elegance of being held together with a silver pin. Then the doctor told him that it was an ordinary galvanized nail.

Byrd referred to his first term of service in the Navy as "Five wasted years." [10] Wasted they seemed to a man of fierce ambition,

8. Richard E. Byrd, *Skyward*. Blue Ribbon Books, New York, 1938.
9. *Year Book*, Class of 1912. U. S. Naval Academy, Annapolis, Md.
10. Byrd, *Skyward*.

who dreamed of great accomplishments and who seemed to have come, at this point, to a dead end. Yet he accomplished a great deal and won several citations and a medal for bravery—not an easy thing in a peacetime navy. On July 6, 1914, when he was serving aboard U.S.S. *Washington,* he was in command of a swimming party off Cape Haitien. Seaman Nuttal got a cramp and sank. Byrd went overboard with all his clothes on and with the help of Seamen Taylor and Eldridge "after considerable struggle and difficulty" managed to keep Nuttal afloat until a boat came to the rescue.[11] A month later, on August 15, Byrd again went overboard in full uniform to haul a sailor out of the shark-infested waters off Puerto Plata, San Domingo; it was the third life he had saved. Eight years later the United States Government awarded him the Silver Life Saving Medal of Honor.

After service in the *Washington,* Byrd was transferred to Secretary of the Navy Josephus Daniels' yacht *Dolphin* and a year later to the Presidential Yacht *Mayflower.* These were the pleasantest jobs in the Navy. Occasional short tours of duty cruising the Potomac, the Chesapeake, or Long Island Sound were followed by long periods when the yachts were moored at the Navy Yard. The young officers were invited to all the best parties in Washington, where hostesses, then as now, were desperate for eligible single men. In addition, Byrd could easily go home to Winchester most weekends.

It seemed an ideal situation, but Byrd was thoroughly disgusted; so disgusted that, when he found that because of his injured leg he was ineligible for promotion, he requested that he be retired. On March 16, 1916, Byrd was declared unfit for active duty and placed on the retired list on three-quarters pay. In *Skyward* Byrd laconically describes his frustration: "Career ended. Not enough income to live on . . . temperamentally disinclined for business. A fizzle."

11. Report of Captain Louis E. Fagan of U.S.S. *Washington* to the Navy Department.

III · A BYRD TAKES TO THE AIR

DURING THE "wasted years" Richard Evelyn Byrd, Jr., took an important step which, in a peripheral way, contributed to the success of his great enterprises, and most directly to his own happiness. On January 20, 1915, he married Marie Donaldson Ames, the daughter of Mr. and Mrs. Joseph Blanchard Ames of Boston.

He had known her since they were children. Marie Ames often came to Winchester with her grandmother, who suffered from asthma and chronic bronchitis in Boston's harsh climate. Dick Byrd, who was not usually fond of little girls, found her so companionable that he even read her the secret thoughts that he constantly jotted down in the little black notebook he always carried. They were a strange mixture of fantasy and practical ambition. One note that Marie remembers well said, "I want to be the first man to reach the North Pole." This was about 1901, six years before Peary discovered the Pole.

Another note which he made when he was a midshipman read, "War is obsolescent. But if it is abolished it will leave a vacuum which must be filled by some other form of activity." Byrd may have had exploration and pioneering in mind.[1]

---

1. Admiral Byrd's widow in conversation with the author.

Marie Ames grew up to be a very pretty young lady—the word lady is used advisedly—with merry brown eyes, a nice wit, and considerable musical talent. She studied the violin, and although she never went on the concert stage, she frequently appeared at charitable benefits. Her family were as well known in Massachusetts as the Byrds in Virginia and they were far more affluent. Falling in love with her, as over the years she grew up and became more beautiful, was undoubtedly a gradual process for Dick Byrd. It was a natural thing. Like him she was shy and very reserved except among her close friends, when she sparkled with fun and high spirits. She was quite different from the belles of Winchester, who were obviously quite mad for him.

Being no fool, nor even particularly modest, Byrd had to be aware of his good looks and his charm. He was slim and strong and very masculine with perfectly modeled features, curly brown hair, and gray-blue eyes that reflected the fire of his spirit. Indeed, this, more than physical perfection, was the source of his extraordinary beauty. The psychic dynamo within him not only bowled women over but was the secret of his leadership quality. Men would follow him to the ultimate of exhaustion or danger and onward one step beyond the limit of human endurance.

Yet he was a remote person, despite his obvious heroics; a mystic with a hidden reserve of spiritual force; a secret person who did not give himself casually to others, though he basked in their obvious admiration. It was natural, then, that the shy, reserved Bostonian girl, who kept her secrets, too, should become the woman with whom he chose to spend his life. She more than reciprocated his love. Whatever the difficulties—and they were many—of life with Richard Byrd, Marie accepted them joyfully, never doubting her good fortune in having married so great a man.

Their wedding in Winchester was one of the great gala occasions to which the extrovert Virginia Byrds could contribute style and exuberance. Mr. Dick and Miss Bolling gave a dance the night before. The wedding took place in Christ's Protestant Episcopal Church, and Mr. and Mrs. Ames gave the reception at the big house they had rented for the winter in Winchester, with a caterer and a big-name band imported from Washington.

All the groomsmen were Byrd's shipmates. Captain Ralph Earl of the *Dolphin* gave leave to all his officers. If the Secretary of the

Navy had needed a yacht in a hurry, he would have had to whistle up a battleship. They came to Winchester in high spirits, handsome young fellows in their blue dress coats, golden epaulettes, cocked hats, and gold-hilted swords, to bring salty fresh air to that somewhat closed society; raising a normally joyous occasion to a Pike's Peak of gaiety. For all his moodiness no one could be gayer than Dick when the playful spirit was on him, as it was that day. No one was more ecstatic than his bride, who made no Bostonian effort to conceal her joy.

Then Ensign and Mrs. Richard E. Byrd, Jr., went to live in Washington and cope with the financial difficulties of existence on an ensign's pay, and with the discontents of a ragingly ambitious young man whose career was about to end in a fizzle.

"The war saved me," Byrd wrote.[2] Perhaps it did, though one may conjecture that he would have saved himself had it never occurred. With the nations of Europe locked in the bloody stalemate of the trench warfare of World War I and the United States maintaining a precarious neutrality, preparedness was the slogan of the hour. The rapidly expanding Navy with so many new recruits to be trained could ill afford to lose an efficient Annapolis graduate. Byrd was on the beach only two months when he was asked if he would accept the post of Inspector Instructor of the Naval Militia of Rhode Island. Gladly he returned to the service on May 24, 1916, with a promotion to Lieutenant, junior grade (retired).

Byrd combined a very real talent for organization with his spirit of derring-do. He revitalized the Rhode Island militia so effectively as to earn the personal commendation of the Governor. To fill in his "spare time" Byrd took a course in commercial economics at the Harvard Graduate School, driving the round trip of one hundred miles every weekday.

When America entered the war in April, 1917, Byrd was ordered to a desk job in the Personnel Bureau of the Navy Department in Washington. He was soon promoted to executive secretary of the Navy Commission on Training Camps under Dr. Raymond B. Fosdick. He admired Dr. Fosdick enormously and hated his own job as "a high class clerk." By the summer of 1917, Byrd's classmates were

2. Byrd, *Skyward*.

serving in the destroyers operating out of Queenstown, or aboard battleships with the British Grand Fleet in the North Sea, or, most glorious of all, commanding small, storm-wracked subchasers in the dangerous patrol of the English Channel.

Byrd was frantic. He worked day and night to organize the commission so he could get on to active duty. Meanwhile he fretted and griped so much that he lost twenty-five pounds and was on the verge of a nervous breakdown. He pulled every wire he could lay his hands on to get into the fight. "By conspiracy," as he put it, he came up before a naval medical board. They told him he was in terrible condition and should take leave. Byrd begged them for a chance to learn to fly, promising that if he did not regain his health within a month, he would do whatever they said. Powerful forces went to work on that board—perhaps Congressman Flood, who had the President's ear, or Senator Charles Faulkner of West Virginia, but definitely not Mr. Dick.

The board cleared Byrd for flight training at Pensacola. When he told his father the good news, the latter said, "You're a damned fool. Good-bye. I'll probably never see you again." [3]

In the autumn of 1917, the Byrds started for Pensacola. They had just bought a new automobile which they could not bear to leave behind, so they took it to Savannah by ship and drove from there to the base over dirt roads that were hardly more than tracks through the pine woods. Byrd reported in and installed Marie in a boardinghouse with a number of other young wives. Then he went off to look the place over.

He was in high heart. Though he had been up in a plane only once before for five minutes, he knew this was what he was meant to do. He walked toward the bay front in the Florida sunshine, grinning with delight at the sight of the seaplanes drawn up along the sea ramp, or taking off and landing on the ruffled blue water. The pretty picture was suddenly shattered. Byrd heard a shout, looked upward. A tiny plane was fluttering like a drunken moth at a great height. Then it went into a perpendicular dive. Down it came; slowly, it seemed, because of its altitude; then faster and faster, straight down

3. Richard E. Byrd of Rosemont in conversation with the author.

until it hit rock-hard water with a rending crunch, white spray flying upward mixed with bits of canvas and wood. The crash boat raced out to the wreckage and, after interminable minutes, came back with a terribly still figure, face covered.

As Byrd stood stunned and sickened, an Annapolis classmate, Nathan Chase, greeted him joyously. Byrd motioned toward the wreck and asked if that sort of thing happened often. "Every day. Sometimes two or three times a day," was the answer. Then Chase, who knew the cure for the sort of shock Byrd had suffered, asked him if he wanted to take a hop.

Right then it was the last thing Byrd wanted to do, but he had to say yes. Twenty minutes later he was airborne. Chase gave him the full treatment—diving, rolling, sideslipping, and ended with making him take over the dual controls. When they landed, Byrd was psychologically a veteran, sobered but serene again.

After only six hours of dual instruction, Byrd was declared ready to solo. His instructor, Ensign Gardiner, suggested that twenty minutes was enough for the first time. Characteristically Byrd flew for an hour and a half, making landing after landing. After that he practiced every day for as long as he could keep a plane—they were in short supply. He flew double-float planes, single-pontoon jobs and Curtiss flying boats. He made hundreds of landings a week from every altitude between fifty feet and five thousand, under all possible weather conditions, trying to perfect his technique and prepare for any contingency. He had completely regained his health. Early in 1918, he won his wings as Naval Aviator Number 608.

When he was not flying, Byrd, a member of the Crash Board, made an intensive study of the daily accidents to learn their causes and invent procedures for preventing them. There was at Pensacola a holocaust comparable to a battlefield. Whenever the crash siren shrieked its dismal warning, wives, children, and servants poured from their houses asking, "Who is it now?"

In some degree the slaughter was due to the imperfect state of the machines. Seaplanes had been invented only six years before. Those at Pensacola were mostly little biplanes—adaptations of the Army Curtiss JN4 (Jennie), mounted on pontoons. They were more cumbersome and trickier to fly than land planes. In addition, their OX6 power plant was unreliable. The rocker arms that actuated the valves often flew off, cutting out a cylinder. Sometimes one of the pilots would climb up and repair it in flight. But mostly the accidents were due to the pressure and haste of wartime training; the fact that the seat-pack parachute had not yet been invented; and most of all to reckless, overconfident young men, who did not know enough to be afraid. The spirit that wins wars does not lead to longevity.

Marie suffered with the other wives. At the restaurant where they usually lunched while their husbands were flying, friendships were quickly made, but they were often all too temporary. "One never knew who would be there the next day," she said.

Once she had a terrible scare. One of her friends came in and said, "Dick's been in a crash. There were three men in the plane. One of them was killed, but I think Dick's all right. He's been taken to the hospital. I'll take you to see him if you will break the news to the dead man's wife."

Marie performed her duty and was driven to the hospital, where she found her husband merely shaken up. "The other man was decapitated," she said.

When her son, Richard E. Byrd, Jr., suggested that her anxieties at Pensacola were good preparation for her later worries when her husband was flying to the poles, Mrs. Byrd said calmly, "I never had that fear. I always had the feeling that he would do it right, that if there were trouble he would know how to get out of it.

"The only time I was really worried about him was when he spent five months alone at Advance Base on the Ice Barrier in Antarctica. The children and I were spending the summer [1934] at Manchester on the North Shore of Massachusetts Bay. Though he kept sending cheerful messages to Little America, I sensed that there was something terribly wrong. That was, of course, the time he nearly died of carbon monoxide poisoning." [4]

At Pensacola, Byrd began the series of innovations and experiments for which he became well known in Naval Aviation long before the American people ever heard of him. One of these was what is believed to have been the first night landing on water. Since no proper floodlights were then available, he had drums of flaming gasoline anchored at intervals a hundred yards off the beach. He invited

4. Mrs. Byrd and her son in conversation with the author.

Marie to sit on the shore opposite the place where he proposed to land.

She *was* nervous that night. She could hear the plane coming down, but could not see it, for it had no lights. Then there it was—lighted by the flaring gasoline, touching the water between wings of rainbow spray, and immediately taking off again. "I thought he had not been able to land properly," Mrs. Byrd says. "He came in several more times right in front of where I was sitting. I became quite anxious, but later he told me that the first landing had been perfect and he made the others to make sure it was not just luck and that he could do it every time." [5]

By May, 1918, Byrd began to fret again. He had learned all there was to learn at Pensacola; he felt that he was going around in routine circles; he wanted to fight. Since orders for overseas did not come, he dreamed up another scheme for the advancement of aviation, the glory of the United States Navy, and his own personal satisfaction. He knew that the Navy was building a "giant" flying boat to be powered by three 400-h.p. Liberty motors. He believed such a machine would be capable of crossing the Atlantic in a series of hops—Labrador, the Azores, England. The idea of delivering it to the front by air was irresistible.

Byrd was by now too wise in the ways of the Navy to go through channels. Instead he wrote to Walter Camp, the great football star and Yale football coach, whom he knew slightly, asking him to back the idea for such a flight. Camp did more than Byrd had hoped for. With Admiral Robert E. Peary, the discoverer of the North Pole, he went to the Navy Department and suggested that such a flight be made.

Greatly encouraged, Byrd wrote a formal proposal to the Navy Department which was approved and forwarded by the Commandant of the Naval Air Station at Pensacola. He also took his friend Lieutenant Walter Hinton into his confidence. Together they made an intensive study of the capabilities and fuel consumption of Liberty motors. They also got permission to install compasses on some of the little seaplanes and practiced aerial navigation out of sight of land. This gives an extraordinary insight into the primitive state of avia-

5. *Ibid.*

tion. It seems incredible that planes flying over waters where sudden fogs, though unlikely, were not unknown, should not routinely have been equipped with compasses.

In the course of these experimental flights, Byrd found that planes needed a special navigational instrument to measure drift caused by changing wind-speed and direction. So he invented the drift indicator. He always believed that this was the first practical step toward transoceanic aerial navigation.

Then came a telegram ordering him to Washington. As he boarded the train north, he was in a euphoric state of mind that envisioned flying to Europe "by October first at the latest." [6]

Washington in wartime was the place to dash a young man's hopes. At the Navy Department, amid the crowds and confusion in the badly designed, temporary buildings on Independence Avenue, Byrd could not find a single person who knew anything about a proposed transatlantic flight. Instead, he got orders to set up a naval air station at Halifax, Nova Scotia. Glumly he began methodical preparations. It was not until he received specific orders from Chief of Naval Operations Admiral W. S. Benson for the establishment of a refueling station on the east coast of Newfoundland that he realized that it might be a step toward his objective.

For this mission Byrd was promoted to the rank of lieutenant commander. It required all his skill in organizing and wangling to assemble the men and the innumerable supplies necessary for his task. Arranging transportation for them and for the big, delicate planes in their huge crates was even more difficult. He finally reached Halifax with two planes, eight men, and one other officer—Hinton. Driving the men as only he could, he built a makeshift base on a deserted shore of the bay in three days, hoisted the flag, and went into commission. However, his primary mission—to search out and attack enemy submarines—could not be carried out because the aerial bombs had been lost in transit.

Byrd solved that problem by borrowing depth charges from the regular Navy. These "cans," with their unwieldy shape and delicate firing mechanism, were terribly dangerous to carry in planes, but they

6. Byrd, *Skyward*. Although Byrd believed he had initiated the transatlantic project, Glenn Curtiss had it in mind when he and his engineering staff designed the NC flying boats.

were better than nothing. Because of the careful training of the pilots there were no accidents.

Men and planes began to pour in. A city of tents arose on the bleak shore of the bay. The Navy even sent some sausage-shaped observation balloons, for what purpose no one knew. Just as the base became a well-organized fighting force, the war ended. Byrd was ordered to turn the base over to the Canadians and ship his men and planes home. However, he had one major accomplishment to his credit. Working with Hinton, he had invented a sextant with an artificial horizon leveled by a bubble in liquid similar to an ordinary carpenter's level. Known as the Byrd Sextant, it became the standard tool for aerial navigation.

On his way home from Halifax, Byrd received word that plans for the transatlantic flight were still on. He was so excited that he went straight through to Washington without even pausing in Boston to see Marie and his family. When he got to the Navy Department, he learned that Commander John H. Towers (naval aviator Number 2) had been appointed to command the transatlantic flight. Then Byrd received a crushing blow. The order came through that no personnel who had seen foreign service would be eligible for the flight— including those who had been on the Canadian detail. Those long, dreary months in Halifax had robbed him of his great ambition.

A few days later Byrd received orders to report to Pensacola. This was too much! All the months of study and planning gone for nothing. He called Jack Towers and asked if he still wanted him to help plan the overseas flight. Of course Towers did, for he knew that Byrd was the most knowledgeable man in the Navy on the subject. Then Byrd went to see Captain N. E. Irwin, Director of Naval Aviation. Captain Irwin was a broad-shouldered, genial six-footer with the immense leverage of rank. Byrd, bursting with anguish, talked to him as no lieutenant commander should address a captain, but Irwin was a big man in more ways than one. He knew how hard Byrd had worked on the project, how desperately disappointed he was. Orders to Pensacola were canceled. Byrd became one of eight officers assigned to the Trans-Atlantic Flight Section of the Naval Aeronautics Division.

On April 21, 1919, the Trans-Atlantic Flight Section was sent from Washington to the Naval Air Station at Rockaway Beach, Long Island. It was a cold and dismal place with makeshift wooden barracks built on sand dunes, a few hangars, and concrete ramps extending into Jamaica Bay. Three NC flying boats were housed in an airship hangar. To Byrd they must have looked immense. Their box-kite, heavily braced biplane wings stretched 126 feet. From their bows to the tips of their incredible, cross-braced, cantilevered, flying-jibboom tail assemblies they measured 72 feet. Originally they had been designed for three 400-h.p. Liberty motors, with puller propellers anchored high up between the wings to keep them clear of salt spray; but for this flight, a fourth engine had been added behind the center one which drove a pusher propeller to give them a total of 1600 h.p. A hydroplane boat body housed the crew of six men in three cockpits. An NC's weight fully loaded was 28,000 pounds. With their struts, bracing-wires, uncovered engines with huge radiators, they were, from the point of view of modern streamlining, a designer's nightmare, but they were very strong. On one occasion fifty-one men were jammed into NC1 and taken aloft, a record that stood for some years.

The following month at Rockaway was a time of meticulous preparation and enormously hard work. Byrd was concerned principally with problems of navigation, but everyone gave a hand to everyone else. They were a splendid group. Commander Towers was reserved, methodical, studious, and generous; he commanded NC3, the flagship. Lieutenant Commander P.N.L. (Pat) Bellinger, a rugged seafaring type, had NC1; and Lieutenant Commander A. C. (Putty) Read, slim, quiet, and alert, was in NC4.[7] Of Byrd at that time a fellow officer said, "He seemed unsociable and imperious, but he had that 'look of eagles.' "[8]

On May 8, 1919, the three flying boats took off for Halifax. Because of the kindness of Commander Towers, Byrd flew with him in *Three* on the first leg of the trip. What he remembered about that historic take-off was not the cataract of solid green water pouring over the ship before she lifted onto the step, or the long, dangerous, bumpy run across Jamaica Bay before she pulled herself reluctantly

7. There was no NC2. NC1 had been wrecked on the ground by a sudden storm, and the wings from NC2 had been put on her.
8. Edward M. Shields, Naval Aviator Number 452, in conversation with the author.

into the air. What he remembered best was the ear-shattering, bone-shaking, soul-satisfying roar of those four great engines at full pitch.

According to Towers' report, Byrd spent that afternoon "vibrating" between the forward and after cockpits, trying out smoke bombs (to measure wind direction and drift), and taking innumerable sights with his special sextant, checking his position against known points on land. Towers' small forward cockpit was jammed with charts, sextants, chronometers, and miscellaneous gadgets. Telephone wires, in which he and Byrd were frequently entangled, trailed from his earphones.

The planes flew up the coast in a wild-duck vee until Read in *Four* radioed that one motor had gone out. He spiraled down and landed on the water off Cape Cod. *Three* and *One* flew on, hitting Halifax at exactly 7 P.M. EST. Byrd noted his pleasure at seeing the familiar, desolate shoreline and the seaplane base he had built, as if for this very landing.

The next morning the planes flew on to Trepassey, Newfoundland, where the minelayer *Aristook*, the tanker *Hisco*, and a floating machine shop named U.S.S. *Prairie* waited to mother them. Byrd flew in *One*, to which Towers had transferred for this leg. The air at 5,000 feet was icy and Byrd suffered in the open cockpit. Curiously enough, all his life he hated being cold. This by inverse reaction may have been one of the reasons for his fascination with the polar regions, since he had a continuing compulsion to test his manhood against the most adverse condition possible.

In the distant, desolate harbor of Trepassey, the Navy Department with its bureaucratic regulations seemed infinitely far away. Byrd had high hopes of being allowed to continue on the flight in defiance of the official directive. But Commander Towers sympathetically handed him a radiogram from Captain Irwin, containing the specific order that Byrd should not, repeat *not*, continue on the flight. Byrd's wry comment was, "My nemesis was still on duty." [9]

In this case nemesis may have worn the familiar features of his father; for, according to family tradition, Mr. Dick stamped into the office of Secretary of the Navy Daniels and said, "I want you to stop my son going on that damn fool flight." Fortunately for the future relations between father and son, Byrd did not learn of this exercise of political pull until after Mr. Dick's death.

9. Byrd, *Skyward.*

On May 16, 1919, Byrd stood forlornly on the bridge of the *Aristook*, watching the three [10] planes take off on the great adventure he had planned. Between them and their next landfall at the Azores, the Navy had flung a bridge of fifty destroyers, deployed at fifty-mile intervals along their course. Byrd had written a memo advising the Navy Department that this was an entirely unnecessary precaution. It was well that he was disregarded.

Contrary to the primitive meteorological predictions, a dense fog enveloped the ocean for the last half of the flight. Hopelessly lost, Pat Bellinger in *One* landed on the open sea. His plane broke up in the huge waves, but the whole crew were rescued by a passing freighter. *Three* also came down on the ocean, but Commander Towers brought her safely through two hundred miles of heavy seas to Ponta Delgada in the Azores, in what was probably the most remarkable feat of seamanship ever performed in an airplane.

Only Putty Read in *Four* had luck; he always admitted it was luck. He flew in the bright sunshine above the fog for hours. Though he could talk with the destroyers by radio, he had only the foggiest idea of where he was. That beautiful, deadly blanket of undulating mist, white as a snowfield in the sunshine, stretched from horizon to horizon. Then off to his left Read saw a vagrant hole in the gleaming floor. He headed for it and, peering down, saw, "the most beautiful sight my eyes ever beheld—a white house on a green hillside." [11]

Four landed at Horta in the Azores at 9.25 A.M., New York time, on May 17, 1919. Two days later Commander Towers brought the flagship in to Ponta Delgada, where Read joined him. The NC3 was too badly battered to continue the flight. There was talk of Commander Towers transferring his flag to NC4 for the final, easy leg to Spain, but he refused to do so. "Read has earned the glory," he said, "let him take her in."

The flight of the NC boats seemed to prove that aerial navigation was not as far advanced as Byrd had believed. A one-in-three chance of arriving safely was not good enough. Byrd's ardent spirit and imagination always pushed the technology at his disposal beyond its

10. NC4 had rejoined at Trepassey.
11. Rear Admiral A. C. Read in conversation with the author forty years ago.

probable capabilities. The indications here were that he had mis-judged them badly.

And yet Byrd was not aboard any of those planes. As he was later to prove, several times over, he was an inspired navigator. When mechanical aids were washed out and all else failed, he still reached his destination. Whether it was luck or a sort of homing-pigeon instinct, or a combination of both, he got where he wanted to go. So there is always the possibility that, had he been navigating one of those wandering NC's, it might have changed the odds against them.

IV · THE LUCK CHANGES

BYRD WAS swept into the politics of interservice rivalry as soon as he returned to Washington. Brigadier General William Mitchell was hard at work lobbying for an independent Air Force, modeled after the British R.A.F. Mitchell's Air Force was conceived as having a Secretary with Cabinet rank equal to the Army and Navy. It would control both land and sea aeronautics, and civilian aviation as well. The young naval aviators violently opposed this concept. They were anxious to have Congress establish a Bureau of Aeronautics in the Navy Department. The ensuing internecine battle for the minds of the legislators was one of the bitterest ever fought between the armed services.

Billy Mitchell was a prophet ahead of his era. He had a fanatical dedication, a flair for publicity, and strong arguments on his side. The time would come when the growth of air power would make a separate Air Force imperative. On the other hand, it was equally essential for the Navy to control its own aeronautics because of the basic difference in its functions and capabilities, and the necessity for close cooperation between planes and ships.

In the fight for a Bureau of Aeronautics the Navy was badly handicapped by being divided against itself. The old admirals were dead set against giving more than a minimum of their precious appropriations to a branch of the service that they considered pure frippery. As late as 1927, the author recalls an old sea dog, Captain William N. Jeffers, Commandant of the Norfolk Navy Yard, saying to him, "Planes are no good except for scouting. We have to have them because the other fellows do. But they're just a damned nuisance." This was the attitude of a large percentage of the high command of the Fleet less than fifteen years before our entire battleship force in the Pacific was sunk or put out of action by Japanese planes at Pearl Harbor.

There could be no question as to where Byrd stood. He was a flyer by instinct and conviction, a Navy man by training and loyalty. He understood the situation. Since no one else seemed to be doing anything, he decided to act. At a meeting of young naval flyers at the Bureau of Navigation, he helped to organize them to block Mitchell's plan to grab the Navy Air. An idealistic and enthusiastic group, they were not actuated by selfish motives, but by their convictions of what was best for the future of aviation as an arm of sea power.

A Bureau of Aeronautics was an essential step in their plan because it would give Naval Aviation equality with other branches of the Navy. In what he described as a "moment of expansion," [1] Byrd volunteered to draw up an act creating the Bureau. It was a remarkable performance for a neophyte in legislation. Being loyal Navy men, the group did not go directly to Congress as Billy Mitchell had. Byrd and three fellow flyers took the proposed bill to their superior, Captain Irwin. Irwin was a Naval Academy man, thoroughly indoctrinated with the Navy's distaste for politicians. He poured buckets of cold water on the idea and advised Byrd not to get himself or Naval Aviation embroiled in politics. Byrd was crushed—a condition to which he should have become accustomed.

But, as to Putty Read over the Azores, a hole suddenly appeared in the clouds. Billy Mitchell's Army bombers were practicing against floating targets in Chesapeake Bay, making a great stir in the press; and Mitchell himself was battering at Congress with considerable chance of success. The Admirals suddenly realized that he was trying to take something away from the Navy. However little they valued Naval Aviation, they were damned if they were going to let it be taken over by an outsider.

The first break came when Captain T. T. Craven replaced Irwin

1. Byrd, *Skyward*.

as Director of Naval Aviation. Like most other ranking officers, he had thought little about the Navy's air arm. Byrd and his cohorts went to work on him and gained their first convert. With his cooperation they moved on the Admirals. Admiral Benson, who was still Chief of Naval Operations, began by telling them to go to the devil and ended by supporting them enthusiastically. The next step was to win Assistant Secretary of the Navy Franklin D. Roosevelt. A man of the future with an imaginative grasp of naval strategy, Roosevelt came in strongly from the first. Secretary of the Navy Daniels, his mind probably prepared by a briefing from his Assistant Secretary, required little persuasion. He agreed that a Bureau of Aeronautics was a good idea and asked the young enthusiasts what they proposed to do next. When Byrd answered, "Get Congress to pass the bill," the seasoned old politician smiled gently at his naïveté in making it sound so easy. But he promptly dictated a strong letter of endorsement.

Because of Byrd's powerful political connections and his persuasive manner of presenting his arguments, it was decided that he should carry the ball in what he called "The Battle on the Hill." [2] Knowing nothing about politics, at first he bulled his way in where more sophisticated men would have maneuvered. Because of his naïveté and enthusiasm, it worked. His first move was to call on Senator Carroll Smalley Page of Vermont, Chairman of the Naval Affairs Committee. The Senator listened intently to his exposition of the proposal and, to Byrd's surprise, asked some intelligent questions. Then he asked what the young naval officer wanted him to do. Byrd suggested that he call a meeting of the full committee and give him a chance to appeal for one of its members to sponsor the bill. He waited for a reply, awestricken by his own audacity. The Senator, watching the expression on Byrd's face, took his time. Then he asked, "Would Friday do?" [3]

For the next few months Byrd was probably the most active lobbyist in Washington. After winning the support of the Senate Naval Affairs Committee, he had to tackle the House of Representatives. Here also his logical arguments, reinforced by his good looks, earnestness, and charm won him supporters. They proposed tacking the

2. Charles J. V. Murphy, *op. cit.*
3. Byrd, *Skyward.*

Bureau legislation onto the Naval Appropriations Bill as a rider to make sure it would reach the floor of the House.

This was good progress, but there were snags ahead. General Mitchell, realizing that a Bureau of Aeronautics would make his united air force more difficult to obtain, threw some roadblocks in the way. Byrd had to counter them by talking personally to as many congressmen and senators as he could reach. He used all his political and social connections to become acquainted with them; played golf and tennis with them; argued, flattered, charmed, and cajoled them, and in the end won them over—at least enough of them. After the final vote was taken, the Navy had its Bureau of Aeronautics, with Admiral William A. Moffett as its first chief; and Byrd had a liberal education in political techniques and many new friends in both houses of Congress.

To move a little ahead of chronology, Byrd had succeeded so well that for the next four years the Navy used him as its unofficial liaison man with Congress. He hated the job, but performed it with enormous vigor and dedication because of his belief in his cause and his loyalty to the Navy.

That loyalty was put under a severe strain when, like all other officers with temporary wartime rank, he was demoted from lieutenant commander to his regular rank of lieutenant, with consequent loss of status and pay. His classmates were soon due for promotion again, but because Byrd was officially on the retired list, and on temporary active duty, he was ineligible for normal promotion. It would take a special act of Congress to advance him, and he knew that was impossible. Once again he tried to retire completely, but his superiors begged him to continue his good work. Loyalty triumphed over self-interest.

In 1924, the impossible happened. In recognition of his services, the Secretary of the Navy instigated a bill in Congress to promote Byrd. The Naval Affairs Committee looked over his record carefully; for example, the report from the Chief of the Bureau of Aeronautics, December 30, 1921:

Lieutenant Byrd is an exceptionally loyal, capable and efficient officer. For his age and length of service he has remarkably good judgment. He is zealous, has tact and ability to cooperate with others; and is indefatigable in the performance of duty and persistent in accomplishing the end in view. I have no hesitation in saying that he, more than any-one else, by his own qualifications had much to do with getting passed the legislation creating the Bureau of Aeronautics.

Of course, Byrd did not—could not—lobby for his own promotion. The Naval Affairs Committee of the House unanimously reported the bill out with a strong recommendation calling attention to his twenty-two detailed reports of fitness and seventeen citations for "service performed over and above the call of duty." The passage of the bill was a most unusual honor. Byrd again became a Lieutenant Commander (retired). That final word was rather ironical as there were few officers in the Navy more active or less retiring.

One of Byrd's most useful political efforts on behalf of his fellow naval officers and the whole personnel of the Navy was to fight a foolish proposal in Congress to cut back the pay of naval personnel to the pre–World-War-I scale. Because of the great inflation of prices that war had caused, this would have decimated the Navy. It was impossible any longer to live or support a family on such a minuscule salary. Byrd won that round.

The biggest battle of all was against General Mitchell's Air Force Bill. The General had proved the value of air power by sinking some old German warships in Chesapeake Bay. He had the backing of most of the Army Air Corps officers, a powerful group in Congress, and a large section of public opinion. He was also in the right, at least for the distant future, except in his insistence that the Air Force must embrace Naval Air as well as land-based planes.

In the final hearing in 1925, before a Joint Committee of the Congress, Byrd was one of the star witnesses against the Mitchell plan. In part he said:

For forty centuries . . . there have been two objectives in warfare. The towns and the ships. This great division of the armed forces of nations is natural since cities are usually attacked and defended by armies and ships are attacked by sea craft.

Cities and ships can now be approached through the air, but the air does not provide a third objective. Therefore no reason exists for a third division of the armed forces of a country. A city can be bombed but it cannot be captured by aircraft. . . . Ships can be bombed, but the ships and their personnel cannot be taken prisoner by aircraft. The Navy must do that.

There is nothing in the air to attack unless it is put there—then it is only temporarily there. . . . It does not supply an enemy with a third objective.

Until there is a third objective no reason for a third military department exists.

Our conclusion is clear. Experience shows beyond peradventure that if the Navy is to reach its maximum war efficiency it must entirely control its air arm in peace as well as war. . . .

Byrd ended his presentation with a politically canny argument to the economy-minded Republican Congress that a separate Air Force would be enormously expensive.

Though he argued so forcefully against a separate Air Force, Byrd, in his own mind, did not entirely discount its value. His real objections to it were that the time for it was not yet; and that Navy Air should not be comprised in it. That he foresaw a need for it in the future is shown by his statement: "The trouble was [General Mitchell] was ten to twenty years ahead of aviation." [4]

Ahead or not Billy Mitchell might well have carried the day had he been a better politician and less of a zealot. His ruthless pertinacity made even his friends into enemies. Nor could he accept defeat and recoil to try again. Instead he continued wildly to attack his superiors in the Army, Navy, and even in Government, which finally resulted in his court-martial and disgrace. [5]

Throughout all the argument Byrd remained on friendly terms with General Mitchell and later paid tribute to his sincerity and foresight. He agreed with many of the General's ideas; and took the stand he did partly from loyalty to his service and his superiors, and partly from his conviction that the Navy must control its own air arm.

There can be no doubt that Byrd's lobbying, his clear logical statement and well-informed replies before the Joint Committee of Congress played a significant role in the tragedy of Billy Mitchell. He would have had it otherwise, but Mitchell forced the issue to Byrd's deep regret. The final irony was that after the General's premature death, Admiral Byrd's brother, Tom, married Billy Mitchell's widow.

These political activities forced the Byrds to live much of the

4. *Ibid.*

5. Only recently General Mitchell's name has been cleared and the court-martial's verdict reversed.

time in Washington. However, their real home was now the ivy-covered brick house at 9 Brimmer Street in Boston where Marie had grown up, and which she had inherited from her father. Though in the midst of the city, it was a serene place. Brimmer Street, lined with old-fashioned brick houses, is but one block long and goes nowhere in particular, so there is little traffic. Due to the configuration of the land Number 9 was pie-shaped. It had a narrow frontage on the street but broadened out in the back, where there was a walled garden with trees and flowering shrubs overlooking the Charles River. Through the tall windows of the drawing room on the second floor one could step out onto a balcony shaded by an awning. There, in later years, Admiral Byrd loved to sit while he dictated his books.

In that house the Byrd children grew up. There were four of them in all, son Richard E. Byrd, Jr., who regarded his father as a demigod; and three daughters—Bolling, Catherine, and Helen. Although Byrd was necessarily away from home so much, they all adored him. With them he was never the lonely aloof commander, but a boon companion of their own age, whatever that age happened to be. When he came home, he lighted up their lives.

During Byrd's political interlude, he continued his regular duties in the Navy Department. He was quite as zealous and pertinacious as Mitchell—though more politic—in his determination to fly the Atlantic. Soon after the Naval Bureau of Aeronautics was activated in 1921, he approached Admiral Moffett, who became his close friend and warm admirer, with a proposal to make a solo flight from Newfoundland to England in one of the new Navy JL single-engine planes. Although the distance from St. Johns to Clogher Head Island was 1909 miles, and the plane's most favorable range only 1650 miles, Byrd pointed out that the prevailing winds were westerly, which he optimistically reckoned would give him a safety margin of 270 miles. He wanted no destroyer escorts.

The purpose of the flight, he said, was to prove that a pilot could fly and navigate at the same time, and thus demonstrate a single-seater airplane's ability to perform long-range reconnaissance flights.[6]

6. Byrd's memorandum to Chief of the Bureau of Aeronautics with accompanying endorsement. Dated July 30, 1921.

Its real purpose was to let Byrd achieve his ambition to fly across the Atlantic.

Admiral Moffett let himself be talked into endorsing the project against his better judgment. The matter went before the new Assistant Secretary of the Navy, Theodore Roosevelt, Jr. Although Roosevelt agreed to approve the request if Byrd insisted, he fortunately succeeded in talking him out of it. To solace him, Admiral Moffett appointed Byrd U. S. Navigation Officer on the British Airship ZR2,[7] which had been purchased by the Navy and was scheduled to be delivered by air in late August or September. One can imagine the Admiral thinking, "If we let this lunatic fly the Atlantic in *something* perhaps he will be satisfied."

The venture did not seem especially dangerous. The smaller British dirigible R34 had made two successful transatlantic crossings. The ZR2 was much larger and more powerful. She was 700 feet long with a diameter of 85 feet, which gave her a capacity of 2,720,000 cubic feet of hydrogen gas. She was by far the biggest aircraft in the world.

Ten hours after he received his orders Byrd left for England, supercharged with enthusiasm. He reported in to the U. S. Naval Attaché in London on August 20, 1921, and learned that ZR2 was to make a trial flight two days later. He telephoned his friend Commander Louis Maxfield, commanding the American contingent, and arranged to go on the flight.

The ZR2 was based at Howden. Byrd was ordered to take the morning train there from London. He missed it. There has never been any explanation of how this came about. Byrd was the most punctual of men; as far as is known he never missed a train in his life except that one. It was the beginning of his luck; it was downright providential.

He arrived at Howden by the afternoon train to find that his place aboard ZR2 had been filled for the trial flight. Somewhat dashed, he mingled with old friends and new, among them Commander Maxfield and Lieutenant Commanders Emery Coil and Valentine Bieg. There was a strange atmosphere at Howden. Byrd expected to find everyone as excited and enthusiastic as he was; instead they were glum and jittery. Byrd spent the evening with Coil

7. Her British designation was R38.

and his pretty English bride. Coil was obviously forcing a gaiety he did not feel. About midnight he confided in Byrd that he felt there was something wrong with the ship, perhaps a weakness at frame 10. The others did, too, he said. Pulling Byrd aside, Mrs. Coil told him her husband had a premonition that the ship would never make it across the ocean. Byrd put it down to pre-flight jitters.

The next morning early he went aboard the airship. She was as long as an ocean liner and nearly a hundred feet high from the floor of the forward navigating cabin to the flattened top of her great, gray envelope. Gleaming in the slanting sunshine of a rarely beautiful English dawn, she was a sight to lift one's heart. Byrd's wire-pulling had got him permission to replace a crewman on the flight. The only man who could be spared was Mechanic's Mate W. J. Steele. When Byrd and Coil broke the news to him, he looked as though they had kicked him in the stomach. So pitifully did he plead to go that Byrd had not the heart to disappoint him; he was always far more considerate of enlisted men than of his equals or superiors.

Feeling "so grouchy" that he did not even go over to speak to lovely Mrs. Maxfield, who was his cousin, Byrd stood on the field watching the great ship slowly lift off and slant majestically up the sky. Then he took a train back to London, cursing his luck.

The ZR2 (or R38) was to cruise for two nights and land at another airship base at Pullham. The following evening, as Byrd came out of his hotel to take the train to Pullham, he noticed grim looks on people's faces, heard the pseudo-hysterical shouting of newsboys, hawking calamity. Huge headlines confirmed his sudden fears:

R38 EXPLODES IN AIR
OVER HUMBER RIVER

The ZR2 had broken in two as she tried a sharp turn. Sparks from rending steel fired the highly flammable hydrogen gas. Of nearly one hundred men aboard only five survived; only one enlisted man out of thirty-six Americans on board. Lieutenant Commander Coil's body was found beside frame 10, which he had been watching.

Back in Boston, where she was living in her family home on Brimmer Street, Marie Byrd received a dreadful blow. Harry Byrd telephoned her from Virginia that the Navy Department believed that Lieutenant Richard E. Byrd had been lost aboard the ZR2. Fortunately before that long night was over a cable came stating that he was safe. In the end this false alarm may have strengthened Mrs. Byrd's remarkable equanimity when her husband was off on one of his perilous adventures and taught her not to fret about rumors of disaster.

Byrd worked with the British for days at the gruesome task of recovering the bodies and endeavoring to deduce the cause of the accident from clues discovered in the twisted heap of metal lying like a beached whale in the Humber. He returned to America in the U.S.S. *Olympia,* sad and sobered—but as determined as ever someday to fly the Atlantic.

However, Byrd's next adventure was in a different direction which pointed him on his true course of exploration. In January, 1924, he received orders to join the planning group for a proposed flight of the Navy Dirigible *Shenandoah* across the Arctic Ocean from Point Barrow, Alaska, to Spitzbergen. The flight was soon canceled by cautious President Calvin Coolidge. Byrd was not so easily put off.

Joining forces with Peary's former associate, Captain Bob Bartlett, he began to organize a private expedition to fly over the North Pole in one of the new Army amphibian planes recently invented by Grover Loening. Byrd talked Edsel Ford out of $15,000 and got $10,000 from John D. Rockefeller, Jr. Then he learned that Donald B. MacMillan was already forming an expedition backed by the National Geographic Society for aerial exploration of the Arctic Ocean and the Polar Sea northwest of Greenland to discover if land existed there. The Navy Department ordered Byrd to join the MacMillan Expedition in command of the three planes and the naval unit which was to do the flying.

The expedition sailed from Wiscasset, Maine, on June 20, 1925, in two ships, the graceful, yachtlike schooner *Bowdoin* and the small steel steamer *Peary.* On that trip Byrd learned that wooden ships had an advantage over steel in the Arctic because, when bucking ice, steel can be bent and rivets loosened, whereas wood, if it is not crushed, springs back into shape when released from ice pressure. However, the *Peary,* in which the naval unit sailed, had her bows reinforced by triple plating and packed with concrete. She was a fairly efficient icebreaker.

Byrd got his first experience of the polar ice pack in Melville Bay off the west coast of Greenland. The hard blue ice five feet thick extended as far as the eye could see. The *Peary* smashed into it with a crunching, wracking sound, while trying to break a lane for the two ships. When the *Bowdoin* tried the same maneuver, her bow slid right up on the ice. Finally both ships came to a halt, and many members of their crews went off for a seal hunt on the ice. When the tide changed, leads of open water appeared in the pack and the ships steamed slowly ahead, dodging and twisting through the ice.

On August 1, 1925, they sailed under the Crimson Cliffs into Smith Sound between Ellesmere Island and Greenland. In the early morning of August 2, they anchored off Etah, Greenland, in a snow-storm. Except for a few weirdly shaped icebergs the anchorage was free of ice. Greenlanders came out in *kyacks* to beg for tobacco. Their women rowed out in a clumsy *umiak,* a big canoe made of sealskin. They were dressed in their best—beautiful white leather boots, over tight sealskin trousers with polychrome, mosaic insets composed of a hundred tiny bits of dyed leather. They all wore deep collars shaped like berthas made of bright-colored beads in elaborate designs, and round woolen hats above their smiling round faces.

Byrd lost no time getting the three planes ashore, using the wing crates to make a ramp for them on the rocky beach. They were Loening Amphibians, borrowed from the Army. They had a single boatlike pontoon into which their wheels retracted. A Liberty motor which drove a four-bladed puller propeller was mounted high above the water, and the two-man crew—plus one passenger if necessary—rode in open cockpits between the biplane wings. The planes' service designations were NA1, NA2, and NA3. Working round the clock in freezing wind and occasional snow flurries, Byrd and his men had the planes ready to fly by August 4.

During this work Byrd particularly noticed an obscure Navy petty officer named Floyd Bennett. He was lanky and blond with very light blue eyes. Oddly enough he had been born on October 25, as had Byrd. When Bennett got his chance, he turned out to be a superb pilot, always steady, always calm, with the sure, instinctive touch that got the best out of any craft he flew. Byrd came to love him dearly.

Except for a few short trial flights, gales, snow, and fog kept them grounded until August 8. Because the ships would have to leave by late August to avoid being frozen in the ice pack, there were but fifteen days left for exploration. Out of that time only three and three-quarter days were good for flying; two were fairly good and one indifferent. As Byrd commented in an article in the *National Geographic Magazine*, it was a short "summer." [8]

With the midnight sun lighting their way, the planes took off at 9:10 P.M. on August 8. Lieutenant Schur piloted NA2 with Rocheville as mechanic and MacMillan as passenger. NA3 was piloted by Lieutenant Reber with Byrd as relief pilot and navigator. Bennett piloted NA1. As the motors started a herd of angry walruses reared out of the water shaking their tusks, then dived to attack them. The pilots gunned their ships and left the frustrated beasts in a storm of spray.

Byrd set their course for Cannon Fjord on the Polar Sea. They flew over the ice-flecked waters of South Sound to Cape Sabine and on over the magnificent icy peaks of Ellesmere Island with their glittering glaciers trailing down to the sea. Navigation was extremely difficult. In those latitudes, far north of the magnetic pole, an ordinary compass hardly functions. To fly northwest Byrd had to steer due east. Though he had a sun compass, invented by Alfred H. Bumstead, it was useless because of the heavy overcast. Searching anxiously for a place to land in case of engine failure, Byrd found none in that desolate, chaotic terrain. Indeed in all his flights from Greenland, only twice did he see a safe landing place, for even the open water was filled with floating ice cakes several feet thick that would have smashed a plane's pontoon.

Halfway across Ellesmere the western range of mountains pushing up into the clouds barred their way. Behind them the weather was closing in, so Byrd reluctantly ordered the planes to steer for Etah. The clouds closed down to meet the high plateau, so he took the planes into the sunlight above them and flew by the sun compass and dead reckoning. As he calculated that they were over Smith Sound, he spotted a hole in the clouds. They came down through it near enough to see their ships at anchor and the little frame cabins of Etah. Immediately after the flight Byrd called a meeting of his unit and told them that never again would he order any man to fly over Ellesmere because of the extreme danger. They unanimously volunteered to go anywhere he did.

8. Vol. XLVIII, p. 520, November , 1925.

Though there were so few days of flying weather, numerous flights were made over the unexplored western range of the Greenland ice cap and Ellesmere. In all, the planes flew over five thousand miles, and from an altitude of three thousand feet, overlooked thirty thousand square miles of territory, most of which had never been seen by any man. But Byrd was again frustrated. After a particularly hazardous flight through the incredible turbulence over the unexplored region of Grinnell Land, a howling blizzard struck and Etah Fjord froze. Fearful that his ships would be frozen in for the winter, MacMillan told Byrd that no more flights should be made and that they should prepare to sail for home.

This produced an angry conflict between the civilian and naval sections of the expedition. The gung-ho naval flyers, led by Byrd, wanted to push on to the Arctic Ocean even if they had to walk over the ice. Byrd, controlling his temper, went to MacMillan's cabin and quietly told him that he proposed to fly NA3 unescorted over Ellesmere to the Cape Hubbard on the Arctic Ocean. MacMillan was adamant against it. That afternoon he radioed the Navy Department: "I am convinced that far northern Arctic work is extremely hazardous in heavier-than-air planes simply because landing places are few and food caches cannot be relied upon." He stated that the work of exploration should be done by airships and added that if Navy officials could see the conditions from the air, he was sure that orders would be issued to stop all work at once.[9]

This was a terrible blow to Byrd, completely sabotaging all his beliefs and hopes. He shot off his own dispatch, directly contradicting MacMillan's opinions. On that same afternoon he received a direct order from Secretary of the Navy Wilbur to: "Withdraw with MacMillan and make such flights in secondary exploration as expedition returns south as you deem practical."[10]

On August 22, the expedition sailed for home. Once again Byrd's fine dreams had been shattered. Sadly he accepted defeat for the time being and in a final radiogram stated that he did not question Commander MacMillan's judgment and "sympathized" with his position. In fact, he felt that their great labors had been mostly in vain and that he could hope for little further help from the Navy.

Nevertheless, he had learned a great deal. The experience he

9. Dispatch from Donald MacMillan to Navy Department, August 20, 1925.
10. Secretary of the Navy to Lieutenant Commander Byrd, August 20, 1925.

had gained of Arctic conditions was of immense value in the future. Moreover, he had reached a conclusion that was the keystone of success. In the future he would rely on private enterprise to sponsor his work. Not again would he be subject to orders from men sitting in snug offices in Washington. He and he alone would be in command.

V · THE POLE

No sooner did Byrd reach the United States than he began planning his first great adventure. Drawing on his new knowledge of Arctic conditions and his old skills in aerial navigation, he began meticulous preparations for an assault on the North Pole itself the following summer. All the years of bad luck, failure, and disappointment contributed to his final success. In this work Floyd Bennett was his indispensable aide and loyal supporter.

Byrd's polar expedition was sponsored by the National Geographic Society and privately financed. Much as he hated begging, he went hat in hand to such affluent friends as Edsel Ford, John D. Rockefeller, Jr., and other tycoons to raise $100,000. The Shipping Board loaned him the old thirty-five-hundred-ton coal-burning steamer *Chantier*. The single plane on which his hopes rested was a secondhand Fokker monoplane powered by three 200-h.p. Wright Whirlwind engines with a top speed of 120 m.p.h. Her fuselage was 42 feet 9 inches long and her wingspread 63 feet 3 inches. She carried 410 gallons of gasoline in her tanks, plus extra five-gallon cans in her cabin, which she burned at the rate of 28 gallons an hour. As the flight would take a minimum of sixteen hours, even if all went well, this was a slim margin of safety. Byrd named her the *Josephine Ford* after the three-year-old daughter of his principal backer.

Though the plane looked huge to Byrd and the members of his party, she was a fragile thing in which to face the tempests that sweep so suddenly across the polar seas. Her entire 600 h.p. was less than one-sixtieth of the power of a single modern jet engine. But those were the days when, in Kipling's phrase, "Men flew in kites with oil engines." [1]

There were about fifty members of the expedition in addition to Byrd, almost all of them volunteers. A few were borrowed from government sevices; a metcorologist, from the Weather Bureau; a doctor, from Johns Hopkins University. Several Army officers served as ordinary seamen. The rest were naval reservists or young adventurers. There was one stowaway who more than earned his way. In the first decade following World War I, when peace seemed to have permanently settled in and America was surging forward on a great tide of prosperity, young men sought adventure where they could. Even a chance to share vicariously such a feat as a flight over the North Pole was enough to bring them out in droves.

For pilot, companion, and friend, Byrd took Floyd Bennett, of course. His second pilot was Lieutenant George A. Noville, U.S.N.

Though a great deal of the material and food was donated by different corporations, the Expedition went flat broke before it ever sailed. Byrd had to go on the mendicant road again to raise more money. At that he owed nearly $40,000 when the *Chantier* finally sailed from New York.

On April 29, 1926, the *Chantier* steamed between the round, snow-covered headlands of Kings Bay on the Arctic island of Spitzbergen. Byrd had chosen this place for his take-off because it was only 750 miles from the Pole, and was the nearest harbor where he could hope to find open water so early in the spring. Roald Amundsen and his American backer, Lincoln Ellsworth, with part of their crew were already at Kings Bay, momentarily expecting the arrival of the Italian airship *Norge* in which they hoped to be the first to fly over the Pole. The race was on.

As Captain M. J. Brennan conned the *Chantier*, bumping and scraping through the drifting ice floes in the bay, Byrd saw the gray Norwegian gunboat *Heimdahl* moored to the only dock. The *Chantier* was forced to anchor nine hundred yards off shore. Hot with

1. The expedition also had a small Curtiss Oriole, good for scouting, but useless for a polar flight. She was never used.

anger because he had reserved the dock by cable, Byrd rushed ashore and asked the captain of the *Heimdahl* to clear the landing. The Norwegian refused on the ground that it was too dangerous to anchor his ship among the moving ice floes in the bay. His real intent was probably to delay Byrd so that the Norwegians could be first over the Pole. It was the only example of poor sportsmanship shown by either side.

Though Byrd always contended that he was on a scientific expedition and not in a race to the Pole, his every act showed his fierce competitive spirit. His shipmates despaired of landing the fuselage and the huge wings of their plane without a dock. Byrd thought of a way. He had his men construct a big clumsy raft by laying heavy planks across the *Chantier's* four lifeboats. He well knew the danger of trying to ferry his only suitable plane to shore through ice-strewn waters on that contraption. It was an absurd risk to take if his object had been merely scientific exploration. Scientific fiddlesticks! He— and all his crew—were out to win the polar race come hell, high water, and five-foot-thick cakes of ice. But it was not just egotism. Byrd was intensely patriotic. He and his company of adventurers truly felt that they represented America in a great contest for world prestige.

Working like Dante's devils in a blizzard, the men built the raft on the bobbing boats, and lowered the heavy fuselage of the plane onto it. As they hoisted the big wings out of the ship's hold, an icy half-gale struck. The floe ice began to move and a small iceberg bore down upon them. They leaped aboard it, chopped a hole in it, and with dynamite blew it into manageable pieces.

As the wind slackened, they fitted the wings to the fuselage on the heaving raft. Then they began the perilous trip to shore, rowing that impossible craft through the shifting, grinding floes while a small boat cleared a lane ahead. It was a wildly exciting, comic scene. Half the men had never rowed a boat before. They pulled ahead when they should have backed water, caught crabs splashing wildly, fended off the ice with butt and blade. Despite strain, anxiety, and intense physical effort, Byrd's antic mind flashed an absurd picture of Washington crossing the Delaware.[2]

Somehow they made it. As the raft grated on the rocky shore, Amundsen and the other Norwegians stood cheering on the beach.

2. Byrd, *Skyward*.

Unordered the gunboat's band lined up on deck and played "The Star-Spangled Banner."

Without a pause, skis were fitted on the *Josephine Ford*. Then began the difficult job of manhandling the heavy plane up the slope which a working party from the *Chantier* had partly cleared as a runway. No one thought of sleep; the midnight sun lighted their labors. The men were fed from a field kitchen; they rested in a pit dug in the snow. The temperature hovered around zero.

Byrd foregathered briefly with Amundsen, Ellsworth, and the Norwegian party. Though the captain of the gunboat had been uncooperative, the leaders of the expedition were splendid sportsmen, free with helpful advice and material assistance. Amundsen insisted on lending Byrd a light Eskimo sled in case he came down on the ice and had to walk home but there was not much chance of making it back on foot.

Four days after their arrival, on May 3, the *Josephine Ford* was ready for a trial flight; the snow runway was as smooth as the men could make it. Byrd and Bennett took their places in the cabin. The motors roared and the plane lumbered down the slope. No one had ever tried to take a tri-motored plane off on skis before; it was a matter of guesswork. Halfway down the runway a ski broke. Bennett quickly killed the motors.

They strengthened the skis and tried again. This time they hit a bump in the runway and the plane went nose down into a snowdrift. By a miracle, nothing was broken but the skis. Obviously they were too light to stand the strain. Byrd came near to despair. If his plane could not take off lightly loaded, what chance would there be with a full ten-thousand-pound load?

Chips Gould, the carpenter, worked through two days and two nights making new skis, strengthening them with oar handles. A blond Norwegian Viking named Bernt Balchen strolled over and suggested waxing the skis with a mixture of paraffin and resin to cut drag. On the third attempt the *Josephine Ford* took the air. Bennett flew her around for two hours. Gas consumption was lower than Byrd had expected.

On May 6, while Byrd was loading his plane, the *Norge* sailed majestically over the white horizon and was moored by many ropes between the curving walls of an unroofed hangar about two hundred yards from the *Josephine Ford*. If the Americans had worked hard before, they now labored like maniacs. Because of the plane's low gas consumption and probably due to the airship's arrival, Byrd decided to give up his plan to establish an advance base at Cape Jessup in northern Greenland, and shoot the works on a direct dash for the Pole.

On the morning of May 8, everything was ready. The *Josephine Ford*'s gas tanks were full, her cabin crammed with five-gallon cans of extra gas, concentrated food for ten weeks, a tent, rifles, and other supplies. The meteorologist, W. C. Haines, predicted good weather. It had warmed up a bit to 10° Fahrenheit. Byrd and Bennett, wearing colorful Eskimo parkas of polar-bear skin over their flying suits, climbed aboard. They opened the throttles wide and the plane started slowly down the runway.

That was an agonizing fifty seconds. Try as he might, with all his skill, Bennett could not lift the plane off. She staggered and yawed and refused to break loose. She was just too heavily loaded. In his desperation Bennett held on a bit too long before he cut the engines. The plane overshot the end of the runway, bumping horribly over rocks under the snow. As she stopped at a tipsy angle, Byrd and Bennett were out in a flash, burrowing under the deep snow to examine the landing gear. The whole crew came running down the mile-long slope utterly exhausted, haggard with despair. They found Byrd alight with enthusiasm. His incredible luck had held. Nothing vital was broken.

Under his orders the ship was lightened. Some of the extra gasoline was put off. Nearly two hundred pounds of souvenirs the crew had sneaked aboard—flags, pictures, coats, shirts, knickknacks of all kinds—were found and pitched out. Supplies were jettisoned; the load was pared to the bone.

As the crew prepared to haul the plane laboriously up the hill again, Byrd said there was no time. "Damn it, I'll taxi her up," he said.[3] He did. While minor repairs were made, he went aboard the *Chantier* to catch a little sleep, his first in thirty-six hours. Bennett would not leave the plane. He curled up in the fuselage and slept.

Just after midnight the *Josephine Ford* was ready again. Byrd and Bennett conferred and agreed that this time they would go full ahead to the end; either take off or crash. They iced the runway in

3. Charles J. V. Murphy, *op. cit.*

front of the plane. They tied the tail to a stake in the frozen ground so that the motors could be revved up full before she moved. Then they took their places in the cockpit, checked the pitifully few instruments, and revved up the motors.

At 1:58 A.M., May 9, 1926, with the motors roaring and shaking the plane, Byrd waved his hand to signal "Go!" Tom Mulroy [4] swung a sharpened ax blade against the taut rope. The plane shot forward down the slope. The crew watched her disappear in the blizzard of snow kicked up by her propellers; watched that whirlwind move faster and faster. At glorious last they saw bright wings rise from the boiling snow cloud, tilt in a long easy turn, and head due north.

It was one thing to head due north and quite another to maintain that course. In those latitudes, nearly a thousand miles north and east of the magnetic pole, the compass was almost useless. Byrd had a newly invented gyroscopic compass, which was only a little more accurate; and the Bumpstead sun compass, which worked like a sun dial in reverse—if the navigator knew the exact time, he could tell his direction from the angle at which the sun hit the instrument. Of course if there were clouds, it ceased to function. Byrd also had the special artificial-horizon sextant that he had invented himself for aerial navigation. He froze his face and one hand taking sights through the open hatch above him.

At an altitude of two thousand feet, they crossed the strip of blue water along the rugged coast and flew over the polar ice pack glittering in the slanting sunshine, stretching endlessly ahead. In addition to checking the compasses and taking sights with his sextant, Byrd had to check the drift every three minutes because, with a change of wind direction, a plane that was pointed due north might actually be going northwest or northeast. Every so often Byrd relieved Bennett at the controls, while the latter checked the gauges and figured gas consumption. Byrd, flying with one hand, holding the sun compass in the other, noted a slight tail wind.

In those days many geographers believed that there was land near the North Pole. One of Byrd's scientific objectives was to dis-

4. Chief engineer of the *Chantier*.

cover it, if it was there. From a plane at two thousand feet the range of vision was enormously greater than that of Admiral Peary, who had reached the Pole on foot. Once Byrd mistook a cloud formation for a snow-capped mountain; but as the excitement of discovery rose, the Arctic mirage faded.

After a time the flight became almost monotonous: the drone of motors, the flat glaring ice below, ribboned by blue leads of open water or the greenish hue of new skim ice. Then quite suddenly, about an hour's flight from the Pole, the flags of danger flew. They took the form of yellow globules of oil splashing on the cabin window. Looking out, they saw oil seeping from the starboard motor. No one who has not flown over inhospitable country in a little plane can realize the skin-pricking terror of such a sight. When a motor is throwing oil, it means that as soon as it runs dry, it will overheat and stop. The Fokker was supposed to be able to fly on two out of three engines, but not with such a load as the *Josephine Ford* was carrying. Byrd did not need the note Bennett scribbled: "That motor will stop." [5]

Bennett then suggested that they try to land on the ice and make repairs. Byrd shook his head. The pack ice that looked so flat from two thousand feet above was actually like frozen waves, with pressure ridges up to forty feet high crossing and crisscrossing it at all angles. Even if they got down safely, they would never get off again. From long experience Byrd knew that the only sensible thing to do was to turn tail, and run for home base; to get as near it as possible before the plane came down. If Peary with his dogs and sledges, his caches of supplies along the trail, had taken nearly three months to fight his way back from the Pole, what chance was there for two men with one little sled? Practically none unless they managed to get much nearer Spitzbergen. Holding his own life cheap, yet responsible for Bennett's as well, Byrd must have known what he should do. But with the Pole now only fifty-five minutes away by his reckoning, he would not, could not, turn away. His ardent spirit, or foolhardy daring, whichever you choose to call it, impelled him to go on. The chances were a hundred to one the motor would stop before they even reached the Pole, let alone getting back. Yet he held on. Bennett was in full agreement. Great deeds are seldom done by sensible men.

5. Byrd, *op. cit.* Speech was impossible because of the roaring motors.

Byrd now took over the controls and flew the plane, constantly flicking his eyes from the motor to the oil-pressure gauge. When that began to fall the motor would stop. He expected it momentarily. But the gauge held steady.

At 8 hours 58 minutes 55 seconds Greenwich time Byrd took an observation that showed them to be at 89°55'3" north latitude or 4.7 miles from the North Pole.[6] Bennett was piloting. At 9:02 Byrd clapped him on the shoulder and shouted, "The Pole!"

The flat expanse of ice looked exactly the same as it had for the past six hours, but both men were in a state of wild exhilaration. Making absolutely sure, Byrd ordered Bennett to hold on course for a minute or two. Then they turned to the right and took two sextant observations; then to the left, taking two more. All observations confirmed the previous position. Finally Bennett flew the plane in a four-mile circle around the imaginary point Byrd believed to be the Pole while Byrd took moving pictures. Flying at three thousand feet in brilliantly clear air, they had a view of a circle 120 miles in diameter, an area no other men had ever seen.

Then they turned homeward. Whichever way they flew was due south, but it had to be the *right* due south to bring them back to Spitzbergen—a tricky business. Byrd chose to fly directly down the fifteenth meridian of longitude.

The return trip seemed endless. Both Byrd and Bennett suddenly felt relaxed. Drowsiness overcame them; they kept falling asleep at the controls. But the luck held. That motor not only kept running, but the oil leak stopped. Later they found that it had been caused by a loose rivet near the top of the tank. When the oil fell below that level, it stopped seeping out. Not only that, but the drift indicator showed that the wind had swung right around the compass and was blowing hard from the *north*—a tail wind going and coming!

At some point a slight jar sent the Byrd sextant sliding off the folding chart table, smashing the artificial horizon. Now they had only the sun compass. However, "At the moment when the sun would be crossing the 15th meridian, [Byrd] had the plane steadied, pointing directly toward the sun, and observed at the same instant that the shadow on the sun compass was down the middle of the

6. Report of the Special Committee of the National Geographic Society to examine Byrd's charts and records.

hand, thus verifying his position as being on that meridian." [7] Byrd wrote a note to Bennett: "We'll hit at Gray Hook."

Hours later the shining mountains of Spitzbergen glinted on the horizon. As they drew nearer, they saw a rocky gray headland dead ahead—Gray Hook.

Admiral Byrd was probably the greatest navigator of his time, not perhaps in scientific knowledge or mathematical ability, but from the pragmatic viewpoint of getting from where he was to where he wanted to be. It amounted to a sort of genius, or perhaps pure instinct such as guides the migrating swallows from South America to Capistrano. Even so, hitting Gray Hook on the nose after flying for more than seven hours over totally unmarked territory without even a sextant was so wildly improbable as to exceed the fantastic imagining of science-fictioneers.

Bennett swung the *Josephine Ford* to the west to fly along the coast, then lifted her over the snowy peaks. Beneath was long, narrow, fjordlike Kings Bay with the *Chantier* at anchor and the *Norge* still huddled in her hangar. As Bennett set the ship down on the snow, figures came running from both camps, among them Amundsen in a flying suit and a round wool hat, his narrow, wrinkled face beaming in genuine delight as he grasped Byrd's hand.

They had a tremendous party that night. The shouts of *Skol* echoed off the hills as they drank toast after toast. At one point Amundsen asked Byrd, "Where to next?"

"The South Pole," said Byrd.

Though Byrd always pretended to disparage the kudos heaped upon him after one of his daring feats, in reality he delighted in them. He read with relish the cables of congratulations that poured in from world leaders. When he reached London in the *Chantier* on May 27, 1926, wharves all along the Thames were sagging under wildly cheering crowds. The British honored him as one of their own. With American Ambassador Alanson Houghton chaperoning him, Byrd attended a series of luncheons, banquets, and receptions, climaxed by the Earl of Derby's traditional ball after the running of the Derby. Since the King and Queen were to attend, court costume was required. The

7. *Ibid.*

New York *Times* for June 4, 1926, headlined an account of the affair:

BYRD IN SILK KNEEBREECHES
EXPLORES LONDON SOCIETY

Lieutenant Commander Richard E. Byrd explored last night one of London's fashionable strongholds in silk kneebreeches that made him resemble his ancestor Col. William Byrd who went to Virginia in 1641 [sic]. . . . He was taken to the town residence of Lord Derby to meet Queen Mary and Princess Mary at the annual Derby Day reception. He had been invited to attend the race but instead had luncheon with A. R. Hinks, Secretary of the Royal Geographical Society. . . .

Behind this highly inaccurate dispatch was a wild scene at Ambassador Houghton's residence when they tried to outfit Byrd to meet royalty. He wore a pair of black silk stockings borrowed from an unwilling secretary, breeches borrowed from an embassy footman, somebody's tail coat trimmed with brass buttons cut from Byrd's own uniform, and Ambassador Houghton's silver buckled pumps three sizes too large. This jury-rigged costume might have embarrassed an ordinary citizen, but not a Byrd of Virginia. Completely unselfconscious, he had a whale of a time dancing with all the prettiest girls and an occasional grande dame. Even when one of his shoes flew off as he romped around the floor with a duchess, he did not quaver, but stood laughing as she obligingly retrieved it.[8]

The dispatches from London heightened New York's enthusiasm for their hero. When Byrd and Bennett finally arrived in the slow old *Chantier* on June 23, the City gave them one of those rousing ticker-tape receptions for which the 1920's were so famous. Marie Byrd joined her husband in New York. That afternoon, accompanied by Bennett and Admiral Moffett, they went in a private railroad car to Washington where, at a packed reception in the Washington Auditorium, President Calvin Coolidge presented Byrd with the National Geographic Society's Hubbard Gold Medal. In his laudatory address, the laconic President, for once, pulled out all the stops. Byrd responded in a pleasantly modest speech in which, as convention demanded, he gave credit to Bennett and all the other members of his

8. Charles J. V. Murphy, *op. cit.*

party; and made a strong argument for the future of aerial Arctic exploration.

But it remained for Secretary of the Navy Wilbur to honor the unsung heroine of the occasion. He described how, before giving Byrd permission to make the flight, he had asked, "Has your wife consented to your expedition?" to which Byrd answered, "Yes, sir, she said she was willing that I should do whatever I considered my duty."

Then the Secretary asked Marie to stand up so that all might see her. He could not have known what agony such publicity cost her. Fortunately for her sanity, six thousand people stood up at the same time, so virtually no one saw her.[9]

Throughout that summer Byrd and Bennett continued their triumphal tour. Richmond was riotous; Winchester went wild. So it was throughout the country. When Congress reconvened, they passed an act promoting Byrd to Commander and awarding him the Congressional Medal of Honor, one of the few ever given in peacetime. Americans had suddenly realized that they belonged to the greatest nation in the world. They wanted heroes to prove it to themselves and to all mankind. Byrd, with his slight, straight figure, his good looks, his courage, and that charming shyness which overlay his egotism, was the perfect symbol of their national hubris.

The hero enjoyed it all immensely; so much in fact that he began to worry. Was there too much egotism in his nature? Was he really vainglorious? Finally he rationalized it. He was carrying the invisible banner of "the superb world-conquering fire which is the American spirit." [10] That was what the crowds were cheering, the banner not the man, as they had saluted when he had carried the colors as a midshipman at Annapolis. So, in receiving the plaudits, he was just playing his role in the American drama. He could relax and enjoy it to the full; until he passed the invisible banner along to the next national hero, whose name, though he had never heard it then, was Charles A. Lindbergh.

9. *National Geographic Magazine*, September, 1926.
10. Byrd, *Skyward*.

VI ᐧ THE AMERICA

COMMANDER BYRD had toyed with the idea of mounting an Antarctic expedition in the autumn of 1926; but he soon realized that there was not enough time if he were to meet the demands of the American public to see him and Bennett; and thus make enough money to pay off that $40,000 debt.[1] So he returned to his old dream of a nonstop transatlantic flight. On the way home in the *Chantier*, he and Bennett talked it over night after night. They agreed that although a single-engine plane would be more efficient, they would use a tri-motored Fokker like the *Josephine Ford*. Byrd did not want the flight to be just a stunt, but a precursor of the day when planes would carry passengers across the ocean on scheduled flights. He also wanted the safety factor which three engines would give him.

This time he did not have to go begging for money. Not entirely by accident, he found himself seated next to Mr. Rodman Wanamaker at one of the welcome-home banquets. As early as 1912, Wanamaker had financed the building of the plane *America* to attempt such a flight. Fortunately for Wanamaker, the war had prevented it. Now he was eager to try again and he offered Byrd all the money he needed for the attempt. A great francophile, he insisted

---

1. On this and other lecture tours, and from his books, Byrd earned over $1,200,000 in the years 1926–38.

that the destination must be Paris. Wanamaker set up the Atlantic Aircraft Corporation to finance the plane and the flight.

In the autumn, Byrd and Bennett, with Anthony Fokker, went to work designing the plane. It was to have a slightly larger wing-span than the polar plane—71 feet instead of 63 feet. In addition the Wright Whirlwind Engines had been beefed up to deliver 220 h.p. Byrd calculated that this would give the extra lift needed to carry an additional 3,000 pounds. The laminated wooden wings were built in Holland to Fokker's specifications; the fuselage and engines, in the United States. Wanamaker named the new aircraft the *America* after his earlier plane.

Since this was to be a demonstration of an airplane's ability to do more than just get across the ocean, Byrd allowed for a four-man crew and 800 lbs. of extra equipment, including a specially built radio set, emergency food, and safety devices of all sorts—Very pistols for night signaling, self-igniting flares, and two inflatable rubber boats which he had designed himself.

The cabin of the plane was almost entirely filled by an enormous, specially made tank with a capacity of 1,200 gallons of gasoline. For the first time, the tank had a dump valve which could empty it in two minutes to prevent fire in case of an impending crash. For the same reason Bennett designed a special switch that could cut all three engines at once. Catwalks were built from the cabin to the wing engines so that minor repairs could be made in flight. To man the plane and prepare it for the flight Byrd had gathered many of his former companions of the polar expedition. He had added the sandy-haired Norwegian, Bernt Balchen, who had advised him to rub paraffin and resin on the *Josephine Ford's* skis.

Leaving nothing to chance, Byrd arranged with the U. S. Weather Bureau for a special forecasting service. He persuaded the Radio Corporation of America to supply weather reports from all ships in the North Atlantic. The Weather Bureau put Doctor James H. Kimball in charge of this meteorological service and for the next decade he was to be the weather god of airmen.

The final job was to prepare a runway suitable for the take-off of a heavily loaded tri-motor plane. It is difficult to recall that in 1927 there was not a decent airport in all America. The best one was Roosevelt Field near Hempstead, Long Island—a mile-long field of rough grass with dips and rolls and bumps, and a few hangars at its edge. The French pilot René Fonck had attempted to take a Sikorsky tri-motor plane off from it on a transatlantic flight the year before. That plane had crashed before it ever got into the air.

Grover Whalen, the dapper and dynamic official greeter for New York City, who was Mr. Wanamaker's representative, had rented Roosevelt Field. At Byrd's suggestion he put contractors to work for months grading and rolling it. Even then it was hardly an ideal runway. It was far too short and since it was bounded by two main highways, it could not be extended. This problem was the subject of many anxious conferences in Byrd's camp. Finally Fokker thought of making a little hill of earth 30 feet high at the start of the runway with a sloping ramp to give the plane a downhill start. Byrd figured it would give him the equivalent of 500 feet more runway. He needed an extra 2,500, but this would have to do. The work on the field and Byrd's hillock cost Mr. Wanamaker $30,000.[2]

As springtime approached, Byrd learned, with no surprise, that he was not the only man who wanted to fly the ocean. In fact it looked as though there would be heavy traffic over the Atlantic. The French Ace, Charles Nungesser, and François Coli proposed to make an east-west flight from France against the prevailing winds. In the United States, Noel Davis and Stanton Wooster had built the tri-motor plane *American Legion* for the flight. Clarence Chamberlain, backed by Irving Levine, was getting a single-engined Bellanca monoplane ready; and Charles A. Lindbergh, financed by a group of St. Louis businessmen, was having a small Ryan monoplane built for the attempt. Because Raymond Orteig had offered a prize of $25,000 for the first plane to fly from New York to Paris, the newspapers called it "The Great New York to Paris Air Derby." Byrd had purposely not entered the competition, but he was an odds-on favorite to win.

Fortune always favored Byrd in the polar regions, but his transatlantic attempts were jinxed. From the flight of the NC's onward, there seemed to be a malevolent design to prevent his achieving this ambition. Strictly speaking he never quite attained it, for on his flight to France he rowed the last fifty yards.

Bad luck began on the trial flight of the *America* on April 20,

2. Byrd to Charles J. V. Murphy.

1927. Anthony Fokker was at the controls; Floyd Bennett in the co-pilot's seat, while Lieutenant Noville and Byrd crouched beside the huge gasoline tank in the cabin. The plane took off splendidly from the rough little Fokker factory field at Hasbrouck Heights, New Jersey. As it circled around, all four men were grinning with delight. Then Fokker prepared to land. As he cut back the engines, the nose of the plane dropped almost straight down. Fokker gave her full power and caught her before she hit. Around they went and Fokker again throttled back the engines. Again the nose dropped; once more Fokker caught her and took her up.

It was a grim moment. Every man abroad realized that the *America* was so nose heavy it had the gliding angle of a flat rock. It seemed almost impossible to make a safe landing. Byrd could see that Floyd Bennett was aching to take over [3]—he was a far better pilot than Fokker—but the little Dutchman had no intention of yielding the controls. He brought the plane around again, and this time flew it to within a hundred feet of the ground. As he cut back the engines, the plane seemed to fall out from under them. When the wheels hit the ground, Byrd, clinging to a steel girder, saw Fokker abandon the controls and jump for the hatch in the cabin roof. The great machine wheeled wing over wing in a terrifying arc ending in a tremendous splintering crash. Byrd felt a double impact that snapped his arm. Then everything was silent.

Byrd and Noville were lying in a tangled mess of broken rods, seats and gear, hopelessly trapped. Their one thought was fire! Noville staggered up, smashed a hole through the fabric wall of the cabin with his fist, and dived out head first. He lay moaning on the ground. Byrd followed him and ran around the plane to find Bennett hanging from his seat, head down with blood pouring from him. As Byrd bent over him he said faintly, "Guess I'm done for, Commander. I'm all broken up. I can't see and I have no feeling in my left arm."

Byrd, too, thought Bennett was finished, but lied quickly, "Nonsense, old man." [4]

Tenderly he wiped the oil from Bennett's eyes, and found that he could at least see.

Ambulances came screaming. Both Bennett and Noville were

3. Charles J. V. Murphy, *op. cit.*
4. Byrd, *op. cit.*

badly injured; for a time neither was expected to live. Fokker had been thrown clear and was only shaken. Byrd's arm was broken in two places. He set it himself in a car on the way to the hospital. His typical comment was, "Beyond being something of a nuisance for a few weeks it did not interfere with our plans." [5]

Ten days after the *America* was wrecked, Davis and Wooster were killed when their plane crashed on a test flight. Then Nungesser and Coli took off from France in the *White Bird* and disappeared forever in the Atlantic mists. The newspapers began to roar warnings against the folly of attempting transoceanic flights. Byrd was upset because this publicity brought aviation into disrepute. Beyond his own compulsive appetite for danger and glory—which he always denied even to himself—was a sincere desire to advance the science of aeronautics. Naturally he had no intention of giving up the flight, but he was no longer the favorite in the Great Air Derby. Repairs to the *America* took nearly a month. It was found that Noville was not too seriously injured, but poor Floyd Bennett was badly smashed up. Byrd replaced him with Bertram Acosta, a fine pilot, who had recently set an endurance record of fifty-one hours with Clarence Chamberlain in a Bellanca. Finally, the rebuilt *America* was successfully test-flown, and taken to Roosevelt Field.

Meanwhile Chamberlain was ready for his attempt with his Bellanca, *Columbia,* held up only by legal squabbles among his backers. Lindbergh flew the *Spirit of St. Louis* in from St. Louis a few moments before Bernt Balchen brought *America* in from Hasbrouck Heights. Though Mr. Wanamaker controlled all rights to Roosevelt Field, Byrd insisted on offering the use of it and his hillock to his rivals. Not only that, he made his meteorological service available to them and advised them on problems of navigation.

He would not rush his own meticulous preparations. Again and again he test-flew the *America* with different loads, carefully calculating fuel consumption under all conditions. The results were favorable. He was getting a great deal of fan mail, most of it critical. People who had bet on him were infuriated by his delay; letter after letter called him a coward. He affected to be unconcerned, but they hurt, though not enough to force him into a premature take-off. Byrd's re-

5. *Ibid.*

fusal to yield to the racing spirit as he had the previous year in Spitz-bergen showed his growing maturity. However, as Secretary of the Navy Claude A. Swanson wrote in his foreword to *Discovery*,[6] "His personal activities do not encourage me to believe that the leopard has changed his spots or that Dick Byrd, the man, is any less willing to take chances than Dick Byrd, the youth. . . ."

The press was also a constant source of annoyance and nervous tension to Byrd. Almost all the flyers were staying at the Garden City Hotel, a big, red-brick, white-pillared hostelry, whose corridors and public rooms teemed with reporters. Every time Byrd appeared, they swarmed around him, chattering like starlings attacking a crow; asking innumerable questions, and one question numberless times, "When will you be ready to take off, Commander?"

Byrd fended them off with the answer, "When all the tests are satisfactorily completed and I am confident of our ability to reach France. I am *not* in a race."

At three o'clock in the morning of May 20, 1927, Byrd was awakened by the news that Lindbergh was about to take off. He rushed over to the field just in time to shake the shy young pilot's hand and wish him luck. Then he stood watching the little white plane plunge down the ramp and struggle across the field. It staggered into the air at the last possible moment. As its wheels just cleared the telephone wires along the road Byrd felt a genuine lift of heart.[7]

Those two great publicity hounds, Rodman Wanamaker and Grover Whalen, had set the following afternoon for the great christening ceremony of the *America*. At five o'clock several thousand people were gathered around the plane; its golden wings glistening in the sunshine; French and American flags snapping in the breeze. The usual orations flowered in purple adjectives—"Franco-American friendship," "gallant band of adventurers," and so forth. Just as Byrd was about to speak a reporter in the crowd shouted, "Lindbergh has landed in Paris!"[8]

There was instant chaos, the crowd cheering wildly, everybody congratulating everybody else. Of that moment, Byrd was to write that he could think of nothing but how the splendid news would

6. Richard E. Byrd, *Discovery*. G. P. Putnam's Sons, New York, 1935.

7. Byrd, *Skyward*.

8. The news was premature. Lindbergh had just crossed the coastline of France.

arouse enthusiasm for aviation and the wonderful effect on international relations.[9] Pride and patriotism did indeed fill his heart, but he would have been less than human had not a shadow of disappointment chilled his brain. He was a good sport, but a great competitor. And he had lost. He realized instantly that the christening would be anticlimax; he threw his speech away and turned the ceremony into a celebration of Lindbergh's feat. He described the heart-stopping take-off of the *Spirit of St. Louis* and the perils he knew so well that Lindbergh had conquered.

Though Lindbergh's accomplishment undoubtedly took the edge off the *America's* attempted flight, it remained for Clarence Chamberlain to put a real blight on it. Soon after Lindbergh's flight that young man had his Bellanca hauled onto Byrd's hillock and casually stepped into it. Just as he was about to take off, Levine, dressed in a business suit, jumped into the plane beside him and away they went, leaving Mrs. Levine howling hysterically on the field. Thirty-odd hours later Chamberlain and Levine landed in Germany. It made flying to Europe look as easy as a Sunday drive in Central Park.

However, some of the pressure was now off Byrd. The race was over. The only thing that remained was what Byrd has always emphasized, the scientific and safety aspects of his flight. He proposed to Mr. Wanamaker that, in order to be different, he should fly to Rome, which his gasoline consumption records showed was possible. But Wanamaker's heart was set on Paris; he vetoed the suggestion.

In mid-June everything was ready except the weather. The clear skies that had favored Lindbergh and Chamberlain gave place to continuous storms. Night after night Byrd and his crew sat up with Doctor Kimball nearly all night, hoping for a break in the dreary succession of lows that chased each other across the Atlantic. During this trying period, as in their boyhood, Byrd's brothers rallied to support him. Harry, who was by now Governor of Virginia, came and went; Tom was there almost continually. Marie had been with her husband all the time, though she loathed the inevitable publicity.

Finally at one o'clock on June 29, Kimball telephoned that conditions on the flight course, though far from ideal, were possible. Byrd made his decision. Perhaps he should have waited for a better

9. Byrd, *Skyward.*

prognosis. His rationalization was that he felt the transatlantic plane of the future could not wait for ideal conditions and that science would be better served by experiencing stormy weather.[10] He was probably just bone-weary of waiting.

Byrd telephoned the crew to get the plane ready. When he reached the field about 3 A.M., having had one hour's sleep, the *America* was sitting on top of his little hill and the men were working on her. It was a dark and dismal morning, but a large crowd was standing around in the drizzle. As Byrd conferred with his crew, photographers kept flashing final pictures. They showed Byrd and Noville wearing leather jackets and the high-laced field boots and riding pants that officer aviators still affected. Acosta and Balchen were wearing comfortable tweed trousers.

The flyers took their places in the plane. Bert Acosta was at the controls with Balchen beside him. Noville sat just behind them with his hand on the dump valve. Byrd was in the navigator's place behind the great gas tank. As in the polar flight, the *America* was tied to a stake to let the engines reach full power, and Tom Mulroy stood ready to cut the rope.

The engines were warmed up. Acosta opened them up wide to test their condition and synchronization. The plane trembled and rattled like a beach shack in a hurricane. The rope snapped and they were involuntarily off.

After all those weeks of testing and calculating it was, perhaps, foolish to continue that involuntary start without the engines fully revved up. Byrd in the rear could not have been heard if he had ordered the plane back. Apparently he did not. Acosta, who could have stopped, decided to go for broke. The overloaded plane was terribly sluggish on the soggy field. Acosta jockeyed her, trying to break her loose. Fokker tore along beside them in a racing car filled with fire extinguishers. As the gulley at the end of the field rushed at them, Acosta started to raise his hand to signal Noville to dump the gas; then he gave one powerful pull on the wheel that seemed to lift the plane by brute force. Bumping wheels gave place to the blessed smoothness of flight. Clearing the deadly wires by hardly more than Lindbergh had, the *America* was finally off and flying.

It was as miserable a trip as four men ever made. Doctor Kim-

---

10. Richard E. Byrd, "Our TransAtlantic Flight." *National Geographic Magazine*, September, 1927.

ball's crystal ball was badly cracked—the weather was foul. At four hundred feet they went into the overcast; rain clouded the windows, fog swirled beneath them. Byrd got only occasional glimpses of sodden earth or leaden sea by which to calculate drift. At three thousand feet, he found the winds slightly advantageous; but the three motors, at full speed to keep the overladen plane in the air, were gulping gasoline like thirsty dinosaurs. Noville kept pouring gas into the main tank from the extra five-gallon cans and throwing the empties out through the hatch. Byrd communicated with the men up forward by notes stuffed into a can on a clothesline trolley like those in an old-fashioned department store. When he wanted to see them face to face, he had to crawl like a snake on his belly in the curve of the fuselage under the tank. Even then they could not talk because of the roar of the motors.

Over Nova Scotia the weather cleared for the only time in the next twenty-four hours. They flew in bright sunshine over rugged forested hills and hundreds of little, deep blue lakes. As they passed over Halifax, they were still in sunlight above the clouds which concealed the city. The shadow of the plane on their tumbled white surface was ringed by a rainbow, which Byrd thought a good omen.[11] Over Newfoundland the fog rolled in, ruining Byrd's last chance to get a fix on a known point before starting over the ocean. For the next two thousand miles they saw nothing that was beneath them; often they could not even see the tips of the wings.

At about 2 P.M., Noville emptied the last five-gallon can into the tank and checked fuel consumption. He reported to Byrd, who calculated that, at the rate it was going, they had not enough left to reach France if there were even a slight head wind. Here was a command decision: Keep on or turn back? Byrd wrote a note to Noville, asking his opinion. The latter urged him to keep on. This was what Byrd wanted to hear. He staked their lives on his theory that he could find favorable winds if he flew high enough. At the cost of more fuel he ordered the plane to climb; but he did not tell Acosta and Balchen of his worries: "They had enough troubles of their own." [12]

As darkness fell, they were flying nearly two miles high, still in the clouds. It was icy cold. Through the paper-thin walls of the cabin, through windows made of isinglass to save weight, the bitter wind

11. Byrd, *Skyward.*
12. *Ibid.*

poured. Shaking and shivering, moaning and roaring, tossed up and blown down over the invisible chasms and rising columns of an unchartered ocean of air, the plane lurched on. Byrd noted that it was impossible to navigate with no point of reference. The only solid information he had was that they were in the vortex of an Atlantic storm.

Ice began forming on the wings; in minutes it could deform the curve of lift, bringing them down. Byrd urged Acosta to go higher, to clear the clouds at all costs. For brief moments they broke through the ceiling, skimming above the wooly white floor among towers of cloud that reached far above them, plunging through them in darkness so thick they could barely see the wing tips lit by the flickering blue fire from the engines at thirty thousand flashes a minute.

From time to time Byrd crawled forward and took over the controls to let the pilots rest. On one trip he stuck in the passageway and had to tear his sweater off to get through. The gas tank began to leak and he patched it with putty. Once when Balchen was at the wheel, the plane went into a screaming dive that set the primitive blind-flying instruments whirling madly. All sense of balance, of up or down, was lost. The Norwegian pulled out of it, flying in the old-fashioned phrase "by the seat of his pants."

That was probably the worst moment until the last moment. Shortly after the dive, Noville got a radio fix on a streamer somewhere below them, then another on the French liner *Paris*. By crossing the lines on his map Byrd fixed his position—not exactly, but near enough. They had been blown far south of their great-circle course. Byrd decided to ride the wind, heading straight for Cape Finistère on the west coast of France. His maxim was that the shortest route in a plane was the way the wind would take you. Noville made another check of the gas and came up with marvelous news. Due to the tail-down position of the plane, he had miscalculated. They had far more fuel than he thought—enough to take them on to Rome if the Commander so ordered. Byrd scribbled, "Wish I'd known that 18 hours ago." [13]

The second day dawned in opaque gray, cloud-mist streaming past the windows. They were all groggy with fatigue. Balchen caught occasional cat naps in his seat. Acosta crawled aft to doze in the navigator's cramped compartment while Byrd flew the plane. Of them all!

13. *Ibid.*

he was in the best shape. Whatever his cranks and foibles, he had the indomitable spirit of a leader who can keep on and on and on beyond the recognized limits of human endurance.

They had seen neither land nor sea for nearly twenty-four hours when the solid cloud-field broke up. Through the holes they could see an angry ocean. The sun broke through above. Byrd got a sight with his sextant and knew where he was—dead on course for Cape Finistère. Noville at the radio was swamped with messages. All Europe seemed to be calling them.

The second day crawled by. Late in the afternoon they crossed the coast of France, in their eyes the most beautiful landfall since Columbus sighted San Salvador. They flew over Brest and set their course for Paris. But the weather was thick ahead; soon they were back in the soup. Messages from Paris told of low clouds, fog, and rain. Byrd knew he could skirt the disturbance and go on to Rome. But Wanamaker had his heart set on Paris and Byrd felt a moral obligation to his generous backer to make an attempt to reach it. The plane ground along through the overcast. At this point, luck took its worst turn. When Byrd reckoned they were approaching Paris, they saw the lights of a town ahead. He scribbled a jubilant message to Wanamaker: "Paris in sight." It was never sent. As they drew nearer, they saw a revolving light on the coast, which must be at least a hundred miles from Paris. Byrd discovered that the earth-induction compass by which they were steering had suddenly gone haywire; they had flown in a huge circle.

When Byrd communicated this news to Bert Acosta at the wheel, the big man suddenly collapsed. He had been at the controls for the better part of the thirty-seven hours they had been in the air; he was totally spent. He throttled the motors, then pushed them full ahead, and went into a steep bank. As the others watched, horrified, he seemed to collapse like a pricked balloon and fell sideways into the narrow space between the seats. Before he hit the floor he was sound asleep. [14]

Byrd climbed over the back of the seat and grabbed the controls while Balchen and Noville pulled Acosta partly out of the way. Then Balchen took over while Byrd, checking with the magnetic compasses and the chart, calculated the exact position of the lighthouse and gave Balchen the course to Paris. Once more they were buffeted by

14. Charles J. V. Murphy, *op. cit.*

the storm, which by evil chance was centered directly over their objective. The plane bucked and pitched in the rough air; rain slashed against the windows. Byrd checked all the compasses every few minutes. Finally, dead reckoning showed them to be over Paris. They could see nothing, not even a reflection of light in the thick clouds. For half an hour they circled around while people waiting in the rain at Le Bourget Airport heard the sound of their motors. They knew it must be Byrd for no other plane would be up on such a night.

By now the fuel was running low, barely enough left to get back to the coast. Byrd dared not order the plane lower for fear of hitting the surrounding hills or even the Eiffel Tower. The storm had knocked out the radio; Noville could get nothing but the crackle of static. At this point Byrd made a desperate decision, but the only right one—he would try to find that lighthouse again and land on the beach or in the water. He ordered Balchen to head back for the coast.

During that long last leg in their storm-buffeted craft the strain on all of them was tremendous. No one had ever landed a big trimotor land plane in water; expert opinion held that the wheels would trip it into a fatal somersault. Byrd concentrated on navigation, but that thought never left him. They were flying so low that Noville had to reel in the radio antenna for fear of hooking onto something below. Finally the moment came when Byrd told Balchen to start a gentle descent through the fog. Neither he nor they knew for sure whether they were over land or sea. If they crashed into a mountain, they might never know. That long, shallow glide was the worst moment of all. After what seemed an interminable time, they broke out of the overcast at a few hundred feet altitude. Almost directly below them were the lights of a town with the same lighthouse flashing on its headland.

That was probably Byrd's greatest feat of navigation. To fly blind for nearly two hours, circle blind for thirty minutes, and then return through fog and rain to the precise point from which they had started four hours before was nothing short of incredible. Though science and skill played its part, they were not enough to account for it. Pure chance would have called for odds of a thousand to one. Byrd had done similar things before; he would do them again; but this was his most extraordinary feat. Against logic and known human capabilities there still remained his birdlike instinct.

They circled the town of Ver-sur-Mer and flew over the beaches. In the darkness and pouring rain, they could discern nothing of their character. With all its perils, a landing on the sea seemed safest. Byrd told Balchen to head seaward, crossing the beach at a right angle. As he did so Byrd and Noville dropped self-igniting flares in a straight line.

For the last time Balchen swung the *America* in a wide circle and headed straight for the line of bobbing flares on the water. They had waked Acosta, and all hands braced themselves. As they skimmed the crested waves, Balchen cut the motors. A second later the stoutly braced landing gear sheared off with hardly a jar. Then the *America* hit water as solid as cement and skidded to a crashing stop.

Byrd had been looking out of the open window. He was thrown through it and found himself outside the wreck. After hearing the roar of the motors for forty-two hours, the silence was deathly. Noville crawled through the window; Balchen struggled free. Byrd swam around looking for Acosta. He dove back into the flooded cabin to see if Bert was trapped under water. Suddenly he appeared swimming around the submerged cabin. Grunting and groaning, they hauled themselves up on the wing which was level with the water. While they rested briefly, Byrd found that his companions were stone deaf from the continuous roar of the engines. He could hear because he had worn ear protectors most of the time. Bernt Balchen was talking a mile a minute though nobody listened; the rest were silent. Then Noville, carrying out orders given him before the start, ripped open the after compartment, hauled out the rubber boats, and began inflating them. He was so exhausted he kept falling down every moment or so. Byrd got the most precious cargo—the U. S. mail and a scrap of the first American flag as a present for France—out of the compartment in the curve of the wing. They got into the rubber boats and rowed ashore in the rain.

By Byrd's own standards, his transatlantic flight was a failure. Though the following morning, when the tide went out, they were able to haul the *America* up on the beach and rescue all the important documents and observations, that was only partial comfort. So were the great celebrations in honor of Byrd and his companions. Huge crowds greeted them in Paris. The French Government made Byrd an *Officier de la Légion d'Honneur,* a higher class of the decoration than that given Lindbergh.[15] On their return, New York staged one of its spectacular welcomes. Byrd, slim and jaunty in his white uniform blazing with decorations, his curly hair just barely grizzled at the temples—he was thirty-nine that year—his blue-gray eyes sparkling in his tanned face, was an ideal hero. As long as he flew, and dared, and came back alive, people loved him.

But though he told himself that he had accomplished great things, contributing far more than Lindbergh or Chamberlain to scientific knowledge of the conditions of transoceanic flight, he must have known in his heart that he had failed. For he had set out to show that the capability of regular passenger-carrying transatlantic flights was not far away. All he did prove was the exact opposite. He had wanted to prove that meticulous preparation, the most modern equipment available, and scientific navigation greatly increased the safety factor and virtually assured success. What he proved—with an assist from Lindbergh and Chamberlain—was that the most-advanced aeronautical techniques then available were no substitute for good luck.

In this connection it is interesting to read his sober predictions for the future of regular passenger flights over the ocean in *Skyward,* written immediately after the flight of the *America.* They are altogether too pessimistic. Though he foresees the coming of variable wing surfaces to help planes take off and land, his prediction that landing speeds must become slower is far off the mark: The *America* could land at 60 m.p.h. Modern jet liners land at 180 m.p.h. He believed that with the 525 h.p. Wright Cyclone motor, then being tested by Charles L. Lawrence, engines were nearing their ultimate capability and that future progress would be slow. Within fifteen years, similar engines were made that delivered more than 4,000 h.p., and a single jet engine can deliver more than 40,000 h.p. Finally he suggested that, perhaps, the air freight of the future would be carried in airships. His friend C. J. Murphy, who reflected his views, wrote, "For all the tall talk of the optimists, fast and efficient passenger-and-freight service over the Atlantic seems doubtful for a long time at least." [16]

15. Lindbergh was made *Chevalier.*
16. Murphy, *op. cit.* Only eleven years after Murphy wrote those words Pan American Airways inaugurated such a service.

All this shows the sobering effect of Byrd's experience, yet he never lost his enthusiasm for the future of aviation. His feet had hardly touched the sidewalks of New York before he began organizing a flight over the South Pole.

VII · NINETY DEGREES SOUTH

THE ANTARCTIC Expedition was by far the most elaborate Byrd had undertaken. Its budget was estimated at $750,000, but eventually it cost over a million. As before, this trip was sponsored by The National Geographic Society and Byrd had the enthusiastic backing of its President, Doctor Gilbert Grosvenor. Oddly enough he had little more difficulty raising $750,000 than the $140,000 for the north polar flight.

However, Byrd was a very busy man. Not only did he have to travel all over the country giving lectures and meeting possible contributors, he also had to oversee assembling the enormous amount of equipment which filled two ships; and select personnel from about ten thousand young adventurers who wanted to go. Of course, old comrades of his other adventures were his first choice and he made Floyd Bennett, who had apparently recovered from his injuries, his second in command. In addition, many scientists went along to study conditions in the Antarctic about which far less was known than about the northern polar regions.

This expedition was to be no dash for glory like the north polar flight, but a genuine attempt to enlarge man's knowledge of an ice-age continent as large as the United States and Mexico together. Byrd sought out meteorologists, geologists, and specialists in electrical phenomena, zoology, oceanography, and, of course, geography.

Each expert made an agenda of the scope of his work and a list of the instruments he would need. Byrd saw to it that these were provided.

One unusual member of the expedition was Eagle Scout Paul Siple.[1] Because Byrd loved youth, he sponsored a contest to choose a Boy Scout to go with him to Antarctica. Paul, a big, handsome nineteen-year-old, was one of six finalists. He was selected as the winner by the Selection Committee and Byrd heartily endorsed their choice. It was the beginning of a friendship that became ever closer and endured until Byrd died while Paul was again in Antarctica.

The most important single piece of equipment for the expedition was, of course, the plane. The South Pole is located on a vast plateau roughly 10,000 feet high, surrounded by peaks up to 19,000 feet high, encased in eternal ice which is 5,000 feet thick on parts of the plateau. Its weather, therefore, is far fiercer that that of the Arctic. Sudden blizzards driven by hurricane-force winds sweep over it even during its brief summer, and temperatures average more than forty degrees lower than at the North Pole, sometimes reaching 100° below zero. Compared to this contemplated flight, Byrd's north polar trip had been a pleasure jaunt. He needed a far more advanced plane to have even a fair chance of making it.

Fortunately one had been designed. The Ford tri-motor was the first commercially viable plane ever built. An all-metal, high-wing monoplane[2] its range, useful load, and reliability outdistanced everything then on the market. In fact, some of those old tin geese flew right on into the Jet Age. The first Fords for commercial use were designed to be powered by three Wright Whirlwinds. Since Edsel Ford was again one of his principal backers, Byrd worked closely with Ford's engineers and with Charles L. Lawrence of Wright on a Ford especially designed for his purpose. The nose motor was the new 525 h.p. Cyclone, with Whirlwinds for the wing motors. This gave the machine much greater lift and about 10 m.p.h. more speed than the commercial model. Its wing spread was 70 feet; length 49 feet 10 inches, and it could lift a total weight of 15,000 pounds.

Byrd took along two other planes to back up the Ford: a Fokker Universal monoplane powered by a single 425 h.p. Pratt and Whit

1. The late Doctor Paul A. Siple.
2. Wings and fuselage were made of corrugated duralumin, landing gear and bracing of steel.

ney Wasp, and a smaller Fairchild folding-wing monoplane, also powered by a Wasp.

His next great concern was the ships he needed to transport the expedition to the edge of the Great Ice Barrier that partly rimmed the shores of Antarctica, a floating wall of ice hundreds of feet thick. On the advice of Amundsen, he cabled Tromsee, Norway, and bought the *Samson,* an auxiliary bark with square sails on fore and main masts, fore-and-aft rig on the mizzen. Launched in 1882 as an Arctic sealer, the *Samson* was very strongly built with a hull of spruce and oak, with oaken ribs spaced inches apart, and sheathed with heavy planking inside and out. The wooden garboards along her keel were 41 inches thick. Her wedge-shaped hull was designed so that if caught in the ice, she would be lifted up by its pressure instead of cracked like an egg. The *Samson* was a little ship, 170 feet long and 31 feet beam, rated at 515 tons.[3] Her auxiliary power was a 200-h.p. coal-burning steam engine, which could drive her at 6 knots on a good day. As Byrd remarked, "We were fortunate that an engine built in 1882 would run at all." [4] He christened her the *City of New York.*

Byrd's second ship was a little old iron freighter of 800 tons. She also had a 200-h.p. engine which sent her merrily along at 9 knots. Byrd named her for his mother, the *Eleanor Bolling.* In addition, two splendid Norwegian whalers, the *Sir James Clark Ross* and the *C. A. Larsen,* helped to transport personnel and supplies as far as Dunedin, New Zealand.

Purchasing the supplies became a full-time job for a staff, working under Byrd's personal supervision in offices loaned by the Hotel Biltmore in New York. They procured such items as boots and parkas of reindeer skin, and polar-bear pants from Greenland; sleeping bags, woolen underwear and socks for ninety men; a big radio transmitter and three knock-down steel towers for the aerials, presented by Adolph Ochs of the New York *Times;* a radio beacon; portable radios; huge quantities of gasoline and oil; Eskimo sleds; 93 Husky and Malamute dogs from Alaska; and a Ford snowmobile. (The dogs, incidentally, beat the snowmobile all hollow.) To give some idea of the quantities of provisions there were 5 tons of beef, 2 tons of

3. Captain Cooke's ship, *Resolution,* was larger.
4. Richard Evelyn Byrd, *Little America.* G. P. Putnam's Sons, New York, 1930.

ham, 500 cases of eggs, 15 tons of flour and all sorts of other foods by the ton. A ton of cooking utensils was assembled, in addition to 150 cans of face cream, 1,200 sticks of shaving cream, 8,840 cakes of soap and tons of medical supplies.[5]

Naturally, the money ran out, and Byrd went begging for $250,000 more to get them started. During the year Byrd was organizing the Antarctic Expedition, he allowed himself hardly more than four hours' sleep a night. It was a rare and happy day when he could spend a few hours with Marie and his children in their comfortable old-fashioned brick house in Boston. Marie was as dedicated as he. Though her heart must have sunk each time he announced a new venture, she never tried to stop him. This was his way of life; without it he would not have been the man she had married and loved so dearly. So she accepted the anxieties and helped in every way she could. When her husband was away, Marie had the final word on the business affairs of the expedition. Though they saw him so rarely, his children, especially Dick, Jr., utterly adored him; and he them.

During that strenuous year of preparation Byrd was struck by a very personal tragedy. In the spring of 1928, two German-Irish transatlantic flyers were marooned on Greenly Island off Labrador. Though he was feeling far from well, Floyd Bennett offered to fly a relief plane there. When he reached Murray Bay, Province Quebec, he collapsed with pneumonia and was taken to a hospital in Quebec. Dropping everything, Byrd caught the first train to Canada. For the last thirty-six hours of Bennett's life, Byrd sat almost constantly in his hospital room. When Floyd Bennett died, Byrd lost the dearest friend he ever had. Because of the perils and glory they had shared, and the remarkable affinity which made them think alike and, in moments of stress, act in concert without having to communicate, they shared the ultimate degree of friendship, complete and utter trust in each other.

Another sadness came that summer. Byrd's friendly rival, Roald Amundsen, was lost in the Arctic as the big Italian dirigible *Italia* went down on the polar ice pack.

The *City of New York* sailed from her namesake city on August 25, 1928. The *Eleanor Bolling* got away shortly afterward. Another con-

---

5. Richard Evelyn Byrd, "Conquest of the Antarctic." *National Geographic Magazine*, August, 1930.

tingent left in the *Ross;* and Byrd, with the final group of men and his fox terrier, Igloo, sailed from San Pedro, California, in the *Larsen* on October 10. During the voyage to New Zealand, Byrd charmed Captain Nilsen of the *Larsen* into agreeing to tow the *City* through the ice pack provided she was able to rendezvous with him by late November. The captain did not want to delay longer than that because every day lost hunting whales meant a loss of $30,000 worth of whale oil. It was a wonderful break for Byrd, for it not only meant that the ice-breaking power of the big Norwegian whaler— 17,000 tons, 8,000 h.p.—would clear the way for his little ship; it also meant a great saving in coal which would free space for precious cargo in the *City.*

There was a mad rush to reload the ships at Dunedin, but try as they might they could not get away before December 2. Towed by the *Bolling,* the *City* was literally loaded to the gunwales; her holds were cram-jammed; her decks littered with boxes and gasoline drums; the Fairchild was lashed down between the masts; and the howling dogs were in crates on her poop deck and cabin tops.

As the ships struck the high latitudes, rolling in the great seas, half the amateur crew of the *City* were seasick. A fifty-knot gale drove green water aboard. The *Bolling,* hidden by the huge waves, staggered on. The steel towline alternately sagged, then tautened with a terrific jerk. Once, the *City,* coming up fast under sail, almost crashed into the *Bolling.* Finally the towline broke. When the wind dropped, mist closed in. Through it, Byrd could see a procession of weirdly shaped icebergs stretching along the horizon.

In spite of the very real perils, the *City* did rendezvous with the *Larsen,* on December 10 because Captain Nilsen waited for her at the edge of the pack. Surrounded by floe and pack ice in heavy seas, she took on coal from the *Bolling,* which then started back to New Zealand for more supplies. A message from the *Ross* stated that she was stuck fast in the pack, which was unusually heavy that year. While the *Larsen* and the *City* drifted with the ice, the *Larsen's* chaser boats harpooned an enormous blue whale that weighed 80 tons.

Finally, just after midnight on December 15, the anniversary of Amundsen's discovery of the South Pole, the *Larsen* pushed into the ice pack with the *City* bobbing along behind her like a fishing skiff. Their way was, of course, lighted by the southern midnight sun. The powerful whaler would nuzzle up to a floe, then suddenly go full ahead, crushing it, while the *City* followed, hoping to get through before the ice closed in behind. This stop-and-go procedure was extremely dangerous. Captain Frederick C. Melville of the *City* had to be constantly alert to avoid a rear-end collision. The weather was clear and at midnight, when the sun was lowest, sky, air, and ice were suffused in marvelous shades of rose, gold, green, and crimson.

After five days of slamming through the pack, they passed into the blue water of the Ross Sea between a range of flat-topped icebergs, some of them 10 miles long. The *Larsen* cast off the tow and, tooting farewell, went off after a school of whales. The *City*, under sail, crossed the 180th meridian of longitude—the International Date Line—on December 26, which thereby became December 25 again, giving them two Christmases in one year to celebrate. But the real celebration was the second one when they sighted the Great Ice Barrier floating on the sea, guarding that part of the Antarctic Continent with perpendicular cliffs of ice from thirty to two hundred feet high. After a brief stop at Discovery Inlet, the *City* coasted along the Barrier toward the Bay of Whales which, following Amundsen's advice, Byrd had selected for their base. The wind conditions there were comparatively good for aircraft and it was in the midst of unexplored territory. The bay was well named, for when the ice finally went out, Byrd saw eighty of those great creatures in one day.

Meanwhile, he organized the command structure, making geologist, Doctor Lawrence M. Gould, his second in command. He had not had the heart to appoint one since Bennett's death. Bernt Balchen was put in charge of the aviation unit. His fellow pilots were Captain Alton N. Parker, Harold G. June, and Dean C. Smith. In addition, Byrd posted a list of safety rules to which he had given a great deal of study. Few of his men had any knowledge of the treacherous nature of Antarctic conditions—the sudden fierce storms; the deadly crevasses in the ice cap, often concealed by snow bridges that collapsed under the weight of a man; the danger of floes detaching themselves from the bay ice and drifting out to sea; and a dozen other special conditions on which he had made himself an authority by hours of research and long talks with men like Amundsen who had experienced them. These safety rules were so rigidly enforced that Byrd came to be considered a martinet, but because of them not a man was lost.

On December 28, the *City* came to the Bay of Whales. Byrd had hoped against hope that the ice would have begun to break up as it usually did in the Antarctic summer. But the bay was still covered by a solid mass of thick ice. There was nothing for it but to moor the *City* to its edge by special, sharp-fluked ice anchors. The ship was greeted by a stately flock of emperor penguins, bowing a courteous welcome, and crowds of playful Adélie penguins. There were also herds of somnolent seals, who would not even wake when men came to kill them as food for dogs and humans.

Moored far out in the bay, the *City* was at least eight miles from any possible base. Byrd immediately set out on skis with half a dozen men and two dog teams to look for a place for his main base. They crossed the heavily ridged ice of the bay and found a place where the Barrier was broken by a gentle slope of snow. Once on the ice cap, they went looking for traces of Framheim which had been Amundsen's camp when he discovered the South Pole. No sign of it remained. That night, they camped in the dead stillness of a rare windless Antarctic night. On January 1, 1929, Byrd found another slope up the Barrier. Beyond it in the ice cap was a huge hollow or basin, about a mile in diameter, which he instantly decided was the place for his base. Then and there he named it "Little America."

The next day they began unloading the *City* onto the bay ice. Planks were laid from her bulwarks, and down them poured the heterogeneous assortment of supplies. A trail to Little America was made and marked with bright orange flags. Seven dog teams were assembled to ferry the stuff the eight miles from the ship to the base. The dogs went wild with joy at the prospect of work. For the men, it was hard physical labor, which became rather risky when the bay ice began to break up. As it did so, the *City* was moved closer to shore. Byrd toured around in an outboard whaleboat, looking for leads of open water. On one trip he and Paul Siple were actually chased by a herd of killer whales and leaped to safety on the ice as the whales shot under the boat.[6]

The Fairchild was unloaded, assembled on the ice, and named *The Stars and Stripes*. On January 15, Byrd, with June and Smith copiloting, made his first exploratory flight. As the light plane fairly leaped off the ice, a magnificent prospect of the rolling Barrier opened up before him. That was a short flight, but on January 27,

6. Dr. Siple in conversation with the author.

with Balchen piloting, Byrd took the Fairchild on a long sweep over
the mainland, passing the small Alexandra Mountains, discovered by
Captain Robert Falcon Scott; on over the terraced glaciers, dropping
pale blue to the sea; through snow squalls and clouds until they
sighted a superb mountain peak of slate-gray, bare rock never seen by
anyone before. As Balchen headed the plane toward it, other sharp
peaks appeared. For the first time Byrd knew the thrill of discovering new land. He named the range the Rockefeller Mountains after
John D. Rockefeller, Jr., who had helped him so much; the area between them and the Alexandra Mountains, he named Marie Byrd
Land. He had a lot of fun immortalizing people he was fond of by
giving their names to places he discovered—Floyd Bennett Bay,
Chamberlain Harbor, Hal Flood Bay and, in fond memory of a
friendly French Village, Ver-sur-Mer Inlet. He claimed all the
newly discovered land for the United States.

Good news awaited him back at Little America—the *Bolling* had
returned from New Zealand with a large cargo. By now the *City* was
almost unloaded; the dog teams had transported several hundred
tons of material to Little America, running an incredible thirty-two
miles, or two round trips, a day. Two specially designed, prefabricated wooden houses had been built in troughs dug in the névé snow [7]
of the Barrier; aerial masts were going up. The next day, the *Bolling*
sheered through the last of the bay ice and was moored at the foot of
the Barrier with the *City* beside her. Among many other things, she
brought the Ford, which Byrd had christened the *Floyd Bennett;*
the Fokker, and 7,500 gallons of aviation gasoline.

During his surveys of the Barrier, Byrd had often seen enormous
pieces of ice break off it and float away as icebergs. It was far from an
ideal dock, but he had to risk it. While the unloading was going forward, there was a crack of doom. Thousands of tons of Barrier ice fell
into the bay. Fortunately only part of it crashed down on the deck of
the *Bolling;* had it hit her fairly, she would have been obliterated.
The vessel heeled over so far under the weight of snow and ice that
Byrd thought she would capsize. But she held just short of her critical angle. Benjamin Roth was flung into the heaving, freezing water
amid great chunks of clashing ice. Arthur Harrison was left hanging
on a rope from the remaining edge of the Barrier.

7. This eternal snow has a crystalline consistency like coarse hand-packed
sand.

Tremendous confusion ensued. Benny Roth, who could not swim, was floating in the bay, using two cakes of ice under his arms as water wings. Because of the *Bolling*'s heavy list, none of her life boats could be lowered. The chief radio operator, Malcolm Hanson, using his head, lowered the tiny captain's gig from the stern davits of the *City*. Byrd in his heavy clothing dived overboard followed by another member of the crew. Arthur Creagh, the cook, bent on fame, tore out of the galley, shouting to Hanson, "I'm going with you."

Hanson yelled, "Stop! There isn't room." But Creagh slid down the falls into the gig and Hanson went overboard. Now there were four people swimming around in water so cold that a man could live in it only a few minutes. Somehow they were all hauled out; encased in solid ice, they rushed into the galley. Harrison, too, was rescued from his precarious rope. No one even caught cold! [8]

By February 2, 1929, the *Bolling* had been unloaded and she sailed to New Zealand for another cargo. She did not return that year because the ice pack closed in. A twenty-seven-dog team hauled the fuselage of the *Floyd Bennett* to Little America. A fourteen-dog team dragged the wings on a sledge. She was berthed for the winter in a huge igloo—a hangar made of blocks of snow.

On February 22, the *City* was ready to sail. To keep her any longer would risk her being frozen in and smashed like a rotten watermelon by ice pressure. Every man of the eighty-three members of the expedition wanted to stay through the winter, but only forty-two could remain. Byrd stated later that one of the hardest things he had to do was to order the others back to the comforts of Dunedin.[9] At least one of them wept when he heard he could not stay. Next day, in the dusky morning light, with all sails set and black smoke pouring from her funnel, the *City of New York* moved slowly off into the frost smoke caused by zero air hitting the warmer sea.

There was a great deal still to do before the Antarctic night made it impossible to accomplish much out of doors. Most of the supplies from the *Bolling* had yet to be transported from the bay ice to *Little*

8. Doctor Siple in conversation with the author. The account in *Little America* purposely leaves out Byrd's dive into the bay.

9. *Ibid.*

America and that village on the ice cap had to be completed. Meanwhile parties of men with dog teams were sent out to establish caches of supplies on the way to the Rockefeller Mountains and the route to the South Pole, marking their trails with flags at half-mile intervals. On March 8, Lawrence Gould took a party in the Fokker (which Byrd had named the *Virginia*), on a geological survey of the Rockefeller Range. At the base of the mountains they were pinned down by a blizzard driven by a 120-mile gale. Though the *Virginia* was well anchored, the wind picked her up like an old newspaper, carried her a mile and completely smashed her.

When the weather cleared, Byrd, in the Fairchild, rescued Gould's party. While the plane was taking Gould's people home, Byrd, Harrison, and Gould spent two nights in sleeping bags on the open ice cap at 25° below zero.

Little America became the most amazing habitation in the world. There was the Main Administration Building, Mess Hall, Norwegian House, Block House, Magnetic Station, Meteorology Station, Photographic House, Biology House, Radio House, Medical House, General Supply House, Aviation Hangars; also a machine shop, dog shelters, and innumerable caches of supplies. By April 19, when the red ball of the sun danced along the horizon and vanished until August, all these buildings had disappeared under the snow. The only things to be seen above the smooth white surface were the radio towers, some stovepipes, ventilators, and a flagpole.

Under that immaculate shield, life teemed like a gopher colony. All the buildings and supply caches were connected by a maze of man-size tunnels, which formed a subway system over a quarter of a mile long beneath the snow. The main buildings were crowded with tiers of bunks in which forty-two men lived in astonishing amity. Since it was far too cold to bathe, their smell must have been appalling, though numerous chroniclers are too delicate to mention it. Splendid beards flourished because of the difficulty of shaving. Byrd kept his face clean, but allowed his hair to grow shoulder length. Combed back from his forehead and ears, falling in smooth glossy waves, it made him look like a young medieval philosopher.

He was the only one who had a room to himself; it was just behind the library in the Administration Building. There he read and worked with yeoman Charles Loquin, who acted as his secretary. Once every day, when it was at all possible, he would poke his head into the library and invite one or two men to go for a walk. Keeping fit was a necessary preoccupation. In heavy furs over wool, and with face coverings shaped like catchers' masks with breathing tubes, they would tramp over the Barrier in temperatures of —55°F. Byrd believed that the reason Amundsen's party had been in such poor shape when the spring finally came was that they had slept with heaters going full blast. Not only was this unhealthy, there was always the danger of fire and of carbon-monoxide poisoning from kerosene fumes. Therefore, he ordered all heaters and fires put out every night except the one in the library. He also had the doors to the exit tunnels opened, so by morning, if one could call it that, the temperature within the houses fell to —35°.

For relaxation, the men read, played Byrd's old-fashioned Victrola in the library—"The Bells of St. Mary's" was the favorite record—and listened to the radio telling of an almost unimaginable world where summer temperatures in New York hit 94°. Bridge was a popular game. Byrd is said to have won thirty thousand points in one night—but that night was four months long.[10]

Practical jokes, of which Byrd dreamed up some beauties, also enlivened things occasionally, as did the arrival of puppies, which had to be taken into comparative warmth to survive. In all but the worst weather the adult dogs slept in unheated shelters at temperatures of —50°.

Some of the men found other entertainment in the alcohol supply. The expedition, starting as it did in the depths of prohibition, was basically dry, but there were in the doctor's stores medical alcohol and a large quantity of grain alcohol to be used as a preservative for biological specimens. It became a game, and a source of needed relief, to pilfer the alcohol. Young Paul Siple, who was tremendously interested in biology, had preserved a rare fish in alcohol which convivial spirits soon drank with relish, leaving the fish unprotected.

In despair, Siple asked Doctor Coleman what he could use that was not potable. Coleman gave him some very strong lemon extract. But again Siple's fish found itself high and dry. At Coleman's suggestion Paul then put it in formaldehyde. That, no one drank.[11]

10. Doctor Siple to the author.
11. Dr. Siple to the author. On his second expedition to Antarctica, Byrd, realizing the men needed some relaxation, took along two thousand gallons of whiskey.

However, all was not fun and good fellowship. Inevitably tensions built up. Men cooped up under such rigorous conditions were bound to get on one another's nerves. There were quarrels and factions were formed which have never been mentioned in any of the books, though Pilot Dean Smith did fire some unjustifiable barbs at Commander Byrd in his autobiography.[12] Smith was a superb pilot of the old school who did, in fact, fly by the seat of his pants. He knew and cared little about the maintenance of aircraft and less about navigation, so he could neither understand nor appreciate Byrd's rigid safety rules and precautions or his extraordinary expertise as a navigator. One of the wild breed of barnstorming pilots, he deeply resented the Commander's strict discipline, and took his resentment out in some very disagreeable innuendos, among them the absurd implication that Byrd was so fearful of flying on a comparatively minor expedition that he kept a plane waiting with its engine running for eight hours while he prayed in his room.

Smith appears to have been particularly irritated by Byrd's absolute control over all news emanating from Little America. Every member of the expedition was required to sign a contract not to write or lecture about it for a period of two years after their return to the United States. This was only reasonable, since Byrd relied on his lectures and books to pay off the huge debts and supply funds for future expeditions. However, Byrd's insistence on censoring every dispatch to the outside world was unnecessarily autocratic. He was extremely sensitive to public opinion and inclined to be suspicious of people who implied that Little America was anything less than Utopian. Smith states that Russell Owen, the New York *Times* correspondent, was so shocked by Byrd's censoring of his dispatches that he took to his bed for several days.[13]

Smith was not the only man who regarded Byrd as a martinet. Some of the unpaid adventurers from civilian life found him equally irritating. His natural aloofness and meticulous attention to detail combined with his assumption of supreme authority sat ill with them, unaccustomed as they were to naval discipline. Thus an anti-Byrd faction grew up in Little America, at swords points with the Commander's loyal supporters.

Though Byrd never mentioned it in any of his writings, he was

12. Dean Smith, *By the Seat of My Pants*. Atlantic Little Brown, Boston, 1961.
13. *Ibid.*

fully aware of this situation. He handled it by avoiding any direct confrontation with the malcontents because, as they were not bound by the Articles of War, it might have led to a loss of dignity and prestige essential to successful command. Instead he conveyed his orders or rebukes through other loyal officers of the expedition. Since the loyalists were in a large majority, there was nothing much the disaffected could do but grumble. No doubt there would have been some extremely bitter recriminations had things gone wrong. But the remarkable success of the expedition and the fact that Byrd brought every man back alive stilled them.

So much for pleasure and petty quarrels—mostly it was hard work, and lots of it. W. C. Haines, the weatherman of the North Pole flight, made an intensive study of Antarctic meteorology, sending up at regular intervals hot-air balloons—kept aloft by a fat candle under their bags—and big box kites. In the nonmagnetic hut, the physicists tended their instruments, gaining important information about the mysterious currents that course through the earth, while the radiomen and electronic specialists studied the peculiar Antarctic conditions and the Aurora Australis, the Down Under version of the northern lights. And everybody worked hard at preparing for the great moment when the returning sun would again make possible the business of exploration. In addition, just by observation, a great deal of knowledge was gained concerning the effect of intense cold on all sorts of material from kerosene, which froze solid at $-55°$, to the human body.

Byrd closely followed all these varied activities. Though he knew less about meteorology than the weathermen, less about magnetism and electronics than the physicists and engineers, less also than the other specialists, his over-all knowledge of the entire operation and of Antarctic conditions thereby became more comprehensive than that of any other man on earth. With each addition to the sum of human knowledge, his enthusiasm for the purely scientific aspect of the expedition soared.

August 22 was the great day when the sun came back to Little America. So eager were the men to see it, that on the previous day some of them had laboriously climbed the steel radio masts to get a preview. The red ball of light and hope, skipping momentarily above the horizon, touched off a great celebration. Byrd ordered the American flag hoisted, followed by the Norwegian and British emblems in memory of the great explorers who had come that way—of Amundsen and Shackelton, Nansen and Captain Scott.

Though the weather got worse,[14] everyone got even busier. The main preoccupation was getting ready for the sledge-borne geological expedition to the foot of the towering Queen Maud Mountains where the Axel Heiberg Glacier swept down a gorge from the ten-thousand-foot-high South Polar Plateau. Larry Gould proposed to climb fifteen-thousand-foot Mount Fridtjof Nansen whose steep sides were bare of snow and therefore accessible to geological examination. With the support party, that expedition consisted of eleven men and ten sledges loaded with 5,368 pounds, 14 ounces of supplies and equipment.[15]

The supporting party left on October 15, very early in the Antarctic spring. On the gray afternoon of November 4, 1929, Larry Gould with five men and three nine-dog teams hit the trail which the advance group had marked by orange flags placed a quarter of a mile apart. When they were finally off, Byrd could concentrate all his energy on the South Pole flight.

Unlike the Arctic flight, the "stunt" aspect of this venture was completely submerged in Byrd's mind by its scientific value. In part this was due to lack of competition, but mainly it was because of his increasing maturity and interest in pure science. In addition, the South Pole on its high plateau, surrounded by as-yet-undiscovered mountain ranges, was far more interesting than the flat ice of the Arctic Ocean. Of course the "stunt" had publicity value, which he needed to raise money to pay off debts and to finance future expeditions, and he still enjoyed the kudos it would bring him, but these had become secondary considerations.

Because of this scientific interest, he insisted on taking Captain Ashley C. McKinley and his heavy photographic equipment even

14. The average temperature in September was —44° against an August average of —27.8°.

15. Richard Evelyn Byrd, "Conquest of the Antarctic." *National Geographic Magazine*, August, 1930.

though the added weight—which he calculated to be about six hundred pounds [16]—would preclude a nonstop round-trip flight to the Pole. The alternative was a dangerous landing on unknown snows, to establish a depot at which they could stop and gas up on the way home.

The *Floyd Bennett* was hauled out of its sunken igloo by its own roaring center motor and most of the remaining men straining on a block and tackle. All three motors had received constant care during the long night, but they required complete overhauling and replacement of all the parts that seemed to have deteriorated.

On November 19, after a series of test flights, Byrd took her on the base-laying flight, loaded with 14,300 pounds. Dean Smith was the pilot, Harold June, co-pilot and radio man. Byrd, of course, was navigating and McKinley was aboard with his camera. Because of the proximity of the South Magnetic Pole, ordinary compasses were as useless as they had been in the Arctic. Byrd, once again, relied mainly on the Bumpstead sun compass.

For the first two hours he followed the Grosvenor Trail [17] made by the geological party. From two thousand feet they could see the orange trail flags zigzagging around crevasses and crazy ice formations. About two hundred miles out, they passed over the geologists struggling through deep snow. In the rough going, men were hitched to the sledges with the straining dogs. Byrd told Smith to bring the plane down to three hundred feet, and they dropped mail and supplies.

Soon after, mountains rose from the flat plain of the Barrier ice. As they drew nearer, "Peak after peak sprang into view until the horizon [ahead] was one immense gallery of mountains . . . like jealous ramparts guarding the solitude of the Pole." [18] Between the mountains, ice-blue glaciers pushed down to the Barrier plain. Byrd, with Amundsen's rough maps spread out on the chart table, identified the Axel Heiberg in a pass to the Polar Plateau, and told Smith to land near the foot of the glacier. They dropped four smoke bombs in a row to give them wind direction and perspective. (The white

16. McKinley plus his hundred-pound camera plus his survival food and other equipment in case of a forced landing.

17. Named after Gilbert Grosvenor, President of The National Geographic Society.

18. Byrd, "Conquest of the Antarctic," *op. cit.*

refracted light of the snowfields can fool a pilot into "landing" fifty feet in the air.) Smith circled and flew along the line of smoke. This was a chancy moment, for if the snow were not as smooth as it looked, the expedition would end in a crash. With infinite care Smith eased the heavily loaded plane toward the surface. She touched down in a series of appalling bumps, but nothing broke.

Quickly they set up the little depot: several hundred gallons of fuel, 350 pounds of food, a gasoline stove, and miscellaneous supplies. Byrd sentimentally named the base for Josephine Ford. Then, as quickly as possible, they took off and headed for home. It looked like a nice easy flight in clear sunshine, but there had been a miscalculation due to a leaky fuel pump. About one hundred miles from Little America they ran out of gas. All three engines stopped dead. Smith was faced with a dead-stick landing on an area of the Barrier the dog teams had reported was impossible for planes. Down they came, eyes strained to pick the smoothest surface. They hit hard, bumped, and rocked madly along over the undulating ice; then came to rest undamaged. Byrd noted simply, "We were lucky." [19]

After they had spent a miserable thirty-six hours in a tent on the ice, Bernt Balchen and Carl Petersen turned up in the Fairchild. Having guessed the trouble, they had with them one hundred gallons of gas in five-gallon cans. Within a couple of hours they were all safely back home (Little America was by then very much home). The next step was the big one.

The *Floyd Bennett* took off for the South Pole at 3:29 P.M. on November 28, 1929. Aboard were Bernt Balchen at the controls, Harold June, Captain McKinley, and Commander Byrd. Loaded with extra gasoline in five-gallon containers, 750 pounds of food for six weeks, a sledge, survival gear of all sorts, and McKinley's photographic equipment, she weighed approximately 15,000 pounds. The last thing Byrd put aboard her was an American flag wrapped around a stone from Floyd Bennett's grave.

The weather was cloudy, but Larry Gould had radioed from the geologists' camp near the Queen Maud Range, "Perfect visibility; no clouds anywhere." At Little America, Bill Haines said, "Things

19. *Ibid.*

could be more nearly perfect, but you had better go now. Another chance may not come." [20]

Despite its heavy load, the *Floyd Bennett* took off easily enough. Byrd looked down affectionately at the shouting, dancing men along the runway who had cheerfully endured all the hardships and were having none of the fun. The plane was out of their sight in thirty seconds. Clouds above, white snow below obliterated the horizon. In Byrd's expressive phrase, "It was like flying in a bowl of milk." [21] He picked up the faint broken thread of the Grosvenor Trail. A southeasterly wind pushing them off course cut down their speed and fuel reserve.

Soon blue sky showed ahead; then the Queen Maud Range. Less than four hours out, they passed over the geologists, who had taken twenty-four days to get this far. A bag with supplies, mail, and photographs was parachuted down to them, and Gould radioed Byrd his exact latitude and longitude. The *Floyd Bennett* was now about one hundred miles from the Polar Plateau. Balchen gave the engines full throttle and began to climb. The passes through the mountain rampart were over ten thousand feet high. There were two: the Axel Heiberg Glacier, which Amundsen had used and mapped, and the Liv Glacier. Here was Byrd's first command decision: Should he go through the first, the known, or try the second which, from where he sat at nine thousand feet, looked wider and a little lower? He decided to tackle the unknown.

The plane was filled with violent activity—June dumping the last five-gallon cans of gas into the cabin tank and throwing them out through the hatch in the floor; Balchen coaxing the plane upward (she was close to her ceiling); McKinley hauling his camera from side to side, poking it through holes cut in the cabin, and shooting the mountains towering above them in fantastic shapes, glittering ice, or bare, black vertical pinnacles.

As they neared the bluish ice slide of the Liv Glacier, looking like an enormous frozen waterfall, the plane began to mush; she had reached the limit of altitude and was still below the top of the pass. Balchen yelled above the motors, "It's drop two hundred or go back!"

Two hundred pounds of what? Gasoline, which they needed to

20. *Ibid.*
21. *Ibid.*

reach the Pole, or food for survival if downed. There was never a doubt of Byrd's decision, the leopard had not changed his spots. He ordered June to drop a 150-pound bag of food. The plane bounded upward, tossed about in the violent currents from the peaks like a mosquito in a gale. Another thousand feet and she felt mushy again. Balchen yelled for another drop. Over went 100 pounds of possible survival, scattered, smashed on the rocks below.

Now they were between peaks that mounted to fifteen thousand feet, the black walls of Nansen on their left, Mount Fisher on their right; engines roaring full out in the rarefied air; Balchen jockeying with all his skill, fighting the down drafts for a few feet more altitude. It looked as though they would not make it. Byrd states that he would have dropped no more food.[22] It would be reasonable to doubt that. But he did not have to. The *Floyd Bennett* staggered over the pass clearing it by 500 feet. The level Polar Plateau, inclining gently upward, lay clear ahead.

Byrd set the course due south almost on the line followed by Amundsen. But the Norwegian on foot could have seen at most 50 square miles, whereas in a plane at 10,000 feet the range of vision according to Byrd, can be 50,000 square miles. A new mountain range appeared far to their right, until then unseen by any man. McKinley mapped it with his camera. Because of the head wind they were only making 90 m.p.h., and the motion of the plane made the use of the sextant difficult. But at half an hour after midnight Byrd got a good shot at the sun that placed them fifty miles from the Pole. He took a second observation which confirmed the first. But clouds were approaching.

At 1:14 Greenwich time, Byrd sent a radio message to Little America that they were over the South Pole. Gravely they opened the trapdoor and dropped the flag-wrapped stone from Floyd Bennett's grave. Then they performed evolutions similar to those over the North Pole, flying right, left, and around. The mountain ranges had long since been left behind, and the flat snowfield extending to infinity looked not unlike the featureless Arctic ice except that it was ninety-six hundred feet high. The plane, lightened because of the fuel it had used, was flying at eleven thousand feet above sea level but only fourteen hundred feet above the ground.

The flight home was a canter. With a tail wind, they stormed

22. *Ibid.*

down the 168th meridian. As they neared the mountains, clouds were forming around them. Balchen opened the throttles wide and streaked for the passes at 125 m.p.h. They squeaked through ahead of trouble and glided down the Axel Heiberg Glacier between Ruth Gade Mountain and Dom Pedro Christophersen. Beyond the pass Byrd made a detour to photograph more unmapped territory, then swung back and, without too much difficulty, found their cache at the foot of Axel Heiberg. June, who had been there before, landed them smoothly.

Then it was gas up fast and get on with it. Pouring two hundred gallons of fuel into the high wing tanks was heavy labor for exhausted men. It took an hour and thirteen minutes. By then the clouds were chasing them over the mountains. They took off light and fast, and dallying no more, headed straight for Little America. Byrd hit it dead on the nose. At the sound of their engines, men came tumbling out of their burrows like rabbits on a rampage, to watch the *Floyd Bennett* wheel over the Administration Building. Sun flashing on her corrugated wings, she came in steady and sweet. Snow dust spurted from the skis as she slid to a stop. It was 10:08, November 29, 1929, G.M.T.

All that remained was a clean-up operation. With Captain Parker, Harold June, and McKinley, Byrd made a long exploratory flight over the ice sheet at the eastern edge of the Ross Sea on December 4. McKinley mapped the mountains they had discovered in the Fairchild the year before. Far to the east, spreading northward and southward along the coast line, they found another tremendous range which McKinley also mapped. A surprising discovery was a chain of small lakes, their sparkling blue water unfrozen for some unknown reason. Lack of gas forced them to return before reaching the end of the mountain range, but they had mapped 150 miles of hitherto undiscovered territory which now belonged to America. The round trip flight was over seven hundred miles.

In December, Paul Siple laboriously chopped a hole through eighteen feet of ice at the foot of the Barrier about a hundred yards from Little America. When he got through to water, he dropped a scoop like a clam shell fastened to a mile of piano wire on a reel. The line went out and out finally hitting bottom at nearly sixteen hundred feet. This showed that the great, solid-seeming Ice Barrier was floating on deep water. In fact, had there been a severe enough storm to crack it loose, Little America might have floated out to sea on an iceberg.[23]

On January 19, the geological party appeared over the southern slope of the Barrier led by George Thorne and Larry Gould, tall and gaunt, with a long black beard under his peaked woolen cap and a red and white sash around his waist. His expedition had traveled a total of over thirteen hundred miles by sledge, climbed parts of the Queen Maud Range, and detoured to Marie Byrd Land where they ceremoniously hoisted the American flag, thereby becoming the first men to set foot on American soil in Antarctica. Gould's studies of glaciology, geology, and meteorology were an invaluable addition to human knowledge of that vast, mysterious continent.

Byrd made one more flight in the *Floyd Bennett* over the western part of the Barrier, pinpointing the jutting points of land that anchored the enormous ice mass to the Antarctic continent.

It was time and past time for the *City of New York* and the *Bolling* to return to pick up the explorers. But this year conditions were very bad. In 1929, the ice pack had been 290 miles across. In the Antarctic summer of 1930, it was 400 miles across and much thicker. Even some of the great Norwegian whalers could not get through. Had this situation prevailed the year before, the whole expedition would have failed. As it was, the *Bolling* never got back to Little America. The *City* cruised back and forth at the edge of the ice pack until February 13. It took her three days to smash her way through. Then she was caught in a violent gale and nearly sank from the weight of ice accumulated on her deck, spars, and rigging. On the evening of February 18, she sailed into the Bay of Whales, glittering with ice like a spun-candy ship on a birthday cake.

It was already almost too late to get out. The bay was beginning to freeze again. Tons of the most precious material had been transported from Little America to the bay ice. Byrd had to chance their sailing away on a detached floe. The moment the *City* tied up to the ice, men and dogs began the most strenuous work of the whole trip, urged on by the sight of ice freezing in small floes around the ship. If

23. Paul Siple, *A Boy Scout with Byrd*. G. P. Putnam's Sons. New York, 1931.

she stuck fast, it meant another ghastly winter-long night. Driven by so sharp a spur, they completed the loading—dogs, captured penguins, and all—in ten hours. Radio WFA, which had handled fifteen thousand messages, signed off the air. Captain McKinley lowered the flag for the last time. Byrd wrote in his diary, "At 9.30 o'clock the following morning, February 19 [1930]—just in time—we left Little America." [24]

24. Byrd, "Conquest of the Antarctic," *op. cit.*

VIII · ADVANCE BASE

YRD CAME home to America to find himself at the very
height of his fame—and justly so. Not only had he flown over the
South Pole and carried the American flag a thousand miles farther
south than it had been before; he had also shrunk the blank white
blob of unknown territory at the bottom of the globe, had etched it
with coastlines, mountain ranges, and vast plateaus. The Navy had
offered to propose him for commodore after his return from the
transatlantic flight. He had refused. Now Congress made him a rear
admiral (retired!!!) virtually by public acclamation.

The National Geographic Society brought Admiral Byrd and
seventy-nine members of the expedition, as well as Marie and young
Dick, the Admiral's mother, brothers, and various other Byrds from
New York in a special train. There was another great reception in
the Washington Auditorium, whose proscenium arch was hung
with Navy signal flags Y.W.X., meaning "Well done." Doctor
Gilbert Grosvenor characterized the expedition as "one of the most
comprehensive, dramatic and productive explorations of modern
times."

President Herbert Hoover, presenting Admiral Byrd with the
National Geographic Society's Special Gold Medal of Honor, said:

His daring and courage have thrilled each one of us, because he has proved anew the worth and power and glory of qualities which we believe are latent in our people. . . .

Knowledge, too, has been enriched by Admiral Byrd's expedition. New coasts of the Antarctic Continent have been mapped. . . . Geological data have been increased which contribute to our knowledge of the earth. New knowledge of magnetic currents and of weather changes has been gained. The store of the world's knowledge may not be priced in money, for money we make and spend, but knowledge remains always with the race.

All these achievements are the capstone of a career whose progress Americans have watched with interest and pride. Admiral Byrd has conquered the difficulties of reaching the Poles by heavier than air flying. . . . Success has followed upon success in his life, and this is the greatest of all.

As with all consistently successful issues, his accomplishments have been built upon painstaking preparation, foreknowledge of the special problems . . . thoughtful plans to meet them and infinite patience in preparation and infinite patience in execution. He has demonstrated the traits of the born commander—boldness at the right time, comradeship, those heroic qualities that endear the captain to his men. And he is beloved by the American people. . . .[1]

Marie Byrd had gone to New Zealand for the long sail home with her husband. It was one of their happiest times. She now enjoyed the unique experience of having him home for more than three years. He was not in Boston all that time, of course. Much of it was taken up by the Admiral's lecture tours across the country and his efforts to raise money for another expedition to Antarctica to continue the work of exploration and scientific research, which he felt had just begun. Nevertheless it was a comparatively peaceful interlude.

Byrd had returned from Antarctica at the beginning of the great depression, which deepened through the following years. The toll of bankruptcies and unemployment rose; farmers fought for their farms with shotguns against sheriffs serving dispossess warrants; long bread lines in the great cities crawled through rain and snow for a meager ration to keep them alive. Finally, in 1933, every bank in the country

1. Address by President Herbert Hoover, June 20, 1930.

was closed because of the panic conditions which would have broken the strongest of them.

At such an ebb tide of the economy, only a fanatic would have attempted to raise money for a purely scientific expedition to the Antarctic; and only a man of Byrd's enormous persistence and power of persuasion could have succeeded. His ardent belief that the value of such work to humanity transcended economic considerations was the compelling force that overcame apparently insuperable obstacles. One of his favorite maxims was, "Nothing is impossible"; and, more than his successful explorations, the fact that he was able to mount such an expedition in those times proves it.

In the course of his fund-raising, he roused a good deal of public antagonism. The hero of 1930 appeared to many as a heartless egotist in 1933. Byrd received many letters condemning him for stupidity and selfishness. Though he could not believe that people could think of the rigors of Little America as "a haven for spirits too sensitive to endure the economic agonies of civilization," [2] that is exactly what his acerbic correspondents did think; some also felt that he was out to grab more glory at any cost. They were certainly wrong. Admiral Byrd had glory enough for any man and there were no more Poles to conquer. There remained only his complete dedication to finishing the job he felt he had only begun.

Even Byrd could not wring any great amount of money from his hard-pressed fellow countrymen. In comparison to the million-dollar stake of his first Antarctic Expedition, the actual cash donations only amounted to $150,000 from thousands of small givers and a few big ones. The rest was made up of material and stores, given or merely loaned, and payments by CBS for anticipated broadcasts. The expedition was sponsored by the National Geographic Society and Byrd had the support of President Franklin D. Roosevelt and Secretary of the Navy Claude A. Swanson.[3] Of course, the manufacturers who supplied their products free expected some return in the form of advertisements of how well they performed under adverse weather conditions. As Byrd remarked, "Even Columbus worked on a percentage basis." [4]

Most of Byrd's old comrades joined up for little pay or none. It

2. Byrd, *Discovery.*

3. R. E. Byrd "Exploring the Ice Age." *National Geographic Magazine,* August, 1935.

4. Byrd, *Discovery.*

is extraordinary that so many men who had endured that desperately uncomfortable, winter-long night in Little America were so eager to return. As they were leaving Antarctica on the first trip, Haines had said to Byrd, "I won't come back." Byrd answered, "Yes you will." He did. The explanation lies partly in Byrd's ability to induce loyalty among his people and to grapple them to his soul; and partly in the inexplicable lure of the polar regions. As the Admiral's niece, Mrs. Stimpson put it, "The Antarctic is like heroin. You get hooked on it."

Despite the paucity of funds, the expedition was the most lavishly equipped so far. Byrd took four airplanes. His main reliance was a Curtiss Condor. This was the last biplane ever designed in the United States as a commercial passenger plane. Its wing span was 82 feet, which with its double wings gave it an unusually large lift surface. Powered by two souped-up Wright Cyclone engines of 750 h.p. each, it was roomy and very comfortable. It failed utterly as a transport because it was too slow and uneconomical, but for Byrd's purpose it was ideal. It could lift a gross weight of nineteen thousand pounds from either pontoons or skis, and its majestically steady progress through the air made it an ideal platform from which to make observations and map terrain photographically. Byrd could not afford such an expensive plane and no one could make him such a big present. He ingeniously solved this problem by inducing the manufacturers of different component parts to present them to him. He had to pay only for assembling them and for a few odd pieces. William Horlick gave him a special donation for this purpose, so the plane was named after him.

The other planes were a Fokker single-engine monoplane loaned by Alfred P. Sloan of General Motors; a small Pilgrim monoplane contributed by American Airways, and a Kellett autogyro from the Pep Boys of Philadelphia. This curious contraption had rotating blades like a helicopter except they were not power-driven but revolved freely, driven by the slipstream of the propeller and the machine's forward progress through the air. It could not ascend vertically like a helicopter; rather it sprang into the air after a brief run and climbed at a steep angle.

Ships were no problem. There were hundreds of ships—anchored in rusting rows in the Tappan Zee, the Delaware; off San Diego and Mare Island—ships that nobody wanted because there were no cargoes to move, while bananas rotted on the wharves of

Guatemala, swelling wheat burst the elevators of Kansas, and half
the world starved while the other half ate very carefully. Byrd could
have his choice of ships for the asking. One was an oil-burning discard
from the West Coast lumber trade. It was called the *Pacific Fir*, but
he rechristened it the *Jacob Ruppert*, after the beer baron who had
put up a large stake.

Locating an efficient ice ship was more difficult. On a tip from
Bob Bartlett, Byrd found her in Oakland, California. She was the
barkentine *Bear*—an icebreaker built in 1873, with an honorable
record of service. Known as the White Angel of the Whaling Fleet,
she had rescued six men of Greely's fatal Arctic thrust at Cape Sabine, Alaska, in 1884. Very strongly built of oak, sheathed with Aus-
tralian ironbark, she was 200 feet long, 32 feet beam and 703 net
tonnage. Like the *City of New York*, she had an ancient auxiliary
coal-burning steam engine. The City of Oakland owned her and was
perfectly willing to give her to Byrd, but they could not do so
legally. So they put her up at public auction, with everyone quietly
told not to bid. A junkman did not get the message, and bid $1,000.
People rushed at him from all directions. Byrd's representative bid
$1050. The junkman said no more.

Perhaps as important to the success of this expedition as the
planes were the newly designed tractors. Edsel Ford gave Byrd two
light snowmobiles. The Cleveland Tractor Company presented an
extraordinary machine called a Cletrac, which Byrd describes as a
"snow dreadnought." [5] Mounted on tanklike caterpillar treads, it
had an enclosed cabin and a body like a farm fodder wagon, and a
load capacity of 20,000 pounds. It could tow a long line of sledges.

André Citroën, whom Byrd had met in France, completed the
mechanization by sending him three intermediate Citroën tractors. In
addition, Byrd took along 153 dogs and 100,000 pounds of Ralston's
Purina Dog Chow presented by the company. The other livestock included three Guernsey cows loaned by the American Guernsey Association, and a calf born on the voyage.

On January 7, 1934, while Byrd in the *Jacob Ruppert* was fighting
his way through the ice pack, he received a message from his friend,
Lincoln Ellsworth, whose ship the *Wyatt Earp* was already in the

5. *Ibid.*

Bay of Whales. Ellsworth had financed his own expedition. It seemed that, as always, luck was no lady to him. His efforts to fly the Atlantic had failed; he had been *second* over the North Pole in the *Norge,* and now his only plane was destroyed by a catastrophic ice slide in the Bay of Whales. It was a remarkable contrast to the good fortune that attended Admiral Byrd.

Ellsworth radioed that Bernt Balchen and Christoffer Braathen, both old Byrd men, were going to try to ski to Little America. Byrd awaited the next message with intense anxiety. So much depended on whether his main base had survived three Antarctic winters; whether it had been crushed by moving ice, buried unfathomably deep in snow, or even floated away on an iceberg. The next day he got wonderful news. Little America appeared to be intact.

On January 17, 1934, the *Jacob Ruppert* entered the Bay of Whales. A motor sailer was launched and Byrd, with Charles J. V. Murphy, Commander Noville, Bill Haines, and Carl Petersen, started for the ice shelf. They crossed the Barrier on skis, closely followed by another party with the former Boy Scout, Paul Siple, joyfully driving a dog team.

As he mounted the rim of the wide, shallow basin in which was Little America, Byrd could hardly believe his eyes. The towers of the radio masts still stood, though one was tipped at a crazy angle. Stovepipes, ventilators, even the meteorologists' anemometer pole poked through the snow. Off to the left the rudder of the Floyd Bennett stuck up out of a drift. As fast as their weary legs would take them the party headed for the place the Administration Building should be. Measuring from the weatherman's pole, they began digging like mad. In thirty minutes they broke through to the tunnel. They slithered down through the hole and walked along the tunnel, past ice stalactites, through the sticky door, into the main room. It was lighted by a faint glow from the snow-covered windows. Byrd found an old kerosene lamp and lit it. The yellow light showed the whole place in an awful mess. In the frantic departure of 1930, everyone had simply abandoned what they could not take with them. Old papers, books, shoes, socks, shorts, and dirty underwear were scattered all over. A roast of pork stood on the Mess Hall table, looking singularly unappetizing. On snow-covered bunks lay a section of the roof of the Administration Building which the weight of snow had caved in.

As they surveyed the junk pile, the intercom telephone rang. Everybody jumped. It was someone calling from the Mess Hall. Petersen idly flipped a switch. To their amazement a bulb glowed dimly. The batteries had lasted through three Antarctic winters.

Barring that roast of pork, all the food they had left behind was found to be in perfect condition, kept so by the deepest freeze on earth. They got a fire going in the stove in the Administration Building and dined well off three-year-old seal steaks. Someone wound up the Victrola which promptly played "The Bells of St. Mary's."

Unloading the ships was slow and difficult. Pressure ice, tumbled and tossed like a stormy sea that had been quick-frozen, blocked the direct route. The enforced detour was seven miles long and very precipitous. They named it Misery Trail. But at least they did not have to build a base from scratch. The *Bear of Oakland* sailed in and was moored to the bay ice near the *Jacob Ruppert*. Planes were assembled on the ice and flown over the pressure ridges to Little America. (While his ship was in the ice pack, Byrd had already made two exploration flights in the Condor mounted on pontoons.) Tractors and dog teams hauled the supplies. A few new prefabricated buildings were put up to accommodate the enlarged personnel and the additional scientific instruments. In a surprisingly short time, Little America was again habitable, but the unloading took two months.

Byrd had a bad scare when all the bay ice went out to sea, and cracks and crevasses began to appear in the Barrier all around Little America. The three-hundred-foot-thick ice on which it was built heaved perceptibly up and down with the swell of the sea. For a time he thought Little America might be the first city ever to drift out to sea on an iceberg, but the deepening March cold sealed the cracks with fresh ice and that danger was averted.

A series of near-fatal accidents tautened nerves. The Fokker plane crashed. It was a total wreck though no one was badly hurt. The medical hut caught fire during an appendix operation on Photographer J. A. Pelter. John Dyer fell forty-five feet from an aerial mast. He landed in soft snow, but could have been killed. These mishaps seemed like ominous portents to Byrd and his comrades.

Because of the lateness of the season Byrd was eager to get on with his project for establishing a manned inland scientific observatory where throughout the long winter night meteorological studies could be made and observations taken of the Aurora Australis. He believed they would be of great scientific value because weather conditions inland were far more rigorous than at the edge of the Barrier. The portable hut for three men had been planned by Victor Czegka, and built in a Boston loft by a cabinetmaker named Ivor Tinglof. Into a tiny space, 9 feet by 13.8 feet, were crowded three bunks, scientific equipment, supplies, and an ordinary railroad-caboose stove for heat and cooking. It had been designed for coal, but Byrd had it converted to burn a mixture of gasoline and kerosene called "Stoddard solvent." A jerry-built contraption it was. The shack was given a dry run of six weeks at Little America. First Paul Siple and Charlie Murphy tried it for two weeks. They complained of headaches from carbon monoxide, so a new burner was put in the stove and Byrd lived in the hut for a month with no discomfort.

An expedition was sent out to establish a fuel depot almost due south of Little America at 80°08′ south latitude on the Barrier. In the course of this trip, the big tractor broke down, making it impossible to transport to Advance Base supplies for three men for seven months. Pondering the matter carefully, Byrd reached a decision, which he appears to have been considering all along: that only one man should occupy Advance Base. That man would be himself. His reasoning, or rather rationalization, was that two men, cut off from all human companionship and cooped up in so small a space under such rigorous conditions, would soon find each other intolerable. Each small peculiarity might become a source of intense irritation, sufficient, perhaps, to induce madness, murder, or suicide. It was a risk he did not care to take.

The alternative of a man alone in the howling Antarctic night, with no chance of rescue in the event of accident or illness, appeared to him a more acceptable risk. If his logic seems somewhat strained, it was. The truth of the matter lies in a sentence he wrote in "Exploring the Ice Age": "Besides, I wanted to go, and welcomed the opportunity to go alone."

In his description of that long fearful "night" [6] Byrd more fully outlined his reasons. Like his father, Mr. Dick, and almost all that gentleman's male descendants, Admiral Byrd had a compulsive

6. Richard E. Byrd, *Alone*. G. P. Putnam's Sons, New York, 1938.

need for solitude. During most of his adult life and especially since the North Pole flight, this craving had been completely frustrated. He had lived among adulating, demanding crowds in America; on his expeditions there were fewer people, but those few were cram-jammed into small uncomfortable quarters where privacy was impossible. There had been hardly a moment alone in which to meditate, to appraise himself and his work, to read and study without fear of interruption. Sometimes in America the pressure had literally driven him to drink, but on expeditions the responsibilities of command foreclosed this method of escape.

Now he saw his great opportunity to savor the experience of total aloneness, beyond reach of any demands or any succor, "to know that kind of experience to the full, to be by himself for a while and to taste peace and quiet and solitude long enough to know how good they really are. . . ." [7]

In addition, there was the challenge. Dick Byrd was psychologically incapable of refusing a challenge. It went far back to being the smallest boy at home, in the village gangs, on the football team. Forever he must prove his manhood. It was not that he seriously doubted it any longer, but that he welcomed the opportunity, "to try a more rigorous existence than any I had known." [8]

In short, Byrd was determined to man Advance Base by himself; and his friends, his angels, and all the devils in hell could not stop him.

Byrd had originally intended to locate Advance Base at the foot of the Queen Maud Range, but the worn-out condition of the tractors decided him to place it at the One-Hundred-Mile Depot at 80°08′ south latitude. By the twisting trail it was 123 miles from Little America. The base-building party left in early March, headed by Paul Siple, Captain Alan Innes Taylor and Harold June, with Ivor Tinglof—a long way from his loft in Boston—Petersen, and several other men. Byrd spent the next few days reorganizing the command structure of the expedition. He appointed the senior scientist, Doctor Thomas C. Poulter, as second in command to himself. His old comrade William Haines was third in command; Harold June became

7. *Ibid.*
8. *Ibid.*

Chief of Staff, and George Noville, veteran of the transatlantic and South Pole flights, was Executive Officer. With such men as these to run the show, Byrd had no anxiety about conditions at Little America during his absence.

On March 22, 1934, Byrd flew in the Pilgrim plane to Advance Base. Following the trail by the marks of the tractor treads and the orange trail flags required no navigational skill. W. M. Bowling, the pilot, landed alongside the camp of tents, dogs, tractors, and men on the flat, snow-desert of the Barrier. The plane took off almost immediately for home base and Byrd went with Paul Siple and Innes-Taylor to see how the work was progressing.

The trail party was in poor shape. For over three weeks they had camped and worked in the open Barrier in temperatures sometimes lower than fifty degrees below zero. Lips cracked, faces yellowed by frost-bite, they were exhausted. In the névé snow of the Barrier they had dug a pit fifteen feet long, eleven feet wide and eight feet deep in which to erect Byrd's portable shack. The floor sections were down. With Byrd working beside them, they soon got the walls up. Night fell, but by the light of pressure lanterns and the faint warmth of primus stoves they got the roof almost on. At −61° the kerosene and flashlight batteries froze, so the lights went out. Two gasoline blowtorches were substituted. Byrd's nose and cheeks froze; so did Innes-Taylor's feet. Byrd described the scene as being like Dante's Ninth Circle of Hell. At 1 A.M.—and −63°—the roof was on the shack. They tumbled into it. Paul Siple, ex-Boy Scout, got a fire going in the stove.

In the morning, Harold June and E. J. Demas turned up with three beeping Citroën tractors. After that the work went fast. They dug supply tunnels thirty-five feet long, branching out from the hut, and stocked them with gasoline, kerosene, candles, fire bombs, fire extinguishers, spare parts, quantities of food, and hundreds of miscellaneous objects. The toilet pit was placed at the far end of one tunnel, thirty-five feet from the hut. By the end of that second day, March 23, the aerials were up, scientific equipment located, the stove and stovepipe were installed (badly). Advance Base was finished. They held a farewell dinner party—turkey thawed out with blowtorches. The next day a blizzard made the party premature. Byrd was desperately anxious to get them off—they snored "heroically."

After one false start, the trail party was ready to leave for Little

America at noon on March 28. Byrd had twisted his right shoulder badly when he fell with a heavy box. "It was hurting like the devil," [9] but he mentioned it to no one; they might have insisted on remaining. He repeated his final orders—even if communications failed, no one was to attempt to rescue him until the sun returned. Then he stood in the trapdoor of his hut, watching the tractors, with their gay red hoods and canvas covers, diminish in the distance of that vast, flat white plain; listening to the rattle of their machinery and the beep beep of their horns, carried for miles by the crystalline air. When he could hear them no longer, the Admiral went into his hut and closed the trapdoor. He was alone at last—without doubt the alonest man in all the world.

Of the first two and a half months at Advance Base in the Antarctic night Admiral Byrd later wrote, "This was one of the greatest and most satisfying periods of my life." [10] He was content in a deep, soul-satisfying way. The world did not feel as happy about him. Byrd had slyly forbidden any word of his plan being sent to the outside until he was settled at Advance Base. When the news broke, Charlie Murphy, who was in charge of public relations, was overwhelmed by literally thousands of messages from people all over the world, protesting Byrd's decision and demanding that he be brought back to Little America. Even President Grosvenor of The National Geographic Society sent a peremptory message ordering Byrd back. Murphy thoughtfully did not mention the messages during the tri-weekly radio contacts with Advance Base. He knew Byrd well, knew his determination, and did not propose to shake his serenity by forwarding useless pleas to return.

During those months Byrd was extremely busy. He had a regular schedule for his scientific tasks—outdoor observations at 8 A.M., 10 A.M., and 8 P.M. Change paper, ink, pens in the automatic temperature- and barometric-pressure recording apparatus in the hut at 12 to 1 P.M.; reset the other instruments; climb the anemometer pole (once or twice a day when possible) to free it from ice, using his left arm only; the right one was almost useless. He also spent hours in the snow tunnel rearranging the boxes of food, fuel, and other

9. *Ibid.*
10. Byrd, "Exploring the Ice Age," *op. cit.*

supplies and generally neatening up. The trail party had left things in reasonably good shape, but not nearly orderly enough to please an old Naval Academy graduate.

In addition, Byrd fastidiously took a sort of bath every evening, washed his underwear frequently, shaved once a week, and took a walk for an hour or two every day that it was humanly possible to do so. He always carried a bundle of staves which he stuck in the snow at thirty-foot intervals so he would not get lost. One day he did get lost; he was meditating and forgot to place the markers. Suddenly he found himself on that vast icy plane with no sure knowledge of where his snow-covered base lay. It was terrifying, even to him, but he did not panic. He made a little mound of snow at the point where he was and walked in different directions from it, marking his path with sticks until, an eternity of thirty minutes later, he found a trail flag. He was not that foolish again.

In his spare time Byrd wrote in his diary, read the books he had always planned to, played solitaire against an imaginary bank, and listened to classical records or "Home on the Range" and his favorite, "Carry Me Back to Old Virginny." On Sundays, Tuesdays and Thursdays, at 10 A.M., he talked with Little America by radio. His set was powered by a generator driven by a gasoline engine. Getting it going in time to meet the schedule was extremely laborious. It had to be started like an old-fashioned outboard motor by pulling a cord wrapped around the flywheel. Because the transmitter was not powerful enough to send voice, Byrd hesitantly tapped out his messages by Morse Code, which he had just learned. Little America replied by voice. In spite of his difficulty in sending, Byrd discussed all the details of the plans for the spring explorations and scientific expeditions and made the decisions on all important changes. The Admiral was still in command.

The polar night was not always dark, even when the sun set for good. At its farthest north, on June 21, a faint finger of color still touched the northern sky. On clear nights the stars looked brilliant and so close that Byrd felt he could reach up and gather them in like shiny pebbles. When the moon shone, its light, reflected from the enormous circular snow mirror of the Barrier, was brighter than many a noon in London. When the Aurora Australis was at its peak, half of the southern sky was covered by a pulsing curtain of colored fire. There were, in fact, many things to instruct and delight a lover of beauty. Beyond all of them was Byrd's mystically ecstatic response to a situation perhaps unparalleled in human experience.

On the other hand, there were times of blizzards and gales that were like hurricanes, with seventy-mile winds that drove the stinging snow like a sandstorm and shook the cabin under its carapace of snow. At such times Byrd felt lonely and beleaguered. Even on still nights, it was a bit terrifying to hear a loud report, or a roaring avalanche as the instable crust of ice and snow on which he was perched shifted or cracked open in new crevasses, sometimes hundreds of feet deep. He could only hope that one would not open under Advance Base.

Mornings were the worst time. Because he always turned the stove off and left the door open a crack when he went to bed, the temperature in the hut was frequently $-30°$ when he awoke. He would lie in his sleeping bag gathering courage to open it. Finally, as will prevailed over inertia, he sprang out, threw on his outer clothes, and lit the dim oil lantern which barely illuminated the far corners of the room. Then he started the balky stove, which took quite some doing. A hunk of snow was put to melt in a bucket on the stove while he took his morning observation. It would be hours before the shack warmed up to zero—and this, remember, was a man who hated to feel cold!

What Admiral Byrd came to think of as the idyllic era of his stay at Advance Base came to an abrupt end on the morning of May 31, 1934. He was holding a long radio conversation with Charlie Murphy, Harold June, Dr. Poulter, and various others, giving minute instructions on everything from a message to his wife about cutting down expedition expenses at her end to hiring a new ice pilot for the *Jacob Ruppert* next spring. After an hour and a half the generator engine began to miss. Byrd tapped out "Hold" and went into the tunnel. It was choked with gas fumes. He bent over the carburetor and fell flat on his face.

The next thing he remembered was crawling on his hands and knees back to the transmitter and signing off. After that he had only the haziest recollection of what he did. He lay for a while on his bunk, then became conscious enough to hear the generator engine still going. He knew he must stop it or die. Crawling through the exhaust smoke in the tunnel, he threw the ignition switch.

The rest of the day passed like a fever dream—"skyrocketing pain" in his forehead and eyes, nausea, his heart beating wildly, "the illusion of being a thin flame drawn between two voids." [11] Somehow he managed to change the paper in the weather recorder. Then he collapsed in his sleeping bag.

When Byrd's mind finally cleared, he knew exactly what had happened to him—carbon-monoxide poisoning. He realized, too, that it was not just from the generator. That stove, with its badly fitted stovepipe, had been seeping the gas into the room all along. He remembered vague warnings—terrible fits of depression, violent headaches. The diagnosis was not much help. The stove had done it, but without the stove he would freeze to death. His life must be a compromise between freezing and asphyxiating.

In his condition every move was laborious; to walk set his heart pounding. But he could not lie in the bunk. The stove went out. With infinite effort, tottering like an old man, he took the empty oil tank to the tunnel and filled it. Getting it back on the stove must have taken almost an hour. He hardly slept that night because of the pain in his head, back, and legs. When he did, he had a dream of horrors. He awoke weaker than ever. Lying in his sleeping bag in that sub-zero room, he assayed his condition. He concluded that he had a very small chance of survival—all he could hope for was to prolong his life a few days. He determined to fight for those few days.

He must have heat. Working extremely slowly, resting at intervals, he took at least forty-five minutes to get the stove going. His thirst was a raging fire. He melted some dirty snow from the floor, drank it, and threw it up. He finally kept some down by taking small sips. Hours later, feeling a little stronger, he tried to make an outdoor observation and collapsed. When he got back to his bunk, great waves of fear swept over him. Bitter remorse for being such a fool alternated with terror. He blamed his own selfishness in seeking peace, enlightenment, enrichment of life. He was "a fool lost on a fool's errand." [12] In that most bitter hour he told himself the exact truth, sparing nothing.

How Byrd got through those first few days neither he nor any man knows. Even to make a thermos jug of warm milk was so great

11. Byrd, *Alone.*
12. *Ibid.*

an effort that when he drank it, he vomited and fainted. At one time he gave up hope. Even bitterness left him. With what he thought was his last strength, he wrote letters to Marie and to his mother. He fell back again into his bunk, and gave way to hallucinations. When he regained consciousness, he fingered his bottle of sleeping pills, almost yielding to temptation. Instead he pulled himself together again and wrote a brief statement of his philosophy: A Supreme Intelligence all pervading the Universe, whose major purpose was the achievement of universal harmony. Striving for peace puts one in accord with that Intelligence. The human race is not alone in the universe. Therefore I [Byrd] am not alone. Belief in that Intelligence is the one point on which all religions agree. "It has been called by many names. Many people call it God." [13]

Having written that in his freezing hut, he got into his bunk and fell asleep.

Sunday was his great day of testing; on Sunday he had a radio engagement with Little America. He knew if he did not keep it, they would wonder. If no word came from him for several days, knowing those brave men, he was certain they would disobey his orders and set out on a desperate venture across the crevass-riven ice in blackness and blizzards to attempt a rescue. He had to stop them at all costs to himself.

That Sunday morning he somehow found the strength to slide the thirty-five-pound engine into the shack to heat up; to push it back into its tunnel; to get it started. In came Little America "KFZ calling KFY." For the first time Byrd was glad he did not have to talk; his voice would have betrayed him, the telegraph key would not. J. N. Dyer came on first, and, as always, said, "We hope that everything is well with you."

Making the key sound firm and strong, Byrd tapped out the letters "O.K."

That was the most blazing lie of his life; the most heroic deed of his valiant career. The great flights were extreme daring. But that lie —told by a man who believed that without help he would soon die— was gut courage of the highest order.

13. *Ibid.*

That afternoon Byrd ate some salted crackers, his first solid food since Thursday. The next day he ate a curious mixture of malted milk, crackers, almonds, and dried apples soaked in hot water. He was always cold. Ice formed on the floor and walls of the hut because he dared not keep the stove going too long. But in the afternoon he found strength to crank up the phonograph and play a song from the *Bohemian Girl*, the drinking song from *Heidelberg*, and "Adeste Fideles." The music and the glorious voices roused a faint spark of hope that said, "You are on the mend. You really have a chance. One in a hundred, perhaps, but still a chance." [14]

For nearly three months more Byrd lived on alone. His survival was a miracle of sheer determination and physical stamina. All that time he kept the recording machine going, and made almost daily outside observations, though he was so weak he had to climb the ladder one step, rest five minutes, climb another step, rest again. He kept up the radio schedules, too, though the effort almost cost him his life. Even when the motor broke down and he had to crank the hand generator furiously with his good left arm and work the key with his right, he kept the schedule except when atmospheric conditions made it technically impossible. Those men back there, those dear friends and comrades, must not suspect that anything was wrong.

In time, though, as his sending got ever more erratic, they did suspect. Charlie Murphy was the first to realize something was wrong. He had worked with Byrd on *Skyward* and then written the story of the Admiral's life. Under such circumstance, a good biographer gets to know his subject so well, to identify with him to such an extent that he begins to *think* like him, to have an empathy that may almost amount to extrasensory perception. Charlie Murphy called it a hunch, based on his own mystical sensitivity and on little things like the slowness of Byrd's sending, long pauses before he began a reply, a certain indecisiveness that was very uncharacteristic. When Murphy told the others, they did not believe him at first. He wanted to make an immediate dash to Advance Base; but the others objected that it was against the Admiral's orders.

Meanwhile, however, Demas had been working on Number One tractor turning it into a sort of house trailer with a wooden body,

14. *Ibid.*

bunks, a stove, and radio. In it, the crew could travel and yet be protected against the cold. At the same time Doctor Poulter, having observed large numbers of meteors ordinarily hidden by the hazier atmosphere of the temperate zones, conceived the idea of taking the tractor twenty miles or so south in the darkness to get a longer base line for his observations. Then, because of Murphy's hunch, they developed the idea of taking it to Advance Base, in case Charlie was right that Byrd was in trouble. A very carefully worded message from Byrd, inquiring as to which kind of fuel and lamp produced the most carbon monoxide, helped to convince some of the others that the Admiral might be ill.

On June 14, Doctor Poulter described to Byrd the new tractor and the idea for an expedition in July. The Admiral was noncommittal, but did not forbid it. Three days later Byrd suffered a severe setback that laid him low. He knew he could not last until October when the relief was scheduled to arrive. Again he almost abandoned hope. Then a thought struck him. If Poulter were going to start operations in July with the newly equipped tractors, why should he not come to Advance Base? Hope revived.

On his next radio contact Byrd suggested this and added very casually, "I may come back with you sooner than I expected."

That was enough for Murphy. Now he knew the Admiral was in trouble.

June 27 was a great day for Byrd. Poulter came on the radio to tell him that the trial run of tractor Number One had been a great success. They had easily avoided the crevasses; many of the trail flags were still standing. Poulter went into great detail concerning the meteor-observation trip, which he proposed to start in July. Then he asked, "What do you think of it?"

What does a drowning man think of a raft that suddenly appears, a condemned prisoner of a reprieve? But Byrd would not be hurried. He tapped out "Wait," and thought hard. He was still in command. If disaster struck a premature thrust across the Barrier, it would be his fault. Yet if he "went down" there would be a terrible mess. The whole fabric of Antarctic exploration would be set back many years because it was his name that had made it possible. His death would make further exploration impossible for a long time. He had great confidence in Poulter. If the scientist thought it not too great a risk just to observe meteors, it might be all right.

Trying to calculate the risk objectively, Byrd spent that whole afternoon with charts and logarithm tables, calculations of fuel consumption in the tractors, and temperature probabilities. The real problem was whether the tractor party could follow the trail and avoid the crevasses in the brief, dim reflected light of a sun still below the horizon. But there would be a full moon the last week of July!

Back in Little America a row was going on. Murphy, Poulter, and some others were for taking off with a tractor as soon as possible. But according to the rules Byrd had decreed, such a drastic change of plan had to be approved by the Staff Council, consisting of sixteen officers of the expedition. The majority were dead set against it. They pointed out that Byrd's orders were that under no circumstances were spring operations to begin before the return of the sun on August 22. They refused to disobey his directive upon a mere hunch, and insisted that Byrd be queried directly as to his condition before they would approve. Murphy would not agree to this. He knew that no matter how desperate Byrd's situation, he would lie about it rather than allow his men to take an unnecessary risk.

Both sides were lying. Little America kept informing Byrd that everything was going smoothly and that Poulter's reason for the proposed July dash across the Barrier was purely scientific. Poulter always maintained that this was true. Although Byrd believed it at the time, in retrospect he thought that, "Knowing his gallantry," [15] Poulter's real motive was to rescue him. In early July, tension mounted in Little America and tempers flared. The pros accused the cons of caring so little about the Admiral's life that they would not break a rule or take a risk to save him. The cons accused Murphy, Poulter, and company of deliberate evasion of an explicit directive that might lead to disaster. After four days of discussion so heated that it was a wonder the snow did not melt, the staff reluctantly yielded to Murphy's intuition and Poulter's assessment of the scientific value of establishing a longer base line. On July 1, Byrd sent a message, approving in principle the July expedition.

Meanwhile conditions were desperate at Advance Base. Had not June been a "mild" month with average minimum temperatures no lower than —23°, Byrd would certainly have died. The "warm weather" enabled him to keep the stove turned off much of the time. July came in roaring like a bull walrus. The temperature dropped

15. *Ibid.*

into the sixties below zero, and one day hit —80°. The five-hundred-foot-deep Barrier ice cracked and groaned under the intense cold, and the hut shivered and shook in the icequakes. Byrd had one ear frozen while *in his sleeping bag.* He had to keep the stove going fifteen or sixteen hours a day to survive. The poisonous monoxide seeped into his system.

On Thursday, July 5, the generator engine broke down. Byrd took it apart and found it was irreparable. He missed the scheduled contact with Little America. In the next two days he assembled the hand-generator set. Ordinarily one man would crank the generator while the other sent the message. He had to do both, but he finally established contact. Laboriously he sent a long message detailing the safety precautions the tractor expedition must take. They were so rigid as to make the trip almost—but not quite—impossible.

The tremendous effort, plus the accumulation of monoxide in his system were too much for him. He vomited and collapsed in his sleeping bag. It was his third relapse. "It nearly did me in."[16]

The cold did not let up. From July 1 to July 7, the thermometer never got above —45°. From July 7 to July 17 it hovered between —64° and —71°. The ice crawled up the walls of the shack and met on the ceiling. Byrd was living in a room of ice. When he found strength enough to go outside, his breath froze with a rippling, crackling sound. Still he enjoyed the beauty of the aurora, the colors glowing in the sky at noon as the sun moved up behind the curve of earth.

On July 18, there was glorious news that Doctor Poulter's tractor would start at six o'clock the next morning. Byrd was awake at five-thirty to send the men a weather report: clear but very cold. The tractor started at 2:30 P.M. on the nineteenth. Byrd, his heart pounding with hope, kept in frequent painfully difficult radio contact with Little America. The next day the thermometer hit —74°. Byrd was almost dead from the cold, but he radioed to Little America that Poulter must turn back and await warmer weather.

They never got the message, but, nevertheless, Poulter was forced to turn back when he reached Fifty-Mile Depot and could not find the flagged trail through the crevasses. A blizzard buried the tractor on the return run. It did not get back until July 23. Meanwhile, on July 20, Byrd had lost radio contact with Little America. He was frantic between hope and anxiety for Poulter and his men.

16. *Ibid.*

Every night he lit a gasoline beacon at the prearranged hour, but
there was no answering flare. Bitterly he blamed himself for the disaster he feared had overtaken Poulter. Keeping on, in the blackness
of despair and shattered hopes and self-reproach, stretched his thin
reserve nearer the breaking point.

On July 26, six days after losing radio contact, Little America
came through. Poulter was safely back after four frightful days on
the open Barrier. He would start again soon. The next day the temperature rose nearly to zero.

In Little America, everyone had finally realized that Byrd was
in desperate trouble. Brave Poulter decided to make a direct dash
for Advance Base. He took only two other men—Pete Demas and
A. H. Waite, Jr. On August 4 they started once more. The tractor
broke down. They started again on August 7 in Number Three tractor. A bad oil pump turned them back. Meanwhile Byrd was hopefully burning guiding lights from 3 to 8 P.M. every day. Radio communication was so bad he did not know what was happening. He kept
tapping out "O K here!" Only once he slipped a little and asked
"What is the matter? . . . Use all resources." Then he suffered bitter remorse, fearing that he had given away the real condition and
that Poulter would risk all to save him.

On August 8 at 1:25 A.M., Poulter started out again, having had
no sleep. Sitting on top of the tractor in the fearful cold in order to
see the trail flags he signaled the two men inside how to steer. They
made thirty miles that day and camped on the Barrier. The next
night they were at Fifty-Mile Depot again. On August 10 they
started the last dash. The ignition system was giving out, but they
kept it going with paste-and-glue repairs.

The alternation of hope and despair, coming as they did after
two months of terrible illness, had almost finished Byrd. That he survived them, kept the lights burning, and the scientific records up to
date is a measure of the character of the man. While Poulter was on
the trail, Byrd tried to make radio contact with Little America every
four hours except at night. Cranking the generator utterly exhausted
him. In addition he felt he must go up into the icy night to set off
beacons. If Poulter's party overshot the camp, they would be lost on
the uncharted Barrier to the south.

On the morning of August 10, Byrd actually succeeded in flying
a kite, with a fiery, gasoline-soaked tail, to guide Poulter in. In his

terrible tension he wasted strength pacing the icy floor of the shack, three strides forward, three back. At 4 P.M., Charlie Murphy called in great excitement to say that Poulter was ninety-three miles south and right on the trail. Byrd noted that it was, "like knowing you would be reborn again without the intermediate obliteration of death." [17]

At five o'clock Byrd climbed to the trapdoor, and again at six. This time he saw a vertical beam of light sweep up the sky. He had been fooled many times by false lights, lit by hope, but he knew this was the real thing—Poulter's searchlight. Running, falling, and running again to the kite, he tied a flare to its tail and got it seventy-five feet in the air. Eagerly he looked for a return signal, but there was none. Strength gone, he crawled back down into the hut and collapsed.

But he could not lie still. In half an hour he was topside again; no light, no anything. Despair again blacked out hope. In sheer exhaustion he slept for a little while. When he awoke, he had not strength enough to climb the ladder. He searched the medicine chest and took an energizing shot of strychnine compound. Then, grabbing a flare and a length of flexible wire, he went up again. He threw the wire over the radio aerial, lighted the fuse, and hauled it up to the top of the mast. The light was blinding. When it died, he stared into the blackness. As his eyes refocused he saw the searchlight. Its beam moved up and down, signaling, signaling. . . .

Poulter, sitting on the top of the tractor, had seen that bright blue light, and headed straight for it. At the crawling pace, which was the best the crippled tractor could manage, it was two hours before it topped the final rise and the men in it saw a great burst of flame from a gasoline beacon. They stopped about a hundred yards off and jumping out of their machine, ran toward it.

Silhouetted against the light, they saw a cadaverous figure swaying beside the hatch that led to the shack. In a faint, rusty voice—but jauntily—Admiral Byrd said, "Hello, fellows! Come on below. I have a bowl of hot soup waiting for you." [18]

17. *Ibid.*
18. Byrd, *Alone* and *Discovery.*

IX · AMERICA FILES A CLAIM ON ANTARCTICA

THREE TIMES Admiral Byrd had come home to gather a hero's laurels. This time he found himself a legend. As the story of his incredible vigil on the Barrier became known, people realized that this had been far more than an act of gallantry to be acknowledged by Congressional Medals or Victoria Crosses. It had been rather a great spiritual testing, a classic trial of one man's strength of character in the tradition of Job or Gautama or St. Augustine—and perhaps more rigorous. For Richard Byrd had spent nearly four times forty days in the wilderness. His ultimate accolade was not in the speeches or the cheers, but in an almost unnoticed five-word message that Doctor Poulter sent to Little America from Advance Base the day after he arrived, "The meteorological records are complete."

It was two months before Admiral Byrd was fit to travel back to Little America. His weight had dropped from 185 pounds to 125. He was a barely animate skeleton. Only devoted nursing by Poulter, Demas, and Waite enabled him to survive. But he did not lose touch with the preparations for the spring campaign; he was still in command. He returned to Little America by plane on October 12, 1934.

Of all Byrd's privately financed expeditions this one was the most fruitful in expanding man's knowledge of Antarctica. Twenty-two different branches of science from astronomy to zoology benefited by the data they brought home. In addition to Byrd's own observations at Advance Base, important contributions were made by the Queen Maud Geological Party led by Doctor Quin A. Blackburn. Exploring the Leverett Plateau only 210 miles from the South Pole, Doctor Blackburn discovered fossils of trees a foot in diameter that proved the region had once been subtropical. Another party, led by Doctor Ervin Bramhall and Charles D. Morgan, contributed valuable scientific data on magnetism and seismologically plumbed the depths of the polar ice cap.

When aerial exploration became possible on November 5, flights were made over numerous unknown regions, many new mountains and plateaus were discovered and over a thousand miles of coastline mapped. Despite the stringent orders of Doctor Louis H. Potaka, Byrd, who had by no means recovered his health, took part in some of these flights.

Loaded with enough data to keep American scientists busy for years, and all the material they could salvage from Little America, as well as the dogs, the cows, and a flock of penguins, the *Bear of Oakland* and the *Jacob Ruppert* sailed out of the Bay of Whales on February 7, 1935. Byrd again could write, "Above all else—what means more to me than anything—is that we left not a single man in Antarctica, and for that we give thanks to Providence.[1] Strangely, these are almost the same words used by his forebear, the "Second William," on his return from the Wilderness. Byrd had never read them.

It is the opinion of many of his friends that Admiral Byrd never completely recovered from his ordeal at Advance Base. In the sense that it may have put so great a strain on his constitution that he invisibly aged this is quite possibly true. Certainly it matured and deepened his philosophy of life and in that context changed his nature. But if it is meant that it put a permanent crimp in his spirit of adventure, his ability to enjoy the good things of life, and the prospect of facing yet other perils and serving his ideals, the answer is an unequivocal no.

1. Byrd, "Exploring the Ice Age," *op. cit.*

A month or so of recuperation in Boston, and in Maine during the summers of 1935 and again in 1936, effected a complete restoration of Byrd's sense of well-being and his physical appearance. His curly hair was only a little grayer and, though there were more lines in his face, his cheeks were ruddy and his lively blue eyes still had "that look of eagles."

His debutante niece, Margaret Byrd, invited him to the Richmond Cotillion in 1938. "He came in his full dress uniform with all his medals," she said. "He was the handsomest thing you ever laid eyes on, and he had a wonderful time dancing with all the beautiful girls." [2]

Admiral Byrd, like all the Byrds, still loved to take long walks, and he did his setting-up exercises religiously. He said to his niece, "Margaret, if you do these exercises every day, you'll never have a pot."

But he had an abiding hatred for cold, as should he not? His brother, Senator Byrd, was just the opposite. The Senator never wore an overcoat in winter and he kept his beautiful house, Rosemont, definitely in the frigid zone. On one frosty morning, the Admiral stormed out of his room at Rosemont, wearing a heavy overcoat over his pajamas, beating his chest to keep warm, and shouting in his best bridge-in-a-storm voice, "My God, Harry, can't you put that thermostat up a bit!" [3]

On another occasion, his nephew, Beverley Byrd, was driving him to the airport on a very hot day when the Admiral asked him to shut a window because he might catch cold in the draft. Grinning, Beverley said, "You must have caught cold a lot at the South Pole."

"Never do," the Admiral said. "No germs down there. Too cold for them to live." [4]

This he firmly believed and in a way proved it by the extraordinary good health enjoyed by the members of his expeditions.

During the time he was supposed to be recuperating, the Admiral wrote *Discovery*, his account of the expedition, and he crisscrossed the country on lecture tours. As much as possible he kept to

2. Mrs. Stimpson to the author.
3. Richard E. Byrd of Rosemont to the author. The Admiral's son, Richard E. Byrd, Jr., says that on the contrary, his father did not mind cold and wore thin suits out of doors all winter. He thinks the Admiral was teasing the Senator.
4. Beverley Byrd to the author.

himself on these trips, though it was very difficult. In Colorado Springs he had the good fortune to find his cousin Joseph Massie from Winchester at the railroad station. Shaking off the Mayor and a delegation who had come to meet him, Byrd drove with Massie to the Broadmoore Hotel. When they reached the Admiral's suite, he said, "Joe, will you be my secretary here? I don't know a soul in Colorado Springs and I don't want to talk to anyone."

Byrd went to the bedroom to lie down while Massie coped with numerous telephone calls. There was a knock on the door. Massie opened it to find a young woman and a small boy. The woman explained that she was the widow of a Navy pilot and wanted to see the Admiral in the hope of arranging an appointment at the Naval Academy for her son when he grew up. Massie decided this was a different situation and went in to tell the Admiral, who said, "Let her come in."

He received her with his usual courtesy and the warmth he usually reserved for his intimates, and promised the boy an appointment to Annapolis in due time if he could pass the examinations.

Massie says that the Admiral's aloofness among crowds was self-defense, but that to any person whom he felt deserved his help he was "most compassionate and kind." [5]

After resting awhile at the Broadmoore, Byrd took his cousin for a long walk in the foothills of the Rockies. The next day they went up Cheyenne Mountain to lay a wreath on Will Rogers' grave. The driver was taking the hairpin turns on the icy road in show-off style. Finally Byrd shouted, "Slow up!"

The driver looked over his shoulder and said, "What you scared of, Admiral? You've flown over the North Pole and the South Pole."

"Yes," said Byrd, "but I knew who my pilot was." [6]

Although he had wandered so far from his native Virginia, Byrd loved to go back to Winchester and jumped at every chance of doing so. In 1938, he was invited to crown the Queen of the annual Apple Blossom Festival for the second time; he had done this first in 1931. Dropping all his other commitments, the Admiral went to Winchester and stayed with his mother in the rambling old house on Amherst Street where he had grown up. Fashion had moved on, leaving the

5. Joseph Massie in conversation with the author.
6. *Ibid.*

Byrd home in a deteriorating neighborhood, but despite the advice of her friends, Eleanor Bolling Byrd would not budge. She loved that house as her son did.

The Admiral had a grand time crowning the Apple Blossom Queen, but his enjoyment was nothing compared to the pleasure he gave the young ladies of Winchester. For in Virginia he felt at home; the armor of aloofness which marked his public appearances in other places was replaced by easy affability and old-fashioned courtesy. These, combined with his striking appearance and legendary fame, had a devastating effect upon women of all ages.

Knowing that the Admiral, despite his residence in Boston, regarded Virginia as his home, his friends, John D. Rockefeller, Jr., and Edsel Ford, felt that there should be a permanent memorial to him in the state, where his papers and memorabilia could be kept. They offered to buy Westover and give it to him for life. After his death, they would present it to the people of Virginia. Byrd liked the idea, but Marie vetoed the plan. The Admiral's close friend, Doctor James Mooney, once asked her why she had done so. "Indeed, I would not agree," Marie said, "because I would not like tourists peeking at me over the fence." [7]

The fact that Westover stands two miles from the nearest public road made the chance of such an invasion small indeed. However, Marie Byrd had so fiercely defended her privacy for all those hectic years that the thought of living in the public domain, however well sheltered and guarded, was completely abhorrent to her.

That same year the Byrds acquired Wickyup, on Tunk Lake in Maine. It was here that their happiest memories were thereafter centered. It had been a millionaire sportsmen's club. A wickyup, literally a tent of sticks, was an Indian hunting shelter, in contrast to a tepee which was a more permanent abode. The millionaire sportsmen had so named it, but it was a lavish sort of tent.

The big house, built on several levels in conformity with the ground, was made of whole round logs, peeled and polished so that every log shone in the sunshine. There were large rustic rooms for lounging and dining, and twelve bedrooms, each with a private bath. There was also a big hotel kitchen. The property included the entire shoreline of the lake except for one distant enclave on which stood another camp. There was, of course, a dock with various types of

7. Doctor James Mooney in conversation with the author.

boats. Blueberries grew around the lake, ripening in late summer. Though it was deep in the Maine woods, it was only fifteen miles from Mount Desert Island and the sea.

In 1937, even some millionaires were not feeling very affluent, and the members decided to sell Wickyup. Admiral and Mrs. Byrd went there for a picnic in honor of Mary Roberts Rinehart and fell in love with it. When they got home, they "added up their check books" and found the total came to nothing like the asking price.

But Marie could be as persistent as her husband. With his consent, though greatly to his embarrassment, she wrote to the secretary of the club, making a much smaller offer. Word came back that the offer was being considered, but that all the trustees of the club must be consulted.

Mrs. Byrd says that the whole family spent the winter alternating between hope and despair. The children were as anxious as they to have Wickyup. Finally, in the spring of 1938, her offer was accepted. Mrs. Byrd believes that this was partly due to the great affection people had for Admiral Byrd, whether they knew him or not. The club members knew he would love Wickyup and cherish it, and they wanted him to have it.[8]

Love it Admiral and Mrs. Byrd did. It became their enchanted land, their Avalon, sealed in serenity by wild, wooded hills, granting the privacy they both liked.

Of course privacy did not exclude the family. All the nephews and nieces were invited up at one time or another; together with the four Byrd children they made a continuous house party of noisy young. As one of them said, "Lots of people and lots of fun."

Byrd was a great organizer, but at Wickyup he apparently did not overdo it. People swam or fished or picnicked as they liked, but when things slowed down, they could always count on the Admiral to start something—a game, or cooking and singing around a campfire, a chase through the woods, or a race on the lake—and carry it through with his enormous, youthful zest and joy of living.

He would go to extraordinary lengths to stir things up. Once when there was a whole crowd of children at Wickyup, the Admiral somehow acquired an inflatable rubber figure of a man. Before dawn he sneaked off into the woods, pumped it up with a bicycle pump and set it adrift in a canoe, carefully calculating its probable course and

8. Mrs. Byrd in conversation with the author.

speed. At breakfast that morning he "sighted" it and announced that a strange object was on the lake. After examining it through the telescope, the Admiral gravely announced that in his opinion it was a visitor from outer space. Each child took his turn at the telescope and agreed with the Admiral that it was, indeed, "A man from Mars or somewhere."

When the canoe finally drifted in, there were roars of delighted laughter. Nobody minded being had by Uncle Dick.[9]

There were also long philosophical discussions in the evenings, during which the Admiral let his imagination roam the universe, enchanting adults and children alike, keeping his words on a level the youngsters could understand without ever talking down to them. In one of these talks he asked if they had ever tried to think about infinity, of space going on and on with no end ever, and time that neither began nor stopped. When he had them all concentrating furiously, he roared with laughter and said, "Everybody who has ever envisioned it has gone crazy."[10]

When he was away, Byrd corresponded with his young relatives in the manner of this charming letter he wrote to Ricky Byrd, the five-year-old son of the Rosemont Byrds:

Dear Ricky:

I am sending you three of my books. . . . Some day when you're grown up you may want to read these books. Now I think you can, perhaps, enjoy the pictures. . . .

I have seen Santa and he sends his best wishes. . . . I sometimes fly around the poles. Santa Claus lives near the North Pole and his house is made of big blocks of snow. He has a large workshop and little men smaller than you who make toys for him. They wear red and green suits and have shoes with toes turned up, and funny green hats with tassels on them. I have asked Santa Claus to write to you and you should get a letter very soon.

I have written in the books for you and I hope they will arrive soon.

Love from your godfather to you and your father and mother and the baby.

Uncle Dick

If the Admiral loved his young kinfolk, he fairly adored his only son, who in turn worshiped him. There was an unusually friendly re-

9. Told to the author by Mrs. Richard E. Byrd of Rosemont.
10. Mrs. Stimpson to the author.

lationship between them, due to Byrd's ability to meet people of any age on their own ground. When they walked and talked together, it was as equals, sharing their experiences and their secret thoughts. This kept their mutual devotion from becoming overly sentimental. When young Dick, aged eight, gave his father $4.85 he had saved to help finance one of the expeditions, Byrd thanked him in just the same manner as he thanked Edsel Ford for fifty thousand.

In 1939, the Admiral had two main preoccupations. One was, of course, a third expedition to Antarctica and the other was the Moral Rearmament Movement (M.R.A.). Founded by Doctor Frank N. D. Buchman as the Oxford Movement, M.R.A. was originally a nonsectarian attempt to lead people, especially young people, away from the materialistic philosophy of the 1930's, toward the spiritual values of a Christian life. It had strong pacifist leanings and Admiral Byrd's espousal of it brought the usual storm of criticism upon him. On one occasion he remarked, "I would have lost fewer friends if I had murdered Santa Claus." [11]

Byrd's reasons for joining M.R.A. came from the spiritual enlightenment of his vigil at Advance Base. One day he had written in his diary, "If I survive I shall devote what is left of my life to help further the friendship of my country with the other nations of the world."

Byrd had returned from Antarctica to find the nations of Europe preparing for a second world war, and his own country so busily engaged in attempting to work out of the great depression that it appeared to have forgotten the basic faiths upon which it was founded. M.R.A. appealed to him strongly because of its international character and its Christian principles. His thoughts concerning it were beautifully expressed in a broadcast he made from his home in Boston in October, 1939, shortly after Nazi Germany had started World War II and just before Byrd's third departure for the Antarctic:

I speak from Boston. Greetings to all of you who are listening no matter what country you may be in.

It was on my lonely vigil during the long polar night that I learned the power of silence, of a quiet time. The values and problems of life sorted themselves out when I began to listen.

11. *Coronet* magazine, August, 1948.

I went exploring because I was fired by those pioneers of history who felt the urge of charting uncharted seas and discovering unknown places. However, today, with the crisis that threatens to destroy freedom and civilization, the most pioneering to be done is in the realm of the spirit.

America's first line of defense is the character of her citizens. Character cannot be taken for granted. If we are going to preserve freedom it has to be battled for by every man, woman and child, every day and every generation. Without character man does not deserve freedom, so he loses it. . . .

The building of character is Moral Rearmament. It is the fight of America and of the world. That is the only armament that can stop armament for destruction.

On the eve of my departure for the Antarctic I want to say that I believe in this way lies the hope.

Moral Rearmament, the fight for a new world, strong, clean, united, should fire the hearts of all red-blooded Americans and stir their wills to action.[12]

Though Admiral Byrd deeply believed in the ideals of M.R.A., even going so far as to express on numerous occasions his conviction that the United States should under no circumstances rush to the rescue of Europe as she had done in 1917, he had not become blindly ensnared in pacifist idealism. He still believed that principles were worth fighting for, and his patriotism was no less ardent.

The Admiral's expedition to Antarctica in 1939–41 was triggered by the news that a German expedition was on that continent, presumably for the purpose of establishing territorial claims. In addition, Great Britain, New Zealand, Australia, France, Norway, Chile, and Argentina had made claims to different sections of Antarctica. Most of these territories were not only unmapped but unseen. Byrd did not relish having Hitler, or anyone else, encroach on territory he had discovered. He felt obligated to establish America's position more firmly. To this end he went to his old friend, President Franklin D. Roosevelt, for assistance. Roused to action, Roosevelt declared that it was time for the United States to make good its claims in Antarctica, and he proposed to establish colonies there. "Only Admiral Byrd can run such a program," he said.[13]

12. Broadcast by Admiral Byrd on behalf of Moral Rearmament. October 31, 1939.

13. Alfred Steinberg, *Admiral Richard E. Byrd*. G. P. Putnam's Sons, New York, 1960.

Roosevelt set up the United States Antarctic Service in the Division of Territories and Island Possession of the Department of the Interior and designated Admiral Byrd as commanding officer of the proposed expedition. The Executive Committee consisted of a representative of the departments of State, Treasury, Navy, and Interior, and Admiral Byrd, ex-officio. Roosevelt asked Congress for $450,000 for an expedition "to substantiate United States claims to about 1,000,000 square miles of polar waste."

Testifying before the House Appropriations Sub-Committee Admiral Byrd said, "That peninsula called Palmer Land, the northernmost land of the Antarctic, is nothing more than an extension of South America. It is only about 575 nautical miles from the tip of South America. So this land falls naturally within the scope of the Monroe Doctrine, as should also most of Antarctica that lies in the Western Hemisphere." [14]

Congress appropriated $350,000 in 1939 and $171,000 the following year, making a total of $571,000. Byrd needed nearly a million. He put in $300,000 of the money he had earned from lectures and books and once again went to his friends for help. Charles Walgreen, William Horlick, the Kohler plumbing family, and several others made handsome contributions. With this additional money, Byrd overhauled the old *Bear of Oakland* at a cost of $120,000, and sold her to the Navy for one dollar. He also renovated the famous Condor and purchased a Beechcraft. The Armour Institute of Chicago contributed a $150,000 snow cruiser, 55 feet long, 20 feet wide and 15 feet high with wheels 10 feet in diameter. It carried a small airplane on top. Inside it was a small but complete Antarctic camp and it carried fuel enough for five thousand miles. Byrd had high hopes for this machine, but it failed miserably on the névé snow of the Ice Barrier.

Because the United States Government was backing the expedition, Byrd found it far more difficult than before to get donations of supplies. Businesses which had given goods to him or sold them to him at cost for his previous expeditions now demanded the full price. In spite of these difficulties, he succeeded in mounting the expedition in amazingly short time. The *Bear* under Lieutenant Commander Richard N. Cruzen sailed in the early autumn of 1939. Admiral Byrd was piped aboard the U.S.S. *North Star* at Panama in October and reached New Zealand late in December, 1939.

14. Congressional Record, June 15, 1939.

The President's orders to Admiral Byrd were to explore Antarctica between 78° and 140° west longitude, that is from the Antarctic zone south of Cape Horn to the Bay of Whales. He added, "Members of the [Antarctic] Service may take appropriate steps such as dropping written claims from airplanes, and depositing writings in cairns, etc., which might assist in supporting a sovereignty claim by the United States Government. . . ." As Byrd pointed out in his preface to the *Report on the Scientific Results of the United States Antarctic Service Expedition of 1939–1941* [15] this was "the first United States Government expedition to go to the Antarctic since the famous United States Exploring Expedition one hundred years before under the command of Lieutenant [later Admiral] Charles Wilkes, U.S.N." The great American discoveries in the Antarctic since then had been mainly due to private enterprise, "ranging from the voyages of Connecticut sealers, particularly Nathaniel B. Palmer, to the expeditions undertaken by Sir Hubert Wilkins under American sponsorship, and by myself and Lincoln Ellsworth."

Byrd added: "It is incumbent on us to be prepared with information for whatever policy concerning territorial rights the Government may decide upon." Even then he hoped that Antarctica would be internationalized as "a great white continent of peace" [16] for all nations. This was eventually brought about, largely through his efforts.

While the *North Star* was establishing Paul Siple, Doctor Alton Wade, and the main part of the expedition at Little America III on the Bay of Whales, Byrd cruised far to the eastward in the *Bear*, making numerous exploratory flights in the little Beechcraft to find a suitable site for East Base. He selected a small rocky island in Marguerite Bay, which he named Stonington Island after the port in Connecticut from which Captain Nathaniel Palmer had sailed on the voyage on which he became the first man to sight the Antarctic Continent. The island was connected to Palmer Peninsula by a drifted snow slope leading to the quiescent glaciers of the continental ice cap. There, Byrd established a base with twenty-six men under the command of Richard B. Black (now Admiral Black, Ret.) and Commander Finn Ronne, U.S.N.R. For their work of exploration he left

15. Published by The American Philosophical Society of Philadelphia. 1945.
16. Richard E. Byrd, Jr., to the author.

them seventy-five dogs, one light armored tank, and one artillery tractor. Most of the exploration of the virtually unknown Palmer Peninsula was done by dog sledge.

Byrd then returned to West Base. By March 21, 1940, with winter fast approaching, both ships had been unloaded. Because of the uncertain condition of the world, Admiral Byrd felt that he could be more useful in the United States and he sailed for home in the *Bear*.

The Antarctic Service Expedition attained its major objectives, mapping five mountain chains, a thousand miles of coastline, and making numerous discoveries which were unofficially claimed for the United States by placing American flags, claim sheets, and bronze bench-marked monuments according to President Roosevelt's directive. The word *unofficially* is emphasized because official claims were deliberately held in abeyance. A vast amount of scientific data was added to the world's store of knowledge. Twenty-five papers were afterward published by various scientists on subjects ranging from the geographic and geological features of hitherto unexplored lands to the general principles governing the selection of clothing for cold climates, the biology of East and West Bases, zoological data, cosmic ray observations and many other scientific subjects.[17]

Though the expedition was successful in its primary objectives and contributed so much scientific data to the world's store of knowledge, it had to be aborted before accomplishing Admiral Byrd's dream of establishing permanent colonies in Antarctica. When he reached the United States in the late spring of 1940, Nazi panzer divisions were rolling through Europe while the Luftwaffe spread death and destruction with, until then, unparalleled ferocity. As Norway, Denmark, Holland, Belgium, and finally France surrendered to Hitler, President Roosevelt and the American people realized that the United States must concentrate all its available resources on building up the Armed Services to defend herself against so dangerous a potential enemy. There was nothing more to spare for Antarctic exploration. Even the *North Star* had to be recalled, leaving only the *Bear* to supply the expedition. Though Byrd was bitterly disappointed, he recognized this greater necessity.

17. *Ibid.*

But if Americans were united on the subject of defense, they were sharply divided as to whether we should help England to withstand the Nazi challenge. Isolationist sentiment was strong and vociferous. Never again, its proponents swore, must American troops fight in Europe. Admiral Byrd had once held this view, but he was too wise, too humane, and too patriotic not to change his mind in the face of Hitler's tremendous challenge to democracy. On August 19, 1941, at Madison Square Garden in New York, he addressed a huge mass meeting of the Council for Democracy as follows:

We as a nation will survive this crisis, or we will perish—the outcome depends on us. Let us face the first truth boldly. This is a war between two ideas. This is the age-old struggle between democracy and tyranny, between freedom and slavery, between good and evil.

This is everybody's war. Adolph Hitler has declared that the world is not large enough for Nazism and democracy. Well, we of the democracies believe in the dignity and equality of man. We believe that reason and truth and compassion in the end can be weapons mightier than any bombing. . . .

There is a second great truth. . . . The world has shrunk in size. But there are Americans who don't realize what modern transportation and communication mean. They deny the catastrophe or disease of a war erupting in one region affects all regions. They believe we can hide in our own little cabin and let the forest fire rage around us. . . . A foolish feeling of security may play into the hands of Hitler's agents. We cannot stand aside. . . .

If we rise today with all our might and a single purpose of doing our utmost to save our freedom, what on the face of the earth need we fear? What dictator would dare to fight us? What economic disaster could possibly lick us when we once again prove to the world that democracy, backed by unity, sweat and sacrifice is the most potent idea in the history of mankind?

We are faced with the greatest of all choices. At the end of one choice lies hell. At the end of the other lies peace and freedom in which all men may repeat with the psalmist:

"Behold how good and pleasant it is for brethren to live together in unity."

Here at Madison Square Garden tonight you are enjoying the four freedoms of our Bill of Rights. . . . What are we going to do to repay democracy for these freedoms? Are we going to sit back and enjoy them? Are we going to divide our national house against itself through dissension, or are we going to stand united behind the President . . . with an unconquerable morale?

Americans! What is your answer? [18]

Immediately after the Japanese attack on Pearl Harbor, Admiral Byrd closed out all the business of the expedition, canceled all lecture dates and other commitments, and offered his services to President Roosevelt in any capacity in which the President felt he might be useful.

18. Admiral Byrd's Speech at Madison Square Garden. New York *Times*, August 20, 1941.

X · ON ACTIVE DUTY

URING THE first chaotic days of war, Admiral Byrd worked closely with President Roosevelt on various missions to unify the country behind the President and the war effort. For example, there was a strike on at Boeing's great aircraft factories in Seattle. Byrd flew out to talk with management and labor leaders and to address the workers in a rousing speech in which he said in effect, "You know I have no ax to grind. I come to beg you to settle your differences and unite behind the President and the vital business of winning this war."

The strike was quickly settled.

As soon as this special work was finished, Admiral Byrd went on active duty on the staff of Admiral Ernest J. King, Chief of Naval Operation. The situation in the Pacific was desperate. The whole American line of battle had been sunk or put out of action at Pearl Harbor. There remained a few aircraft carriers, cruisers, destroyers, and submarines to counter the victorious Japanese fleet. Singapore, the Dutch East Indies, and the Philippine Islands fell, as did the American bases at Guam and Wake Island. The Japanese held effective control of the Southwest Pacific. Even Australia seemed in danger. As the Admiral's son said, "King had virtually nothing. He had to build from scratch." [1]

1. Richard E. Byrd, Jr. to the author

In the battles of the Coral Sea and Midway, the Japanese advance to the eastward was checked, but American island bases were desperately needed in the South Pacific. Specially tailored units were sent out to construct different classes of naval and air bases. The work went forward so slowly that Admiral King was greatly disturbed. He appointed a special inspection board to report on the difficulties and speed things up. Admiral Byrd headed the board, which included representatives of all Navy Department bureaus concerned with logistics. Their orders were to inspect all proposed sites and make recommendations for their utilization. "The tours of inspection were made in May and June, 1942. The board's report, dated 15 August 1942, one week after the start of the Guadalcanal Campaign [the first American counter attack in the South Pacific] laid out a plan for development that was in the main followed." [2]

Thus even before the Japanese Fleet was checked at Midway, Byrd found himself in the steaming, tropical islands about as far, climatically speaking, as it was possible to get from his beloved Antarctica. In the course of the trip he not only inspected American bases in being but flew over Japanese-held islands to reconnoiter them for future operations.

The report, which weighed eight pounds, bore the hallmark of Byrd's meticulously methodical approach to any problem. Not only were the harbor depths, land characteristics, climate and the conditions and attitudes of the native inhabitants and American morale, or lack of it, minutely surveyed, but the locations of future airstrips were mapped with records of the prevailing winds and all other needful data for aeronautical operations.

There were, however, lighter moments. In his report, Byrd particularly mentions the warm cooperation of Queen Salote at Tonga Batu, where a Seabee battalion was already at work on a large fuel base and staging area for aircraft at Nukualosa Harbor. He did not, however, report the extent of Her Majesty's efforts to be civil. Queen Salote was an enormous woman, who had not left her "palace" for many years. However, feeling that a special effort should be made to honor Admiral Byrd, whose fame had flowed from sub-zero Little America to her overheated land, she determined to go out and greet the Admiral. As her attendants tried to get her through the

2. Samuel Eliot Morrison, *History of the United States Naval Operations in World War II*, Vol. 4. Little Brown & Co., Boston, 1944.

doorway of her palace, she stuck fast. But the Queen was not to be balked so easily. She ordered the doorway torn out and a larger one built.

In her conversations with Admiral Byrd, Queen Salote confessed that, though she was heart and soul for the American cause, she was greatly anxious on one point. She feared that the presence of so many Americans on her island paradise would corrupt the purity of her race. The Admiral promised to do his best.[3] But careless as boys and girls are of racial purity, by the time the American presence was withdrawn the blood of the Tongan race was thoroughly polluted.

In 1943, Admiral Byrd made a second trip to the South Pacific to report on the tremendous progress and to reconnoiter more Japanese-held islands. President Roosevelt also asked him to go to New Zealand to help coordinate that country's war effort with American strategy. He was an ideal ambassador not only because of his fame and charm, but also because his knowledge and determination were tempered by Virginia courtesy.

The report which Admiral Byrd submitted to the Chief of Naval Operations (CNO), on March 31, 1944, not only evaluated the use of 130 Pacific islands for the war then being waged against Japan, but contained a long-range forecast of American policy and defense needs in the Pacific. He assumed that the prevention of another great war would be "the most important objective of the post-war era." Therefore he recommended that: "To prevent war this nation will, when the time is propitious, put its weight behind the formation of a world-wide organization based on reason and justice, of which all peace-desiring nations will be members. Further, it would be folly for this nation to expect to reap the benefits of civilization without doing its fair share to preserve it. . . ." However, he added, "Though we cannot avoid our responsibilities as a member of a peace-desiring family of nations we will reserve the right . . . of independent action when our national preservation is seriously threatened."[4]

The Admiral went on to describe probable American postwar commitments in the Pacific, including the protection of an independent Philippine Republic, and to forecast the danger points. He hoped that Russia would remain friendly, but pointed out that, "China's future form of government and internal conditions will be

3. Richard E. Byrd, Jr., to the author.
4. Report of Admiral Byrd to the CNO. Dated March 31, 1944.

among the few issues that may bring about a conflict of interest between the United States and Russia" (in the Far East). He added, "This nation will be very determined in its efforts to isolate any embers of war wherever they might smolder in the world. The only certain way to keep this nation out of war is to prevent wars everywhere."

The Admiral then evaluated at great lengths the different island groups as strategic bases for the long-range policy he envisioned, and for commercial aviation. However, he warned: "It is imperative not to rock the boat of international unity by seeking too aggressively the control of strategic islands or by otherwise laying this nation open to the charge—whether justified or not—of territorial aggrandizement or imperialism." [5]

Considering that Byrd's report was written while the Nazis still held most of Europe, and the Japanese had the Philippines and a majority of the Pacific islands, it was remarkable for its balanced judgment and prophetic foresight. Events in the Far East might have been far more favorable had it been more closely adhered to.

On his return from the Pacific in 1943, Byrd attempted to leap from the ship's launch to a dock. The boat sheered off and he landed on a big iron cleat, injuring his foot. The Admiral was unduly upset by this accident, not by the pain or inconvenience, but because of a peculiar facet of his character. He would never, if possible, appear in public in anything less than bounding good health. His perfectionist theory of leadership required that the leader must always be strong and in perfect physical condition. He knew he must report to the President on the result of his trip and the thought of appearing at the White House on crutches was as distasteful to him as would be any publicity concerning his accident. In this emergency he turned to his distant cousin, Colonel Harold E. Byrd of Dallas, Texas. Harold Byrd, who was immensely influential, arranged for him to enter a Dallas hospital under an assumed name. No word leaked out of the Admiral's injury and in due time he walked into the White House as fit as ever. [6]

In the interim between trips Byrd had an opportunity to show

5. *Ibid.*
6. Richard E. Byrd of Rosemont to the author.

that he had not lost his expertise in getting needed legislation through Congress. Early in the war the American generals and admirals were consistently outranked by their British opposite numbers because their top commanders were field marshals and fleet admirals whereas there was no five-star rank in the American Armed Services. Only Congress could create it. This caused considerable inconvenience and diminished American prestige. At a dinner in Washington the President's Naval Adviser, Admiral William D. Leahy, and Major General Patrick Hurley, who were about to leave on a mission to Russia, discussed this with Admiral Byrd. Leahy said, "I wish we could hurry the five-star bill through."

"When do you want it?" Byrd asked.

Hurley put in, "By the time we get back."

"All right."

"You say that," Hurley remarked, "but I'll bet you can't get Congress to move that fast."

"Will you bet a first-class Russian dinner?"

"It's a bet!"

It is almost unnecessary to add that before Hurley and Leahy returned the Five-Star Bill was passed and signed, and Hurley paid his bet with a superb feast also attended by Marie and the Admiral's son, Dick, who was on leave from the Navy.[7]

In Washington, the Admiral served as adviser to the Bureau of Naval Operations and the Army General Staff on clothing and foot gear for the winter campaigns from the Aleutian Islands to Europe. In the course of this assignment, he instigated the manufacture of the light, cotton, windproof material known as Byrdcloth.

Unfortunately, the Armed Services did not take his advice on footwear for cold weather, with the result that trench foot reached epidemic proportions. During the winter campaigns over fifty thousand officers and men were incapacitated. Byrd's son still fulminates about this stupidity. He said, "Not only in Europe but in the Korean War as well they would not take our advice, with very bad results. It is interesting that in Korea, while our troops were suffering from excessive foot trouble, the armies of industrially underdeveloped North and South Korea had no such problems. Lack of manufactured shoes forced them to improvise footwear such as burlap wrappings which were far more suitable for intense cold."[8]

7. Richard E. Byrd, Jr., to the author.
8. *Ibid.*

During the campaign in France and Germany in the winter of 1944, the condition of the American troops became so serious that Admiral Byrd was sent over to inspect the situation at first hand and make recommendations, as well as to report on how to improve liaison and cooperation between air and ground forces. He made a hedge-hopping foray thirty-five miles behind the enemy lines and his reconnaissance plane flew through puffballs of bursting antiaircraft shells with never a scratch. The flak disturbed him not at all. He may even have been rather pleased to have been under fire at last.

While in Europe, Byrd went to great lengths to discover the whereabouts of his nephew Richard Byrd, the Senator's son, who was serving as a sergeant with the 10th Armored Division, then part of General George S. Patton's Third Army. Young Byrd describes how one cold and dreary night he and his buddies were sitting around a bivouac fire when a stranger with a major's oakleaf on his helmet walked into the flickering light and sat down, saying nothing. After a while young Dick Byrd became a little annoyed and said, "What do you want, sir? What can we do for you?"

The Major said, "I don't want anything," and continued to sit motionless.

Dick, becoming more and more irritated, studied the man intently. Finally he looked him straight in the eye and said, "Damned if you don't look like my Uncle Dick!"

The Admiral burst into his familiar roar of laughter and said, "Good to see you, Dick! Come over to my jeep. I've got a driver I think you know."

The driver was Dick Byrd's brother Beverley, who had been badly wounded on D-Day when he parachuted into Normandy with the 101st Airborne Division.

To this day neither Dick nor any other member of the Byrd family knows whether the Admiral had borrowed a major's helmet in order to surprise his nephew or if he had assumed the lesser rank in order to move less conspicuously among the troops and get inside facts on their condition.[9]

As a result of the Admiral's recommendations an immediate check-up was ordered on the feet of all officers and men on the Western Front. Quite unexpectedly, when Dick was examined, he was found to have such a bad case of trench foot that he was invalided out of the service.

9. Mr. Richard E. Byrd of Rosemont to the author.

In the spring of 1945, shortly before Germany surrendered, Admiral Byrd was ordered to the Pacific on the staff of Fleet Admiral Chester W. Nimitz. He had clearance to the topmost of secrets. His work took him to many of the islands newly occupied by the Marines. During the long tropical nights, he delighted to play a few rubbers of bridge with new friends and old. A special pal was Eddie Bracken, the comedian, whose job was putting on shows to improve the morale of the bored and listless troops. One night in August, 1945, on Tinian Island, when Bracken had been asleep for several hours, he awoke to find the Admiral shaking his shoulder. A glance at the clock showed it was three o'clock in the morning. Bracken said crossly, "For Pete's sake, Admiral, you can't want to play bridge at this hour."

"No," said Byrd. "I'm going to show you something you'll never forget in all your life."

Bracken dressed and drove with the Admiral to the airport, where the latter's special pass got them through the tight security. Byrd parked the jeep near the runway. Judging by the activity near the hangars a small mission was preparing to start. In the faint luminescence of false dawn Bracken saw three B-29 bombers roar down the runway. The middle plane seemed overloaded, for, at the cliff that ended the runway, it dipped down toward the sea and fairly staggered into the air.

"What's so great about that?" Bracken asked.

"You won't forget it," said Admiral Byrd.

Some hours later Bracken learned that the overloaded plane had been the *Enola Gay*,[10] on its way to Hiroshima.

When Japan surrendered, Admiral Byrd was aboard the *Missouri* to witness the signing of the historic document. He was the first American officer, after Colonel Turner Joy of the Amphibious Forces, to set foot on the conquered land. His orders were to inspect the bomb damage at Hiroshima and Nagasaki. He was among the first Americans to visit those stricken cities, which were still radiation-hot. The terrible impact of acres of rubble where people had lived and worked and laughed until they were incinerated in one ghastly second, and of the dazed, horribly mutilated and soul-scarred survivors profoundly

10. Eddie Bracken to the author.

affected Admiral Byrd. Though the devastation was not as complete as at Hiroshima, Byrd was more deeply distressed by Nagasaki because he had visited it as a young boy and remembered well the pretty wooden houses, the curve-roofed, scarlet and gold temples, and the exquisite miniature gardens of Japan's age of innocence.[11]

Long discussions with General Douglas MacArthur were followed by a comprehensive report to Washington. But Admiral Byrd never found words adequate to express his own feelings—they were, indeed beyond words. He returned to Washington in October, 1945, more determined even than after his vigil at Advance Base to devote his life to the cause of peace among men.

Because of the most secret nature of Admiral Byrd's missions, little was heard about him by the public during the war except that he had received for his services various decorations, including the Legion of Merit. On November 8, 1946, Fleet Admiral Nimitz presented him with a gold star in lieu of a second Legion of Merit, with the citation:

For exceptionally meritorious conduct in the performance of outstanding services to the Government of the United States as Confidential Adviser to the Commander in Chief, United States Fleet and Chief of Naval Operations. . . .

[Admiral Byrd's] thoroughness, attention to detail, keen discernment, professional judgment and zeal which produced highly successful results in the execution of his exacting assignments, together with wise counsel, sound advice and foresight in planning constituted material contributions to the war effort and to the success of the United States Navy. . . .

Knowing very well that the public seldom reads citations, Admiral Nimitz proceeded to put the record straight in a charmingly humorous comment at the ceremony:

From the many questions asked about Rear Admiral Byrd I know that there is widespread interest in this country as to what has become of him since he vanished from the news columns . . . after his last expedition ended in 1940. Some think he has departed for the next world, and, strangely enough, many people think he is still at the South Pole, so it is high time that we show he has been alive and well and going strong as this decoration shows.

11. Richard E. Byrd, Jr., to the author.

Now it can be told.

He disappeared from view in 1941, first because he chose, and insisted, upon completely subordinating himself in teamwork as good naval officers believe in doing.

I am happy to tell you that Dick Byrd did a job in the war that his fellow citizens would expect him to do. This is his *fourth* citation for war work. He was overseas four times, having been at both fronts in connection with aviation and other matters. He won the respect of his fellow officers and men.

So I am glad to be able to tell you that he has not been frozen in at the South Pole during all these years, but has been serving his country as usual.[12]

12. Navy Department Press Release of Fleet Admiral Chester W. Nimitz's Speech. Dated October 8, 1946.

XI · HIGH JUMP

S OON AFTER his return to the United States in October, 1945, Byrd began agitating for a new naval expedition to Antarctica. This time his task of persuasion was comparatively easy. The cessation of hostilities left the Navy with thousands of ships and millions of men at loose ends, whom it would have been unwise to demobilize all at once. James V. Forrestal, the brilliant, hard-driving Secretary of the Navy, and Admiral Nimitz, now Chief of Naval Operations, agreed with Byrd that exploring and mapping the still-unknown areas of Antarctica would be an ideal way to occupy some of them. Of its almost six million square miles only about one million had even been seen by man, and over three-quarters of its sixteen-thousand-mile coastline was still uncharted. The expedition was not officially authorized until August 26, 1946, which meant a tremendous rush to begin operations by the Antarctic summer in December.

In the new jargon of the Armed Services the expedition was known as Operation High Jump. It was originally called Pole Vault, but that sounded too imperialistic. It was entrusted to Task Force 68 under the immediate command of Captain Richard M. Cruzen, who was promoted to Rear Admiral at Byrd's request. Cruzen had been captain of the *Bear* in the 1939–41 Expedition. High Jump was by far the greatest assault on the Antarctic ice-fortress ever mounted until then. Under Admiral Byrd's over-all command were four thousand men and thirteen ships including the Aircraft carrier *Philippine Sea;* the coastguard's 10,000-h.p. icebreaker *Northwind,* and the Navy's brand-new *Burton Island,* both of which could smash through ordinary three-foot ice at ten knots. Also assigned to him was the submarine *Sennet,* which proved so vulnerable to the ice pack that she was towed to the safety of the open sea by the *Northwind,* and thereafter acted as a weather ship for the expedition.

In addition to naval personnel there was a large group of civilian scientists and many of Byrd's old comrades, among them Lieutenant Colonel Paul Siple, who headed a group of sixteen Army Observers and was also Byrd's Scientific and Polar Adviser. Another officer in whom the Admiral was especially interested was Lieutenant Richard E. Byrd, Jr., who was aboard the Command Ship *Mount Olympus.*

The expedition was equipped with nineteen airplanes and four helicopters. There were six big Martin flying boats (PBM's) and six twin-engine R4D's, known to the Air Corps as the C47 and to the traveling public as the DC3. In addition there were several varieties of mechanized transport perfected during the war, including several amphibious weasels, which could travel over water, land, and snow. They proved their worth on a 250-mile trip into the interior. Finally, but never to be forgotten by Admiral Byrd, there were the dogs, including Rickey, a Husky born in Little America in 1934.

Admiral Byrd was in high heart as he sailed in the *Philippine Sea* early in January, 1947. The thought of returning to his beloved land of eternal ice after six years' absence filled him with excitement. His emotions are made evident in the unusually poetic language of the opening paragraphs of his account of the expedition in the *National Geographic Magazine:*

At the bottom of this planet lies an enchanted continent in the sky like a pale sleeping princess.

Sinister and beautiful she lies in her frozen slumber, her billowy white robes of snow weirdly luminous with amethysts and emeralds of ice, her dreams iridescent ice halos around the sun and moon, her horizons painted with pastel shades of pink, gold, green and blue.

Such is Antarctica, luring land of everlasting mystery. . . .[1]

1. Richard E. Byrd, "Our Navy Explores Antarctica," *National Geographic Magazine,* October, 1947.

When the Admiral sailed to take command, part of Task Force 68 was already slogging through the ice pack. Despite its tremendous size and lavish equipment, High Jump, like all South Pole expeditions, was a perilous enterprise. For one thing, thin-skinned Navy ships had never before attempted to challenge the ice pack. Even with the *Northwind* breaking a path for them and Admiral Cruzen scouting ahead in a helicopter for open leads, it was a tricky business as young Lieutenant Byrd soon found out. As the *Mount Olympus* moved through the narrow lane cleared by the icebreaker, a jagged piece of ice slashed an eight-foot gash in her side. "We never even knew we had hit anything until some wiring shorted out and we went to investigate," he said.[2]

Another serious problem was whether the R4D's could be launched from a carrier. The *Philippine Sea* was far too fragile to go through the ice, so the planes she carried would have to be launched from her deck on the open sea six hundred miles from the rendezvous at the Bay of Whales. To this end, they had been equipped with a unique combination of short skis, with wheels protuding just three inches through them. Captain Delbert S. Cornwell, commanding the carrier, wanted six inches of wheel, but Admiral Byrd feared that more than three would trip the planes when they landed on the névé snow of the Barrier.

No plane as large as an R4D had ever taken off from a carrier. The B-25 bombers in which General James Doolittle took off from the carrier *Hornet* for his famous raid on Tokyo had a shorter wing span. The wings of Byrd's planes would not clear the "island" (conning tower) at one side of the carrier's deck, so there were only four hundred feet of deck for planes that normally required twenty-five hundred feet for take-off on land. To solve this problem Byrd proposed to use JATO (Jet Assisted Take Off), which consisted of two rocket-propulsion tubes fastened under each wing.

By the time the *Philippine Sea* reached the area selected for the take-off, four of Admiral Cruzen's ships, the *Northwind*, the *Mount Olympus*, and two freighters were moored to the ice in the Bay of Whales, and Little America IV was functioning. Because the expedition was a hit-and-run operation which would not remain through the Antarctic winter, it consisted of a tent city pitched near the edge of

2. Richard E. Byrd, Jr., to the author.

the Barrier—cold comfort but adequate shelter as long as daylight lasted. Two or three prefabricated wooden buildings were erected to house scientific equipment. A rough landing strip had been bulldozed on the snow. Everything was ready except the weather.

In order for the flight of the six big planes to have a chance of success, meteorological conditions had to be right, not only at Little America but in the take-off area. There, a comparatively smooth sea and perfect visibility were essential so that the carrier could make a run of thirty miles or more at thirty knots into the wind for the launching.

It was not until January 29 that this happy combination of circumstances occurred. Byrd decided that the planes should fly in pairs for maximum safety. Since both take-off and landing presented unknown hazards, there was no question in his mind as to who should command the lead plane. It was piloted by Commander William M. Hawkes of the RD Unit with Admiral Byrd as copilot, navigator, and commander. Four other men completed the crew.

As the *Philippine Sea* turned into the wind, they climbed into the plane and sat waiting until the carrier could gain speed. Byrd knew by the vibration of her great engines when she reached the required thirty knots. The signal was given and the plane moved forward, fairly crawling it seemed to Byrd. Then Hawkes fired the four JATO rockets. With a tremendous roar and neck-snapping acceleration, the big plane leaped into the air as though shot from a cannon. Byrd noted with relief, "Our first river was crossed." [3]

It was an easy flight to Little America over the ice pack which had taken Admiral Cruzen fifteen days to penetrate. Byrd navigated mainly by his beloved sun compass, for they passed close to the South Magnetic Pole which set magnetic compasses whirling. As they crossed the deep blue open water of the Ross Sea and sighted the Ice Barrier, Byrd noted that his companions seemed drunk with excitement, and he, too, felt exhilarated. But the sight of the landing strip at Little America quickly sobered them. It was ridged and roughened by bad sastrugi, drifts of frozen snow from a recent storm. They circled and circled, looking it over. In view of the short, wheel-pierced skis, it did not look promising. Finally Hawkes let the plane down as

3. Byrd, "Our Navy Explores Antarctica," *op. cit.*

gently as possible. It touched ground and ran along, jumping and jerking over the ridges, metal clashing and banging like a junk yard in an earthquake, but it came to rest undamaged.

The other five planes also arrived safely. Byrd, looking at them lined up with military precision, noted how imposing they seemed compared to the one small tri-motor Ford of his first flight. But there was little time to admire the planes. Meteorological indications were that, in a land of short summers, this one would be of record brevity. The ice pack was wider than Byrd had ever seen it, and the optimum season for aerial exploration (November–December) was already long past. Admiral Cruzen was frantic to get his precious ships out of the Bay of Whales and through the pack before they should be frozen in and crushed like eggshells by the pressure of expanding ice. He left on February 6, a little over a week after Byrd arrived. The *Northwind* would return for the rest of the party. Even so, they had only six weeks at the longest, and they did not yet know if the R4D's could take off from the sandlike névé snow on the short skis.

While the planes were being readied, Admiral Byrd and Paul Siple had the pleasure of showing the Admiral's son through the old Little Americas, which had moved on the slowly creeping Ice Barrier a mile and a half from their original position. They were now buried under snow so deep that the tops of the steel aerial towers which had stood seventy feet tall in 1929, were only eighteen feet high. In the ice-walled rooms everything they had left behind was in its expected state of perfect preservation, and the party ate a beefsteak six years old. The moving ice had also changed the Bay of Whales. Its entrance had been twelve miles wide in 1928. Now it was less than two hundred feet wide, and the Barrier had moved forward until the body of water was now less a bay than a small harbor.

Meanwhile the wheels had been taken off the planes and the slits in the skis filled with duralumin. On February 9, one plane was loaded heavily for a discovery flight. Byrd and a crew of five were aboard. Hawkes opened the throttles wide. The engines roared, the plane shivered and shook and did not budge one inch. They jacked it up and slid boards under the skis. This time it moved forward very slowly. Then Hawkes fired the JATO rockets and she took off like a frightened partridge. But that flight was aborted by a sudden shift to bad weather and a gasoline leak caused by the violent vibration of the first attempted take-off.

Soon, however, all the planes were making exploratory flights. In fourteen days of flying weather they flew 27,500 miles and explored 200,000 square miles of the Polar Ice Cap. Three new mountain ranges were discovered, one of which had peaks up to 20,000 feet high, comparing favorably with the Himalayas. Each plane was equipped with four trimetrogon mapping cameras set at different angles from which a complete map of the terrain covered could be assembled.

The longest flight was Byrd's thrust into the unknown wastes beyond the South Pole. In preparing for this mission, he exemplified his whole philosophy of exploration. "There are many occasions," he wrote, "when explorers have to take hazardous chances to succeed. When such chances have to be taken I believe in calculating the risk with the greatest care." [4]

For the polar flight two planes were used. The lead plane was piloted by Lieutenant George H. Anderson and Byrd's old associate Lieutenant Commander J. C. McCoy, whom he described as "resourceful, level-headed, conservative, a splendid companion and a gallant gentleman." [5] Lieutenant (j.g.) Robert P. Heekin was officially the navigator, but breathing down his neck and checking every move was Admiral Byrd. Radioman J. E. Valinski and Photographer K. C. Swain completed the crew. In the second plane were Commander Clifford M. Campbell and a Marine Corps crew.

Both planes were greatly overloaded: "That is the thing an explorer is always forced to contend with." [6] Extra gasoline and equipment brought their gross weight up from a safe maximum of 25,000 pounds to 32,000 pounds. Despite their tremendous weight JATO shot them into a cloudless, purple-blue sky. At 10,000 feet visibility was nearly 150 miles in the crystal clear air. It was almost midnight and the red ball of the sun was rolling along the southern horizon.

Outward bound their course was only a little west of the first South Polar flight. But this was a very different situation. Where Bernt Balchen had struggled to jockey the tri-motor Ford through the Liv Glacier Pass of the Queen Maud Mountain, the R4D's soared easily over the Wade Glacier. For part of the way, Admiral Byrd, wearing his lucky old suit of caribou skin, lay on his stomach on

4. *Ibid.*
5. *Ibid.*
6. *Ibid.*

the big gasoline tank in the cabin, checking their course with his sun compass.

But even in this comparatively modern plane there were moments of peril. Once, as it was gaining altitude, one of the engines cut out, no one knows why. When they switched to another gas tank, it started again and gave no further trouble. But in the increasing cold the automatic pilot stopped working and the heating system, congealed by cold, gave up. It was so cold in the plane that Lieutenant Anderson's ears began to freeze. Vibration loosened the fittings of the extra fuel tanks and the cabin aft of the cockpit filled with gasoline fumes.

Then they were over the South Polar Plateau, heading due south along the 180th meridian. Byrd took his place in the copilot's seat beside Anderson. Because of the failure of the heating system, ice began to form on the windows. He and Anderson were kept busy scraping it off with their knives. The temperature inside the plane was -- 40°. When Byrd went aft to check their course with the sun compass from the back compartment where Swain was photographing the terrain, icy air was pouring through the camera openings. Byrd admitted, "We got a bit chilly." [7]

They were flying at between eleven thousand and fourteen thousand feet. It became necessary to use alcohol to defrost the windows. There was no oxygen aboard the plane, so the alcohol fumes plus the altitude gave some members of the crew anoxia. They talked in an uncoordinated way, staggering around, and appeared slap-happy. There were roars of laughter. At the time Byrd, too, thought it was very funny, but he was not sure this was not due to the heady atmosphere.

At almost exactly 5 A.M. (Greenwich Time), February 16, 1948, both planes crossed the South Pole. They circled it and Admiral Byrd ceremoniously dropped a cardboard box containing the flags of the United Nations, and sent off a radio message to Fleet Admiral Nimitz in Washington.

Then the planes continued on into the unknown area beyond the Pole. Though they were on the same course, because they had passed the Pole they were now heading due north, and, instead of the 180th meridian, they were flying up zero meridian, that of Greenwich, England. East had become west. They flew approximately one

7. *Ibid.*

hundred miles beyond the Pole without seeing the slightest change in the terrain of the vast plateau that is the bottom of the world. Then they turned right and flew almost a hundred miles to the 45th meridian so as to fly back over unexplored territory. The sky remained completely cloudless, the visibility unlimited. As they neared the edge of the Polar Plateau, the mountains rimming it towered into the sky, some of them coal-black or brick-red, others sheathed in glittering ice that refracted the sunlight into the full spectrum of colors. Byrd recorded that it was the most breathtakingly beautiful sight he had ever seen and called it "The Avenue of Frozen Rainbows." [8]

At a little before noon, something over twelve hours after take-off, both planes landed safely at Little America.

Though the time grew short as the sun declined, a number of other flights were made toward the southwest, exploring beyond the Beardsley Glacier up which both Sir Ernest Shackleton and Captain Scott went to the Plateau. A plane commanded by Commander Hawkes flew over the exact spot where Scott and his fellow explorers had died of cold on their return trip from the South Pole. At this point the heater in Hawkes' plane was working so well that Lieutenant Anderson actually opened the window because it was too hot.

Hawkes continued much farther west, mapping a belt of mountains from fifty to seventy-five miles wide, extending westward from the Ross Sea. Among them were ice-free oases like that discovered by Byrd in 1929. On another westward flight, Hawkes discovered a huge river of ice flowing at least eighty miles from the Continental Plateau through the mountain ranges of Victoria Land, which Byrd believed to be the largest glacier in the world. Byrd, piloted by Major Weir of the Marine Corps, made a flight far to the southeast on which he, too, discovered a large new glacier and "new mountains every few minutes." Because of the steep declivities down which they flow, these rivers of ice exert enormous pressure on the Barrier, producing in it the deep, horseshoe-shaped crevasses that could swallow up unwary men and, indeed, large tractors and their trains of sledges.

8. *Ibid.*

Important as the explorations from Little America were, they were almost matched by two other sections of Task Force 68, which between them almost circumnavigated the Antarctic Continent, charted almost the entire coastline, and penetrated its mountainous rim in many places. The Western Group, commanded by Captain Charles A. Bond, consisted of the seaplane tender *Currituck,* the tanker *Cacapon* and the destroyer *Henderson.* There were three big PBM's (Martin flying boats) with three crews. The planes were flown from the open sea beyond the ice pack, which is not very wide in this area. They mapped the coastline from Victoria Land on the Ross Sea all the way around to the hitherto unknown coast of Queen Maud Land where the Indian Ocean touches Antarctica. Their penetrations inland from Queen Mary Coast found another large, ice-free area with blue and green lakes and brown hills. These lakes took their color from the blue-green, red, and brown algae that grow in countless billions in their waters, since there is no other form of life, except a few Antarctic birds in summer, to consume them. One of the PBM's landed on a grass-green lake three miles long. Its crew trailed their hands in the water and reported it to be "comfortable," far warmer than the ocean beyond the ice pack.

This oasis in the eternal ice was about three hundred square miles. Around it the ice cap rose, in hundred-foot cliffs on two sides, sloping gently upward on the others. Admiral Byrd and all the scientists were unable to adduce a satisfactory explanation of this phenomenon.

Meanwhile the Eastern Group, under the command of Captain George J. Dufek (who had been an officer in the *Bear* in 1940), in the seaplane tender *Pine Island,* with two other ships and three more PBM's, had explored and mapped the coastline from the Amundsen Sea, just east of the Ross Sea, on around the Palmer Peninsula to the Weddell Sea. He, too, discovered new mountain ranges, enormous glaciers and a bay 150 miles wide.

However, despite Captain Dufek's experience of Antarctic conditions, his group suffered the first casualties on a Byrd expedition, though it should be noted that the Admiral was not in personal command, and had no direct control over the Eastern Group. Indeed, at the time, he had not yet left the United States. Quite early in the cruise a PBM piloted by Lieutenant Paul LeBlanc, with Lieutenant

William H. Kearns as copilot, Captain Henry Howard Caldwell of the *Pine Island,* and six crewmen, took off to explore the Thurston Peninsula, the eastern shore of the Amundsen Sea. It was a cloudy day. When they reached land, they suddenly flew into a "whiteout." Although there was no fog or frost smoke, they were lost in a white glare, "a bowl of milk." There was no horizon, no up or down.

Lieutenant Kearns, who had taken over the controls, made a 180° turn toward the sea. The bottom of the plane grated along something like hard sand. He pushed the throttles forward to full power to climb. It was too late. There was a rending crash, a violent explosion as the plane hit a snow slope he could not see. Pieces of plane and people skidded over the glazed surface of the snow, then lay motionless.

Hours later some of the men began to recover consciousness. They were battered and broken, but somehow they managed to survive until Captain Dufek found them with scouting planes and organized the difficult rescue operation. But Ensign Maxwell A. Lopez, Machinist's Mate Frederic W. Williams, and Radioman First Class Wendell K. Harrison died on the snow lying beside the broken wing of their plane.

Admiral Byrd blamed himself bitterly for this disaster, though he had briefed all the top commanders on the danger of this particular phenomenon peculiar to the Antarctic, which Paul Siple once described as "the antithesis of darkness." Siple believed it was caused by light bouncing back and forth in multiple reflections trapped between snow and sky. Knowing that LeBlanc and Kearns, like most of the Navy pilots, had no experience of Antarctic flying, Byrd felt that it was his fault that the warning did not reach the pilots in Dufek's group; that somehow he should have managed to talk to all of them personally, to keep control—even though to have exercised personal command over such numerous, far-flung operations seems beyond human capacity.

Though darkened by this tragedy, Operation High Jump was successful beyond all expectations. It ripped the veil of mystery that surrounded Byrd's "sleeping princess" and left but few blank spots on the map of the bottom of the world. In a statistical sense, as Richard E. Byrd, Jr., truly said, "It accomplished more than all the previous Antarctic expeditions put together."

XII · LAST FLIGHT

IT HAD BEEN the intention of James V. Forrestal, who had become the first Secretary of Defense, and of Admiral Byrd to follow the great gains made by High Jump with a second expedition to establish permanent scientific bases in Antarctica. Before this could be accomplished, Forrestal died and President Harry S. Truman appointed Louis B. Johnson as Secretary of Defense. Johnson was so economy-minded that he starved all the Armed Forces to a point where their efficiency was compromised. Certainly there was need for drastic economies after the spending binge of World War II. But the fact that Johnson carried it much too far was shown by the deplorable condition of American defenses when the next international crisis occurred.

Under such a penny-pinching policy, there was no money for High Jump II. Also, the fact that President Truman was feuding with Senator Harry F. Byrd did not help. Admiral Byrd was still working to get High Jump going again when the Korean War broke out in June, 1950. For its duration there would be no more government aid for Antarctic exploration.

Meanwhile, the Admiral had never forgotten his vow to further the cause of international amity. He renewed his support of the Moral Rearmament Movement. Though he was not completely convinced that M.R.A. was the ultimate answer to the world's problems, he felt that since the best efforts of conventional diplomacy had failed, it offered at least a chance for friendship among nations. If the peoples of the Western world would lead a truly Christian life and would honestly believe in the brotherhood of man, he believed that the world would be infinitely better off. The movement appealed strongly to the mystical side of his character. In 1948, he became Chairman of M.R.A.'s National Committee of Invitation. For the time being he put the weight of his great reputation and international friends behind M.R.A. He helped to sponsor a musical road show played by a multi-national cast of M.R.A. members. They planned to tour the world, combining entertainment with appeals for international amity and the Christian way of life. Though he was now sixty years old, he worked hard for M.R.A. in addition to his other activities. As he traveled all over the United States on his lecture tours, he endorsed M.R.A. principles, and urged people to see *The Good Road,* as the show was called.

Many people thought his enthusiasm absurd if not irrational. Others criticized him venomously. Gales, blizzards, leaky engines, or "impossible" conditions never stopped the Admiral, neither did jeers nor imprecations deflect him from his charted course.

What did divert him was the end of the Korean War, bringing with it the possibility of a renewed assault on Antarctica. At first he had hopes of financing it privately and conducting it without Government interference, as he much preferred. However, his friends, particularly Professor Mooney, convinced him that this had become impracticable. The tremendous advances in technology had made polar exploration infinitely easier and more efficient, but taking advantage of them was as infinitely more costly. An expedition that could be financed for a million dollars in 1928 would cost ten million by 1953; and to do it properly would cost three times that amount.

So Byrd was forced to seek Government assistance. Dwight D. Eisenhower had been elected President and with the change in administrations had come a more favorable attitude toward polar exploration. Great Britain, Norway, France, New Zealand, Australia, Chile, and Argentina were making claims in Antarctica, some of them conflicting. Several nations had established more or less temporary bases there. The United States, which, due to Byrd, had the soundest claims, had made no official move to validate them and was being left out. The United States Navy was working on plans for a new expedition, but it had not gone far.

In these circumstances Admiral Byrd and his friend and adviser, Professor Mooney, called on Secretary of the Navy Thomas Gates and then on President Eisenhower. They both looked favorably on the idea of another expedition led by Byrd, as did other Cabinet members. The difficulty was to find a gimmick that would make it sufficiently appealing to Congress to get the necessary appropriations. At this point someone suggested tying it in with the program of the International Geophysical Year, scheduled to run from July, 1957, to the end of 1958.

Byrd leaped at the idea. Because of its international aspect, with a dozen or more great nations cooperating in the search for knowledge in Antarctica, it tied together the two main themes of his life—Antarctic exploration and amity among nations. He had long cherished the ideal of internationalizing Antarctica. He had seen rival Chilean and Argentinean expeditions in the Palmer Peninsula argue heatedly about who was on whose territory, then seen the argument end as one group said to the other, "Well, anyhow, come into the cabin for a cup of coffee and a game of chess." His favorite maxim was: "Men cannot fight each other in the Antarctic because the one universal enemy is the cold." [1]

The opportunity to give his ideals concrete form set Byrd ablaze with enthusiasm. He immediately approached the leading American IGY organizers with the idea. To his surprise the scientists were skeptical and indifferent. They were already preparing many IGY experiments in other parts of the world. They were appalled by the immense cost and difficult logistics of establishing observation bases in Antarctica.

After many discussions, Byrd finally convinced Doctor Joseph Kaplan of California Tech., who was chairman of the United States National Committee for the IGY, of the immense value of an Antarctic progam because "Here has been set up by Nature herself a titanic physical, chemical, and biological laboratory where phenomena, impossible of duplication elsewhere, are in progress. . . ." [2]

Though convinced, Doctor Kaplan pointed out that the Commit-

1. Richard E. Byrd, Jr., to the author.
2. Richard E. Byrd, "All Out Assault on Antarctica," *National Geographic Magazine*, August, 1956.

tee was advisory and had no funds. "Where's the money coming from?" he asked.

"I'll get it for you," said Byrd. "All you need." [3]

Admiral Byrd became Honorary Chairman of the Antarctic Committee of the IGY. Now for the last time, his expertise and experience in lobbying with Congress proved useful. In fulfilling his promise, he worked with such friends as Senators Lyndon B. Johnson, John F. Kennedy, and others. But mostly he relied on the loyal co-operation of his brother, Senator Harry F. Byrd of Virginia, who was approaching the peak of his great influence in the Senate. The Admiral also proposed that the Navy's plan for a national expedition be merged with the IGY effort. The result was even more spectacular than he had hoped. The first appropriation from Congress was $9,000,000, later increased to $25,000,000. This money went to the National Science Foundation and did not include the great numbers of ships, planes, mechanized transport, and personnel furnished by the Navy. Speaking in retrospect in 1961, Doctor Kaplan said, "Admiral Byrd gave courage and hope for this program. I don't think there would have been an IGY project in the Antarctic without Admiral Byrd." [4]

In 1953, various scientific area committees for IGY were formed. In November, Doctor Lawrence Gould, who had been Byrd's deputy commander in 1929, was named Chairman of the Antarctic Committee. Doctor Paul Siple became a committee member (in addition to his regular post as head of the Army Research Program); so did Bernt Balchen. Byrd, the Honorary Chairman, was also acting as an unpaid adviser to Admiral Arthur W. Radford, Chairman of the Joint Chief of Staff, but he had a firm grip on the organization.

It was decided that the bases of the IGY Antarctic program must be set up during the South Polar summer of 1955–56 so they would be working smoothly by the time the IGY began. Though a number of bases would be used, including Byrd Station in Marie Byrd Land, the most exciting project was a base at the South Pole itself. Because of the tremendous difficulties of maintaining men on that mile-high, hurricane-and-blizzard-swept plateau, in temperatures down to a hundred degrees below zero, no one knew if it could be done. But Byrd was determined to try.

3. Richard E. Byrd, Jr., to the author.

4. Speech by Doctor Joseph Kaplan at the presentation of the Byrd Memorial to Virginia in June, 1961.

To set up the bases a great naval task force must be assembled. This operation was named Deep Freeze I to be followed by Deep Freeze II in support of the actual IGY operation the following year. Admiral Byrd wanted Captain George J. Dufek to command the task force because of his Antarctic experience. This required considerable political maneuvering. The task force commander must have the rank of Rear Admiral. In order to promote Dufek without injuring naval sensibilities and the sacred rules of seniority, Byrd worked out an ingenious solution. Dufek retired with the rank of rear admiral, which hurt nobody's feelings, since he was now out of the seniority tables. Then a special bill was put through Congress, enabling Dufek to command ships even though on the retired list. He was appointed Commander of Task Force 43, and promptly made Paul Siple its Director of Scientific Projects.

On March 28, 1955, President Eisenhower gave out a press release, announcing that the United States would send an expedition to the Antarctic to build bases in connection with the International Geophysical Year. The concluding paragraph states:

"Rear Admiral Richard E. Byrd, USN (Retired) will be designated by the Defense Department as Officer in Charge, the same title he held in the last Navy Antarctic expedition in 1946–47." [5]

The actual order from the Defense Department was not issued until October, but this did not noticeably slow up Admiral Byrd. The Presidential order gave him authority over the entire program except the direct command of Task Force 43. Byrd promptly fitted another hat on Paul Siple's overworked head by appointing him his personal deputy.

The work of planning this vast expedition, coordinating civilian and naval functions and cooperating with eleven other nations who were taking part in the IGY Antarctic project was staggering. Though Admiral Byrd was now sixty-seven years old, he attacked the task with all his old vim if not quite the old vigor. One of his assistants was his son. Frequently young Dick, coming into the office on Jackson Place at midnight to finish up some work after going to a Washington party, would be greeted by the watchman saying, "Your father just left." [6]

The Admiral was growing weary. He had been working for three years to bring this great joint Government-civilian enterprise

5. White House Press Release, March 28, 1955.
6. Richard E. Byrd, Jr., to the author.

into being—talking, urging, buttonholing people, making speeches, writing innumerable letters, arguing that "nothing is impossible." Now he had the ultimate responsibility of making it work. But his physical exhaustion did not impair his judgment or cause him to slacken the meticulous attention to detail which had always marked his leadership. The strength of character which had enabled him not only to survive the ordeal at Advance Base but also to maintain the scientific records was in no way eroded. It kept him going long hours after physical strength was spent and weary flesh and common sense alike called quits.

Early in December, 1955, Admiral Byrd and Paul Siple started on a commercial flight to New Zealand to join the ships of Task Force 43. Their plane stopped at Dallas where the Admiral was highly amused by pretty Texas girls carrying placards: BYRD UNFAIR TO WOMEN. This was because he had recently said that the reason Little America was the quietest place on earth was because there were no women there.[7]

The flight across the Pacific was long, hot, and tiring. The Aide the Navy had assigned to the Admiral was drinking all the way, while Byrd and Siple reminisced about old times. There was no rest for Byrd in New Zealand; the whole country turned out to do him honor. At Aukland, the press was clamoring for an interview and the New Zealand Air Force held a review in his honor. At Wellington, he spent the night with the Governor General, who gave a formal reception and a state dinner for him; and he conferred with New Zealand Prime Minister S. G. Holland. Then he was off on a quick crowded tour of speech-making banquets and receptions. It made things no easier that his Naval Aide became ill. He was replaced by Air Force Major Murray Weiner. Young Dick also joined his father in New Zealand.

Finally Byrd boarded the new Navy icebreaker *Glacier* at Lyttelton. There was a brief contretemps when he found he had been assigned a small single cabin way down in the bowels of the ship. For a few minutes the Byrd temper flared, and rightly so. Apart from the fact that one does not put an Admiral below the waterline, he needed space to work in. However, a few quiet words to Captain Eugene Maher put things quickly to rights.

7. Paul Siple, *90° South*. G. P. Putnam's Sons, New York, 1959.

On December 10, the *Glacier* sailed from Lyttelton. She was a brand-new ship on her maiden voyage. Her displacement was 8,625 tons and her 21,000-h.p. engines could drive her at 19 knots as compared to the *City of New York*'s 502 tons and 200 horsepower. She carried two bright orange helicopters on her afterdeck. As Byrd noted, "Quite a difference." [8] Even the *Glacier* was far from the perfect passenger liner. Her rounded bottom made her bob and jerk around eccentrically in a seaway. It was a rough trip but Byrd enjoyed it immensely. His blood began to sing again in his veins, his eyes sparkled as he stood on the *Glacier*'s bridge in the clean, sharp, ice-tanged wind. On December 15, when she butted her powerful bow into the ice pack he felt "the old sense of excitement." [9]

The Air Operating Unit was to be established on Ross Island far back in McMurdo Sound, where Captain Scott had made his first Antarctic base. On the evening of December 17, through the frost haze and wind-torn clouds, Byrd saw the glittering icy peak of Mount Erebus (the only known active volcano in Antarctica) with a plume of steam and smoke curling above it, and Mount Byrd, trailing its blue-gray robes of glacial ice. The *Glacier* docked against the ice in the Sound with her bow pointed straight at Mount Erebus.

Byrd watched the unloading process and wrote joyfully of "the clatter of tractor trains, the whir of helicopters, the shouts of men wrestling with vehicles and gear. Yes, and the howling of huskies, too; they're still needed for rescue work." Gaily he greeted old animal friends, the seals lolling on the ice, whales gamboling in the lanes of open water, mewing skua gulls and bowing penguins—"symbols of life's triumph in a lifeless land." [10]

Hut Point on Ross Island, where the pyramid-roofed cabin built by Scott on his first expedition still stood, was chosen for the Air Operations Base. An 8,500-foot airstrip was bulldozed on the snow nearby. Soon two twin-engined Neptunes (P2V's) and two four-engine Skymasters (R4D's) flew from New Zealand and landed on the strip. The Skymasters were the first four-engined planes to land in Antarctica, and the first to land on wheels instead of skis.

Meanwhile the *Glacier*, with Byrd aboard, smashed back through the ice pack to bring in the rest of the convoy—a tanker and

8. Byrd, "All Out Assault on Antarctica," *op. cit.*
9. *Ibid.*
10. *Ibid.*

three cargo ships, including the *Arneb*, flying Admiral Dufek's two-starred blue flag. After that, followed by the *Arneb* and the *Greenville Victory*, she cruised along the face of the Ice Barrier toward Little America. There was nothing left of the Bay of Whales. The arms of Barrier ice that had enclosed it had smashed together, while a huge piece of the Barrier two hundred miles long and ten miles wide had broken off and drifted out to sea.

However, all the Little Americas were still there. At four o'clock in the morning, Admiral Byrd, with his son, took off in a helicopter from the *Glacier*'s deck and flew over the Barrier. Byrd saw in the eye of his mind the long lines of sweating men and straining dogs hauling supplies from ship to camp twenty-eight years before.[11]

They flew low over the third and fourth camps and saw the abandoned tents and aerials. Then they landed at Little America I. They could now stand on the top of the seventy-foot aerial masts which barely protruded above the surface of the snow. Little America, of course, was buried seventy feet deep. Old friends from former expeditions flew in to join them, among them Paul Siple and Admiral Dufek. A new flagpole was set up and Admiral Byrd, wearing the lucky suit of caribou skin, his fur cap, and the high-laced boots in which he first flew over the South Pole, raised the American flag in a nostalgic ceremony.[12]

The shifts in the Barrier had made the place unsuitable for a new base, so the *Glacier* coasted along the cliff of ice. Thirty miles northeast in Kainan Bay, Paul Siple, scouting by helicopter, discovered a viable place, where snow sloped up the Barrier's face. The *Glacier* smashed out a good-sized harbor in the bay ice, to which the cargo ships were moored. The Seabees bridged some awkward crevasses with light, stainless-steel trusses and the work of unloading began, hastened by thirty-five-ton D8 tractors instead of dog sledges.

On January 4, 1956, Admiral Byrd, in his old fur suit, in the presence of Admiral Dufek, young Richard Byrd, Paul Siple, and many of his old shipmates, formally commissioned Little America V as two seamen in bright yellow Byrdcloth suits hoisted the American flag on a new steel flagpole.[13]

11. *Ibid.*
12. Richard E. Byrd, Jr., to the author.
13. Byrd, "All Out Assault on Antarctica," *op. cit.*

The *Glacier* steamed swiftly back to McMurdo Sound, for the Admiral had one more task to perform. Of all the objectives of Deep Freeze I, establishing a base at the South Pole was probably nearest to Byrd's heart. The project was threatened by the report of a young Marine Corps lieutenant who had flown over the site and stated that in his opinion the snow was too soft and deep to bear the weight of an R4D on skis. Byrd did not believe a word of it. He was determined to go and see for himself.

It was inevitable that an expedition with a split personality—Navy and IGY—should engender tensions. In addition, all the bright young men, filled to their sinciputs with scientific knowledge, regarded the old Antarctic hands as fogies to be treated kindly but ignored, though this attitude was not generally applied to Admiral Byrd except by the most callow fledglings. Nevertheless it put difficulties in the way of utilizing the experience of the older men and occasionally resulted in some acerbic confrontations. This feeling as well as ignorance may explain the young lieutenant's report.

Early in the morning of January 8, 1956, Admiral Byrd began his third and final flight to the South Pole. For the first time Paul Siple flew with him. Byrd wanted to land at the Pole and take some temperature readings deep in the snow, which would show the average temperature because it was a constant in both summer and winter. However, the Navy insisted that he fly in a Skymaster which was not equipped with skis so a landing was impossible.[14]

Siple says that the Admiral was as excited as a schoolboy as the great plane took off. His eyes sparkled and his cheeks were rosy. "Let's take a look at the spots where the Russians are planning their inland IGY stations," [15] he said to Squadron Commander Gordon Ebbe and the pilot Lieutenant Commander Henry P. Jorda.

The Russians planned several bases, among them Vostock Station at the axis of the earth's magnetic field—the Geomagnetic South Pole—and Sovietskaya at the "Pole of Inaccessibility" in Wilkes Land at Latitude 82° 30′ South, Longitude 56° East where the Polar Plateau rises to 11,500 feet. Byrd flew over the proposed site of Vostock and appraised it. Then he headed for Sovietskaya.

14. Richard E. Byrd, Jr., could not make the flight as he was on duty as Geographic Officer at McMurdo Base.
15. Siple, *90° South*.

Heavy clouds blocked the way, but not before he had acquired a general idea of the terrain. Then his plane headed directly for the South Pole along the 90th Meridian East Latitude.

The navigator of the Skymaster overshot the Pole by forty miles because broken clouds interfered with the sun compass, but there was plenty of gas. Indeed, there was plenty of everything, including a heated cabin and hot pork chops for lunch. Again—quite a difference!

The plane turned back and located the Pole. As they circled it, going from January 8 to January 9 and back to January 8 three times, Commander Ebbe jokingly asked, "How could we count this in our per diem?" [16]

Then, the plane was taken down to only two or three hundred feet above the snow so that Byrd could study the surface. He could tell by the light, fan-shaped sastrugi, or snowdrifts, that the névé snow underneath was as hard as usual. In fact there was surprisingly little loose snow at the Pole, possibly due to very high winds blowing it away. He and Siple were in complete agreement that landings by ski-equipped R4D's were both practical and safe. Even heavier P2V's were able to land there when Byrd had their skis faced with Teflon to prevent sticking to the ice.

Then they flew back to McMurdo by way of the Beardsley Glacier, which appeared to Byrd to be shrinking. They landed at the base about 10:30 P.M., having flown 2,310 miles in eleven hours ten minutes. The Admiral noted, "I had never made a polar flight under such comfortable conditions." [17]

Soon after landing, Byrd radioed the Russian IGY Expedition: "Welcome to Wilkes Land. Hope you are having good luck finding your IGY Base Site. We recently flew over interior in vicinity of your planned inland bases. Surface does not appear rough, but glacial plateau ranges from 11,000 to 13,000 feet elevation. We would like to exchange weather information. Siple joins me in sending our best wishes for success of our international effort for science."

This was Byrd at his diplomatic best, for it was a courteous and helpful gesture combined with a gentle remainder that he was there first; and it emphasized the international aspect of the IGY.

By February, the McMurdo Base and Little America V were well established. Navy planes were making long exploratory flights

16. Byrd, "All Out Assault On Antarctica," *op. cit.*
17. *Ibid.*

from McMurdo and a series of short training flights for pilots new to Antarctic conditions was begun. In Navy jargon these were known as "flight familiarization," but the pilots called them "fright familiarization."

On February 3, 1956, Admiral Byrd and his son sailed for New Zealand in the *Arneb*. The Admiral was in tip-top physical condition, glowing with a sense of achievement and the prospect of greater things to come. There was no sign or premonition that he was looking at his "enchanted continent in the sky" for the last time.[18]

In New Zealand the round of receptions, banquets, and speech-making began all over again. Byrd's son said, "They had a tremendous program for Father. It was extremely exhausting, but he took it all in his stride. I could not keep up with him. He wore out all his staff including Paul Siple [a huge and powerful man weighing 250 pounds]. He had to get people from other naval units to replace those who fell by the wayside." [19]

As always, when the Byrds reached the United States, Marie was on hand to meet them. The Admiral was immediately plunged into another exhausting round of festivities: in New York, where Mayor Wagner gave him the Keys of the City; in Philadelphia, where he received the Poor Richard Award; and in Boston. In Washington, when he addressed the Daughters of the American Revolution, Byrd did not talk about the Antarctic at all, but opened his speech with a poem on chivalry. "The ladies loved it." [20]

There is a photograph of him at a Pentagon conference on this visit to Washington. Though his hair was almost white, he was still straight and slim, with ruddy cheeks and the old sparkle in his blue-gray eyes. On the breast of his uniform there was hardly room for the ribbons he was entitled to wear—almost every medal his country could give him and many from other nations.

Yet these exhausting programs eroded much of the renewed energy Antarctica had given Byrd. When they were temporarily over, he went back to the grind of organizing the second phase of the program—Deep Freeze II. Though his physical examinations

18. Richard E. Byrd, Jr., to the author.
19. *Ibid.*
20. *Ibid.*

showed nothing seriously wrong, he fought an almost overpowering weariness. His doctors—and his family—begged him to take a "let up." He himself wished he could. But temperamentally and in honor he could not while so much remained to be done and he was still Officer in Charge.

There were further triumphs to lift his spirits. On October 31, 1956, Admiral Dufek and a party landed in a ski-equipped plane at the South Pole, conclusively proving that Byrd's estimate of conditions there was correct. Early in 1957, Ansel Talbert on the first commercial flight over the South Pole radioed, "I am thinking of your first flight."

Admiral Byrd had persuaded Paul Siple to take charge of the civilian effort in building the South Pole Station. Eighteen men were to winter there at a cost, Siple figured, of $1,000,000 each. There was a split command between Navy and IGY which threatened trouble, but Siple managed to get along well with the Navy Commander, Lieutenant (j.g.) Richard A. Bowers, and later with Lieutenant (j.g.) John Tuck, Jr. However, in his book *90° South,* Siple gave vent to many gripes about slights and non-cooperation of the Navy brass.

On October 3, 1956, Paul Siple had lunched with the Byrds at 9 Brimmer Street just prior to leaving for Antarctica. He reported, perhaps with hindsight, that the Admiral looked delicate, but "still exuded his usual boyish enthusiasm and puckish humor." [21]

After lunch those two old comrades talked for a long time about the new project and old times. As a lazy red sun was setting over the Charles, Siple rose to take leave. The Admiral presented him with a superb navigator's wrist watch. On its back was engraved: *To my old comrade, Paul Siple from Dick Byrd.*

The two men stood silent; Paul seemed unable to speak. The Admiral said, "Paul, living at the South Pole would have been the high point of my life. But since I can't go, there is no one I'd rather see taking my place than you." [22]

Paul Siple succeeded in setting up the South Pole Station in spite of great difficulties. To begin with, the Navy miscalculated slightly, landing the first construction party eight miles from the Pole. All the

21. Siple, *90° South.*
22. *Ibid.*

material had to be hauled over the snow. Even then, meticulous observations showed the new situation was still half a mile off. Siple set up a flagpole in a circle of empty gasoline drums at the exact spot.

The South Pole Station was officially commissioned on January 10, 1957. Messages came from all over the world and there were ceremonies in New Zealand and the United States. Admiral Byrd named it the Amundsen-Scott Station in an emotional speech in which he recalled the inspiration that Captain Scott, who died so gallantly on his way back from the South Pole, had been to his own youthful spirit; and the help that Amundsen, who in his words "breathed greatness," had been to him on the North Pole flight and in preparing for his first expedition to the Antarctic.

On February 21, 1957, the Chief of Naval Operations, Admiral Arleigh Burke, acting upon the recommendation of President Eisenhower, presented Admiral Byrd with the Medal of Freedom, the last of the glittering awards he received from his country. The Presidential citation stated that: "This decoration was awarded to [Admiral Byrd] in recognition of his outstanding accomplishments as Officer in Charge of the United States Antarctic Programs (1955–1957), and his humanitarian contributions to the world."

Admiral Byrd enjoyed both of these immensely moving occasions, but they were a further drain on his waning strength. However, his enthusiasm was undimmed. He was particularly pleased by the fact that, in addition to the United States, eleven other nations had set up bases until a total of 46 IGY bases were operating in Antarctica and 15 more on adjacent islands. He was working hard to bring about a treaty making this unique example of international cooperation a permanent arrangement in Antarctica, outlawing war and, especially, atomic weapons there. He did not want to go through the United Nations because he felt that this would bring in many nations which had no possible interest in Antarctica. Rather he sought to bring together those nations with a legitimate stake in the Continent, whether or not they actually had bases there, in a pact for mutual cooperation and good will. This effort was, of course, in addition to his supervisory role as Officer in Charge of the American IGY Antarctic program. It cost him his last ounce of strength.

All those last months he kept promising that he would arrange "a let up" in his rigorous schedule, but he did not. Early in March, 1957, in an interview he said, "I am trying desperately to get a let up." He never succeeded in slowing down.

But his incredible luck held to the end. There was no long twilight period of declining powers, no diminution of mental acuity, or even an erosion of his good looks or youthful zest. On March 11, 1957, Admiral Byrd, at the peak of his reputation and the summit of accomplishment, died in his sleep.

Throughout this story mention has often been made of Admiral Byrd's incredible good fortune in his perilous enterprises. No derogation of his magnificent accomplishments is thereby intended. Great men make their own luck, as the Admiral made his, by courage, foresight, and taking the infinite pains of genius. All these qualities the Admiral had, in addition to the one indispensable attribute, an instructive, almost mystic, feeling for the limits of the possible and a sense of how the tide is flowing. Somehow he knew when to say, "Hold, enough!" and when to command, "Damn the torpedoes! Full ahead."

When Admiral Byrd died, the leaders of many nations and men renowned for their gift of words paid him tribute. But the epitaph he would have liked most was pronounced by his brother Tom, who said, "Dick was born courageous."

Though he did not live to see it, Admiral Byrd's greatest ambition was realized, in part at least, in the Antarctic Treaty, which was signed and ratified by twelve nations, among them Russia, the United States, Great Britain, France and Norway.[23] In it they pledged that, "Antarctica shall be used for peaceful purposes only. There shall be no establishment of military bases . . . [or] the testing of any type of weapons." The area embraced by the Treaty was declared to be any land or ice-shelf lying within 60° South Latitude. Freedom of scientific investigation and cooperation to that end among the signatory nations was assured, as well as a free exchange of scientific information. Nuclear explosion in Antarctica and disposal there of radioactive waste were forbidden, and, *for the first time*, Soviet Russia agreed to on-site inspection of their bases by international inspection teams.

Incidentally, on the occasion of the first inspection in 1963, the Russians could not have been more cooperative. They showed the ob-

23. Sixteen nations are now signatories.

servers their installations and with sly humor even invited them to "look under the beds." [24]

The Treaty, which became effective on June 23, 1961, assured the continuation of the enormously successful joint international effort begun during the International Geophysical Year. Today some sixteen nations work in Antarctica in amity and cooperation. Of course the rapid advances in technology have made the Antarctic bases far more comfortable and efficient than even Admiral Byrd could have visualized. For example, instead of the jerry-built, oil-fired horror of a stove which laid Byrd low with carbon-monoxide poisoning at Advance Base, the United States South Pole Station is heated by atomic energy. A lead-encased packet of uranium 38 no more than two feet square contains sufficient fuel to heat it comfortably for a year.

When he was Officer in Charge of the American IGY Program, Admiral Byrd wrote, "I am hopeful that Antarctica, in its symbolic robe of white, will shine forth as a continent of peace as nations working together there in the cause of science set an example of international cooperation." [25]

That hope came true. In 1966, the Assembly of the United Nations approved the text of a treaty, modeled after the Antarctic Treaty, stating that, "The exploration and use of outer space, including the moon and other celestial bodies shall be carried out for the benefit and in the interests of all countries irrespective of their degree of economic or scientific development, and shall be the province of all mankind."

The treaty barred all military weapons from outer space and provided for inspection of orbiting objects. It assured the cooperation of all the signatory nations in the free exploration of space and free exchange of scientific data. It was signed by the great majority of the nations of the world. Most importantly it was ratified by the United States and Soviet Russia. Now a similar treaty is proposed for the depths of the oceans.

There can be no doubt that the Space Treaty, as well as the more recent Nuclear Non-Proliferation Treaty, stemmed from the success of the Antarctic Treaty and, as such, owed their affirmation in no small degree to Admiral Byrd's vision of a "Continent of Peace."

24. Richard E. Byrd, Jr., to the author.
25. Byrd, "All Out Assault on Antarctica," *op. cit.*

BOOK FIVE

The Senator

I · HARRY FLOOD BYRD
OF VIRGINIA

WHILE HIS brother, Admiral Byrd, was winning fame at the ends of the earth, Senator Harry Flood Byrd, considerably less flamboyant, was content to make the Commonwealth of Virginia his domain. He loved his state with a rare passion, from the sand dunes on her Atlantic beaches, to the flat, history-soaked meadows of Tidewater and the rocky, pine-covered peaks of the Blue Ridge. Especially he loved the Blue Ridge. He loved the land and its people and Virginians returned this love full measure.

From the sure political base of his state, Harry Byrd wielded an influence that, for better or worse, probably left as great an impression on the history of his country as all of the Admiral's scientific achievements. Even the Senator's most vigorous political opponent in Virginia, Colonel Francis Pickens Miller, admitted that, "It is true that Senator Byrd was greatly beloved. He embodied the very essence of Virginia." [1]

Colonel Miller was not referring to the Virginia of romantic fiction. Harry Byrd was a practical fellow, even though he stoutly defended many a lost cause. His dreams did not chase Aurora up the sky, but he did have dreams. And principles, especially principles. He also had power.

1. Colonel Miller to the author.

Senator Byrd was a rich man. He got his money the hard way, by working sixteen hours a day, six days a week from the age of fifteen until he died in his eightieth year. None of it was inherited. The lack of cash money in his youth conditioned his thinking on fiscal matters throughout his life; that, and having been born only twenty-two years after the Civil War when the Shenandoah Valley was still a place of genteel poverty. Paint was peeling off the noble Corinthian columns of the great mansions; roofs were leaky, or obviously patched. And every man over thirty he knew could remember the Federal troops, the carpetbaggers, and going hungry because of devastated fields, stolen cattle, and the wreckage of the economy.

Harry Byrd never lacked food; but he had no money for luxuries. No one had any money. If a man got into debt, there was small chance of getting out of it. The Commonwealth itself was in debt; and it seemed as though it would never be paid off. So owing money was a terrible thing, a lifelong burden and a stain on honor. Byrd never forgot the misery it brought. He had an almost pathological abhorrence for borrowing that went beyond reason to the realm of deep emotion.

However, Byrd's political power was inherited in some degree. He belonged to the closely interrelated group of families who had governed Virginia under the King and the Republic ever since the Dominion was founded in the seventeenth century; but family influence provided only the launching platform. Byrd achieved his national importance by his own qualities. In politics he was as indefatigable as his brother, the Admiral, was in the pursuit of science and glory. After being Governor of the Commonwealth, Harry Flood Byrd was United States Senator from Virginia for thirty-three years, during which time he worked as hard for what he considered her interests and those of his country as he ever had on his own behalf.

The Senator's outstanding quality, which endeared him to the electorate, was his integrity. Even his most ardent enemies—and he had some bitter ones—never questioned that. Whatever the temptations or political advantages of another course, he never wavered from his conservative principles of fiscal responsibility and limitation of Federal power. This made him the most popular politician in Virginia and most unpopular with the ardent reformers in the social-minded Federal governments, Democratic and Republican, which succeeded one another while Byrd held sway as the Chairman of the

Senate Finance Committee. He was either a bulwark of financial integrity or a roadblock in the path of progress, according to the point of view; an unbiased estimate seems to indicate that he was both. His austerity in his personal habits and in his public policies once led Forrest Davis to refer to him as "A Puritan sport on a cavalier tree." [2]

So tenacious was Byrd's grip on the State of Virginia that a not completely mythical monster known as the "Byrd Machine" decided who would hold almost every important office in the State. The power of the Byrd Machine was sometimes ruthlessly applied by the Senator's satraps, but, generally speaking, it rested less on patronage and pressure tactics than on the Senator's personal popularity. The Machine fell apart when he died.

An important factor in Byrd's success was that a majority of his fellow Virginians saw eye to eye with him and trusted him. It may not have been sensible of them to agree with him so completely; for example, his financial fetish against borrowing money left Virginia with an extremely inadequate school system. Since Byrd never had time himself to acquire a formal education, he was inclined to regard this deficiency too casually. However, Virginians were certainly right to trust him. Thomas Schlesinger, son and brother of the historians, once said, "The Byrd Machine governed Virginia with grace and integrity, but it was not democracy." [3] That is a very fair statement.

Obviously Senator Byrd lost most of his battles with the Federal Government. His was a rear-guard action against the overwhelming forces of technology, of necessary social progress, and of the appalling complexity of modern economics. Except for his excellent record as a reform Governor of Virginia, Byrd's influence on history had to be negative—not what he did but what he succeeded in preventing overenthusiastic devotees of progress from doing. Had he not been there the Federal machine might have plunged beyond control down the declivity of burgeoning bureaucracy and fiscal adventure. At the very least, his careful scrutiny of expenditures from stamps to battleships saved the American people a great deal of money that might otherwise have been wasted.

Once, in one of his famous furies, President Harry S. Truman

2. Forrest Davis, "The Fourth Term's Hair Shirt," *Saturday Evening Post,* April 8, 1944.

3. Mr. Schlesinger to the author.

said, "There are too many Byrds in the Senate." *Life* magazine, summing up the Senator's career after his death in 1966, observed, "In Virginia, and in every other state, there will always be too few, not too many, Harry Byrds. Men like him, not his fetishes, are what keep freedom alive."

II · YOUNG MAN IN A HURRY

HARRY was the most companionable of the Byrd boys—at least his father found him so. Just as Dick was his mother's favorite, Harry was his father's. When his eldest son was about nine or ten years old, Mr. Dick began to take him up to Byrd's Nest, his cabin at Skyline, to share his periods of solitude and, incidentally, his drinking bouts. Harry was never obtrusive or demanding, nor did he raise an eyebrow when his father drank excessively. He seemed to accept the drinking as an unalterable part of the older man's character, but it was probably seeing his idol and mentor reduced by alcohol to childlike helplessness that gave Harry an un-Byrdlike aversion to alcohol. Though, except during prohibition, he served liquor to his friends, he was a teetotaler all his life. Oddly enough, when his father, Mr. Dick, was Speaker of the House of Delegates, he passed Virginia's first prohibition law, an act denying licenses to saloons in remote parts of the state where there was no police protection.

Those days in the rough cabin at Skyline, in what was then an unmarred wilderness completely cut off from civilization, fostered Harry's inherited love of solitude and his abiding love of mountains, above all, the Blue Ridge. When he was in his seventies and crippled by arthritis, he still climbed Old Rag, his favorite mountain, every year on his birthday.

The warm relationship between father and son was partly due to their compatibility and partly to a charming side of Mr. Dick's character. He loved children and they returned the compliment. When he walked down Amherst Street in Winchester toward his office on the Courthouse Square, children followed him as they had the legendary piper in Hamlin. True, he always had a pocketful of candies, but he and they knew that this was not the real attraction.

Like his brother Dick, Harry developed the main elements of his character very early. He hated waste and had a remarkable aptitude for business. In 1903, the Winchester *Evening Star*,[1] which Mr. Dick owned and used to promote his own political career, was bankrupt. Its owner, who was a poor businessman, had more interesting things to think about—such as becoming Speaker of the House of Delegates. Besides, Mr. Dick had an aversion to dunning his friends, which meant virtually everyone in Winchester owed him money for advertising. Harry could not bear to see this potentially profitable business go under. When he was barely fifteen years old he went to his father and asked to be allowed to leave the Shenandoah Academy and put the newspaper on its feet. His brother Dick had just returned from his much publicized trip around the world and this may have had something to do with Harry's haste to quit fooling around with education and do something useful; but his primary motive was probably financial.

Mr. Dick agreed to let the boy try. That he would consent to his son's leaving the Academy at the age of fifteen, without even a high-school diploma, is surprising enough; but the really extraordinary thing is that he believed Harry could do what he proposed. Everyone in Winchester undoubtedly thought Mr. Dick was crazy. However, he knew Harry better than anyone else. He always had complete confidence in his son's judgment and backed him to the hilt in any enterprise he ever undertook.

The *Star* was in the worst sort of trouble a newspaper can have. It owed $2,500 to the Antietam Paper Company, across the Potomac in Maryland. Seeing no prospect of being paid, the company refused to ship any more paper on credit. Donning his first suit with long trousers, Harry crossed the river to talk to the paper company's officials. He had nothing to sell but himself—but that he could always do. The deal he proposed was that the paper company ship

1. Now the Winchester *Star*.

one day's supply of paper every day, which he would pay for in cash. This was the first appearance of Byrd's famous pay-as-you-go policy. The Antietam people liked his forthright style and, despite his youth, thought he looked like a go-getter. They accepted the deal, saying in effect, "All right! We will ship the newsprint C.O.D. every day. If you pay for the shipments in cash, you can forget about the debt." [2]

Then Harry went after the businessmen who owed money for advertising. In his quiet, courteous way he pointed out that if the *Star* went under, it would leave them only one place to advertise their wares, the *Star*'s bitter rival, *The News Item* owned by George Norton. This monopoly situation would be bad for them in the long run, Harry said, and he asked for payments on account. Hereafter, he said, the *Star* would accept advertising only on a pay-as-you-go basis. Most of the merchants agreed to go along. Harry and the *Star* were back in business, but on many a morning he scurried around town collecting five dollars here, two there, selling an extra advertisement or so, and reaching the station just in time to pay cash for the newsprint for that afternoon's edition.

Under his cost-conscious management the situation gradually improved to the point where the *Star* was actually making money, and Harry could afford to buy a small inventory of paper sufficient to assure that the *Star* would come out even if the creeks rose and cut rail communications with Maryland. He also insisted on paying off the "forgotten" debt for $2,500 to the Antietam Paper Company.

However, it was still a struggle; for Winchester was not big enough to support two newspapers. James Thompson, a far more prosperous newspaperman who lived in Summit Point, just over the state line in West Virginia, suggested to Harry that he buy the *News Item*. "That's impossible," Harry said. "Norton is Father's political enemy. He'd never sell to me."

"Let me talk to him," Thompson said.

The upshot was that Harry bought the *News Item* for $2,500 and closed it down. Now the *Star* had a monopoly. Harry once told Mr. Thompson, "That was the beginning of my good fortune." [3]

Meanwhile Byrd looked around for ways to improve his own finances. Reckoning that he could manage the *Star* in his off hours, he

2. Gray Beverley (Byrd's brother-in-law) in conversation with the author.
3. Mrs. Massie's memoirs and Mrs. James Thompson to the author.

took a full-time job as local manager of the Southern Bell Telephone Company at $60 a month. Still he had energy to spare. In 1908, when Harry was twenty-one, he talked his way into the presidency of the Valley Turnpike Company which owned the Valley Pike, the only paved intercity highway in Virginia. This was the same road on which the third William Byrd had fought the Indians in the French and Indian War. A hundred years later General Philip Henry Sheridan had galloped along it to rally his demoralized army at Cedar Creek. In 1908, it was a stretch of macadamized road running from Winchester to Staunton, Virginia, with toll gates every few miles. The cost of a trip between the two cities was $4.75, an enormous toll for those days, but well worth it to a motorist or even a heavily loaded farm wagon when the alternative was trying to slog through eighty miles of red Virginia mud. At chosen spots on other roads, farmers waited with their teams of mules ready hitched to haul helpless motorists out of a quagmire at a cost of $10.00, which made the toll on the Valley Pike a bargain.

Byrd's presidency paid him $33 a month and entailed driving the length of the Turnpike at least twice a month to inspect it and to arrange for necessary repairs. He must have considered it worthwhile, for he held the position for ten years.

Even before that, when he was nineteen, Harry Byrd had drifted into the business which was to become the foundation of his fortune. Then, as now, the Shenandoah Valley was a splendid place to grow apples. Around Winchester there were many small orchards of two to ten acres whose owners were too busy with other occupations to care for or harvest the fruit properly. Young Byrd saw in this an opportunity to add to his income. In June, when the danger of frost was past and the small, green apples, no bigger than Ping-Pong balls, clustered thickly on the trees, he approached the owner of such an orchard just beyond the railroad tracks in Winchester and offered to buy and harvest his crop. The owner jumped at his offer. It was good business for him, since it relieved him of a great deal of bother, and it was good business for Harry because half the speculation in apple-growing in the Valley comes in the hazardous period in late April and May when a heat wave may force the delicate blossoms too early permitting untimely cold to shrivel them. All Byrd had left to worry about that year was drought, excessive rain, and insects.

Having made one deal, Byrd went on to make others. He

bought a spray rig and recruited a crew from the Negroes and whites who hung around the streets of Winchester looking for odd jobs. Right after sun-up and in the evenings he worked beside them thinning, spraying, nurturing his apples. Every evening he paid the men off in cash. Gray Beverley, who later became Byrd's brother-in-law, reports that, "In those days Harry worked eighteen hours a day." [4]

It was not necessary for him to work so hard. Mr. Dick, though far from rich, would have seen his son through high school, college and, had he desired, law school, as he did for Harry's brother Tom. It was the nature of the man, an inner compulsion compounded of ambition and a desire to make things grow, that drove Harry into these activities, as the Admiral was driven to his more spectacular accomplishments.

In both cases the Byrd drive paid off. Harry took on more and more orchards. Throughout the summers he had a small permanent crew of workers, who lived in a "sort of big house on wheels," a truck, which also carried the spray rig, ladder, and tools.

By 1911, Byrd had saved enough capital to buy a piece of land for an orchard of his own. It lay in the open country just north of Winchester on what is now Hawthorne Drive. With his crew, Byrd planted apple trees on this land himself. In 1912, in partnership with the Reverend William Smith, the Episcopal minister, he bought his first bearing orchard, the Rosemont Orchard nine miles to the east near Berryville. He loved this orchard most of all because part of it was land from the Cottage Farm on which Thomas Taylor Byrd had settled in the Shenandoah Valley in 1786.

By then, through a combination of intensive study and practical experience, Byrd knew more about apple-growing than many a Cornell graduate in pomology. Unlike the limited nature of today's crops, there were sixteen varieties of apples in Byrd's burgeoning orchards. He grew Ben Davises, Albermarle Pippins, Grime's Goldens, Staymans, Yorkshires, Winesaps, Wealthies, and Smokehouses to mention a few. Each variety had its special quality of flavor, tart or sweet; it was firm-fleshed or mealy; early or late bearing; of a unique color, durability, and resistance to pests. Beauty of appearance did not correspond to flavor. The current Byrds declare they could grow much more delicious fruit if people did not insist on buying big red or golden apples.

4. Gray Beverley to the author.

Much of Byrd's first crops were shipped abroad, especially to England where appearance counted for less than flavor. Though politically conservative, Byrd was an innovator in apple-growing, alert to follow changes in public taste, to introduce new varieties and abandon old ones, to switch markets or introduce new labor-saving devices and new methods of spraying. To keep track of his multiplying orchards he bought a horse and runabout—a smart, one-seater trap that had evolved from the farmer's buggy. When he needed more speed, he got a motorcycle on which he whizzed, bumping and jumping over the rutty roads and between the long rows of burgeoning trees, the very prototype of a young man in a hurry. He had to be quick to remain solvent in that precarious business.

With all his jobs and business interests, Harry Byrd had little time for the normal pleasures of youth. While the other young men of Winchester were leaving work early to play tennis and staying out late to take their girls on picnics, or to the movies, or just buggy-riding through moonlit, fragrant lanes, Harry was either tearing from job to orchard to job on his sputtering motorcycle or sleeping the dreamless sleep of exhaustion in his big, cool bedroom in the house on Amherst Street. However, on the seventh day he rested.

Everyone who possibly could observed Sunday in those early days of the century. It was part of the pattern of life. In social customs Harry was a conformist. Fortunately, Sundays in Virginia were not like the joyless Sabbaths of New England. Most of Harry's friends were, like himself, devout Episcopalians. They went properly to church on Sunday mornings, but after that observance, Episcopalians considered it no harm to have a little fun, being in that more like Catholics than the stern disciples of the Puritan ethic.

The younger crowd in Winchester usually met in the afternoon at Robert and Davis Conrad's big hospitable house with its tennis court and large, shady lawn. The house was like a country club with no dues and congenial company; lemonade or iced tea was drunk under the tall trees and there was a Victrola to dance to if they felt so inclined. It was a simpler scene than Westover in the eighteenth century, but in the same hospitable tradition.

Harry Byrd was welcome whenever he could come. Though as different in appearance from Dick as two brothers could be, he, too, was good-looking with his big blue eyes, red-gold hair and round, apple-cheeked face. He always wore an immaculate white linen suit in summer, and freshly blancoed white tennis shoes. Despite his experience and essential toughness in business, he had a rather touching innocence, especially where women were concerned. His unsophistication may have been due in part to the proprieties of rural Virginia and partly to his lack of formal education. He simply had no time to read the avant-garde literature from England and abroad that was, almost imperceptibly as yet, readying American youth for their great leap forward in sophistication after World War I. To his pleasant unworldliness was added the good manners of his upbringing and birthright, and a liberal endowment of Byrd charm. Among themselves the girls called him "Handsome Harry." [5]

In 1912, Anne Douglas Beverley and her brothers, Westwood Gray and Bradshaw Beverley, were among the regulars at the Conrads'. Nicknamed "Sittie," as the only sister of four brothers, she was a tiny girl with golden hair and blue eyes and a gentle nature. Devoted though Harry Byrd was to his strong, outspoken mother, it was natural that he should find Sittie's sweetness and conformity extremely attractive. He began finding time to go courting her in the customary way, taking her for rides in his horse-drawn runabout—motorcycles were considered vulgar as conveyances for ladies—to baseball games and dances. Quite soon they were thought of as a couple. As naturally as apple blossoms attract honey bees they became engaged.

Both families were delighted. The match was in the best tradition of the Virginian aristocracy, for Sittie was descended from Robert Beverley and Ursula Byrd—the first William's little Nutty.

A splendid wedding was planned for October 7, 1913. There were to be eight bridesmaids and eight groomsmen, all of them kinfolks of the bride or the groom or both; also two flower girls and a small page. Harry could not choose between his beloved brothers to be his best man, so he asked both of them. His mother, "Miss Bolling," extravagantly bought a gown of "white rhinestone cloth over white charmeuse imported from France." The bride's mother, Mrs. James Bradshaw Beverley, decided to wear "pink charmeuse with gold passamentry-trimming and diamond ornaments." The bridesmaids wore green charmeuse under shadow lace; and the bride chose white charmeuse under shadow lace, and a tulle veil with diamond

5. Mrs. Massie's memoirs.

ornaments in her hair.[6] The fathers got their tailcoats out of moth-balls and rubbed up their high silk hats. Harry bought a new dress suit, but compromised on a derby.

Harry Byrd had great good fortune in his marriage, but the luck was out the day of his wedding. Shortly before the big day a Mr. Joseph Wright, a cousin of Mrs. Beverley's by marriage, died. According to Virginia usage mourning was almost as strictly observed as among the French aristocracy, whose women spend half their lives wearing black for distant cousins. Mrs. Beverley decreed that although the wedding could go on as scheduled, the elaborate reception afterward and the ball beforehand must be canceled. All the fine clothes, the bridal gown and lovely bridesmaids' dresses would be seen for at most twenty minutes in church.

To add to the disappointment October 7 was, in the words of one of the bridesmaids, "The rainiest days there ever was." [7] Somehow they all got to Christ's Episcopal Church that evening. Sittie walked solemnly up the aisle on her father's arm. Harry appeared flanked by Ensign Richard E. Byrd, Jr., splendid in his dress uniform with the first of his many decorations on his breast, and Tom, towering genially over both of them. The reporter for the *Star* wrote: "The bride is a lovely little girl, as beautiful in character as she is in person. . . . Surrounded by the groom and his two brothers and her superbly dressed bridesmaids, she was married at eight o'clock in the evening . . . [by] the Reverend William D. Smith."

Miss Bolling took pity on the wedding party with no place to go after the ceremony and gave a reception for them at the house on Amherst Street. The bride and groom did not attend it, for Sittie's ideas about mourning were as strict as her mother's. However, Harry, already the good politician, gave a stag dinner for his disappointed guests at the Fairfax Club where, "He appeared for a short time and received the congratulations of his friends."

According to the *Star*, Mr. and Mrs. Byrd boarded a midnight train at Martinsburg for Washington, New York, and Atlantic City. But according to their family and friends the happiest moments of their honeymoon were spent at Byrds' Nest on a peak of the Blue Ridge.

The Harry Byrds first lived in an apartment his parents ar-

6. Winchester *Evening Star*, October 8, 1913.
7. Mrs. W. Nelson Page to the author.

ranged for them in their home on Amherst Street, perhaps to save money but more likely because Harry loved the old house. He was as busy as ever with his jobs and his ever-expanding orchards. Within three years he was able to build a big, two-story log house in the Rosemont Orchards. It had a main room forty feet long warmed by a great stone fireplace and plenty of guest rooms for his friends. He and Sittie lived there in the summertime. In winter they went back to Winchester.

In addition to the orchards, Harry was beginning to make very shrewd investments in America's booming industries. Had he concentrated on making money, he undoubtedly would have become very rich indeed; but that was not his main goal. At first he worked hard at it to give himself, and his family, a reasonably comfortable way of life. Later he played the game for the fun of it, as he might play a few rounds of solitaire in the evening. Harry Byrd's great game, the focus of his life and the delight of his soul, was politics.

III · THROUGH THE RED
VIRGINIA MUD

ARRY BYRD was elected to public office before he ever voted. In 1908, when he was just twenty-one, he won election to the Winchester City Council. Even before that he had, of course, been a worker for the Democratic party.

If Byrd's formal education was somewhat sketchy, his political education was conducted by experts and he graduated *magna cum laude*. His mentors were his father, who in 1908 had just become Speaker of the Virginia House of Delegates; his uncle, Congressman Henry Delaware Flood of Appomattox, who was soon to become Chairman of the House Foreign Affairs Committee; and his kinsman, United States Senator Thomas Martin of Charlottesville, Virginia, who was head of the powerful political machine known as the "Organization." This small group of men ran the Democratic party in the Commonwealth. In other words they ran Virginia. In addition, young Byrd was on friendly terms with virtually all of the local Winchester party leaders. What the elders in his own family did not teach him, these men did.

During the years when he was getting on his feet financially, Harry Byrd was content to remain a member of the City Council and a good party worker, while his relatives became increasingly powerful. In 1912, his father was a delegate to the Democratic National

Convention where, as we have seen, he earned the gratitude of Woodrow Wilson by defying Senator Martin and swinging part of the Virginia Delegation to Wilson.

Riding the campaign train through Virginia with Wilson and having a considerable voice in Federal patronage in Virginia after Wilson's election made Mr. Dick even more powerful in the Commonwealth. When Wilson appointed him United States District Attorney for Western Virginia, in 1914, Mr. Dick resigned from the House of Delegates and opened a law office in Richmond with his son Tom, recently graduated from the University of Virginia Law School. Possible conflict of interest was not then a matter of public anxiety; nor need it have been with a man of Mr. Dick's integrity.

Harry, who had been waiting for the right time to begin a political career, seized upon this moment. With his connections, he had no great difficulty in getting elected to the State Senate in 1915 at the age of twenty-seven.

Young State Senator Byrd was an energetic legislator. He served on the Finance, Roads and Privileges, and Elections Committees. His first years in the State Senate were a serene era in Commonwealth politics, though not so on the national scene. The Organization was functioning as quietly as a Rolls Royce and there were no controversial local issues. The outbreak of World War I in Europe riveted the eyes of all Americans on the international and national scene. The sinking of the *Lusitania* by a German submarine on May 7, 1915, began the long, heated debate as to whether or not America should enter the war on the side of the Allies. This, together with the flood of prosperity engendered by the war orders from England, France, and Russia, kept labor, management, and even the farmers quite contented with the status quo.

Byrd's best friend in the State Senate was Willis Robertson, a very tall, lanky young man who had been elected at the same time Byrd was. They had more than that in common, for Robertson had also been born in Martinsburg only two weeks earlier than Harry; and the same doctor had taken care of their mothers. Though they had not known each other particularly well before entering the Senate, they became inseparables in politics and friendship, a relationship that endured throughout Harry Byrd's life.

Byrd and Robertson were known as liberals within the comity of the Organization. They supported a law for the protection of working children, the Workmen's Compensation Act, and legislation for improving the schools. They were both interested in Virginia's roads, or lack of them, and made a tentative start at doing something about them.

When peace-loving President Wilson, in an agony of spirit, finally asked Congress for a declaration of war against Germany in April, 1917, it was Byrd's uncle, Hal Flood, Chairman of the Foreign Affairs Committee, who sponsored the bill in the House. A great surge of idealistic patriotism swept the country. Soon Dick Byrd was a naval aviator at Pensacola and Tom went to officers' training camp and served as lieutenant of infantry in France. Harry Byrd was no less patriotic than his brothers but with a wife and two small children —Harry, Jr., and a daughter, Westwood—he felt that he must remain at home. In the years to come his political enemies made some capital of this.

After the war, in 1920, Harry Byrd was elected Chairman of the Virginia State Democratic Committee, though "appointed" might be a better word, in view of the authoritarian control exercised by the party leaders. He was now recognized as one of the power elite, a "comer" who could aspire to the highest offices in the Commonwealth. The party chairmanship did not, however, make him as powerful as it sounded. Though United States Senator Claude A. Swanson was by now the titular boss of the party, effective control of the Organization was grasped by Methodist Bishop James Cannon, a fanatical prohibitionist, a male Carrie Nation in clerical garb. He seized power by using the misguided idealists in the state and the nation who fastened the Eighteenth Amendment to the Constitution during the emotional upheaval of wartime.[1]

Harry Byrd, a teetotaler himself, did not quarrel with the Bishop's antialcoholic views. Indeed, he voted for a state prohibition law and ratification of the Eighteenth Amendment. He was one of the few members of his class who strictly observed both state and Federal law. It was on an entirely different issue that he challenged the Organization, and emerged from comparative obscurity.

The roads in Virginia were called the worst in the nation with

1. *Virginia Record*, January, 1956.

only slight exaggeration. The Valley Pike was now toll-free due to a bill proposed by Byrd in 1918, who thereby legislated himself out of a job. It was still the only paved intercity highway in the state. With the postwar influx of automobiles, the situation had become intolerable. North Carolina, which Virginians had considered backward ever since the days of the second William Byrd, had authorized a $50,000,000 bond issue to build a network of new highways. Could Virginia do less?

Harry Byrd was vitally interested in better roads. In 1918, he and Willis Robertson had introduced a bill to create a State Highway Commission. The next year he supported a bill to start road construction with funds to be advanced by the counties, who were to be reimbursed by the state. The counties put up $12,000,000. A long-needed bridge across the Rappahannock was built, and work on the roads begun.

A majority of the legislature favored a $50,000,000 bond issue to repay the counties and construct more roads. Byrd was against it. To his almost pathological horror of going into debt was added the recollection of the long struggle of Virginia to pay off $35,000,000 in pre-Civil-War bonds issued in 1835. The task had been made more burdensome when West Virginia became a separate state. Northerners, who were then in control of the Boundary Commission, had favored West Virginia in allotting the debt and Virginia had received a highly inequitable share. That old debt had hung like a rotting albatross around the neck of Virginians struggling to rebuild their ravished homeland. It had not yet been entirely paid off by 1922. Byrd figured that interest and other charges had cost Virginia more than four times the amount of the original debt.

As Chairman of the Senate Roads Committee, he led the fight to defeat the bond issue in the General Assembly, proposing instead a 4½ cent tax on gasoline. His group lost by one vote in the Senate. In accordance with the Virginia Constitution, the proposed bond issue was then placed before the voters in a referendum in 1923.

Byrd took to the campaign trail. Back and forth across the state he went, by train, by Model-T Ford and, when that could not get through, by horse and buggy, sloshing along those awful roads to plead with the farmers to vote against the bond issue. Harry Byrd was no great orator and he knew it. He used to go alone into the orchards and practice speaking to the rustling apple trees. On the bond issue he sounded no high-flown phrases, but talked quietly, plainly, giving his audience the facts and the figures.

On Election Day the rain came down as it had not since Noah launched the Ark. In Winchester, Byrd could picture to himself the conservative farmers, upon whom he depended to defeat the bond issue, looking out at the solid downpour through which they must struggle to the polls, shaking their heads, and closing their doors. It did not happen that way. Cursing and griping, they hitched up their teams, cranked up their Model-T's and slogged through the red-mud morasses to vote against the fair promise of a hard surface upon which to travel to town. They did not want the improvement if they had to go into debt. The bond issue was soundly defeated by a majority of over 46,000 votes.

Harry Byrd was the hero of the hour, catapulted into the spotlight of state politics. Congratulations poured in upon him from allies and opponents alike, for he was popular with all factions. It was heady stuff, and his ambition stirred. He looked toward the gubernatorial campaign of 1925. The Constitution of Virginia states that a governor may not serve more than one four-year term, so Governor Lee Trinkle could not succeed himself. The way was open for another man. Furthermore the bond issue was down but not out. Its powerful proponents would try again after the next election; and again and again. So Byrd had not only ambition but a cause, an issue on which he had won once and might again. He let it be known that he was in the running and quietly began sounding out his friends in the Organization. The response was generally favorable, but the big question was what the inner ruling clique, headed by Swanson and Cannon, would say. He got his answer in New York.

Byrd was a delegate to the Democratic National Convention of 1924 held at Madison Square Garden in New York. The convention lasted for nearly two torrid weeks while the partisans of Al Smith and William G. McAdoo fought a grim, no compromise battle for the nomination that tore the National Democratic party into tatters. During that time, with politicians huddling in a hundred smoke-filled rooms, many other things were settled beside the sad fate of the

Democratic party. One of them was the future of Harry Byrd—or so it was thought.

On one stifling evening Byrd came out of his hotel to find Bishop Cannon waiting for a taxi. When he got one, he invited Byrd to ride with him to the Garden. As they drove through the heavy traffic on Madison Avenue, the Bishop spoke in a kindly, paternal, but definitely ex-cathedra manner. "Young man," he said, "I understand that you will be a nominee for Governor. You're a nice fellow and have done a great many good things. You have a fine character and all that; but we have decided your time is not yet. We're going to elect Walter Mapp. Your turn will come perhaps next time, perhaps later than that."

When Harry got home to the house on Amherst Street, he repeated the Bishop's words to his father. Every gray tuft of hair on Mr. Dick's head bristled like an angry dog's; his eyes shot sparks through the thick spectacles. "Did that son of a bitch say that to you?" he growled. "Now you've got to run!" [2]

The Democratic nomination for Governor of Virginia was tantamount to election, so the real political battle took place in the primaries. Throughout the summer of 1925, while his brother Dick was flying over Greenland's glaciered peaks, Harry Byrd tore up and down and across the sunbaked plains and piney hills of the Old Dominion, speaking at every crossroads and hamlet where he could get a crowd together. Unlike most Virginia politicians, he devoted a lot of attention to the rugged Ninth Election District in the southwest corner of the state, where the tough, unpredictable miners with coal dust seeping from their pores stood and listened in scowling silence while Mr. Dick fondled his little derringer, just in case. Byrd's oratorical style was still hopelessly low-keyed and matter of fact, but the people seemed to like it—even the miners. He ran on the debt issue and probably made the same speech with local variations a hundred times. Mr. Dick went with him most of the way. He would support his son to hell and back.

On Monday, August 3, Harry came home to Winchester for the

2. Gray Beverley, Senator Willis Robertson, and Richard Byrd of Rosemont to the author. The quote differed slightly, but the gist of it was the same.

final rally of the campaign. Placards on telephone poles, trees, and fences and headlines in the *Star* urged:

Come to the Empire Theatre Monday, August 3,
to welcome Harry Byrd home

Despite the counterattraction of the arrival of the circus, the people came in thousands. The manager of the theater had to strike the scenery and put three hundred extra seats on the stage. As Byrd walked out on the platform, a solid soul-satisfying roar greeted him from his fellow townsmen. They were all for him, confident of victory, ready to cheer and laugh.

It had been a rough campaign. Knowing that the roots of power were at stake, the leaders of the Organization, with the exception of Carter Glass who backed Byrd, stopped at nothing. At one point the Virginia Highway Contractors' Association sued him for $100,000, for alleged slander in one of his pay-as-you-go speeches. One hundred thousand farmers subscribed one dollar each to pay the damages if assessed, but the case was thrown out of court.

That night in Winchester, Byrd described some of the other tactics used against him. He told the laughing audience that he had been variously depicted as a man of great wealth unsympathetic to the poor, and a bankrupt who never paid his debts; a teetotaler and a drunkard, an infidel and a friend of commercialized vice. "I'm glad," he said, "that the campaign is almost over as I am sort of worried about the next bad character my enemies will try to make me play."

More seriously, Byrd said that he had tried to conduct his campaign so that he could look every man and woman in the face without being ashamed of anything he had done. Then for half an hour he talked about the issues of the campaign and for the hundredth time renewed his pledge to equalize land taxes, oppose all bond issues, and build good roads on the pay-as-you-go plan. It was as the *Star* said, "A night of triumph for a Winchester boy returning home. . . ."[3]

The greater triumph came next day when Byrd beat Walter Mapp and the Organization by over forty-five thousand votes, the largest majority ever polled until then in a gubernatorial primary. He carried every election district except two and every city except

---

3. Winchester *Evening Star*, October 4, 1925.

Roanoke and Lynchburg. In Winchester, only seventeen votes were cast against him.

The actual election campaign was, as it usually is in Virginia, an anticlimax. Although the Organization's support was far from enthusiastic, Virginians had not yet broken the habit of voting Democratic. In addition they knew they had a candidate worth voting for. The Republican candidate, S. Harris Hoge of Roanoke, never had a chance.

But Harry's triumph was dimmed by sorrow. His father, who had been his good companion and staunchest supporter, died on the evening of October 23, 1925, in Richmond. Until a few days before his death, Mr. Dick had appeared to be in splendid health. In addition to campaigning with his son, he had written hundreds of letters, talked to innumerable people, and made dozens of speeches with a flourish and emotional impact that far surpassed his son's rather mundane efforts. His political expertise made him Harry's most valuable adviser. Possibly he had worn himself out, but if he had any regrets, one may be sure it was only that he did not live to see his son inaugurated as Governor of Virginia. At least he knew that his work was well done; his greatest ambition accomplished.

Though Mr. Dick had operated within the power structure of Virginia politics until his son challenged it, he had been no ordinary politician. He had kept his integrity and his ideals intact. He loved nothing better than a good fight, and was ready to challenge anyone who opposed the things he believed in. He never hesitated to champion the underdog in the cause of justice. Gray Williams pronounced his best epitaph when he wrote, "Like Jefferson, Mr. Byrd hated every form of tyranny over the mind of man." [4]

Less than two weeks after his father's death, Harry F. Byrd was elected Governor of Virginia by a majority of over 70,000 out of 120,000 votes cast. At thirty-eight, he was the youngest Governor of Virginia since Thomas Jefferson.

4. Winchester *Evening Star*, October 24, 1925.

IV · REFORMING GOVERNOR

IT HAS BEEN said that the election of Harry Byrd marked the beginning of the "Byrd Machine." It was, in fact, only changing the guard.

The Organization which controlled Virginia politics for over seventy years had its origin back in 1893. From the end of Reconstruction and the rout of the "Black Republicans" and carpetbaggers, political power had been in the hands of the old Confederate heroes and their families. In the 1890's a group of younger politicians, under the leadership of Thomas S. Martin of Scottsville, were becoming restive under the kindly, paternalistic rule of those backward-looking gentlemen. The "Young Turks," as they have been anachronistically called by modern historians, had the financial backing of the railroads—the Chesapeake and Ohio, B & O, and Southern—who wanted to get the Commonwealth moving in the direction of industrial progress. Thomas Martin was a local attorney for the Chesapeake and Ohio.

For a number of years young Martin worked quietly behind the scenes, organizing his cohorts, never offering himself for public office. He had two objectives: to become United States Senator from Virginia and to assume control of the Democratic party in the state. In those days senators from Virginia—and most other states—were elected by the State Legislature. The candidate was previously chosen at a caucus of the Democratic members of the legislature, and all were bound by the majority vote of the caucus.

Martin raised the standard of revolt at the Democratic caucus held in Richmond on December 8, 1893. His campaign manager was Hal Flood of Appomattox. The leading contender for Senator was General Fitzhugh Lee, a former Governor and a nephew of Robert E. Lee. Fitzhugh Lee did not take Martin very seriously; it seemed insanity for an obscure, small-town lawyer to challenge so eminent a candidate. To General Lee's amazement and chagrin, he did not receive the necessary clear majority of votes for nomination on the first ballot, though he had more votes than anyone else.

What happened then belongs in the arcane obscurity of backroom politics. Dark rumors were later circulated that a dozen legislators each received $1,000 of railroad money to switch to Martin. An official investigation uncovered no proof whatever of such venality. The only definite fact is that enough legislators did switch to Martin to elect him United States Senator from Virginia. He remained in office until he died twenty-six years later. He also became the unchallenged boss of the political machine he had built so carefully and he tended it solicitously for the rest of his life.

The absolutism of the machine was further strengthened by the revised constitution which Martin and his colleagues rammed through in 1901. At that time, all the former Confederate states were devising schemes to nullify the Federal Constitution and deprive Negroes of the vote. In the deep South the Grandfather Clause was popular. This requirement confined the suffrage only to those whose grandfathers had been eligible to vote, thus eliminating most Negroes, since their grandfathers had been slaves. The Supreme Court eventually struck the clause down, but it took many years.

Virginians thought of a better and more constitutional device. They simply put a poll tax in the constitution, with the proviso that it must be paid *three years in advance* before a man could vote. This not only eliminated all Negroes, but many poor whites as well. The Virginia electorate became a small, elite body that would almost have met the aristocratic standards of William Byrd of Westover. The Organization became firmly entrenched.

It did not abuse its power. Apart from his political maneuvering, Martin was a blunt and honest man, who did what he thought was

right and said what he thought was true even to Presidents. When
Woodrow Wilson asked his advice about going to the Versailles Peace
Conference in 1919, Martin said, "Don't go!"

"I am going," President Wilson said.

Martin started for the door of the Oval Room. "Mr. President,"
he said, "why the hell did you ask my advice?" [1]

The elected officials, appointed judges, and others put in office by
the Organization were generally honest and efficient. There was surprisingly little graft or injustice, but they all knew that they owed
their positions to the Organization. In 1925, Governor Byrd stepped
into the driver's seat.

Though he used the machinery of the old Organization, Governor
Byrd brought an era of youthful hope and idealism to the people of
Virginia. Frances Strothers, in an article entitled "Youth Takes the
Helm," pointed out that the Governor was only thirty-eight years
old; the editor of the Richmond *News Leader*, Douglas Southall
Freeman, but forty, and the President of the State Chamber of Commerce only thirty. Strothers wrote, "In sixty days he [Byrd] had put
on the statute books of Virginia more constructive legislation than
any previous governor had got there in four years of office." [2]

William Byrd of Westover also would have approved of the way
his descendant governed Virginia. Official business was conducted in
the same incorruptible, conscientious, and courteously decisive manner in which the eighteenth-century Councilor had exercised similar
power. Even his most bitter opponents concede that Byrd was the
best Governor Virginia had in the twentieth century. He was a peculiarly honest man, who even went to the extreme length of taking
his campaign promises seriously. He had pledged himself "to build
roads with speed, efficiency and economy; to develop the schools
which are the dynamos of democracy; to enforce the laws; make the
best use of our great natural resources and let the world know by
means of an effective advertising campaign the riches and opportunities that here await and attract development. . . ."

He added that he considered his election a mandate for economy

1. Marshall W. Fishwick, *Virginia: A New Look at the Old Dominion.* Harper and Brothers, New York, 1959.

2. Quoted in Fishwick, *op. cit.*

and promised to institute "the best methods of efficiency and economy"; abolish useless offices, consolidate duplicate services, and to dedicate himself "to this service for the state I love." [3]

All these things he did except for "the dynamos of democracy" which developed a good deal fewer kilowatt hours than he had hoped.

Byrd began by breaking tradition on his very first day in office. Shortly before Inauguration Day, January 1, 1926, a rural constituent said to him, "I hope you ain't going to become a Silk Hat Harry." [4]

This made Byrd think. He was sworn in wearing the traditional frock coat with a *derby* hat.

It was a bitterly cold day, but despite that, as the Governor made his inaugural address—wearing a heavy frock coat, but no overcoat—his friends observed the sweat pouring down his face.

The only time Byrd ever wore a silk hat was when President Calvin Coolidge came to Williamsburg in 1926. After the official luncheon, Byrd confided to the President that he had bought his first topper in his honor. "Well, Governor," said Coolidge, "it isn't what's on your head, it what's in it that counts." [5]

Governor Byrd's first business was those roads. He got his proposed 4½ cent gasoline tax through the legislature. It yielded $25,000,000 for roads within the first two years. Much to the distress of local politicians who wanted the job, he imported Henry G. Shirley from Maryland to be Highway Commissioner. Shirley was a brilliant man, who had shown great ability in his home state. He made an even greater name for himself in Virginia. In that connection there is an amusing story of the time Governor Byrd stopped at a strange gasoline station with the old beat-up Chevrolet he still drove.

"How is it you've got license plate number one?" the attendant asked, not recognizing him.

"Who do you think should have it?"

"Commissioner Shirley, of course."

"I guess you're right," said Governor Byrd.

Shirley, with Byrd's enthusiastic backing, did such an outstand-

3. Harry F. Byrd's victory speech at Winchester on August 4, 1925. Winchester *Evening Star*, August, 5, 1925.
4. An uppity cartoon character of the era.
5. Judge William M. Tuck, a former Governor of Virginia, to the author.

ing job of road building that, from being close to the worst, Virginia's road system became one of the best in the nation. Eventually Byrd decided that maintaining the secondary roads was too great a burden on the counties, which were not handling them efficiently, and he proposed to Commissioner Shirley that the state take them over. Shirley's reply was, "Are you crazy, Governor?" [6]

The Commissioner's question was justifiable, for it meant doubling the mileage for which the state was responsible. He stated that the financial burden would be too great. Byrd thought otherwise and persuaded or dragooned Shirley into going along. Naturally the proposal threw the county commissioners into an uproar. They hastily got together, formed an association to oppose the bill on state control, and descended on Richmond. By the time they got there, the bill had passed the House and Senate, and was the law of the Commonwealth.

The changeover was accomplished successfully. So that the counties would not lose a capital investment, Byrd arranged for the state to take over their road-building machinery at a fair valuation. It turned out that Shirley was too pessimistic. A great deal of duplication and waste was eliminated as well as a fine source of graft. The county roads were vastly improved. And all these things were accomplished without the state assuming one cent of bonded indebtedness.

Byrd suggested to the county commissioners that they spend the money they saved from the roads on improving their schools. Unfortunately few of them did so.

In spite of the many things Byrd accomplished on the national scene, Senator Robertson considered Virginia's splendid highway system Byrd's finest memorial and sentimentally quoted:

> "Careless of monument by the grave
> He built it in the wilderness so men might see
> Not where he died but where he lived." [7]

Off to a good start on the road system, the Governor went to work on his other pledges. One of the most important was to revise the antiquated tax structure. There was a jungle growth of taxes—county, city, village, property taxes, income taxes; taxes on money in

6. Former Commissioner for Revenue of Page County, M. J. Menefee, to the author.

7. Former Senator Willis Robertson to the author.

the bank, on bonds, securities and personal property. There were enormous inequalities from place to place because local officials appraised the property to be taxed. Property in one county might pay $1,000 in taxes, while property of the same real value might be taxed only $500 in another. Land bore a disproportionate share of all taxes. In addition, the county revenue commissioners had to count every horse, cow, pig, and chicken a farmer owned.

Byrd considered this system of taxation very unfair to the farmers. To correct it he proposed tax segregation, whereby certain sources of taxation were to be reserved to the state and others to the counties and cities for their local expenses. His plan was to finance the state by such methods as the gasoline tax; an increased tax on physical properties, such as public utilities and railroads (which fought it bitterly); intangible taxes; and certain others. At the same time he persuaded the legislature to repeal the 10 mills per $100 of the land tax which the counties and cities had been obliged to pay the state Government so they could use the whole land tax locally. He gradually eliminated many of the nuisance taxes and consolidated others. When these fiscal changes were made new industries began to come into the state, greatly increasing the total revenue.

To carry out some of his other campaign pledges, Governor Byrd needed to revise the Constitution of Virginia. He appointed his kinsman, Gray Williams, to head a commission to advise on the revision. In the end, Byrd wrote a good part of the new constitution himself and edited every period, semi-colon, and comma. The new Constitution made two especially important changes in the basic law of the Commonwealth. The article closest to Byrd's heart was the provision that the Commonwealth of Virginia was prohibited from incurring any bonded indebtedness or borrowing any sum of money larger than $1,000,000, to meet a temporary emergency. With this prohibition in the Constitution, it was virtually impossible for any improvident administration suddenly to plunge the state into debt.

Though this section has been retained through the years, many Virginians think that its benefits have been outweighed in recent times by the disadvantages to the state. True, it has prevented the sort of blue-sky financing that has sent many states floundering in a morass of debt. Of the fifty, Virginia is the only one without a mortgage on her future. On the other hand, it has been expensive in subtle ways. For example, bonds for turnpikes, bridges, college dormitories and other self-liquidating projects have been forced to pay a higher-than-average rate of interest because the credit of the Commonwealth could not be placed behind them as in other states. The effect on educational institutions has been particularly disastrous. Even so ardent a Byrd fancier as Senator Robertson says, "Byrd did not do as well with the schools as with the roads because there was no special fund, like the gasoline tax, that could be applied to them. Although I was dedicated to the pay-as-you-go system, a proper distinction can be drawn between a bond issue for capital outlay for schools that can be used for half a century, whereas highways are worn out in a few years and must be bettered." [8]

Another important reform of the constitution was the adoption of the highly controversial "Short Ballot," substituted for the foot-long paper ballots used prior to Governor Byrd's administration, when the entire Cabinet and many other officials were elected, rather than appointed. This system made it very difficult for a governor to administer the business of the state efficiently because cabinet members not appointed by him could simply refuse to go along with the Governor's policy decisions, no matter how worthwhile they might be.

In the Byrd Constitution only the Governor, the Lieutenant Governor, and the Attorney General were elective officials; the rest were appointed by the Governor. This, of course, put great power in his hands. The man he chose to head the State Compensation Board, for example, fixed the salaries and expense allowances of all local and state officials. His was the power of financial life or death over them. How this power was used depended primarily on the Governor who hired and therefore could fire the Board. At the same time the short ballot fixed the responsibility for errors. As Judge Tuck observed, "Under the old system if things went wrong the Governor could always pass the buck to an elected official. After we had the short ballot he had to take the blame."

Administration had been such an amorphous thing under the old system that most Virginians still feel that the short ballot was a great improvement. Certainly Byrd made it so while he was Governor. He had no difficulty in getting the revised Constitution through the General Assembly. In the referendum that followed the voters approved it by a smashing majority.

Governor Byrd then went to work on the wilderness of bureauc-

8. *Ibid.*

racy which had grown up around the old laws and customs. A Commission on Simplification had reported to former Governor Lee Trinkle. Byrd took this report and reworked it himself, in consultation with the General Assembly and a Citizens' Committee headed by William T. Reed. As a result of their energetic pruning over one hundred bureaus, boards, and commissions financed by forty-eight special funds outside of and in addition to the State Treasury were consolidated into fourteen departments.[9] In all, Byrd's reforms required forty-seven changes in Virginia's Constitution, all of which were approved by the voters.

The Governor's constituent who feared he might become a "Silk Hat Harry" did not know him very well. Despite his high-powered administration, Harry Byrd's personal life and public manner remained as easy as one of the dusty old brogans he delighted to wear even in Richmond, or, for that matter, in Washington when he became Senator. His liking for old clothes and old cars led to some amusing contretemps. On one occasion when he and his son, Harry, Jr., were speeding down to the Capitol, a motorcycle policeman stopped him. "Officer," he said, "I'm Governor Byrd and I'm late for an important appointment."

"Oh, no you ain't," the policeman said. "Governor Byrd is much better-looking than you." [10]

When Byrd was first inaugurated, the big, old Governor's Mansion was undergoing much-needed repairs, so he and Sittie lived at the comfortable Jefferson Hotel. They finally moved into the Mansion with their children, Harry, Jr., Westwood, Richard Evelyn (Dick), and Beverley. They were a gay rambunctious lot like their father and uncles.

In the early summer of 1927, Governor Byrd virtually commuted to Mineola, Long Island, to be with his brother, who was preparing to fly across the Atlantic. In his most engaging manner Harry pleaded with Dick to take him along. But cajoleries which melted hard-bitten politicians had no effect on the Commander. Again and again Dick told his brother that he could not accept the responsibility for endangering the life of the Governor of Virginia. It was his

9. Fishwick, *op. cit.*.
10. Related to the author by Harry F. Byrd III.

courteous way of refusing Harry. The truth was that every one of the *America*'s four-man crew had to be an expert in the job he had to do. Harry's idea was a charming fantasy, for despite Irving Levine's joy-ride in Chamberlain's Bellanca, the time for aerial transatlantic passengers had not arrived.

Many men of prominence came to stay at the Governor's Mansion in Virginia while Byrd inhabited it. Perhaps the most interesting —and the most difficult—was Winston Churchill. Admiral Cary Grayson asked Byrd if he would put Churchill up, so that Douglas Freeman could show the historic Virginia battlefields to the British statesman who was doing research for his *History of the English Speaking Peoples*. Even then, in his years of apparently declining political fortunes, Churchill was one of the greats of this world and was well aware of the fact. For him and only for him, Byrd broke a law of the land.

Churchill arrived with a party which included Lord Faversham. Faversham had a girl in California to whom he telephoned every day —at the Governor's expense, for Byrd would never have thought of charging such calls to the State. The bill was two hundred fifty dollars. Admiral Grayson had warned the Governor that Churchill must have a minimum of a quart of brandy a day. In considerable embarrassment because of the Prohibition law, but for the sake of Anglo-American relations and the hospitality he felt was due to a distinguished Briton, Byrd called his friend Stuart Bryant, who owned two leading newspapers, and said, "Stuart, I am in a terrible fix. I need you to deliver a quart of French brandy to the Mansion every day this week."

It was done and no questions were asked.[11]

Though Governor Byrd had voted for prohibition and believed in it—at first—he was neither a hypocrite about it nor a prisoner of the Drys as so many politicians were. When he became Governor, the state prohibition-enforcement officers were operating in plain clothes. This practice did not coincide with Byrd's ideas of the rights of citizens or the dignity of the Commonwealth. Contrary to the wishes of ardent prohibitionists, he ordered the officers to wear uniforms.

Another famous visitor to the Mansion was Commander Byrd's friend, Charles A. Lindbergh, who arrived in Richmond on his 1927 tour of the United States in *The Spirit of St. Louis*. Harry Byrd,

11. Richard E. Byrd of Rosemont and Mrs. Massie's Memoirs.

who had wished to fly the ocean with his brother, now wanted to fly in Lindbergh's famous plane. Harry Guggenheim, who had put up the money for Lindbergh's tour to promote interest in aviation, was also staying at the Mansion at this time. Knowing how keen Byrd was on it, Guggenheim said to Lindbergh, "Why don't you take the Governor up for a flight?"

"You know it's only a single-seater," Lindbergh objected.

"Well," said Guggenheim, "you took Edsel Ford up, why can't you take the Governor?"

Rather unhappily Lindbergh agreed to do so. They all drove out to the little airport, which was only a rough field with two or three hangars and a windsock. Hardly anyone was there. Lindbergh had the plane brought out and, as always, meticulously inspected it before he warmed up the engine. The Governor crawled in and wedged himself half on the seat and half on the pilot's lap. It must have been a miserable flight for both of them, because Byrd was beginning to put on quite a bit of weight, and *The Spirit of St. Louis* had no forward visibility. Byrd's nose was jammed against the instrument panel in front of the pilot's seat and he could only catch fleeting glimpses of the ground at odd angles through the small side windows.

During the brief moments they were in the air, word of Lindbergh's presence had spread. When they landed, the airport was crowded, and people in all sorts of vehicles were tearing along the road from Richmond. When Byrd and the famous aviator climbed out of the plane, Lindbergh was mobbed. There were no police. No matter how friendly the crowd, such a situation could become serious. Nelson Page, Guggenheim, and the Governor managed to shove Lindbergh into the comparative safety of the office shack and lock the door. He seemed quite shaken and said, half apologetically, half irritably, "I've got a complex about crowds."

Several years later Lindbergh stayed with the Byrds at Rosemont. This time he took Mrs. Byrd for a flight in a more comfortable plane. Sittie did not want to go, but when Lindbergh invited her she felt she must accept. Starting from the tiny field at Winchester, they headed straight for Berryville. Lindbergh buzzed the great house, flying low over its pillared portico while the luncheon guests waved. Sittie, frozen in her seat, was unable to respond to their greeting.[12]

Young reformist Governor Franklin D. Roosevelt of New York

12. Mr. W. Nelson Page to the author.

and his wife came to visit the young reformist Governor of Virginia at the Mansion in 1929. Roosevelt could not walk a step without braces, crutches, or a strong friendly arm, but he could whiz around like a circus cyclist in his wheelchair. Byrd could not help admiring his spontaneous gaiety and his brilliant, compassionate mind. Roosevelt, just beginning his term, appears to have been much interested in Byrd's streamlining of Virginia's Government and his fiscal reforms. In fact, the two Governors got on so well that the Byrds paid a return visit to the Victorian-Gothic Mansion in Albany. The enormous vitality of the Roosevelts and their five children filled even that gloomy house with gaiety and laughter.

The year 1928 had been a year of disaster for the Democratic party. Herbert Hoover was running for President on the Republican ticket against Governor Alfred E. Smith of New York. Though Al Smith was a fine man, extremely popular with the people of the big Eastern states, he never had a chance. Riding the enormous wave of prosperity that was cresting toward its appalling smash, the American people were far too euphoric to consider rocking their accelerating boat by a change of administrations. In addition, the fact that Al Smith was a Catholic rang the final knell upon his hopes. Though Mr. Hoover was far too good an American to capitalize on religious bigotry, many of his supporters were less scrupulous. There were comparatively few open references to Governor Smith's religion, but the underground campaign of vilification and terror tactics to garner Protestant votes was appalling. It was particularly effective among large numbers of Baptist and Methodist voters in the Southern and Midwestern states.

Governor Byrd, as an experienced and pragmatic politician, realized that the national campaign was lost before it ever began, but when his advisers reported that the Republican candidate was likely to carry Virginia by forty thousand votes or more it came as a terrible shock. Never since the dreadful days of Reconstruction had the Old Dominion gone Republican. Byrd went out on the campaign trail with all the élan, vigor, and charm of which he was capable. Doubtless he used pressure tactics as well. It was to little avail. The best his all-out effort could accomplish was to cut down the predicted Republican majority. Herbert Hoover carried Virginia by about 28,000 votes. He also carried North Carolina.

Byrd was badly shaken and humiliated. He was a traditionalist and a partisan and he regarded the first break in the solid South as a calamity. From a personal point of view he was anxious lest the loss of the state to the Republicans have an adverse effect on his own political career.

Two or three weeks after the election, President Coolidge slyly rubbed salt in his wounds. At the football game between the Universities of Virginia and North Carolina the President occupied a box with the Governors of both states. With the dead-pan humor that endeared him to the American people Coolidge said softly, "I don't know which side to cheer for, sitting as I am between the Governors of two Republican states."

After the election, Byrd's first work was to repair the damage and woo errant voters back to the Democratic party. A gubernatorial election was coming up in 1929. According to Virginia's Constitution, Byrd was ineligible to succeed himself. He must choose a strong candidate, who would make such a powerful showing that the debacle of 1928 would be forgotten.

However, the choice was not entirely in his hands. Though he had gained a leading position in the Organization, Senators Carter Glass and Claude A. Swanson were its titular leaders and still exercised considerable power. Bishop Cannon had regained prestige with the Drys in the successful fight against Al Smith who was very Wet.

With Willis Robertson, Commissioner for Game and Fisheries, and other close advisers, Byrd canvassed the field carefully, weighing the qualifications of possible nominees. It was finally decided that John G. Pollard would be their best candidate. He had an unlikely combination of professions, being both a farmer and President of William and Mary College, appealing, therefore, to very different types of voters. Pollard was a strong temperance man, and a close friend of the Byrds.

The decision made, Byrd drove to Washington to propose Pollard's nomination to Senator Swanson. To his dismay and anger Swanson said, "No." He had decided that the Organization would back Patrick H. Drury of Petersburg. The last thing Byrd wanted was a bitter primary fight; but he thought Drury a weak candidate. He reasoned with Swanson, argued and cajoled. The Senator would not yield; neither would the Governor. When he saw that further talk was useless, Byrd, temper rising but courtesy controlling it, said simply, "All right! You back Drury, I'll back Pollard." [13]

13. Former Senator Robertson to the author.

The battle of the primary was less a contest between two candidates than a fight for control of Virginia between the kingmakers. Byrd went flat out, campaigning across the state with his usual energy and dry, matter-of-fact speech-making, his warmth and earthy affability. Behind him also were the levers of power of his office and the many friendships, favors and ties he had made during three and a half years as Governor. He used these assets with the skill learned from his uncle and father and, especially, during his own long apprenticeship. In addition he appears to have chosen the best man, or at least the most appealing candidate.

Swanson's old regulars countered with every device they could recall or imagine, but the issue was not seriously in doubt. Pollard was easily nominated and handsomely elected. That election night as the ballots were counted the Organization became in fact the "Byrd Machine." Glass and Swanson continued to reign, but they no longer ruled.

In appraising Harry Byrd's governorship of Virginia, the striking paradox is that the man who became known as the greatest conservative of his time was the greatest innovator in the Commonwealth. Not only did he streamline the gothic governmental system, smooth the way for Virginia's wheels and reorganize the tax structure, but he was the first governor to take an interest in conserving the state's great natural resources. He had sponsored the bill creating the Game and Fisheries Commission and had begun the move to create what later became Shenandoah National Park in his beloved Blue Ridge. The first steps in this project required $2,000,000. Byrd persuaded the General Assembly to appropriate $1,000,000 and raised the rest by public subscription. Ever opposed to the paternalistic state, he put his faith in community action and voluntary endeavor.

Byrd also advocated the establishment of a liberal arts college for women. He increased the state appropriation for education and welfare—though the allocation was not nearly enough. In 1928, he got the General Assembly to pass the harshest antilynching law of any state in the Union. It ended lynching in Virginia.

Despite Byrd's devotion to tradition, he gave Virginia a new direction, bringing many new industries into the state by a policy of tax reductions and economic stability. The flood of big payrolls and capital investments brought with it large increases in state revenues that made up many times over for the tax concessions he used to lure industry to Virginia. Thus from a stagnant, agrarian economy Virginia moved toward modern industrialization without damaging—rather improving—the condition of the farmers, who were naturally Byrd's first concern. Instead of saying, as some state liberals cynically had, "Thank God for Mississippi," because it was even more backward, Virginians, once again as before the Civil War, began to take pride in the progress of their state and think of it, not as a piece of hallowed ground, but as a dynamic partner in the Union. In short, Harry Byrd can be said to have led the Old Dominion into the twentieth century.

However, the accomplishment of which he was proudest was that when he took the reins, Virginia was running a deficit of $1,258,000. When he yielded to Pollard, he left a $2,596,000 surplus.[14]

14. Fishwick, *op. cit.*

V · BYRD FOR
PRESIDENT

GOVERNOR BYRD faced his temporary retirement from public office with considerable equanimity. There were many things for him to do, and he certainly would not miss the salary. By now he was definitely affluent if not quite as rich as his opponents claimed. He had accumulated a considerable fortune outside of the apple business. Throughout the 1920's, when income taxes were minimal and opportunities maximal, he had made some very profitable investments in America's booming industries. His rising political prospects and personal charm brought him many friends among the leaders of finance as well as in politics. These gentlemen gave him expert advice and useful tips. There is no implication whatever that they acted in hope of political favors; they knew Byrd better than that. They helped him because they liked him, and foresaw a brilliant future for him.

However, two financiers seldom give a man the same advice. Harry Byrd's own shrewdness in choosing whose advice to take and his instinctive feeling for when to jump into a situation and, much more important, when to get out was the key to his success.

Whatever his other financial ventures, apple-growing remained the foundation of his fortune. Throughout his whole life he continued to expand this operation, buying land, leasing orchards, building packing plants and canning factories. In 1920, when Harry became active in politics, Tom Byrd had closed up his law office in Richmond and gone home to mind the store. This huge, genial man, whom his daughter described as "six foot two and strong as a bull," was, perhaps, more popular with his neighbors than either of his brilliant brothers. His friends were inclined to commiserate the fact that he was always in their shadow. "Poor sweet Tom always gets the short end of the stick," was a favorite saying.

Tom did not feel that way. He had no desire for fame or political power, and envied his brothers not at all. He preferred to live quietly and happily in the lovely valley that was his home, hunting through his expanding orchards in the fall, fishing in spring or summer; laughing a great deal; and possibly enjoying life more than his self-starting, hard-driving siblings.

Tom ran the intricate affairs of the huge apple business extremely well. Though Harry made the important policy decisions, he prized Tom's advice, both in running the orchards and in legal matters of a political as well as a business nature. As his brother's partner, Tom, too, became quite rich and bought the Cliff, a beautiful old house looking toward the Blue Ridge.

Tragedy touched his life early. He married lovely Margaret Lewis, who died giving birth to his daughter, Margaret. Tom Byrd was desolate for several years. He was a splendid father to Margaret, who adored him, though even she talks more enthusiastically about her glamorous Uncle Dick. She was brought up largely by her dynamic grandmother, Miss Bolling, in the shaggy old house on Amherst Street.

In 1938, Tom was married again to Elizabeth Miller Mitchell, famous General Billy Mitchell's widow. She was still a beautiful, vital woman; a magnificent horsewoman who loved to tear across the deep grass fields with the Blue Ridge Hunt sitting sidesaddle on her thoroughbred hunters. Her stepdaughter says, "She was afraid of nothing except aeroplanes." It appears that General Mitchell liked to take her up in a little, two-place biplane and fly into thunderstorms, "because they were so beautiful." It gave her an abiding distaste for aeronautics.[1]

Though earthborne, her brother-in-law, Harry Byrd, also loved thunderstorms. When the blue-black clouds came over the Blue Ridge to drench the parched valley with healing rain, he sometimes

1. Mrs. Stimpson to the author.

walked barefoot over the soaking grass. Then he would come home to hold Sittie's hand as she sat in her room trembling at every crash of thunder.

While Governor Byrd was battling for Pollard in the summer of 1929, he was looking for a place to live. Apart from the big but unheated Log House, he and Sittie had never had a home of their own. That summer, Byrd acquired the house he wanted most of all and loved until he died. Rosemont stood on a hilltop in Berryville in the midst of orchards he already owned. Built by George Norris, the first High Sheriff of Clarke County, in 1804, Rosemont was an archetypical white Southern mansion with a few Yankee additions. Under a classic portico, supported by enormously tall fluted columns, a broad terrace looked eastward down a steeply sloping wild garden with the brilliant color of azaleas and other flowering shrubs backed by towering black-green pines. Berryville, crouched under the hill, was completely hidden by the foliage so the eye leaped beyond it over the orchards to the ever-changing Blue Ridge—often as blue as its name, sometimes lavender in the sunset, light or dark green on a cloudy noon, and flaming red in autumn. The Norris family lived at Rosemont until 1902. After a quick succession of owners, Mr. and Mrs. J. Low Harriman bought it in 1910, brought the plumbing up to date and added a big, but surprisingly inconspicuous wing with ten bedrooms, making a total of forty rooms in the house.

The main part of Rosemont had a large airy two-story hall with a balcony part way around it reached by a broad, easy staircase. From the front door, one could see right through the house to the shimmering mountains. On the left was a formal drawing room and on the right a pleasant library and an oak-paneled dining room capable of seating twenty people. An enclosed breakfast porch beyond it overlooked the formal garden. The house was furnished with a heterogeneous but pleasing collection of furniture, acquired in one way or another through a couple of centuries and ranging from a small exquisite writing desk from Westover to the Senator's big double bed which was a copy of the one his uncle Hal Flood slept in.

Governor Byrd's upstairs office had a small balcony cantilevered out under the portico. He and his wife loved to sit there and look at the mountains. The office was usually in wild disorder with papers, documents, and letters heaped on the desk and all the chairs.

The grounds at Rosemont were even more beautiful than the house. There were over sixty acres of lawns with fine old trees and rare shrubs. The formal gardens had been designed by an Italian landscape gardener. The driveway wound between tall oaks and maples up a gentle hill. In springtime, white and pink dogwood and azaleas made a delicate drift of color under taller trees standing in fresh green grass.

Governor Byrd bought Rosemont in the summer of 1929, from the widow of Doctor G. W. Smith, who had bought it from the Harrimans. His son, Dick, who now owns it, wryly remarked, "If Father had waited until the next year he would have paid a great deal less."

One of the first things Harry Byrd did after moving into Rosemont in 1930, was to put a sign in front of the big stone gateposts, surmounted by eagles like those at Westover. The sign said: VISITORS WELCOME. He really meant it. At any hour of the day tourists dropping in were warmly greeted by the Governor, if he was there, and given a personally guided tour of the estate. If they happened to arrive when Byrd was giving one of the big luncheon parties which became famous, they were usually invited to the meal and met a bewildering group of statesmen, politicians, and society people who had motored out from Washington. The guests might include anyone from the current President of the United States through a whole range of Cabinet officers, ambassadors, senators, congressmen, aviators, artists, actors, bankers, industrialists, and neighbors.

Some years later the VISITORS WELCOME sign had an embarrassing result. Very early one morning Byrd and his favorite grandson, Harry F. III, went skinny-dipping as usual in the secluded swimming pool. Some early-rising and for once not-so-welcome visitors found them there. As young Harry tells it, he and his grandfather clung to the edge of the pool like leeches—"Luckily it was in shadow." The visitors talked and talked, enchanted by the Senator's wit and courtesy. Katz, the Byrds' old cook, rang the breakfast bell, then shouted, "Breakfast!" The visitors kept right on talking. The two Harrys shivered and shook with cold, but dared not move out of the shadow. Young Harry says that the ordeal lasted for over an hour.

Mrs. Byrd never approved of her husband's promiscuous hospitality. Like many other good housewives, she thought her house should be in apple-pie order, with every floor dustless and every table polished before visitors saw it. Her objections did no good. At an early-morning knock at the door, the Senator would heartily shout, "Come in!" Then a couple of strangers walking in would find the Senator in his orchard clothes, eating a huge breakfast and throwing pancakes over his shoulder to Pam, his cocker spaniel. He had a long line of cockers named Pam.[2]

Whatever Byrd paid for Rosemont, he got his money's worth. He loved it perhaps more than his ancestors had loved Westover. In truth, it was a bigger, gayer, and more comfortable house, and if not as classically proportioned as the mansion on the James, it commanded an infinitely more beautiful view. The only thing lacking was hummingbirds to fan his cheeks.

The great depression that began with the stock-market crash of 1929 hit the inhabitants of the Shenandoah Valley as hard as it did the rest of the nation. The collapse of the American economy had a domino effect on all the countries of Europe. The foreign market for apples, which had taken forty to fifty per cent of the Virginia crop, completely collapsed. Byrd could not give away the small, flavorful apples he had been growing for export.

After assessing the situation with his brother Tom, Byrd moved swiftly to tailor his crop to the domestic market. Tens of thousands of trees were ripped out and the Byrds began growing the beautiful-looking Red and Golden Delicious apples suitable for selling on city sidewalks and to American housewives who bought by eye rather than by bite. He was also the first, in that part of the world at least, to begin packaging apples in crates rather than the traditional barrels, and the first to shift from crates to cardboard boxes. It was tough going for a few years, but the Byrds' flexibility—in business matters at least—enabled them to come through with all their lands intact.

In 1938, the Byrds made what was probably the largest single planting in pomological history, setting out fifty thousand new trees in a single orchard on their own land. By then, with a total of two hundred thousand trees on five thousand acres of land, they were be-

2. Harry F. Byrd III to the author.

lieved to be the largest individual apple-growers in the world. As their cousin, Joe Massie, said, "Trees always grew for the Senator. It seemed like he'd put a twig in the ground and next year it was bearing apples." [3]

Byrd always paid his workers the full going wage. When, as Virginia's Senator, he had become anathema to Roosevelt's New Dealers, the story was put out that he had said, "A dollar a day is plenty for any laborer." It was further rumored that he paid his apple-pickers only nine or ten cents an hour. Byrd's friends urged him to bring the rumor mongers before a Senate committee, but he told them he would not use the Senate for a personal purpose. The truth was that in 1937 his one hundred and twenty-five year-round employees started at forty cents an hour. He took care of them and their families if disaster struck. During the picking season, he hired one thousand itinerant workers, who were paid ten cents a box, not an hour. This enabled a fast worker to make as much as ten dollars a day—a very good wage in depression times.

In 1932, the Byrds sailed to Cuba for a brief vacation. While they were staying with Ambassador Harry Guggenheim at the Embassy there, Sittie suffered a slight heart attack. It was the first of several that occurred throughout the years. Though she lived until 1964, she was never again completely well and became increasingly fragile. Her illness limited Harry's social life, since he did not like to go to parties without her. Though the doors of Rosemont were still hospitably open to all, the Byrds' formal entertaining was confined to the series of great luncheons which Byrd gave in the spring, and to the annual apple picnic on the last Saturday in August.

Young State Senator Harry Byrd had begun these picnics in 1923, by asking two or three hundred neighboring apple-growers to the Rosemont Orchards to have a picnic luncheon, sample the new crop, and talk about raising apples. Throughout the years they became a Shenandoah institution. From a few hundred people, they grew in size to three or four thousand. Byrd always invited the Governor, some congressmen and other political bigwigs. He had experts come from various universities to lecture on fertilization, sprays, changing public tastes, and all the latest developments in pomology.

3. Mr. Massie to the author.

He would wind up the program with a political address on the State of the Commonwealth—and the Union. He called it, "A Byrd's Eye View."

The apple picnics were held annually from 1923 through 1964, the year Sittie died. In all those forty-two years it rained on no picnic day—until the last one.

The depression had a profound and totally unforeseen effect on American politics. After the debacle of 1928, political soothsayers and historians alike were almost ready to bury the disintegrating National Democratic party along with the Federalists, Whigs, and Know Nothings. Three years of diminishing incomes, enormous unemployment, mounting bankruptcies, farm-foreclosures and a rising revolt against the paralyzed Republican administration and, indeed, against the capitalistic system itself, changed all that. By 1932, the Democratic party was the liveliest corpse in American political history. It was evident to virtually all unbiased observers that the man nominated for President at the Democratic National Convention in Chicago would become the next President of the United States.

In these circumstances there was a plethora of candidates. The leading contender was Governor Franklin D. Roosevelt of New York, an old friend of Harry's, whose mother and Mrs. Roosevelt, Sr., the formidable Widow of Hyde Park, had known each other for many years. Other leaders were that "Happy Warrior," Al Smith, who was down but not out; John Nance Garner of Texas, backed by Senator William Gibbs McAdoo of California and William Randolph Hearst; and Newton D. Baker of Ohio, Woodrow Wilson's Secretary of War. A group of favorite sons, included Senator James Reed of Missouri, Alfalfa Bill Murray of Oklahoma, Governor Albert C. Ritchie of Maryland, and half a dozen more.

In the councils of the Old Dominion it was decided, not unexpectedly, that former Governor Harry F. Byrd should be Virginia's favorite son candidate. As usual with such candidacies, this was mainly a holding action to see which way things were going, and to give the state bargaining power in drawing up the platform and in the passing out of political plums. Neither Byrd nor his supporters thought that he had more than an outside chance for the nomination.

But like all those other "sons," Byrd could hope that in a deadlocked convention the unpredictable lightning might strike.

That hope was not entirely illusory. Byrd could point to a remarkable record as Governor of Virginia. His financial reforms and the fact that the depression had neither shaken Virginia's credit nor plunged it into debt were strong arguments in his favor. Amid the general hand-wringing and desperate deficit financing of forty-seven states, many people thought of him as a rock of fiscal integrity and a financial genius. The country sorely needed such a man.

Before the Convention, Governor Roosevelt came to Rosemont to ask Harry Byrd for Virginia's votes. Gray Beverley, peering from an upstairs window, saw a big touring car drive up and three men helping a fourth up the broad, shallow steps. Gray, not knowing Roosevelt was expected, thought it was some drunk being put to bed in that hospitable house. Byrd received Roosevelt with Virginia courtesy and the warmth of old friendship. But he made no promises.[4]

The Virginia delegation at Chicago was led by Senator Swanson, who supported Byrd ardently, less from love than from the fear that if Byrd were not kicked upstairs he would run against him for Senator in the primaries in 1934. Harry, Jr., who was seventeen, traveled with his father as aide and errand boy. Admiral Byrd, recently back from the South Pole, loyally joined them in Chicago to lend the glitter of his fame. Financed by William T. Reed of Richmond and Colonel Henry Breckenbridge of New York, the entire band of the Richmond Light Infantry Blues came along to add its brassy clamor to the demonstration for Byrd.

That was a wild convention. Franklin D. Roosevelt came into it with a majority of the votes, but over a hundred less than the two thirds necessary to nominate according to the rule then prevailing in Democratic conventions. The other leaders, Al Smith, Cactus Jack Garner, Governor Ritchie, and Newton D. Baker, together with the "sons," banded together to stop Roosevelt. Among the prominent candidates, Byrd favored Baker because of his financial conservatism and his record of efficiency and integrity in handling the huge sums appropriated for the Army in World War I.[5]

4. Gray Beverley to the author.
5. Senator Harry F. Byrd, Jr., to the author.

Before the nominations, a platform had to be adopted. The main battle was over the prohibition plank. Wets and Drys fought it out. Byrd, always realistic, had modified his dry stand and spoke for a national referendum on the issue. However, a plank demanding outright repeal of the Eighteenth Amendment was voted in. Byrd was not displeased; he realized that the "noble experiment" had been a dismal failure.

The plank which he favored most enthusiastically was the unrealistic proposal, written by Carter Glass, to balance the Federal budget by cutting Government expenses by 25 per cent and pledging "a sound currency to be preserved at all hazards." [6] In fact, though the Rooseveltian liberals had a majority of the delegates, the platform as adopted was not particularly radical. Everything would depend upon the nominee.

The nominations began in the customary uproar of real and manufactured enthusiasm. Each name set off a demonstration that was carefully timed by the pundits to gauge the popularity of the nominee (though they knew it meant nothing.) The permanent Chairman, Senator Thomas J. Walsh of Montana, almost split a gavel restoring order. When Byrd's turn came, his followers, backed by the Richmond Blues Band wildly playing "Carry Me Back to Old Virginny" and "Dixie," made up in enthusiasm what they lacked in numbers. A press photographer caught a picture of Admiral Byrd in civies, dutifully carrying a Byrd banner and looking as though he wished he were sitting on the South Pole.

On the first ballot Roosevelt got 666¼ votes, a clear majority. But it took 770 to nominate. On the second ballot he gained 11¼ votes to 677¾. That was not enough to start a bandwagon. Up in room 1702 of the Congress Hotel, his strategic high command, headed by Louis McHenry Howe and James A. Farley, were becoming desperate. They knew that if Roosevelt did not win by the third or fourth ballot, his delegates would begin dropping away. The Convention would be deadlocked. While Louis Howe sat like a spider in the center of a web of telephone lines talking to the powers behind the powers at the Convention, Jim Farley tore around from delegation to delegation, pleading, promising them anything if they would switch to Roosevelt. At some time during that long hot night he came to Harry Byrd and offered him the Vice-Presidential nomina-

6. Democratic platform 1932.

tion if he would deliver the Virginia delegation to Roosevelt. Whether he would have made good or not no one will ever know, for Byrd refused.

"I think you should have taken it," Willis Robertson said to Byrd. "It could lead to the Presidency. Why didn't you?"

Byrd replied, "For one thing Reed and Breckenbridge put up all that money to send the band here for me. They are bitterly opposed to Roosevelt and would never forgive me if I sold out." Byrd added that in any event he considered Baker a better man for the Presidency.

The night-long session of the Convention ended after the third ballot in which Roosevelt gained only five more votes. Walsh railroaded through an adjournment, for fear Roosevelt's strength would begin to erode on the fourth ballot. During the recess, Louis Howe's sleepless vigil on the telephone paid off. By promising Garner the Vice-Presidency he succeeded in winning him over, together with his backers, Hearst and McAdoo. When the Convention reconvened and the roll call of the states on the fourth ballot reached California, Senator McAdoo stood up and shouted, "California came here to nominate a President of the United States. She did not come here to deadlock the Convention. . . . If the contest were prolonged it would only lead to schisms. When a man comes here with almost 700 votes . . ." [7]

A tremendous crash of cheers, the wild roaring noise of victory, drowned all else he had to say. Hardly anyone heard McAdoo shout, "California, forty-four votes for Franklin Delano Roosevelt." Other states as they were called jumped on the Roosevelt bandwagon, though Massachusetts held stubbornly for Smith. Then came the words that clinched it: "Texas for Roosevelt!" In that wild melee, Swanson yelled, "Virginia for Roosevelt."

Whether he consulted Byrd or not is in doubt; there are no written records of such moments. Harry Byrd, Jr., says, "Father released his delegates." [8] Other accounts seem to indicate that Swanson acted unilaterally. In any event, Roosevelt was nominated by 945 votes to 229. Al Smith's cohorts were too bitter to make it unanimous.

Though Roosevelt was far from Harry Byrd's first choice among the candidates, he thought he could live with him. Roosevelt

7. Alden Hatch, *Franklin D. Roosevelt.* Henry Holt & Co., New York, 1947.
8. Senator Harry F. Byrd, Jr., to the author.

began smashing precedents by his dramatic flight to Chicago to make his acceptance speech. However, the speech itself was hardly revolutionary, and Roosevelt's resounding call for a "New Deal" for the American people seemed to be just good campaign oratory. Byrd became Roosevelt's Finance Manager for the campaign and worked very hard for his election. He still put foolish faith in the economy plank in the platform and Roosevelt's earlier speeches encouraged him to believe the candidate would implement it. Some of the later speeches may have troubled Byrd; for example, Roosevelt's address at the Commonwealth Club in San Francisco in which he said that "private economic power . . . is a public trust as well," and spoke of "the greater social contract" implying Government control over business. Then there was the agricultural speech, master-minded by radical Henry Wallace; and Roosevelt's advocacy of the use of Federal credit for unemployment relief; expansion of the Federal program of construction; and his plan for re-establishing the purchasing power of wage earners as a step toward recovery, with its implication of deliberate inflation. Byrd may well have wondered how Roosevelt was going to accomplish all these things within the balanced budget that he proclaimed as his goal. But like many conservatives, Byrd probably also put these things down to campaign oratory and hoped Roosevelt would forget about them after his election. As everyone now knows, he did nothing of the sort.

In the four-month interim between Roosevelt's election and his inauguration on March 4, 1933, there was a deadly pause; deadly because the economy drifted yet further downward while Government was paralyzed, unable to take any steps to relieve the situation. Yet, businessmen were fearful of what the new regime would bring. The final economic collapse occurred on the very day of Roosevelt's inauguration.

Though the economy stagnated, politics went merrily on during the interregnum. In naming his Cabinet, Roosevelt paid off several political debts. That some of the men he appointed were less than competent did not matter very much to him, as he intended to run the whole show himself with the assistance of his Brain Trust—that group of brilliant and rather radical intellectuals who had advised him during his campaign.

It was in February or thereabouts that Senator Claude Swanson came to Byrd with a message from the President-elect offering him the post of Secretary of Agriculture. With his love of the land, his knowledge of farming, and his compassion for farmers, Byrd would have made a good Secretary. It is interesting to speculate on the different course American agriculture might have taken had he held the position instead of Henry Wallace, but it is a very moot question.

Byrd replied to Swanson, "I am full of anger. He [Roosevelt] promised to put you in the Cabinet in Chicago when you ran out on me. Let him! I'm going to the Senate." [9]

Swanson went back to Roosevelt. He had a heart condition and had also lost touch with the people. Knowing that he would have no chance against Byrd in the primary, he persuaded Roosevelt to appoint him Secretary of the Navy. There was some justification for the appointment because Swanson had been on the Naval Affairs Committee of the Senate and had considerable knowledge of naval matters. However, he made a singularly poor civilian head of the Navy. Roosevelt was not upset. The Navy had been his lifelong love and was, in particular, one of the things he intended to run himself.

When Swanson resigned his Senate seat to go into the Cabinet, Governor Pollard immediately appointed Byrd for his unexpired term. On March 4, 1933, the day of Roosevelt's inauguration, Harry Byrd took the oath of office as United States Senator from Virginia. That same day Willis Robertson took the oath as a member of the House of Representatives from Virginia.

9. Former Senator Robertson to the author.

VI · THE LAST
NEW DEALER

SENATOR BYRD said, "I went along with the New Deal for the first ninety days." [1] Many years later he described himself as "The last of the New Dealers." By that he meant he was the last of those who held to the principles enunciated in the Democratic Platform of 1932, and the doctrines expounded by Franklin Roosevelt in his campaign speeches. Byrd also regarded himself as a Jeffersonian Democrat, a true liberal, who believed in Jefferson's doctrines of states' rights and limitation of the powers of the central government, strict interpretation of the Constitution of the United States, and as little interference as possible with the liberties of the people. Economically he relied on the advice of his friend Bernard Baruch, who frequently dropped in on him.

Though Byrd talked of ninety days, this was a slight exaggeration. No more than thirty days had passed before he began to be dissatisfied with the acts and demands of the Roosevelt administration. On Saturday morning, March 4, when Roosevelt—and Byrd—took office, the entire banking system of the United States collapsed. The great central banks in New York and other large cities closed their doors because to open them for even the half day then usual on Saturday, in the face of the panicky public withdrawing its deposits,

1. Senator Byrd, Jr., to the author.

448

would have meant instant bankruptcy. The New York Stock Exchange and all the other security exchanges suspended trading. American finance was flat on its back.

At President Roosevelt's request, his Cabinet was unanimously confirmed en masse by the Senate without any hearings or committee action. They were sworn in that evening at six o'clock, immediately after the inaugural parade. Roosevelt then held a Cabinet meeting at which he announced that he was going to proclaim:

1. A four-day banking holiday throughout the country.
2. An embargo on the withdrawal or transfer for export or domestic use of gold or silver.
3. A maximum penalty of $10,000 and/or five to ten years' imprisonment for violation of the proclamation.
4. Power for the Secretary of the Treasury to make exceptions to the proclamation.

This was done under the dubious legality of the 1917 Trading with the Enemy Act which subsequent congresses had forgotten to repeal since the war. The President called Congress into special session on Thursday, March 9.

Though the President thus unilaterally took the United States off the gold standard, Senator Byrd found no fault. He realized that the situation was desperate and that rich men here and abroad were hoarding gold in the belief that the Government would be forced to devalue the dollar. He believed it to be a temporary measure calculated to preserve a sound currency.

When Congress met on Thursday, the House and Senate passed an act ratifying the President's proclamation, extending wartime authority over gold and silver currency and authorizing his plan for reopening the banks and permitting the Federal Reserve Banks to print fiat money to finance this operation. The Emergency Banking Act, as it was called, was drawn up largely by the Senior Senator from Virginia, Carter Glass, and Secretary of the Treasury William Woodin.

Incidentally, Roosevelt had begged Carter Glass to become Secretary of the Treasury, as he had been in President Woodrow Wilson's Cabinet. Glass did not want to leave the Senate, but the real basis of his refusal was that Roosevelt would not give him a firm commitment not to devalue the dollar. Woodin had a much more flexible financial philosophy, in keeping with Roosevelt's.

Immediately after the passage of the Emergency Banking Act, Roosevelt sent Congress a bill cutting Federal expenses by $500,-000,000. This was accomplished by cutting over $100,000,000 of Government salaries, including his own and those of Congress, and shaving $400,000,000 from Veterans' pensions and compensations which through the years had burgeoned and exfoliated outrageously due to the pressure tactics of the Veterans' Lobby. This move to economy delighted Byrd's soul and probably marked the high point of his brief honeymoon with President Roosevelt.

Byrd also went along with many of the other bills that poured out of the White House Brain Trust. Roosevelt by his inspiring inaugural address—"The only thing we have to fear is fear itself"— and his quick decisive actions had lifted the hearts of his countrymen. The banking crisis ended. But there was no denying that much more must be done. Farm prices were at an all-time low. Because of the intense deflation, money the farmers had borrowed in good times was now worth twice as much in terms of the things they had to sell. They could not pay their debts. The same thing was true of small businesses and even big ones. For example, the railroads were not even earning the interest on their bonded indebtedness. More than seventeen million workers were unemployed.

To relieve the farmers, a Farm Bill, staggering in scope and confusing in complexity, was proposed. One feature of it was payments to farmers not to produce certain crops—wheat, cotton, hogs, and so on. Payments were to be made for acreage taken out of production. Incidentally, under this and other farm bills, Byrd was entitled to a subsidy of two dollars an acre on from four to five thousand acres; but he never applied for it. His independence and integrity forbade it.

Other Roosevelt bills tackled other problems: the Civilian Conservation Corps to put unemployed young men to work conserving the forests; the regulation of the stock markets and stock promotion; $500,000,000 for relief; the Federal Home Loan Bank to relieve mortgage-oppressed homeowners; the bill giving the economy and the people a shot in the arm by legalizing 3.2-per-cent beer; the Federal Land Bank Bill to lend money to farmers at low rates of interest. All these things cost a great deal of money. How to square such a program with the platform promise to balance the budget? Roosevelt's machiavellian and inventive mind supplied an answer. Henceforward there would be the ordinary budget, consisting of the normal expenses of running the Government, and the extraordinary budget embracing capital investments and emergency expenditures. His brilliant semantics satisfied a lot of people; they did not fool Harry Byrd. The first rift opened.

It appeared to Keynesian economists that inflation was essential to combat depression—a principle now widely accepted, but at that time viewed with horror by orthodox economists. In addition, enormous pressures were at work against the dollar in international finance. England had devalued the pound in 1931 and her economy had improved. The franc clung precariously to the gold standard, after the great devaluation of the 1920's. In April, 1933, international speculators attacked the dollar. Gold was shipped to Europe to stabilize it, but the effort failed. In a few days the country lost $100,-000,000 in gold. At the same time, representatives from the farm states were backing an amendment to the Farm Bill, giving the President the power to devalue the currency; and the silver states were pressing for the unlimited coinage of silver. In the New York *Herald Tribune* Walter Lippman wrote:

> Either the Administration . . . will take charge of inflation and manage it or Congress will produce inflation by statute . . . or we should still get it by budgetary deficits and the undermining of Government credit. . . . There is a choice among several methods of producing inflation and controlling it. But there is no longer any choice between inflation and no inflation. This choice has been abolished by economic developments and by the political sentiments they now reflect.[2]

On April 19, 1933, Roosevelt announced that he would accept from the inflation-minded Congress the power to devalue the dollar by 50 per cent, to make the Federal Reserve Bank issue up to $3,-000,000,000 in fiat currency, the free coinage of silver, and other inflationary powers. Roosevelt only announced that he accepted them; he did not employ them immediately. Nevertheless, with this announcement went the gold standard, the "sound dollar" and other sacred cows of orthodox banking. And with it, too, went Harry Byrd's confidence in the Roosevelt administration.

Even as a freshman Senator, Harry Byrd achieved a position of some power and had considerable influence over the course of events. This

2. April 19, 1933.

was no doubt because of his recent status as Virginia's favorite son. It was enough to get him on three choice committees, the Finance Committee on which he served for thirty-three years, the Naval Affairs Committee, and the powerful Rules Committee.

In fiscal policy Byrd followed the course of his revered colleague Senator Glass, who was a fanatical sound-money man. Fragile and wispy though he appeared, Glass had a steely backbone. However, in those first Roosevelt years Byrd and Glass could hardly do more than watch, eyes bulging with horror, as the revolutionary bills implementing the New Deal whizzed through Congress.

The whole "alphabet soup of government agencies," as conservatives called it, came into being—among others the Agricultural Adjustment Act (AAA); The Tennessee Valley Authority (TVA), which put the Federal Government into the utilities business in competition with private enterprise; and the National Industrial Recovery Act (NIRA), under which industry-wide codes of fair practice, wages, and prices were set up by big corporations under government supervision of the National Recovery Administration (NRA), and given the force of law. This last agency was administered by idealistic but autocratic General Hugh ("Iron Pants") Johnson. Of all Roosevelt's remarkable financial improvisations Byrd most detested NRA because it represented direct Government interference with the management of industry and was in his thinking a Brobdingnagian step toward socialism.[3] The Supreme Court eventually declared NRA unconstitutional.

In 1935, Senator Byrd got a new desk mate on the Senate floor, the recently elected Senator Harry S. Truman of Missouri. There was a certain dubiety about Truman because he was known to be a protégé of Boss Michael Pendergast who ruled the Democratic party in Missouri in a distinctly unsavory manner. However, Truman himself was a man of integrity. He was a lively, pugnacious little man with a first-class brain. Although Truman was a dedicated Roosevelt man who at first followed New Deal policies almost slavishly, Byrd became very fond of him. The Virginian recognized Truman's worth and ability, and the fact that he said just what he thought in a most direct, though undiplomatic manner. In addition he had a keen country wit that often made Byrd roar with laughter.[4]

3. Senator Byrd, Jr., to the author.
4. *Ibid.*

Senator Byrd's political differences with President Roosevelt did not at first compromise their friendship. On at least one more occasion Roosevelt went to Rosemont and Byrd was frequently invited to the White House. There the President lavished his charm on the Senator, partly in the hope of softening his political opposition, but also because he really liked him and wanted to be liked in turn. Byrd responded with the courtesy and warmth with which he usually treated political adversaries and allies alike. He felt for Roosevelt a genuine friendship, which took a long time to erode. On one occasion, when Byrd was lunching alone with the President, Roosevelt reminisced about the friendship between their mothers and said, "Those are two great ladies. We must get them together—here at the White House." [5]

Though the proposed meeting never came about, there was a genial glow as they parted that day, a genuine cordiality between the Senator and the President.

But after the Supreme Court overthrew the Railroad Retirement Act, the NRA, and part of the new Bankruptcy Act, Roosevelt, in fury, swung far to the left. He was pushed there partly by his indignation at the "horse and buggy" philosophy of the "nine old men"; somewhat by the advice of the new New Dealers, who had largely displaced the old Brain Trusters; and partly because he feared that Senator Huey Long of Louisiana would steal progressive leadership with his radical "share-the-wealth" program. Byrd himself once tangled with the Senator from Louisiana when the rabble-rousing Long attacked Carter Glass in a speech on the Senate floor. Afterward Byrd cornered him in the cloakroom and with icy fury warned him never to mention Senator Glass's name again in any connection. So venomous was Byrd's expression that the Kingfish fled to the men's room and locked himself in a toilet not to emerge until everyone but the cleaning women had left the Capitol. [6]

Roosevelt replied to the Supreme Court and his business critics with his "Soak the Rich" tax program of 1936, which was greatly emasculated in Congress. He also introduced the much-needed Social Security Act. Byrd, whose influence was by now increasing markedly, opposed this Act but later, in 1939, played a considerable part in get-

5. *Ibid.*
6. Forrest Davis, "The Fourth Term's Hair Shirt," *Saturday Evening Post,* April 8, 1944.

ting Social Security put on a sound actuarial basis, with contributions by employers and employees, rather than having it financed out of general revenues.

In the Presidential campaign of 1936, Roosevelt declared war on business, the "malefactors of great wealth"—a phrase he borrowed from his cousin President Theodore Roosevelt—and the "economic royalists"—his own words. He included in his attacks virtually the entire press of the United States. Byrd loyally but unenthusiastically supported the Democratic ticket. Evidently Roosevelt knew what the American people wanted, for Republican Candidate Alfred M. Landon suffered the greatest defeat in the history of the Republican party. He carried only two small states—Maine and Vermont. Republican representation in the House was reduced to a pitiful 88 out of 432. There were only 16 Republican Senators.

Riding the flood tide of popularity, Roosevelt planned a program for 1937. He sent for Byrd and talked warmly again of their mothers. Then, when he reckoned the warm glow of friendship had softened Byrd up, he said, "Harry, here is the act implementing the reorganization of the Federal Government on more efficient lines. In view of the splendid job you did in reorganizing the Virginia Government and our old friendship, I'd like you to sponsor it in the Senate."

"Well, Mr. President," said Byrd, "I don't know what's in it. I'll have to read it first."

Still warmly, but definitely, Roosevelt said, "You'll have to tell me right now. Take it or leave it!"

"I'll leave it," Byrd answered. "I will not agree to handle any bill I have not read."

Byrd's refusal to sponsor the Reorganization Bill was the beginning of President Roosevelt's personal break with him. As presented to the Congress, the Reorganization Act gave more power than ever to the Federal Government, and eliminated the Congressional Audit of executive expenditures. When it came before the Senate, Byrd bitterly opposed it. He became a member of the Joint Committee on Government Reorganization despite Roosevelt's rather forceful opposition.

Harold Ickes wrote:

There is more or less talk about the hard sledding the President's Reorganization Plan will have in Congress. . . . Byrd has a plan of his own and is Chairman of the Special Senate Committee which is conducting its own investigation through the Brookings Institute. He wants to cut off a lot of independent agencies and proclaimed over the air that a very real saving in Government expenditures can be made. . . .

In the fight on the Reorganization Bill he has attempted to undermine or actually restrict the President's power by an amendment. The proponents of this amendment said it was preserving the rights of Congress and resisting dictatorship. . . . But after all it was a political fight. Sen. Byrd admitted to me on more than one occasion . . . that there can never be reorganization unless the Executive is given the power to shift departments . . . but he is lined up with the Wheeler [Senator Burton K. Wheeler] forces. . . . They are playing politics of a particularly low order. [7]

No doubt Ickes believed this, but Byrd was not playing politics. He was following the Jeffersonian principle of limiting the power of the Executive. In addition, he no longer trusted Roosevelt and would use any fair means to curb him.

The final break between Byrd and Roosevelt came over what was known as the Court Packing Plan. Roosevelt's tremendous victory in 1936 had given him an almost papal complex; he seemed to believe that his ideas for the welfare of the American people were infallible. The Supreme Court stood like a stone wall in the path of progress; therefore, in his view, the Court must be circumvented. Attorney General Homer S. Cummings came up with an ingenious plan. The number of justices on the Supreme Court was determined not by the Constitution but by Act of Congress. There had been as many as ten, as few as five. Cummings proposed that Roosevelt send Congress a bill increasing the number of justices to fifteen. He could then appoint six liberals who, with those already on his side, would constitute a majority willing to declare the President's radical legislation to be constitutional. The bill was drawn up and presented to Congress as a reform of the Federal judiciary—which was, in fact, badly needed. The section dealing with the Supreme Court was only part of a larger plan. It exactly suited Roosevelt's penchant for ingeniously intricate solutions to his problems. With the enormous Democratic majorities in the House and Senate, he was sure the act would be quickly passed, the remaining teeth of the nine old men be drawn. He sent the bill to Congress on February 5, 1937.

What Roosevelt and his advisers had forgotten was that in the

7. *The Secret Diary of Harold L. Ickes*, Vol. II. Simon & Schuster, New York, 1959.

hearts of most Americans, next to the Bible, the Constitution of the United States was the most sacred writing on earth. Generations had been taught that the Supreme Court was the Guardian of the Constitution. They might have accepted an attempt to amend it in the prescribed manner—that had been done, and undone, often before. But such a palpable attempt to circumvent the Court without due process made them fearful for the very foundations of the Republic. Like Horatius they sprang to defend "The ashes of their fathers and the temples of their gods."

The roar of anguish, the bellows of rage that arose truly dumbfounded the President and his advisers. But they did not dismay Roosevelt. He could no longer imagine defeat. When Senator Joseph T. Robinson, the Majority Leader, suggested compromise, he roared with laughter.[8] Robinson went unhappily to work to shepherd the bill through the Senate.

The opposition quickly coalesced, strengthened each day by a tremendous adverse reaction of the citizens in the form of tens of thousands of letters and telegrams. Of course, the sixteen embattled Republicans fought the Court-packing bill and they found they were not alone. Conservative Democrats joined them whooping. Senators Glass and Byrd of Virginia were among the leaders of the fight, as were virtually all their colleagues from below the Mason-Dixon line as well as many from above it. Thus was born that coalition of Republicans and conservative Democrats which for thirty years, off and on, has frustrated Democratic Presidents in their attempts to push progressive—and frequently badly needed—legislation through Congress.

On June 14, 1937, the Democratic majority of the Judiciary Committee reported the bill out with these words:

"We recommend the rejection of this bill as a needless, futile and utterly dangerous abandonment of constitutional principle. . . .

"It is a measure that should be so emphatically rejected that its parallel will never again be presented to the free representatives of the free people of America."[9]

It was.

Roosevelt, stunned and infuriated, hoped to revenge himself on the leading opponents of the bill the following year by purging

8. Raymond Moley, *After Seven Years*. Harper & Brothers. New York, 1939.
9. Congressional Record, June 15, 1937.

them. He only succeeded in one case. Byrd was, of course, immune, because he was not running in 1938, and also because he was by then so clearly invincible in Virginia that the President would not waste ammunition on him. But never again did Roosevelt invite Byrd to the White House for a cozy little chat about their mothers.

This account of Byrd's differences with Roosevelt on fiscal policy and the Supreme Court makes him appear an old-fashioned reactionary, and so he was in financial matters. However, he continued to go along with the New Deal in such progressive legislation as rural electrification and soil conservation, though he loathed the AAA. In regard to labor, he upheld the workers' right to organize and favored collective bargaining. He got along very well with responsible labor leaders, but not with those who, in his opinion, fomented strikes for their own aggrandizement. Byrd opposed such men as James Petrillo, communist-leaning Harry Bridges, and the coal miners' John L. Lewis. He particularly detested Lewis, with his black beetle brows, rough demagogic speech, and ruthlessness. In this Byrd was, perhaps, less than fair; for at that time Lewis was fighting to organize and improve the condition of one of the most downtrodden groups of industrial workers in the United States. To get anywhere, the leader of the coal miners had to be both hard-nosed and ruthless. Furthermore, Lewis was a man of honor and integrity, who never profited by his position, and whose word, once given, was scrupulously kept.[10]

Taken all in all, Byrd did not oppose social progress for the sake of maintaining the status quo. He merely wanted to put it on a pay-as-you-go basis.

10. The testimony of such leaders of the coal industry as the late Ralph Enis, Vice President and General Counsel of the Delaware Lackawanna Railroad.

VII · THE BUDDHA
OF BERRYVILLE

A s a United States Senator, Byrd was no more inclined to be a Silk Hat Harry than he had been as Governor. He and Sittie lived quietly in a small apartment in the Shoreham Hotel in Washington. Partly because of her fragility and partly out of their shared inclination, the Byrds hardly went out at all in Washington society and seldom if ever entertained there. The Senator liked best of all to get up very early in the morning and walk through Rock Creek Park with his cocker spaniel. For these expeditions, he wore his orchard clothes, khaki pants, a rough, faded shirt and stout, dusty brogans.

On one occasion in the 1940's, a policeman caught him trying to crawl under the gate to the grounds of the National Zoo, which are under supervision of the National Park Service. Naturally, the Senator had no identification with him or even any money. The officer did not believe a word of his explanation that he was Senator Byrd of Virginia and carted him off to the station house. It took Byrd several hours to establish his identity.[1]

After this incident—so he would not get caught like that again—the National Park Service presented him with a pass key to all the National Parks in the country and made him their only honorary

1. Harry F. Byrd III, to the author.

458

ranger, with silver badge number 777 as a tribute to his untiring work for conservation.

Of course the Senator went back to his beloved Virginia as often as possible—every weekend and during the intervals when Congress was not in session. As Mrs. James Thompson remarked, "If you gave the Byrds a choice between heaven and Virginia they'd say, 'We'll take Virginia.'"

When he was back home, the political center of the Commonwealth was Byrd's office at the Winchester *Star*. It was a messy little room to be the seat of power. Up a steep, bare flight of stairs from the reception room and composing room, shaken by the rumble of machinery when the press was rolling, it was as bare and plain as any country editor's office. The walls, a sickly shade of green, were enlivened by unflattering cartoons of the Senator. The windows looked out on the police station across the street. Masses of letters, bills, and other papers were suspended by clothes pins on a wire stretching across the room—the Senator's personal filing system. He could pick out any needed document with the precision of an English setter pointing a covey of quail in the underbrush. At the end of the day the floor was knee-deep in newspapers, which the Senator read very rapidly and tossed on the floor. His memory was like microfilm. He could read a paper or the page of a book with hardly more than a glance and ten years later quote it accurately.

In that office, behind a big cheap table cluttered with piles of documents, Byrd sat in the swivel chair presented to him by the Virginia General Assembly when he became a Senator. His visitors sat on old apple crates. He had grown stouter with the years but not fat; his poundage was all hard muscle. When the reporters and his much younger friends tried to follow him up Old Rag or some other Blue Ridge peak, he left them gasping in his wake. He could still make the climb when he was in his seventies.

In Washington, he worked out every afternoon in the Senate gymnasium in addition to his morning walks. Full-bodied and florid, bright blue eyes twinkling, the high color of health in his cheeks, red-gold hair thinning and graying, he sat ready to greet any caller with the broadest smile in the Valley; and gently, very gently, he guided the destiny of the Old Dominion. He never gave orders, merely suggestions. To some less than admiring columnists he was known as "The Buddha of Berryville."

Byrd ran for his Senate seat in 1934. He did not have to run very hard. He had won the all-important primary handily and, of course, the actual election was a breeze. Three years later, in 1937, the Byrd Machine did not function so perfectly. An opposition candidate for governor, James H. Price, won the Democratic primary against Byrd's man. Byrd loyally supported him in the election, but Governor Price had a wretched four years in the Mansion. Large majorities in the General Assembly were Byrd men, and it would appear that they effectively frustrated his efforts to govern. Price was the only opposition candidate to slip by during the Senator's lifetime.

How much the Senator actually ran the state is an unresolvable question. Former Governor William Tuck says that Byrd scrupulously avoided interfering with his administration, though he was ready with advice if asked.[2] Colonel Francis Pickens Miller says that his successful opponent, Governor John Battle, never made a move without telephoning Byrd.[3] One can take one's choice between these testaments. Or perhaps they amount to the same thing since both agree that Byrd was free with advice if asked.

The same disparity exists in descriptions of the functioning of the Byrd Machine. Its high command always described it as simply a group of like-minded people.[4] On the other hand, there appears to have been a hand of steel under the Senator's extra-soft velvet glove. Control was effected through the county courthouses. The upper echelon, including Byrd, would meet at the Commonwealth Club in Richmond or perhaps at Rosemont or in Winchester, and decide who would be the candidates for the state offices. Then E. R. Combs, Chairman of the Compensation Board, would telephone the different courthouses and tell the judge or county executive, "It will be so and so for Governor; such a one for Attorney General. . . ." The list would even include state senators and delegates. Each local judge would pass the word along and all good Byrd men would accept the *obiter dicta.*

The functioning of the machine cost very little money. The lower echelons were kept in line by the three Byrd men who made up the State Compensation Board. This Board fixed the net salaries and

2. Judge Tuck to the author.
3. Colonel Miller to the author.
4. Speaker E. Blackburn Moore, and others, to the author.

expense allowances for every office in the Commonwealth down to the level of clerks and local school commissioners. It did not take any particular brilliance for a young state employee to realize that if he were a good boy, his remuneration would go up and if he defied the ukase, it would go down.

Another leverage was the social one. A young lawyer just starting out wanted—indeed *needed*—to be invited to the judge's Christmas party or wherever else he might mingle with the power elite to gain new clients and impress the ones he already had by his intimacy with the leading lights of his community. Rebels were seldom welcome at such functions. These pressures were subtly exercised. No one was threatened and no one openly coerced—but the pressures were very real.

The extraordinary thing is that there was virtually no corruption in Virginia throughout these years. The judges, who were appointed, were generally fair and merciful. Few people, however lowly—or however openly opposed to the Organization—could complain of injustice. Even though the other person was rich and powerful, Senator Byrd was as scrupulous as his ancestor, the Second William, to prevent anything that "did not consort with his idea of justice." Any judge who thought to gain favor by jiggling the blind goddess' scales soon found himself in trouble.

The state and county officials, commissioners of revenue, school commissioners, and so forth, were also honest men. If, by chance, a man was elected who dipped his hands in the public till or took a bribe, he did not last long. There was no scandal, no one went to jail; the greedy were just quietly persuaded to resign and turned out to an extremely barren pasture.

The organizational mechanism functioned so smoothly and quietly that Virginians were only dimly aware of its power. Men who were more liberal than Byrd, or who held different views on such matters as education and social welfare, did not have a chance at public office. Even so, there is still some validity in the definition of the Byrd Machine as "a group of like-minded people." They were, indeed, of the same mind in their effort to govern Virginia honestly, efficiently, economically, and for the good of the Commonwealth and the Nation as they saw it. They were also loyal to Harry Byrd, not from fear, but from admiration and, though it sounds sentimental, from love. No man can occupy a position at the apex of political power for forty years without the support of the people. Inevitably the men immediately below him are ambitious; they are ready to tumble the King off the Mountain if they have any reason or even a good excuse to do so. Byrd was secure, not because of the perfection of his political technique or his lieutenants' pressure tactics, or any fear they inspired, but because a large majority of Virginia voters were "like-minded" in their admiration and affection for him.

Oddly enough, though Senator Byrd wielded such power in Virginia, he was for many years the only former Governor whose portrait did not hang in the Capitol. It is the custom to have a portrait painted immediately on the Governor's retirement and this was done in Byrd's case. But when he brought his mother to see it, Miss Bolling said, "I hate it!" and personally took it down from the wall.

Years later when Harry, Jr., was walking through the Capitol with Governor Tuck, they found the Senator's picture in the guardhouse. "Do you want it?" asked Governor Tuck. "I'll give it to you."

"You can't give it to me," young Harry said. "It's the property of the State of Virginia. Besides, I dislike it as much as my grandmother did." [5]

In those last years before the Second World War the Senator had a very happy life. His children were growing up very satisfactorily indeed. Harry, Jr., who was almost a replica of his father at the same age, followed his uncle, the Admiral, at V.M.I. and graduated from the University of Virginia. He started work on the *Star* in 1935. Like his father, he loved politics best, but next to that he enjoyed journalism, in which he was to become quite a figure. In 1941, he married the girl he had loved since the time he was nineteen and she sixteen. Gretchen Thomson was the daughter of Paul J. Thomson of Summit Point, just over the West Virginia line. She was a lovely blonde with fair delicate skin, big blue eyes, corn-silk hair and an unexpectedly good mind. The year she had been chosen Apple Blossom Queen, young Harry was her escort.

The Senator's only daughter, Westwood, was a Greek sculpture of a girl, with long reddish blonde hair piled on her head and the

5. Senator Byrd, Jr., to the author.

classic Byrd features. She was very forthright, stubborn, and courageous. Mrs. James Thompson described her as "Harry [her father]
in petticoats." She was devoted to her father and to her brother
Beverley, though he was four years younger. Westy loved riding and
followed the Blue Ridge Hunt skillfully and boldly—too boldly. She
married Harry R. Kern, Jr., a charming gentleman, whose principal
accomplishment was owning a dashing yellow La Salle convertible.
The feeling in the Valley was that it had not been a grand passion;
rather that Westy drifted into it because all her friends were getting
married and because she had been brought up surrounded by four
hearty men, her father and her brothers. The marriage was doomed
and did not last.

The younger boys, Beverley and Dick, also were growing up.
Beverley looked like the Admiral, with a thin, tanned face, brilliant
blue-gray eyes and regular features, while Dick evidently would become a big, easy-going man very much like his Uncle Tom. The
three boys were, in fact, startlingly like the Byrd brothers who had
been the terrors of Winchester.

Before the break between them, President Roosevelt took one action
that contributed greatly to Byrd's happiness. Ever since his term as
Governor, Byrd had been pushing to preserve the wild mountainous
range of the Blue Ridge, south of Front Royal. A large amount of
acreage was acquired by the Commonwealth for $2,000,000. Half of
this sum was appropriated by the General Assembly and the other
half raised by private subscriptions. On one occasion late in 1934, the
Senator was driving with President Roosevelt over the twisting, narrow gravel road that had been hewn out along the skyline of the
Blue Ridge. The air was sharp with the tang of autumn and sweet
with the scent of towering pines. Seizing the moment, Byrd said,
"Mr. President, we ought to make this a national park."

Roosevelt's eyes sparkled at the thought. "Harry, that's a great
idea," he said. "But I've got a better one. We ought to run it all the
way from Maine to Georgia." [6]

Byrd laughed joyfully at Roosevelt's fantastic imagination, but
he continued to push the plan for Shenandoah National Park. With

6. Richard E. Byrd of Rosemont to the author.

Roosevelt's backing, a bill was put through Congress and Byrd's dream came true. Virginia presented the land to the Federal Government which assumed the responsibility for its development and maintenance as a national park. President Roosevelt dedicated the park on July 3, 1936.

Shenandoah National Park now consists of about 189,000 acres of virgin timber along the spine of the Blue Ridge. At least 2,500,-000 persons visit it every year. Only one other national park, the Great Smokies, exceeds this figure. Just south of Shenandoah National Park lies Blue Ridge National Park, and beyond that the Great Smokies. Thus, though the parks never approximated Roosevelt's grandiose conception, it is possible to drive, with two minor breaks, for 469 miles through superb primeval wilderness.

However, even in this happy accomplishment, Byrd ran afoul of the Federal bureaucracy. Secretary of the Interior Harold L. Ickes had over-all authority over the Park Service. He decided to tidy up the new park by evicting the mountain people, who lived in lonely, ramshackle cabins scattered among the almost inaccessible peaks, and settling them in a new town with fine $8,000 houses complete with modern plumbing. This did not consort with Byrd's idea of justice. He knew those wild free men and women, knew they would hate semi-suburban living in the lowlands. When the Commonwealth had taken over the park site, he had seen to it that the old folks who had lived all their lives among the great trees were verbally assured that they could continue to inhabit their small homes until they died. It now turned out that Ickes cared nothing for the given promise of the Commonwealth.

Calling on a few of his friends in the deep woods, Byrd confirmed his belief that they were miserable at the prospect of moving. He introduced a bill in the Senate to forbid the Government from harassing them, but it was defeated by the "do-gooder" vote.

Ickes then built Tugwell Town [7] and sent the Park Service men to bring the mountain people down to earth. The trouble was that as soon as the guards were gone, the mountain men climbed back up to their old homes. Ickes solved that problem by ordering all the little, dilapidated cabins burned.

So it came about that, in the opinion of Byrd and his friends, the mountain folk lived unhappily ever after in the splendid houses a

7. Named after Rexford Tugwell, an ardent New Dealer.

paternalistic government had freely presented to them. It was agreed that there was one thing they liked. The gleaming white toilet bowls were a good place to mix home-brewed alcohol with juniper berries to make gin.

VIII · BYRD & TRUMAN

EVEN HIS close friends in the Senate spoke of Harry Byrd's lack of education. He could not cap a quotation from Seneca with a riposte from Cato or compare Plato's *Republic* with de Tocqueville's description of the young United States. But education embraces a good deal more than classical learning. In his knowledge of American history, of politics and economics, and of current world events, Byrd had no need to yield to anyone. His omnivorous reading and retentive mind made him one of the best-informed men in the Senate on the subjects with which they dealt.

His knowledge was particularly impressive concerning the worsening situation in Europe. In the late 1930's the drive toward fascist dictatorships and the insatiable appetites of the dictators for land and glory clearly presaged another world war. The American people were deeply divided on the issue of internationalism versus isolationism. Neutrality was thought to be the way to keep America safe in her continental fortress from the tragic mistake of World War I. To make certain of this, the Neutrality Act of 1937 imposed a ban on the export of arms, ammunitions, and munitions of war to any belligerent and prohibited credits and loans to belligerents. It also gave the President discretion to prohibit American ships from carrying to belligerents the essential commodities of modern war such as cotton, copper, oil, and steel.

The act had the support of a majority of Americans at the time. However, as the European crisis deepened, many Americans began to wonder if we could afford to stand aloof.

The reactionary conservatives were generally strongly isolationist. They were joined by unexpected allies of the extreme left—Communists, fellow-travelers and ardent New Dealers who feared that the new social gains would be imperiled by money spent on defense.

Real liberals were uncertain. They saw that England, France, and the smaller democratic countries of Europe were too weak to withstand the powerful fascist armies without arms drawn from the industrial potential of the United States. President Roosevelt, with his wide knowledge of European affairs, his patriotism and humanistic philosophy was powerfully persuaded of this viewpoint. But he could only do what was politically possible.

Senator Byrd was, by now, typed as a great conservative leader and strongly anti-Roosevelt. This, together with his preoccupation with economical government, it might be supposed would put him in the isolationist camp. Wars cost a great deal of money. On the contrary, after pondering the situation for a long time and not without anguish, Byrd came to the conclusion that he must go along with Roosevelt's foreign policy of supporting the democracies against the Axis Powers.

The first vital decision came in September, 1939, immediately after Germany attacked and overran Poland, and England and France declared war. Roosevelt proposed that the Neutrality Act be amended to permit belligerents to buy munitions in the United States on a "cash and carry" basis—that is they must pay cash and send their own ships to collect what they bought. Since England and France controlled the seas, it was a most unneutral proposal. Senator Byrd, foreseeing the danger to America if the Nazis got control of all Europe and organized its tremendous industrial and military power with Germanic efficiency, voted for the bill, though he did offer an amendment of his own first. According to Harold Ickes, the Byrd measure would have watered the act down too much. When it was defeated, Byrd voted for the changes the President wanted. They were enacted.

Byrd also supported Roosevelt's early inadequate efforts to strengthen America's defenses. Pacifist sentiment in the 1930's had allowed them to fall into a dangerously dilapidated state. When, in 1940, the Nazis loosed the blitzkrieg that swept over Norway, Denmark, Holland, and Belgium, and finally brought France to her knees, Roosevelt called for adequate measures to defend the United States. In May, 1940, he asked Congress for appropriations to build fifty thousand airplanes and for $1,182,000,000 to strengthen the Army and Navy. When France fell in June, the President asked for $4,000,000,000 more and a Draft Act to provide an Army of 1,300,000 men, the first peacetime draft in American history. Despite his allegedly pinch-penny mind, Byrd enthusiastically supported both of these great appropriations and conscription, as did a great majority of other Southern congressmen and senators. Virginia had suffered terribly in the Civil War and her people had vivid recollections of those awful years. Cost what it might, Harry Byrd was determined that his beloved country should be spared even a remote chance of foreign invasion.

The fact that Senator Byrd supported Roosevelt's foreign policy did not imply that he was any less opposed to the President in domestic matters. He glumly heard Roosevelt's announcement that he would run for an unprecedented third term in 1940. Many other good Democrats, including Democratic National Chairman James A. Farley and Vice-President Garner, were opposed to a third term, but they were helpless.

The Democratic National Convention in Chicago was called merely to ratify the President's decision to run again. When Carter Glass made the nominating speech for Jim Farley, a forlorn conservative hope, he mentioned the name of Thomas Jefferson. The pro-Roosevelt delegates booed. Byrd was genuinely shocked by this incivility to Glass, a man who had devoted a lifetime to the service of his state and the nation, and to his idol, Jefferson. When Roosevelt's name was put in nomination, a wild and genuinely enthusiastic demonstration sent the delegations from all the states but one marching, dancing, howling, and swirling around the rostrum. Virginians sat silent in their seats. The standard of the Old Dominion never moved. It was firmly grasped in the hands of Harry Byrd.

The only real contest was over the Vice-Presidential nomination. Roosevelt picked Henry Wallace as his running mate. It was not a popular choice. Harry Hopkins and the Roosevelt floor managers had to use all the jokers in the political pack to put it over. Their every move was directed by the master politician over an open line from the White House. Needless to say Senator Byrd was, again, most unhappy.

There was little doubt about the outcome of the election, though it was no such sweep as 1936 had been. The Republicans nominated Wendell Willkie, a liberal-minded idealist to whom many men of good will from both parties rallied. The majority of Americans however thought that Roosevelt was the best man to lead the country through the dangerous days that lay ahead. Whatever his sympathies, Senator Byrd did not openly break with the National Democratic party, but his support of its candidates was extraordinarily silent. The ballot being secret, no one is quite sure how the Senator voted; but members of his family believe that this was the first time, though not the last, that Harry Byrd voted for the Republican Presidential candidate.

Running unopposed for his own Senate seat, Byrd polled over 40,000 more votes than Roosevelt in Virginia.

By January, 1941, the situation of England was desperate. She stood alone in Europe against the tremendous power of Nazi Germany and her Axis ally, Italy. Nazi bombing raids had devastated England's great cities and greatly reduced her ability to produce the planes, guns, and ships essential to her survival. U-boats were taking a fearful toll of her shipping. In addition, she was bankrupt, and in a matter of weeks, she would no longer be able to pay for the American munitions, supplies, and food that alone kept her going. In President Roosevelt's thinking, the frontiers of freedom had been thrown back from the Rhine to the shores of the English Channel. If Britain surrendered, the front line would be on the beaches of Long Island. As soon as he was re-elected, Roosevelt determined that England must be given much further assistance.

How to accomplish that was a complex political problem. Isolationist sentiment was still so strong in the United States that the President knew that any proposal to make an outright gift to England would raise a great clamor of protest and be defeated in the Congress. On the other hand, to lend England the billions she needed to purchase American supplies would result in an enormous unpayable debt, like those which had plagued our relations with Europe and played havoc with the economy of the whole world after World War I.

Roosevelt ingeniously devised a solution by a semantic *tour de force* which he called Lend-Lease. The United States would lend not money, but the materials themselves, the guns, ammunition, tanks, planes, ships, and whatever else England needed to survive. What was used against our common "enemy"—though we were still theoretically neutral—would be regarded as having been expended in our own defense; those items that remained would be returned after the war. Roosevelt, with his love of historical echoes and his gift for public relations, had the Lend-Lease Act numbered HR1776.

Senator Byrd supported HR1776 as he had almost all of Roosevelt's defense measures. He understood as well as the President what the fall of England would mean to America and to the world, but he insisted on a very important amendment. It made clear that none of the moneys appropriated by Congress for the American armed service or the armament bought therewith could be transferred to a foreign nation under Lend-Lease unless specifically authorized by the appropriation bill. In explaining his amendment to the Senate, Byrd said, "I do not believe that the Congress of the United States should enact any law which would give the President, or anyone else, authority to transfer without limit the defense articles provided for in future appropriations." [1]

In thus curtailing Presidential discretion, Byrd made sure that Congress would retain the power to decide how much American armament production would be allotted to England and how much kept for our own defense.

Harold Ickes wrote: "There is some feeling that the Byrd Amendment is deleterious, but notwithstanding this the Administration decided that it would be better policy for the House to accept the Senator's Amendment. This was done quickly and overwhelmingly." [2]

That the President was unwillingly forced to accept Byrd's amendment if he wanted to get the Lend-Lease Act through the Sen-

1. Congressional Record, February 26, 1941.
2. *Ickes Secret Diary*. Vol. II.

ate, shows the force of Harry Byrd's influence in that body. In that same year, 1941, he became Chairman of the powerful Rules Committee of the Senate.

Almost at the same time Byrd's deskmate, Harry Truman, moved into prominence by organizing and becoming Chairman of the Senate Committee to Investigate the National Defense Program. The first hearing of the Truman Committee, as it was called, was held on April 15, 1941, with Secretary of War Henry L. Stimson as the first witness. As it probed into the expenditure and management of the huge appropriations for the Armed Services, the Truman Committee uncovered all sorts of deficiencies and mismanagement. The waste in the vast camp construction program was in Truman's own word, "appalling." [3] Other instances of inefficiency were almost as bad. The Truman Committee saved the American taxpayers billions of dollars. More important, the increased efficiency in war production and in the use of materiel by the Armed Services that it brought about saved unknown thousands of American lives.

The period of the Truman Committee represented the high point in the friendship between Harry Byrd and Harry Truman. Byrd's admiration for Truman's achievements soared with the savings he saw realized. His disgust with the bureaucratic inefficiency Truman uncovered reached a new high.

In the confused summer of 1941, Byrd was also incensed by the strikes which, in his opinion, the Administration's policy of pandering to Labor permitted to hamper vital war production. Industry continued to pour out a plethora of consumer goods and the New Deal's social services continued at full blast, while defense needs were unmet and Lend-Lease commitments went unfilled. On August 19, 1941, Byrd made a full-dress Senate speech in which he blasted the Administration for its inefficiency and the public for its apathy; and described lagging defense production.[4]

The President, just back from the Atlantic Charter Conference with Churchill, was very upset and said, "Someone has sold Harry Byrd down the river." He countered Byrd's statements with some soothing figures. However, a few days later William S. Knudsen, the hard bitten head of Industrial Mobilization, indirectly admitted that

3. Harry S. Truman, *Memoirs*, Vol. I. Doubleday, Garden City, New York, 1955.
4. Congressional Record, August 20, 1941.

Byrd's figures were correct. Whereupon Byrd again took the floor to demand a single head for the office of War Production, reform of bureaucratic confusion, and a temporary end to new social measures and to strikes in defense industries.

The final event that sent Byrd on the warpath was the strike John L. Lewis called late in October, 1941, against the steel companies' coal mines, throwing fifty-five thousand men out of work and threatening the whole defense program. Roosevelt protested to Lewis, who replied so contumaciously that Byrd said, "I know of no more disgraceful or humiliating episode in American history than John L. Lewis' act." [5]

A few days later, less than a month before Pearl Harbor, Roosevelt asked Congress for the authority to arm American merchant ships carrying Lend-Lease supplies through U-Boat-infested waters to England. Byrd in a grand gesture of dissent voted against it, though he approved of the move. In fact, it is certain that he would not have voted "No," if there had been any doubt of the bill's passage. Explaining his vote, Byrd stated that he would not vote for another step toward war until the Administration cracked down on strikes in defense production, took other steps to improve the faltering rearmament program, and eliminated conflicting New Deal measures for social progress.

That autumn Byrd proposed the formation of his famous Joint Committee (of the House and Senate) on the Reduction of Nonessential Federal Expenditures.

The Japanese attack on Pearl Harbor on December 7, 1941, ended the period of complacency. America went all out to win the war. The Joint Committee on the Reduction of Nonessential Federal Expenditures was activated without opposition under Byrd's chairmanship. He was a tough man to serve under, driving his committee members and staff harder than old William Byrd ever drove his slaves. Every department of the Government was subject to minute inspection for possible financial excrescenses. Byrd gleefully axed such New Deal favorites as the Civilian Conservation Corps, the Works Progress Administration, and many others. He kept a sharp eye on military expenditures but never tried to reduce essential appropriations. In its

5. "The Fourth Term's Hair Shirt," *op. cit.*

first two years the Byrd Committee saved taxpayers an estimated $2,100,000.[6]

The Senator was as economical in running his committee as in pruning Government departments. Quite early in its existence a secretary brought Byrd a long telegram to sign. Byrd went over it rapidly and crossed out one word saying, "We don't need that one." He saved the Government ten cents with the same care as he saved ten million dollars. At one point the Byrd Committee went so far as to recommend a law providing penalties of a year in jail or a $1,000 fine for the unauthorized use of a Government car.

Immediately upon the Declaration of War, Harry Byrd, Jr., enlisted in the Navy. The fact that he had just been married did not make him hesitate. He served in Navy Public Relations for a time, but he had not joined the Navy to see Washington. He got himself transferred to the South Pacific where he served as Executive Officer of a patrol bombing squadron until 1946.

As we have seen, Beverley Byrd became a paratrooper in the 101st Airborne Division. He landed in a Normandy apple orchard in the early hours of D-Day. It was as fragrant as the serene orchards surrounding Rosemont, but within minutes it became an annex of hell. Almost as soon as Beverley landed, his scattered group were heavily attacked. Beverley was shot in the hand. In spite of his wound, he fought one-handed from a ditch throughout that desperate night and morning, and was credited with saving one boy's life and probably several others.

It was a short but glorious war for Beverley, followed by a long recuperation. Military doctors worked on his hand for two years before they got it as right as it could ever be.

Meanwhile, his brother Dick, a sergeant in the Tenth Armored Division, went through France with Patton's Third Army until he was invalided out with frozen feet in early December, 1944. He, too, was in and out of army hospitals for many months.

Westy got a job in Washington in the O.S.S. She lived with her parents in their small apartment in the Shoreham and took care of her mother who required increasingly diligent nursing. Washingtonians still remember her striding through Rock Creek Park in the

6. *Ibid.*

early morning with the Senator, her harlequin Great Dane, Arno, towing her along.

Though Byrd unfailingly voted for the great appropriations necessary to carry on the war, he continued to fight extravagance and waste at every turn. He also rallied conservative opinion against Roosevelt's attempts to make wartime taxes an instrument of social revolution—the President's favorite scheme of redistributing wealth by taxation. Byrd succeeded in defeating the most onerous provisions of Roosevelt's tax bill of 1943.

By doing this he assumed the leadership of the Southern conservatives in the Senate, until then badgered, bewildered, and torn between their patriotic duty to support the war effort and their aversion to the socialist state at which the President seemed to be aiming. In December, 1943, to Byrd's amazement and consternation, Senator Ellison D. (Cotton Ed) Smith suddenly interrupted a debate to make a speech proposing him as the ideal Democratic candidate for President in 1944. Cotton Ed's "rebel yell" was a pathetically futile gesture. Byrd hastily leaped to his feet to decline the empty honor. Nevertheless it set people thinking. During the months before the convention Byrd succeeded in crystallizing the conservative Southern opposition. He became its acknowledged leader.

When the Convention met in Chicago on July 17, 1944, there was no question but that it would nominate Roosevelt for President. Though Byrd was definitely not a candidate and refused to allow the Virginia Delegation to make him a favorite son, he received eighty-nine votes on the first and only ballot.

The Vice-Presidential nomination was another matter. The President wanted Vice-President Henry Wallace renominated. Wallace had swung further and further to the left, and had become very unpopular, not only in the South but in the Senate, over which he had presided, and among the politicians who ran the Party machinery throughout the country. In view of the President's failing health under the enormous burden of conducting the war, and his gallant disregard of his personal safety, the Wallace nomination seemed a terrible risk not only to conservatives but even to some left-of-center liberals. Though a Presidential nominee is traditionally supposed to choose his running mate, Byrd felt it was time to say "Stop!" He succeeded in rallying almost the entire South, and many Northern conservatives as well, against Wallace. So strong was his faction that Robert Hannegan, the Democratic National Chairman, telephoned the President that Wallace's nomination, if not impossible, was certain to tear the Democratic party apart.

Roosevelt agreed to a compromise and suggested Senator James F. Byrnes of South Carolina as a unifying choice. The Senate majority leader Alben W. Barkley also announced that he was available. Byrd and his colleagues would have been delighted with either man. However, Philip Murray of the CIO, William Green (AFL), A. F. Whitney, Sidney Hillman, and other labor leaders with tremendous behind-the-scenes power vetoed both Byrnes and Barkley.[7]

An enormous amount of back-room politicking went on. Roosevelt's lieutenants rushed back and forth from labor leaders to Byrd to Byrnes and Barkley and the head-men of the great industrial states, seeking a viable compromise candidate. Finally, Bob Hannegan telephoned Roosevelt again. This time Roosevelt was in a private car in the railroad yards at San Diego, California, just prior to sailing to Hawaii for a conference with General Douglas MacArthur and Admiral Nimitz. Hannegan told the President, "We can get an agreement on Harry Truman." Roosevelt thought a moment and replied, "Well, he's honest." [8]

Byrd, as the leader of the fairly solid South, had agreed to Truman. He had not succeeded in getting the nomination for either of his preferred candidates. But he had, as it turned out, prevented Henry Wallace from becoming President of the United States.

Senator Byrd played no further historic role in wartime politics apart from his steady support of the war effort. His continued concern for unnecessary Federal expenditures earned him the title of "The Watchdog of the Treasury." In this connection he had one last clash with President Roosevelt.

Byrd was chairman of the Joint Committee for Roosevelt's Fourth Inaugural on January 20, 1945. He asked the President if he wanted the customary $100,000 for the Inauguration expenses. Roosevelt replied that he had no intention of spending such a large

7. Harry S. Truman, *op. cit.*
8. Alden Hatch, *Franklin D. Roosevelt.*

amount in wartime, and that $25,000 would be enough. To his friends, he remarked that for once he would teach Byrd a lesson in economy.

The $25,000 appropriation was duly passed. A few days later the President's close friend and doctor, General Edwin M. (Pa) Watson, telephoned Byrd that the $25,000 would not be enough. Byrd said he would be glad to increase it if the President would write him a letter to that effect. Two days later Pa Watson called to say that the President was unwilling to write the letter because he felt Byrd might publish it. The Senator said, "The President need not have any doubts about it. I'm certainly going to read it into the *Congressional Record*."

In effect Roosevelt answered, "The hell with you." He held the Inaugural ceremonies on the South Portico of the White House. Roosevelt was probably happy about this arrangement because he was desperately tired and it saved him from the exhausting effort of the traditional ceremony on the Capitol steps with all the walking, speech-making and taking the salute of the Inaugural Parade. The Fourth Inaugural cost $526.02. Roosevelt returned $24,473.98 to the Treasury. If by doing so he hoped to make Byrd feel small, he was disappointed. Byrd was delighted.[9]

As Byrd was driving back to the Capitol from that strange little Inaugural, he said sadly to Menefee, "Franklin looks like a ghost. I'm afraid he won't last long."[10]

Two days later, on January 22, 1945, President Roosevelt sailed for Yalta.

Like all Americans and half the population of the world, Harry Byrd was stunned by the death of President Roosevelt on April 12, 1945. Though he had fought the President on so many issues that their friendship had curdled to bitterness, the memory of it was still in his heart. In addition, he had recognized that the President was a great wartime leader and he was a strong advocate of Roosevelt's plan for the United Nations. He could not have helped wondering how his former deskmate would handle the grave perils and tremendous opportunities he now faced.

If ever there was a lost soul in the White House it was Harry

9. Senator Byrd, Jr. in the Washington *Post*, May 19, 1968.
10. M. J. Menefee to the author.

Truman in the first months of his Presidency. Roosevelt had given no one his full confidence, least of all his new Vice-President. After the strained, dramatic swearing-in ceremony in the Cabinet Room of the White House, the new President sat down at the head of the huge odd-shaped table to hold his first Cabinet meeting. When it ended, Secretary of War Henry L. Stimson lingered behind. He told President Truman that an immense project looking to the development of a "new explosive of unbelievable destructive power" was under way. Truman had not the faintest idea what he was talking about. It was several days later that Doctor Vannevar Bush told him about the atomic bomb. Admiral William D. Leahy, who was present, showed the thinking of Navy top brass by saying, "That is the biggest fool thing we have ever done . . . The bomb will never go off." [11]

Like all the new President's former colleagues, Senator Byrd was deeply sympathetic and did all he could to help. Harry Truman had been very popular with the Senators, whether they agreed with him or not. Again and again during his first months in the White House President Truman would say sadly, "I was so happy in the Senate.[12]

But the momentum of great events could not stay its course while the new President found his footing. The war in Europe was drawing to its close as Eisenhower's armies streamed almost unopposed through defeated Germany, and the Russians closed their ring of steel around Berlin. Hitler killed himself in the shell-rocked bunker outside the ruins of the Reichkanzlei, and the puppet German generals came, stiff with despair, to the schoolhouse in Rheims to surrender what little was left of the "Thousand Year Reich." Meanwhile in San Francisco, the United Nations were meeting to draw up a Charter and hopefully to build a new and better world.

Senator Byrd was deeply troubled by the provision in the proposed charter that any of the five great nations on the Security Council (the United States, Russia, Great Britain, France, and China) would have the power to veto its decisions. He foresaw that in practice this would nullify any action the Council might take contrary to their interests and reduce it to impotence. President Roosevelt, with bitter memories of the refusal of the Senate to ratify President Wilson's League of Nations Treaty, had originally proposed this provi-

11. Harry S. Truman, *op. cit.*
12. President Truman to the author in May, 1945.

sion as necessary to obtain Senate approval of the United Nations Charter. So strongly did Byrd feel about the veto that he made a special trip to San Francisco to use his influence on Secretary of State Edward R. Stettinius, Senator Arthur H. Vandenberg, and other leading members of the United States Delegation to persuade them to drop the veto provisions. It was a useless effort. The Russian Delegation was strong for the veto and the Americans were equally insistent on it. Like Roosevelt, they were convinced that it was essential to Senate ratification of the Treaty. In his memoirs, President Truman stated flatly, "Without such a veto no arrangement would have passed the Senate." [13]

Quite possibly Truman was right; and even if he were not, the Russians, by then, would never have accepted the Charter without it. Yet it is interesting to speculate on how much grief and frustration would have been avoided had Harry Byrd's opinion prevailed.

Realizing that henceforward the United States would play an increasingly important role in world affairs, Byrd made his first trip to Europe with a group of Senators two weeks after the German surrender. He was keenly aware of the limitations of his education in respect to foreign affairs and he proposed to remedy this by firsthand observation, which to him was always the best way of learning. He visited England, France, and the wreckage that had been Germany. Natural curiosity took him to Hitler's Eagle's Nest at Berchtesgaden. A mountain man himself, he must have delighted in the superb view of those rugged peaks and deep ravines.

For the rest, Byrd concentrated less on sightseeing than on enlarging his understanding of Europe and its problems and getting the feel of it by personal contact with its people great and small. In the rubble of Berlin he had a long talk with Allied Supreme Commander Dwight D. Eisenhower. The Senator was especially perturbed by the thought of East Berlin being turned over to the Communists. When he expressed this view to Eisenhower, the General characteristically scratched his head and said, "I can push them out if I'm told to, but you'll have the Russians on your necks." [14]

13. Harry S. Truman, *op. cit.*

14. E. Blackburn Moore, Speaker of the Virginia House of Delegates, to the author.

In view of Senator Byrd's misgivings, it was natural that he should be horrified by President Truman's actions at the Potsdam Conference in July, 1945. Despite Eisenhower's emphatic objections, Truman agreed with Josef Stalin to a Soviet Zone of Occupation far to the west of the Elbe River where the Russian and Allied armies had originally met. He thus fixed the present border of East Germany. When General Eisenhower (who became increasingly friendly with Byrd) returned from Europe, he said nothing to revise the Senator's estimate of the Potsdam Agreement. He once remarked that neither Truman nor his new Secretary of State, James F. Byrnes, knew what he was doing there. "It was a case of the blind leading the blind." [15]

Byrd became increasingly disenchanted with his former desk-mate. When the Atomic Bomb forced Japan to surrender in August, 1945, President Truman immediately began to make plans for demobilizing the Armed Forces, for implementing a program of social gains and *peacetime* price and wage controls, for a great housing program, and for generally enlarging Government control of the economic life of the nation. He christened his program the "Fair Deal." While Senator Byrd recognized that wartime government controls over prices and wages, and priorities in the production of essential commodities could not be relinquished all at once, he ardently desired to see a gradual withdrawal of Government interference in business rather than a continuation or increase in wartime restrictions. Furthermore he was appalled by the cost of the Government subsidies for new housing and other social advances. The enormous cost of the war had left the United States with a staggering debt of $279,200,000,000. Byrd felt that instead of further deficit financing, draconian measures should be taken to balance the budget and at the very least make a beginning at paying off the debt. Some reduction was made in it, but it was not sufficient to meet the Senator's requirements. He used his very considerable influence to chip away at the large sums the administration requested for its programs.

Byrd's resistance to Fair Deal programs provoked some decidedly acrimonious debates in the Senate. In one such debate liberal Senator Claude A. Pepper of Florida made a personal attack on him. Byrd rose to ask if the Senator from Florida would yield for a question. Pepper yielded. Byrd's "question" was, "My father always told me never to argue with a skunk."

15. General Eisenhower to the author in 1947.

The following day Byrd was riding down to the Capitol in a taxi with Senator Homer Ferguson of Michigan. "Don't you think you were a little rough on Pepper?" Ferguson said. "Perhaps you might make some form of apology."

"You're quite right, I should," Byrd said. "I will ask for time and if the Senator yields to me I'll apologize to the whole skunk family." [16]

Byrd's most important service in 1946 was in regard to atomic energy. The Armed Services wanted the administration of atomic development put under their control as a weapon of war. Senator Byrd, a member of the Special Committee on Atomic Energy, helped to draw up the legislation which kept it in civilian hands and created the Atomic Energy Commission.

The Congressional elections of 1946 were a staggering blow to the Democratic administration. The fact that the Democrats had been in control of the Federal Government for so long, together with war weariness and disenchantment with postwar policies, had the usual effect on the voters. They gave the Republicans control of both houses of Congress for the first time in sixteen years. Though Senator Byrd thereby lost his chairmanship of the Rules Committee and the Byrd Committee, he was not altogether displeased.

At this time his warmest friends in the Senate were his co-leaders of the conservative Southern group, Senators Richard Russell and Walter F. George. Willis Robertson, Byrd's teammate in so many political battles, came to the Senate in 1947. Byrd had previously offered to make Robertson the Governor of Virginia, but Robertson declined the honor. "I can't afford it," he said. "I'd be like those horses from the short grass country—too slow to race and too proud to plow." [17] When Senator Carter Glass died, Robertson took his place.

In addition to these old friends Byrd was close to several Republican Senators who were far more compatible to his basic philosophy than most of his Democratic colleagues. Among his intimates were Senator Arthur H. Vandenberg, who now became Chairman of the Foreign Relations Committee, and the new Senate Majority Leader Robert A. Taft.

It is interesting to note that although Senator Taft was called "Mr. Republican" and was considered the great conservative, his

16. Former Senator Ferguson to the author.
17. Former Senator Robertson to the author.

financial thinking was more flexible than Byrd's. For example, though Keynesian economics and deficit financing always remained anathema to Byrd, Taft believed in Keynes' principle of using deficit financing and inflation to combat a depression.[18]

The Republican victory in 1946 had been in part due to the series of nationwide strikes which had erupted after the war. The Wagner Act of New Deal days had given labor some much-needed reforms, but it had also provided unscrupulous labor leaders with a tremendous leverage that upset the balance of labor-management relations. During the war labor had patriotically refrained from pushing this advantage, but with the coming of peace and the relaxation of government controls the unions went all out. Strikes in the coal, automotive and meat-packing industries that idled over five hundred thousand workers were followed by a railroad strike of three hundred thousand workers that threatened to paralyze the nation, to literally starve it into accepting the striker's demands. President Truman asked a joint session of Congress for the power to draft striking railroad employees into the armed services. As he was halfway through this speech, he received a message that the unions had accepted the findings of the unofficial arbitration board he had set up.

The last straw came when John L. Lewis called a strike of four hundred thousand miners in the bituminous coal fields. Since President Truman had taken over the mines in May to end a previous strike, this strike, in effect, was against the Government itself. Lewis' demands seemed beyond all economic reason or possibility of acceptance.

Truman succeeded in ending that strike by the use of harsh court action and he proposed to curb the labor leaders. However, his labor proposals were not acceptable to the Republican 80th Congress which wrote its own labor legislation. The House passed a severe act, sponsored by Representative Fred Hartley, Jr., of New Jersey. In the Senate, Robert A. Taft produced a more reasonable bill. The differences between the two bills were worked out in conference and the result, generally known as the Taft-Hartley Act, was passed and sent to the President.

Senator Byrd played an important role in the Taft-Hartley Act. Though a conservative he was definitely not antilabor. He always upheld the right of labor to organize and favored collective bargain-

18. Senator Taft in an interview with the author in 1947.

ing. He urged the incorporation of labor unions, with mutual labor-management responsibility under contracts for the protection of the workers themselves against exploitation by unscrupulous labor leaders who dipped into their union funds (as in the case of the Teamsters' Union). His advice on and support of the Taft-Hartley Act was important to its moderation and passage.

When President Truman vetoed the Taft-Hartley Act on June 20, 1947, Byrd's support became essential because a two-thirds majority was required to override the veto. He summoned all his influence to bring like-minded Democrats to the support of the bill, which was passed over the President's veto on June 23.

Though the Act has been anathema to organized labor, it has proved its usefulness many times over. With its provisions against secondary boycotts and jurisdictional strikes and its key provision that the President may appoint a fact-finding board and decree an eighty-day cooling-off period in strikes that affect the national health and safety, it has undoubtedly contributed to more peaceful relations between management and labor, saving hundreds of millions of dollars in lost wages and production.

While Congress and the Administration were at odds over domestic legislation, harmony reigned in regard to foreign affairs. This was due to a continuation of the wartime agreement on a bipartisan foreign policy and in particular to the wisdom and patriotism of Senator Vandenberg, Chairman of the Foreign Affairs Committee. This accord on foreign policy was extremely fortunate for the nation and the free world, for a series of crises was averted and dangerous problems were solved because of bipartisan support of the President.

The first crisis after the convening of the Eightieth Congress was touched off by Great Britain's announcement that she could no longer afford military or financial support for the democratic Government of Greece against the communist revolutionaries who were being supplied by Russia and her satellite countries. Without British assistance, the Greek Government would surely fall. General Eisenhower, who was then Chief of Staff, called Greece "a vital bastion of the free world." If Greece were lost to communism, he said, Turkey would fall.[19]

President Truman courageously called upon Congress for $250,-000,000 in military aid to Greece and $150,000,000 for Turkey.

19. General Eisenhower's report to President Truman.

Strongly supported by Vandenberg and other Republicans in the Senate and a large majority in the House, the bill was passed. This was the beginning of the Truman Doctrine of supporting the free nations of the world and halting the flooding tide of communism. Senator Byrd shortsightedly opposed this policy.

Another instance in which Senator Byrd's judgment was questionable was in his opposition to the Marshall Plan later that year. In 1947, many nations of Europe, particularly France and Italy, were bankrupt as a result of the war. In a brilliant speech at Harvard University on June 5, 1947, Secretary of State George C. Marshall proposed that the countries of Europe agree on a cooperative plan for recovery, which would be supported by the United States. The Iron Curtain countries, at Russia's insistence, declined to participate. Virtually all the European democracies accepted and worked out plans for their economic rehabilitation. The Marshall Plan cost the United States about $13,000,000,000, but it made Europe once again financially viable and it halted the advance of communism.

In his opposition to the Marshall Plan, Byrd seemed illogical. He was never an isolationist. He voted for direct relief and military assistance to Europe, and later voted for the NATO Treaty. But he was so convinced that people and nations must stand on their own feet economically and earn their way by their own sweat, and so fearful that the United States was spending itself to financial ruin, that the large sums necessary to implement the Marshall Plan seemed frantic folly to him.

Indeed, Byrd had an unbroken record of voting against foreign-aid bills. Later failures of some of these projects, due to maladministration and corruption among officials of some of the countries assisted, might seem to justify his attitude. However, in view of the success of the Marshall Plan, Byrd would seem to have been penny-wise.

IX · REVOLT IN VIRGINIA

DESPITE HIS political battles, the defeats of his economic policies, and his distaste for the National Democratic party's policies, Senator Byrd was a happy man. When he sat under the portico at Rosemont with his friends, it was said that you could hear his hearty booming laughter clear across the valley. Though in the Senate he usually wore an immaculate white suit with a red necktie, as he had in Winchester when he was "Handsome Harry," his customary costume at Rosemont was more disreputable than ever. His grandson Harry described bringing a girl out to Rosemont a few years later. "Father, Uncle Tom and Grandfather came walking through the snow. Grandfather was wearing an old suit of blue quilted underwear with a rope around his waist to keep the pants up. It did not work very well and every few steps he stopped to pull them up. My girl's expression was something. After that day, I never saw her again." [1]

On another occasion, as Byrd arrived at his plant in Berryville, a migrant worker was just coming out of the door. In friendly fashion he said to the Senator, "No use going in. They ain't hiring today."

The Senator's sons were all safely home from the war. Harry, Jr., has taken over the management of the papers and built a new brick

1. Harry F. Byrd III to the author.

building to house the *Star*. The Senator's new office soon looked just as messy as the old one.

Harry, Jr., became a director of the Associated Press and later its first vice-president. He traveled much more than his father had, interviewing the political leaders of many lands for articles that were widely syndicated. In 1947, he was elected to the Virginia Senate in which he served for nineteen years.

Beverley and Dick were serving their apprenticeship in the orchards, preparing to take over when their time came. Beverley married Martha Robinson. She was a gay, society-loving girl, while Beverley had his father's dislike of getting all dressed up, and the reclusive intellectual habits of his grandfather, Mr. Dick. Like Westy he loved fox-hunting and rode boldly and well, serving as Master of the Blue Ridge Hunt in 1949 and 1950.

Inevitably, with such a clash of temperaments, Beverley's first marriage ended in divorce. In 1963, he married Shirley Deane, the lovely daughter of a British diplomat, whom he met when she was working at the United Nations. Shirley loved fox-hunting as much as he did and enjoyed the bookish, farming, country-squire existence in the Log House. Though it was now fortunately provided with central heating, it was still very cold by American standards, but that suited them both.

Incidentally, in his fondness for a frigid atmosphere, Beverley took after his father. The Senator kept Rosemont just above the freezing point in winter. All the radiators in his Washington office were turned off. Coming into it from the overheated corridors of the Senate Office Building was a little like entering Admiral Byrd's cabin at Advance Base. The Senator's faithful secretaries, Miss Meta Dick and Miss Martha Crop, wore sweaters and woolies all winter.

Indeed, the Senator seemed quite impervious to climate. The hot Virginia summers affected him as little as the icy Shenandoah winters. He hardly ever wore an overcoat. In Washington, he seldom used the Senators' underground railway between the Capitol and the offices, but in a business suit walked gaily through ice or snow to and from the Capitol, reaching out to touch the tall trees that he passed.

The Senator's youngest son, Richard E. Byrd II, married Helen Bradshaw of Massachusetts, a beautiful young woman with enormous blue eyes, golden hair, and an apple-blossom skin. With all those attributes Helen had an excellent mind and an intrepid spirit.

Brought up in the New England tradition, she was somewhat taken aback on her introduction to her husband's grandmother. Miss Bolling looked her firmly in the eye and said, "Do you believe that Robert E. Lee was the greatest American who ever lived?"

Helen gasped and murmured, "What? Who? Of course."

She, too, is a diplomat.

The Senator's grandchildren began arriving in due time and they contributed enormously to his happiness, but shadows were falling across the sunlit lawns of Rosemont.

Westy had never remarried. The sense of serving and her interest in her work had inspired her during the war. Afterward there was a let-down. Like Beverley, who was her best friend as well as brother, she cared nothing for social life. As Sittie became ever less active, Westy played the part of her father's hostess with grace if not enthusiasm. And she went to infinite pains to make Christmas at Rosemont a joy for all the family. But her friends say she was not a happy person.

All she appeared to care about was fox hunting, and she rode ever more boldly. In 1946, her hunter made a mistake and fell upon her, breaking two vertebrae in her back. For months she lay in a plaster cast in a great deal of pain. The doctors said she must never hunt again, but of course she did. She got away with it for five more years until the winter of 1951, when she had another bad fall that further damaged her back. After that she was never entirely free from pain and relied on pain-killers and sleeping pills to make her life bearable. Despite the pain, she was hunting again that autumn, though it must have been torture to her.

In the spring of 1952, Westy Byrd either groggily took too many of the pills that were her staff, or she decided life was no longer worth the effort. Westy died on March 20, 1952.

In 1948, almost the only person in the Democratic party who thought President Truman could be re-elected was President Truman. He was at the nadir of his popularity with a rating of 29 per cent in the Gallup Poll. This was not displeasing to Senator Byrd. A concerted effort, backed by many liberals as well as conservatives, was afoot to dump Truman as the Democratic nominee for President. Overtures were made to General Eisenhower who had retired from the Army to become President of Columbia University. If Ike had so much as crooked his little finger, he could have been President that year. Instead, he made a Shermanesque [2] refusal to run. An attempt to nominate Senator Russell at the Democratic National Convention in Philadelphia failed by 947½ votes to 263.

After Truman was nominated, Senator Byrd, who had backed Russell, broke almost openly with his party saying he was "too busy picking apples" to take part in the campaign. In the Senate, he continued to hack away at Truman's program. Truman, of course, confounded the pundits by beating Republican candidate Thomas E. Dewey, and carrying the Congress with him. Byrd again became Chairman of the Byrd Committee.

The liberal resurgence led to the only serious challenge to the Byrd Machine in the Senator's lifetime. The Organization candidate for Governor of Virginia was John S. Battle. Colonel Francis Pickens Miller announced against him in the Democratic primary. Colonel Miller was a tall, rangey man whose family was almost as aristocratic as the Byrds. A graduate of Washington and Lee, he had taken postgraduate courses at Oxford. Miller was a liberal idealist, who had been a member of the House of Delegates from Fairfax County. At that time, before World War II, he made quite a reputation as an orator. Noting this, Byrd sent him a message by State Senator Harry Carter Stewart, "The Senator sends his compliments and invites you to join him."

Had Miller done so, he believes that he would have been Governor of Virginia and perhaps Senator. Instead he replied with formal courtesy, "Present my compliments to the Senator and tell him that I appreciate his offer but I feel that I can serve Virginia better in other ways." [3]

After serving in World War II, Colonel Miller moved to Charlottesville as a better base for political operations than Fairfax County, and began his campaign against the Organization. Even twenty years later he was still emotional about his reasons: "The epitaph on a tomb in Dublin Cathedral," he said, "reads 'Here lies the body of Dean Swift, his heart lacerated with furious indignation.'

"That could be mine. My heart was lacerated about the poor

2. General William T. Sherman said, "If nominated I will not run, and if elected I will not serve."
3. Colonel Miller to the author.

schools, the poor public services, and most of all because Virginia was getting out of the main stream of American politics—Virginia who had been the *leader* in an earlier day!

"Byrd isolated it because he was so opposed to the trend of the times. It resulted in stagnation. . . ." [4]

There was a good deal of truth in Colonel Miller's contention. As a result of the poll tax, there were only about 130,000 voters in Virginia out of a population of 3,000,000 in 1940. There was also the lowest *white* adult percentage of population voting of any state in the Union, perhaps in the world. In one primary only 7.7 per cent of the *eligible* electorate voted. In the matter of schools and public services Virginia was indeed low on the roster of the states. The Commonwealth was an enclave of conservatism in a nation moving toward social progress. But even Colonel Miller never charged that she was not governed with integrity and grace.

It was a rough primary campaign. Miller succeeded in raising a standard of revolt to which many voters rallied. The Organization had to go all out to defeat him. They manipulated all the levers of power. "The Courthouse Gang" and the State Compensation Board put social and financial pressure on the waverers. John Battle campaigned furiously, financed by William T. Reed. He labeled Miller a radical and a tool of labor because the CIO backed him. Miller replied by attacking Byrd as a dictator who had run Virginia for nineteen years *after* he had left the Governor's chair. He said, "The chief overseer of this absentee landlord has been Mr. E. R. Combs, Chairman of the Compensation Board . . . [and] the operating boss of the Byrd machine . . . a machine as ruthless and powerful as any in the United States. . . ." [5]

On the constructive side, Miller promised Virginians all the social gains that more progressive states were making. He was a charming candidate, immensely appealing in his evident sincerity, his immaculate idealism—a very gentle man. He influenced a great many votes, so many that Senator Byrd had to call out his Republican shock troops. [6] The method was for Byrd to go to Republican Boss Henry A. Wise and ask him to have his people cross over and vote in the

4. *Ibid.*

5. Speech by Colonel Miller over Radio Station WRNL, Richmond. February 10, 1949.

6. State Senator Ted Dalton (Republican) in a speech in the Virginia Senate, February 12, 1952.

Democratic primary. A formal invitation was issued by Wise to Republicans to do so, a perfectly legal procedure in Virginia. Miller lost to Battle by only 24,000 votes. Since the normal Democratic primary vote was only 292,276 (in 1944) and 316,000 voted in 1949, Miller claimed that Battle's 24,000 majority was made up of conservative Republicans who crossed over. This may not be entirely accurate. The normal primary in Virginia was not much of a contest, so the voter ordinarily did not turn out; but a good fight will bring them flocking to the polls. However, it seems likely that a good many Republicans did join the fray.

Colonel Miller was badly lacerated by the campaign. Such staunch friends as Martin Hutchinson (who ran against Byrd in 1946), Tom Gill of Danville, as well as Miller's campaign managers in Norfolk and the Ninth District were either politically ruined or left the State.

Oddly enough, the thing that hurt Miller most was a comparatively mild epithet hurled by John Battle in the heat of action. After the dust of defeat had settled, Miller rather pathetically said to Randolph Perry, who was Battle's campaign manager in Charlottesville, "There's one thing that bothers me. I didn't think that John [Battle] would be so low as to say of me, 'It's an evil bird that fouls its own nest.'"

"But Pickens, you were criticizing Virginia," Perry said.

"I was not criticizing Virginia," Miller expostulated, "I was criticizing Byrd."

Perry said, "Byrd *is* Virginia."[7]

Groggy but still on his feet, Colonel Miller took on the old champion himself in the senatorial primary of 1952. Again he was deeply wounded by a poster which Senator Byrd had blazoned on every billboard, fence and rock in the state:

VOTE AMERICAN:
RETURN HARRY F. BYRD, SR.,
TO THE UNITED STATES SENATE.

The implication that a vote for Miller was un-American was the unkindest thrust that lacerated Miller anew.

Miller dredged up the interesting information that in the Senate, Byrd had voted more frequently against the Democratic Admin-

7. Colonel Miller to the author.

istration in 1951 than "Mr. Republican" (Senator Taft) himself. Byrd rejoined, "Because my name begins with B, I vote first. The Republicans vote with me." Byrd won the primary easily—216,131 to 128,869.

After the primary campaign, Byrd said, "Miller is a real gentleman. He never hit me below the belt." When this remark was repeated to Colonel Miller, he said, "But I thought I *had* hit him below the belt." [8]

In the general election, the Republicans did not even bother to run a candidate against the Senator. As even Colonel Miller sometimes admitted in private, Byrd *was* Virginia.

Though Senator Byrd fought most of President Truman's program so bitterly, he supported him on the Korean War, and voted for the huge military appropriations to carry it on—which is not to say he was happy about it. He was delighted when President Eisenhower was able to achieve a reasonably satisfactory peace. During the conflict, the Byrd Committee was exceedingly active in eliminating unnecessary Government expenses.

Senator Byrd also had a run-in with General Omar Bradley, when the latter was head of the Veterans' Administration. Bradley wanted to build a hospital on some Government land near Arlington. Byrd realized that the hospital was necessary, but he studied the location carefully. Then he said to General Bradley, "You have made a mistake. Listening to the buglers blowing taps over soldiers buried at Arlington will not have a therapeutic value for the patients, nor will the planes taking off from the National Airport improve their dreams. You will not build a hospital there." [9]

Though the Senator had no authority in this purely administrative matter, General Bradley gave up the idea.

As might be expected, Byrd was a great friend and admirer of General Douglas MacArthur. On the night Truman decided to dismiss MacArthur for insubordination, General Bradley called Senator Byrd to tell him as a matter of courtesy. The Senator was asleep so his assistant, M. J. Menefee, took the message. "I woke the Senator at six o'clock in the morning and gave him the message," said

8. *Ibid.*
9. Mr. M. J. Menefee to the author.

Menefee. "Though he must have been much distressed he never said a word. You see he was the ranking member of the Armed Services Committee and he never discussed military matters with anyone, not even with me." [10]

When MacArthur came to Washington, he went first to Senator Byrd's office, where he stayed for some time talking to the Senator. From there he went straight to the Joint Session of the Congress to make his famous "Old Soldiers Never Die" speech.

The National Democratic Convention of 1952 was the last one Senator Byrd ever attended. He was always elected a delegate in subsequent conventions, but he realized that the tide in the National party was running too strongly against his views for him to have any influence, so he elected to go mountain climbing with his young friend E. Blackburn (Blackie) Moore, who was one of the coming men in the Byrd Machine, and became Speaker of the House of Delegates in 1950. So subtle were his methods that there was a saying in Virginia that "Blackie could walk through dead leaves three feet deep and never make a sound or leave a trail." Blackie went to Chicago with Byrd in 1952, as did young Harry. They battled unsuccessfully against the nomination of Adlai Stevenson.

Stevenson's nomination was the occasion of Byrd's first formal break with the National Democratic party. His close association with the Republican candidate, General Eisenhower, led him to believe that the General would be a better President than Stevenson; certainly his views were more compatible with Byrd's. On October 17, 1952, Byrd was scheduled to make a radio address over the largest network ever arranged in Virginia. Shortly beforehand Eisenhower called him up and said with a grin in his voice, "Don't be too hard on me."

"I won't," Byrd replied.

In the speech the Senator said that Trumanism is "a definite and precise trend toward socialism and away from the free enterprise system. . . . [It] is contrary to the basic principles upon which America was founded and has grown great. . . . To those who say that Governor Stevenson . . . will change the trend from Trumanism I ask that one single measure be named wherein there exists a

10. *Ibid.*

difference in fundamental policy between Mr. Truman and Governor Stevenson. . . .

"I will not, and cannot, in good conscience, endorse the National Democratic platform or the Stevenson-Sparkman ticket. . . . Endorsement means to recommend. That I cannot do." [11]

In November, Virginia gave Eisenhower a majority of 80,000 votes.

Though Senator Byrd's influence in the National Democratic party had declined, his prestige and power in the Senate was rising toward its apex. The Eisenhower sweep in 1952 again gave the Republicans control of the House and Senate, though by a slim margin. By that token Byrd should have yielded his chairmanship of the Joint Committee on the Reduction of Nonessential Government Expenditures to a Republican. Instead, in an almost unprecedented action, the Republican majority voted to retain him as the Committee Chairman. Even from 1947 to 1951 when he had not been its chairman, it had still been known as the Byrd Committee. Whatever may be thought of Byrd's extremely conservative principles, there was little question in either party that under his leadership the Committee was serving an extremely useful purpose. The most ardent liberals had no desire to see funds appropriated for social progress wasted. They recognized that, however much they might deplore Byrd's old-fashioned philosophy of government living within its means and his opposition to what he considered socialistic measures, his watchfulness against waste and unnecessary extravagance had not only saved the tax-payers uncounted billions during his long tenure, but also had left the Government agencies more money to spend for the alleviation of hardships and for social reform.

It was not only the many instances in which the Byrd Committee uncovered actual misuse or careless handling of Government funds; the knowledge that the old Watchdog of the Treasury had his X-ray eyes constantly scanning every department of the Government indubitably gave pause to free spending heads of agencies. Since it is impossible to reckon this imponderable deterrent effect, it is equally impossible to calculate the amount of money saved. It was certainly a huge sum.

11. Quoted from transcript of Senator Byrd's address.

During the comparatively peaceful years of the Eisenhower administration, Senator Byrd did a good deal more traveling than he had previously. Blackie Moore was a favorite companion on these jaunts. Together they ranged from British Columbia to the Caribbean and to Switzerland. They visited all the national parks. Yellowstone, in the early spring, before the tourists came was one of the Senator's favorites. It was there that he wrenched his knee when he fell climbing some loose rocks to get around a fallen tree. It was a serious injury and when he got home the doctors wanted to operate, but Byrd would have none of that. They wanted him to keep off his leg, but he would not do that either. His cure was to go out and climb Old Rag. The Senator admitted that "It hurt like hell," but somehow he made it. Though the knee never recovered, the rough usage Byrd gave it seemed to strengthen it. He once showed how muscles had grown up around the joint making it lumpy and twice as large as his normal knee. Halt as he was, the Senator could still leave younger men gasping in his wake when he went climbing. Even in his seventies he insisted on carrying his own heavy pack on overnight trips.

Speaker Moore says that sharing a room with the Senator was a rugged experience. Byrd would keep the light on all night reading paperbacks with lurid covers for relaxation until he fell asleep. "He read with incredible speed," Moore said, "and when he finished one he would throw the book on the floor and start another." Moore described one trip to Emerald Lake in Canada. "We were in a little cottage that only had a wood stove to heat it, but Senator still shaved in cold water and took his cold bath. When he got out of the tub he looked all red, his body glowing, the picture of health. In his pajamas he would get down on his knees and say his prayers no matter how tired he was. I often said, 'Say mine for me.' Then Senator opened all the windows and got into bed with the icy wind blowing across him. That's why I always tried to get a separate room. I could not take it."

Moore said that even before Byrd hurt his knee he liked to walk with a stick—afterward he depended on it—but he did not want to be photographed with it as he thought it affected his image—not that he would have used that term. On one trip to Glacier Park his son Dick and he both carried canes. When they saw the press waiting at the airport they both handed Blackie their canes and went down to meet the photographers. Blackie said, "As I followed them off the plane the stewardess said solicitously, 'May I help you?' I remarked shortly, 'I don't need any help.' But there I was with two canes. It was kind of hard to explain." [12]

No matter where he wandered the Senator always loved Shenandoah best. The Skyline Corporation, which had cottages to rent to campers, offered to build one for him at a place he would choose. He and Blackie selected the site in a formation of hills that made a natural chimney up which cool winds blew no matter how hot the day. Byrd named it Winchester Cottage. It had one bathroom, next to the Senator's room. His guests had to walk through his room to get to the bathroom. There was only cold water and no stopper in the tub. To take a bath one was obliged to find something to stuff in the drain. There was a lovely mountain lake in which Byrd liked to swim. Former Governor Tuck said, "Harry used to swim the whole length of the lake. I would drive around and meet him at the other end. I wouldn't have gone into that lake for anything. Man alive it was cold!" [13]

Though Winchester Cottage was for rent like the others, the Skyline people held it for Byrd every week until Thursday night to see if he wanted it. On most Fridays he would drive out from Washington, check in at Rosemont to see Sittie, put on his old clothes and head for the hills, usually alone. There, in the rough little shack, he was content. He would sit on the porch in the very heart and center of his beloved Blue Ridge watching cloud shadows chase each other swiftly across the timbered hills, drawing refreshment and strength from the wilderness. On Sunday he would leave, renewed for battle on that other much lower "Hill" under the lactescent dome of the Capitol.

12. Blackburn Moore to the author.
13. Former Governor Tuck to the author.

X · POWER

IN 1954, the Democrats regained control of the House and, by the defection of Senator Wayne Morse of Oregon, of the Senate as well. It mattered little to Byrd. His coalition of conservative Southern Democrats and Republicans was functioning perfectly. In the House, Congressman Howard W. Smith, a Byrd man from Alexandria, had been carried up the slow escalator of seniority to become Chairman of the Rules Committee, which gave him the enormous power of deciding which bills would be taken up by the House. Smith simply bottled up legislation of which he did not approve. Of course, he could not keep the cork in forever but he delayed many bills and killed some.

Also by seniority, Byrd became Chairman of the Senate Finance Committee in 1955. In this position, he could delay or severely pare money bills. He and Smith made a formidable team. Though they could not halt the tide of social reform they most certainly slowed it down.

Byrd worked extremely hard on the Finance Committee. His secretary, Martha Crop, said, "Our work was very heavy. The Senator was at it all day long, and sometimes late in the evening. As he grew in seniority and became head of the Finance Committee bags and bags of mail came in. He had a photographic memory and could handle a stack of mail a foot high in a few minutes. He had an open-door policy; he kept all the doors of the different offices open. When he went out to the Senate or a Committee meeting, his dog used to lie in the hallway waiting for him, and then follow him into his office. We could never lie to the reporters. If they did not see the dog in the hall, they knew the Senator was in.

"The Senator was so quiet. When he walked into the office there was no turmoil, no matter how great the rush, even in the midst of a campaign. He might freeze with anger but he never blasted out.

"The great figures from England came to talk with him. Heywood Bell said that never was there a great financial wizard came before the Committee that Byrd could not chew down." [1]

At the very start of the Eisenhower administration, Byrd's delicate sense of public honor caused a celebrated row. Eisenhower named Charles E. Wilson of General Motors Secretary of Defense. It was an excellent appointment of which Byrd approved. But the Senator refused Senate confirmation—and he had influence enough to make it stick—until Wilson sold all his stock in General Motors lest there be a conflict of interest. "Engine Charlie" huffed and puffed, and made the famous gaffe, "What's good for General Motors is good for the country." But nothing shook Byrd. In the end Wilson sold his stock. It cost him millions in unrealized future profits.

This incident did not impair Byrd's pleasant relations with Eisenhower. The President attended the Woodrow Wilson Centennial at Staunton, Virginia, largely on Byrd's urging. It was a remarkable thing to get a Republican President to join in a tribute to an idol of the Democratic party.

However, as with all the Presidents he knew well, Byrd soon opposed Eisenhower politically. His disenchantment began when the President appointed Earl Warren Chief Justice of the Supreme Court in 1953. Warren had been an extremely popular Governor of California, nominated by both the Republican and Democratic parties in his state. In 1952, he swung California to Ike. [2]

Byrd was certainly not enthralled with Warren, but he was not violently opposed to him either until Monday, May 17, 1954, when

1. Miss Crop to the author.
2. On the vote to seat the pro-Eisenhower delegation from Texas instead of the Taft delegates. This tipped the balance to Eisenhower.

the new Chief Justice announced the decision of the Court in the case of Brown versus the Board of Education. Speaking for a unanimous Court, the Chief Justice said, "In the field of public education the doctrine of 'separate but equal' has no place. Separate educational facilities are inherently unequal." A year later an order was issued that desegregation of schools must proceed "with all deliberate speed."

That was Black Monday for Senator Byrd. Friends who were with him say that he was literally stunned by the decision of the Court to reverse its long-standing ruling that separate but equal educational facilities met the requirements of the Fourteenth Amendment of the Constitution. There is no denying that Byrd was a racist in the modern sense of the term. He believed that the races should be kept pure for the benefit of both. This does not mean that he believed in Jim Crow in all areas of life. In his orchards crews composed of black men and white worked together and ate together, and he worked and ate with them; he comforted their families in sorrow and paid for their illnesses. In all his dealing with Negroes he was scrupulous never to favor one race above another. He paid the same wages to black workers as to white. He believed ardently in equal justice for every man under the law and equal opportunity. But he had no relationships with Negroes as his equals, on a social level. All the traditions of his people and of his beloved state, the environment of his youth and the chivalric code of his manhood had formed his thinking on race relations in an inflexible mold.

Even so, it was not the actual prospect of desegregation that troubled Byrd most deeply; it was the fact that the Federal Government, through the Supreme Court, had commanded it in a sovereign state. He said that to him this was the ultimate outrage. It recalled all the bitterness of Reconstruction days, of Federal troops in occupation and Virginia as Military District Number 1. He believed that the action of the Court was as illegal as the usurpation of a tyrant. As he said later, "To say this decision is the law of the land is to give the Warren Court the divine right to be wrong." [3]

Former Virginia Congressman Howard W. Smith put it this way: "With people like Byrd and myself it was basically a fight for the survival of the constitutional system. When the Supreme Court

3. Transcript of speech by Harry F. Byrd at the Orchard Picnic at Rosemont on Saturday, August 30, 1958.

assumes to make the laws of the land then you have a system of judicial dictatorship." [4]

Disregarding for the moment the moral issue in which the Supreme Court seems to a majority of the people to have been right, there is the matter of legality in which Senator Byrd's stand has far stronger support. Whether, under the Constitution, the Supreme Court has the right to legislate is very dubious. In 1959, forty-eight chief justices of all the forty-eight states protested that it had not. And beyond the legalities lay a political ideology that has been argued about ever since the birth-pangs of the Republic. Byrd always considered himself a Jeffersonian liberal. As his son Beverley said, "So you have the old clash between Jefferson and Hamilton, between Calhoun and Daniel Webster, the difference between the ideal of state independence [in local affairs] and federal control." [5]

For once Senator Byrd had no clear conception of how to act. His every instinct was to resist, but what form could resistance take? What should Virginia do? He gathered a group of friends and neighbors together at Rosemont to find out what Virginians were thinking, how they would react. The discussion at Rosemont turned on the 7th District, the Valley. Byrd's cousin, Joe Massie, says, "They got nowhere because everyone had a different idea. It was something entirely foreign to us. There was no problem in Clarke County because of the tiny percentage of Negroes in the population. In neighboring Frederick County there were only 129 Negroes in the whole school system. Desegregation was therefore not so vital a matter that our people were prepared to take on the whole United States Government to avoid it."

Senator Byrd felt differently; he represented the whole state not just his own 7th District. But he did not try to press his ideas upon his neighbors. However, down in Warren County, with its great textile mills and much larger Negro population, the feeling was quite different from Clarke and Frederick. The strong Textile Union, in spite of having some Negro members, backed segregation and were ready to fight. Eventually the union opened a private school which is still in operation. But in view of his neighbors' feelings and his own indecision, Byrd waited for nearly two years before he decided what should be done.

4. Former Congressman Smith to the author.
5. Beverley Byrd to the author.

In 1955, the National Association for the Advancement of Colored People filed desegregation suits in seventeen states. But it selected Virginia as its main target. Its leaders probably adopted this strategy partly because Byrd had made Virginia the bellwether of the Southern states, and partly because feeling did not run as high in a state where only 22 per cent of the population was black as in the Deep South where the percentage of Negroes was so much greater. Suits brought in the names of Negroes were prosecuted with vigor in Virginia. As local Federal judges rendered decisions favorable to desegregation, Byrd decided to act.

On February 25, 1956, he held a press conference in Washington at which he called upon the states of the old Confederacy for "massive resistance" to the Supreme Court's order for public school integration. He made it perfectly plain that he was not advocating or condoning violence. Rather he wanted the Southern States to stand together in declaring the Court's order unconstitutional.

"If we can organize the Southern States for massive resistance to this order," he said, "I think that in time the rest of the country will realize that racial integration is not going to be accepted in the South.

"In interposition," he continued, "the South has a perfectly legal means of appeal from the Supreme Court's order." [6]

Senator Byrd had reached far back in history for a legal quibble first proposed in 1799 when the states of Virginia and Kentucky proposed interposition against the Alien and Sedition Act rammed through Congress by Federalist President John Adams. According to those who uphold it, interposition enables the several states to refuse to implement a Supreme Court decision they believe to be unconstitutional. Though it had been put forward several times since 1799, it had never been fully tested in the courts because circumstances, or war, had rendered it moot before it was adjudicated.

Byrd was not alone in his stand. It was the result of a study undertaken by a group of eighteen Southern Senators. Backing him were such Southerners as Senators Walter F. George and Richard B. Russell of Georgia, John C. Stennis of Mississippi and Samuel J. Erwin of North Carolina.

It was a lost cause, and Byrd probably knew it. But that stopped him no more than it stopped the Virginians who charged across the

6. A.P. dispatch in the New York *Times*, February 26, 1956.

wheat field at Gettysburg. That it was also a bad cause never for one moment entered Byrd's head. For in all his life he never defended a thing in which he disbelieved, and no temptation of personal gain or political convenience could make him do so. He was utterly, tragically convinced of the justice of his cause even as were those yelling boys who followed Pickett against the massed cannon on Cemetery Ridge.

Byrd invented the tag of the "Warren Court." It was a shrewd political gambit, for it seemed to depreciate the Supreme Court from a respected institution to the personal instrument of a single man. Right-wing conservatives took up the phrase and Byrd, himself, really appeared to blame Warren for what he considered the malpractice of the Court. He launched a personal vendetta against the Chief Justice.

This produced a difficult situation. Byrd was Chairman of the Jamestown-Williamsburg-Yorktown Celebration Commission to plan the festivities in connection with the 350th Anniversary of the first successful English Colony in Virginia in 1957. As the time for the celebration drew near, President Eisenhower announced that he would be unable to attend and designated Chief Justice Warren as his representative. It suddenly dawned on Byrd that as Chairman of the Commission he would be seated next to the Chief Justice. For two weeks he studied protocol, consulted the State Department, and everyone else, trying to find a way out of this distasteful situation. In the end, he adopted the only possible solution. He refused to attend the ceremonies of which he had been the chief planner.

As the "Warren Court" continued to hand down decisions affecting the rights of the states in other matters, such as those concerned with police procedures and the Konigsburg and Schware cases, which denied the states the right to set standards for those who wished to practice law before state courts, Byrd became increasingly bitter. Like his ancestor, the third William, he was hopelessly fighting the trend of the times and the consensus of national opinion, and like that Tory he was doing it from loyalty to an outmoded ideology. But *unlike* William, it did not bring down upon him the opprobrium of his fellow Virginians; quite the contrary, as was dramatically made evident in 1958.

That year Sittie, who had had a stroke and was becoming increasingly helpless, begged her husband to give up politics so that he could spend more time with her and not wear himself out fighting political battles in and out of the Senate. As she pointed out, he was now in his seventy-first year and his forty-three years of public service entitled him to a less arduous life. There were few things the Senator could refuse his beloved wife. In addition he *was* wearying of rear-guard actions against a world that seemed to him to be willfully departing from the standards of economic integrity and personal honor which he held dear. Rather sadly he sat down at his desk at Rosemont and wrote a letter to his colleagues telling them of his personal situation and definitely announcing that under no circumstances would he run for re-election in 1958. Then, to avoid the fuss and supplications which he knew would ensue, he took off for New Mexico leaving no forwarding address, though, as always, wherever he was, he telephoned Sittie every night.

The letter reached Richmond while the General Assembly was in session. Had it been an announcement of an impending atomic attack on the city, it could hardly have caused more consternation. The world seemed upside down. In this situation the General Assembly took action which as far as can be ascertained is unique in the history of the United States.

Joint Resolution No. 58 of the General Assembly of the Commonwealth of Virginia commended Harry Flood Byrd for his long service to the Commonwealth, and his outstanding contributions as a member of the General Assembly; as Governor, making the Government of Virginia "a model for economy and efficiency"; and stated that his achievements as United States Senator "in reducing non-essential government expenditures and opposing those who would throw the country into socialism, waste the wealth of this country in foreign and domestic extravagance, and tax the American people to such an extent that private enterprise would be destroyed, and other accomplishments too numerous to mention, have been without equal. . . ."

The key paragraph noted with regret Byrd's decision not to offer for re-election and added, "Be it further resolved that the members of this body . . . wish him every happiness and a long, well-earned retirement, with the hope, however, that, if it is possible, consistent with his own personal situation, he reconsider his announced intention to retire from the United States Senate. The general welfare of the entire United States and Virginia demands his continued service. . . ."

What makes this resolution unique is that it was unanimously passed by the House of Delegates and signed by everyone of its hundred members, Democrats and Republicans alike. It then went to the Virginia Senate where it was passed and signed by thirty-nine of the forty members. The only one not signing was Ted Dalton. He went to Harry Byrd, Jr., saying that he wanted very much to sign, but that in view of the fact that he had recently run for Governor on the Republican ticket he "did not think it would look quite right." Young Byrd agreed with him.[7]

Governor J. Lindsay Almond, Jr., wrote in his own hand on the document:

"I wholeheartedly join in this highly deserved tribute to Virginia's beloved son and most faithful public servant.

"I pray that he will find it possible to accede to the appeal of the General Assembly to reconsider his decision and once again offer his services to Virginia and the nation."

"J. Lindsay Almond, Jr."

When this extraordinary document with its 140 signatures reached Rosemont, Sittie, ill as she was, wrote a reply in her shaky handwriting saying that, in view of the honor they had done her husband and their opinion of his indispensability, she would withdraw her objections and urge him to run for re-election.

Naturally Senator Byrd was re-elected without opposition. He was by now one of the three senior members of the Senate, being junior only to Senators Russell and George. Most of his old friends were gone, but he had made new and influential ones, among them Senator Lyndon B. Johnson, the Majority Leader, and young Senator John F. Kennedy of Massachusetts. Though he was frequently in opposition to Johnson, Byrd liked and admired the Texas Senator. His feeling was warmly reciprocated. He was even more frequently opposed to Senator Kennedy, but again their personal relations were remarkably close, considering the difference in their ages and points of view. Byrd was less enchanted with Senator Hubert H. Humphrey. When

7. Senator Byrd, Jr., to the author.

the Minnesotan was a freshman Senator, he called the Byrd Committee an example of "waste and extravagance." Byrd took the floor and poured on the brash young man a chilly torrent of acidic language that went on and on until it covered five pages of the Congressional Record. Some time later when they became more friendly, Humphrey admitted to Byrd, "That was the worst mistake I ever made." [8]

The Senator's relations with President Eisenhower chilled considerably when for 1959, the Administration proposed a budget with a deficit of $12,400,000,000. One of Byrd's favorite cartoons, the original of which hung in his Winchester office, depicted the Senator reading the document with eyes popping out of his round face. The caption was : "Budget for the Byrds."

Although the Senator did not attend the Democratic National Convention of 1960, he let it be known that he favored Lyndon B. Johnson over John F. Kennedy as a more stable character. When Kennedy won the nomination, Byrd again refused to support the National Democratic ticket, saying, "I have found at times that silence is golden." Although Republican Candidate Richard M. Nixon lost the election, he carried Virginia by over forty-two thousand votes.

The Kennedy administration was as financially adventurous as Byrd had feared. A proposal to cut taxes in 1962, in order to stimulate the economy and eventually bring in more revenue, was killed with a comment from the fiscally orthodox Chairman of the Senate Finance Committee that it was "a damned absurdity."

When the Medicare Bill was sent to the Finance Committee, Byrd did not bottle it up; he did not believe in that sort of maneuver. But he scheduled ahead of it such lengthy hearings on tax revisions that it was evident that Medicare would not come to a vote before the session ended. The Kennedy strategists tried an end run by tacking it on to another bill as an amendment. Though the Democrats had in the Senate a large majority who would have carried Medicare if it had been brought to the floor in the normal way, the gentlemen of the Senate were not about to allow one of their very own to be thus circumvented. The amendment was defeated 52 to 48.

Byrd, in fact, made a shambles of much of Kennedy's New Frontier program. He cut the section requiring businesses to withhold

8. *Time* magazine, August 17, 1962.

taxes due on dividends or interest out of the Tax Revision Bill because he was firmly opposed to the idea of the Government using business as a tax collection agency. He further cut down or eliminated many spending bills.

Byrd's obdurate opposition to the administration programs for once did not cause any coolness between him and the President. The Senator said of Kennedy, "He's a very attractive person. He's got ability, no doubt about that."

The President said, "Harry Byrd is the most gracious person you'd want to meet. But he does give us fits." [9]

The friendship was made plain at one of the Rosemont luncheons, which had now become legendary functions. Since Sittie could no longer manage them, Helen Byrd and various female relations took charge of the arrangements. One of these ladies was Mrs. James Thomson who said, "We would get a preliminary list from the Senator's Washington office on Monday, but we never paid much attention to that. Then Thursday night or Friday morning the real list would come. It would always be much larger; we'd have a frantic time. On Sunday the guests would come through the house and have cocktails on the terrace. Then there would be a luncheon for 150 persons or more, seated at small tables all through the lower floor. Sometimes there would be so many that even Rosemont could not accommodate them all and some of us would eat lunch sitting on the stairs." [10]

At one of these luncheons the guests were all out on the terrace when the rackety pop-popping of a helicopter made them look up. Red, white and blue Air Force colors and the gold and blue Presidential insignia told them who was aboard. Senator Byrd stumped rapidly down the lawn as the machine settled noisily in the clear space near the swimming pool. He came back walking between the young President and his lovely wife, all of them laughing in sheer high spirits. Never was Rosemont gayer than on that sunny afternoon.

9. *Ibid.*
10. Mrs. James Thompson to the author.

XI · RECESSIONAL

IN ITS cover story on Senator Byrd in August, 1962, *Time* magazine wrote: "It is an irony that as he nears the end of his political life Harry Byrd has arrived at a crest of effective power and influence. He has, in fact, become a symbol of the Capitol Hill revolt against the young activist who lives at 1600 Pennsylvania Avenue." [1]

The anonymous *Time* writer seemed rather surprised that this should be true; but it was, in fact, perfectly natural. Byrd's seniority was only one of the reasons for it. Despite the fact that he was now seventy-five years old, he was apparently as energetic as ever. He still climbed Old Rag on his birthday, as he had every year since his fifteenth. When seniority in the Senate is combined with such vigor and determination, it is bound to exercise great influence.

In addition, his warmth, his courtly manners, and his integrity made him, perhaps, the best-loved and most-respected member of a body, the majority of whose members frequently disagreed with him but always listened to him. When Byrd was scheduled to speak, the usually empty seats filled up. Even now, he was no great orator, but his fellow Senators found it decidedly refreshing to hear a man say exactly what he thought in simple, blunt language with no concern for political advantage. As *Time* put it, "Byrd stands in the center of the

1. *Time* magazine, August 17, 1962.

innermost circle, but he is far from being one of the boys. . . . He dislikes and avoids cloakroom politics but many of the cloakroom politicians are now holding his coat." [2]

That year the Senator attended the NATO Conference in Paris —at his own expense. He was vitally interested in the defense of Europe which, ever since 1939, he had recognized as essential to the security of the United States. He returned to tell his neighbors of disillusionment and disgust. Not one of the NATO powers was keeping its military commitments except America. "There is a NATO deficit," he said. And he compared it to all the other deficits from foreign trade to the budget in which he saw the country and the world on the high road to hell.

In 1963, Byrd reached, perhaps, a peak of personal happiness. An editorial writer for the Richmond *News Leader* recalled him climbing Old Rag on his birthday, "his blue shirt wet with perspiration, his blue eyes twinkling in delight, as he hiked a flock of bureaucrats into the ground. And he stood on top of the world that evening, reminiscing of bygone wars while a campfire flickered and a country fiddler played." [3]

October 7, 1963, was the Byrd's Golden Wedding Anniversary. They gave a dinner that night at Rosemont for forty members of the family and their closest friends. Unlike the great luncheons, which represented the current power structure, it could have been at Westover in the eighteenth century and the Second William would have recognized most of the names. Beside a flock of Byrds there were Grays, Beverleys, Carters, Armisteads, Pages, Douglases. . . . Sittie was feeling well that evening. As the Senator pushed her wheelchair into the great hall to greet her guests, someone took a photograph of them—Sittie lovely in a shimmering, formal evening gown, her cheeks delicately flushed, her eyes sparkling with pleasure. Her husband's round, wind-burned face wore a smile as broad as the James River. He tenderly maneuvered her chair through the clusters of kinfolk to her place at the head of the long table in the candle-lit dining room.

There was a splendid dinner with lots of champagne; even the

2. *Ibid.*
3. June 10, 1966.

Senator sipped some. The air was filled with gay talk of people of all ages in the ease of perfect compatibility. Then came the graceful toasts to the bride and groom of fifty years; Byrd, at the peak of his form and powers, responding genially. For a few hours the lusty, gutsy, changing world retreated beyond the sloping lawns and the tall trees turning to red and gold. Rosemont's magic circle enclosed their whole world with an illusion of permanence that stretched backward to great houses on a broad river at the edge of a vast, untouched wilderness; and forward to a fantastic future where, amid the beauty of gleaming silver reflected in polished mahogany, softly burning candles, graceful rooms and spacious lawns, gallant men and lovely ladies lived and laughed forever.[4]

Like Queen Victoria's Diamond Jubilee, the Golden Wedding marked the apex of an empire and almost the exact moment at which it began to decline. Like Victoria, Byrd was never a dictator, though like her he exercised great power. His friends compared him to a constitutional monarch—a monarch enthroned on a rickety swivel chair with his courtiers seated on apple crates. As such he necessarily had to rule with popular approval, and the character of his people was changing. All those new suburbs on the Virginia side of Washington were filling up with voters who did not give a damn for Virginia traditions or fiscal orthodoxy. The industries which he, as Governor, had brought into the Commonwealth were booming and expanding all around the quiet old cities, attracting a new type of blue-collar worker with plenty of money to pay the poll tax and the political consciousness to take the trouble to do so. The battle against the desegregation of schools was gradually being lost even in the most adamant section of all, Prince Edward County. Things were, in short, changing fast in Virginia and everywhere else.

A little more than a month after the Byrd's golden wedding came the insane horror of that day in Dallas which altered the history of the United States, and perhaps the world, so profoundly. As deeply as any man, Byrd mourned the young President, whom he had opposed so vigorously.

The new President, who had been his choice in the Convention of 1960, was a jarring shock to Byrd. Not only was Lyndon Johnson

4. Beverley Byrd and other guests to the author.

quite as socially minded and financially improvident, by Byrd's standards, as his predecessor, but he was a lot more successful in getting his program through Congress. Byrd opposed the measures he considered socialistic or financially unsound quite as stubbornly as before, but he found his power had eroded.

As in President Kennedy's case, their political differences did not affect the friendship between the Senator and the President. In the spring, a Presidential helicopter again landed at Rosemont, and Byrd escorted the President and Mrs. Johnson up the lawn. Knowing that the President's famous beagle, Him, was also to be his guest, the Senator had shut up his cocker spaniel, Pam—the last and perhaps best-loved of the line—in his second-floor study.

The Senator's guests greeted the Johnsons with polite enthusiasm. But Pam was very rude to the Presidential beagle. She came out on the little balcony under the high portico, growling and barking at the intruder, making such a row that conversation was impossible. "Let's take Him up and introduce them," the President suggested. "Perhaps it will calm Pam down."

The Senator foolishly thought it a good idea. He and the President escorted Him up the broad stairway and let him out on the balcony. It was not a good idea. The worst dog fight in the history of Berryville broke out. Growls, barks, yelps of pain and roars of rage riveted the guests' eyes to the balcony. They saw the Senator and the President valiantly trying to separate the dogs, shouting suggestions at each other, as they pulled at their pets regardless of flashing canine teeth. Someone asked, "Who is fighting? The dogs or the people?" [5]

Eventually peace was restored with the assistance of the nervous Secret Service, and the last of Senator Byrd's famous luncheons proceeded with suitable decorum.

Contrary to the expectations of most of the politicians and the press, Senator Byrd decided to run again in 1964. In a brief statement he said:

I shall offer for re-election to the United States Senate.

This has been a difficult decision for me to make. In arriving at this conclusion I have been influenced by numerous requests from all parts of the State that I run again for the office to which the people of Vir-

5. Nelson Page and Senator Byrd, Jr., to the author.

ginia have so generously elected me on five previous occasions. I cannot adequately express the depth of my appreciation. . . .

If nominated and reelected. . . . my allegiance—as in the past—will be to the people of our Commonwealth and the Constitution of the United States. . . .

My platform will be my record of nearly fifty years in public service.[6]

Even with the changing electorate, Byrd did not have to campaign very hard. Though the new voters disliked the Byrd Machine, they loved and respected Byrd. It was no contest; the Senator did not even bother to have a campaign manager. One of the few political speeches he made that summer was at the forty-second Orchard Picnic, which was held on Saturday, August 15. In his crisp white suit and red necktie, he stood up on a flatbed apple truck to greet four thousand of his neighbors, fellow apple-growers, and political colleagues with the words: "This is a happy day for me." The day of the picnic was always a happy one for him. He dismissed his candidacy for the Senate in a single paragraph: "Candidate comes from the latin word meaning shining or white. The old Roman candidates appeared in the Forum in white togas. I have on a white suit, but that is because it's a hot day."

Then he went on to give them his "Byrd's-Eye View" of the State of the Nation which, as usual, he considered perilous. Near the end, he recited his political, fiscal, ideological beliefs. It was a simple creed—almost simplistic in the complex era into which he had survived. But he had lived by it, unswerved by personal, political, or financial considerations. If it sounded old-fashioned, so was he. And so were many of those old Romans in white togas who fought against the decline of the Republic into Empire.

Senator Byrd said:

I believe sound progress is the source of individual and national strength. . . .
I believe progress is not sound if it is based on unsound financing. . . .
I believe our form of representative democracy through dual governments is capable of providing the best government the world has ever known. . . .
I believe that good government flows from separation of powers and that concentration and consolidation of power breeds corrupt and despotic rule.

6. Transcript of Senator Byrd's statement, dated March 14, 1964.

I believe in separate but equal and coordinate branches of government at all levels.

I believe—with Jefferson—that States should act in their own right, generally, with respect to matters purely domestic. And

I believe—with Jefferson—that States should act as one through the Federal Government as to everything connected with foreign relations. . . .

I believe that our system of government is based on these fundamentals; and that they guarantee our liberty and nourish the competitive enterprise which makes sound progress possible.

I believe our strength has been sapped by federal bureaucracy grown too big, and by the Federal Supreme Court grown too mighty.

I believe centralization of power in the Federal Government has undermined our system, changed our attitudes, and hobbled our liberty.

I believe—with our Virginia Declaration of Rights—that: No free government, or the blessings of liberty can be preserved to any people but by firm adherence to justice, moderation, temperance, frugality, and virtue, and by frequent recurrence to fundamental principles.

I believe that—with responsible citizenship, good government, and fiscal soundness—there can be no fear for the future. And

I believe that without these there can be neither solid progress nor security with military preparedness.

I believe, as a representative of the people of Virginia in the United States Senate, I owe my allegiance to the people of our Commonwealth and to the Constitution of the United States—partisan political platform planks to the contrary and notwithstanding.

This, generally, is my philosophy of government. It has governed every vote I have cast in the nearly fifty years that the people of Virginia have honored me with the privilege of serving them in the Virginia Senate, as Governor, and as United States Senator.

Then Senator Byrd said, "I shall end . . . by saying I hope you are having a good time. You have my very best wishes.

"Good luck! God speed! Come again next year." [7]

They did not come next year.

Sittie had failed rapidly after the Golden Wedding. Most of the time she stayed in the downstairs bedroom suite to which she and her husband had moved after her stroke.

7. Transcript of Senator Byrd's speech at the 42nd Orchard Picnic, Saturday, August 15, 1964.

Right after the last Orchard Picnic, Senator Byrd went to Maine for a brief vacation. As always, he telephoned Sittie every evening though some evenings she was not strong enough to talk with him. In that case he talked with her nurse. He always asked first how Sittie felt; then if Pam was all right; and finally for his children and grandchildren. Dick Byrd remarked, "I guess that was the order of his affections." [8]

On Monday, August 24, the Senator telephoned his wife as usual. She felt much better and chatted with him gaily. The following afternoon, she died suddenly of a heart attack.

Though he must have lived with the possibility for many years, Senator Byrd was shattered. He came home to the great, still house that was suddenly empty, even though relatives were gathering from all over the Old Dominion. One of the most important was not there. The Senator's favorite grandson, Harry III, had gone west as a migrant worker in the great Washington State Orchards to learn how they did things out there. No one knew where he was. The Senator's son called one of the big apple-buyers and got the names of large orchard-owners in that state. Then he methodically called them until he got one who said, "Is that Byrd kid yours? He's been sleeping in his car. That's awful, I had no idea. . . . We'll get him on a plane right away." [9]

People came from all over the country for Sittie's funeral—by automobile, by bus, by train and plane. And one came in a helicopter. Under the double pressure of a hot election campaign and his executive functions, President Lyndon Johnson found time to fly to Winchester to pay tribute to the wife of an old friend and staunch opponent. After the ceremony, as Senator Byrd sat outside Christ's Church in the big, black, funeral Cadillac waiting for the motorcade to start for Mount Hebron Cemetery, there was a tap on the window. Byrd opened it and extended his hand for a farewell handshake with President Johnson. His strained, lost-little-boy look must have touched a chord in the emotional Texan's heart. Overcome by affection and sorrow for his friend, the tall President bent down and kissed the Senator's hand.[10]

8. Richard Byrd of Rosemont to the author.
9. Mrs. Harry F. Byrd, Jr., to the author.
10. Richard E. Byrd of Rosemont to the author.

Many of his friends attributed the rapid decline of Senator Byrd's health to shock and sorrow. Among them was Admiral Lewis L. Strauss who said, "I believe that Sittie's death began the undermining of the Senator's health. When you have a great sadness like that, you give up. If you have cancer, it makes it go faster. Harry tried to keep fit even after Sittie died. He continued to go to the Senate gym three days a week. But his heart was not in it." [11]

For a time things went on almost as before. Harry III spent a great deal of time with his grandfather. They had always been very close. Years before, when Harry was in school in Winchester, he took the bus to Berryville almost every Friday night to spend the weekend at Rosemont. His eyes shine as he recalls splendid autumn mornings walking through the orchards with the Senator, with guns under their arms and preceded by a pointer or two or a beautiful golden retriever; the dogs pointing coveys of quail, then flushing them; the Senator getting off two quick shots that brought down two birds. On the first day of hunting the Senator often got his limit in an hour—ten birds with ten shots.

They would have a tremendous breakfast afterward—fried apples, quail, scrambled or fried eggs, hotcakes, fried tomatoes and coffee.

"An amazing thing about Grandfather was his great sense of humor," Harry said, "and, furthermore, even when things were not going well he was always pleasant—even in the morning. He would have nice things to say to everybody, especially, of course, to the people who worked on the place. I think that was the reason why I tagged along after him so much."

Harry's happy recollections often ran to food. "Every night for supper," he said, "Grandfather would have a tremendous pot of small raw onions—tiny things just out of the garden in cold water to keep them fresh. He and I would eat thirty or forty of those small sweet onions apiece. If I had a date with some girl and held back, the Senator would flip his hand at my chest and say, "Come on, you've got to eat 'em. The girl will want to kiss you anyway." [12]

In Washington, the Senator, now in his sixth term, continued to cause trouble with almost his old verve. But he now indulged himself

11. Admiral Strauss to the author.
12. Harry Byrd III to the author.

to the extent of taking Pam onto the floor of the Senate, an unheard of thing. When Senator Robert F. Kennedy imitated him by bringing a favorite setter, another ferocious dog fight ensued. It was evident that Pam thought she owned the Capitol as well as Rosemont.

On March 1, 1965, Byrd sent a well-thought-out letter to Secretary of the Treasury Douglas Dillon and Secretary of State Dean Rusk, with a copy to President Johnson. In it he wrote:

> You know of my long-standing concern over our balance of payments deficit and the outflow of our gold.
>
> If it has not been done, would it serve a worthwhile purpose to review all of the treaties, contracts and arrangements under which we own and generate foreign currencies with a view to renegotiation for more constructive use under current circumstances?
>
> It is not my intention here to be critical of earlier policies which were involved. The fact is that conditions have changed, and, if it would help, renegotiation may be justified and acceptable.

This produced a long answer from the President, stating that he had ordered some steps to be taken in this direction and explaining the reasons why more could not be done—the poverty of some of the countries involved, etc. In short there was very little result beyond showing that the old Watchdog was still watching.

On his birthday, for the first time, Byrd rode up the mountain in a four-wheel cart instead of walking. Then he dedicated one of the stone shelters for campers, called "Byrd's Nest," one of which he had presented to the people of Virginia each of the past three years. That summer his son Dick commissioned Gib Crockett to paint a portrait of the Senator. The result was extraordinarily felicitous, as though the Senator himself were sitting in the sunshine on the portico at Rosemont in his fresh, white suit, his ruddy face and lake-blue eyes expressive of the warmth and kindliness his friends knew so well. But despite his genial appearance one senses the inflexible character that gave him the strength to say "No" to the temptations of political expediency; and also the ruthless power to command.

In July, Byrd and a group of fellow senators made a final appeal against passage of the Medicare Bill. They proposed what they considered a more rational approach to the problem. They sought a solution that would not, as they feared this bill might, put a brake on the economy by its $6,000,000,000 estimated collection of additional taxes; and injure private insurance companies. Byrd's plea was largely ignored, for the conscience of an affluent nation could not rest easy unless proper medical care was assured to its elderly citizens.

As late as September 6, 1965, Senator Byrd made a brief statement of opposition to the proposed repeal of the right-to-work provisions of the Taft-Hartley Act. He believed as ardently as ever in the right of any man to join a labor union. "But," he said, "it is unAmerican for the Federal Government, by law, literally to force people to join *any* organization—labor, fraternal, political, religious or other— as a condition for taking a job.

"Enactment of this proposal would betray and overthrow a fundamental liberty for which this country was founded and which our form of government was designed to protect . . .

"This proposal has not been justified, and there is no justification for it." [13]

Despite these flashes of the old Byrd, his colleagues, his friends and, especially, his heart-broken office force, Mr. Menefee, Miss Dick, and Miss Crop, realized that the Senator's fine brain and vital force were fading. Sometimes, now, he would go to sleep in the midst of a conversation with an important visitor. In the Senate, he occasionally lost the thread of a debate and had to be told, sometimes by a friendly opponent, whether he wanted to vote aye or no. At first, people thought that these lapses were merely due to age; Byrd was seventy-eight. But as his condition worsened, it became evident that something more serious was involved. Byrd's doctors, suspecting a tumor on the brain, urged him to go to the University of Virginia Hospital for a thorough examination and an operation if necessary. The Senator was too busy.

Finally he realized that, as he said, "Physically and mentally I can no longer carry out my duties as a United States Senator." [14] He had always said he would not remain in the Senate until he had to be wheeled in. On Saturday, November 6, 1965, he sadly wrote to Virginia Governor Albertis S. Harrison, Jr.:

It was fifty years ago this month that I was first elected to the Senate of Virginia. Since then, through the generosity of the people of Virginia, I have served as Governor of our Commonwealth and, for nearly thirty-three years, I have served in the United States Senate. [Byrd had served longer than any other Virginia Senator].

13. Transcript of Statement by Senator Byrd, September 6, 1965.
14. Gray Beverley to the author.

The people of Virginia have been so very good to me and I have over-whelming gratitude for the confidence they have shown in me through so many years. I have sought to merit this confidence by dedicating my-self to those programs and policies which in my judgment were in the best interests of all the people of our state and nation. I am fully con-scious, of course, that I have made errors of judgment; but I have sought as best I could to conscientiously discharge my responsibilities to the best of my ability.

Continuing, "I have always tried to be frank with the people of Virginia," the Senator described his increasing exhaustion under the strain of long committee meetings, the advice of his doctors to retire and the fact that he felt obliged to resign the burden to younger shoulders.

I hereby submit my resignation as a member of the United States Senate to become effective upon receipt of this letter.

While this letter is addressed to you, Albertis, as the Chief Executive of our Commonwealth, I would be pleased for you to make it available to the people of Virginia for whom, in my heart, I have enduring grati-tude. . . .

Governor Harrison was so distressed that he did not, in fact, make Byrd's letter public until five days later, on November 11, 1965. When he did, the Commonwealth and many people beyond its borders were stunned. Editors and columnists, of whatever shade of opinion throughout the United States, wrote regretfully of Byrd's re-tirement from the political scene and in praise of his great qualities. In a sense, Senator Byrd had the rather unique pleasure of reading his own obituaries. A column which William S. White wrote was typical:

Harry Flood Byrd is leaving the Senate of the United States. . . . More than Byrd is leaving. Going with him are irreplaceable qualities rarer and bigger than all manner of ideological and partisan jawings. His retirement . . . is like a parting of the rope of time and tradition.

For Byrd, the great conservative, will be missed as no Senator has been missed since Robert A. Taft. This is not because of the views of Byrd of Virginia, nor because Byrd of Virginia has been among the right-minded and the winners. It is because however wrong he has been . . . he has been so gallantly wrong, so bravely among the losers . . . to the end against all odds he fought with skill and valor, without hatred or intolerance, to restore a world that once was but will never be again.

. . . No man [in the Senate] has so embodied absolute honesty, absolute honor, absolute integrity.

Endlessly the liberals and the moderates despaired of him—and equally endlessly they respected and valued him. . . . Endlessly the far rightists sought to capture him; but endlessly they mistook their man. . . . He was their tireless opponent; he never for a moment embraced a politics of mere bitterness, a politics of spite and destruction. . . .

. . . This same Byrd [who fought school integration] as Governor of Virginia put through the first tough anti-lynching law. This same Byrd, a generation ago, brought the Ku Klux Klan to its knees in Virginia. . . .

Harry Flood Byrd never burned a witch nor put a dissenter to the rack. He is a man who goes far back beyond that Confederate South of which many suppose he is the automatic champion. He goes back to the British colonial Cavaliers, men gaily untroubled in the full exercise of their privileges, but bound by hoops of iron to the Spartan discharge of their responsibilities as they saw them. [15]

The day after he announced that Senator Byrd had resigned, on November 12, 1965, Governor Harrison appointed Harry F. Byrd, Jr., to the United States Senate in his father's place. This act brought general approval from the Virginia press, though there were, of course, some mutterings about dynastic succession. Young Harry had waited a long time in the shadow of his father, making his own reputation in a quiet way. He was stymied rather than helped by parental fame. Those who had worked with him for nineteen years in the Virginia Senate had a high regard for his ability as a statesman and politician. As the Danville *Register* put it: "All familiar with Virginia public affairs . . . have been aware that Harry F. Byrd, Jr., worked under rather heavy wraps. He was restrained from seeking statewide office, for which he has been mentioned often over the past dozen years, by his own sensibilities." [16] For example, he had been offered the Governorship in 1961, without the Senator's knowledge. When he told his father, the latter said, "Good for you, Harry. I'm delighted. But I don't think it's right for one family to hold two of the highest offices in the Commonwealth. I shall resign."

Needless to say Harry could not permit that.

He had run the newspapers profitably on his own ever since 1946. Of course, he had inherited the job, but he had been made first

15. The Washington *Post*, November 15, 1965.
16. Danville *Register* quoted in Winchester *Star*, November 30, 1965.

vice president of the Associated Press on his own. That is not an organization that is impressed by names or subject to nepotism. Harry had gained the post through sheer ability with no obligations to anyone.

Because of his annual trips to the crisis places abroad—Berlin, Spain, Yugoslavia, Cuba—for first-hand investigation and interviews with their leading statesmen, he had a greater knowledge of foreign countries than his father and, perhaps, a better understanding of America's world-wide role. On internal affairs, though he followed the Senator's basic principles, he was more flexible, especially on school integration. In fact, they had many hot arguments, which did not in the least impair their affectionate relationship. The old Senator was never a man to carry a political difference to a private grudge. He liked a good fight and respected his son for standing up to him.

At long last, Senator Byrd was operated on at the Virginia University Hospital on March 4, 1966, exactly thirty-three years to a day after he had taken the oath as a United States Senator. The doctors opened his skull and found a malignant tumor that had grown beyond the bounds of surgical treatment. They could do nothing but send him home to Rosemont.

From that time on the Senator went downhill rapidly. He began losing consciousness for considerable periods. In June, 1966, he sank into a coma from which he emerged only in occasional brief flashes to recognize one of his sons or some old friend.

Perhaps it was as well that he could not follow the Virginia primary elections in the summer of 1966, for the political structure he had engineered disintegrated. As Gray Beverley said, "The Senator was the captain of the ship all the way through. When he took his hand off the throttle everything went down." [17]

While the Senator lay unconscious at Rosemont, his son was running for his political life, because Virginia law required that in the next general election he must stand for election for the remainder of the unexpired term to which he had been appointed. Senator Robertson was also running, as were Howard Smith and many other Byrd men.

It was a hard-fought campaign. The Supreme Court's one-man

17. Gray Beverley to the author.

one-vote decision had radically altered the boundaries and character of many election districts. Hitherto in Virginia, as in many other states, the representation had been heavily weighted in favor of rural districts. In accordance with the ukase of the Court, boundaries were redrawn to give urban populations a fairer representation. Above all was the sudden release of the liberal spirit that resulted from Senator Byrd's removal from the political scene. Now that his great prestige, his hold on the affection of Virginians, and his extremely effective campaigning no longer weighted the balance against them, the young progressives saw a chance to overturn what they considered an archaic financial and political system. They went out to smash the Byrd Machine.

In their speeches and broadsides they pointed out that while the Commonwealth was, indeed, free of debt this was "an economic deception" because most of the counties were overburdened with debts on which they were paying a much higher rate of interest than would the State if it assumed their obligations. The same was true of self-liquidating projects. An example of this, they said, was the Chesapeake Bay Bridge Tunnel. Its series "C" bonds paid an interest rate of 5¾ per cent. If it had been possible to put the credit of the State behind them, they would have paid at most 3¾ per cent, which would have meant a saving of $80,000,000 over a twenty-year period. Pay-as-you-go must go they proclaimed, and adduced the admittedly inferior schools and general lack of social progress in the Old Dominion.

It was "time for a change," was the theme of the new generation. They said, "Virginia has been run so long by an aristocracy that she has lost consciousness of the fact." New faces, new blood, new ideas and new representation in the Congress were what Virginia needed they proclaimed. The people seemed to agree with them.

The night of the Primary election was a cliff-hanger for the little group of loyalists gathered in young Senator Byrd's headquarters in Winchester. The news coming in from the urban districts was all bad. Majorities were piling up for Harry's opponent, Armistead Boothe. Other Byrd men were in worse trouble. By nine o'clock they thought they had lost. Then the slower-counted rural returns began to come in. The farmers were overwhelmingly loyal to the old order. Even so, it was a close thing. Congressman Howard W. Smith was defeated in his expanded district around Alexandria by about 500 votes.

Senator Robertson lost to William Spong by not much more. But the love of Virginians for the man who lay dying at Rosemont was reflected in a small plurality for Harry F. Byrd, Jr.

Senator Byrd died on October 20, 1966, without knowing any of these things. Had he been conscious, courtesy undoubtedly would have prompted him to apologize, like his ancestor's friend King Charles II, for "taking so unconscionably long in dying." Beverley and Dick were with him. Harry, Jr., racing down from Washington, arrived just too late.

Though so long expected, the news of Senator Byrd's death was a shock to friends and opponents alike. Even people who had never known him, or been consciously influenced by him, felt a sense of loss, as the laudatory articles in all the great newspapers, the nationally syndicated columns, and the weekly news magazines made them aware of America's loss.

In the Senate the morning Byrd died, Senator after Senator, representing every region of America and the whole spectrum of opinion, from Senator Strom Thurmond of South Carolina to liberal Senator Wayne Morse of Oregon, rose to eulogize him. Those whom he had so vigorously opposed were, perhaps, more affected than those whom he had supported; for a generous foe, who can be loved and respected while in the heat of battle, is rarer than an ally who earns the same regard.

Senator Everett Dirksen of Illinois used the most felicitous phrase when he said, "There are gentle men in whom gentility finally destroys whatever of iron there was in their souls.

"There are iron men in whom the iron corroded whatever gentility they possessed.

"There are men—not many to be sure—in whom the gentility and the iron were preserved in proper balance, each of these attributes to be summoned up as the occasion requires.

"Such a man was Harry Byrd. . . ."

A rare consensus appeared not only in that feisty body in which Senator Byrd had served so long, but in the press and all the other media of communication. There was no question that Harry Byrd had ennobled American politics. By his courtesy, his courage, by his very intransigence he had personally raised the level of the national political scene. For he embodied, in a decadent day, the virtues— even though accompanied by the prejudices—of the founders of his state and his country. As the curtain slowly fell on his long life, it inexorably ended not just an era but a whole span of American history. That span extended back beyond the Civil War, beyond the Revolution, back three hundred years to a time when Americans were first learning to govern themselves and men were daring to defy their King and all the power of his scarlet troops, and becoming aware that they were citizens of a new country with its own needs and loyalties.

The curtain fell for the same reason that it had risen on young America; because the old ways would no longer serve the complexities of a changing world. But even those who profited by the new order realized that something infinitely valuable had been lost. Though they were glad to see the road of progress open wide ahead, they could, the best of them, pause in their triumphant march toward the future for one brief moment of regret for what the ancient Romans called *Virtus*.

EPILOGUE

THE HISTORY of the Byrds of Virginia stops here, but does not end. Fortunately, there are a good many of them left to carry on according to their abilities. In addition, there are the Boston Byrds, for so the descendants of the Admiral must be classified, since they have become completely naturalized in Marie Byrd's home town. The Admiral's only son, Commander Richard E. Byrd, Jr., since his retirement from the Navy, has devoted his life to furthering his father's ideals of international amity and exploration. Commander Byrd has shifted his interest to the exploration of space, which he feels offers the sort of challenge the Admiral would have accepted had he been living today. His contribution lies in applying lessons learned in the Antarctic to the even more frigid and demanding conditions of space.

There are also Texas Byrds, headed by Colonel Harold Byrd of Dallas. If the Boston Byrds have taken on the coloration of New England, the Texas branch has exfoliated in the flamboyant style of their adopted State.

Colonel Byrd's story is not rags to riches but from moderate circumstances to enormous wealth. His family was able to send him to Trinity University at Waxahachie and then to the University of Texas, where he improbably specialized in theology. He came down to earth immediately after graduation, taking various jobs in the oil fields to learn the business. Then he set up on his own as a consulting geologist and drilling contractor at Brownwood, Texas.

The Colonel's own efforts to find oil were extraordinarily frustrating. He drilled fifty-seven wildcat wells that were as empty as Mother Hubbard's cupboard, and became known throughout the State as, "Dry Hole Byrd." Persistently, he dug a fifty-eighth well which came in with a glorious roaring, skyscraping explosion of rich, black oil. The Colonel was on his way.

In true Byrd fashion, Harold augmented his fortune in 1935, by marrying Mattie Caruth, whose father had acquired a small spread of a few thousand acres of cotton land. As in the old joke, the acreage turned out to be, not in downtown, but in uptown Dallas.

No man enjoys his money more than the rambunctious Colonel who flits from here to yon in either his Lear Jet or his Lockheed Lode Star. He is a devoted alumnus of the University of Texas to which he has contributed millions of dollars as well as the largest drum in the world. Every year, on the occasion of the Texas-Oklahoma football game, the Texas Band marches through Dallas to the Tower Petroleum Building, wheeling the drum on a cart—a man cannot carry it. There they serenade Colonel Byrd with "The Eyes of Texas Are Upon You," accompanied by the biggest *booms* ever heard by man.

The Colonel maintains the traditions of Southern hospitality in Texas. One year, at that same football game, he rose in his seat in the stadium and shouted in his tremendous, bull-horn voice, "Now you all, everyone who can hear me, I'm having a little party at my house after the game and I want all of you to come!"

He got fifteen hundred guests. Even the Second William was not that hospitable.[1]

Other Byrds in other places have become almost as numerous as the flocks of passenger pigeons that once darkened American skies. The concern here is with the Byrds of Virginia. The Senator's sons now represent the direct line. Senator Harry Byrd, Jr., is the oldest male

1. John William Rogers, *The Lusty Texan of Dallas.* E. P. Dutton and Company, 1960.

heir to his cousin William Byrd of Princeton, who is the head of the house, but has only two daughters.

In his three years in the Senate, Harry has quietly earned the respect of his colleagues. He is a member of the Armed Services Committee and the Agriculture Committee and has maintained his interest in foreign affairs. In March, 1967, he flew to Southeast Asia. In Vietnam he watched from a helicopter an assault landing in the face of enemy fire, a night-strike launch from an aircraft carrier, and dropped in at field hospitals and lonely outposts of marines and infantry north of Da Nang. Of course, he conferred with the Vietnamese leaders, the American Ambassador and all the top brass. Then he went on to Thailand and Taiwan for further conferences. On his return, he presented a thoughtful and at times emotional report to the Senate in which he bitterly described the great numbers of ships from countries which were receiving American foreign aid, bringing supplies into North Vietnamese ports. He also condemned the administration for its diplomatic failures to enlist more military support from friendly Asian nations. Later he proposed an amendment to the Foreign Aid Bill denying aid to nations which traded with North Vietnam. He also implied that Haiphong should be bombed to halt the flow of supplies to North Vietnam.

In January, 1968, Senator Byrd, Jr., made a trip to Greece, Cyprus, Israel and the United Arab Republic, talking to the leaders of those countries, the ambassadors of other countries to them, and to everyone else who could give him first-hand information. In his report to the Senate he was optimistic concerning relaxation of tension between Turkey and Greece over Cyprus, but extremely pessimistic about any Israeli-Arab settlement. He said that the United States might have to provide Israel with our latest fighter planes to counter the Soviet build-up of Arab war-making capacity. In short, the young Senator is definitely hawkish on all fronts.

On internal affairs, he generally follows his father's line of curtailing Presidential power; and of retrenchment, economy, and government living within its means, though he is, perhaps, more cognizant of the realities of modern fiscal necessities and theory. His amendment to reduce the proposed new debt ceiling from $365,000,-000,000 to $355,000,000,000 lost by a single vote. He is also less adamant on foreign aid. In 1967 he supported a grant of three million tons of food-assistance to the people of India. Testifying before the Senate Foreign Relations Committee in November, 1967, he supported a proposal made by Admiral Lewis Strauss to construct nuclear desalting plants in the Middle East as a way to provide needed fresh water to both Arab countries and Israel. He said, "Certainly there is a need for a bold and imaginative plan to help alleviate the two great problems of that strategic area, namely water and displaced population." [2]

Senator Byrd does his homework diligently, is freely accessible to his constituents and indeed to all comers, and works long hours. Without being hidebound by the principles and ideals of his father—whose appearance he resembles more than either of his brothers—he tries to exemplify them. He is well liked, but not loved as was the old Senator.

It is far too early to know how much of a mark he will make in the Senate, or even if he will be re-elected when he runs again in 1970. As Mr. Menefee says, "After long years in his father's shadow, Harry is just coming out into the sunlight."

Beverley and Richard E. Byrd II collaborate in running the great apple orchards. Beverley lives happily in the Log House, which he rechristened Westwood after his beloved sister. The Richard Byrds live at Rosemont, which his father left to him, because Harry has his own handsome house in Winchester and Beverley prefers the simple life in the Log House.

The Richard Byrds maintain the historic hospitality of their beautiful mansion even more lavishly than his father did. They give the traditional luncheons, which, though not as large, are more frequent. Senator Harry has his big political luncheons in Winchester. In addition, the Rosemont Byrds, with grace and gaiety, give an occasional fine old-fashioned ball, and frequent informal evening parties for young people around the swimming pool.

This brings us to the younger generation. The present Senator's eldest son, Harry III, at twenty-five consciously emulates the grandfather whom he adored. With his ruddy face, bright blue eyes, and curly red-gold hair he is "Handsome Harry" all over again. Like the old Senator he proposes to establish himself in business before taking to politics. He works long hours in the orchards learning the business

2. Transcript of testimony furnished by Senator Byrd, Jr.

from the roots up. As to politics he said, "Maybe, later on." He has the qualifications and the charm.

The Senator's second son, Thomas Thomson, has just graduated from college and is serving in Vietnam. His daughter, Beverley, a red-haired vibrant girl, aims at a career in journalism. With youthful intolerance, she considers politics "a dirty business." [3]

Beverley Byrd of Westwood has two young daughters, Anne Robinson and Westwood Beverley by his first marriage, and a four-year-old son Beverley, Jr. Known as Huffy-Puffy, he is as beautiful and charming a little boy as can be found between the Shenandoah and the James. His great delight is his father's famous outdoor zoo where he plays fearlessly with llamas, Himalayan goats—they butt—buffalo, yaks, camels, reindeer and other exotic beasts, not to mention seventeen peacocks, several dogs of assorted sizes and two tame woodchucks.

The Richard Byrds have a son Richard III or IV, no one seems quite sure of the number. Ricky goes to the University of Texas. He recently attended his first Democratic Convention—Chicago '68. Their daughter, Lucy, is at college. The youngest son, William Benton Byrd, is only eleven. He has the Byrd good looks, a bright inquiring mind, and a precocious interest in politics, which foreshadows his future.

With so many young Byrds coming along, it would seem the family tradition of three hundred years of unbroken public service to the Commonwealth and people of Virginia may well be maintained. The younger generation will not have much help from the Byrd Machine, which is functioning like a rusty lawn mower. They will have to face a far different, perhaps hostile, electorate, who are tired of tradition, orthodox fiscal policies, and lack of progress in many areas; an electorate which may be as bored with the name of Byrd, as a certain Athenian who voted against Aristides because he was tired of hearing him called "The Just."

Perhaps the political cards are too heavily stacked against them; or perhaps they will ride the flooding tide of liberalism to positions of power and service in a political environment that would have horrified their forebears. Virginia needs a change, but it would be encouraging to think that in a more dynamic future she will still be governed with grace and integrity.

3. Miss Beverley Byrd to the author.

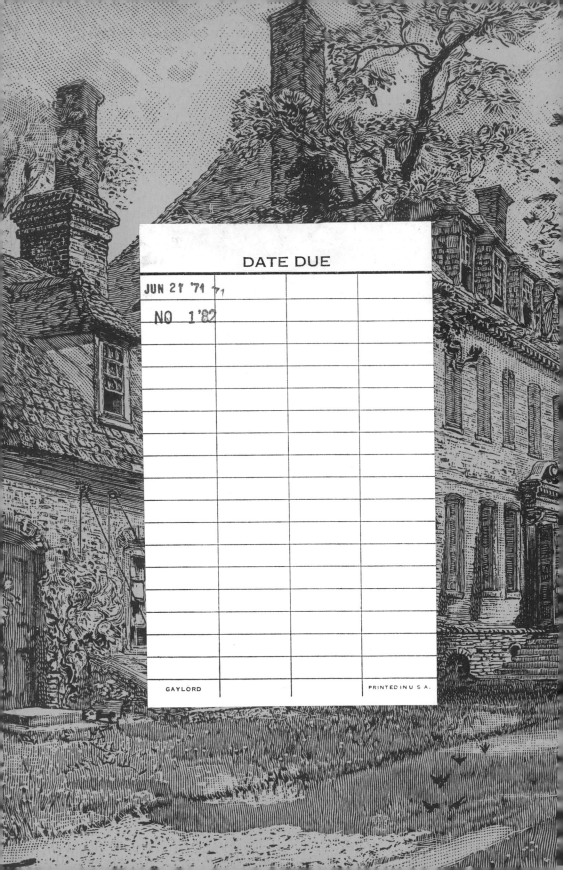

DATE DUE

JUN 21 '71 '71		
NO 1'82		
GAYLORD		PRINTED IN U.S.A.